Implementation Modules

Data Type	Implementation	Page	Representation	Meets Specification
ReversibleStrings	1.1	24	Array	1.3
LinkedList	2.1	82	Linked	2.4
Stacks	3.1	107	Array	3.1
StackPairs	3.2	110	Array	3.2
Stacks	3.3	115	Linked	3.1
Queues	3.4	121	Array	3.3
Lists	4.1	146	Array	4.1
Lists	4.2	150	Linked	4.1
SortedList	4.3	168	Array	4.3
BinaryTrees	5.1	220	Linked	5.1
BinarySearchTrees	5.2	239	Linked	5.2
Heaps	5.3	269	Array	5.4
PriorityQueues	5.4	271	Heap	3.4
StructuredSets	7.1	343	Hash Table	7.2
Strings	8.1	390	Array	8.1
Graphs	9.1	410	Lists	9.1
Graphs	9.2	417	Array	9.1
Maze	B.1	499	Array	B.1
Random	C.1	518	Array	C.1

Program Modules

Program Module	Function	Page
Palindrome	Finds palindromes	22
CheckParens	Checks parentheses matching	104
CharFreq	Letter frequency analysis	184
InternalExample	Example of internal module	479
FindMazePath	Find path through maze	500

[a]Other larger applications can be found in Appendix C. A diskette, available from the publisher, contains the modules in the text as well as small program modules to test them.

Data Structures
with Abstract Data Types and Modula-2

Data Structures
with Abstract Data Types and Modula-2

Daniel F. Stubbs and Neil W. Webre
California Polytechnic State University, San Luis Obispo

Brooks/Cole Publishing Company
Pacific Grove, California

To Our Parents

Brooks/Cole Publishing Company
A Division of Wadsworth, Inc.

© 1987 by Wadsworth, Inc., Belmont, California 94002. All rights reserved.
No part of this book may be reproduced, stored in a retrieval system, or transcribed,
in any form or by any means—electronic, mechanical, photocopying, recording
or otherwise—without the prior written permission of the publisher,
Brooks/Cole Publishing Company, Pacific Grove, California 93950,
a division of Wadsworth, Inc.

Printed in the United States of America

10   9   8   7   6   5

Library of Congress Cataloging-in-Publication Data

Stubbs, Daniel F., [date]
    Data structures with abstract data types and Modula-2.

    Bibliography: p.
    Includes index.
    1. Data structures (Computer science)   2. Modula-2
(Computer program language)   3. Abstract data types
(Computer science)   I. Webre, Neil W., [date]
II. Title.
QA76.9.D35S76   1987   005.7″3   86-26423
ISBN 0-534-07302-6

Sponsoring Editor: Cynthia C. Stormer
Marketing Representative: Cynthia Berg
Editorial Assistant: Corinne Kibbe
Production Editor: Candyce Cameron
Manuscript Editor: Meredy Amyx
Permissions Editor: Carline Haga
Interior and Cover Design: Jamie Sue Brooks
Art Coordinator: Michele Judge
Interior Illustration: Tim Keenan, Reese Thornton, Carl Brown, David Aguero
Typesetting: Bi-Comp, Inc., York, Pennsylvania
Cover Printing: Phoenix Color Corp., Long Island City, New York
Printing and Binding: R.R. Donnelley & Sons Co., Crawfordsville, Indiana

Preface

This text represents a fresh approach to the study of data structures. During the past several years, researchers have developed a new method of designing data structures, the new forms of which are called abstract data types. In the original papers, abstract data types are quite formal and unsuited to the beginning student. When the formality is removed, however, there remains a basic and easily understood essence.

Our major objectives in this book included a clear presentation of "classic" data structures as well as the integration of the notion of abstract data types into the study of the subject. As students complete the course, we want them to have not only a toolchest of data structures and a good knowledge of their characteristics but also skills in the use of abstraction, specification, and program construction using modules. These skills prepare students to use modern languages such as Ada, Modula-2, and Mesa. They are an excellent complement to the techniques of top-down design, successive decomposition, and structured programming. Students will be prepared for advanced courses in which the methods are formal logic and mathematics. Finally, these skills serve as an important—perhaps necessary—first step toward object-oriented programming.

Can these skills be attained by students who are early in their careers of study? The Pascal-based sibling of this book has been used successfully in many universities and colleges, and students appear to have no particular problems in using data abstraction. Indeed, they seem to be delighted to have a framework into which to fit the study of data structures and a means of defining and specifying data types precisely. The approach is analogous to the introduction of top-down design, successive decomposition, and structured programming in a first course in algorithms and programming.

This text can be considered to be a second edition of an original—*Data Structures with Abstract Data Types and Pascal*. An important difference from the first edition is the programming language used to illustrate the concepts. The original used Pascal, a language well suited to writing structured programs, but one that has no features to support the recently developed concepts of data abstraction. This book uses Modula-2, a language designed by Niklaus Wirth, the designer of Pascal. The bulk of it is quite similar to Pascal, and those who know Pascal are quickly at home with Modula-2. It improves upon Pascal's strengths in structured programming, while providing three important new features:

1. Modules, which provide support for abstract data types;
2. Co-routines, which provide support for concurrent programming;
3. Access to system-level objects such as words, bytes, ports, files, and the functions of the operating system.

It is the first of these upon which we will concentrate in this text.

Although Modula-2 is used throughout the book, it is not the primary focus. This is a book about data structures. The language used to illustrate and implement them is an important but secondary consideration. Modula-2 is a better language than Pascal for that purpose, but the latter was also used successfully in the earlier book.

In addition to the use of Modula-2, this book incorporates the following improvements over the original:

- Several simple applications of the data types studied appear throughout the body of the text. They are intended to demonstrate the use of abstract data types and to provide students with complete operational units in Modula-2. A number of more complex applications are gathered in Appendix C so that they are available but do not disrupt the flow of the basic material.
- Appendix B introduces recursion. Recursion is used in many places in the book. The appendix is an introduction to the subject for those who are not familiar with it. It can be covered at any point, but its content should be understood before covering Chapter 5.
- Appendix E contains notes by the authors that examine the issue of pre- and postconditions and their relationship to error checking during execution.
- Source code for all the modules in the text is available on a diskette in IBM PC® format. The files are text files and can be easily transferred to other systems. The diskette also includes drivers for most of the modules. These drivers permit students to exercise the data structures and observe the effects using data of their choice. They also provide examples of Modula-2 code to utilize the data structures. The diskette is free to all who receive review copies of the text, and unlimited copying of the diskette is encouraged. The sale of copied diskettes is forbidden.

• **Methods used in the text**

The discussion of each data structure begins with its specification, which includes a description of its elements, structure, domain of possible values, and operations. An important point is that the specification of a data structure is separate from and independent of its implementation. As a result, each data type is described using a format that is simple and concise and has only the details necessary to use it. This facilitates an understanding of the essence of the data type, as well as comparing different data types.

The specification of each data type is given as a Modula-2 definition module. The syntactic aspects of the specification are interwoven with semantic specifications in the form of Modula-2 comments. For example, the *Enqueue* operation of a priority queue is specified as follows:

```
PROCEDURE Enqueue (VAR PQ: PriorityQueue; e: Element; p: Priority);
(* pre  — PQ is not full.
   post — PQ contains element e with priority p. *)
```

The PROCEDURE statement specifies the syntax of the operation. The comment (* **pre** . . . *) specifies the semantics. The precondition states what condition must be met for the operation to execute correctly. The postcondition states the result of successful execution. These techniques are introduced in Chapter 1.

The semantics of procedures are written in English. They could have been specified more precisely using formal notations such as the predicate calculus and set theory. A formal specification of *Enqueue* might be

```
PROCEDURE Enqueue (VAR PQ: PriorityQueue; e: Element; p: Priority);
(* pre  — Cardinality(PQ) <MaxSize.
   post — PQ=PQ'U {<e,p>}. *)
```

We do not use formal notation in this book, except in Chapter 10. We feel that a first course using abstract data types is best covered using English for specifications, as in the former specification of *Enqueue*.

After specifying a data structure using a definition module, we normally follow with one or more Modula-2 implementation modules, each of which contains data structures and code written to meet the specifications. The student thereby sees a unit that is complete and self-contained and gains a working knowledge of modules. We urge instructors to make modules available to students and to assign exercises that use the modules. As easy way to do this is to use the modules provided on the diskette available from the publisher. Of course, writing implementation modules, given specifications in the form of definition modules, is an important exercise also. We demonstrate the power of and use of modules in problem solving in several applications throughout the book and in a number of larger applications gathered in Appendix C.

Each implementation of a data type has its own performance characteristics. We present these in two ways. The first is by an analysis of operation counts, often stated as order-of-magnitude estimates. The second is by timing the implementations' actual executions on a computer. One problem in particular is solved by using a variety of data structures as they are encountered in the text. It is a frequency analysis of the occurrence of single letters and pairs of letters in some English text. The use of a single problem allows a direct comparison of the data structures used to solve it. Although the timing results are for a specific language, compiler, and computer system, they introduce the use of empirical techniques in computer science and indicate that care must be exercised not to place too much reliance on order-of-magnitude estimates.

When we started writing this book, we expected to make heavy use of stepwise refinement to design and implement many complex algorithms. We were pleasantly surprised to find that the use of abstract data types, a careful choice of operations and their specifications, and the considered use of pre- and postconditions often led to procedures whose implementations were too simple to need stepwise refinement. In effect, these techniques taken together provide a data-oriented design method for solving problems. They do not replace stepwise refinement; rather, they provide the designer and programmer with a powerful complementary problem-solving tool.

• Special features

This book has been specifically tailored to the study of data structures and makes use of the following features:

- Modula-2 programming language
- detailed illustrations
- margin notes and figures
- annotated computer algorithms
- exercises at the ends of sections
- chapter summaries

The book concludes with five appendixes: (A) Modula-2 syntax and comparison with Pascal; (B) introduction to recursion; (C) several large applications; (D) specifications of three standard Modula-2 modules—*SYSTEM, STORAGE* and *InOut;* and (E) notes on checking preconditions.

• Chapter organization and suggestions for teaching

The prerequisites for this course are one course in algorithm design and construction and a working knowledge of a structured programming language, preferably Modula-2 or Pascal. We assume no knowledge of either modules or pointers; they are both covered at an introductory level in the book.

Chapter 1 introduces many of the key concepts used throughout the remaining chapters and should be read by everyone (a possible exception is Section 1.5.3, whose material may have been studied in other courses). The introduction to Chapter 1 describes a fast path through the material for a first reading, with a complete reading to follow as experience is gained with the material of other chapters.

Chapter 2 covers two fundamental data types that students will have studied in prerequisite courses: arrays and records. Although the material might be covered quickly, we suggest that it not be skipped since it contains specifications of these two important data types, as well as details of their implementations. The later sections of Chapter 2 include a tutorial on the use of pointers, which may be new to many students entering a data structures course. Students familiar with them should still study the specification and implementation of linked lists (Section 2.4).

Chapter 3 is very important and should be studied carefully. It introduces stacks, queues, and priority queues. Many texts describe stacks and queues as linear structures. Our approach permits a more general view.

Chapter 4 centers on data types with linear structure and discusses rings, sequences, and a variety of types of lists—chronological, sorted, frequency-ordered, and self-organizing. The frequency analysis problem is introduced and timing studies are presented for various list solutions. The chapter also discusses files through the example of Modula-2's *Stream* and *InOut* modules. If files are to be covered as part of the course, the instructor may continue the discussion with more advanced Modula-2 file modules, which are not included in this book.

Chapter 5 is about trees, one of the most important, efficient, and widely used data types of computer science. Sections 5.1 through 5.5 cover the basics of binary trees and binary search trees and should be studied by all. Material from other sections can be added as the instructor sees fit, though we suggest including Section 5.7, which extends the timing studies of the frequency analysis problem introduced in Chapter 4, and Section 5.8, which discusses heaps and their use in implementing priority queues.

Chapter 6 is based upon algorithms rather than a data structure. It covers internal sorting methods; that is, sorting methods that are efficient for data stored entirely in a random access memory. Sorting techniques for data stored in files are not covered.

Chapter 7 discusses two types of sets. Sets of atomic objects are a type built into Pascal and Modula-2. Sets of structured objects are also covered, as is hashing, an implementation technique especially well suited to implementing sets.

Chapter 8 covers one of the most widely used data structures—strings. Strings are really a special type of linear structure, but they are different enough and important enough to be treated separately.

Chapter 9 is about graphs (in the graph theory sense). The discussion of graphs completes the coverage of the four most common structures—set, linear, tree, and graph. The search algorithms for breadth, depth, and priority first searches are introduced and then applied to find shortest paths, minimal spanning trees, and topological order.

Chapter 10 covers three topics relating to data abstraction. The first is a brief discussion of the data typing facilities of Ada. The second is a demonstration of the use of formal methods for specifying abstract data types. The third is an elementary example of the use of data abstraction in object-oriented system design.

Appendix A presents the syntax of Modula-2 and contrasts it with that of Pascal. Appendix B is an introduction to recursion and its implementation on digital computers. When reading this appendix, remember that it is only an introduction. More advanced applications of the techniques are found throughout the text, especially in Chapters 5, 6, and 9. Appendix C has a number of more complex applications of the data types studied than are found in the text. These applications are gathered in an appendix in order to avoid interrupting the flow of the basic material. They may be read at the same time as the data types that they use are covered in the text. Appendix D contains the definition modules of three standard Modula-2 modules that are used throughout the book. They are *SYSTEM,* the module containing definition of basic system-level objects and the operations that act upon them; *Storage,* a module that deals with the dynamic allocation of memory; and *InOut,* the text file I/O module. Appendix E discusses some of the aspects of pre- and postconditions.

• Acknowledgments

We would like to thank Zane Motteler, Bob Dourson, Pasha Rostov, Keti Anderson, Hannah Chauvet, Len Myers, and Bob Schuerman, each of whom taught from or read Pascal versions of the manuscript and provided encouragement and valuable suggestions for improvement. We are indebted to Philip Dorin, Loyola Marymount; Robert Gann, Hartwick College; Peter Greene, Illinois Institute of Technology; Richard Sutcliffe, Trinity Western University; and Hoyt Warner, Western New England College, all of whom read the Modula-2 manuscript.

The production editor for this text was Candy Cameron. Candy is charming, intelligent, tactful, and has a wonderful sense of humor. She led us through production of our part of this text, and its predecessor, with always the right encouragement to meet just one more deadline. Copy editor Meredy Amyx did a great job with a challenging manuscript, and Cindy Stormer, the sponsoring editor, did a perfect job of coordinating the entire process.

We believe that this is the most attractive data structures text on the market. Credit for its exemplary design and appearance goes to Jamie Sue Brooks, designer; Michele Judge, art coordinator; and Reese Thornton and Tim Keenan, artists.

Dan Stubbs & Neil Webre

Contents

1   **Introduction**   **1**

1.1   **Introduction**   **2**
     1.1.1   *Down-to-Earth Analogy*   *2*
     Exercises 1.1   4

1.2   **Data Types and Data Structures**   **4**
     1.2.1   *Data Types*   *5*
     1.2.2   *Abstraction Levels of a Data Type*   *7*
     1.2.3   *Native Data Types*   *9*
     Exercises 1.2   11

1.3   **Abstract Data Types**   **12**
     1.3.1   *Specifying an Abstract Data Type*   *12*
     1.3.2   *Specifications in Modula-2*   *16*
     1.3.3   *Implementation Using Modula-2*   *23*
     1.3.4   *Advantages of Abstract Data Types*   *26*
     Exercises 1.3   29

1.4   **Elements and Structure—An Overview**   **29**
     1.4.1   *Data Elements*   *29*
     1.4.2   *Structure*   *30*
     1.4.3   *Linear and Ordered Structures*   *32*
     1.4.4   *Data Structures and High-Level Languages*   *33*
     1.4.5   *Representing Abstract Structure*   *34*
     Exercises 1.4   35

1.5   **Virtual and Physical Data Types**   **36**
     1.5.1   *Memories*   *37*

1.5.2   *Processors*   *38*

1.5.3   *Representation of Common Atomic Data Types*   *40*

1.5.4   *Complexity, Performance, and Metrics*   *46*

Exercises 1.5   50

1.6   Summary   51

2

**Arrays, Records,
and Simple Linked Lists**   **53**

2.1   Introduction   54

2.2   Arrays   57

2.2.1   *Array Characteristics*   *61*

2.2.2   *Array Mapping Functions*   *63*

2.2.3   *Array Descriptor Records*   *65*

2.2.4   *Special Arrays*   *65*

2.2.5   *Dynamic Arrays and Open Array Parameters*   *68*

Exercises 2.2   69

2.3   Records   70

2.3.1   *The Record Abstract Data Type*   *71*

2.3.2   *Record Characteristics*   *73*

2.3.3   *Record Description and Memory Mapping*   *73*

2.3.4   *Variant Record Schemes*   *74*

Exercises 2.3   76

2.4   Pointers and Simple Linked Lists   77

2.4.1   *Pointers*   *77*

2.4.2   *A Simple Linked List*   *79*

2.4.3   *Design of Linked Lists*   *88*

Exercises 2.4   91

2.5   Composite Structures   92

2.5.1   *Records of Arrays*   *92*

2.5.2   *Arrays of Records*   *93*

2.5.3   *Arrays of Pointers*   *93*

Exercises 2.5   96

2.6   Summary   96

3   Stacks and Queues   99

3.1   Introduction   100

Exercises 3.1   101

3.2   Stacks   101

3.2.1   Multiple Instances of a Data Type   103

3.2.2   A Simple Use of Stacks   104

3.2.3   An Array Implementation   106

3.2.4   Stack Pairs   108

3.2.5   An Application: Memory Management   111

3.2.6   A Linked Implementation   114

Exercises 3.2   117

3.3   FIFO Queues   118

3.3.1   Array Implementation   119

3.3.2   Linked Implementation   123

Exercises 3.3   123

3.4   Priority Queues   124

3.4.1   Implementations   126

Exercises 3.4   127

**3.5   Application of Queues:
Scheduling I/O Requests on a Magnetic Disk   128**

3.5.1   Disk Scheduling   129

3.5.2   An Abstract Schedule   133

Exercises 3.5   134

3.6   Summary   135

4   Linear Structures   137

4.1   Introduction   138

4.2   Lists   139

4.2.1   List Specification   139

4.2.2   List Array Implementation   143

4.2.3   List Linked Implementation   149

Exercises 4.2   157

4.3   Ordered Lists   157

4.3.1   Chronologically Ordered Lists   158

Exercises 4.3.1   160

4.3.2   Sorted Lists   161

Exercises 4.3.2   172

4.3.3   Frequency-Ordered Lists   172

Exercises 4.3.3   175

4.4   Rings   176

Exercises 4.4   178

4.5   Sequences   178

4.5.1   Sequence Specification   178

4.5.2   Modula-2 Files   180

Exercises 4.5   183

4.6   An Application: Single-Letter and Digraph Frequencies in English Text   183

4.6.1   The Frequency Analysis Program   184

4.6.2   Timing Studies   186

4.7   Summary   190

5

Trees   191

5.1   Introduction   192

Exercises 5.1   194

5.2   Ordered Trees, Oriented Trees, and Terminology   194

5.2.1   Elements of Trees   194

5.2.2   Structure of Trees—Hierarchical Relationships   195

Exercises 5.2   200

5.3   Abstract Binary Tree   201

5.3.1   Structure   201

5.3.2   Specification and Operations   205

Exercises 5.3.2   212

5.3.3   Linked Representation and Implementation   214

5.3.4   Sequential Representation   225

Exercises 5.3.4   226

5.3.5   Threaded Trees   226

Exercises 5.3.5   228

5.4 **Abstract Binary Search Tree** **228**

5.4.1 Specification and Operations 229

*5.4.2 Binary Search Tree Representation and
         Implementation 234*

Exercises 5.4 242

5.5 **Enumeration and Performance** **243**

Exercises 5.5 250

5.6 **AVL Trees** **250**

5.6.1 AVL Tree Representation and Implementation 253

Exercises 5.6 260

5.7 **Frequency Analysis Revisited** **261**

Exercises 5.7 264

5.8 **Heaps and Priority Queues** **264**

5.8.1 Heap Data Structure 264

5.8.2 Heap Implementation of a Priority Queue 271

Exercises 5.8 272

5.9 **B-Trees** **273**

5.9.1 Insertion and Deletion Illustrated 274

*5.9.2 Algorithmic Descriptions of Insertion
         and Deletion 276*

5.9.3 Specification 278

Exercises 5.9 282

5.10 **Summary** **283**

6 Internal Sorting   285

6.1 **Introduction** **286**

6.1.1 The Sorting Problem 287

6.1.2 Specification of Sorting Algorithms 289

Exercises 6.1 290

6.2 **Simple Sort Techniques** **290**

6.2.1 Selection Sort 290

6.2.2 Exchange Sort 291

6.2.3 Insertion Sort 293

6.2.4 Insertion Sort—Implemented for a Linked List 295

6.2.5 Performance of Simple Sorts 297

Exercises 6.2 299

6.3   Advanced Sort Techniques   301

6.3.1   *Quicksort   301*

6.3.2   *Treesort   308*

6.3.3   *Heapsort   308*

6.3.4   *Mergesort   310*

Exercises 6.3   314

6.4   Radix Sort   316

6.4.1   *Example of a Radix Sort   317*

6.4.2   *General Process for a Radix Sort   317*

6.4.3   *Drawbacks of a Radix Sort   318*

Exercises 6.4   319

6.5   Summary   320

7

Sets   **323**

7.1   Introduction   324

7.2   Sets of Atomic Types   324

7.2.1   *Set Specification   325*

7.2.2   *Implementation Using Bit Maps   328*

Exercises 7.2   330

7.3   Sets of Structured Objects   330

7.3.1   *Set Specification   330*

Exercises 7.3   332

7.4   Hashed Implementations   333

7.4.1   *Hashing Functions   335*

7.4.2   *Collision-Resolution Strategies   340*

7.4.3   *Perfect Hashing Functions   353*

Exercises 7.4   355

7.5   Hashing Performance   356

7.5.1   *Performance   357*

7.5.2   *Memory Requirements   358*

7.5.3   *Deletion   359*

7.6   Frequency Analysis of Digraphs   359

7.6.1   *Hash Function   359*

7.6.2   *Frequency Analysis Summary   361*

7.7   Summary   362

8 Strings 365

8.1 Introduction 366

8.2 Characters 366

8.2.1 *Fixed-Length Representations* 366

8.2.2 *Embedded Shift Instructions* 369

8.2.3 *Embedded Mode Shift Instructions—An Application* 370

8.2.4 *Representing Characters with a Variable Number of Bits* 371

Exercises 8.2 375

8.3 Strings 376

8.3.1 *Specification of a String Data Type* 377

8.3.2 *Representation of Strings* 381

8.3.3 *Array Implementation of Strings* 383

8.3.4 *Linked Implementation of Strings* 393

8.3.5 *Comparison of Array and Linked Implementations* 395

Exercises 8.3 396

8.4 Summary 398

9 Graphs 399

9.1 Introduction 399

9.2 Terminology 401

Exercises 9.2 403

9.3 Graph Data Structure 404

9.3.1 *Specification* 404

9.3.2 *Representation* 405

9.3.3 *Implementation* 407

Exercises 9.3 421

9.4 Traversal 421

9.4.1 *Graph Traversal Algorithms* 421

9.4.2 *Implementation* 424

Exercises 9.4 427

9.5 Applications   428

9.5.1   *Abstract Solutions   428*

9.5.2   *Implementation   430*

Exercises 9.5   *432*

9.6 Directed Graphs   434

9.6.1   *Transitive Closure   434*

9.6.2   *Topological Sorting   435*

Exercises 9.6   *438*

9.7 Summary   438

10   Abstract Data Types Revisited   441

10.1 Introduction   442

10.2 Generic Data Types   443

Exercises 10.2   *445*

10.3 Data Typing Facilities of Ada   446

**10.4 Problem-Level Objects
and Data Abstractions   449**

**10.5 Formal Specifications
of Abstract Data Types   453**

10.5.1   *Abstract Model Method   453*

10.5.2   *First-Order Predicate Calculus   454*

10.5.3   *Formal Specifications   456*

10.5.4   *Correctness Proofs   460*

Exercises 10.5   *460*

10.6 Summary   461

APPENDIX

A   Comparison of Pascal and Modula-2   463

A.1 Program/Program Module Structure   464

A.2 Identifiers   465

A.3 Comments   465

A.4 Block Structure   465

A.5 Declarations   466

A.6   **Label Declaration**   **468**

A.7   **Constant Declaration**   **468**

A.8   **Type Declaration**   **469**

A.8.1   *Standard Types*   *469*

A.8.2   *Simple Types*   *470*

A.8.3   *Pointer Types*   *470*

A.8.4   *Array Types*   *471*

A.8.5   *Record Declaration*   *472*

A.8.6   *Set Type Declaration*   *474*

A.8.7   *File Type Declaration*   *474*

A.8.8   *Procedure Type Declaration*   *474*

A.9   **Variable Declaration**   **475**

A.10   **Procedure Declaration**   **477**

A.11   **Internal Module Declaration**   **477**

A.12   **Definition Module**   **480**

A.13   **Implementation Module**   **482**

A.14   **Statements**   **483**

A.14.1   *Assignment*   *483*

A.14.2   *Compound Statement*   *483*

A.14.3   *Statement Sequence*   *483*

A.14.4   *If Statement*   *484*

A.14.5   *Case Statement*   *485*

A.14.6   *While Statement*   *485*

A.14.7   *Repeat Statement*   *486*

A.14.8   *Loop and Exit Statements*   *486*

A.14.9   *For Statement*   *487*

A.14.10   *With Statement*   *488*

A.14.11   *Return Statement*   *488*

A.14.12   *Procedure (or Function) Call*   *488*

APPENDIX

B

Recursion   491

B.1   **Recursive Functions**   **492**

B.2   **Some Sample Recursive Functions**   **493**

B.2.1.   *Factorials*   *493*

B.2.2.   *Fibonacci Numbers*   *493*

B.2.3 A Recursive Search Procedure   494

B.2.4 A Recursive Sort   495

B.2.5 Passing Through a Maze   496

B.3 How Recursion Is Implemented   500

B.4 Performance Issues   503

B.5 Alternatives to Recursion   504

B.5.1 Iteration   504

B.5.2 Stacking   504

APPENDIX

C   Selected Applications   505

C.1 Finding Patterns in Files   506

C.2 A Random Number Generator   517

C.3 Insertion Algorithm for a B-Tree   519

C.4 Printing a B-Tree   525

C.5 Printing Binary Trees   528

C.5.1 Tree-Printing Issues   528

C.5.2 Basic Operations   530

C.5.3 Wprint   530

C.5.4 Vprint   532

APPENDIX

D   Modula-2 Reserved Words, Symbols, Identifiers, and Modules   539

D.1 Reserved Words   540

D.2 Special Symbols   540

D.3 Standard Identifiers   540

D.4 Standard Modules   540

APPENDIX

E   Notes on Checking Preconditions   545

References   549

Index   554

Introduction 1

1.1 Introduction
    1.1.1 Down-to-Earth Analogy
    Exercises 1.1

1.2 Data Types and Data Structures
    1.2.1 Data Types
    1.2.2 Abstraction Levels of a Data Type
    1.2.3 Native Data Types
    Exercises 1.2

1.3 Abstract Data Types
    1.3.1 Specifying an Abstract Data Type
    1.3.2 Specifications in Modula-2
    1.3.3 Implementation Using Modula-2
    1.3.4 Advantages of Abstract Data Types
    Exercises 1.3

1.4 Elements and Structure—An Overview
    1.4.1 Data Elements
    1.4.2 Structure
    1.4.3 Linear and Ordered Structures
    *1.4.4 Data Structures and High-Level
        Languages*
    1.4.5 Representing Abstract Structure
    Exercises 1.4

1.5 Virtual and Physical Data Types
    1.5.1 Memories
    1.5.2 Processors
    *1.5.3 Representation of Common Atomic
        Data Types*
    1.5.4 Complexity, Performance, and Metrics
    Exercises 1.5

1.6 Summary

1.1 Introduction

In this chapter, we will introduce the basic notions, approach, and terminology that will be used throughout the book. In Section 1.2 there are definitions of data type and data structure. The notion of abstraction is very important in computing. We are particularly interested in its application to data stored in a digital computer. In Section 1.3 we will introduce the concept of abstract data typing, discuss its advantages, and give a simple example of the approach that we will take throughout the remainder of the book.

Section 1.4 deals with the data elements that make up data structures and with the structure itself. We will pay special attention to the representation and implementation of data structures in high-level programming languages (Modula-2, Pascal, FORTRAN, COBOL, Ada, etc.). Section 1.5 addresses the kinds of memories and processors available for data structuring, from the machine level up. There is an introduction to the representation of common "atomic" data types, such as integers, real numbers, and characters, as bit patterns in the physical memories of computers. The final topic we will discuss is general concepts of performance and efficiency.

Although this chapter is important to a thorough understanding of the remainder of the text, it contains more information than is necessary in order to continue successfully. The extra material attempts to place the abstract data type approach into perspective. You will find that you are studying material that, while helpful, is not absolutely necessary in order to go on to the following chapters. We suggest a fastpath through Chapter 1 and then a return to read the entire chapter when you are comfortable with the idea of an abstract data type. The suggested fastpath includes the following sections: 1.1, 1.2–1.2.2, 1.3–1.3.3, 1.4–1.4.3, and 1.6.

1.1.1 Down-to-Earth Analogy

Let us start our investigations with a down-to-earth analogy. Suppose we take a dozen eggs. We will consider the eggs to be nondecomposable objects; we do not care that each has a shell, yolk, white, and whatnot. We choose the individual egg, as shown in Figure 1.1, to be our **atomic element**. Beyond that level, we are not concerned with details. A person who will use the eggs for cooking would pay attention to their component parts, so for that purpose they are not atomic. Grocers do not deal in individual eggs, but only in packets of one dozen. Therefore, the entire collection of 12 eggs is the grocer's atomic level. The function that we perform thus tends to dictate an atomic level, and it can be changed to suit the situation.

Every physical object can be decomposed, and modern physics is in a state of uncertainty as to what is the ultimate level of decomposition. There are subatomic quarks, leptons, and muons. Up to the boundary of the limits of our knowledge, we can take any object and decompose it further. We can also take a collection of objects and think of the collection itself as an object. A bridge is a collection of beams, girders, bolts, pilings, and so on. Most people

Figure 1.1
We choose an individual egg as
our atomic element.

would think of a bridge as a single object, not as a collection of parts. We focus our attention on the level of detail necessary for our use of the object(s). A motorist and a structural engineer have different atomic levels when considering the bridge.

Let us get back to our dozen eggs. Suppose that we want to consider these eggs to have individual identities. We will paint a unique number on each, ranging from 1 to 12. We can visualize our dozen eggs floating in space neatly lined up by number. We have given some **structure**—the eggs have certain relationships to each other. They are arranged in a line (linearly) in order of their painted numbers.

We certainly do not want to leave our eggs floating in space. We want to be able to do things with them. For example, we want to be able to pick out any egg by number and remove it from the group. We want to be able to ship the entire dozen (or what remains of it after we have removed some). We may want to add new eggs to the group, but only in the gaps where other eggs have been removed and only if the number painted on the egg being inserted is the same as the one removed. We can imagine any number of **operations** for our collection of eggs.

We will define the **collection of atomic objects** that we have mentally arranged with some structure, and for which we have arbitrarily specified certain operations, to be an **abstract egg structure.** It is not real because, unless we are in a spacecraft, we cannot make our eggs float in space, and, although we have defined *what* we can do with our collection of eggs, we have not said exactly *how* we are going to do it. The whole thing exists only in our imagination. However, if this is going to be more than just a daydream, we have to decide how we are going to accomplish our imaginings using real eggs and real implements. No matter what our **physical egg structure** is to be, we want it to act exactly like our abstract egg structure.

Let us first tackle the problem of physically storing the eggs. Suppose we found a double-rowed egg carton, a triple-rowed egg carton, and an old Easter basket with straw in it, illustrated in Figure 1.2. These are our available **storage media.** If we choose the triple-rowed carton and arrange the eggs regularly in rows of three as shown in the lower half of Figure 1.2, we can find the physical position of any numbered egg in the carton by a simple calculation. The position of egg number k is

$$\text{row} = (k - 1) \text{ div } 4$$
$$\text{column} = (k - 1) \text{ modulo } 4$$

The egg numbers do not have to be showing for us to find the one we wish. In addition, if we want to ship the eggs, we can just close the top and we would have a good shipping container. The triple-rowed carton seems to be a good choice for these operations. The double-rowed carton has much the same characteristics.

The Easter basket is not very good for these uses. If we artistically arrange the eggs in no particular order, we can still find the egg with a given painted number, but it will take some time. We have to rummage through the eggs in

Our eggs are numbered from 1 to 12. These numbers establish a relationship among the eggs—they provide the eggs with a structure.

We can perform operations on our eggs such as picking out the kth egg or shipping the entire dozen.

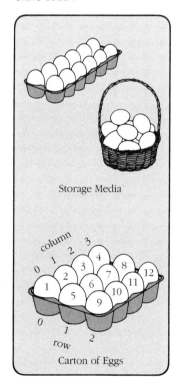

Storage Media

Carton of Eggs

Figure 1.2
We have several different ways of actually storing our eggs. How we store them will affect how efficiently we can perform operations on them.

We have specified an abstract egg structure, which is composed of the following:

1. Atomic elements—the eggs
2. Structure—the eggs are numbered and have a linear structure relationship
3. Operations

the basket looking at each number until we find the one for which we are searching. Shipping the eggs is going to be quite difficult. The Easter basket is not a good storage medium for these operations.

Now, of course, this book is not about arranging eggs, but it is about arranging and operating on collections of objects. The objects we will be interested in are **data objects.** We are not going to use egg cartons. Instead we have several types of **computer memories** as our storage media. We are not going to use people to retrieve and ship eggs, but we will use **computer algorithms** to perform operations on data stored in memories. The overall strategy that we use will be the same as the one we used with our eggs: We will imagine atoms of data arranged with some structure while ignoring the reality of the memories that we have at our disposal. We will define certain operations that we want to perform on our imaginary structured collection of data. We can then write algorithms that use those operations while leaving it to someone else or for ourselves later to actually build an implementation that acts to the outside world just like our abstract one. All of the details of the actual implementation will be buried inside a neat external package, or module, with precisely defined interfaces.

If we combined our abstract egg structure with a method for storing the eggs and an implementation of the operations, the result would be a module. We could call it an abstract egg module.

Exercises 1.1

1. Explain the following terms in your own words:

    atomic element   structure
    operation   storage medium

2. **a.** Describe a physical structure with which you are familiar; include its component parts, the relationships among its parts, and the operations that may be performed.
    b. Do the same for a structure occurring naturally in the physical world.
    c. Do the same for an organization created by people.
3. There are many kinds of structure. The component elements of a bridge have certain spatial relationships to each other, certain load-bearing relationships, and certain "type" relationships (e.g., all beams are related by being of type *beam*). What kinds of structure are there among component parts of an automobile? among employees of a firm? among students of a university?

1.2 Data Types and Data Structures

Before defining the specifics of data types and data structures, let us discuss our terminology. It would be convenient if the computer science community had adopted standard meanings for terms, such as data type, data structure, and abstract data type, that will be important to us. Such is not the case. In fact, each of these terms is assigned many different meanings. Consequently, we must choose definitions that are not at variance with general usage. We will define the terms in a way that will assist us in the process of learning about data structures rather than for a research-oriented approach.

Let us first define a term that will be used throughout this book. A **data value** is a piece of data that we can consider, perhaps only momentarily, as a single entity. We might consider, for example, the integer value 593 as a single data value.

The set

{32.99, −1.04, 0.395}

might be considered in its entirety a single data value. It might also be considered to be composed of three distinct component values that are somehow related. In this case, their relationships to each other are that they are members of the same set. If we decompose a data value as we have done with the set value, we need a term for the pieces that result. Each piece is a value of another data type, in this case *real*. We will call these component values **component elements**, or simply **elements**.

An **atomic data value** is a piece of data that we choose to consider as a single, nondecomposable entity. For example, the integer

62953

may be considered as a single integer value stored on this sheet of paper. We can decompose it if we wish to do so. The integer 62953 could be seen as a collection of digits stored on the page in a left-to-right order. Each digit—6, 2, 9, 5, and 3—could either be considered to be atomic or be viewed as collections of dots of ink (suppose we are using a dot-matrix printer). Each dot is a collection of ink molecules, and so on. We could continue in this vein until the limit of our knowledge of the composition of matter is reached (see Figure 1.3).

We may choose any level to stop the decomposition, and, except for the ultimate level of the basic composition of matter and energy, the level chosen is arbitrary. If we choose to consider 62953 as a single, nondecomposable entity, we may do so. If we wish to decompose it in any of a number of ways, we may do so. The decision to decompose is strictly at our discretion.

1.2.1 Data Types

What is a data type? The essence of a **type** is that it attempts to identify qualities common to a group of individuals or objects that distinguish it as an identifiable class or kind. If we provide a set of possible data values and a set of operations that act on the values, we can think of the combination as a **data type** (see Figure 1.4).

> If a data value can be decomposed into component parts, we call each part a component element.

> A value of an atomic data type is regarded as nondecomposable.

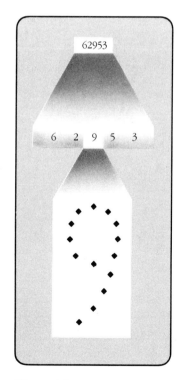

Figure 1.3
Successive decomposition of a data value.

Data Type

1. A set of values
2. A set of operations on those values

Figure 1.4

A type identifies qualities common to a group of individuals that distinguish it as an identifiable class or kind.

•

Atomic Type Integer

Values
. . . , −2, −1, 0, 1, 2, 3, . . .
Operations
  Addition
  Subtraction
  Multiplication
  Division
  Absolute value
  ⋮

•

A data structure is a data type whose values are composed of component elements that are related by some structure.

•

Since a data structure is a data type, it has a set of operations on its values. In addition, there may be operations that act on its component elements.

•

TYPE Sample = ARRAY [1..3] OF REAL;

•

Value 1	Value 2	Value 3	
[1] 0.0	[1] 5.33	[1] 2.16	
[2] 1.9	[2] 2.2	[2] 0.14	⋯
[3] 3.4	[3] 4.2	[3] 6.30	

Figure 1.6
Values of the structured type *Sample.*

•

Value A		Value B
[1] 0.0		[1] 1.9
[2] 1.9	not =	[2] 0.0
[3] 3.4		[3] 3.4

Value A is not the same as value B.

Let us look at two classes of data types. We will call any data type whose values we choose to consider atomic an ***atomic data type.*** Often, we choose to consider integers to be atomic. We are then only concerned with the single quantity that a value represents, not with the fact that an integer is a set of digits in some number system. *Integer* is a common atomic data type found in most programming languages and in most computer architectures.

We will call any data type whose values are composed of component elements that are related by some structure a ***structured data type,*** or ***data structure***. In other words, the values of these data types are decomposable, and we must therefore be aware of their internal construction. There are two essential ingredients to any object that can be decomposed—it must have *component elements* and it must have *structure,* the rules for relating or fitting the elements together (see Figure 1.5).

Data Structure
A data type whose values
  1. Can be decomposed into a set of component data elements each of which is either atomic or another data structure
  2. Include a set of associations or relationships (structure) involving the component elements

Figure 1.5

The operations of a structured data type might not only act on the values of the data type, they might also act on component elements of the data structure. Let us look at an example.

Suppose that we have a data type called *Sample.* Individual values of this data type are made up of three real numbers arranged linearly. Each set of three real numbers together with its order of arrangement is considered to be a single data value of the type *Sample.* We can treat *Sample* as a structured data type by considering each of the real numbers as a component element. We will specify a structure for each element of *Sample* by prescribing each component element to be the first, second, or third. One way to show this structure is by appending the appropriate integer (or ***index***) to each component.

Some values of the structured type *Sample* are given in Figure 1.6, with the relationship between component elements—the structure—shown using appended indexes.

It is important to note that each value of a data structure has an associated structure. The two values of the type *Sample* shown in the margin are different even though their component elements (0.0, 1.9, and 3.4) are the same. Only the structure (relationship among the elements) is different.

Let us consider an operation for the data type. Suppose that we have three variables of type *Sample* and that the addition operator "+" is defined in accordance with the illustration in the margin on page 7. The element values in corresponding positions are added.

The operator "+" operates on a pair of values of data type *Sample* and produces a value of the same type.

A second kind of operator is one that acts on component data elements instead of on the entire composite value. For example, languages that provide for the array data type also provide an operator that allows the user to read out the value of an array element. Let *Sample* be implemented as a Modula-2 array. (Notice the similarity to the abstract type *Sample.*) The assignment statement x := a[2] retrieves the value of the element that is associated with the index value 2 and subsequently moves it by the assignment operator ":=" into the real variable *x*. At first it might not be apparent that indexing on the right side of an assignment statement is such an operator. Indexing on the left side of an assignment statement is a different operator that can be thought of as an update or change operation – a[2] := x.

Thus we see that a structured data type can have operations defined on its composite values, as well as on the component elements of those values. Figure 1.7 distinguishes between two classes of data types.

VAR a,b,c: Sample;

a := b + c

[1] 7.4   [1] 5.3   [1] 2.1
[2] 2.3 ← [2] 2.2 + [2] 0.1
[3] 10.5   [3] 4.2   [3] 6.3

•

VAR a: Sample;
    x: REAL;

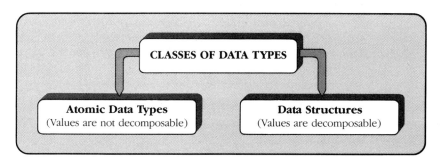

CLASSES OF DATA TYPES

Atomic Data Types
(Values are not decomposable)

Data Structures
(Values are decomposable)

Figure 1.7

1.2.2 Abstraction Levels of a Data Type

We can distinguish among several levels of reality of data types. Recall our egg structure from Section 1.1.1. We started with the abstract notion of a dozen eggs floating in space and ordered by numbers painted on them. This is an abstraction because it exists only in our imaginations and it concentrates only on the properties in which we are interested, excluding others. We can apply the same technique to the study and design of data types. If we have a list of names, we can think of the names floating in space each with a number attached to it. We can think of a set of operations that we might perform on the list (print the list, find the third name, etc.). We can imagine using such an ***abstract data type*** in a program and, in fact, we can write programs using the operations defined on the data and its structure. We can do so, being concerned with neither how the data will be ***represented*** in the computer nor the details of the code that ***implements*** the operations.

If our program is to execute, we have actually to store and operate on the data by means of computer programs. (In an analogous way, we had actually to store our eggs in a carton or basket and to instruct someone on the actions

When constructing an abstract data type we do not concern ourselves with how it will be implemented by a computer.

necessary to make it appear to the user that his or her abstract notion of the eggs was real.) When using a computer, we often implement our data type using some high-level language. Suppose that we choose Modula-2. We use the data types and data structures provided by the language to build others not provided. For example, we might define *a* as an array of three records.

Such a structure appears to exist on a ***virtual machine***, which appears to execute Modula-2 instructions and implement Modula-2 data types and structures. The Modula-2 machine exists only as a combination of software (perhaps an interpreter or a run-time system for compiled Modula-2 code) and the operating system and hardware of the host computer. We will call this kind of data structure a ***virtual data type***.

Eventually any data structure has to be stored in a physical memory and has to be operated on by a ***physical machine*** (computer). As we will see in the following sections, most random access memories (RAM) are simply a one-dimension array of bytes. No matter how exotic our abstract data type or how elegant our virtual representation, they must all eventually be represented in the one-dimension array of bytes that is the computer's random access memory. The actual physical operations that the machine can perform are limited to those in its ***machine language***. We will call a data type at this level a ***physical data type***. Figure 1.8 is a summary of the various data types.

Modula-2 appears to the user as a virtual machine that executes Modula-2 commands.

Abstract level
  The user
  Database systems
  Computer-aided design and
    computer-aided manufactur-
    ing (CAD/CAM) systems
  Word processors
        •

Virtual level
  High-level languages
  Assembly languages
        •

Physical level
  Machine language
  Microcode
        •

Abstract data types are implemented with virtual data types.
        •

Virtual data types are translated
into physical data types.

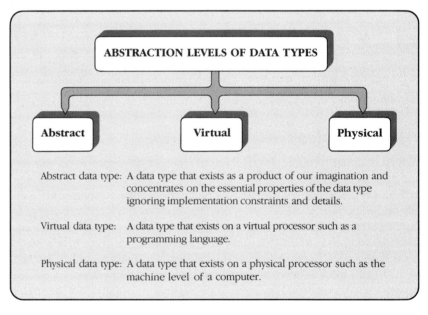

Figure 1.8

The abstraction level and class of data types are orthogonal—they can be considered independently. Figure 1.9 shows some examples of data elements in the various categories. The remaining sections of this chapter are devoted to expanding upon these basic ideas.

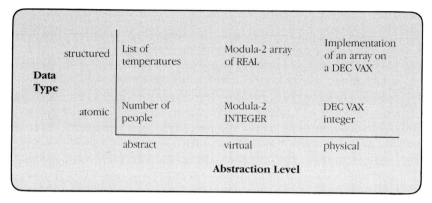

Figure 1.9

1.2.3 *Native Data Types*

A natural level at which to stop the decomposition of data values stored in a digital storage medium is the bit. Logically, we may think of a bit as a data element that must have at any time one of two values, and we will assign these the numeric values 0 and 1. Of course, we may decompose these if we wish. If the value is stored on a magnetic disk, for example, it is represented by an electromagnetic signal recorded on or in the disk surface. Taking the abstract point of view, we will ignore how the values are physically recorded. We might think of this point as one boundary between hardware and software. It is a fuzzy boundary.

All data values in a digital computer are represented as a variety of data structures with only 0's and 1's (bits) as data elements. If the bit level were the only real level provided and every other data structure had to be built from it, the programmer's lot would be tedious indeed. Fortunately, most processors provide certain data types to their users in the form of what we have called abstract data types. The user (ideally) need not know anything about the representation or implementation of the data types in order to use them. Thus, we can write a Modula-2 program without knowing how integers, reals, arrays, and so on, are represented and implemented by the hardware of the computer.

Every processor (high-level language, database system, operating system, computer hardware, and others) has certain atomic data types and data structures that are built in or ***native*** to it. For a given computer's hardware, these are the data types whose operations are implemented directly by its circuitry. The operations are implemented by instructions called ***machine language instructions.*** The collection of all machine language instructions for a given computer forms its ***machine language.*** These operations tend to be particularly efficient since the instructions are implemented by the circuitry of the host computer. The selection and implementation of a computer's native data types are extremely important because any other data types to be manipulated by that computer must be constructed using them as building blocks.

Some native data types for an Intel 8080 processor are

> *byte*
> *address*
> *integer*
> *binary-coded decimal (BCD)*
> *stack*

Some native data types of
Modula-2 are

> *BOOLEAN*
> *CHAR*
> *INTEGER*
> *REAL*
> *POINTER*
> *ARRAY*
> *RECORD*
> *SET*

We have built up a vocabulary to assist us in discussing data elements, data types, and data structures. We will now build a similar vocabulary describing operations and instructions at the physical machine level.

A machine language instruction is logically a sequence of 0's and 1's. One example is the sequence 01000111, which tells an Intel 8080 processor to move the content of register "A" to register "B." Another example is the sequence 0001101101010111, which tells an IBM System/370 (IBM S/370) processor to subtract the content of register "7" from the content of register "5" and put the result in register "5." The contents of registers "5" and "7" are presumed to be integers. There was a time when most programs were written using binary sequences of 0's and 1's, such as those shown above. Such programs were difficult for people to write, read, debug, and modify. These difficulties led to the development of assembly languages.

Typical native data types for mini
and maxi computers are

> *integer*
> *floating-point real*
> *BCD real*
> *character*
> *boolean/logical*
> *bit*
> *byte*
> *word*
> *pointer*

If a machine language instruction is replaced by a mnemonic—which is intended to make it more understandable to people—the result is an ***assembly language instruction.*** The collection of all assembly language instructions for a processor is that processor's ***assembly language.*** The sequence 01000111, for example, is replaced by the mnemonic *mov* B,A for the Intel 8080 processor, and the sequence 0001101101010111 is replaced by *SR* 5,7 for IBM processors. People do not like machine language, and computers cannot execute assembly language. The result is that assembly language must be translated into machine language before it can be executed. This is usually done by a translation program called an ***assembler.***

Assembly language usually represents the lowest-level interface between a programmer and a computer. Assembly language presents the most primitive operations that the computer can perform (ignoring microcoding). A computer's native data types and data structures provide the basic building blocks from which all other data to be manipulated by that processor must be constructed. The process is usually carried out by a high-level language or, more accurately, by the collection of programs that is called a high-level language.

A program written in a high-level
language must be translated into
a program consisting entirely of
machine language instructions
before the program can be
executed.

A ***high-level language*** provides a user with data types at a virtual level. The high-level language operations are translated into a lower-level language and eventually into the machine language of the computer that will execute the program. Each high-level language instruction is translated into one or more (usually more) machine language instructions. By providing programs—called ***compilers*** or ***interpreters***—that do the translation into the machine language instruction sets of several distinct computers, a high-level language can provide a machine independence not provided by assembly languages. (There are programs to translate one assembly language into another, but this is infrequently done.) In fact, there is frequently more than one compiler that translates one high-level language into the machine language of a single computer. One of these compilers may execute rapidly but produce inefficient machine language code. Another may execute slowly but produce results that execute more efficiently.

Just as we speak of the native data types of a particular computer system, so we can speak of the native data types of a particular high-level language. The native data types provided by a high-level language must be represented using the data types native to the computer that will execute the program. Once again, different translators must be provided for different target machines. The ease with which the translation can be accomplished and the efficiency of the results produced depend on the machine language instructions and the data types available on the target processor.

An assembly language provides data types that are machine specific. High-level languages, being independent of specific processors, provide a selection of data types and structures that can be used on a wide variety of computers but that often do not match the native data types of the computer system upon which the program is to be executed. It is very common to find the data type *real* in high-level languages, but many micro- and minicomputer systems do not have hardware that can support it. The translator must provide software routines that allow representation and manipulation of data of this type.

All computers have an atomic data type bit, but very few high-level languages provide it as a data type. Every high-level language has its own particular set of data types, and each computer architecture has its own set of data types. (If one manufacturer makes a computer that sells particularly well, however, it is possible that others will make a computer that executes the same machine language instructions and has the same data types and data structures.)

If a computer's native data types are not built into a particular high-level language, they are usually not accessible to programmers using that language to execute programs on that computer. (The language prevents the user from accessing the data types of the machine on which the program is executed—unless the high-level language can be linked to machine language.) Data types native to a language but not native to the host computer must be implemented in software in order to permit the programmer to use them when writing programs in that language for that host computer.

> The data types and structures of a high-level language must be implemented using the data types and structures native to the target computer.

> Typical data types and structures native to high-level languages are
>
> | | |
> |---|---|
> | *integer* | *character* |
> | *floating-point* | *boolean* |
> | *real* | *pointer* |
> | *BCD real* | *string* |

Exercises 1.2

1. Explain the following terms in your own words:

value	data type
atomic data type	structured data type
component data element	abstract data type
virtual data type	physical data type
native data type	machine language
assembly language	high-level language

2. What is the domain of Modula-2's data type CHAR? What are the defined operations (see Wirth, 1985)?

3. What is the domain of Modula-2's data type BOOLEAN? What are the defined operations?

4. What is the domain of the following structured Modula-2 data type:

> **TYPE** X: **ARRAY** [1..3] **OF** BOOLEAN

List two allowed values of type *X*. What operations of type *X* are provided by Modula-2? Which of them result in a value of type *X*? Which result in a component element value?

5. Define some abstract data types at the user level. Give at least two alternate ways of representing the data using the virtual data types provided by Modula-2.

1.3 Abstract Data Types

We defined abstract data type in Section 1.2. How do we put this concept to use? What are the advantages of using it? In Sections 1.3.1 and 1.3.2 we discuss the design and specification of abstract data types. In Section 1.3.3 we show how the abstractions are implemented using a programming language. Finally, in Section 1.3.4, we review the advantages of using abstract data types.

1.3.1 Specifying an Abstract Data Type

• Atomic type

Recall that an atomic data type includes a set of possible values (its domain) and a set of operations on those values. Suppose that we define an abstract data type whose values are colors. We call the abstract type *Color*. Its specification is shown in Specification 1.1. The form is one that we will use for specifications throughout the text.

The domain includes values that are the primary colors—red, yellow, and blue—and the secondary colors that can be formed by mixing two primary colors. The operations are chosen simply to illustrate the points. The operation *Assign* is, however, necessary because there must *always* be an operation or sequence of operations that enables variables of the type being specified to take on any value in the domain of possible values; *Assign* does so for color.

Specification 1.1   Abstract Atomic Type *Color*

Domain: The set of possible values is *(red, yellow, blue, green, orange, violet)*

Operations: We define four operations:

PROCEDURE Mix(c1,c2: Color): Color   (* *Make a color from c1 and c2.* *)
    pre – c1 and c2 are primary colors.
    post – Mix is the color formed by mixing colors c1 and c2 in equal
        amounts.

continued

Specification 1.1, continued

```
PROCEDURE Primary(c: Color): BOOLEAN                    (* Is c a primary color? *)
    pre  — None.
    post — If c is a primary color, then Primary is true else Primary is false.

PROCEDURE Form(c: Color; VAR c1,c2: Color)             (* Which colors form color c? *)
    pre  — c is not a primary color.
    post — c1 and c2 are the two primary colors that form c.

PROCEDURE Assign(VAR c1: Color; c2: Color)             (* Assign value c2 to c1. *)
    pre  — None.
    post — c1 has the value of c2.
```

What are the statements labeled pre and post? The term **"pre"** is an abbreviation for **precondition.** Simply stated, it is an **assertion** that must be true in order for the operation to execute correctly. Function *Mix,* for example, has a precondition that *c1* and *c2* are primary colors. If either *c1* or *c2* or both are not primary colors, then the effect of executing *Mix* will be undefined. Anything may happen: The program may stop. An incorrect value may be returned. An error message may appear. There will simply be no agreement between the designer who writes the specifications and the programmer who implements them by writing code.

There are also implicit preconditions. The values of *c1* and *c2* must be valid values of the type *Color.* We will always make the assumption (assertion) when passing arguments that they contain valid values.

Suppose that the precondition is true. What can we say? The term **"post"** is short for **postcondition.** It is the assertion that prevails upon completion of the operation. It is a description of the results of the actions performed by the operation. It must be accurately and precisely stated. Note that it does not state *how* the results are achieved, but only *what* the results are to be.

Both the pre- and postconditions can be precisely stated by using a mathematical notation such as the **predicate calculus.** This topic is discussed in Chapter 10. However, in the other chapters of this book, English is used. It is less precise and less formal than the predicate calculus. It is, however, reasonably precise and less confusing to those not skilled in formal methods.

Notice the precondition of procedure *Form.* It specifies that *Form* is defined only for cases in which the value of *c* is not a primary color. How does a user avoid using *Form* on a primary color? Notice that the operation *Primary* allows the user to test the value in *c* before using *Form.* It is a convention that says when a precondition is specified, there should be another operation that allows a user to test for that precondition. Thus, since the precondition of *Form* is that the color be nonprimary, the operation *Primary* is provided to allow the user to test the "primaryness" of a variable's value before passing it to *Form.* The kind of code that must be written to use *Form* correctly is given in the margin.

It is illegal to execute an operation when its precondition is not met. The results of doing so are undefined.

Using Procedure *Form* Correctly

```
(* Assign c a value *)
    ⋮

IF Primary(c)
    THEN c1 := c; c2 := c
    ELSE Form(c,c1,c2)
END;
```

We could have defined *Form* to return $c1 = c2 = c$ if the value of c was primary. In that case, the specification of *Form* would be

```
PROCEDURE Form(c: Color; VAR c1,c2: Color)
    pre   —  None.
    post  —  If c is primary,
             then c1 = c2 = c
             else c1 and c2 are the two primary colors
             that form color c.
```

The decision as to which specification of *Form* to use depends on how the module will be used. Making decisions like this is a typical task of designers of abstract data types.

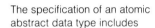

The specification of an atomic abstract data type includes

A domain of allowable values
A set of specified operations

We have written a specification for the abstract data type *Color*. It includes the specification of its domain and its operations. The next step is to implement the data type in an available programming language. Great care would be taken to assure that any implementation meets the specifications. Since we are more interested in structured types, we will discuss that now and will delay an example of implementation until Section 1.3.3.

• Structured abstract type

Suppose that we wish to define an abstract data type called *ReversibleString* whose values are sequences of characters. Suppose that we also specify that the number of characters in such a string is no more than 80. The terms "list" and "sequence" will be discussed in Chapter 4 but can be taken for the moment to imply a linear arrangement of the characters.

Recall that *component element,* or just *element,* refers to the components of the values of a structured data type. In this case, those elements are characters.

Since the data type is to be structured, we must also specify a structure. We can do so informally as follows. There is a first (leftmost) character and a last (rightmost) character. Each character except the first has a unique **predecessor** immediately on its left; each except the last has a unique **successor** immediately on its right. We can think of the characters as being strung together like a string of beads—they have a linear structure.

Thus, any collection of 80 or fewer characters arranged according to the structure specification is an allowable value for the type *ReversibleString*. The set of all possible values of this kind forms the **domain** of the structured type. (See Figure 1.10.) Though it is large, it is not infinite.

What sort of operations should we specify? In this case we choose to specify six operations. *Append* adds a character to the string, whereas *LeftChar* removes one from it; *Length* lets us know at any time how long the string is; *Equal* allows us to test whether two strings are identical; *MakeEmpty* sets a string to the null string (0 length). The last operation, *Reverse,* gives the type its name. It reverses the order of the characters in a string. Specification 1.2 is the specification of data type *ReversibleString*.

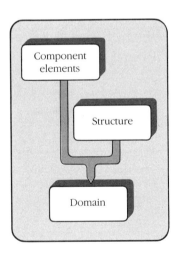

Figure 1.10
The component element type and the structure specification together help specify the domain of the abstract data type.

Specification 1.2   Abstract Data Type *ReversibleStrings*

Elements: The data elements are of type CHAR.

Structure: There is a linear relationship among the characters of each value of a reversible string.

Domain: There are between 0 and 80 characters in any reversible string value.

Operations: In specifying operations, we occasionally have to refer to the value of a reversible string both before and after execution of an operation. We refer to the former as RS-pre and to the latter as RS-post.

PROCEDURE Append(**VAR** RS: ReversibleString; ch: CHAR)
>   **pre** — The number of characters in RS (i.e., RS-pre) is less than 80.
>   **post** — RS (i.e., RS-post) is longer by one character than RS-pre, and the character ch is its last (rightmost) character.

PROCEDURE LeftChar(**VAR** RS: ReversibleString): CHAR
>   **pre** — The number of characters in RS is greater than 0.
>   **post** — LeftChar is the first (leftmost) character of RS-pre; RS is RS-pre less its first character.

PROCEDURE Equal(RS1, RS2: ReversibleString): BOOLEAN
>   **post** — If RS1 and RS2 are equal in length and have the same characters in the same sequence, then Equal is true, else Equal is false.

PROCEDURE Length(RS: ReversibleString): CARDINAL
>   **post** — Length is the number of characters in RS.

PROCEDURE Reverse(**VAR** RS: ReversibleString)
>   **post** — RS is RS-pre with its character sequence reversed; the first and last characters have changed places, the second and next-to-last, and so on.

PROCEDURE MakeEmpty(**VAR** RS: ReversibleString)
>   **post** — RS has 0 characters.

Notice that we have specified the data type of the component elements, the structure among those elements, and the domain of possible values. The cumulative effect of the three is to specify all possible values that an instance of the data type can assume. Operations are specified using the same pre- and postcondition method that we introduced with atomic data type *Color*.

The appearance of *RS* in a precondition unambiguously refers to its value just prior to execution of the operation being specified. An ambiguity arises in stating some postconditions. Certain operations modify the value of the data type; *Append* and *LeftChar* both do so. In the postcondition of these two operations, we need to refer to both the value of *RS* just prior to execution and the resultant value of *RS* just after execution. We use the notation *RS-pre* (*RS'* is often used in the literature) to mean the former, and simply *RS* to mean the

The specification of a structured abstract data type includes

A component element type

A structure that relates the component element values

A domain of allowable structured values

A set of operations on the values in the domain

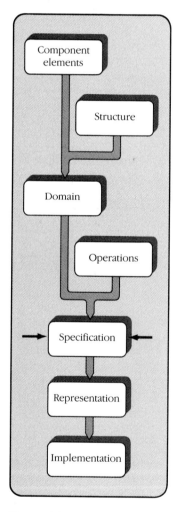

latter. Thus the single notation *RS* refers to different values in the pre- and postconditions.

We are using the programming language Modula-2 throughout this book. Specification 1.2 is written in a language-independent form. In Section 1.3.2, we apply the same notions but use Modula-2's **module** construct to write the specifications, and that is the form that we follow thereafter.

The specifications of an abstract data type (see Figure 1.11) to some extent correspond to the blueprints of a building. The building exists only in the imagination of the architect, and the blueprints are a precise description of it. The contractors who actually build it are both guided and constrained by the blueprints. In this way, the architect's objectives are met.

Like most other analogies, however, this one breaks down. Blueprints are often very detailed and tell the builder what materials to use. The functional specifications, in contrast, seek to constrain the implementor as little as possible. The implementor is free to choose among the native data types of the programming language, the logic of the program, and possibly one of several techniques for doing the same job. Certain choices might produce more efficient algorithms. It is the job of the implementor to make the proper choices.

Specification is a broad concept. What we have done in the *Color* and *ReversibleString* types is to write **functional specifications.** We can also write specifications about other aspects of the abstract types. We might have specified that speed of execution is of paramount importance for an implementation and that the amount of memory used is of no consequence. Though our attention in this text is focused on functional specifications, we spend a great deal of time discussing the relative efficiencies of different implementations of a given abstract data type.

1.3.2 Specifications in Modula-2

We have seen in the previous section how an abstract data type can be specified. Since we will use Modula-2 as the programming language in this book, let us introduce some of the features of Modula-2 that support abstract data typing.

• **Modules**

Modula-2's module construct directly supports the notion of abstract data typing. A module is a collection of constants, types, variables, procedures, and code packaged together as a single unit. Let us refer to those things packaged inside a module as **objects.**

There are three kinds of modules that are separately compilable (see Appendix A):

Program MODULE
DEFINITION MODULE
IMPLEMENTATION MODULE

Figure 1.11
The symbol "→ ←" represents the interface between the user and the implementor.

A fourth module type, which exists only by being embedded within a program or implementation module, is a

Local MODULE

We primarily use the first three module types in this book and will not discuss local modules at this point. Please refer to Appendix A, Section 11, for details of local modules.

A program MODULE is equivalent to what is considered in most programming languages to be a main program. A small example is given in Figure 1.12.

```
MODULE Main;                    (* A main program MODULE.  *)
(* post — Two integers are read from the terminal and
          their sum appears on the terminal. *)

FROM InOut IMPORT Done, ReadInt, WriteInt, WriteLn;

VAR i,j: INTEGER;

BEGIN
  ReadInt(i);
  IF Done
    THEN ReadInt(j);
         IF Done
            THEN WriteLn; WriteInt(i + j, 5)
         END
  END
END Main.
```

Figure 1.12   A program module.

As you can see, with one important exception, this looks quite similar to an equivalent program in other common programming languages such as Pascal or FORTRAN. (Appendix A describes modules and differences between Modula-2 and Pascal.) Though it wasn't necessary in this simple case, types, constants, and procedures could also have been included.

An important statement in Figure 1.12 is

```
FROM InOut IMPORT Done, ReadInt, WriteInt, WriteLn;
```

IMPORT statements inform module *Main* that it is to find another module, one named *InOut,* and that it is to use four objects from *InOut.* One object, *Done,* is a BOOLEAN type variable. The other three objects are procedures. This information is not available from the IMPORT statement alone. We cannot tell if the procedures are function type procedures or what their argument lists are. In order to find the details of the imported objects, we must look at the **DEFINITION MODULE** of *InOut.*

Figure 1.13 has excerpts from the definition module of module *InOut.* The entire module is somewhat large, but all the important points are contained in the pieces excerpted.

```
DEFINITION MODULE InOut;
(* Text file, including terminal, I/O *)

EXPORT QUALIFIED
   EOL, Done, termCH,
   OpenInput, OpenOutput, CloseInput, CloseOutput,
   Read, ReadString, ReadInt, ReadCard,
   Write, WriteLn, WriteString, WriteInt, WriteCard,
   WriteOct, WriteHex;

CONST EOL = 36C;                 (* End of line character. *)
VAR   Done  : BOOLEAN;  (* Operation success/fail flag. *)
      termCH: CHAR;
         .
         .
         .

PROCEDURE ReadInt(VAR x: INTEGER);
(* Read string and convert to integer,
   integer = ["+"|"-"]  digit {digit},
   Leading blanks are ignored,
   Done = "integer was successfully read". *)

PROCEDURE WriteLn;
(* Write end of line marker. *)

PROCEDURE WriteInt(x: INTEGER; n: CARDINAL);
(* Write integer x with (at least) n characters on file
   "out". If n is greater than the number of digits
   needed, blanks are added preceding the number. *)
         .
         .
         .

END InOut.
```

Figure 1.13 Excerpts from definition module *InOut* (from Wirth, 1985, with comments slightly modified).

Module *InOut* is provided to transmit text files to and from I/O devices, including terminals. In order to use it, we must know what objects it has made visible to us. A list of visible objects is given in the **EXPORT** statement. A mixture of constants, variables, and procedures is exported. Types can also be exported, but there was none in this case.

What is each of the objects listed in the EXPORT statement? We find out by reading further in the DEFINITION MODULE. We are interested in *Done, ReadInt, WriteLn,* and *WriteInt,* since those are the objects we chose to import from *InOut* to *Main.*

Done is a boolean variable that is used to indicate the success or failure of certain operations, as we see when looking at the procedure specifications. Reading further, we see that *ReadInt* is a procedure with a single VAR type integer argument. The PROCEDURE statement provides us with the **syntax** of the *ReadInt. ReadInt*'s syntax is the formal rules for using it. The PROCEDURE statement does not, except for the suggestion contained in the name *ReadInt,* tell us what the procedure does.

The comment following the PROCEDURE statement is an attempt to provide the **semantics** of *ReadInt*. It is what we do by stating pre- and postconditions. Wirth (1985) has used a somewhat different convention. The semantics of an operation describe what it does when executed. Thus we can see when reading the comment that it defines what an integer is and what *ReadInt* will do with the integer. A similar construction is used for *WriteLn* and *WriteInt*.

Notice that there are no statements defining the body of each procedure; that is, there is no code following the PROCEDURE statement. Definition modules give only specifications of how to use the operations of the module and, through comments, what the operations do, but not how they will do it. That comes later in an associated **IMPLEMENTATION MODULE.** Thus there can be one definition module, and several implementation modules, each using different techniques to represent the data and to implement the operations. In addition, definition modules export (make visible) to users only what is absolutely necessary for the user to use the module. This idea is called **information hiding.**

The syntax diagram for a definition module is shown in Figure 1.14, which is the same as Figure A.32 in Appendix A, where further details may be found.

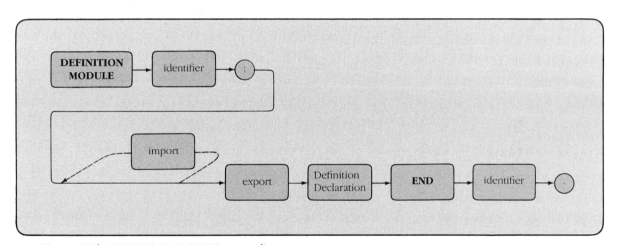

Figure 1.14 • DEFINITION MODULE syntax diagram.

We will see other definition modules shortly, but first let us summarize the major points. In Modula-2, a DEFINITION MODULE

- is used to provide a specification;
- imports objects from other modules as needed;
- tells us which objects are to be made visible (exported) to users of the module;
- specifies the syntax of the objects by formal declarations in Modula-2, such as TYPE, CONST, VAR, and PROCEDURE statements;
- specifies the semantics of the objects informally using Modula-2 comments.

The next question is how modules are related to abstract data types.

• **Modules and abstract data types**

We will use Modula-2's modules in much the same way as we have seen in the example of the module *InOut*. We will use DEFINITION MODULEs to specify the abstract data types that we wish to study. We will specify the semantics of the operations of a data type by comments following the PROCEDURE statements, but we will use pre- and postconditions in those comments.

Let us look at a concrete example. We have seen a language-independent specification of the data type *ReversibleString* in Specification 1.2. We will now recast that specification into a Modula-2 DEFINITION MODULE, the form we will use throughout the remainder of the book. Specification 1.3 is the Modula-2 form of the *ReversibleString* specification. A discussion follows.

Specification 1.3   ReversibleStrings

```
DEFINITION MODULE RevStrings;

(* Elements: The data elements are of type CHAR. *)

(* Structure: There is a linear relationship among the characters of each
      value of a reversible string. *)

(* Domain: There are between 0 and 80 characters in any reversible string
      value. *)

EXPORT QUALIFIED ReversibleString, Append, LeftChar, Length, Reverse,
                 Equal, MakeEmpty;

TYPE Index = [1..80];
     ReversibleString = RECORD
                   size  : CARDINAL;
                   string: ARRAY Index OF CHAR
              END;

(* Operations: In specifying operations, we occasionally have to refer in
      the postcondition to the value of the reversible string before
      execution of the operation.  We refer to that value as RS-pre. *)

PROCEDURE Append(VAR RS: ReversibleString; ch: CHAR);
(* pre  - The number of characters in RS is less than 80.
   post - RS is longer by one character than RS-pre, and the character
          ch is its last (rightmost) character. *)

PROCEDURE LeftChar(VAR RS: ReversibleString): CHAR;
(* pre  - The number of characters in RS is greater than 0.
   post - LeftChar is the first (leftmost) character of RS-pre;
          RS is RS-pre with its first character removed. *)

PROCEDURE Length(RS: ReversibleString): CARDINAL;
(* post - Length is the number of characters in RS. *)
```

continued

Specification 1.3, continued

PROCEDURE Reverse(**VAR** RS: ReversibleString);
(* **post** — RS is RS-pre with its character sequence reversed; the first and
　　　last characters have changed places, the second and next-to-last,
　　　and so on. For example, if RS-pre is 'abcde', then RS is
　　　'edcba'.*)

PROCEDURE Equal(RS1, RS2: ReversibleString): BOOLEAN;
(* **post** — If RS1 and RS2 are of equal length and have the same characters
　　　in the same sequence, then Equal is true, else Equal is false. *)

PROCEDURE MakeEmpty(**VAR** RS: ReversibleString);
(* **post** — RS has 0 characters. *)

END RevStrings.

The EXPORT statement lists all objects that we wish to make visible to
users of the module. In this instance, we export type *ReversibleString* and six
specified operations. The only object declared that is invisible to the user is
type *Index*. A modification to Modula-2 has been proposed (Wirth, 1985a) that
eliminates the EXPORT QUALIFIED statement and exports all objects declared
in the DEFINITION MODULE. Compilers implementing this change are not
available at the time of writing.

The operations of the abstract data type are defined as Modula-2 procedures. The syntax of each is specified by a PROCEDURE statement. The semantics of each are defined by a comment immediately following the PROCEDURE
statement. We use the precondition/postcondition form of specifying the semantics of operations. To reiterate Section 1.3.1, the precondition is a statement (predicate) that must be true for correct execution of the operation. If
the precondition is true, then after execution of the operation the postcondition is true. If the precondition is not true and execution of the operation is
attempted, then that execution is illegal and anything might happen. It is a
serious error to execute an operation when its precondition is false.

We will specify all the data types that we cover in this book—lists, stacks,
queues, trees, sets, and others—with Modula-2 definition modules using the
general form shown in Specification 1.3.

A user of data type *ReversibleStrings* needs only its DEFINITION MODULE
in order to write a module that uses the type. Figure 1.15 is a small program
module that uses *ReversibleStrings* to find out whether strings of characters or
names entered from the terminal are palindromes (are the same character
string when written backwards). Although we could write *Palindrome* using
only the definition module of *ReversibleStrings,* we need an implementation
module for *ReversibleStrings* before we can execute *Palindrome*.

```
MODULE Palindrome;
(* post — The palindromes in a series of strings entered from the terminal
           are identified. Terminates if a string is over 80 characters. *)

FROM InOut      IMPORT EOL, Read, WriteString, WriteLn, Write, ClearScreen;
FROM RevStrings IMPORT ReversibleString, Append, Length, Reverse,
                       Equal, MakeEmpty;

VAR str, rev: ReversibleString;
    ch: CHAR;

BEGIN
   ClearScreen;
   WriteString('Enter one string per line.'); WriteLn;
   MakeEmpty(str);

   LOOP
      Read(ch); Write(ch);                      (* Read and echo a character. *)
      IF ch = EOL THEN EXIT END;                (* Quit on zero length string. *)

      WHILE ch # EOL DO             (* End-of-line char (EOL) marks end of string. *)
         IF Length(str) = 80
            THEN WriteString(' String too long.'); WriteLn;
                 RETURN                          (* "Graceful" program exit. *)
         END;
         Append(str,ch);                          (* Build up the string. *)
         Read(ch); Write(ch)
      END;

      rev := str;                                (* Copy string into rev. *)
      Reverse(rev);
      IF Equal(str, rev)          (* If the string and its reverse are equal. *)
         THEN WriteString('!!Palindrome!! '); WriteLn
         ELSE WriteString('--Not a Palindrome--'); WriteLn
      END;
      MakeEmpty(str)
   END; (* LOOP *)

   RETURN
END Palindrome.
```

Figure 1.15   Palindrome.

Writing specifications and definition modules is only part of the process of abstract data typing. The specifications are only useful if we can implement them. Let us now look at the process of implementation in Modula-2.

1.3.3 Implementation Using Modula-2

Specifications, like blueprints, are only abstractions. In order to carry through the process, we must implement them by using the native data types of some programming language to *represent* the specified types, and by using the constructs of the language to write code to *implement* the operations. We will continue with the *RevString* example given in Specification 1.3 and with the module facilities of Modula-2.

• Representation

The **representation** of an abstract data type is the combination of other data types that we employ in order to store and manipulate it on the processor we are using. In our example, we are using Modula-2. We have chosen to represent type *ReversibleString* as shown in the **TYPE** statement of Specification 1.3:

```
TYPE Index = [1..80];
     ReversibleString = RECORD
                           size  : CARDINAL;
                           string: ARRAY Index OF CHAR
                        END;
```

This representation of *ReversibleString* is a combination of the native data types of Modula-2. It could also include other abstract data types, though it does not in this case. This mixture of types is typical of Modula-2 (and of other languages).

• Implementation

Next, we have to write the code that implements the abstract operations. The collection of algorithms is called the **implementation** of the abstract type. (When there is no danger of confusion, we will shorten the terminology by using the term "implementation" to mean the combination of representation and implementation as they are defined above.)

Module 1.1 is a Modula-2 IMPLEMENTATION MODULE containing algorithms that implement the operations specified in the DEFINITION MODULE (Specification 1.3). The implementation is simple and straightforward in this case. The DEFINITION MODULE of Specification 1.3 must be compiled prior to compiling either *Palindrome* or Implementation Module 1.1, both of which need it. Implementation Module 1.1 must be compiled prior to execution of *Palindrome* since *Palindrome* calls its procedures while executing. It is generally true that **modules can be compiled separately from, but not independently of, each other.**

Enter one string per line.
ROBERT
--Not a Palindrome--
BOB
!!Palindrome!!
ANNE
--Not a Palindrome--
ANNA
!!Palindrome!!
ABCDEFGFEDCBA
!!Palindrome!!
!@#$%↑&*()_+_)(*&↑%$#@!
!!Palindrome!!

Figure 1.16
Results from *Palindrome*.

Implementation Module 1.1 *ReversibleStrings*

```
IMPLEMENTATION MODULE RevStrings;                        (* Meets Specification 1.3. *)

PROCEDURE Append(VAR RS: ReversibleString; ch: CHAR);    (* Append ch to the *)
BEGIN                                                    (* end of RS.       *)
   WITH RS DO
      size:= size + 1;
      string[size] := ch
   END
END Append;

PROCEDURE LeftChar(VAR RS: ReversibleString): CHAR;      (* Delete and return the *)
VAR i : Index;                                           (* first character of RS. *)
    ch: CHAR;
BEGIN
   WITH RS DO
      ch := string[1];
      FOR i := 2 TO size DO
         string[i-1] := string[i]
      END;
      size := size - 1;
      RETURN ch
   END
END LeftChar;

PROCEDURE Length(RS: ReversibleString): CARDINAL;    (* Return the length of RS. *)
BEGIN
   RETURN RS.size
END Length;

PROCEDURE Reverse(VAR RS: ReversibleString);         (* Reverse the sequence of *)
                                                     (* characters in RS.       *)
VAR i    : Index;
    temp: CHAR;
BEGIN
   WITH RS DO
      FOR i := 1 TO (size DIV 2) DO
         temp := string[i];                                (* Swap characters. *)
         string[i] := string[size-i+1];
         string[size-i+1] := temp
      END
   END
END Reverse;
```

continued

Implementation Module 1.1, continued

```
PROCEDURE Equal(RS1, RS2: ReversibleString): BOOLEAN;      (* Are RS1 and RS2 of *)
VAR i: Index;                                  (* equal length and do they have the same *)
BEGIN                                          (* characters in the same sequence?        *)
    IF RS1.size # RS2.size
       THEN RETURN FALSE
    ELSE FOR i := 1 TO RS1.size DO
             IF RS1.string[i] # RS2.string[i]
                THEN RETURN FALSE
             END
         END
    END;
    RETURN TRUE
END Equal;

PROCEDURE MakeEmpty(VAR RS: ReversibleString);             (* Make RS empty. *)
BEGIN
    RS.size := 0
END MakeEmpty;

END RevStrings.
```

Note that Implementation Module 1.1 did not need to redeclare types *ReversibleString* and *Index* since they are available from the compiled definition module. Also note that procedure *Append* makes no special provision for executing when the input string *RS* is full (RS.size = 80). It does not even check to see that that is the case. The precondition states clearly that the procedure is not to be executed if *RS* has 80 characters. The task of ensuring that *RS* has fewer than 80 characters is assigned by the precondition to the user, who is provided with an operation to perform the test (*Length*). If the user executes *Append* while violating the precondition, then the program will be in error regardless of whether *Append* detects the condition. (See Appendix E for a more complete discussion of the reasons.)

Each implementation module must have a corresponding definition module that specifies it. The definition module must be compiled before the implementation module can be compiled. If a definition module is changed, then all implementation modules that have been written to meet the specifications must also be changed and recompiled. Modula-2 compilers have mechanisms that police the correspondence of implementation and definition modules. If an implementation module is changed but the corresponding definition module is not changed, then modules that import from the definition module need *not* be rewritten. Users are insulated from changes in implementations but not from changes in specifications.

Throughout this book we will use Modula-2 definition modules to specify data types and follow with one or more implementation modules that implement the data type, often in a number of alternate ways. With this approach we can clearly separate the abstraction of a data type from its implementation and then study a variety of implementation techniques.

One of the major objectives of abstract data typing is to hide all unnecessary details of representation and implementation from the user. In order to use the abstract type *ReversibleString,* the user need not know that it is represented as an array nor the details of the code that implements the operations. We **encapsulate** those details inside the module to achieve information hiding.

We will use a graphic device to emphasize this point. Figure 1.17, which looks similar to an integrated circuit chip, summarizes the module's interface. On the left are the operations. Functions are denoted by a ($\diamond$), symbolizing that a value is returned for the procedure name. Values passed in arguments to and from the module are shown on the right. We call this graphic device a **capsule.**

Only those objects that are shown as lines entering or leaving the module are accessible to the user. In later chapters, we will hide the data structure itself inside the module.

The visibility of the data is an important matter, and the only way in which a user is allowed to access or manipulate the data is through the specified operations. The data are protected from the undefined manipulations, and we can therefore be far more certain that their use is free of errors.

In summary, we have seen how an abstract data type is defined and specified. The specification forms an interface between the user of the data type and the creator of a module that implements it. The module encapsulates and hides all implementation details from the user. Many different modules can be written that implement the same abstract type. All must conform to exactly the same specifications. Each will have certain relative efficiencies and performance characteristics.

A module hides the data and algorithms by encapsulating them.

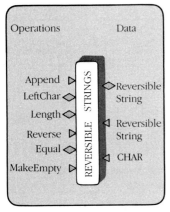

Figure 1.17
ReversibleString capsule. Symbols on left: $\diamond$, function; $\triangleright$, procedure. Symbols on right: $\triangleleft$ input value only; $\diamond$, input and output value; $\triangleright$, output value only. These arrows are used in the capsules throughout this book.

1.3.4 Advantages of Abstract Data Types

There are several important advantages associated with approaching the study of data structures from the point of view of abstract data types. In Sections 1.3.1, 1.3.2, and 1.3.3 we saw several of them—precise specifications, modularity, and information hiding. We will now look briefly at three others—***simplicity, integrity,*** and ***implementation independence.***

• Simplicity

This text is organized around the study of abstract data types—their specification, representation, and implementation. An initial problem with this approach is the use of the word "abstract." Unfortunately, many people infer that if something is abstract it is theoretical, abstruse, and therefore difficult to understand. In computer science the process of **abstraction** is intended to have just the opposite effect. The goal is to simplify by separating the essential

An abstraction is an idea that concentrates on the essential properties of something rather than on concrete realizations or actual cases.

qualities of data, their structure and operations, from the inessential details of their representation and implementation.

One of the basic problems in computer science is that the amount of complexity that the human mind can cope with at any instant in time is considerably less than that embodied in much of the software that we might wish to build. This is even true of the data structures that we wish to study in an introductory text such as this. Our approach is therefore to begin the study of each data structure by considering only the specification of its abstract data type, independent of its representation and implementation. This has the effect, as has been noted by computer scientists for some time, of simplifying the study of the data structure.

It would be incorrect to infer that the study of representation and implementation is ignored or given secondary consideration. After the specification of each abstract data type, we carefully consider, usually from more than one point of view, representations, implementations, and associated performance issues.

Thus we attempt to bring the power of abstraction to bear on the study of data structures. In order to do that, we provide a template or consistent approach, which we use to view and discuss each data structure. Our template is called an abstract data structure and consists of three components: specification, representation, and implementation. Specifications are written using Modula-2 definition modules. Representations are developed using the data types of Modula-2. Implementations are given using Modula-2 implementation modules.

• Integrity

Let us refer to the abstract egg structure described in Section 1.1. Suppose that we have implemented the abstract structure so that we have a dozen eggs, numbered from 1 to 12, stored in some container. We are now ready to let users perform operations on the egg structure. What operations will be permitted? One possibility is to let users invent and implement their own operations. Any operation that they invent will be allowed. Another possibility is to allow only those operations that we have both specified and implemented.

It is certainly true that if k is any integer between 1 and 12, we do not want to allow, at any time, more than one egg in the container whose number is k. This condition is an ***integrity constraint*** that applies to our abstract egg structure. Another constraint is that we do not want to allow more than 12 eggs in the same box at the same time. Attempting to add a 13th egg may have a disastrous effect! The question is how to enforce these and other similar constraints.

If we specify an *Insert* operation, we can implement that operation in such a way that any attempt to insert an egg whose number is the same as an egg already in the box will fail. If we give users direct access to the box of eggs and if we permit them to implement their own operations, then we have no way of assuring that the integrity of our box of eggs will be maintained. (Some

The abstract data type approach lends itself in a natural way to separating the specification of a data type from its implementation. The implementation can then assure that the integrity of the data structure is protected.

disgruntled user may implement the operation *Smash k!* He or she might even put it in a loop!!!)

Our approach is to implement data structures using Modula-2 implementation modules. They act as "black boxes" with push buttons—one for each defined function or procedure—and data lines. The user cannot see into the interior but can only use the box by pushing the available buttons. Data can enter and leave the box only on the data lines. The user has no direct access to the data structure. The data structure and the algorithms that implement the operations are encapsulated within the implementation module. The integrity of the data structure that is hidden within the box (module) is protected because the user only accesses it through operations that are separately specified and implemented. If the operations are all implemented correctly (and if the user does not subvert the rules in some illegal way), then the integrity of the data structure can be guaranteed.

Note that the abstract data type approach lends itself in a natural way to separating the specification of a data type from its implementation. The specification defines an interface that is done first with (ideally) no attention paid to the way in which the representation and implementation will be carried out. The implementation is then done very carefully and in such a way as to assure preservation of the integrity of the data structure. Users of the data structure whose only access to it is through the defined operations can never compromise its integrity.

• Implementation independence

Let us return to our abstract egg structure. Suppose that there are several people who are performing operations on our container of eggs. We may not know what they are all doing, but we do know that each user is only permitted to perform operations listed in the specifications and implemented so as to guarantee the integrity of our box of eggs.

Implementation independence frees the user from nonfunctional details. The implementation may be changed with no effect on the way in which the program executes. It may, however, affect the performance—that is, time, space, maintainability.

Suppose further that it is desirable—perhaps even imperative—for us to change the way in which we implement the abstract egg structure. Perhaps we can no longer obtain cartons organized like the ones we have been using. Or perhaps we have discovered that it would be more efficient to implement some operations in a different way. What effect will changes in our representation and implementation have on people already using the abstract egg structure? There should be no change apparent to the users. The operations should all act functionally the same as they did before the change. The performance that a user experiences or the details of how some operations are carried out may change, but the results will not.

For example, if we change the technique used to perform an operation—without changing the operation performed—then the user may see a change in the performance of the module containing that operation but will not see any change in the results produced. The user is protected from changes in the way in which operations are implemented.

In Modula-2 a program accesses operations whose details are given in an implementation module by linking to the corresponding definition module.

Although a change in the implementation module does *not* require programs that use it to be recompiled, it *does* require that the program be relinked to the new compiled implementation.

Exercises 1.3

1. Explain the following terms in your own words:

precondition	implementation independence
domain	postcondition
specification of an abstract data type	component data element
representation	module
implementation	information hiding
encapsulation	integrity
simplicity	

2. We have seen that the use of an operation when its precondition is not met is illegal. It is the duty of the user of the operation to ensure that this does not happen. However, users can make mistakes. Discuss the extent to which an implementation of an operation should check the validity of its own precondition. What should it do if the precondition is found to be false?
3. We have seen that for structured abstract data types, the data type of the component elements and the structure definition join together to help define the domain. What other factors may enter into the domain definition? Give an example.

1.4 Elements and Structure—An Overview

1.4.1 Data Elements

We begin the specification of every abstract data structure by describing its data elements. An element in computer science is frequently information about an actual physical object. We started the discussion in this chapter with an abstract egg structure and a representation of eggs stored in cartons. Of course, we cannot store eggs in a computer memory. What we can store is data describing the eggs. If we say that our elements are eggs, what we really mean is that each of the elements in our computer model is a collection of information about an egg. For example, we might have data elements that consist of an egg number, weight, and color. We speak (metaphorically) of this collection of information as an egg.

What we store in computer memories is not the actual objects of interest, but rather information about them.

  A potential problem arises immediately. What if the information in one of our elements is not sufficient to specify exactly one object of the type being described? In the above example suppose that the element (9,42,brown) describes three distinct eggs. Life becomes more complicated. For example, what does the operation *Retrieve* (9,42,brown) mean? Does it mean to *Retrieve* all three eggs, or does it mean to *Retrieve* the first one found, or does it mean that an error should be reported?

We assume in most cases throughout this book that each data element has the unique identification property.

We will assume in most cases throughout this book that each element (actually the information that comprises an element) has the ***unique identification property.*** The information content of each element uniquely identifies precisely one corresponding object. In fact, we carry the idea one step further.

It is usually the case that some subset of the information comprising an element has the unique identification property. For example, *egg number* might be assigned so as to have a different value for each individual egg. We will partition the data element into two parts—a key part and a data part. The ***key part*** must have the unique identification property; the ***data part*** contains additional information about the unique object specified by the key part.

Each element is partitioned into a key part and a data part.

•

The key part of an element must have the unique identification property.

This approach to treating the component data elements of data structures is used throughout this book. We use a "standard" element type:

```
TYPE StdElement = RECORD
                    key : KeyType;    (* Unique identifier. *)
                    data: DataType    (* Element data items. *)
                  END;
```

Of course, in each case, KeyType and DataType must be described. In the case of data describing eggs, we might have

```
CONST MaxEgg = 10000;

TYPE  KeyType   = [1..MaxEgg];
      ColorType = (brown, white);
      DataType  = RECORD
                    weight: [1..100];    (* In grams. *)
                    color : ColorType
                  END;
```

Either the key component or the data component of an element may be made up of any number of atomic elements.

Note that in our egg example the data component has two components—weight and color. The key component is atomic. In general, however, either or both can be made up of many components. We will call these components ***items*** or ***fields***.

The structural aspects of data structures determine the basic organization of this (and most other) data structures texts.

1.4.2 Structure

One of the components of the specification of a data type is the relationship among its elements. Several aspects of these relationships occur so frequently and are of such general applicability that they are worth mentioning in this introductory chapter. In fact, the structural aspect of a data structure is so important that most (if not all) data structures are basically organized around it.

The four basic structural relationships discussed in this text are

Set
Linear
Tree or Hierarchical
Graph or Network

There are four basic structural relationships illustrated in Figure 1.18 and discussed in this book. A structure in which there is no relationship among the elements other than their belonging to the set of elements comprising the data structure is closely related to the mathematical notion of a **set.** Structures in which each element is related to one other element (a one-to-one relationship) are said to be **linear.** Those in which the relationships are one-to-many are called **tree** or **hierarchical** structures. Sets of elements in which the relationships are many-to-many are said to have a **graph** (in the graph theory sense) or **network** structure. The chapters of this book are loosely organized according to these categories of relationships.

In addition to these basic relationships, the elements of a data structure may be **totally ordered.** What does that mean?

We are interested in relationships between elements. In almost every case of practical interest, relationships between elements will be determined by the relationships between the key values of those elements. Throughout this book we assume that the relationship among any collection of elements is the same as the relationship among the key components of those elements.

We know and are comfortable with the fact that the integers, when combined with the **comparison operator,** $<=$, form an ordered set. If $a, b,$ and c are integers, the following are true:

1. $a <= a$
2. If $a <= b$ and $b <= c$ then $a <= c$
3. If $a <= b$ and $b <= a$ then $a = b$

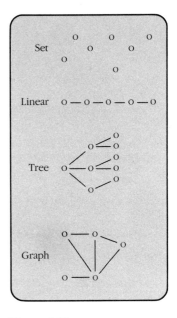

Figure 1.18
Basic structural relationships.

Since items (1), (2), and (3) are true, we say that the integers are **partially ordered** with respect to the operation $<=$. In addition, we know that any two integers can be compared in the sense that

4. Either $a <= b$ or $b <= a$

Adding (4) enables us to say that the integers are totally ordered by the operator $<=$. We can easily generalize all this to any set of elements—for example, S, and any relation—for example, $<=$, defined on pairs of elements of S. If $a, b,$ and c are arbitrary elements of S, and if (1)–(4) are all true, then S is said to be totally ordered (we will henceforth simply say ordered) by $<=$. The elements of S could be of any data type for which the comparison operator $<=$ is defined.

What does this mean for the elements that are the basis of the data structures in this book? In an intuitive sense, a set of elements is ordered if any two elements can be "compared" and if, as a result of that comparison, we can establish either that one element is "larger" than the other or that the two elements are the same. This is certainly true for integers if saying that b is larger than a means that $b > a$.

Let us look at our egg data structure as an example. As above, let an egg element consist of an egg number (which is the key), a weight, and a color. Since the egg numbers are integers, our egg elements are ordered by the relation $<=$.

In many cases the key component of an element is either an integer or a real number. In such cases the operator $<=$ provides a useful ordering of the set of elements. It is also frequently the case that the key component of an

Intuitively, a set is ordered with respect to a relation if any two elements of the set can be compared (by the relation) and if it can always be concluded either that one of the elements is "larger" than the other or that they are the same element.

element is a sequence of characters such as a name or a word or a description of an object. In this case, the operator that orders the elements must be different. Let S_1 and S_2 be two sequences of characters (or character strings). We say that $S_1 <= S_2$ if S_1 is the same as, or alphabetically precedes, S_2. There is another word that comes up in this context. Instead of referring to the alphabetical ordering of character strings, we can refer to their **lexicographic ordering**.

Finally, what is the difference between an **ordered set** of elements and a **linear set** of elements?

Our intuition about ordered sets is likely to be based on attributes of the integers (together with the operator $<=$) since the integers are such a familiar example. This is unfortunate in our present setting because the integers comprise a set that is both ordered and linear, whereas an ordered set does not always have a linear structure. Let us consider two examples. The first is particularly simple and begins with the set of elements $S = \{a, b, c, d\}$. These four elements are shown in Figure 1.19 linked together by directed arcs. Let x and y be any pair of these elements. We will say that $x <= y$ if there is a directed arc or sequence of directed arcs that originates at x and terminates at y. We will also say that $x <= x$. S, together with the operator $<=$, forms an ordered set.

Let us define y to be the **successor** of x if there is a directed edge from x to y. The essence of linearity is that successors are unique. In our example element a has two successors and therefore S, together with the prescribed notion of successor, is not a linear set.

The second example of a set in which elements are ordered but not linear is the set of real numbers together with the operation $<=$. We are tempted to say that if r is any real number, the successor of r is the smallest real number greater than r. The problem is that such a real number does not exist since between any two real numbers there is an infinite number of other real numbers.

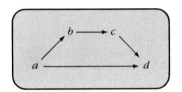

Figure 1.19

A finite set of elements is linear if the set is empty, or if the set contains a single element, or if the following four conditions are met:

1. There is a unique element called the first.
2. There is a unique element called the last.
3. Every element, except the last, has a unique successor.
4. Every element, except the first, has a unique predecessor.

•

Native Modula-2 data types that are ordered and that include the relational operators are

CHAR
INTEGER
enumerated
REAL
CARDINAL

Native Modula-2 data types that are linear

CHAR
INTEGER
enumerated
CARDINAL

1.4.3 Linear and Ordered Structures

We have just described two relationships that can exist among the elements of a data type or the component elements of a data structure. Each of these structures gives rise to a set of operations. These structures and the corresponding operations are so common that we frequently use the operations without thinking about the fact that they are tied to the underlying structure.

If a set of elements is ordered, we can specify—and implement—a collection of relational operators ($=, <, <=, >, >=, \#$) for these elements. Most data types that are built into high-level programming languages are ordered, and most of them include the relational operators in their specification.

If a collection of elements has a linear structure, we can specify find-the-successor, find-the-predecessor, and position operations. In subsequent chapters we will call them *FindNext, FindPrior,* and *CurPos.* These operations are possible because the elements to which they are applied have a linear structure.

There is a natural one-to-one correspondence between a finite set of elements with a linear structure and a subset of the natural numbers (see Figure 1.20). The unique first element can be associated with 1, its successor with 2, and so on, until the last element is associated with some integer—say *n*. We therefore can, and frequently do, refer to the *k*th element in a linear structure. This correspondence adds an implicit ordered structure to the elements. That is, we can say that the *j*th element **precedes** the *k*th element if $j < k$.

Modula-2 has a standard function ORD(x) that returns the relative position of *x* in the domain of values of its type; the type must be linear. If, for example, we have a linear type such as an enumeration for Day,

TYPE Day = (Sun, Mon, Tue, Wed, Thu, Fri, Sat);

then ORD(Tue) would return a value of 2. The ordinal value (position) of the first element is defined by Modula-2 to be 0. In contrast, the position of the first element in the linear types that we specify in this book is 1.

ORD can be applied to the following linear types of Modula-2: CHAR, INTEGER, CARDINAL, any enumerated type, and BOOLEAN (which is defined as an enumerated type; see Appendix A). ORD is a function that returns a value of type CARDINAL.

$$e - e - e - e - e - e$$
$$1 \quad 2 \quad 3 \quad 4 \quad 5 \quad 6$$

Figure 1.20
Correspondence between elements (*e*) with a linear structure and the natural numbers.

1.4.4 Data Structures and High-Level Languages

Consider high-level languages. Each language presents the user with a set of native data types. Each language includes predefined operations and atomic data types. The atomic data types usually include *integer, real, boolean,* and *character.* The values that an element of a given data type can take on and the operations are predefined for the type. A Modula-2 variable of type INTEGER can assume only certain values. The allowable range of values depends on which implementation of Modula-2 is being used.

Some languages allow the user to define new atomic data types. For example, Modula-2 allows the programmer to define a new data type by enumeration as follows:

TYPE color = (red, blue, green, yellow);

or as a subrange of an existing data type:

TYPE Sub = [-5..3];

These user-defined atomic data types give rise to an implicit abstract data type, shown on page 34 under the heading "Enumerated Types." Modula-2 requires that any additional operators be defined using functions and procedures.

High-level languages provide a wide variety of facilities for building data structures using atomic data types. Consider the native data type ARRAY. An

High-Level Languages

FORTRAN
COBOL
PL/I
Pascal
C
Ada
Mesa
Modula-2
LISP
Snobol
PROLOG

Enumerated Types

An implicit abstract data type that Modula-2 provides for user-defined atomic data types is as follows:

1. The elements are specified by the user by enumeration or as a subrange of an existing data type.
2. The structure is both ordered and linear.
3. The operations are
   Assignment :=
   Relational =, #, <, <=, >, >=
   Functional ORD, VAL

•

Scheme 1

Names are stored in successive memory locations.

Address	Name
1000	Milton
1008	Dickens
1016	Eliot
1024	Arnold
1032	Conrad

•

Scheme 2

Each name is positioned in memory according to the value of its first letter. The address is given by

1000 + 8 * [ORD(fl) − ORD('A')]

where fl is the first letter of the name.

Address	Name
1000	Arnold
1008	—
1016	Conrad
1024	Dickens
1032	Eliot
1040	—
⋮	⋮
1104	Milton

array might be composed of data elements that are of some more primitive data type such as INTEGER or REAL. All the most widely used programming languages provide for the definition of arrays. The operators provided differ. BASIC has a matrix add operator that will add the corresponding elements of two equal-rank matrices. COBOL has no such operator. An important type of array is an array whose elements are records. BASIC and FORTRAN have no facility for defining the data structure of type record, whereas COBOL, Pascal, Modula-2, and C do.

An appropriate set of built-in data structures and facilities for implementing other programmer-defined data structures is a very important part of high-level languages. Modern languages tend to provide for a wider choice of data structures. It is instructive to compare the data structure facilities of languages in the following chronological order—FORTRAN, COBOL, PL/I, BASIC, Pascal, C, Modula-2, Ada—and note the progressive addition (except for PL/I) of such facilities.

FORTRAN has arrays, but neither records nor pointers; COBOL has both arrays and records, but not pointers; Pascal has all three; Modula-2 has all three, plus a generalized data structuring facility for implementing abstract data types.

1.4.5 Representing Abstract Structure

In this section we will introduce part of the terminology that will be used to discuss the implementation of data structures. The basic terms that are frequently cited are introduced here, in one place. Other terms will be introduced as appropriate throughout the book.

We will base our discussion on a linear list of names. We want to store these names in random access memory. There are several ways that we could do this; Scheme 1 and Scheme 2, shown in the margin, are two of these ways. We have assumed that each name occupies a maximum of 8 bytes.

The logical structure is linear. Scheme 1 implements this logical structure by storing the successor immediately after the name it follows.

The first point to be made, which may seem rather obvious, is that in order to retrieve an element we must first know its address. There are two basic ways to find an element's address. The first way is to calculate it. With Scheme 1, given the address of the ith record, we can **calculate** the address of the $(i + 1)$st record. The required expression is

$$\text{Address} = \text{Address} + 8$$

This expression tells us, given the address of a record, how to find the address of its logical successor. Thus, Scheme 1 implements the logical structure of the data by allowing us to calculate the address of a logical successor. This is possible because of the way in which elements are positioned in memory.

With Scheme 2 we have no way of finding the logical successor of a record. It prevents us from operating on the data using its logical structure.

Suppose our operation is to find the address at which a given name is stored. (If you are wondering why we would want to do this, imagine that additional information is stored along with each name and that we want some of that information for a specific person.) We could perform this operation with Scheme 1, but it would require a sequential scan of the elements. With Scheme 2, we can calculate the required address directly. Once again, determining the address of the target element involves a simple calculation. The calculation does the job because of the way the elements are positioned in memory. (The alert reader will be anxious to point out a potential problem with Scheme 2. What if there are two, or more, names with the same first character?)

In Schemes 1 and 2 we have obtained the address we wanted by carefully positioning the data elements in the memory and then using a simple expression to calculate it. There is a second basic way to get the address of a target element.

Each element in Scheme 3 (see margin) contains both a name and an address. The address is not part of the element, it is part of a superstructure used to relate the stored elements. The address is the address of the element's logical successor. The data can now be accessed according to its logical structure. Given the address of any element, we can find the address of its successor by extracting it from the information whose location we know. The address of our target element is appended to a related element. The structure we have built is a **linked structure.** It is implemented using pointers that are appended to the data elements.

Scheme 3 implements the given logical order by **linking** the elements together in the proper sequence. Scheme 1 implements the logical structure by **positioning** the elements in memory so that target addresses can be calculated.

Scheme 3

The entry at 992 is used to locate the first element.

Address	Name	Successor Address
992	—	1000
1000	Arnold	1016
1008	—	—
1016	Conrad	1024
1024	Dickens	1032
1032	Eliot	1104
1040	—	—
⋮	⋮	⋮
1104	Milton	—

> ***There are two basic techniques for implementing logical structures:***
>
> 1. ***Positioning and calculation***
> 2. ***Linking***

Exercises 1.4

1. Explain in your own words the following terms:

unique identification property	partially ordered
linear relationship	totally ordered
set relationship	lexicographic order
tree structure	ordered set
graph structure	positioning and calculation
linked structure	

2. Which attributes (or combination of attributes) of commonly available data on the following entities have the unique identification property?
   a. Persons
   b. Universities
   c. Corporations
   d. Dogs
3. List some real-world objects or organizations that are organized according to the following structure:
   a. Set
   b. Linear
   c. Tree or hierarchy
   d. Graph or network
4. Is the set of ASCII characters linear? Ordered? Totally ordered?
5. Are the elements of the Modula-2 array

   VAR a: **ARRAY** [1..10] **OF** REAL

   ordered? If so, in what way?
6. Refer to the list of names in Section 1.4.5. Which of the implementation schemes is most efficient for each of the following operations?
   a. Find a given name.
   b. Print out all the names in any order.
   c. Find the fifth name in alphabetical order.
   d. Delete a given name. Assume you know its position or the name to be deleted.

1.5 Virtual and Physical Data Types

If an abstract data structure is to be of more than theoretical interest, it must be implemented. Although the user still deals with the abstract conception of the structure, and, indeed, the notion of abstract data structuring is intended to guarantee that the user need deal with no more than that, the implementor must face the problems of representation and implementation. The abstraction can be treated as the functional specifications of a "black box." The implementor must design the internals of the box so that memory space is not wasted and the operations are performed simply and efficiently. The black box should be compact and execute rapidly. There are other issues. Does the user know in advance how many data are to be expected? If so, certain efficiencies can be gained. If not, the box may have to be made expandable. Are the data elements of fixed and known length, or is the element length unknown until the data are actually received by the program? Does the element size vary within the same data structure?

   The designer can make certain operations efficient at the expense of others. Which operations are important to the user with regard to efficiency of execution? Trade-offs can often be made between efficiency in the use of the storage medium and efficiency in the execution of operations. Which is the more important to the user? All these questions, and others, must be answered before an effective design can begin.

That is only the beginning of the story. An implementor must be familiar with the physical tools available for implementation—memories, processors, and techniques for recording structure—and must have a good knowledge of well-known data structures and their performance characteristics. The remainder of this section is concerned with implementation tools, algorithms, and performance. Well-known data structures and their abstract specification, implementation, complexity, and performance are the subjects of the remainder of this book.

1.5.1 Memories

Computers can remember. Like humans, most have several kinds of memories (although we know far more about computer memories than we do about human memories). Memories come in many forms—large and small; fast and slow; volatile (needing constant power in order to remember) and nonvolatile; random access, direct access, and sequential access; portable and nonportable (attached permanently to the rest of the system). As a rule of thumb, ***random access memories (RAM)*** are fast (micro- and nanosecond access times), relatively small (ranging from a few bytes to a few million bytes), volatile (although some types are not), and nonportable. ***Direct access memories (DAM),*** which are most commonly encountered in the form of magnetic disks, are moderately fast (millisecond access times), possibly very large [ranging from a few hundred thousand bytes (floppy disks) to gigabytes (billions of bytes), with most hard disks having several tens of millions to several hundreds of millions of bytes], nonvolatile, and sometimes portable. ***Sequential access memories (SAM)*** such as magnetic tape are slow (seconds and minutes to access some random element), hold roughly the same amount of data as moderate size magnetic disks (but can be made quite small and compact such as cassettes), and are always nonvolatile and portable.

Most systems use a mixture of memory types. Random access memory is very desirable but is expensive. The faster it is, the higher the cost. ***General purpose registers*** are the fastest and most expensive, so most systems have only a few such registers. ***Cache*** memory (a form of fast, random access memory) is very fast and far more expensive than random access memory. On systems that have such memory, we can typically expect to find several thousand bytes of it. Pages of the random access memory that are being heavily used are shifted into the cache to achieve better performance. All of these memories—random access memory, cache, and register—are relatively small and volatile. Computer systems need other memories that provide for the long-term storage of large volumes of data. Data in these memories are not processed directly, but are transferred to the fast memories—usually random access memory—before processing. Since data structures containing data stored on direct access memories and sequential access memories can be very large, only part of them can reside in random access memory at any one time. Such data structures are called ***files***.

Memory	Speed	Capacity	Cost
Register	Fast	Small	Expensive
Cache	↑	↑	↑
RAM	│	│	│
DAM	↓	↓	↓
SAM	Slow	Large	Cheap

The term "random access" refers to the characteristics of the manner and timing of access to data elements of the memory. By saying that a memory has such access we mean that the time necessary to fetch the data stored in any randomly chosen position of the memory is the same for all cells of the memory. Typically, the times range from several nanoseconds to several microseconds, with the latter being more common. In the remainder of this book we will assume a random access memory that behaves functionally as follows:

TYPE MEMORY = **ARRAY** [0..MemorySize-1] **OF** BYTE

where MemorySize is the number of bytes in the memory.

The type of memory being used has a definite effect on the performance of data structures implemented on it. Some data structures that have excellent performance characteristics in random access memory are hopelessly inefficient when implemented in direct access memories or sequential access memories. Two implementations—for example, *A* and *B*—of the same abstract data structure in random access memory might be compared to find that *A* performs far better than *B*, whereas if implemented in direct access memories, *B* could be far superior to *A*. ***This book concentrates on data structures that are implemented in a random access memory. You should always be aware that the kinds of implementations chosen and their relative performance characteristics are completely dependent on this assumption.*** Although all of the data structures that we will discuss can theoretically be implemented in direct access memories and sequential access memories, many are rendered useless due to poor performance in those types of memories.

Data structures implemented in direct access memories and sequential access memories (files) form such a large and important topic that it is not possible to treat them in only one or two chapters. Although files are mentioned from time to time, we will leave their comprehensive and thorough coverage to another book. For the same reason, a thorough discussion of the characteristics of direct and sequential access memory is also deferred.

1.5.2 Processors

A second important aspect of implementing data structures is the processor to be used. We will use a very broad definition of such devices. A ***processor*** is a device, either abstract or real, that allows for a variety of data types and data structures and that has a well-defined set of operations that it can execute. Examples of real processors are a Z80 microcomputer, a PDP 11/45 minicomputer, an IBM 3033 maxicomputer, and a CRAY-1 supercomputer. Each has a set of native data types and native data structures that the machine's circuitry is built to handle, and each has a precisely defined machine language that it can execute. Operating systems are also processors, albeit abstract ones [although certain architectures such as the Intel iAPX 432 have a large portion of the operating system imbedded in the hardware (Tyner, 1981)]. We can view the **operating system** as a virtual machine having certain data types and structures (typically files, records, and bytes) that it handles and certain instructions that it can execute [the job control language (e.g., IBM's JCL or UNIX's shell commands)], so it can perform processes (sequences of commands) using data. Almost any computer system that we use requires that we know at least a few of the command language instructions. Quite often, especially in the microcomputer area, the underlying hardware is different for the same operating system. The microcomputer operating system CP/M (DRI 1982) and MS-DOS (disk operating system) [Microsoft (MS-DOS)] and the UNIX (Bell Labs 1978) operating system (formerly for minicomputers, but rapidly moving onto the 16-bit microcomputers) are the nearest things to standards that we have, and they are implemented on a variety of hardware architectures.

Programming languages can also be considered to be abstract, or virtual, processors. Modula-2, for example, is a processor. When writing a program in it, we can imagine that we are writing instructions to a machine that understands that language. It has built-in data types and data structures (INTEGER, REAL, CHAR, ARRAY, RECORD, etc.). Modula-2 exists on a wide variety of systems with various hardware/operating system combinations. The programmer can write programs in Modula-2 and remain relatively unaware of which actual system is going to be used to execute the program. It appears as if a Modula-2 processor existed. It would be nice to be able to say that the programmer can be completely unaware of the system being used for executing the Modula-2 program, but it is likely that a few details will change from system to system. Although the programmer does not have to know any details of the host system, he or she will almost certainly have to be aware of certain restrictions and interpretations that the host system places on Modula-2. For example, defining a variable of type INTEGER on an Apple Macintosh system using MacModula-2 results in a range of possible values from $-32,768$ to $+32,767$. Defining the same integer using Modula-2 on a CYBER 173 might result in a range of possible values from -2^{59} to $+2^{59}$. The difference results from the fact that 16 bits are used to hold the integer in a Macintosh, whereas 60 bits are used in the CYBER system.

The processor chosen to implement a data structure has a definite effect on the efficiency of the data structure's operation. It may not even be possible to implement the data structure given the features that a processor provides (or, more accurately, does not provide). The processor determines the built-in data structures provided, the data structures that can be defined and implemented by the programmer, and the efficiency and operating characteristics of the data structures implemented. Modula-2 has a data type RECORD, whereas FORTRAN does not. Modula-2 has a built-in data type POINTER,

Some Processors

SQL (IBM database system)

WordStar (word processor)

Pascal
COBOL
Modula-2

IBM S/370 JCL (job control language)
UNIX (operating system)
CP/M (operating system)

Intel 8080
IBM 370
DEC VAX

which, along with dynamic allocation of memory space, provides the programmer with the tools to define and build a huge variety of dynamic, flexible, and efficient data structures. The use of pointers is not standard in either FORTRAN or COBOL.

At every level—hardware, operating system, and programming language—the processors must be chosen wisely to fit the task at hand. For example, the processor mix used on board the space shuttle *Columbia* is quite different from the processor mix used by your local bank. In this book we are concerned with the definition and implementation of data structures. We are concerned only with the choice of programming language, not with the operating system and hardware. We have chosen Modula-2 primarily because it is widely used, is simple and concise, and has a nice range of facilities for data structuring. It also provides modules that directly support the specification and implementation of abstract data types.

1.5.3 *Representation of Common Atomic Data Types*

An atomic data value is a piece of data that we choose to consider (and perhaps manipulate) as a single, nondecomposable entity.

We will not provide a complete review of common atomic data types. What we will do is look at a subset, paying most attention to those data types commonly used in high-level languages.

Although all data elements can be represented using bits, most programming is done at a level at which the atomic data types of a high-level language or a particular processor can be considered the natural atomic level of data. The following sections will discuss the bit level representation of some of these data types, but this will be the exception rather than the rule. For example, we will be satisfied that the atomic data type associated with the variable i described by the Modula-2 statement

VAR i: INTEGER

is the INTEGER. How that integer is represented by the high-level language and the host system is an implementation issue that will not affect how we think about i and its manipulation.

• **Integer and cardinal**

$$10011010_2 = 154_{10} = 9A_{16}$$
$$= 12201_3$$

Integers are used to represent whole numbers. Our familiarity with the representation of integers in the base 10 system tends to obscure the mechanism that is being used. For example, it seems unnecessary to say that what is really meant by

$$62,953_{10}$$

is

$$6 \times 10^4 + 2 \times 10^3 + 9 \times 10^2 + 5 \times 10^1 + 3 \times 10^0$$

This underlying mechanism is the basis for representing integers with values of only 0 and 1. The binary number

$$10011010_2$$

can be interpreted as

$$1\times 2^7 + 0\times 2^6 + 0\times 2^5 + 1\times 2^4 + 1\times 2^3 + 0\times 2^2 + 1\times 2^1 + 0\times 2^0$$

which is translated to decimal as

$$1\times 128 + 1\times 16 + 1\times 8 + 1\times 2 = 154_{10}$$

In this way, we can show a correspondence between the binary integers and the decimal integers. Every decimal integer (or integer in any base representation) has a unique binary integer corresponding to it. For example, 10011010_2 is the only bit pattern that translates into 154 decimal. Eight bits can be used to represent at most $2^8 = 256$ different integers. They are commonly used to represent either 0 through 255 or -127 through 128.

Binary arithmetic is carried out according to the following rules:

$$0 + 0 = 0 \qquad 0 \times 0 = 0$$
$$0 + 1 = 1 \qquad 0 \times 1 = 0$$
$$1 + 1 = 10 \qquad 1 \times 1 = 1$$

Examples that apply these basic rules to more complex problems are shown in the margin.

Negative integers can be represented by devoting a bit (usually the leftmost) to function as the sign of the number. The 8-bit integer 10011010 can be signed by adding a ninth bit and adopting the convention that 0 indicates plus and 1 indicates minus.

$$010011010_2 = +154_{10}$$
$$110011010_2 = -154_{10}$$

Such a scheme is called a ***sign-magnitude representation.*** Although it is probably the simplest in concept, other methods such as two's complement representation are often used to simplify the design of computer circuitry (Hill and Peterson, 1968).

Native and built-in operations for integers typically include the arithmetic operations of addition, subtraction, multiplication, integer division, and exponentiation, as well as data movement. Modula-2 provides the built-in atomic data type INTEGER and the operators $+$, $-$ (unary), $-$ (binary), $*$, DIV, and MOD. Implicit transformations will change integers into reals when necessary in Pascal but not in Modula-2. The expression

$$3.2 + \text{FLOAT}(5)$$

transforms cardinal 5 into real 5.0 before addition. The built-in function CHR(i) will transform the integer i into a character.

Modula-2 has a second type closely related to type INTEGER. It is type CARDINAL. CARDINALs are nonnegative integers: 0, 1, 2, ... (Because they can be unsigned and their sign bit can be used to represent magnitude, in most implementations they range between 0 and $2 \times$ MaxInt + 1. For example, if sixteen bits were available to represent INTEGERs and CARDINALs, the

---

Margin:

```
1001      9
+0101    + 5
1110      14

1001      9
× 0101   × 5
1001      45
0000
1001
0000
0101101₂ = 45₁₀
```

•

Data Type INTEGER

The data type INTEGER provided by Modula-2 can be viewed as an abstract data type whose specification is as follows:

1. The elements are the whole numbers from *MinInt* to *Maxint*. The values of *MinInt* and *Maxint* are implementation dependent.
2. Integers are both ordered and linear.
3. The set of operations is implementation dependent, but usually includes the following:

Assignment	:=
Arithmetic	$*$, DIV, MOD, +, −
Relational	=, #, <, <=, >, >=
Functional	ABS, ODD, ORD, INC, DEC, CHR

integer's values could range between -32768 and $+32767$, whereas the cardinal's values could range between 0 and 65535.) If an integer variable's value is always to be nonnegative, then the variable should be retyped to CARDINAL.

• **Floating-point reals**

As with whole numbers, fractional parts of numbers are represented in the decimal system as sums of powers of 10, but in this case the powers are negative. Therefore,

$$0.375 = 3 \times 10^{-1} + 7 \times 10^{-2} + 5 \times 10^{-3}$$

A binary fraction is represented in the same way, but using negative powers of 2:

$$0.11010_2 = 1 \times 2^{-1} + 1 \times 2^{-2} + 0 \times 2^{-3} + 1 \times 2^{-4} + 0 \times 2^{-5}$$
$$= 0.5 + 0.25 + 0.0625$$
$$= 0.8125_{10}$$

The correspondence between decimal integers and binary integers does not extend to fractions in the two bases. For example, the simple decimal fraction 0.1_{10} has no finite representation as a binary fraction (it is an infinite series of negative powers of 2). It can be closely approximated given the register sizes of most computers, but there is always some discrepancy since no computer has a register with an infinite number of bits.

An easier problem is that of associating bit patterns with real numbers. Decimal real numbers can be represented as fractions multiplied by an appropriate scale factor,

$$374.62 = 0.37462 \times 10^3$$

which is the basis of representing floating-point real numbers in binary form. If we adopt a convention for decimals that the exponent (3 in the example) is always to indicate the power of 10, then the 10 does not have to be stated explicitly. In addition, let us reverse the order and show the exponent in front of the number. Allowing for signs ($+$ or $-$) on both the exponent and the number (called the mantissa), we can use a form such as

$$\pm ee \pm ddddd$$

to represent the number

$$\pm 0.ddddd \times 10^{\pm ee}$$

Our example 374.62 would become

$$+03 + 37462$$

In order to represent the number in the memory of a digital computer, we do an exactly analogous thing, only this time the exponent is the power of 2, not 10, and the only digits allowed are 0 and 1. Assume that we have a 16-bit representation and that we allot 8 bits to the exponent (one for the sign of the exponent, and seven for the exponent's magnitude), and 8 bits to the mantissa (with a similar breakdown). The number 17.5_{10} would be

---

Floating-Point REALs

Floating-point REALs can be viewed as an abstract data type with the following specification:

1. The values are a finite subset of the real numbers. The actual subset is implementation dependent.
2. The structure is ordered.
3. Typical operations are

   Assignment : =
   Arithmetic $*, /, +, -$
   Relational $=, \#, >, >=,$
                $<, <=$
   Functional ABS, TRUNC,
                FLOAT

$$17.5_{10} = 10001.1_2 = .100011_2 \times 2^5 = .100011_2 \times 2^{101}$$

Putting this into the form

$$\pm ee...e \pm dddd...d$$

where *ee...e* and *dd...d* are in binary, we get

00000101 01000110
$+ 101_2 + .100011_2$

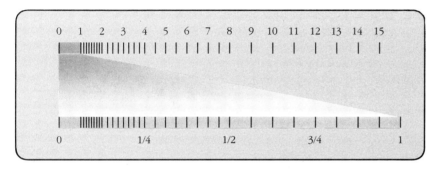

Figure 1.21 The positive real numbers represented by a typical scheme using 8 bits.

Figure 1.21 shows the real numbers that are represented by a typical scheme that stores each real number in 1 byte. Most computers (even micros) store real numbers using at least 16 bits, and 60 bits or more is not uncommon. Figure 1.21 shows why it is desirable to use a large number of bits to represent real numbers. There are gaps—sometimes very large ones—between representable real numbers. Worse yet, the gaps are unevenly distributed. Notice the gap near 0. It is, typically and unfortunately, relatively large!

The difficulties that are associated with representing real numbers are not concerned so much with the mechanics of translating bit patterns into real numbers as with dealing with the inherent fact that there is an uncountable infinity of real numbers to be represented—and only a paltry few bit patterns with which to do the job. Every interval of the real number line contains an infinite number of real numbers. Look at Figure 1.21. Each of the intervals between representable real numbers contains an infinite number of real numbers that can only be approximated. This is true of any representation scheme we choose—no matter how many bits are thrown into the breach. Since we cannot solve the inherent problem by simply throwing more and more bits at it, we must develop a strategy for deciding how to approximate a real number whose value falls in one of the gaps. This is not as easy as it might appear and has been the subject of much study. An introduction to some of the problems and a proposed standard for dealing with them are described in *Signum* (1979).

The study of how arithmetic operations are carried out using floating-point real numbers is interesting, but since it is somewhat off the track for this book, we refer you to *Signum* (1979). We have only shown an example of how a convention can be adopted that can be used to represent real numbers in a digital computer register, in our example a register of size 16. In practice, real machines will devote at least 24 bits to the storage of a floating-point real number, but the way in which they represent the numbers is essentially the same.

Notice that the elements of type *REAL* are ordered by the relational operator $<=$. Although the set of all real numbers is not linear because no real number has a unique successor, the set of digital computer representable real numbers does form a linear set. Each such real number, except the largest (or last), does have a unique successor. The abstract data structure for *REALS* never includes the operation *Successor*. It could be done, but generally is not. There is a good basic reason. Why should we start with a structure that is not linear, approximate it with a structure that is, and then mislead the users (some of whom may not know better) by supplying an operation that is not possible on the data being represented? There are times, especially in numerical analysis, when it is important to know the size of the gaps between representable real numbers. Computing that size could be accomplished by starting with representable r_1, computing r_1's successor, and subtracting the two values. Happily, since linearity is not an inherent property of real numbers, numerical analysts do not think of this computation in the way just described. (See Forsythe, Malcolm, & Moler, 1977, pp. 10–14, for an introduction and example of this sort of computation.)

• **BCD reals**

The *BCD reals* and *floating-point reals* are the same at the abstract level. They are simply different implementations of the abstract type REAL.

The acronym for ***binary coded decimal*** is BCD; ***BCD reals*** are another way of representing real numbers. Suppose that we allocate 4 bits for each decimal digit in the representation of real numbers. We code each decimal digit separately. Therefore, 374.5_{10} would become

0011 0111 0100 0101$_2$

where each 4-bit group represents one of the decimal digits, for example,

$$0011_2 = 1 \times 2^1 + 1 \times 2^0 = 3_{10}$$
$$0111_2 = 1 \times 2^2 + 1 \times 2^1 + 1 \times 2^0 = 7_{10}$$

Such a representation avoids the problem of floating-point reals not being able to represent certain fractional numbers in base 10 exactly in base 2. On the other hand, the range of possible values is much more limited using BCD reals.

• **Boolean**

Boolean quantities have one of two values—true or false. Because of this characteristic shared with the bit, we would think that a single bit set to 0 or 1 would be used to represent them. One bit is in fact sufficient, but because of the difficulty most computers have in isolating a single bit, it is most common to find an entire byte (6, 7, or 8 bits, assume 8 for this discussion) devoted to a boolean quantity. Most computers cannot address a single bit in their memory but must address at least a byte. Therefore, 8 bits at a time are fetched into the fast registers. The single bit representing the boolean quantity would then have to be isolated by masking out all of the others. Most designers have chosen to sacrifice some memory space to avoid this complexity, and typically we find that

$$00000000_2 = \text{false}$$

Anything else = true

• Character

The codes used to represent characters are arbitrary, but with an important practical constraint. If one character is stored in an 8-bit byte, we might choose the bit pattern 01000001 to represent the character A. Such a choice is subject to the condition that the printer must be designed to strike an A when this bit pattern is received. Notice that if we were to encounter the bit pattern 01000001 in memory, we would have no way of knowing if it were the letter A, the boolean value false, the integer 65, or a representation of some other native data type. In fact, if it is the letter A, we could reinterpret it as the integer 65. Now suppose that we chose 01000010 to represent B. It is equivalent to the integer value 66, one larger than the representation of A. Since 66 is numerically greater than 65 and B follows A in the alphabet, comparing the integer equivalents of characters for ordering would give the same result as comparing A and B alphabetically. The integer order is the same as the alphabetical order. Such a tactic is used to simplify the computer's circuitry since an integer comparator can also be used as a character comparator. You will find that character codes are constructed with this in mind.

The two most widely used codes are the ***ASCII (American Standard Code for Information Interchange)*** and the ***EBCDIC (Extended Binary-Coded Decimal Interchange Code)*** codes. Representation of characters is discussed further in Chapter 8.

• Bit

From the software designer's point of view, the ***bit*** is the ultimate atomic level on a digital computer. As we have noted previously, although all information in a computer is composed of bits, the hardware sometimes has difficulty isolating 1 bit. Most memories are addressable in bytes or words.

• Byte

A ***byte*** is a collection of bits, usually 6, 7, or 8, which can be addressed as a single entity. Many random access memories are byte-addressable, and on most computers there are machine language instructions to manipulate bytes. The hardware puts no interpretation on what kind of data the byte contains, and it

---

BOOLEAN

The Modula-2 data type BOOLEAN can be viewed as an abstract data type with the following specification:

1. There are two values—TRUE and FALSE.
2. The structure need not be ordered nor linear, although in Modula-2 it is both. In Modula-2, BOOLEAN is an enumerated type:

    TYPE BOOLEAN = (FALSE, TRUE)

3. The usual operations are

Assignment	:=
Relational	=, #, >, >=, <, <=
Logical	AND, OR, NOT
Functional	ORD, VAL

    •

CHAR

The Modula-2 data type CHAR can be viewed as an abstract data type with the following specification:

1. The elements are a finite set of Latin letters and symbols.
2. The structure is both ordered and linear.
3. The standard operations are

Assignment	:=
Relational	=, #, >, >=, <, <=
Functional	ORD, CHR, CAP, VAL

A byte most often refers to 8 bits, but sometimes to 6 or 7.

is left to the program to interpret the data correctly. Most high-level languages do not provide for explicit access to bytes, but since a character (and sometimes a short integer) is held in 1 byte, it is often possible to manipulate the byte directly.

• **Word**

A ***word*** is a collection of bytes. A PDP-11 word is two 8-bit bytes. An IBM S/370 word is four 8-bit bytes. A CDC CYBER word is ten 6-bit bytes. A word is typically used to store floating-point real numbers and integers. Many computers have memories that are both byte and word addressable.

• **Pointer**

The ***pointer*** is an important data type for data structuring. It is a word or portion of a word in memory, which, instead of containing data, contains the address of another word or byte. Thus, in Modula-2 we are able to define a variable whose value is the memory address of another variable. Because of its importance in data structuring, we will give a full discussion of pointers in Chapter 2.

1.5.4 Complexity, Performance, and Metrics

When we implement an abstract data structure, we will want to know the performance characteristics of our implementation. How thrifty is it in its use of system resources: Does it require a high overhead of random access memory, and does it require an inordinate amount of time to execute certain operations? Is it rigid in its use of memory, or can the amount of memory required be adjusted to the amount of data present? Can it handle data elements of varying lengths, or must all data elements be of one length? Are the algorithms complex or simple? These are only some of the factors that we must consider when evaluating one implementation and comparing it with another.

• **Metrics**

1000	Milton
1008	Dickens
1016	Eliot
1024	Arnold
1032	Conrad

The number of comparisons of one data element with another is frequently an important factor in determining the speed of execution.

There are certain manipulations or operations that occur quite often when executing data structure operations. Suppose we take the list of names in Section 1.4.5 and perform the following operation: Find the relative position of the name 'Eliot.' In order to do so, we can start at the first name and simply search through the list comparing each name we encounter with the name 'Eliot.' One measure of how long we can expect the operation to take is to note that the time taken will be proportional to the number of name comparisons that must be made. Initializing the process and finalizing it once the target name is found will contribute relatively little to the time required (unless the list is short, in which case the contribution from these two processes may be a large part of the total). The major contribution to the time required for a list of any but the smallest size will come from the comparison loop. We will find that with many of our data structures and their operations, the number of comparisons will be one of the major quantities that affects the speed of execution. We will use it as one of our measuring tools, or **metrics.**

A second commonly used metric is the number of data element moves that must be performed in the course of executing the operation. For example, if we wished to delete the name 'Eliot' from our list of names and we did not wish to leave a gap in the list, we might move each name below the deleted one up by one position and then reduce the list size by one. There are no data comparisons involved, but there are many data element moves. In fact, the speed with which the deletion is performed will be determined by the number of data moves required. Data element moves (or the movement of other associated quantities as we shall see later in the text) is another commonly used metric.

There are other metrics that can be used in certain operations on some data structures; none of these shows up as frequently as the two described here.

A different type of metric attempts to measure the complexity of an algorithm. Such metrics are important because they indicate not only the effort required to implement an algorithm, but also the effort required to understand it, to attempt to debug it, to modify it, and to maintain it. The construction and effectiveness of complexity metrics have been active areas of study in computer science for some time. There has been a variety of simple metrics proposed. Among them are the number of statements, the number of levels of nesting, and the number of possible logical paths presented by an algorithm. The books by Halstead (1977); Perlis, Sayward, and Shaw (1981); and Shen, Conte, and Dunsmore (1983) contain in-depth discussions of the problem. In this book, the final section of each chapter has a table that presents simple measures of the complexities of the algorithms of the chapter.

• Effects of memory and processor

Many of the conclusions that we will draw regarding performance will be based on a fact whose importance is easy to overlook. We have assumed that the data types that we will consider in this book are implemented in a random access memory. Let us consider the operation that we performed a few paragraphs ago: Find the relative position of the name 'Eliot.' If the list were stored in an array, *name,* the code to find it would be similar to the code segment shown in Figure 1.22.

The speed with which the operation can be performed will typically be determined by the time it takes to access the *i*th name (test := name[i]) and the time it takes to compare the list name with 'Eliot' [UNTIL (test = 'Eliot')]. The times for each would be roughly comparable on a typical computer, so any effort to improve performance could be equally well directed to either.

Now suppose that the list of names is stored on a disk file. The same process becomes that shown in Figure 1.23. If we assume that each name had to be fetched from a disk when the statement *ReadString*(test) is executed, then instead of being roughly equal in execution time to the comparison statement, accessing each name would be typically 1000 times slower. The

The number of data element moves may also have an important impact on execution time.

The complexity of an algorithm is a measure of the effort required to understand, implement, debug, modify, or maintain it.

•

```
VAR name: ARRAY [1..500]
                OF Surname;
     i    : [0..500];
     test : Surname;
          ⋮

     i := 0;
REPEAT
     i := i + 1;
     test := name[i]
UNTIL (test = 'Eliot')
     OR (i = 500);
```

Figure 1.22
FindName 'Eliot'. List stored in random access memory.

•

```
VAR name: ARRAY [1..500]
                OF Surname;
     i    : [0..500];
     test : Surname;
          ⋮

     i := 0;
REPEAT
     i := i + 1;
     ReadString(test)
UNTIL (test = 'Eliot')
     OR (i = 500);
```

Figure 1.23
FindName 'Eliot'. List stored in a file.

speed with which the operation can be performed would be completely determined by the speed of the *ReadString* statement (the compare statement would be negligible in comparison), and any effort to improve the performance of the operation should be concentrated completely on it.

The logic of the two code segments is essentially identical, but the determinant of the performance is completely different due to the difference in memory characteristics. This is a simple example of a situation that occurs many times. The performance characteristics of a data type can be radically affected by the type of memory (or combinations of memory) used to implement it. We will find some cases in which implementation A is superior to implementation B when the data structure is in random access memory, and other cases in which exactly the reverse is true when the same data structure is implemented using a magnetic disk/random access memory combination.

• Mathematical notations

We will often use the mathematical ***order of magnitude*** notation to give a rough but effective idea of the size of our metrics. For example, in Figure 1.22 if we assume that the name we are looking for is in the list and that every element is equally likely, we can easily show that the expected number of compares is E_c:

$$E_c = (n + 1) / 2$$

We can fairly accurately say that the amount of time that our find operation will be expected to take is E_t (see Figure 1.24).

The actual values of the constants depend on many factors—the computer system being used, the language being used, and the data type of the names. We are not very interested in the values of the constants, but that the amount of time we can expect to use in executing the operation is a linear function of n, the size of the list. Doubling the list doubles the time. In fact, we do not even care that the expression is strictly linear, but are most concerned that the leading or major term, the one that will eventually be the largest in the expression, is $C_1' \times n$. We say that the order of magnitude of the expression is n, and we will indicate this by writing $O(n)$. In the margin are several expressions that we will encounter in analyzing implementations of our data structures and their associated orders of magnitude. Notice that in each case only the dominant term is chosen to represent a crude notion of the size of the entire expression. Comparisons of orders of magnitude of two expressions are an effective means of gauging relative performance without having to address too much detail. Determining lower-order terms will not materially affect the conclusions drawn by comparing the major terms.

Figure 1.25 gives some idea of the relative magnitudes of the orders of magnitude for several values of n. We will find when analyzing sorting methods, for example, that some simple sorts operate in a time that is $O(n^2)$, whereas advanced sorts typically operate in a time of $O(n \log_2 n)$. How much better is the former than the latter? To begin, for $n = 1024$,

---

Margin notes (left column):

$$E_t = C_1 \times E_c + C_0$$

$$= C_1 \times (n + 1)/2 + C_0$$

$$= C_1' \times n + C_0'$$

Figure 1.24
Expected time to find a name.

$$\frac{n(n + 1)}{2} \text{ is } O(n^2)$$

•

$$15\, n \log n + 0.1n^2 + 5$$
$$\text{is } O(n^2)$$

•

$$\frac{6 \log n + 3n + 7}{2n - 5}$$
$$\text{is } O(1)$$

•

$$\frac{17 \log n + 9n}{4n^2 \log n}$$
$$\text{is } O(1/n \log n)$$

$$n^2 \sim 1,000,000$$

whereas

$$n \log_2 n = 1024 \times 10 = 10,240$$

	$n = 8$	128	1024	1,000,000
$O(n)$	8	128	1,024	1,000,000
$O(n^2)$	64	16,192	1,000,000	1,000,000,000,000
$O(n^{1/2})$	3	11	32	1000
$O(\log_2 n)$	3	7	10	20
$O(n \log_2 n)$	24	896	10,240	20,000,000

Figure 1.25 Orders of magnitude for sample values of n.

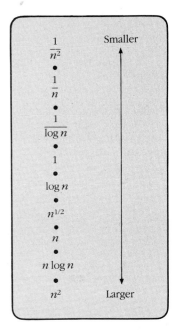

Figure 1.26
Ranking of common orders of
magnitude for large n.

They differ by a factor of 100. It would seem that if the advanced sort took 1 minute, then the simple sort would take 100 minutes. In fact, that is not quite true. We are ignoring the constant multipliers of the two terms. The simple sorts do simple things for each of their 1,000,000 operations, whereas the advanced sorts do something more complex for each of their 10,240 operations. This translates into the fact that the constant multiplying the $n \log n$ term is going to be larger than the constant multiplying the n^2 term, so we probably will not gain a full factor of 100.

Even if it took 100 times more work per operation for the advanced sort so that both methods would require the same time when $n = 1024$, for n greater than 1024 the advanced method would again be preferable. The fact is that no matter what the relative sizes of the constants, for a large enough value of n, the advanced method would eventually be faster. Often we find that an advanced method, although more efficient for a large amount of data, is not as efficient for small amounts. The simpler method should be chosen for small data sets, whereas the more complex method should be used for larger data sets.

We suggest that you do the exercises relating to orders of magnitude to assure that these notions are understood because they will be used quite heavily throughout the book. You will see many examples of various measures of complexity and efficiency being used to compare algorithms.

The use of metrics to compare the execution times (expected, best, and worst cases) of algorithms can easily be misused. Execution times are used because they are quantitative, important to minimize, and produce numbers or orders of magnitude that are easily compared. Other less quantifiable aspects of algorithms may be at least as important. It is a well-documented fact that over the life of a program far more time is spent maintaining and modifying than is spent developing it. Within the development activity itself, more is spent on debugging and testing than on design and programming. In addition, computer time is cheap compared to the cost of people. Choosing the "best" algorithm is a poorly defined and not well understood process. Clear, simple,

"Fast algorithms dramatically decrease run time for certain tasks. Designing them offers not only the promise of better performance but also a better understanding of the problems underlying all computational tasks."
(Bentley, 1979)

but not very efficient programs have the virtue of their simplicity. It is possible that an algorithm that is more easily understood and hence more easily debugged and maintained would result in a reduced total expenditure of effort and money over its lifetime even though it uses more computer resources. We learn a great deal in our efforts to construct more efficient algorithms, and it is very tempting to focus too heavily on the execution times of algorithms as the sole measure of their relative merits. You should be aware when reading this or any book that such comparisons are only part of a very large and poorly understood picture.

> The execution time of an algorithm, though very important, is only one of many measures of its merit.

• **Timing studies**

It is not common—at least in books on data structures—to make specific comparisons on the measured times required to perform an operation for different data types and implementations. We have decided to include the results of numerous timing studies to supplement the order of magnitude comparisons described in the preceding section. These results will be given whenever we feel they will help us make a point. In many cases they provide insights not available from coarser (order of magnitude) comparisons.

Many of the timing studies we present are related. We have selected two simple applications for which we will present the results of timing studies for most of the data structures studied in this book. They are the determination of the number of times each letter of the alphabet and each pair of letters occur in some textual material. The results of such studies have the virtue of being easy to understand. They are simply graphs showing the time required to perform various operations as a function of the number of elements being processed. Different curves show the effects of different data structures and different implementations.

There is a pitfall, mentioned earlier, associated with timing studies. The results depend not only on the data type and its implementation, but also on the programming language, specific compiler, and computer system used. Although such effects cannot be eliminated entirely, the examples we have chosen illustrate the impact of data structure selection and algorithm implementation issues.

Exercises 1.5

1. Explain the following terms in your own words:

memory	file
processor	random access
direct access	sequential access
cache	metric
orders of magnitude	

2. What is the equivalent of the integer values

123
67
4096

in the following bases:
a. Base 2 binary
b. Base 8 (octal)
c. Base 16 (hexadecimal)
d. Base 7

3. What is the equivalent of the fractional values

0.1
0.675
0.25

in the following bases:
a. Base 2
b. Base 16

4. What are the bit patterns that form the ASCII codes for the characters 'g', 'G', ';', 'a', ' = '?

5. What are the orders of magnitude estimates for the following expressions:
a. $4 \times x^2 + 10 \times x + 120$
b. $6.1 \times \log x + x^{1/2} + 5.5$
c. $7 \times x \times ((\log x)/(5 \times x^2)) + 3 \times x^{1/2}$
d. $(5/x) + 0.33 \times x^{1/4}$

1.6 Summary

In Chapter 1 we introduced concepts that are fundamental to our study of data structures. Some of these, which set the stage for the remainder of the book, are as follows:

- Data type
- Classes of data types
    Atomic
    Data structures
- Abstraction levels of data types
    Abstract
    Virtual
    Physical
- Virtual and physical processors
- Processors and native data types
- Abstract data types
    Specification
    Representation
    Implementation

"We believe that the bulk of the problems with contemporary software follow from the fact that it is too complex. Complexity per se is not the culprit, of course; rather it is our human limitations in dealing with it. Dijstra said it extremely well when he wrote of 'our human inability to do much.' It is our human limitations, our inability to deal with all the relations and ramifications of a complex situation simultaneously, which lies at the root of our software problems. In other contexts we (humans) have developed an exceptionally powerful technique for dealing with complexity. We abstract from it. Unable to master the entirety of a complex object, we choose to ignore its inessential details, dealing instead with a generalized, idealized model of the object—we consider its 'essence.' " (Shaw, 1980)

"Abstraction permeates the whole of programming." (Gries, 1979)

- The specification process
    Elements
    Structure
    Domains
    Operations
- Advantages of abstract data types
    Modularity
    Information hiding
    Precision
    Simplicity
    Integrity
    Implementation independence
- Modules, information hiding, and encapsulation
- Modula-2 modules
    Definition modules
    Implementation modules
    Import and export of objects
- Data elements and the unique identification property
- Representation of structure
    Positioning and calculation
    Linking
- Memories and their effects on data types
- Machine level representation of atomic data types
- Computational complexity, implementation performance, and metrics
- Orders of magnitude

An excellent entry into the literature of abstract data types is in the text and bibliography of Shaw (1980). Bentley (1982) discusses the writing of programs. Bentley's (1983a) series "Programming Pearls," which began in the August 1983 issue of the *Communications of the ACM,* is also very readable and informative.

Arrays, Records, and Simple Linked Lists

2

2.1 Introduction

2.2 Arrays
   2.2.1 Array Characteristics
   2.2.2 Array Mapping Functions
   2.2.3 Array Descriptor Records
   2.2.4 Special Arrays
   2.2.5 Dynamic Arrays and Open Array
      Parameters
   Exercises 2.2

2.3 Records
   2.3.1 The Record Abstract Data Type
   2.3.2 Record Characteristics
   2.3.3 Record Description and Memory
      Mapping
   2.3.4 Variant Record Schemes
   Exercises 2.3

2.4 Pointers and Simple Linked Lists
   2.4.1 Pointers
   2.4.2 A Simple Linked List
   2.4.3 Design of Linked Lists
   Exercises 2.4

2.5 Composite Structures
   2.5.1 Records of Arrays
   2.5.2 Arrays of Records
   2.5.3 Arrays of Pointers
   Exercises 2.5

2.6 Summary

2.1 Introduction

Chapter 2 deals with an atomic data type and two structured data types that will form the basis for representing and implementing almost all of the more complex data structures that we shall study. The atomic type is pointer, and the structured types are arrays and records. Their occurrences as built-in data types in most modern general-purpose programming languages such as C, Pascal, Ada, Mesa, Modula-2, and PL/I attest to their fundamental nature. They are at a lower level of abstraction than the other data structures we shall study.

This chapter also introduces linked list data structures. This is done for two reasons. First, linked lists illustrate how pointers are used to construct linked data structures. Second, they serve as a review on the use of Modula-2 pointers.

Arrays and records are among the most fundamental and widely used data structures. Historically, arrays appeared as the primary data structure of FOR-TRAN (indeed, the only data structure of FORTRAN!). Records evolved from the applications of computers to the problems of business data processing and formed the basis of the data division in the programming language COBOL. A more integrated view of computing prevails today, and we realize that both of these data structures are necessary for a wide variety of computation, including systems and applications software.

Both arrays and records are made up of a group of individual elements that may be either atomic or, with some restrictions, other data structures. The similarities between them (and the reason that we have combined the discussion of them in a single chapter) are that they are both fundamental data structures and logically linear in the relationship among their elements. Both are normally implemented by placing their elements in contiguous memory locations so that the physical placement of the elements closely mirrors the logical arrangement. To illustrate this, let A be a one-dimensional array. If element $A[5]$ logically follows element $A[4]$, we will usually (but not necessarily) find element $A[5]$ physically stored next to and after element $A[4]$ in memory. As we shall see, efficient execution of array operations is dependent on such placement. Figure 2.1 shows a simple example.

Differences between arrays and records come from the fact that all elements of an array must be of the same data type, whereas those of a record may be of a variety of data types. Figure 2.1(a) shows an array whose elements are all of type REAL, whereas Figure 2.1(b) shows a record whose elements are of four different data types.

The ability of records to group and handle (i.e., relate, read, write, and move) a collection of data of differing types as a single entity is a distinct advantage. However, this ability also results in a serious disadvantage. A component of an array is identified by specifying the values of its indexes. For example, referring to the array in Figure 2.1,

```
a[i] := 0.0;
```

assigns the value 0.0 to a single element of the array, and the index [i] unam-

Arrays, records, and pointers are fundamental data types that are used as building blocks for many data structures. They are all native to Modula-2 (see Appendix A).

The components of an array are all of the same type.

•

The components of a record may be of different types.

Memory address	Data value	Index value	Memory address	Data value	Element name	Element length (bytes)
500	10.4	[1]				
504	− 13.5	[2]	1000	2351	r.idno	4
508	112.74	[3]	1004	83	r.score	2
512	8.2	[4]	1006	true	r.married	1
516	33.93	[5]	1007	500.45	r.salary	4

VAR a: **ARRAY** [1..5] **OF** REAL;

VAR r: **RECORD**
      idno   : CARDINAL;
      score   : [0..100];
      married: BOOLEAN;
      salary : REAL
   END;

(a)   (b)

Figure 2.1   (a) Memory layout for array *a*. (b) Memory layout for record *r*.

biguously specifies the element. The value of i can be set at any time by the executing program. A component of a record is identified by specifying its name. Referring to the record in Figure 2.1,

```
r.married := TRUE;
```

assigns the value TRUE to a single element (field) of the record *r*, and the name *r.married* unambiguously specifies which element.

It is generally true that programming languages allow indexes of arrays to be variables or expressions as well as constants, whereas the names of record elements must be identifiers. This causes a deficiency of the record data type since the identifiers cannot be varied during the execution of the program. For example, initial values of 0.0 in array *b* can be set by the concise code shown in the margin. This has no counterpart for records. To initialize the values of the elements of record *r*, the programmer must exhaustively name every record element, as shown in the margin.

The programmer may use variable indexes to delay the specification of which array element is to be accessed. The two-line code segment in the margin delays the specification of which array element will receive the value 0.0 until the assignment statement is executed. However, if a record is being used, the programmer must commit to a specific record element at the time of writing the program.

Data structures must have some mechanism for relating their constituent parts. Arrays and records usually (but not always) accomplish this by physical positioning—the *i*th array element immediately precedes the $i + 1$st not only in logical order but also in physical memory. Physical positioning in memory is used to implement an abstract relationship among the elements.

An array component is accessed by specifying a value of its index type. That value may be given as a constant, variable, or expression and hence may be determined at execution time.

•

A record component is accessed by specifying a component identifier. That identifier is given when the program is written.

•

Initialize Array Elements

FOR i := 1 **TO** 2 **DO**
    FOR j := 1 **TO** 3 **DO**
        b[i,j] := 0.0
    END
END;

•

Initialize Record Elements

r.idno := 0;
r.score := 0;
r.married := false;
r.salary := 0.0;

•

Variable Indexes

ReadInt(i); ReadInt(j);
a[i,j] := 0.0;

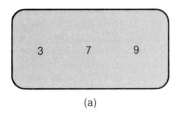

(a)

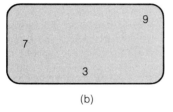

(b)

Figure 2.2
(a) An orderly arrangement.
(b) A scattered arrangement.

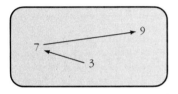

Figure 2.3
A scattered arrangement in
which the ordering is determined by links or pointers.

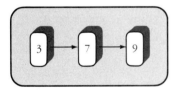

Figure 2.4
The usual illustration of a linked
list.

There is an alternative to this careful and orderly arrangement of elements in memory. The elements may be scattered about memory in any way. Since the abstract relationship among them must be retained, we must have some way of doing this with randomly scattered data. Suppose that we wish to consider the integers 3, 7, and 9 ordered by magnitude. Thus, 7 follows (is greater than) 3, and 9 follows 7. We can store them on the page with the physical left-to-right order indicating the logical order, as done in Figure 2.2(a). If they were stored in a scattered fashion as shown in Figure 2.2(b), their physical placement would no longer indicate their logical order. The logical order can be regained by associating each element with a directed line that points to its logical successor, as shown in Figure 2.3. Data structures implemented in this way are called ***linked data structures.*** Figure 2.4 shows the way linked lists are commonly pictured.

A primary characteristic of linked structures is that each element contains not only data, but also the position(s) in some storage medium of logically related elements. We will call the variables containing locations ***pointer variables.*** Their values are drawn as directed lines. The pointer values are memory addresses, or locations, in whatever type of storage medium the data structure is stored. They can be addresses in a random access memory, or relative record positions on a magnetic tape, or a disk address (surface, track, sector, byte) on a magnetic disk. In this text we are concerned primarily with data stored in random access memory. Modula-2 provides a pointer data type whose values are such random access memory addresses.

Section 2.2 deals with arrays. Each array has a number of characteristics associated with it. The number of dimensions (indexes), the lower and upper bounds of each index, the data type of the constituent elements, and the location in memory at which the array is stored are examples. These characteristic values are fixed by the programmer, the compiler, or the operating system at some time before the array is used. These characteristics are identified and discussed in Section 2.2.1. Array mapping functions, that is, functions that allow random access to an array element's position in memory given the element's index values, are derived in Section 2.2.2. Array descriptor records are discussed in Section 2.2.3.

Not every array fits the normal mold, and two special cases are discussed in Section 2.2.4—triangular arrays and sparse arrays. In Section 2.2.5, issues such as dynamic array memory binding, Modula-2's open array parameters, and the delayed specification of certain array parameters are introduced.

Section 2.3 deals with records. The record abstract data type is introduced in Section 2.3.1. Records, like arrays, have a number of characteristics associated with them; these are identified and discussed in Section 2.3.2. The variation of data types within a record and the use of names rather than index values to identify the individual elements of the record make it impractical to construct simple mathematical functions to map the identifier names of the member elements into their memory addresses. This must be done instead by a table look-up at the time the program is compiling rather than at the time it is executing. These issues are discussed in Section 2.3.3. Section 2.3.4 introduces variant and variable length records.

Section 2.4 discusses pointers and the closely associated concept of dynamic memory allocation. Both of these concepts are used to construct and manipulate data stored in one of the most elementary linked structures—the simple linked list.

Section 2.5 introduces composite structures that are formed by combining fundamental types. We look at several structures such as tables, arrays of pointers, and structures whose data elements vary in length.

2.2 Arrays

A: **ARRAY** [1..3] **OF** INTEGER;

Figure 2.5

Because the ***array*** is a very useful data structure, it is available in most languages and is probably familiar to you. Its specification, however, requires a bit of thought. We begin with a simple example that introduces the basic ideas of arrays in a concrete setting.

Figure 2.5 shows the Modula-2 representation of a simple array whose identifier is A. The array is completely described by its ***component type*** and its ***index type.*** A value of type A contains three integers—one value of its component type for each value of its index type. Figure 2.6 shows a sample value of type A and the three values of its index type, as well as the one-to-one correspondence between the components of A and the values of its index type. It is the two underlying data types, and the relationship between them, that play the central role in specifying an array data structure.

Index-type values	One-to-one correspondence	Sample component values
[1]	⟷	19
[2]	⟷	48
[3]	⟷	11

Figure 2.6

Since all components are of the same type, an array is said to be homogeneous.

We define an ***abstract data type array*** in Specification 2.1.

Specification 2.1   Array

Elements: A component data type is specified, and all component elements are of that type.

Structure: An index type, which must be linear (Section 1.4.1), is specified.   There is a one-to-one correspondence between the values of the index type and the component data element values of each array value.

   TYPE Array: **ARRAY** IndexType **OF** ComponentType

(Figures 2.5 and 2.6 show an example.)

Domain: All index values together with all combinations of associated component values.

Visible Items: User sees the array type, the index type, the component element type, and two operations.

Operations: There are two basic array operations. c is a variable of the component element type, and i is an expression that evaluates to type IndexType.

continued

Specification 2.1, continued

```
PROCEDURE Retrieve(a: Array; VAR c: ComponentType; i: IndexType);
(* post — c has the value of a's component associated with
          index value i. *)
```

The Modula-2 syntax (which is built into Modula-2) that corresponds to Retrieve is c := a[i].   (This is one of the few cases in which the abstraction of a data type seems to complicate things rather than making them simpler.   We are trying, though, to define the essence of the array type — what is the data abstraction for an array.)

```
PROCEDURE Update(VAR a: Array; c: ComponentType; i: IndexType);
(* post — The component element value of array a that is associated with
          index value i is c. *)
```

The Modula-2 syntax for Update is a[i] := c.

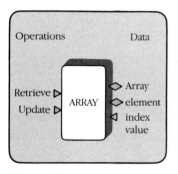

Figure 2.7
A capsule-like view of the array data structure.

•

```
TYPE Index1 = [0..10];
     Day    = (sun, mon, tue,
               wed, thu, fri,
               sat);

     Array1 = ARRAY [−5..5]
              OF REAL;

     Array2 = ARRAY Index1
              OF Day;

     Array3 = ARRAY ['a'..'z']
              OF CARDINAL;

     Array4 = ARRAY Day
              OF BOOLEAN;
```

Figure 2.8
Sample Modula-2 array types.

There can be other important array operations. One that is required in Modula-2 is $A := B$, where A and B are entire arrays of the same type. This operation assigns the value of B to the value of A. It can be simulated, as can many other operations, using our two basic operations—*Retrieve* and *Update*.

The one-to-one correspondence between index values and component elements is important. Given an index value, the array implementation is expected to determine the address of the component associated with that value. Moreover, the time required to convert an index value into a component address is to be independent of the index value. Because of this, an array is said to be a ***random access data structure.*** Index values are converted to component addresses by array mapping functions (AMFs), which we will study shortly.

The index type must be linear. Because of the one-to-one correspondence between values of the index type and components of an array, the array components can be thought of as inheriting the linear structure of the index type. To understand this, remember that there must be a first value of the index type. This value corresponds to a unique component, which can be labeled the first component—a title it inherits from its corresponding index value. It is in this inherited sense that the components of an array can be thought of as having a linear structure.

The component type of an array may be another array—but it cannot be the array itself. An example is shown in Figure 2.9. Using Modula-2 syntax, a reference to a component of S2 is S2[i][j]. Since this notation is cumbersome, a shorthand specification of S2, shown in Figure 2.10, is provided. The component reference S2[i][j] is simplified to S2[i,j]. It is important to note, however, that both specifications describe the same array. This idea can be extended to any level of nesting of arrays as component types. The result is a ***multidimensional array.***

To emphasize notational differences, we will give the specification of a two-dimensional array. Before doing so, consider the array specified in Figure 2.10. Each array value consists of six component values, each of type INTEGER. There are two index types: [1..2] and [1..3]. There is a one-to-one correspondence between all pairs of index values (one of each type) and the components of each array value. The pairs of index-type values, array values, and a one-to-one correspondence between them are shown in Figure 2.11. A more traditional view of the array value is shown in Figure 2.12.

S2: **ARRAY** [1..2] **OF**
    ARRAY [1..3] **OF** INTEGER;

Figure 2.9
•

S2: **ARRAY** [1..2],[1..3] **OF**
    INTEGER;

Figure 2.10
•

Pairs of index-type values	One-to-one correspondence	Sample component values
[1,1]	⟷	42
[1,2]	⟷	29
[1,3]	⟷	67
[2,1]	⟷	88
[2,2]	⟷	52
[2,3]	⟷	11

Figure 2.11

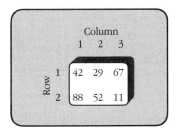

Figure 2.12
This is a more traditional view of the array value in Figure 2.11. It is a two-dimensional display of the components in which the first index value specifies the row and the second specifies the column.

Specification 2.2   Two-Dimensional Array

Elements: A component data type is specified, and all component elements are of that type.

Structure: Two index types, both of which must be linear (Section 1.4.1), are specified. There is a one-to-one correspondence between the values of the Cartesian product of the index types and the component data element values of each array value.

    TYPE Array: **ARRAY** IndexType1, IndexType2 **OF** ComponentType

(Figures 2.10 and 2.11 show an example.)

Domain: All Cartesian product index values together with all combinations of associated component values.

Visible Items: Users see the array type, the index types, the component element type, and two operations.

continued

Specification 2.2, continued

Operations: There are two basic array operations. c is a variable of the component element type, and i and j are expressions that evaluate to types IndexType1 and IndexType2, respectively.

PROCEDURE Retrieve(a: Array;   **VAR** c: ComponentType;
                     i: IndexType1; j: IndexType2);
(* **post** — c has the value of a's component associated with
         Cartesian product value <i,j>. *)

The Modula-2 syntax (which is built into Modula-2) that corresponds to Retrieve is c := a[i,j].

PROCEDURE Update(**VAR** a: Array; c: ComponentType; i: IndexType);
(* **post** — The component element value of array a that is associated with
         the Cartesian product value <i,j> is c. *)

The Modula-2 syntax for Update is a[i,j] := c.

TYPE Index1 = [0..10];
     Day   = (sun, mon, tue,
            wed, thu, fri,
            sat);

   Array5 = **ARRAY** Index1,
            Day **OF** REAL;

   Array6 = **ARRAY** ['a'..'z'],
            Index1 **OF** Day;

Figure 2.13
Some two-dimensional Modula-2 arrays.

Retrieve can fail for two reasons. First, it fails if one or more of the index values specified is not a value of the specified type. The error is often referred to as having an index ***out of bounds.*** An erroneous index may indicate a memory location that is not in the memory space allocated to the array, causing some other variable, constant, or even part of the program to be modified. You might then see some bizarre performance. Such bugs are very difficult to trace. Operation *Update* also fails if an index value is not of the specified type.

Second, it fails if there is an undefined value in the address associated with the index values. Such a situation might occur, for example, if no data had yet been stored in that array component. Some compilers are capable of recognizing such a condition, and hardware to do so has been proposed (Myers, 1982). We will assume, however, that *Retrieve* does not detect undefined values in array elements. On the other hand, many compilers have at least a software switch that the programmer can flip to generate code that will detect subscript values that are not of the specified type. Such code lengthens and slows the program, but during testing it is worth the cost.

The major objective of this section is to study the underlying characteristics of arrays and to investigate the methods that are used to transform index values that are specified by the program into the memory location that contains the desired data. By understanding these issues, you will enhance your ability to design and write high-level language programs more intelligently.

We will show that for most arrays the transformation of a set of index values into a memory address is a linear function of the indexes. For a d-dimensional array the address of a component is given by the ***array mapping function (AMF)***

$$\text{addr} (a[i_1, i_2, \ldots, i_d]) = c_0 + c_1 \times i_1 + c_2 \times i_2 + \cdots + c_d \times i_d$$

where $c_0, c_1, c_2, \ldots, c_d$ are constants whose values are determined before the array is used by the program, and $i_1, i_2, \ldots, i_d$ are the index values of the target array component.

In the following sections we will show that this is an appropriate form for the transforming function and we will show how the values of the constants c_i are determined. For the moment, accept that array mapping functions are of the form shown; there are then three important points that can be made:

Accessing Array Components Based on Their Index Values

1. The memory address of an array component can be calculated from its index values.
2. For an array of d dimensions, the calculation requires d additions and d multiplications.
3. The amount of calculation is the same for all components of the array.

The amount of computation necessary to access an array component, given its index values, is small compared to that required by many other data structures. In addition, only an arithmetic calculation is required. In order to find component a[5,2,4], for example, we do not have to search for it; we only have to compute the value of the AMF for indexes [5,2,4]. The amount of computation is not dependent on the number of components in the array, but rather on the number of dimensions of the array. For example, a one-dimensional array requires one addition and one multiplication to convert an index value into a component address—regardless of whether there are 10 components or 10,000 components in the array. For a two-dimensional array, it requires two additions and two multiplications to convert a pair of index values into a component address, and so on.

The third characteristic, equal access time to all components, is very important. It means that arrays provide **random access** to their member components—each component can be accessed in equal time (i.e., the same amount of computation). The amount of computation is small compared to that required by most other data structures. However, this rapid random access works only for **positional access**—access by index values. **Associative access,** locating an array component by its value, is another matter.

2.2.1 Array Characteristics

There are a number of characteristics associated with an array: its base address in memory, its component element type, its component length, its index type(s), the upper and lower bounds on each of its index types, and its dimension. Each of these is described below, and examples are given. The next section discusses array mapping functions.

The memory address of the first byte of the first array component is called the **base address,** which we denote by b. The time at which the array is assigned to its memory space is called its **binding time.** Binding can occur

The base address of an array, denoted b, is the address of the first byte of its first element. In Figure 2.1(a), $b = 500$.

at a variety of times during the compiling, loading, and execution of a program. We will discuss some issues concerning the binding time in Section 2.2.5; meanwhile we assume that binding is accomplished at some time before an array is first used by the executing program.

The memory required to store an array component is determined by the component type and by the host compiler and computer system. An array whose component type is integer would have an element length of 4 bytes if the host system is a VAX11, but 2 bytes if it is a PDP-11. Two different Modula-2 compilers on the same computer systems might use different lengths for the same data type. For most arrays, the length chosen is not as important as the fact that all components of the array are the same length. We will call this the **component length** and denote it *L*.

It is possible to simulate arrays with variable length elements; these are discussed in Section 2.5.

The memory required to store one component of an array, the component length, is denoted *L*. In Figure 2.1(a), *L* = 4.

Each index type must be an ordered linear type (Section 1.4.2). Each index value therefore corresponds to an integer, which is its ordinal position. For our discussion, we can therefore assume that each index type is a subrange of the integers. Each index type can thus be considered to have a smallest value and a largest value, usually called the **lower bound** and the **upper bound,** respectively. Some older languages require the lower bound to be a given value, usually 1. We will use lo_k and hi_k to denote the lower and upper bound, respectively, of the kth index type. A d-dimensional array will be assumed to be defined as

VAR a: **ARRAY** $[lo_1..hi_1]$, $[lo_2..hi_2]$,..., $[lo_d..hi_d]$
 OF Element;

We will assume for our discussion that an index type is always a subrange of the integers. We will denote the smallest and largest index values of $index_k$ by lo_k and hi_k, respectively. These are also called the lower bound and the upper bound of the kth index.

To illustrate the relationship between general index types and the associated integer values, consider the following example:

TYPE Day = (sun, mon, tue, wed, thu, fri, sat);

VAR a: **ARRAY** Day **OF** REAL;

The values of type day have ordinal positions 0 through 6. The array can be discussed as if it were defined by

VAR a: **ARRAY** [0..6] **OF** REAL;

The integer form can be used internally for computation of the array mapping function, whereas the programmer can use the noninteger form, which has more meaning. The compiler produces code that makes the correspondence. The programmer is thus relieved of the tedium of matching index-type values to integer values (as is done in some of the older programming languages), as well as the possibility of errors, since the compiler takes over the chore of arriving at an internally useful form of the index. Thus, the discussion of array mapping functions in the following sections makes no mention of noninteger index types.

In early versions of FORTRAN there was a limit of three, and later seven, on the dimension of an array. These are the number of index registers on the IBM 704 and 709 series computers, respectively. Designers of languages now try to avoid constraints such as these, which are determined by a particular computer architecture.

The amount of memory required for storage of a multidimensional array can increase rapidly with an increase in the number of dimensions. Assuming that the components are stored contiguously in memory, the number of bytes required by a d-dimensional array is

$$L \times (hi_1 - lo_1 + 1) \times (hi_2 - lo_2 + 1) \times \cdots \times (hi_d - lo_d + 1)$$

We turn now to a discussion of the functions used by arrays to convert index values into memory addresses.

2.2.2 Array Mapping Functions

The simplest case of an array mapping function (AMF) is that of a one-dimensional array, so we begin with that. In the margin there is an example of an array, an example of a set of array parameters, the address of each array component, and the AMF for that example. The AMF for the general case of a one-dimensional array follows. If a is specified as

    a: **ARRAY** $[lo_1..hi_1]$ **OF** StdElement;

then

$$addr(a[i]) = b + (i - lo_1) \times L$$
$$= (b - L \times lo_1) + i \times L$$
$$= c_0 + c_1 \times i$$

so that

$$c_1 = L$$
$$c_0 = b - lo_1 \times c_1$$

Notice that L, b, and lo_1 are necessary to determine the AMF fully. The upper bound, hi_1, does not enter into the AMF.

Our analysis of a two-dimensional array is similar to our treatment of a one-dimensional array. An example is given and worked out in the margin on page 64. The general case is treated below.

We seek an expression for the AMF for the array

    a: **ARRAY** $[lo_1..hi_1], [lo_2..hi_2]$ **OF** StdElement;

We assume that b is the base address and that L units of storage are required for each component. The AMF is

---

a: **ARRAY**
    [1..100],[1..100],[1..26]
    OF REAL;

If $L = 4$ bytes, then the memory required to store the above array is 1,040,000 bytes.

One-Dimensional Array

For the array

a: **ARRAY** [3..7] **OF** INTEGER;

we have

$$lo_1 = 3 \text{ and } hi_1 = 7$$

If we are given

$$b = 500 \text{ and } L = 4$$

the addresses of component values for sample array values are as follows:

Address	Index	Sample component values
500	[3]	-12
504	[4]	7
508	[5]	47
512	[6]	26
516	[7]	-52

The AMF is

$$c_1 = 4$$
$$c_0 = 500 - (3 \times 4) = 488$$
$$addr(a[i]) = 488 + 4 \times i$$

For example,

$$addr(a[5]) = 488 + 4 \times 5$$
$$= 508$$

$$addr(a[i,j]) = b + (i - lo_1) \times (hi_2 - lo_2 + 1) \times L + (j - lo_2) \times L$$
$$= c_0 + c_1 \times i + c_2 \times j$$

so that

$$c_2 = L$$
$$c_1 = (hi_2 - lo_2 + 1) \times c_2$$
$$c_0 = b - c_1 \times lo_1 - c_2 \times lo_2$$

Let us repeat, for emphasis, that the purpose of an array mapping function is to convert a set of index values into a component address. For an array this conversion is simple, fast, and independent of the particular index values. This will be useful information when we want to compare implementations based on arrays with implementations using other data structures.

The general AMF for a two-dimensional array and the example in the margin both depend on the array being stored in what is referred to as **row–major order.** In row–major order components are grouped together by common values of their first index value. Most high-level languages store arrays in row–major order. The outstanding exception is FORTRAN. We will assume row–major order and its analog in three and more dimensions in this text. The basic properties of the AMF are not changed by using other similar orders.

In Exercises 2.2.6 you are asked to derive the AMF in the three-dimensional case. Here, we will derive the *general case.* You can check your answer with the result for the general case of a d-dimensional AMF (for row–major order) that follows.

Two-Dimensional Array

For the array,

a: **ARRAY** [0..2],[4..5]
    OF INTEGER;

we have

$lo_1 = 0, hi_1 = 2$
$lo_2 = 4, hi_2 = 5$

If we are given

$b = 500$ and $L = 15$

the locations of the array components are as follows:

Address	Index values	Sample component values
500	[0,4]	54
515	[0,5]	39
530	[1,4]	72
545	[1,5]	13
560	[2,4]	17
575	[2,5]	45

The AMF is

$c_2 = 15$
$c_1 = (5 - 4 + 1) \times 15$
$\quad = 30$
$c_0 = 500 - 30 \times 0 -$
$\qquad 15 \times 4$
$\quad = 440$

$addr(a[i,j]) = 440 + 30 \times i$
$\qquad\qquad\quad + 15 \times j$

For example,

$addr(a[1,5]) = 440 + 30 \times$
$\qquad\qquad 1 + 15 \times 5$
$\qquad\qquad = 545$

• **General d-dimensional AMF**

$$c_d = L$$
$$c_{t-1} = (hi_t - lo_t + 1) \times c_t \qquad\qquad 1 < t <= d$$
$$c_0 = b - c_1 \times lo_1 - c_2 \times lo_2 - \cdots - c_d \times lo_d$$

$$addr(a[i_1,i_2, \ldots, i_d]) = c_0 + c_1 \times i_1 + c_2 \times i_2 + \cdots + c_d \times i_d$$

AMF d-Dimensional Array; Row–Major Order

VAR a: ARRAY [lo_1..hi_1],..., [lo_d..hi_d] **OF** StdElement

It is the homogeneity of arrays that allows us to derive concise AMFs that give random access to the array elements. In the cases treated so far, we have used the fact that each component is the same size and each row contains the same number of components. If these restrictions are relaxed so that certain lengths are not constant (e.g., the row length of a two-dimensional array) but still have a regularity that can be expressed by a concise mathematical expression, then it may still be possible to derive a suitable AMF. One example is a lower-triangular matrix. The absence of such simplifying regularities usually results in the loss of random access, although an AMF can still be written. In addition, the amount of computation used in evaluating the AMF may become prohibitive.

You should be aware of the terminology often used in referring to the constant c_0 of the AMF. It is sometimes called the ***virtual origin,*** or ***virtual base,*** of the array. Note that if an AMF is evaluated for all indexes equal to zero:

$$\text{addr}(a[0,0,\ldots,0]) = c_0 + c_1 \times 0 + \cdots + c_d \times 0 = c_0$$

the result is c_0, the location of the element whose index values are $[0,0,\ldots,0]$, which may not be a valid member of the array. The location c_0 may be outside of the memory space of the program and even outside the memory space of the computer (e.g., it may be negative).

The syntax of array declarations in Modula-2 is discussed in Section A.8.4 of Appendix A.

2.2.3 Array Descriptor Records

Compilers and run-time systems need to collect information about an array. The constants of the AMF must always be available.

Information about an array must be passed between calling and called modules when using procedures and functions. The information that describes an array is often grouped into a record structure, which is referred to as the ***array descriptor,*** or ***dope vector.*** An example is given in Figure 2.14.

```
TYPE BaseType = (REAL, INTEGER, BOOLEAN, CARDINAL,
                 CHAR, RECORD, ...);

VAR adr: RECORD
            name  : ARRAY [1..8] OF CHAR;       (* Array Name *)
            tcode : BaseType;                    (* Element Type *)
            L     : CARDINAL;                 (* Element Length *)
            b     : CARDINAL;                   (* Base Address *)
            d     : CARDINAL;                     (* Dimensions *)
            bounds: ARRAY [1..d] OF
                       RECORD
                          lo, hi: INTEGER       (* Index Bounds *)
                       END;
            c     : ARRAY [0..d] OF INTEGER  (* AMF Constants *)
         END;
```

Figure 2.14 An array descriptor record. (Note: This is syntactically incorrect Modula-2 because of the use of the variable *d* in defining both *bounds* and *c* and the illegal use of the enumeration.)

An important use of array descriptors is in passing arrays as arguments of procedures and functions.

2.2.4 Special Arrays

Some arrays have special properties that allow considerable savings of memory space. Finding an AMF for such arrays is a matter of case-by-case derivation. We will consider two such special cases to illustrate the kinds of approaches that are used.

$$a_{1,1} \quad 0 \quad 0 \quad \cdots \quad 0$$
$$a_{2,1} \quad a_{2,2} \quad 0 \quad \cdots \quad 0$$
$$a_{3,1} \quad a_{3,2} \quad a_{3,3} \quad \cdots \quad 0$$
$$\vdots \quad \vdots \quad \vdots \qquad \vdots$$
$$a_{hi,1} \quad a_{hi,2} \quad a_{hi,3} \quad \cdots \quad a_{hi,hi}$$

Figure 2.15
A lower triangular array. Elements above the diagonal are zero.

•

We will often use the identity

$$\sum_{x=0}^{n} x = \frac{n(n+1)}{2}$$

•

Memory address	Array element	Row
b	$a_{1,1}$	1
$b + L$	$a_{2,1}$	2
$b + 2 \times L$	$a_{2,2}$	2
$b + 3 \times L$	$a_{3,1}$	3
$b + 4 \times L$	$a_{3,2}$	3
$b + 5 \times L$	$a_{3,3}$	3
$b + 6 \times L$	$a_{4,1}$	4
$\vdots$	$\vdots$	$\vdots$
$b + (N-1) \times L$	$a_{hi,hi}$	hi

Figure 2.16
Dense storage of a lower triangular array.

•

Column	1	2	3	4	5	6
Row						
1	0	0	5.3	0	0	0
2	8.6	0	0	0	−2.1	0
3	0	7.0	0	0	0	0

Figure 2.17
A sparse array.

• **Lower triangular array**

A *lower triangular array* is a two-dimensional array that is square—that is, $lo_1 = lo_2$ and $hi_1 = hi_2$—and for which all components above the diagonal are zero:

$$a[i,j] = 0 \text{ when } j > i$$

For simplicity, we set the lower bounds of the index values to 1. Figure 2.15 shows a lower triangular array. The number of elements on and below the diagonal is

$$hi \times (hi + 1)/2$$

The lower triangle can be stored in memory as shown in Figure 2.16. Such a storage arrangement saves

$$L \times hi \times (hi - 1)/2$$

bytes of memory by not storing the elements whose values are known to be zero. To derive an AMF, note that if the target element is in the ith row, $i - 1$ rows must be skipped to arrive at the first element of the target row. Within that row, $(j - 1)$ elements must be skipped. Since row i contains i elements, we can write the AMF as follows:

$$\text{addr}(a[i,j]) = b + (1 + 2 + 3 + \cdots + (i - 1)) \times L \quad \text{Skip to } i\text{th row}$$
$$+ (j - 1) \times L \qquad \text{Skip to } j\text{th element of the row}$$
$$= b + \left(\sum_{k=0}^{i-1} k \times L \right) + (j - 1) \times L$$
$$= b + L \times i \times (i - 1)/2 + (j - 1) \times L$$
$$\text{addr}(a[i,j]) = c_0 + c_1 \times (i \times (i - 1)) + c_2 \times j$$

where

$$c_1 = L/2, \quad c_2 = L, \text{ and } c_0 = b - L$$

Notice that the arithmetic operations needed to evaluate the AMF are three multiplications and three additions. We may regard the increase, one multiplication and one addition per access, over that required for a full square array as the cost of saving almost 50% in memory space.

There are a number of special forms that occur frequently and allow substantial savings of memory space. The **upper-triangular matrix** and **tridiagonal matrix** are two such cases. Both have regularities in their structure that are easily expressible mathematically, which is the key to deriving an AMF that provides random access.

• **Sparse arrays**

Some arrays, called **sparse arrays,** have the property that most of their elements contain a single value (say zero for purposes of discussion). The few values that are different, in this case, the nonzero elements, are sprinkled about the array in an irregular pattern. We will use a two-dimensional array as an example, but the arguments and conclusions are the same for any number of dimensions. Figure 2.17 is an example of a sparse array.

For a sparse array defined as

VAR a: **ARRAY** $[1..hi_1], [1..hi_2]$ **OF** REAL;

where $L = 4$ and only n_z of the elements are nonzero, the amount of space "wasted" by using the normal form of storing the array is

$$(hi_1 \times hi_2 - n_z) \times L$$

An approach that could save memory is to form a condensed array, or table (one-dimensional array), that contains not only the array elements but also their indexes. An example of such a condensed array is shown in Figure 2.18. The values of the first and second indexes are i and j, respectively, and the value of the corresponding array element is *val*.

Index	i	j	val
1	1	3	5.3
2	2	1	8.6
3	2	5	−2.1
4	3	2	7.0

Figure 2.18   Condensed array form of sparse array in Figure 2.17.

Access to an array element by its index value is no longer a matter of calculation using an AMF; it is a search to find a matching index pair. In Algorithm 2.1, a function *SpFind* is given, which will retrieve the value of the [i,j]th element. Access to the elements is no longer random since a search is required. The expected number of probes required by *SpFind* is

$$\frac{n_z + 1}{2}$$

One difficulty with the use of the condensed array, however, is the necessity of fixing a value of $n_z$max, the upper limit on the number of nonzero elements. This is a general problem with using arrays to hold an amount of data that either is not known in advance of program execution time or varies over time. Some estimate of the maximum amount that might occur must be made. If that amount is exceeded, then drastic measures such as aborting program execution or refusal to accept any more data are required. Arrays are not well suited to such situations.

Another difficulty with the condensed array approach is that in the data stored is no longer only the array element value; it is now also the index values. If we assume that the lengths of i, j, and *val* are all equal to L, the length of each entry is $3 \times L$ and the actual savings in memory space is

$$memory\ saved = (hi_1 \times hi_2 - 3 \times n_z max) \times L$$

```
MODULE Sparse;
(* Constants, types, and
     variables. *)
CONST nzMax = ...;
      hi1   = ...;
      hi2   = ...;
      (* User supplied. *)
TYPE  Sub1 = [1..hi1];
      Sub2 = [1..hi2];
      nzRange = [0..nzMax];
      Condensed =
        ARRAY nzRange OF
          RECORD
            i  : Sub1;
            j  : Sub2;
            val: REAL
          END;
VAR ca: Condensed;
    nz: nzRange;
PROCEDURE SparseFind
(i: Sub1; j: Sub2): REAL;
(* post - SparseFind is
          the value of
          the [i,j]th
          element of a
          sparse array
          stored in the
          condensed
          array ca. *)
VAR k: nzRange;
BEGIN
    k := 0;
    REPEAT
      k := k+1
    UNTIL ( (ca[k].i = i)
          & (ca[k].j = j))
        OR (k = nz);
    IF ( (ca[k].i = i)
       & (ca[k].j = j))
    THEN RETURN
         ca[k].val
      ELSE RETURN 0.0
    END
END SparseFind;

(*    .
      :   *)

END Sparse.
```

Algorithm 2.1
Search a sparse array.

2.2.5 Dynamic Arrays and Open Array Parameters

We have assumed thus far that the characteristics of an array are fixed some time before any element of the array is accessed. This assures that the constants of the AMF have values before the AMF is evaluated. The following discussion is an introduction to **dynamic arrays,** which are provided by programming languages to allow us to delay the assignment for some characteristics.

Dynamic array features allow the programmer to delay specifying one or more array parameters until the program is executing.

Languages such as FORTRAN fix all of the array parameters no later than at the start of program execution. The index bounds and number of dimensions must be set by the programmer (although there is some provision for delaying the specification of array parameters for arrays passed as subroutine arguments). The arrays are usually bound to memory when the program is loaded.

PL/I provides a number of dynamic array features. The element type of the array (and therefore L) and the number of dimensions, d, must be set by the programmer. However, both the binding to memory and the fixing of index bounds can be delayed. PL/I provides a number of variations of such features. For example, consider the array defined in Figure 2.19. (FIXED BINARY is equivalent to Modula-2's type INTEGER.) There are two index types whose bounds are not yet known. In addition, the array is dynamic, which means that the array will not be bound to memory until the program requests it to be. The GET statement reads in values for L1, U1, L2, and U2. The ALLOCATE statement assigns these bounds to the array, requests the necessary space from the run-time system, and binds the array to memory. The index bounds are the values of L1, U1, L2, and U2.

```
DECLARE A(*,*) FIXED BINARY
DYNAMIC
    ⋮
GET DATA (L1, U1, L2, U2);
ALLOCATE (A(L1:U1,L2:U2));
    ⋮
RELEASE(A)
```

Figure 2.19
PL/I array.

ALLOCATE effectively sets the values of L1, U1, L2, U2, and b, thereby allowing determination of the constants of the AMF. After execution of ALLOCATE, the array can be used like any other. Execution of the RELEASE statement cancels the effect of the ALLOCATE, and the array no longer exists. ALLOCATE and RELEASE can be called repeatedly with different index bounds.

The programming language APL probably provides the most flexibility in the use of arrays. Not only can the index bounds be changed, but so can the number of indexes, the component type of the array, and the size of the array, all while the array exists and retains its data.

See Appendix A, Section A.11, for a discussion of the scope and life of variables.

Modula-2 arrays must have their number of dimensions, element type, and index type specified by the programmer so that they are known at compile time. However, most Modula-2 implementations do not bind the array to a memory space until the procedure containing the declaration of the array is called. The binding is canceled when the procedure is exited. Three different invocations of the procedure might involve three different memory spaces for the array. For this reason, the array cannot be expected to retain its value from one invocation to the next.

Modula-2 has a feature that allows the writing of procedures that act on ARRAY parameters when the bounds and type of the array index are not known in advance. This feature increases the versatility of the procedures written in this way. Suppose that we wished to write a procedure that would compute the mean value of any one-dimensional array of REAL values. Algorithm 2.2 illustrates such a procedure and the use of ***open array parameters*** in Modula-2.

```
PROCEDURE MeanValue(a: ARRAY OF REAL);
VAR sum: REAL;
BEGIN
  sum := a[0];
  FOR i := 1 TO HIGH(a) DO sum := sum + a[i] END;
  RETURN sum / (HIGH(a) + 1)
END MeanValue;
```

   Algorithm 2.2

Indexes of open arrays are always considered to be a subrange of type CARDINAL, with the subrange being [0..HIGH(a)], regardless of their actual index type. The function procedure *HIGH* is a standard Modula-2 function that returns the high value of the index subrange. Figure 2.20 shows some examples of the use of *MeanValue*.

Exercises 2.2

1. Explain why an array is said to be (a) random access, (b) static, and (c) linear.
2. What restrictions are placed on the component type of a Modula-2 array? What restrictions are placed on the index type of a Modula-2 array?
3. Let A, B, and C be arrays with index type [1..10] and the same component type.
   a. Write a Modula-2 procedure that uses operations *Retrieve* and *Update* to implement, by transferring one component at a time, the Modula-2 assignment, A := B.
   b. Write a Modula-2 procedure that uses operations *Retrieve* and *Update* to implement the array addition A := B + C.
4. For the array

   ```
   a: ARRAY [3..5], [10..12] OF INTEGER
   ```

   give an example array value, a list of the index pairs, and show the one-to-one correspondence between them. See Figure 2.11.
5. What is an array mapping function?
6. Determine the array mapping function for the following:
   a. a: **ARRAY** [5..15] **OF** Element; $b = 1000$, $L = 12$
   b. b: **ARRAY** [5..15], [6..9] **OF** Element; $b = 1000$, $L = 16$
   c. c: **ARRAY** [5..15], [6..9], [1..10] **OF** Element; $b = 1000$, $L = 18$
7. A logical view of the array

   ```
   a: ARRAY [1..3], [1..3], [0..3] OF INTEGER;
   ```

   is shown in Figure 2.21. Develop a general expression for the array mapping function for a three-dimensional array.

```
TYPE
  Day =
    (sun,mon,tue,wed,thu,fri,sat);
VAR
  a1  : ARRAY [−120..100]
          OF REAL;
  a2  : ARRAY ['a'..'z']
          OF REAL;
  a3  : ARRAY Day OF REAL;
  x,y,z : REAL;
BEGIN
        ⋮
        ⋮
  x := MeanValue(a1);
    (* HIGH(a1) = 220. *)
  y := MeanValue(a2);
    (* HIGH(a2) = 25. *)
  z := MeanValue(a3);
    (* HIGH(a3) = 6. *)
        ⋮
        ⋮
END
```

Figure 2.20
Use of procedure *MeanValue*.

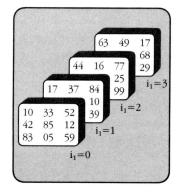

VAR a: **ARRAY**
[1..3],[1..3],[0..3] **OF** INTEGER;

Figure 2.21
Visualization of a three-dimensional array.

8. Determine the values of the components of the array descriptor record (see Figure 2.14) for the arrays in Exercise 6.
9. Find an array mapping function for the following:
   a. An upper-triangular matrix—all values below the diagonal are zero
   b. A tridiagonal array

$$a_{i,j} = 0 \qquad \text{if } |i - j| > 1$$

   c. A band array

$$a_{i,j} = 0 \qquad \text{if } |i - j| > k$$

   for some fixed value of k
10. An array a is specified by

       a: **ARRAY** [1..100,1..100] **OF** StdElement;

   so that it contains 10,000 components. Searching for the component that contains a particular value requires, on the average, examining half (or 5000) components. Plot the number of probes required as a function of p_{nz} if the array is stored as shown in Figure 2.18.
11. Speculate about how you might represent an array whose index values change while the array contains data. Read Standish (1980), Chapter 8, and modify your speculations based on what you have learned.

2.3 Records

An important characteristic of **_records_** is their ability to group individual data elements of different data types as a single unit. This allows a variety of data about something that is to be regarded as a single logical entity. A record describing a person, for example, might include the name, address, telephone number, sex, personal computer owned, and a variety of other data about that person. The information can either be treated as a single data element—stored, moved, retrieved, etc.—or any field can be used separately. The fields need not be atomic elements but can themselves be other data structures. The concept of records contributes greatly to the logical conciseness and ease of programming.

The fact that records are able to group data in the manner discussed, however, leads to a drawback in dealing with components of records. Record components can only be accessed with their **_component identifiers._** They cannot, like array components, be accessed using variables or expressions. A record component must be specified by the programmer at the time the program is written. The programmer loses the option of delaying the exact specification of which element to access. For example, if a is a one-dimensional array of CARDINAL in Modula-2, then

       ReadInt(i);
       WriteCard(a[i],5);   (* Valid.   *)

is a perfectly acceptable code sequence. Modula-2 records have no comparable facility.

The use of records arose in early business data processing applications of computers and became firmly established as the primary data structure of COBOL. COBOL applications tended to involve relatively little computation compared to the activity of transferring records between random access memory and mass storage devices such as disks and tapes. Designers of some languages (e.g., FORTRAN and BASIC) apparently did not realize that records are an important data type in scientific and general systems applications, an oversight that was corrected in languages such as PL/I, C, Pascal, Ada, and Modula-2, which do have the record as a native data type. Of particular importance to the material in this book is the use of records as fundamental building blocks of more sophisticated data structures.

2.3.1 The Record Abstract Data Type

Consider the Modula-2 statement in Figure 2.22 describing an employee record type. A value of this record has four components. The data type of each component is given as part of the record specification. Each component has an identifier so that there is an obvious one-to-one correspondence between identifiers and components. An identifier together with its data type is called a *field*. Together, the fields form a *field list,* which specifies the components of the record.

Figure 2.23 shows a value of the record described in Figure 2.22, the identifiers for that record type, and the one-to-one correspondence between them. Specification 2.3 is a generalization of this example and defines a record abstract data type.

```
TYPE Str = ARRAY [1..20] OF
             CHAR;
     Emp = RECORD
              id:[1000..9999];
              name: Str;
              dept: [1..99];
              rate: REAL
           END;
```

Figure 2.22
Example of an employee record type.

Component identifier	One-to-one correspondence	Field value
id	⟵⟶	2750
name	⟵⟶	Hopper
dept	⟵⟶	56
rate	⟵⟶	6.75

Figure 2.23

Specification 2.3   Record

Elements: A data type is specified for each component element. The types may be different.

Structure: A list of identifiers, each identifying a field of the record, is given; there is one for each component element. The record structure is a one-to-one correspondence between the identifiers and the component elements of a record's value.

```
    TYPE Record = RECORD
                     Identifier list and associated
                     component element types
                  END;
```

(Figures 2.22 and 2.23 show an example.)

Domain: The list of identifiers with all possible combinations of values of the component elements.

continued

Specification 2.3, continued

Visible Items: The user sees the record type, the list of identifiers and their corresponding component element types, and two operations.

Operations: There are two basic operations. Let r be a record, id an identifier from r's identifier list, and v a variable of the type associated with id.

PROCEDURE Retrieve(r: Record; **VAR** v: Variable; id: Identifier);
(* **post** — v has the value of field id of record r. *)

In Modula-2, the syntax for this operation is built in and is v := r.id.

PROCEDURE Update(**VAR** r: Record; v: Variable; id: Identifier);
(* **post** — Field id of record r has the value of v. *)

In Modula-2 the syntax for this operation is r.id := v.

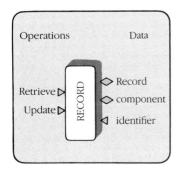

Figure 2.24
A capsule-like view of the record data structure.

If *R1* and *R2* are record identifiers of the same type, then

R1 := R2

assigns the value of *R2* to the value of *R1*. This ability to retrieve and update entire records together with the ability to retrieve and update individual components provides powerful tools for manipulating these data structures. This power is enhanced by the ability to specify either records or arrays as components of records or arrays. The ability to create valuable data structures with various combinations of just these two data types is practically limitless.

Figure 2.25 shows an array of records used to store information about computers. The components of the records include both records and arrays. The interplay between data types in Figure 2.25 is shown in Figure 2.26.

```
TYPE Name       = ARRAY [1..20] OF CHAR;
     DataType   = RECORD
                      wordSize     : [8..64];
                      manufacturer : Name;
                      serialPorts  : [0..10];
                      parallelPorts: [0..3]
                  END;
     StdElement = RECORD
                      key : Name;
                      data: DataType
                  END;

VAR computer: ARRAY [1..100] OF StdElement;
```

Figure 2.25   A data type that is a composite of arrays and records.

Modula-2 provides the ability to retrieve, update, or move any component in the structure. Component identifiers are constructed simply by concatenating additional identifiers on the right end. The *wordSize* of the *j*th *computer* is, for example, given by

> *computer [j].data.wordSize*

and the *k*th character of the *manufacturer* is referenced by

> *computer[j].data.manufacturer[k]*

The process of converting a component identifier into the address of that component must be different for records from what it is for arrays, since the components are of different types and therefore require different amounts of storage. Before we discuss the process usually used, we will present some terminology.

2.3.2 Record Characteristics

The characteristics used to specify a record are base location, field list, and field types. The base address, *b*, of a record is the address of the first byte of the record.

As we discussed in Section 2.3.1, the identifier together with its data type is a field. The fields then form a field list, which specifies the components of the record. The component (field) identifiers of a record must be unique with respect to each other. Ambiguity is permitted, however, as long as the fully qualified name of each component is unique. The record *work,* specified in Figure 2.27, includes two of each of the component identifiers: *mo, day,* and *year.* The fully qualified identifiers such as *work.start.day* and *work.stop.day* are unique. Some languages (e.g., PL/I) allow the use of a simple name if there is no ambiguity. For example, if there is no other variable named *empno* in the program (or more exactly, in the scope of the record *work*), then *empno* may be used. (The scope of Modula-2 identifiers is discussed in Appendix A, Section A.11.) If there is another variable named *empno,* then the field must be referred to as *work.empno.* Modula-2 permits this kind of abbreviation if it is explicitly declared using a **WITH** statement. Referring to Figure 2.27,

```
WITH work.start DO
   year := 1920;
   work.stop.year := 1935
END;
```

Each component (field) of a record has an associated **field length,** which is determined by its data type and the host system. Examples of field lengths for work and for records of type *Date* are given in Figure 2.28.

2.3.3 Record Description and Memory Mapping

All of the characteristics of a record, with the exception of the base address, *b*,

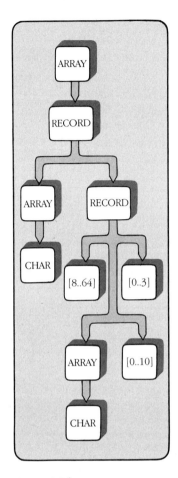

Figure 2.26
The relationship between data types used to form the data structure computer in Figure 2.25. The ability to use arrays and records as components of each other is a valuable tool that can be used to describe complex objects.

```
TYPE
    Date = RECORD
                mo : [1..12];
                day : [1..31];
                year: [1900..2000]
            END;

VAR
    work:   RECORD
                empno:
                [100..999];
                start   : Date;
                stop    : Date
            END;
```

Figure 2.27
Example of a record in which two of its components are records of the same type.

•

Field identifier	Field length
empno	4
start	12
stop	12
mo	4
day	4
year	4

Figure 2.28
Example field lengths.

•

```
TYPE OffSetTable =
    ARRAY [1..noFields] OF
        RECORD
            fieldName:
                ARRAY [1..20]
                    OF CHAR;
            dataType : Type;
            length:CARDINAL;
            offSet:CARDINAL
        END;
```

Figure 2.29

are usually fixed by compile time. When the name of a field is referenced in a program, at least three things must be determined:

1. The data type of the referenced field
2. Its length
3. Its distance, or ***offset,*** from the base of the record

In order to accomplish this, a table of these quantities may be constructed at the time the record characteristics are fixed. A simplified version of the table might look like Figure 2.29, where *Typ* is a scalar type that enumerates the allowable data types. Figure 2.30 shows the offset table, or the record descriptor, for record *work.*

Compilers are built in a variety of ways and may or may not have an explicit table for record fields. However, the information described as being in the offset table is available to the compiler. The offset of a field remains fixed during loading and execution of the program.

A ***memory mapping function*** allows the system to determine the base memory address of a named record field. It is simply the addition of the field's offset to the base address of the record. At that time the field can be manipulated according to its data type and field length.

2.3.4 Variant Record Schemes

Several languages provide features that have the following two major objectives:

1. To allow records of a given type to vary in length according to the data stored in them
2. To allow a delay in the specification of certain field names until execution time

The facilities of COBOL and Modula-2 that allow a partial accomplishment of these objectives are examined briefly.

COBOL provides a simple but powerful facility for variable length records. Consider the following COBOL record definition:

```
01 R.
    02  S   PIC   A(6).
    02  T   PIC   X(4).
    02  M   PIC   99.
    02  V   OCCURS 0 to 99 TIMES DEPENDING ON M.
        03  W   PIC   9(5).
        03  Y   PIC   A.
```

The relationship between these components is shown in Figure 2.31. The definition of *V* states in effect that *V* is an array that can contain from 0 to 99 elements and that the number of elements currently in the array is stored in field *M. M* is also in the record. If $M = 5$, then *V* acts as if it were an array [1..5]; if $M = 0$, then *V* acts as if it did not exist. Different occurrences of *R* can have different values for *M* and therefore different record lengths. In practice,

R is usually allocated enough space in random access memory to store the maximum length ($M = 99$), so memory is not saved. However, if the record is transferred to a mass storage device, only the portion of the record actually holding data is transferred. By use of this simple device, a great deal of economy in the use of mass storage space can be gained. If a record of type R is read from a file, its nonvarying part (S, T, and M) can be examined for the value of M so that the length of the variant portion V can be determined.

Modula-2 takes a different approach. A Modula-2 record is divided into **fixed parts** and **variant parts.** The Modula-2 records we have considered so far have only a fixed part. A variant part of a record consists of a **discriminator** or **tag field** and a list of variants expressed in the form of a **CASE** statement. The tag field specifies a **tag type,** which can be any of the linear, ordered types native to Modula-2 (type REAL is thereby ruled out).

```
TYPE StateType = (solid, liquid, gas, crystal);
     Substance = RECORD
                    name  : ARRAY [1..20] OF CHAR;
                    number: CARDINAL;
                    CASE state: StateType OF
                      solid : hardness: REAL     |
                      liquid: boil, freeze: INTEGER;
                              viscosity   : REAL;
                              CASE  flammable: BOOLEAN OF
                                TRUE : flashPoint: REAL   |
                                FALSE:
                              END
                    ELSE              (* No other fields. *)
                    END
                 END;
VAR data: Substance;
```

Figure 2.32 A variant record.

Look at Figure 2.32. There are two variant parts, one embedded within the other. The first tag field type is *StateType,* and the tag field is *state. StateType* has four values. The CASE statement has four variants specified, two by specified values and two by means of an ELSE clause. (ELSE is used for the sake of illustration; the other values could equally well have been used.)

There is a second variant within the first. The tag field *flammable* applies only to substances in the liquid state, and the record information varies depending on whether or not the liquid is flammable.

There can be more than one variant within a Modula-2 record type, and the variants may be separate and/or embedded within each other. Section A.8.5 of Appendix A covers record declarations.

The variant stored depends on the value of *data.state.* If the value of *data.state* is *solid,* then the variant data fields are as shown in Figure 2.33. Figures 2.34 and 2.35 show the construction of the record *data* if the value of *data.state* is *liquid,* and *gas* or *crystal* respectively. There are two constructions within *liquid,* depending on whether the substance is flammable. Note that *gas*

Field No.	Data name	type	Length	Offset
1	empno	integer	4	0
2	start	date	12	4
3	stop	date	12	16

Figure 2.30
Offset table for variable *work.*

Figure 2.31
Relationships between the components in the COBOL specification in the text.

```
RECORD
    name     : ARRAY [1..20]
               OF CHAR;
    number  : CARDINAL;
    state   : StateType;
                (* solid *)
    hardness: REAL
END;
```

Figure 2.33
Form of *data* when *state* = *solid.*

and *crystal* are treated the same by means of an ELSE clause—there are no other fields of data in both cases.

The following type of code might be used to control references to fields of data (Figure 2.32) :

```
(* Get the record from somewhere. *)
        .
        .
        .

CASE data.state OF
    solid : .....    | (* References to hardness are ok.   *)
    liquid: .....    | (* References to boil, freeze,       *)
                       (* viscosity, and flammable are ok; *)
                       (* references to flashPoint are ok  *)
                       (* if flammable is TRUE.            *)
    gas, crystal: ... (* No variant component             *)
                       (* references ok.                   *)
END;
```

Modula-2 compilers do not generally check references to variant portions of the record to see that they are in conformance with the current value of the tag field. If the value of *data.state* is *solid* and the program accesses the value of *data boil,* the access will probably be allowed. The value retrieved would be garbage unless the programmer knew exactly what he or she was doing and had some reason for the access.

Exercises 2.3

1. Why is a Modula-2 record said to be heterogeneous?
2. Give the type statement for a Modula-2 record that contains information about some object with which you are familiar (e.g., bicycle, sailboard, tree, flower, frog).
3. Each component of a Modula-2 record has a data type. What restrictions are placed on that component data type?
4. Is the following record specification valid Modula-2? Explain.

```
VAR a: RECORD
          a: RECORD
                 a: integer;
                 b: integer
             END
       END;
```

```
RECORD
    name       : ARRAY [1..20]
                 OF CHAR;
    number     : CARDINAL;
    state      : StateType;
                 (* liquid *)
    boil       : INTEGER;
    freeze     : INTEGER;
    viscosity  : REAL;
    flammable  : BOOLEAN;
                 (* TRUE *)
    flashPoint : REAL
END;
```

(a)

```
RECORD
    name       : ARRAY [1..20]
                 OF CHAR;
    number     : CARDINAL;
    state      : StateType;
                 (* liquid *)
    boil       : INTEGER;
    freeze     : INTEGER;
    viscosity  : REAL;
    flammable  : BOOLEAN
                 (* FALSE *)
END;
```

(b)

Figure 2.34
Forms of *data* when *state* = *liquid.*

5. Consider the following data type (which itself is a record) of an array of a record.

```
TYPE C = RECORD
            key : CARDINAL;
            data: ARRAY [1..10] OF CHAR
         END;

VAR  a : RECORD
            b : ARRAY [5..15] OF C;
            d : (fall, winter, spring)
         END;
```

a. Draw a diagram that shows the relationship between the components of *a*. See Figure 2.22 for an example.

b. Describe how the component identifier *a.b*[5].*data*[7] might be converted into an address.

6. Give a type statement for a variant record that is to store information about objects with which you are familiar (e.g., houses, apartments, offices).

7. Compare the Modula-2 data types array and record. Organize your discussion into three parts—components, structure, operations—and describe methods for converting a component identifier into an address.

2.4 Pointers and Simple Linked Lists

Arrays and records both use calculations to locate their component elements. Arrays use an array mapping function based on index value(s). Records add offsets of fields to the base location of the record. **Linked structures** take a different approach. Each data structure element contains not only the element's data value, but also the addresses of one or more other data elements. The fields that contain addresses are called **pointer fields.**

A **linked list** in which each element contains the address of the next list element is probably the simplest linked structure. An illustration of such a linked list is given in Figure 2.36.

In this section we will first study pointers and the closely related concept of dynamic memory allocation. Then, we will see how both concepts are used in the construction of simple linked lists. Finally, we will look at the characteristics of simple linked lists in more detail.

2.4.1 Pointers

A **pointer** is a data type whose values are the locations of values of other data types. For example, if you were to write your home address on a piece of paper and give it to a friend, the piece of paper could be considered to contain a pointer whose value is your home location. In computer systems there are many ways of specifying the locations of objects. For example, we might specify that the data we are seeking is in the *i*th record in a list. It might be in the *j*th register of the system's central processing unit. It might be in the [i,j]th position in a two-dimensional array. Any location, whether it is at the abstract, virtual,

```
RECORD
   name   : ARRAY [1..20]
            OF CHAR;
   number: CARDINAL;
   state  : StateType
                    (* crystal *)
                    (* or gas  *)
END;
```

Figure 2.35
Form of *data* when *state* = *crystal* or *state* = *gas*.

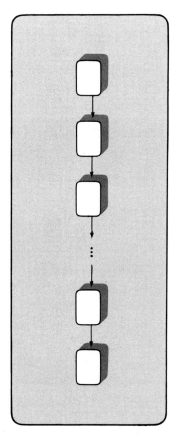

Figure 2.36
Illustration of a linked list.

or physical level, can be a pointer value. In this chapter we will assume pointer values to be memory addresses in random access memory (RAM). The arguments made, the data structures constructed, and the conclusions drawn, however, are all valid for any form of pointer value.

In practice, RAM addresses take forms that are dependent on the architecture of the computer system and the mode of addressing being used (a computer system may have several addressing modes). However, for simplicity, we will assume that RAM is a one-dimensional array of bytes.

A RAM pointer value is simply an index value in the array RAM. A pointer with value 1234, for example, points to RAM[1234]. A pointer can take on values from 0 to $M - 1$, where M is the number of bytes of memory. It can also take the special value undefined. In Modula-2, undefined is called NIL, and we will always refer to it using that term. The value 0 is often used to implement NIL, although other choices are sometimes used. The actual value is of little concern and varies with compiler, language, and host system.

Modula-2 includes an associated type—ADDRESS—to be the memory addresses of the memory's words.

TYPE ADDRESS = **POINTER TO** WORD

Type ADDRESS is exported from the standard module *SYSTEM*. Recall that the contiguous bytes of computer memories are often grouped into a next-larger unit called words. Two- and four-byte words are prevalent, though larger groupings are not uncommon. In many systems, data are fetched from memory in word groups instead of individual bytes.

Two functions exported by *SYSTEM, SIZE*(v) and *TSIZE*(t), return the number of memory words in variable *v* and type *t*, respectively.

The specification of Modula-2's atomic data type POINTER (Appendix A) is as follows:

Domain: The values are the set of RAM addresses together with the value NIL.

Operations: There are five operations:

Assignment	:=
Relational	= and #
Dynamic	NEW and DISPOSE

We will review Modula-2's POINTER data type with a simple example.

Look at Figure 2.37. *Node* is a record type having two fields, *key* and *data*. Another type, *NodePointer*, is also defined. Variables of this type will have values that are memory addresses of (i.e., are pointers to) occurrences of data structures of type *Node*. Identifier *p* is a variable whose value must be the memory address of the first byte of an occurrence of a record of type *Node* (see Figure 2.38) or the value NIL. The elements of the node that *p* points to are *p* ↑ .*key* and *p* ↑ .*data*. The identifier of the entire record is *p* ↑ .

Pointers can be defined for most data types in Modula-2. We can have, for

TYPE
   NodePointer = **POINTER TO**
           Node;
  Node = **RECORD**
       key :CARDINAL;
       data: **ARRAY** [1..20]
               OF CHAR
      END;

VAR p: NodePointer;

Figure 2.37
Declaration of a pointer type.

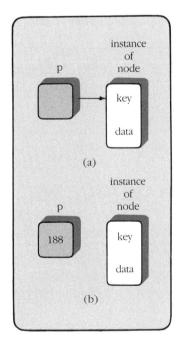

Figure 2.38
(a) Logically, we think of *p* as pointing to a node. (b) Actually, *p*'s value is the address of the node. If the node's address is 188, then *p* contains 188.

example, the definitions shown in Figure 2.39. However, each pointer variable is restricted to referencing data values of a single specified type. In this sense Modula-2 pointers are said to be ***strongly typed.*** In some languages pointers are permitted, at different times, to reference values of different types.

We turn now to our example of the simple linked list. It will serve as the basis for a discussion of dynamic memory allocation.

2.4.2 A Simple Linked List

We will describe a simple linked list by presenting an illustration, giving its specification, elaborating on its operations, discussing the use of pointers, and showing the implementation of the list in modular form.

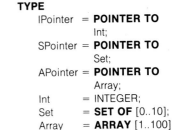

```
TYPE
   IPointer = POINTER TO
              Int;
   SPointer = POINTER TO
              Set;
   APointer = POINTER TO
              Array;
   Int      = INTEGER;
   Set      = SET OF [0..10];
   Array    = ARRAY [1..100]
              OF SPointer;
```

Figure 2.39
Examples of Modula-2 pointer types.

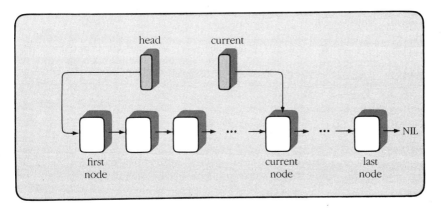

Figure 2.40   Conceptual view of a simple linked list.

The specification of our simple linked list follows.

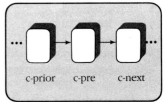

Figure 2.41
Notation for current and adjacent nodes prior to execution.

Specification 2.4   Linked List

DEFINITION MODULE LinkedList;

(* **Elements:** The elements are nodes. Each node contains one standard element and one node pointer. *)

   FROM StdTypes **IMPORT** StdElement;

(* **Structure:** The relationship among the nodes is linear (see Section 1.4.2), and the node pointer in each node points to its successor; the value of the node pointer in the last node is NIL. *)

(* **Domain:** The number of nodes in the linked list is bounded. *)

continued

Specification 2.4, continued

EXPORT QUALIFIED Insert, Delete, Retrieve, Update, FindFirst, FindNext,
                   Empty, Full, Last;

(* **Operations:** There are 9 operations. If the linked list is not empty, then one
     of the nodes is designated as the current node. Occasionally, in the
     postcondition, it is necessary to refer to the linked list or the current
     node as they were immediately before execution of the operation. We use
     LL-pre and c-pre, respectively, for these references. *)

PROCEDURE FindFirst();
(* **pre** – The linked list is not empty.
    post – The first node is the current node. *)

PROCEDURE FindNext();
(* **pre** – The linked list is not empty and the last element is not current.
    post – c-next is the current node. *)

PROCEDURE Retrieve(**VAR** e: StdElement);
(* **pre** – The linked list is not empty.
    post – e contains the value of the element in the current node. *)

PROCEDURE Update(e: StdElement);
(* **pre** – The linked list is not empty.
    post – The current node contains e as its element. *)

PROCEDURE Insert(e: StdElement);
(* **pre** – The number of nodes in the linked list has not reached its bound.
    post – A node containing e is the first node in the linked list, and the
             first node in LL-pre, if any, is its successor; the node
             containing e is the current node. *)

PROCEDURE Delete();
(* **pre** – The linked list is not empty.
    post – c-pre is not in the linked list.
             If c-pre was the first node, then c-next, if it exists, is the
             first node; else c-next, if it exists, is the successor of c-prior.
             If the linked list is not empty then the first node is the current
             node. *)

PROCEDURE Empty(): BOOLEAN;
(* **post** – If the linked list has no nodes then Empty is true, else Empty is
           false. *)

PROCEDURE Full(): BOOLEAN;
(* **post** – If the number of nodes in the linked list has reached the maximum
           allowed (the bound) then Full is true, else Full is false. *)

PROCEDURE Last(): BOOLEAN;
(* **pre** – The linked list is not empty.
    post – If the last node is the current node then Last is true,
             else Last is false. *)

END LinkedList.

The domain statement of Specification 2.4 specifies that the number of nodes in a linked list is bounded. Procedures *Insert* and *Full* refer to this bound. There is no indication, though, of what the bound is. We have seen in Specification 1.2 (*ReversibleStrings*) of Chapter 1 that there was an explicitly stated upper bound of 80 on the number of characters in a reversible string. Yet here we state only that there is some bound. Why?

There is no conceptual limit on the number of nodes in a linked list. The problem is that the list's nodes are stored in computer memories, which are finite in size. Designers of abstract data types must recognize that fact and write specifications to account for it.

Suppose that we had specified an unbounded number of nodes in a linked list. The code segment

```
LOOP
  Insert(e)
END;
```

would eventually fail, not because of a conceptual limit in the size of the list but because memory is finite. In other words, we could not write an implementation on a real computer that meets the specifications. To imagine that we did so would be only an illusion. The loop not only would fail but would do so in some undefined way. Such code is not robust.

If a bound were specified as we have done, then the loop would be

```
LOOP
  IF NOT Full()
     THEN Insert(e)
     ELSE WriteString('Linked list full!');
          EXIT (or RETURN)
  END
END;
```

A program containing the code segment would "fail" in a controlled manner—the code is robust. How *Full* is written in Modula-2 is discussed later in this section.

Almost all the data types that we specify in this book recognize the finiteness of computer memories by specifying bounded domains, and an operation is provided (usually called *Full*) that tests whether an instance of the data type has reached its bound.

Algorithm 2.3 uses the list operations to print all the elements in the list. It is convenient to think of the operations as being divided into three groups. One group includes *Insert, Delete, Update,* and *Retrieve,* which perform **basic operations** on the list. These operations usually act on the list in a way determined by the **current node.** We therefore need operations to set the current node; these operations, *FindFirst* and *FindNext,* form another group. It is important to note that these two operations allow any node in the list to be selected as the current node.

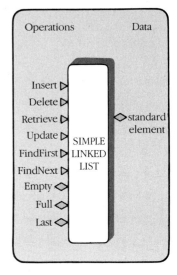

Figure 2.42
A capsule-like representation of a simple linked list.

```
IF NOT Empty()
    THEN FindFirst();
            LOOP
                Retrieve(e);
                Print(e);
                IF Last()
                    THEN EXIT
                    ELSE FindNext()
                END
            END
    ELSE WriteString('Empty')
END
```

Algorithm 2.3   Using list operations to print all elements in the list.

A third group contains three operations, *Empty, Full,* and *Last,* which enable us to test preconditions given in the specifications. More complex data structures will have several preconditions and hence will require more operations in this group. Note that five of the nine operations have the precondition that the list is not empty.

We will now look at a representation of our simple linked list. One possibility is shown in Figure 2.43. There are two points to be made. First, each node contains a pointer, called *next,* to another node. We could add other such pointers, such as to the predecessor node or the first node in the list, but we choose not to in this example. Second, although a *node* is described as a data type, no instances of nodes are allocated by the type statement. Nodes will be allocated and disposed of dynamically by operations *Insert* and *Delete.*

The implementation details are given in Implementation Module 2.1. To explain the use of pointers and dynamic allocation of memory, we will discuss how Implementation Module 2.1 manipulates a linked list.

```
TYPE
    NodePointer = POINTER
                        TO Node;
    Node = RECORD
                el:StdElement;
                next:NodePointer
            END;

VAR head, current, p: Node-
Pointer;
```

Figure 2.43
Representation of a simple linked list holding standard elements.

Implementation Module 2.1   *Linked List*

```
IMPLEMENTATION MODULE LinkedList;
(* LinkedList; meets Specification 2.4. *)

FROM StdTypes IMPORT StdElement;
FROM Storage  IMPORT ALLOCATE, DEALLOCATE, Available; (* Indirectly imports NEW *)
                                                        (* and DISPOSE.          *)
FROM SYSTEM   IMPORT TSIZE;                             (* See the following discussion. *)

TYPE NodePointer = POINTER TO Node;
     Node        = RECORD
                        el: StdElement;
                        next: NodePointer
                    END;

VAR head, current: NodePointer;
```

continued

Implementation Module 2.1, continued

```
PROCEDURE Insert(e: StdElement);            (* Insert e at the head of the list. *)
VAR p: NodePointer;
BEGIN
   NEW(p);                  (* 1 *)   (* Allocate a node for the new data.       *)
   p↑.el   := e;                      (* Move the data into the node.            *)
   p↑.next := head;         (* 2 *)   (* Make the new node point to the old node. *)
   head    := p;            (* 3 *)   (* Adjust head pointer to point to new node. *)
   current := p
END Insert;

PROCEDURE Delete;                           (* Delete the current node. *)
VAR p: NodePointer;
BEGIN
   IF current # head
      THEN p := head;                            (* Find the predecessor of *)
           WHILE p↑.next # current DO            (* the current node.       *)
              p := p↑.next
           END;
           p↑.next := current↑.next              (* Link it to the successor *)
                                                 (* of the current node.     *)
      ELSE head := head↑.next                     (* Delete the first node.   *)
   END;
   DISPOSE(current);
   current := head
END Delete;

PROCEDURE Retrieve(VAR e: StdElement);      (* Retrieve the element in the *)
BEGIN                                       (* current node.               *)
   e := current↑.el
END Retrieve;

PROCEDURE Update(e: StdElement);            (* Update the element in the *)
BEGIN                                       (* current node.             *)
   current↑.el := e
END Update;

PROCEDURE FindFirst;                             (* Make the first node *)
BEGIN                                            (* the current node.   *)
   current := head
END FindFirst;

PROCEDURE FindNext;                         (* Make the successor of the *)
BEGIN                                       (* current node current.     *)
   current := current↑.next
END FindNext;

PROCEDURE Empty(): BOOLEAN;                      (* Is the linked list empty? *)
BEGIN
   RETURN (head = NIL)
END Empty;
```

continued

Implementation Module 2.1, continued

```
PROCEDURE Full(): BOOLEAN;                    (* Has the linked list reached *)
BEGIN                                         (* its maximum size?           *)
    RETURN (NOT Available(TSIZE(Node)))
END Full;

PROCEDURE Last(): BOOLEAN;                     (* Is the last element current? *)
BEGIN
    RETURN (current↑.next = NIL)
END Last;

BEGIN                                         (* Create an empty linked list. *)
    current := NIL;
    head := NIL
END LinkedList.
```

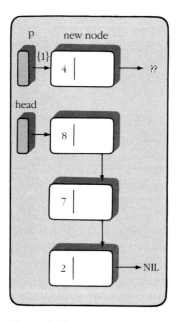

Figure 2.44
A linked list after a new node is
created by {1} but before it is
inserted by {2} and {3}.

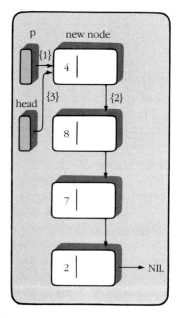

Figure 2.45
The linked list after the new
node is attached as the first
node.

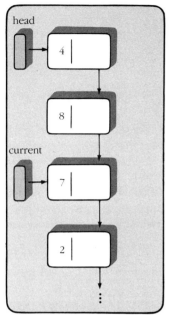

Figure 2.46
The linked list before *Delete* is called.

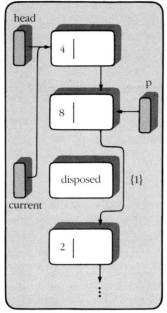

Figure 2.47
The linked list after procedure *Delete*. The value of *p* is set by the while loop.

Figure 2.48 shows the empty linked list created by the BEGIN–END block of the module. Suppose that the key of our standard element is of type INTEGER. If we execute

```
e.el.key := 25;
Insert(e);
```

then the list will appear as shown in Figure 2.49. The statement numbers {1}, {2}, and {3} correspond to statement numbers appended to the procedures in Implementation Module 2.1. The number {1} next to a pointer means that the indicated pointer value was set by the statement labeled {1} in procedure *Insert* in Implementation Module 2.1. This is true, with appropriate changes in procedure name, throughout this discussion, as well as the remainder of the text. This linkage between figures and procedures is intended to help you understand the logic of the procedures.

Refer to Figure 2.43. Note that although *head* is a pointer variable that can be assigned values, *Node* is only a type. One way of creating an occurrence of type *Node* is to define a variable as follows:

VAR x: Node;

Using this approach, programmers must know at the time they write a

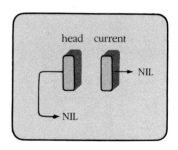

Figure 2.48
The linked list after *Create*.

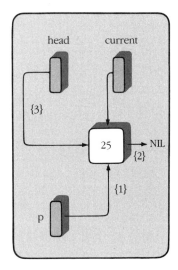

Figure 2.49
The linked list after

p ↑ .el.key := 25;
Insert (e);

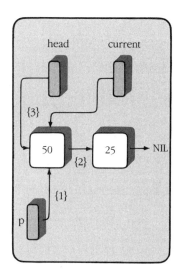

Figure 2.50
The linked list after

p ↑ .el.key := 50;
Insert(e);

program how many occurrences of type *Node* they will need. Suppose that the number of occurrences is not known until the program is executing. For example, suppose that the nodes are to be filled by data from an interactive terminal. The terminal operator may enter any number of nodes of data. How is the number of node occurrences to be matched to the number that is input? One way is through the use of ***dynamic memory allocation.*** Modula-2 contains a built-in procedure called NEW. The statement

NEW (p) ;

in procedure *Insert* (in Implementation Module 2.1) requests Modula-2 to create (i.e., set aside memory for) an occurrence of a record of type *Node.* The space is allocated by the Modula-2 system, and the memory address of the first byte is returned to the calling program as the value of the variable *p.* Figures 2.48 and 2.49 show the situation before and after execution of procedure *Insert.*

A second execution of *Insert* allocates a second occurrence of a record of type *Node* at some other location in memory and returns a pointer to the new occurrence in *p.* If the previous value of *p* were not saved, as it is by *Insert,* reference to the first occurrence of the record would be lost. The first occurrence of the record would still exist, but there would be no way to access it. Figure 2.50 shows the list after the second execution of *Insert.*

Dynamic memory allocation is important to linked data structures. It provides them with the ability to request space for data only at the time and in the exact amount needed. Thus, the program is able to use exactly the amount of memory necessary for a particular set of data. The same program could subsequently be run with a different amount of data, and it will adjust its memory requirements to that amount. You will see many examples of this technique in this text.

Modula-2 also has a function that notifies the system of allocated memory that is no longer needed. The procedure that performs the operation is

DISPOSE (p) ;

where *p* is a pointer to the occurrence of the node being returned. After execution of DISPOSE, the value of *p* is undefined, and the occurrence of the record no longer exists. The memory that is now free is returned to the pool of memory available for future dynamic allocations. Implementation Module 2.1 includes illustrations of the pointer operations. Look at procedure *Delete* for an example of the use of DISPOSE.

When examining the implementation module, remember that the code must faithfully implement the operations as specified. Users of the module need not be aware of its implementation. All that they need to know is given in the specifications. Implementors can use any approach as long as it is faithful to the specifications. The specifications provide the interface between the user and the implementor.

Note that the preconditions have an important effect on the implementation. They simplify the implementation by taking frequently occurring tests from several procedures and centralizing them in a few simple procedures. For example, five operations in the simple linked list module have as a precondition that the list not be empty. Instead of including logic to treat an empty list as a special case in the implementations of each of these five operations, the test for an empty list is isolated in one simple procedure—*Empty*. In fact, all the procedures in Implementation Module 2.1 are simple. This simplicity does not just happen; it occurs because of the careful design of the data structure—both in terms of the operations and of the operation's preconditions.

The operation *Full* has the job of determining whether or not the linked list has reached its bound; that is, is there enough memory left to allocate a new node for the list? Each time operation *Insert* is executed, it executes the built-in procedure *NEW*, which requests space from the pool of available memory that the system is managing. An example of how this is done can be seen in Section 3.2.4, which discusses memory management. It is sufficient now to assume that the operating system is managing a pool of available memory that is being parceled out as requests are made via the procedure *NEW*.

The precondition of *Insert* is that the number of nodes in the linked list has not reached its bound. What determines the bound? In fact it is the combination of executions of *NEW, DISPOSE* (which returns memory to the pool), the amount of memory in the pool, and the strategy used for managing it. The bound may not be fixed, but may vary as memory is allocated and deallocated by different data types and other needs of the executing programs. Given the design of the linked list data type as specified in Specification 2.4, the user cannot know what the bound is at any time, but can tell whether it has been reached by using the procedure *Full*.

NEW and *DISPOSE* are standard procedures of Modula-2 and their names are keywords of the language. However, in order to use them, one must import two lower-level procedures from a standard module *Storage*. That is why you see the statement

FROM `Storage IMPORT ALLOCATE, DEALLOCATE, Available;`

in Implementation Module 2.1. ALLOCATE and DEALLOCATE are necessary for NEW and DISPOSE to execute. (Appendix A discusses these issues.)

Full uses a function-type procedure imported from module SYSTEM. *TSIZE* is a standard function.

```
PROCEDURE TSIZE(some Modula-2 data type): CARDINAL;
(* Returns the number of memory words that would be
   occupied by a variable of the argument data type. *)
```

It is used in *Full* to determine the number of words that would be occupied by an instance of type Node. Thus if *NEW* (Node) were executed, it would use

TSIZE(Node) words from the pool of memory. (This pool is often called the application heap and is discussed in Section 3.2.4.)

The second function used in *Full* is *Available.* This is a nonstandard function that the authors' implementation of Modula-2 exports from module *Storage.* We use it because there is no other way to determine whether the bounds referred to so often in specifications have been reached.

PROCEDURE Available(x: CARDINAL): BOOLEAN;
(* Returns TRUE if x or more words remain in the pool
   of available memory; otherwise returns FALSE. *)

Finally, procedure *Full* contains a single statement:

RETURN (NOT Available(TSIZE(Node)))

You will see this construction used many times throughout this book to determine whether bounds have been reached (from the abstract point of view) and whether sufficient memory remains (from the implementation point of view).

2.4.3 Design of Linked Lists

One of the simplest and most widely used structures using pointers and dynamic memory allocation is the linked list. Linked lists are often found as components of more advanced data structures. For these reasons we will now investigate the design parameters of linked lists.

The software designer has several choices to make when designing a linked list:

- How are the ends of the list to be marked?
- What pointers outside of the list will give access to it? What nodes of the list will they point to?
- How many pointers will be kept in each node to point to related nodes?

These choices are more or less independent of each other, but certain combinations allow for more favorable design and performance characteristics. For the simple linked list described in Section 2.4.2 (Figure 2.40) these choices are shown in the margin.

Let us consider some other possibilities. There will almost always be a *head* pointer to point to the first node in the list. From there any other node can be reached. There are several possibilities for the last node.

Using a NIL pointer as the value of *next* is simple but makes it expensive to locate the last node. Procedure *FindLast* (Figure 2.51) shows the traversal that would be necessary.

If a count of the number of nodes is kept, a procedure similar to *FindLast* can be used to locate the last node. The effort for scanning the entire list is the same. The size of the list provides information that the NIL *next* pointer does not—the number of nodes in the list.

A third approach is to keep a pointer, for example, *tail,* that always points

---

Design Choices for the Simple Linked List in Figure 2.40

- The first node is identified by head, and the last node is designated by a NIL value for its next pointer.
- A current pointer, or cursor, provides access to the current node. It can be set by the user to point to any node in the list.
- One pointer in each node points to that node's successor.

•

PROCEDURE FindLast();
(* **pre** — The list is not empty.
   post — The last node is the
             current node. *)

BEGIN
      current := head;
      WHILE current ↑ .next # NIL
         DO
            current := current ↑ .next
      END
END FindLast;

Figure 2.51

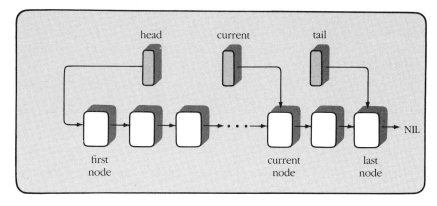

Figure 2.52 Linked list with the last node identified by a *tail* pointer and a NIL *next* pointer. The size of the list may also be kept in a variable such as **VAR** size: CARDINAL;

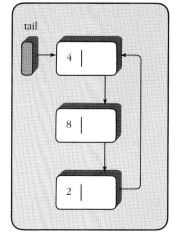

Figure 2.53
Circular linked list with *tail* pointer.

to the last node. By storing and maintaining a single extra pointer, this approach allows direct access to the last node, which neither of the other approaches does. Happily, all three approaches can be combined and have very little impact on storage requirements and program complexity. They provide immediate access to the last node and to the current size of the list. Figure 2.52 illustrates such a list.

A simple process that leads to a number of desirable properties is to make the last node of the list point back to the first node. The list becomes a ***circular linked list*** and can be visualized as shown in Figure 2.53.

The notions of head and tail become irrelevant in this case since the list is now in a circular form that has no head and tail. But assume for the moment that the list still has logical head and tail nodes. Notice that if we keep a *tail* pointer, the *head* pointer is really unnecessary since the tail node points to the head node. That is, *head = tail ↑ .next.*

Insertion of a node at the head of the circular list using only the *tail* pointer to access the list is accomplished as shown in Algorithm 2.4 and Figure 2.54.

```
PROCEDURE CLInsert(e: StdElement);      (* Insert e at the *)
VAR p: NodePointer;                     (* head of a       *)
BEGIN                                   (* circular list.  *)
    NEW(p); p↑.el := e;
    IF tail = NIL
        THEN tail := p                  (* List empty. *)
        ELSE p↑.next := tail ↑.next
    END;
    tail↑.next := p
END CLInsert;
```

Algorithm 2.4

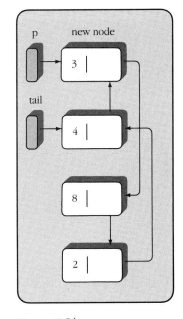

Figure 2.54
Inserting a new node at the head of a circular list. See Algorithm 2.4.

We turn now to a discussion of access pointers. A linked list must provide some means of access to at least one node of the list. Other nodes can be found by following the linkage pointers once the initial access is made. Such **access pointers** are external to the list itself.

For **singly linked lists,** that is, those with only one pointer per node, a first node pointer is required. The lists are traversable only in one direction—the direction of the pointers. Access at any point other than the head node means that all nodes before that node cannot be reached. Circular lists are an exception, since a *tail* pointer effectively provides a *head* pointer.

All of the linked list examples thus far have used only one linkage pointer in each node. Some of the main advantages of linked lists—in fact of linked structures of all types—are gained by the inclusion of more than one pointer field in each node. Important classes of data structures such as trees, multi-linked lists, and graphs are represented using multiple pointer schemes. In this chapter we will only be concerned with singly linked lists. In the remaining chapters, you will see many examples of multiple linkage.

Singly linked lists have a single ordering that is determined by the pointer values of *next*. If an access pointer, for example, *current,* is pointing to a node of the list, then a pointer to the successor or following node, for example, *succ,* is easily found by *succ := current ↑ .next.* Although the predecessor node is also adjacent, there is no direct access to it. It can be found (in the absence of other access pointers) only by returning to the head of the list and traversing forward. That is an inefficient way to get to a logically adjacent node.

One obvious solution is to store in each node not only a pointer to its successor but also a pointer to its predecessor. A node with two such pointers can be represented as shown in Figure 2.55. Figure 2.56 illustrates a **doubly linked list.**

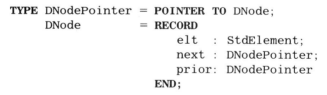

```
TYPE DNodePointer = POINTER TO DNode;
     DNode        = RECORD
                        elt  : StdElement;
                        next : DNodePointer;
                        prior: DNodePointer
                    END;
```

Figure 2.55   Representation of nodes in a doubly linked list.

The constraint that one ordering in a doubly linked list be the logical reverse of the other is certainly not necessary. The second set of pointers could be used to give a wholly different ordering. Even though the list is in a sense doubly linked, the term applied to it is a **multilinked list** of order two, since the two orderings are unrelated.

Figure 2.57 is a multilinked list of order two. Note that the two sets of pointers link the data in two orders. The first pointers, shown on the left, link the nodes so that they are ordered by the value of the integer field. The second pointers, shown on the right, link the nodes so that they are in order by character field. The programmer is able to choose either order simply by

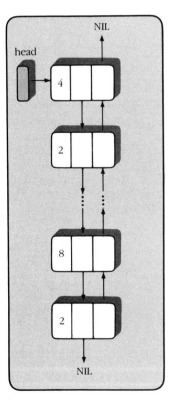

Figure 2.56
Illustration of a doubly linked list.

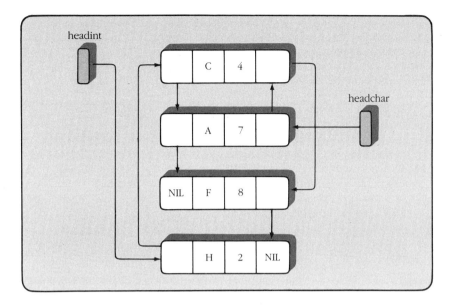

Figure 2.57   Multilinked list of order two.

traversing the list using the appropriate set of pointers. Such a scheme is widely used for exactly that purpose—to keep several different logical orders while having only one physical order—the order in which the nodes happen to be arranged in memory.

Exercises 2.4

1. Describe the Modula-2 pointer data type.
2. Explain the difference between a pointer illustrated as an arc with an arrow-head and a pointer implemented using the hardware of a computer.
3. Describe the action of the Modula-2 operations NEW and DISPOSE.
4. Specify operations for a simple linked list (see Figure 2.40) that does the following:
   a. Makes the ith node in the list the current node.
   b. Makes the node whose element has a specified key value the current node.
   c. Sorts the list in ascending order based on the values of the key field of the elements.
5. Write procedures that implement the operations in Exercise 4 (a) and (b). These procedures should make use of the operations specified for the simple linked list in Section 2.4.2. See Figure 2.40.
6. Write specifications for linked lists that are like that implemented in Implementation Module 2.1 except for the following:
   a. A *tail* pointer to the last node in the list has been added.
   b. The NIL pointer in the last node is replaced by a pointer to the first node, making a circular list.
   c. Each node contains a second pointer, call it *prior,* which points to its predecessor.

7. Give representations for the three linked lists described in Exercise 6.
8. Implement the three linked lists specified in Exercise 6 using the representations developed in Exercise 7.
9. In Implementation Module 2.1, procedure *Insert* adds a new node as the first node in the list. Replace that procedure by one that adds the new node
   a. As the successor of the current node
   b. As the last node in the list
   Discuss the advantages and disadvantages that would arise if these *Insert* operations were to be implemented for the linked lists described in Exercise 6.
10. Write a specification and a Modula-2 procedure that implements each of the following operations for the linked list described in Section 2.4:
    a. Exchange the current node with its successor.
    b. Exchange the current node with its predecessor.
    c. Reverse the order of the nodes in the linked list.
11. The specification of several of the linked list operations includes the precondition

    ```
    (* pre — The list is not empty, which, according to the
             specification, means that there must be a current
             node. *)
    ```

    Replace these specifications by specifications that have no preconditions. This requires additional logic in the postconditions in order to specify what happens if there is no current node.

    Write the procedures (or functions) that implement these new specifications. Compare them with the corresponding implementations in Implementation Module 2.1.

2.5 Composite Structures

Arrays, records, and simple linked lists are very useful data structures, but they become even more useful when we use them in combination. Many data structures use arrays, records, or both as basic building blocks. Dynamic records linked together by pointers are the basis of a wide variety of linked data structures. Arrays of records, although static, provide many effective ways of organizing data for rapid retrieval. Records that contain fields that are arrays are common. Arrays of pointers provide a flexibility not attained with arrays containing actual data elements. Some of the fun of data structuring comes from using interesting combinations of basic data structures. Let us look at three particularly useful composite structures: records of arrays, arrays of records, and arrays of pointers.

2.5.1 Records of Arrays

We have seen several examples of arrays used as fields of records. Any time a repeating group occurs in contiguous fields of a record an array is indicated, although not always recommended. Many levels of nesting can easily be han-

```
VAR r:  RECORD
            event:  ARRAY [1..10]  OF  CHAR;
            place:  ARRAY [1..20]  OF
                      RECORD
                        placeName:  ARRAY [1..15] OF CHAR;
                        date      : ARRAY [1..5]
                           OF  RECORD
                                    mo  :  [1..12];
                                    day :  [1..31];
                                    year:  CARDINAL
                                 END
                      END
         END;
```

Figure 2.58   Example of a record of arrays.

dled. For example, Figure 2.58 shows a record used for recording information about a named event. The event can occur in up to 20 places and on up to 5 different dates in each place. A reference to *r.place[i].date[j].mo* will access the month of the *j*th occurrence, in the *i*th place, of the event named in *r.event*.

2.5.2 Arrays of Records

A one-dimensional array of records is a common composite structure. We call such a structure a ***table.*** Figure 2.59, for example, is a table of information about computer systems. Figure 2.60, an array of records, is a data structure that would hold such a table. We can access the type of the computer in the *i*th position of the table by the reference *computers[i].systype*.

Manufacturer	System	Systype	. . .
DEC	VAX 11/780	Mini	. . .
IBM	PC	Micro	. . .
IBM	3033	Maxi	. . .
APPLE®	Macintosh	Micro	. . .
⋮	⋮	⋮	⋮

Figure 2.59   Example of a table.

```
VAR computers:
  ARRAY [1..100] OF
  RECORD
    co : ARRAY [1..25] OF CHAR;
    system : ARRAY [1..15] OF CHAR;
    systype : ARRAY [1..5] OF CHAR
  END;
```

Figure 2.60
Data structure for the table of computers (Figure 2.59).

2.5.3 Arrays of Pointers

A problem often encountered is that of storing variable length data elements in an array. We have seen that the construction of an efficient array mapping function is dependent on a constant data element length. If each element of the array can have any length (the lengths could even vary over time), then an array is not an efficient data structure.

However, it is often possible to use a simple technique to solve the problems. The solution is not to store the actual variable length data values in the array, but to store pointers to the data values. We thus introduce a ***level of indirection.*** Evaluation of the array mapping function does not produce the address of the data element; it produces the address at which the address of the data element is stored. Figure 2.61 shows an array *head* that contains such pointer values. Each is the *head* pointer to a linked list. We consider the data contents of a linked list to be a single data element value. In this example they are the names of people. The Modula-2 data types involved are given in Figure 2.62.

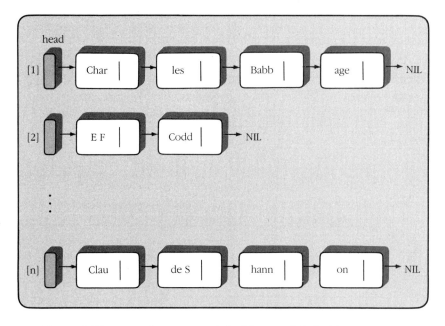

Figure 2.61   Array of pointers to linked lists. Each linked list contains a variable length data element.

```
TYPE NodePointer = POINTER TO Node;
     Node        = RECORD
                       chunk: ARRAY [1..4] OF CHAR;
                       next : NodePointer
                   END;
VAR  head         : ARRAY [1..N] OF NodePointer;
```

Figure 2.62   Representation for the data structure in Figure 2.61.

The key issue is that the pointers are of fixed length, whereas the data elements that they point to are not. In storing the fixed length pointers in the array, we regain the ability to construct an efficient AMF. The value at addr *(head[i])* is a pointer to a linked list that we can then traverse to retrieve the data element value.

We will not mention variable length data elements often in this text. The reason is that almost without exception we can cause any data structure that we discuss to contain variable length data elements by using the method that we have just described for arrays. Pointers to the data elements instead of the actual data are stored in the data structure. Stacks, queues, linear lists, trees, sets, and graphs can all hold variable length data elements by using this method.

Data structures containing pointers have other important advantages. Suppose that we have records containing information about computer systems and they have been dynamically allocated space in memory and, therefore, can be considered to be scattered in memory in any fashion. We might do this with two arrays—*manufacturer* and *systype*. Each array contains pointers to all of the computer system records. If we progress through the array manufacturer from 1 to n, retrieving the computer system's record for each pointer as we encounter it, we find that we have retrieved the systems in order of the manufacturer's name. Traversing systype in the same way, the systems are retrieved in order by type of computer system. The two arrays can be used to make the data appear as if they are ordered in two different ways at once. Such arrays are often called **index arrays** to the data.

Figure 2.63 shows two index arrays with different data element orders. Notice that the process of arranging the pointers in the two arrays into the desired orders need not move any actual data elements, only the pointers.

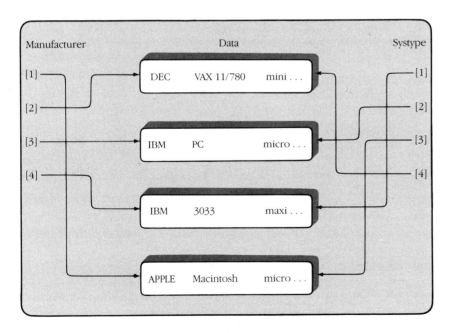

Figure 2.63   Two index arrays with different data element orders.

Exercises 2.5

1. Section 2.5.2 discusses arrays whose components are records. What, if any, restrictions does Modula-2 place on the data type of a component of an array?

2. In a collection of elements, each element is to contain information about an employee. It is to contain the employee's identification number, name, address, age, salary, and department number.

    a. Give a Modula-2 representation of an employee record.

    b. Give a Modula-2 representation of a list of employees using an array of records.

    c. Implement a list of *employees* data structure using the representations in (a) and (b). The operations are those given for the simple linked list in Section 2.4.2. Note that the specification of the *insert* operation will have to be modified to recognize that the array may be full.

    d. Give specifications and a representation for an index data structure that provides direct access to all employees in a specified department.

3. Describe how an array of pointers might be used to store variable length elements. Name other ways you can think of that might be used to store variable length elements.

2.6 Summary

Chapter 2 discussed three Modula-2 data types—arrays, records, and pointers—and one data type that was constructed using pointers—the simple linked list. The first three data types are used to construct most of the data structures described in this text. Linked lists were introduced to illustrate the use of pointers to construct data structures and for readers who are not familiar with the use of the pointer data type.

The component elements of arrays are all of the same type. This, along with sequential location in memory, makes it possible to locate a component using an array mapping function, which converts index values into addresses. The index(es) of the element to be accessed can be a variable of the same type as the index or an expression whose value is among those permitted for the index type.

The component elements of records are also located by an arithmetic calculation—adding the offset of the specified field to the base address of the record. This calculation is performed either at the time the program is compiled or when it is executing. However, the name of the element to be accessed cannot be a variable; it must be completely specified by the programmer when the program is written. This is the price that is paid for permitting components of different types.

Arrays and records provide random access to their component elements by position. This is achieved through sequential placement and arithmetic calculation. An array (or record) has a first component, a second component, a third, and so on. The *i*th component is in the *i*th position. We can calculate the location of the component in the *i*th position so access by position is efficient. Linked structures have no such random access to their component elements. Finding an element in a linked structure entails following a sequence of linking pointers until the target element is reached. For example, finding the *i*th element of a simple linked list involves accessing the head element and then traversing the list via next pointers until the *i*th element is reached. This is contrasted with access by value, or associative access. In this case, we want to access the component with a particular value—no matter what position it occupies. Curiously, the random placement in memory of the elements of a linked structure rules out random access, whereas the regular, contiguous (nonrandom) placement of components of arrays and records results in random access.

One of the most important attributes of linked structures is their ability to adjust their memory requirements to the amount of data currently in the structure. As the amount of data grows or shrinks, so does the memory allocated to the structure. This is achieved through a combination of dynamic memory allocation and pointers. Linked structures are well suited to situations in which the amount of data is not known in advance of program execution.

When implementing more advanced data structures, we shall find that arrays and linked structures often have quite different performance characteristics. Each implementation will typically have a mixture of relatively efficient and relatively inefficient operations.

This chapter contains a single implementation module (Implementation Module 2.1), which implements a simple linked list. One measure of the complexity of this package is given in Table 2.1.

A module with nine procedures averaging 2.4 lines of code per procedure is, of course, a simple one. Part of its simplicity comes from careful selection of operations and preconditions. For example, five of the operations have the precondition that the list is not empty. The logic to check for an empty list is thus removed from all five operations and placed in only one. Simplicity turns out to be a characteristic of all the modules we shall see in this text.

TABLE 2.1 Example of complexity of Implementation Module 2.1.

Module	Data structure	Representation	Operations	Total lines of code	Lines of code per operation	Maximum lines of code
2.1	Linked list	Linked	9	22	2.4	8

Stacks and Queues

3

3.1 Introduction
Exercises 3.1

3.2 Stacks
3.2.1 Multiple Instances of a Data Type
3.2.2 A Simple Use of Stacks
3.2.3 An Array Implementation
3.2.4 Stack Pairs
3.2.5 An Application: Memory Management
3.2.6 A Linked Implementation
Exercises 3.2

3.3 FIFO Queues
3.3.1 Array Implementation
3.3.2 Linked Implementation
Exercises 3.3

3.4 Priority Queues
3.4.1 Implementations
Exercises 3.4

3.5 Application of Queues: Scheduling I/O Requests on a Magnetic Disk
3.5.1 Disk Scheduling
3.5.2 An Abstract Schedule
Exercises 3.5

3.6 Summary

3.1 Introduction

In Chapter 2 we examined three abstract data types that are at a relatively low level of abstraction. The data types *Array* and *Record* are native to many programming languages. By using the *Pointer* data type and dynamic memory allocation, many programming languages also provide the facilities for constructing linked structures. *Arrays, Records,* and linked structures provide the building blocks for implementing what we might call higher-level abstractions. The first two higher-level abstract data types that we take up—*Stacks* and *Queues*—are extremely important to computing.

A **Stack** is a data type whose major attributes are determined by the rules governing the insertion and deletion of its elements. The only element that can be deleted or removed is the one that was inserted most recently. Such a structure is said to have a last-in/first-out (LIFO) behavior, or protocol.

Stacks follow a last-in/first-out (LIFO) protocol.

The simplicity of the data type *Stack* belies its importance. Many computer systems have stacks built into their circuitry and have machine-level instructions to operate the hardware stack. The sequencing of calls to and returns from subroutines follows a stack protocol. Arithmetic expressions are often evaluated by a sequence of operations on a stack. Many handheld calculators use a stack mode of operation. In studying computer science, you can expect to see many examples of stacks. We will study stacks in Section 3.2.

Queues follow a first-in/first-out (FIFO) protocol.

Queues occur frequently in everyday life and are therefore familiar to us. The line of people waiting for service at a bank or for tickets at a movie theater and the line of autos at a traffic light are examples of queues. The main feature of queues is that they follow a first-come/first-served rule. Contrary to a stack, in which the latest element inserted is the first removed or served, in queues the earliest element inserted is the first served. In social settings, the rule appeals to our sense of equality and fairness.

There are many applications of the first-in/first-out (FIFO) protocol of queues in computing. For example, the line of input/output (I/O) requests waiting for access to a disk drive in a multiuser time-sharing system might be a queue. The line of computing jobs waiting to be run on a computer system might also be a queue. The jobs and I/O requests are serviced in order of their arrival, that is, the first in is the first out. We will study FIFO queues in Section 3.3.

There is a second kind of queue that is important. An everyday example can be seen in an emergency room of a hospital. In large emergencies it is common to first treat the worst injured patients who are likely to survive. In certain societies in which less emphasis is placed on equality, people with higher social standing may be treated first.

Priority queues follow a highest-priority-in/first-out (HPIFO) protocol.

In computer systems, events that demand the attention of the computer are often handled according to a most-important-event/first-served, or highest-priority-in/first-out (HPIFO), rule. Such queues are called priority queues; in this type of queue service is not in order of time of arrival but rather in order of some measure of priority. We will study these queues in Section 3.4.

In Section 3.5 we will discuss the use of FIFO and priority queues in scheduling I/O operations on a magnetic disk.

In Section 3.6 we will summarize the material in this chapter.

Exercises 3.1

1. Explain the following terms in your own words:

  a. stack
  b. FIFO queue
  c. priority queue

2. Give two everyday examples of each of the following:

  a. A stack
  b. An FIFO queue
  c. A priority queue

3.2 Stacks

A *Stack* is a data type that exhibits a ***last-in/first-out (LIFO)*** behavior. Elements can be added to the stack. However, the only element that can be retrieved, or removed, from it is the one that was added most recently—the last in. When the last-in element is removed, the next most recently added element becomes the most recently added, or last-in, element. The operation of adding an element to the stack is commonly called ***push.*** That of removing the most recently added element and deleting it from the stack is usually called ***pop.***

An example is shown, in the margin, in which a sequence of stack operations is used to evaluate the expression $10 \times (5 + 7)$. The arithmetic operations add and multiply first pop the two elements from the stack, then operate on the pair, and finally push the result onto the stack.

The result, 120, is the element on top of the stack. This simple mechanism, with the addition of the other arithmetic operators, can be used to evaluate any arithmetic expression no matter how complex.

Data elements being stacked are viewed by the stack as packets of bytes. The stack needs to know nothing about their internal makeup. For consistency, however, we will retain our definition of a data element as consisting of key fields and data fields, with the understanding that there is no real need to separate the two portions. The elements being stacked are assumed to be all of the same data type and all of the same length.

We said in Section 3.1 that a stack is a data structure whose most important characteristic is that elements can only be removed in inverse order of their arrival. We therefore need some mechanism for keeping tabs on the order in which the elements have arrived in the stack. We can, if we wish, conceptualize the stack as a set (in the mathematical sense) of ***time-stamped elements.*** When an element arrives to be added to the stack, the current time is recorded and attached to it. We shall see that the critical operation on this structure is *Pop*, which removes the most recently added element from the set. *Pop* works

Using a Stack to Evaluate

$10 \times (5 + 7)$

push 5
push 7
add
push 10
multiply

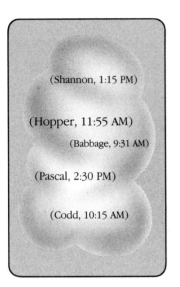

(Shannon, 1:15 PM)

(Hopper, 11:55 AM)

(Babbage, 9:31 AM)

(Pascal, 2:30 PM)

(Codd, 10:15 AM)

Figure 3.1
A stack as a set of time-stamped elements.

by scanning the set and removing the element with the latest recorded time. In Figure 3.1, for example, the operation *Pop(x)* removes (Pascal, 2:30 PM) from the set and assigns the value 'Pascal' to *x*. Remember that this is only an abstraction. Implementors may use any technique they wish to do this, as long as the implementation chosen appears to make *Pop* operate as abstracted above.

It is common to find a stack abstracted as a linear data structure. We can think of the stack as a list of elements that is ordered by times of insertion into the list, with the latest arrival appearing as the first element of the list. (We will see more of the notion of ordered lists in Chapter 4.) Each element has a unique predecessor and a unique successor. In Figure 3.2, we see a cursor, top, that points to the first element. New elements can only be inserted at the top of the list, and the top element is the only one that can be removed.

Which is the better abstraction, sets or lists? It is difficult to say. Each may tend to influence the implementor toward certain kinds of implementations.

The specifications of stacks are given in Specification 3.1 and summarized in Figure 3.3. The specification is for multiple stacks. A discussion is given in Section 3.2.1.

Specification 3.1 Stacks

DEFINITION MODULE Stacks;

(* **Elements:** Although the elements can be of a variety of types, for concreteness we assume that they are of type StdElement. *)

    FROM StdTypes **IMPORT** StdElement;

(* **Structure:** The structure is a mechanism for relating the elements that allows determination of their order of arrival into the stack. *)

(* **Domain:** The number of elements in a stack is bounded. *)

    EXPORT QUALIFIED Stack, Push, Pop, Empty, Full, Create, Terminate;

    TYPE Stack;   (* *Opaque type to represent a Stack.* *)

(* **Operations:** There are six operations. Occasionally in the postcondition we must reference the value of the stack immediately before execution of the operation. We use S-pre as notation for this value. *)

    PROCEDURE Push(**VAR** S: Stack; e: StdElement);
    (* **pre** — The size of S has not reached its bound.
       post — S includes e as its most recently arrived element. *)

    PROCEDURE Pop(**VAR** S: Stack; **VAR** e: StdElement);
    (* **pre** — S is not empty.
       post — e is the most recently arrived element of S-pre;
            S no longer contains e. *)

continued

Specification 3.1, continued

```
PROCEDURE Empty(S: Stack): BOOLEAN;
(* post — If S has no elements then Empty is true else Empty is false. *)

PROCEDURE Full(S: Stack): BOOLEAN;
(* post — If the size of S has not reached its bound then Full is false
          else Full is true. *)

PROCEDURE Create(VAR S: Stack): BOOLEAN;
(* post — If a stack can be created then S exists and is empty, and
          Create is true, else Create is false. *)

PROCEDURE Terminate(VAR S: Stack);
(* post — S-pre does not exist. *)

END Stacks.
```

Certain variations in the operations are common. For example, it is not unusual to define a form of nondestructive retrieval *Top*(**VAR** e: StdElement), which has the same function as *Pop* except that the copied element remains in the stack. We have chosen not to specify this operation. Some abstractions define *Pop* simply as removal of the most recently arrived element, with no retrieval. In that case, *Top* becomes a necessary operation.

An operation is sometimes included that allows the user to retrieve (but not delete) an element in the interior of the stack. We might define *Retrieve*(**VAR** e: StdElement; i: CARDINAL), where the value of the *i*th stack element is copied into *e*. Thus, *i* contains the element's position in order of arrival into the stack, with the most recently arrived element being in position 1.

Pascal ← Top
Shannon
Hopper
Codd
Babbage

Figure 3.2
A stack as a list: The order of arrival is the same as the order of elements in the list, with the latest arrival appearing at the top of the list.

3.2.1 Multiple Instances of a Data Type

Specification 3.1 is written for more than a single stack. There is an argument *S* in every operation that indicates which stack is to be operated upon. There is a data type *Stack,* which is the type of the arguments *S* of *Stacks'* operations. Its details are not visible in the definition module. The operation *Create* brings a stack *S* into existence, and the operation *Terminate* will cause it to cease to exist. Each of the other operations has to be told which stack it is operating on. Each stack of type *Stack* is an **instance** of the type.

The declaration of type *Stack* may seem strange. It is declared as a type, but there are no details. It is an example of a Modula-2 **opaque data type**. It is opaque because, though we can see that *Stack* is a data type, we cannot see its details. Its exact definition will come in an implementation module that is written to the specifications. The intent is twofold:

1. Users are shielded from the details of the type. This both relieves them from having to deal with those details and keeps adventurous users from manipulating the data without using the specified operations.

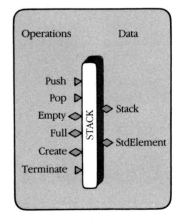

Figure 3.3
Stack capsule.

2. Implementors are free to define the details of the type differently in different implementations without affecting the users. After you have studied them, contrast the details of type *Stack* in Implementation Modules 3.1 and 3.3, both of which satisfy Specification 3.1.

In short, opaque data types provide the benefits of information hiding.

Opaque data types in Modula-2 are usually pointers (see Appendix A). We will see many examples of their use throughout this book.

A constraint in Modula-2 is that all instances of *Stacks* must stack the same kind of element, *StdElement*. It would be handy to be able to specify a generic form of stack that could be told what type of element it was to stack when it is created. *Create* could be used not only to create a stack but also to specify what kind of element is to be stacked in that instance. *Create* could create a stack of reals, a stack of integers, a stack of standard elements, and so on. Data types that have this characteristic are called **generic data types**. Modula-2 has no built-in facility for specifying and creating generic data types, though it is possible to do in an indirect way. Ada does have facilities for generic data types. Section 10.2 discusses generic data types in Ada and the indirect method of achieving them in Modula-2.

Section 3.2.3 contains an implementation of *Stacks*. Consequently, it also covers the second step in the use of opaque data types—the definition of the type and an implementation. Multiple instances of a type are also discussed.

3.2.2 A Simple Use of Stacks

Stacks are widely used. You will see many examples of their use throughout this book. Before looking at possible implementations of *Stacks,* let us now look at the use of its definition module and abstraction (Specification 3.1) to solve a simple problem.

Suppose that we have an expression of the familiar type, grouped and nested using left and right parentheses. Three examples are shown in Figure 3.4. The parentheses in (i) match; in (ii), one of the initial three left parentheses is unnecessary; in (iii), there is a missing left parenthesis. We will write a procedure *CheckParens,* which will examine such expressions to determine if the parentheses match up. If they don't, we want *CheckParens* to indicate the position of an unmatched parenthesis.

Suppose that *e* is a character string representing the expression to be checked. Assume that the expression is terminated by the character ';'. *Check-Parens* is specified as follows:

$$((a + b) + c) * d$$
$$(i)$$

$$(((a + b) + c) * d$$
$$(ii)$$

$$(a + b) + c) * d$$
$$(iii)$$

Figure 3.4

```
PROCEDURE CheckParens(e: ARRAY OF CHAR);
(* pre  - e contains an expression with nested parentheses
          that is terminated by the character ';'.
   post - A message is written that either notes that the
          left and right parentheses of e are matched,
          or notes the position and type of an unmatched
          parenthesis. *)
```

A module that implements *CheckParens* needs to import objects from three other modules as shown. We assume that the *key* field of a standard element (StdElement) is of type CARDINAL.

```
FROM StdTypes IMPORT StdElement;
FROM Stacks   IMPORT Stack, Push, Pop, Empty, Full,
                     Create, Terminate;
FROM InOut    IMPORT WriteString, WriteCard, WriteLn;
```

An implementation of *CheckParens* is given in Algorithm 3.1.

The results of applying procedure *CheckParens* to the expressions of Figure 3.4 are:

(i) All parentheses match
(ii) Mismatched (at position 0
(ii) Mismatched) at position 7.

```
PROCEDURE CheckParens (e: ARRAY OF CHAR);      (* Check expression e for correct *)
VAR k   : CARDINAL;                            (* nesting of parentheses.        *)
    S   : Stack;
    elt: StdElement;
BEGIN
    WriteString(e); WriteLn;
    k := 0;
    IF Create(S)                               (* Attempt to create a stack S.   *)
       THEN LOOP                               (* Have S; loop through expression. *)
               CASE e[k] OF                            (* Treat one character.    *)
                   '(' : IF NOT Full(S)                        (* Treat a '('.    *)
                            THEN elt.key := k;
                                 Push(S,elt)
                            ELSE WriteString('Stack overflow - ');
                                 WriteString('too many parentheses. ');
                                 EXIT
                         END      |
                   ')' : IF Empty(S)                          (* Treat a ')'.    *)
                            THEN WriteString(' Mismatched ) at position ');
                                 WriteCard(k,3);
                                 EXIT
                            ELSE Pop(S,elt)
                         END      |
                   ';' : IF Empty(S)           (* ';' marks end of the expression *)
                            THEN WriteString('All parentheses match. ');
                            ELSE WriteString(' Mismatched ( at position ');
                                 Pop(S,elt);
                                 WriteCard(elt.key,3)
                         END;
                         EXIT
                   ELSE                                 (* Ignore other characters. *)
               END;
               k := k + 1
           END;
           Terminate(S)
       ELSE WriteString('Out of memory - cannot create stack for test. *)
    END;
    WriteLn
END CheckParens;
```

Algorithm 3.1   Check balance of parentheses in an expression.

Note that *CheckParens* begins by attempting to create a new stack. If that fails, then *CheckParens* terminates with an appropriate message. Note also that it ensures that the stack is not full before attempting to push a new element. If the stack is full, then there are too many parentheses in the expression for the size of stack being used, and an appropriate message is written. In both cases, the algorithm "fails" gracefully.

3.2.1 Array Implementation

Let us now turn to the problem of constructing implementations that meet the specifications. A stack represented as an array is shown in Figure 3.5. The bottom of the stack is at stack[1], and the stack grows from there toward the high subscript end (MaxSize). Notice that the time of insertion of an element is not explicitly stored. A new element is always pushed at the top, and popped elements are taken from the top. This scheme avoids having to store insertion times explicitly, and this saves memory. The array index is the mechanism used to determine order of arrival. The cursor, top, in Figure 3.5 points to the position in the stack space of the current top element, and its value is the stack depth or size. The array implementation for a stack is given in Implementation Module 3.1.

Implementation Module 3.1 implements multiple instances of stacks as specified in Specification 3.1. What are the mechanisms it uses to do so?

Type *Stack* is specified as an opaque data type. The implementation module resolves the specification by declaring *Stack* to be a pointer to another type, *StackInstance*. *StackInstance* is a record type with two fields: *top*, which holds the stack's top cursor, and *stack*, which is the storage space for the stack elements (note that *stack* is different from *Stack* since Modula-2 is case sensitive). *StackInstance* is a type, so instances of it must be created by the use of dynamic memory allocation.

Procedure *Create* brings stacks into existence. It uses the procedure *NEW*, which obtains memory space for an instance of *StackInstance* and returns a pointer to the space as the value of *S*. Thus stack *S* is in reality a pointer. Procedure *Terminate* causes stack *S* to cease to exist by deallocating its *StackInstance* record. The other procedures of *Stacks* use the pointer *S* to determine which stack they are manipulating.

These simple mechanisms allow the creation and manipulation of multiple instances of data types and hide their details from the user. You will shortly see Implementation Module 3.3, which is a second implementation of *Stacks*. It uses linked lists for the implementation and a different type of pointer for the opaque type *Stack*. The user who uses *Stacks* is completely unaware of the difference.

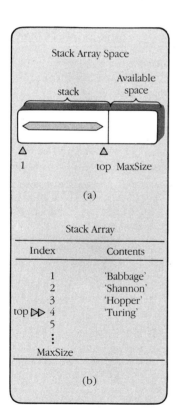

Figure 3.5
A stack represented as an array. (a) Stack array space. (b) Stack array showing subscripts and contents.

Implementation Module 3.1   *Stacks*

```
IMPLEMENTATION MODULE Stacks;
(* Stacks; array implementation; meets Specification 3.1. *)

FROM StdTypes IMPORT StdElement;
FROM Storage  IMPORT ALLOCATE, DEALLOCATE, Available;
FROM SYSTEM   IMPORT TSIZE;

CONST MaxSize      = 10;                            (* Set as needed. *)

TYPE Stack         = POINTER TO StackInstance;
     StackInstance = RECORD
                        top  : [0..MaxSize];        (* Stack top cursor. *)
                        stack: ARRAY [1..MaxSize]    (* Stack space.      *)
                               OF StdElement
                     END;

PROCEDURE Push(VAR S: Stack; e: StdElement);        (* Add new element e. *)
BEGIN
    WITH S↑ DO
       INC(top);
       stack[top] := e
    END
END Push;

PROCEDURE Pop(VAR S: Stack; VAR e: StdElement);     (* Retrieve and remove *)
BEGIN                                               (* most recently added *)
    WITH S↑ DO                                      (* element.            *)
       e   := stack[top];
       DEC(top)
    END
END Pop;

PROCEDURE Empty(S: Stack): BOOLEAN;                 (* Is S empty? *)
BEGIN
    RETURN (S↑.top = 0)
END Empty;

PROCEDURE Full(S: Stack): BOOLEAN;                  (* Is S full? *)
BEGIN
    RETURN (S↑.top = MaxSize)
END Full;

PROCEDURE Create(VAR S: Stack): BOOLEAN;            (* If a stack can be   *)
BEGIN                                               (* created, then do so. *)
    IF Available(TSIZE(StackInstance))              (* Is there memory for *)
       THEN                                         (* a new stack?        *)
          NEW(S);
          S↑.top := 0;
          RETURN TRUE
       ELSE
          RETURN FALSE
    END
END Create;
```

continued

Implementation Module 3.1, continued

```
PROCEDURE Terminate(VAR S: Stack);        (* Terminate the existence *)
BEGIN                                     (* of stack S.             *)
   DISPOSE(S)
END Terminate;

END Stacks.
```

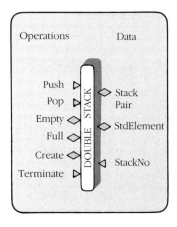

Figure 3.6
Double stack capsule.

Since Implementation Module 3.1 is an array implementation, it suffers from the usual drawback that all of the storage space must be reserved in advance. The maximum depth of the stack is limited to this array's size unless some more dynamic approach is taken. All of the stack operations execute in times that are $O(1)$.

3.2.4 Stack Pairs

Specification 3.2 is an attempt to mitigate the space reservation problem in the case in which there are two stacks. The idea is to put both stacks in one array, letting one stack grow "up" from the bottom of the array while the other grows "down" from the top of the array. In Specification 3.2, the stacks must both contain elements of the same data type. The operations (listed in Specification 3.2) are the same as those defined for a single stack, except that the procedure-calling sequences have been modified to indicate which stack is to be used in the requested operation. For example, the request $Push(x,2)$ will result in the element contained in the variable x being pushed onto stack number 2.

The objective of Specification 3.2 is to allow the two stacks to share the same array. Thus, while one stack grows "up" in the array, the other grows "down." The storage space is exhausted when the two top cursors are adjacent. The depth of one of the stacks is limited by the current depth of the other and the total array space available. Figure 3.7 shows the way in which the array space is used and Implementation Module 3.2 is the code that implements the scheme.

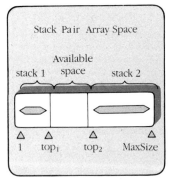

Figure 3.7
Double stacks in a single array.

Specification 3.2 Stack Pairs

DEFINITION MODULE StackPairs;

(* **Elements**: Although the elements can be of a variety of types, for
        concreteness we assume that they are of type StdElement. *)

   FROM StdTypes **IMPORT** StdElement;

(* **Structure**: The structure is a mechanism for relating the elements that
        allows determination of their order of arrival into the stacks. The
        stacks exist in pairs. *)

(* **Domain**: The number of elements on each stack is bounded. *)

   EXPORT QUALIFIED StackPair, StackNo, Push, Pop, Empty, Full, Create,
                   Terminate;

   TYPE StackPair;   (* *Opaque type used to represent a pair of stacks.* *)
        StackNo = [1..2];   (* *Stack identifiers.* *)

(* **Operations**: There are six operations. Occasionally in the postcondition
        we must reference the value of the stack immediately before execution
        of the operation. We use SP-pre as notation for this operation. *)

   PROCEDURE Push(**VAR** SP: StackPair; sno: StackNo; e: StdElement);
   (* **pre** — The size of SP[sno] has not reached its bound.
      post — SP[sno] includes e as its most recently arrived element. *)

   PROCEDURE Pop(**VAR** SP: StackPair; sno: StackNo; **VAR** e: StdElement);
   (* **pre** — SP[sno] is not empty.
      post — e is the most recently arrived element of SP[sno]-pre;
             SP[sno] does not contain e. *)

   PROCEDURE Empty(SP: StackPair; sno: StackNo): BOOLEAN;
   (* **post** — If SP[sno] has no elements then Empty is true, else
             Empty is false. *)

   PROCEDURE Full(SP: StackPair; sno: StackNo): BOOLEAN;
   (* **post** — If the size of SP[sno] has not reached its bound then
             Full is false, else Full is true. (Note that the bound
             varies with the size of the other stack of the pair.) *)

   PROCEDURE Create(**VAR** SP: StackPair): BOOLEAN;
   (* **post** — If a StackPair can be created, then SP exists, SP[1] and
             SP[2] are empty, and Create is true; else Create is false. *)

   PROCEDURE Terminate(**VAR** SP: StackPair);
   (* **post** — SP-pre does not exist. *)

END StackPairs.

Implementation Module 3.2   *Stack Pairs*

```
IMPLEMENTATION MODULE StackPairs;
(* StackPairs; array implementation; meets Specification 3.2. *)

FROM StdTypes IMPORT StdElement;
FROM Storage  IMPORT ALLOCATE, DEALLOCATE, Available;
FROM SYSTEM   IMPORT TSIZE;

CONST MaxSize   = 10;                               (* Set as needed. *)

TYPE StackPair  = POINTER TO StackPairInstance;
     StackTop   = [0..MaxSize+1];
     StackPairInstance
                = RECORD
                     top   : ARRAY StackNo OF StackTop;
                     stacks: ARRAY[1..MaxSize] OF StdElement
                  END;

PROCEDURE Push(VAR SP: StackPair; sno: StackNo; e: StdElement);
BEGIN
    WITH SP↑ DO
       CASE sno OF
          1: INC(top[1]);  |
          2: DEC(top[2])
       END;
       stacks[top[sno]] := e
    END
END Push;

PROCEDURE Pop(VAR SP: StackPair; sno: StackNo; VAR e: StdElement);
BEGIN
    WITH SP↑ DO
       e := stacks[top[sno]];
       CASE sno OF
          1: DEC(top[1]);  |
          2: INC(top[2])
       END
    END
END Pop;

PROCEDURE Empty(SP: StackPair; sno: StackNo): BOOLEAN;
BEGIN
    WITH SP↑ DO
       CASE sno OF
          1: RETURN (top[1] = 0);  |
          2: RETURN (top[2] = MaxSize + 1)
       END
    END
END Empty;
```

continued

Implementation Module 3.2, continued

```
PROCEDURE Full(SP: StackPair; sno: StackNo): BOOLEAN;
BEGIN
    RETURN (SP↑.top[1] + 1 = SP↑.top[2])
END Full;

PROCEDURE Create(VAR SP: StackPair):BOOLEAN;
BEGIN
    IF Available(TSIZE(StackPairInstance))
        THEN
            NEW(SP);
            SP↑.top[1] := 0;
            SP↑.top[2] := MaxSize + 1;
            RETURN TRUE
        ELSE
            RETURN FALSE
    END
END Create;

PROCEDURE Terminate(VAR SP: StackPair);
BEGIN
    DISPOSE(SP)
END Terminate;

END StackPairs.
```

3.2.5 An Application: Memory Management

Variations of stack pairs are found in computer hardware and software systems. For example, many operating systems and run-time systems manage the memory of a microcomputer system using such a scheme. Figure 3.8 shows a typical memory layout.

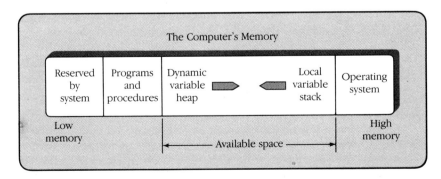

Figure 3.8 Typical memory management scheme.

```
PROCEDURE Main;
VAR p, q, r: . . .;

    PROCEDURE A;
    VAR s: . . .;
    BEGIN
        .
        .
        .
        B;
        .
        .
        .
    END A;

    PROCEDURE B;
    VAR x, y: . . .;
    BEGIN
        .
        .
        .
    END B;

BEGIN
    .
    .
    . ≪← executing
    .

    A;
    .
    .
    .
END Main;
```

Figure 3.9
Nested procedures executing.

In this example the local variable stack has the memory for the local variables of procedures. This memory is not allocated to a procedure until it is called by another routine. When the procedure finishes execution for that call, the memory for its local variables is popped from the stack.

The flow of execution among procedures follows the stack principle. For example, suppose that we had the set of programs and procedures shown in Figure 3.9. The symbol "≪←" indicates the execution is currently in the main program before the call to procedure A. At that time, the local variable stack looks as shown in Figure 3.10.

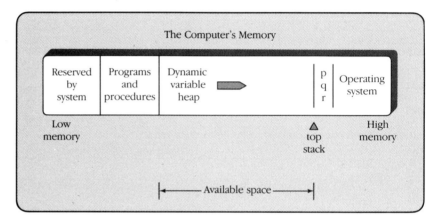

Figure 3.10   Memory space for program *Main* active.

Notice that the variables defined in program *Main* are on the stack, whereas those defined in procedures *A* and *B* do not exist yet.

After the main program has called procedure *A*, procedure *A* has called procedure *B*, and the statement executing is somewhere in procedure *B*, the set of programs and procedures looks like Figure 3.11.

The stack looks as shown in Figure 3.12.

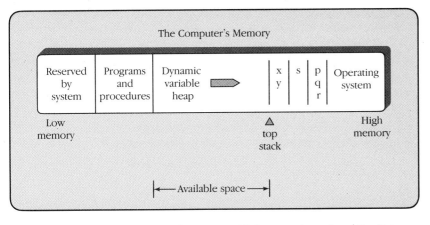

Figure 3.12 Memory space for program *Main,* procedures *A* and *B* active.

The variables defined in the preceding example (*s* in procedure *A; x* and *y* in procedure *B*) in effect come into existence when the procedure is called by another procedure or by the program. As each procedure completes execution and returns to the calling procedure, its variables are popped from the stack and thus cease to exist. Each time a procedure is used it is called an *activation* of the procedure, and the stack element is called an *activation record.* The stack is actually a stack of activation records. The activation records are not necessarily all the same length since, for example, each procedure has its own number and type of variables. A detailed discussion of the contents of activation records is outside of the scope of this book; if you are interested, see Aho and Ullman (1977).

The dynamic variable heap shown in the available memory space in Figure 3.12 need not necessarily be a stack. In the case shown, it is the space for dynamic variables that have been allocated memory space by the *NEW* function. If there were a *POINTER* type as shown in Figure 3.13 and the statement

```
NEW(d)
```

had been executed three times somewhere in *Main, A,* or *B,* then the memory would look as shown in Figure 3.14. The existence of these variables is independent of the activation and deactivation of procedures. They remain in existence until the command

```
DISPOSE(d)
```

is executed. At that time, the instance of *M,* which is being pointed to by *d,* is released.

```
PROCEDURE Main;
VAR p, q, r: . . .;

    PROCEDURE A;
    VAR s: . . .;
    BEGIN
        .
        .
        .
        B;
        .
        .
        .
    END A;

    PROCEDURE B;
    VAR x, y: . . .;
    BEGIN
        .   <<— executing
        .
    END B;

BEGIN
    .
    .
    .
    A;
    .
    .
    .
END Main;
```

Figure 3.11
Nested procedures executing.

```
TYPE Ptr = POINTER TO M;
      M  = ARRAY [1..20] OF
               CHAR;
VAR  d   : Ptr;
     .
     .
     .
     NEW(d);
     .
     .
     .
     NEW(d);
     .
     .
     .
     NEW(d);
     .
     .
     .
```

Figure 3.13

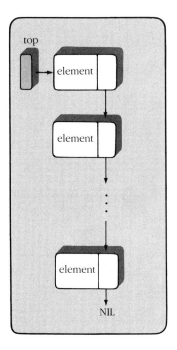

Figure 3.15
A stack as a linked list.

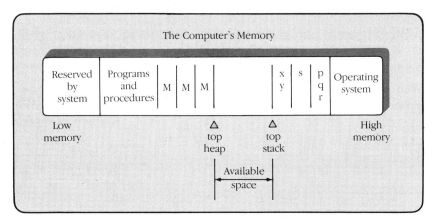

Figure 3.14   Memory space for program *Main,* procedures *A* and *B* active. Three executions of NEW(*d*).

Strictly speaking, this is not a case of two stacks sharing the available space; it is an example of a stack sharing space with another data structure. The heap differs from the stack in that the user may release any of the occurrences of *M* by means of the *DISPOSE* procedure, not just the top one as is the case with stacks.

3.2.6 A Linked Implementation

Linked implementation of stacks has the advantage of dynamic memory allocation; in Modula-2 this is done through the procedures *NEW* and *DISPOSE*. With linked implementation, the stack needs only enough space to accommodate its current depth.

The implementation of stacks with linked lists is simple. For the stack described in Specification 3.1, a singly linked list performs as well as a doubly linked list (the only operations affected are *Push* and *Pop*), so we choose a singly linked list. Next, we have to decide how the element that has been in the stack the longest is to be marked. One approach is to assign its *next* pointer the value NIL. This approach leads to concise algorithms (see Implementation Module 3.3). This is one of those situations in which a design decision is best made by actually implementing several possibilities and observing the differences. Finally, we need to select access pointers. The only one needed is a *top* pointer, which accesses the most recently added element. It is the only one needed because no operation acts on any element other than the most recently added. Figures 3.15 and 3.16 show how a new element is pushed onto a linked stack.

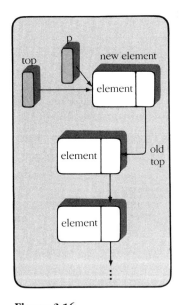

Figure 3.16
Pushing a new element onto a linked stack.

Implementation Module 3.3 *Stacks*

```
IMPLEMENTATION MODULE Stacks;
(* Stacks; linked implementation; meets Specification 3.1. *)

FROM StdTypes IMPORT StdElement;
FROM Storage  IMPORT ALLOCATE, DEALLOCATE, Available;
FROM SYSTEM   IMPORT TSIZE;

TYPE NodePointer = POINTER TO Node;
     Stack       = NodePointer;              (* Points to stack top. *)
     Node        = RECORD                    (* Linked list node.    *)
                     el  : StdElement;
                     next: NodePointer
                   END;
PROCEDURE Push(VAR S: Stack; e: StdElement);  (* Add element e to *)
VAR p: NodePointer;                           (* stack S.         *)
BEGIN
   NEW(p);
   p↑.el:= e; p↑.next := S;
   S := p
END Push;

PROCEDURE Pop(VAR S: Stack; VAR e: StdElement);  (* Retrieve and remove *)
VAR p: NodePointer;                              (* most recently added *)
BEGIN                                            (* element.            *)
   e := S↑.el;
   p := S;
   S := S↑.next;
   DISPOSE(p)
END Pop;

PROCEDURE Empty(S: Stack): BOOLEAN;           (* Is S empty? *)
BEGIN
   RETURN (S = NIL)
END Empty;

PROCEDURE Full(S: Stack): BOOLEAN;            (* Is S full? *)
BEGIN
   RETURN (NOT Available(TSIZE(Node)))
END Full;

PROCEDURE Create(VAR S: Stack): BOOLEAN;      (* If a stack can be  *)
BEGIN                                         (* created, then do so. *)
   S := NIL;
   RETURN TRUE
END Create;
```

continued

Implementation Module 3.3, continued

```
PROCEDURE Terminate(VAR S: Stack);        (* Terminate the existence *)
VAR p: NodePointer;                       (* of stack S.             *)
BEGIN
    WHILE S # NIL DO
        p := S;
        S := S↑.next;
        DISPOSE(p)
    END
END Terminate;

END Stacks.
```

```
PROCEDURE
    Terminate(VAR S: Stack);
BEGIN
  IF S # NIL
    THEN Terminate (S ↑ .next);
        DISPOSE(S)
  END
END Terminate;
```

Figure 3.17
Recursive implementation of
Terminate.

In the margin (Figure 3.17) is a second version of *Terminate*. It is recursive. A structured English version of it is as follows:

IF the end of the stack has not been reached
  THEN terminate the rest of the stack excluding the top node;
      dispose of the top node
END.

The recursive version is no simpler than the iterative version in this case. However, writing simple procedures as recursive procedures promotes a way of thinking that is useful in some classes of problems. Recursion will prove to be useful in certain of the more complex problems encountered later in this book. If you are not familiar with the technique, you may want to cover the material in Appendix B before proceeding further.

Many computers have stacks implemented in the hardware of the machine. These are almost always array implementations using the memory of the computer as the available stack space. Certain registers are devoted to holding the stack's top cursor; these are referred to as stack registers. (See Tanenbaum, 1976.)

Stacks are very efficient data structures. All access to the elements of the stack is at the end of the list of stack elements. All operations of both array and linked implementations execute in a time of $O(1)$, with the single exception of *Terminate* for the linked implementation (see Figure 3.18). It takes $O(n)$ time, where n is the number of elements currently on the stack. The operation *Terminate* must traverse the linked list of stack elements and release the memory for each by using *DISPOSE*. The same procedure in the array implementation only sets the top to zero. However, the array memory space remains allocated to the stack package. The benefit we obtain from the use of linked lists is that the list, when terminated, returns its memory space to the **run-time system**—a set of procedures that are invisible to the programmer but that control the execution of programs. Thus, the less efficient *Terminate* for the linked implementation results in a more flexible use of memory.

The use of dynamic memory allocation may or may not result in a more flexible and efficient use of memory. The burden of making efficient use of dynamic memory allocation is taken from the programmer and placed on the run-time system. The run-time system does jobs such as dynamic memory allocation, I/O, and handling error conditions. It is the responsibility of the compiler designer to make *NEW* and *DISPOSE* efficient. (See Aho and Ullman, 1977.)

Exercises 3.2

1. Using the example of the evaluation of the expression $10 \times (5 + 7)$ in Section 3.2 as a guide, show how the same mechanism might be used to evaluate the following expressions:
   a. $(3 + 5) / (2 - 7)$
   b. $(a \times b)^3 + 20$
2. Rewrite Specification 3.1 for a stack as follows:
   a. Include a *Top*(**VAR** e: StdElement) operation that does a nondestructive retrieval of the current top element.
   b. Modify *Pop* to delete the current top stack element but not return any value. (*Top* and *Pop* together are needed to accomplish what the former *Pop* operation did alone.)
   c. Include *Retrieve*(**VAR** e: StdElement; i: CARDINAL), which returns the value of the element that is the *i*th most recently arrived element. (The top element is at depth 1.) The stack remains unchanged.
   d. Include *Depth:* CARDINAL, which returns the current number of elements in the stack. Why is this operation necessary if *Retrieve* is to be included?
3. Program and test an implementation of your specification from Exercise 2. Use an array representation for the stack.
4. Give orders-of-magnitude estimates of the expected performance of each operation with your array implementation in Exercise 3.
5. In your own words, explain the advantages and disadvantages of stack pairs implemented in a single array. Is there any advantage to implementing stack pairs as linked list(s)? Why?
6. Integers are input to a stack in order 1, 2, 3, ... By interleaving *Push* and *Pop* operations, various outputs can be obtained. For example, the sequence *Push*(1), *Push*(2), *Pop*(x), *Push*(3), *Pop*(x), *Pop*(x) extracts the integers in the order 2, 3, 1.
   a. If the first three integers are input in order, what outputs are possible?
   b. Of the six distinct orderings of {1, 2, 3} one cannot be produced by Exercise 6(a). Explain why.
   c. Extend your explanation of Exercise 6(b) to describe the output sequences that cannot be achieved if the first *n* integers are input in order.
7. In Section 2.4—Specification 2.4 and Implementation Module 2.1—we wrote a specification for a single linked list and implemented it.
   a. Rewrite Specification 2.4 for multiple instances of linked lists using as a model the multi-instance stack specification given in Specification 3.1.
   b. Write an implementation for the specification you have written in Exercise 7(a) above using Implementation Module 3.3 as a guide.

Array Implementation

$O(1)$	$O(n)$
Push	
Pop	
Empty	
Full	
Create	
Terminate	

•

Linked Implementation

$O(1)$	$O(n)$
Push	Terminate
Pop	
Empty	
Full	
Create	

Figure 3.18
Stack performance. The box around Terminate indicates that its performance changed between implementations.

There is a variety of techniques for implementing queues of people. One is to have them form a line. Another is to give each person a tag indicating his or her position in the queue.

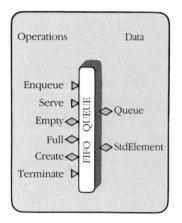

Figure 3.19
FIFO queue capsule.

•

TYPE StdElement =
    RECORD
        key: KeyType;
        data: DataType
    END;

3.3 FIFO Queues

A queue is a data type that exhibits a ***first-in/first-out (FIFO)*** behavior. Elements can be added to the queue. However, the only element that can be retrieved or removed from it is the one that was added least recently, in other words, the earliest arrival. If the earliest arrival is removed, then the next earliest arrival becomes the least recently added element. The operation of adding an element to the queue is commonly called ***enqueue.*** That of retrieving the most recently added element and deleting it from the queue is usually called ***serve.***

Consider the queue of people waiting to be served by a bank teller. They normally form a line in which each person's position indicates his or her relative time of arrival. The person closest to the teller, or at the head of the line, is the first, or earliest, arrival. The person farthest from the teller, or at the tail of the line, is the latest arrival. People who are arriving go to the tail of the line; people who are being served are taken from the head of the line.

Another system of queues is commonly used. Take the example of a busy bakery shop. As people enter the shop they take a number. The numbers are handed out in increasing order. A person arriving sooner will get a lower number than a person arriving later. The waiting customers mill about looking at the goodies in the display cases. When a clerk is free to serve a customer, he or she calls the next number to be served. The person holding the number steps forward and is served. With this method, the waiting customers also form a queue, although the mechanism for recording the order of arrival is different. Physical positioning in the form of a line is not necessary.

In this section we will discuss FIFO queues. The specifications are given in Specification 3.3, a capsule-like summary is given in Figure 3.19, and a

---

Specification 3.3   Queues

DEFINITION MODULE Queues;

(* **Elements:** Although the elements can be of a variety of types, for
      concreteness we assume that they are of type StdElement. *)

    FROM StdTypes **IMPORT** StdElement;

(* **Structure:** The structure is a mechanism for relating the elements that
      allows determination of their order of arrival into the queue. *)

(* **Domain:** The number of elements in the queue is bounded. *)

    EXPORT QUALIFIED Queue, Enqueue, Serve, Length, Full, Create, Terminate;

    TYPE Queue;   (* *Opaque type used to represent a queue.* *)

(* **Operations:** There are six operations. Occasionally in the postcondition
      we must reference the value of the Queue immediately before execution
      of the operation. We use Q-pre as notation for this operation. *)

continued

Specification Module 3.3, continued

```
PROCEDURE Enqueue(VAR Q: Queue; e: StdElement);
(* pre  – The size of Q is less than its bound.
   post – Q includes e as its most recently arrived element. *)

PROCEDURE Serve(VAR Q: Queue; VAR e: StdElement);
(* pre  – Q is not empty.
   post – e is the least recently arrived element of Q-pre;
          Q does not contain e. *)

PROCEDURE Length(Q: Queue): CARDINAL;
(* post – Length is the number of elements in Q. *)

PROCEDURE Full(Q: Queue): BOOLEAN;
(* post – If the size of Q is less than its bound then Full is false,
          else Full is true. *)

PROCEDURE Create(VAR Q: Queue): BOOLEAN;
(* post – If a queue can be created, then Q exists and is empty and
          Create is true, else Create is false. *)

PROCEDURE Terminate(VAR Q: Queue);
(* post – Q-pre does not exist. *)

END Queues.
```

queue that has time stamps to determine order of arrival is shown in Figure 3.20.

As in the case of stacks, we can abstract the queue to be either a list or a set of time-stamped elements. In the list approach an element to be inserted must go at one end of the list, call it the tail end, whereas the only element allowed to be removed is the one on the other end, call it the head end. An element inserted at the tail becomes the new tail. The successor of the removed element becomes the new head. An example is given in Figure 3.21.

Note the similarity between stacks and queues. The only difference other than the change of the names of the operations *Push* and *Pop* and *Enqueue* and *Serve* is that *Serve* returns and removes the least recently arrived element instead of the most recently arrived one. Although the abstract views are quite similar, the implementations are very dissimilar, as we will see in the following sections.

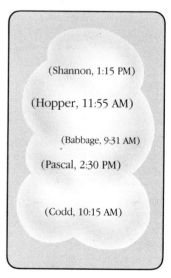

Figure 3.20
A queue as a set of time-stamped elements. The operation *Serve(x)* removes (Babbage, 9:31 AM) from the set and assigns the value 'Babbage' to *x*.

3.3.1 Array Implementation

Figure 3.22 is a snapshot of a queue stored in an array. You can see that serving occurs at the head of the list, and enqueuing occurs at the tail. Figure 3.23 shows the queue at a later time after several elements have been served and a few have been enqueued. Two points are noteworthy:

Pascal ←Tail
Shannon
Hopper
Codd
Babbage ←Head

Figure 3.21
A queue as a list: The order of
arrival is the same as the order
of elements in the list, with the
latest arrival appearing as the
tail.

- The queue crawls through the array from low-to-high index values.
- As the queue crawls forward, it expands and contracts, depending on the relative numbers of enqueues and serves.

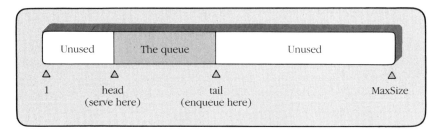

Figure 3.22 The queue in an array.

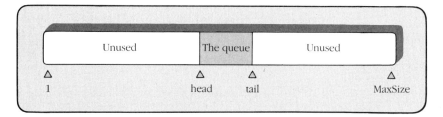

Figure 3.23 The queue in Figure 3.22 at a later time.

The interesting case occurs when the queue crawls to the end of the array space, as shown in Figure 3.24, and another enqueue is requested. The new element cannot simply be attached to the queue as the preceding ones have been, since it would fall beyond the array space. A simpleminded approach is to slide the queue back to the beginning of the array space. The amount of work in doing this is $O(n)$, where n is the number of elements in the queue. If the queue is large, the amount of work is large, and the gain is small. Performance will degrade as the large queue is moved and then quickly crawls back to the end of the array, forcing another move.

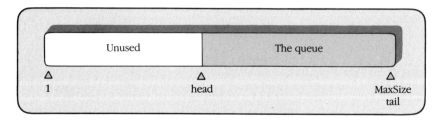

Figure 3.24 The queue at the end of its storage space.

A better solution is to let the queue wrap, whereby the tail is sent to the low index end of the storage space, as shown in Figure 3.25. The storage space in effect becomes circular, as shown in Figure 3.26, which is perhaps a more accurate picture. The queue crawls in a circular space.

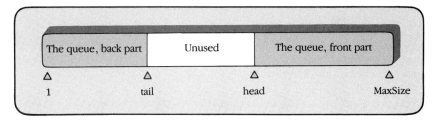

Figure 3.25   The queue in a wrapped state.

Implementation Module 3.4 contains the algorithms that implement a circular queue. The strategy used in Implementation Module 3.4 is preferable to sliding the queue to the low end of the array. With the circular strategy, the queue is never moved.

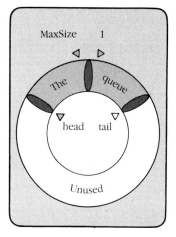

Figure 3.26
A view of a circular queue.

Implementation Module 3.4   *Queues*

```
IMPLEMENTATION MODULE Queues;
(* Queues; array implementation; meets Specification 3.3. *)

FROM StdTypes IMPORT StdElement;
FROM Storage  IMPORT ALLOCATE, DEALLOCATE;
FROM SYSTEM   IMPORT Allocation, TSIZE;

CONST MaxSize       = 10;                              (* Set as needed. *)
TYPE Queue          = POINTER TO QueueInstance;
     QueueIndex     = [1..MaxSize];
     QueueSize      = [0..MaxSize];
     QueueInstance = RECORD
                         head, tail: QueueIndex;
                         n         : QueueSize;
                         queue     : ARRAY QueueSize OF StdElement
                     END;
```

continued

Implementation Module 3.4, continued

```
PROCEDURE Enqueue(VAR Q: Queue; e: StdElement);        (* Enqueue e into Q. *)
BEGIN
WITH Q↑ DO
   tail := (tail MOD MaxSize) + 1;
   queue[tail] := e;
   INC(n)
END
END Enqueue;

PROCEDURE Serve(VAR Q: Queue; VAR e: StdElement);      (* Remove the least *)
BEGIN                                                  (* recently added   *)
   WITH Q↑ DO                                          (* from Q into e.   *)
      e := queue[head];
      head := (head MOD MaxSize) + 1;
      DEC(n)
   END
END Serve;

PROCEDURE Length(Q: Queue): CARDINAL;                  (* Current queue size. *)
BEGIN
   RETURN Q↑.n
END Length;

PROCEDURE Full(Q: Queue): BOOLEAN;                     (* Is the queue full? *)
BEGIN
   RETURN (Q↑.n = MaxSize)
END Full;

PROCEDURE Create(VAR Q: Queue): BOOLEAN;               (* Create a new queue. *)
BEGIN
IF Allocation(TSIZE(QueueInstance))
   THEN
      NEW(Q);
      WITH Q↑ DO
         head := 1;
         tail := MaxSize;
         n    := 0
      END;
      RETURN TRUE
   ELSE
      RETURN FALSE
END
END Create;

PROCEDURE Terminate(VAR Q: Queue);                     (* Terminate Q. *)
BEGIN
   DISPOSE(Q)
END Terminate;

END Queues.
```

3.3.2 Linked Implementation

There is nothing noteworthy about the linked implementation of queues. The representation (nodes and the linked list) is the same as Implementation Module 3.3 (linked implementation of stacks), with the addition of a *tail* pointer to facilitate enqueuing at the list tail and a *count* variable for the number of elements currently in the queue. The implementation is left to you (see Exercise 3.3, 1 below).

All of the operations of the array implementation execute in times that are $O(1)$. The linked implementation, as is the case with stacks, has only one operation whose execution time is $O(n)$–*Terminate*.

Exercises 3.3

1. Write a program for and test a linked implementation of the queue specified in Specification 3.3.
2. Queues are often specified with another operation—*Cancel*. The idea is to be able to delete a given element from the queue. The element is identified by its unique key value:

```
Cancel(tkey: KeyType)
```

A second related operation, *InQueue,* inquires whether a given element is in the queue. The statement

```
InQueue(tkey: KeyType): BOOLEAN
```

returns a value true if an element in the queue has its key value equal to *tkey.* Write the specification of these operations. Are they most easily implemented for the array or for the linked representation? Why?
3. Implement the *Cancel* and *InQueue* operations of Exercise 2 by modifying Implementation Module 3.4 to include them. (This is a good exercise in the use of modulo arithmetic.)
4. A **deque** (pronounced "dek") is a form of double-ended queue (or stack, depending on how you view it). Take the abstraction to be a set of time-stamped elements as we have in Sections 3.2 and 3.3. The deque's *Enqueue* or *Push* operation is the same as those of queues and stacks. The time-stamped element is added to the deque. It has, however, both *Serve*-like and *Pop*-like operations. It can choose at any time to retrieve and delete either the most recently added element or the least recently added element. Other operations are the same as those of queues (Specification 3.3).

Write specifications for a deque, and program and test an array implementation.
5. Write specifications for a variable length element queue. Program and test for an array implementation using a circular array space.
6. Explain how stacks are used to store the return addresses associated with procedure calls.
7. Why are stacks often abstracted as lists? What shortcomings are there to this approach?

8. Use the operations specified in Specifications 3.1 and 3.3 to print the content of a stack or a queue. The stack or queue is to be restored after its content is printed.

  a. Print a queue in order from least recently added to most recently added.

  b. Print a queue in order from most recently added to least recently added. Use a stack as an auxiliary data type.

  c. Print a stack in order from most recently added to least recently added. What auxiliary data type, if any, is needed?

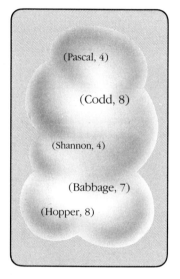

Figure 3.27
A priority queue as a set of name, priority value pairs. The operation *Serve(x,p)* removes either (Codd,8) or (Hopper,8) from the set and assigns the value 'Codd' or 'Hopper' to *x* and 8 to *p*.

```
Hopper,    8←Head
Codd,      8
Babbage,   7
Shannon,   4
Pascal,    4←Tail
```

Figure 3.28
A priority queue as a list. The order of priorities is the same as the physical order of the list, with the highest priority at the top, or head, of the list.

3.4 Priority Queues

The queues that we discussed in Section 3.3 follow a first-in/first-out protocol. We will now take up an important variant—***highest-priority-in/first-out queues (HPIFO).*** We have already mentioned several examples of such structures—the hospital emergency room in which the sickest patients are treated first and the events requesting service by a computer system in which the most critical events are handled first. There are many situations in which ***priority queues*** are applicable.

Priority queues differ from stacks and FIFO queues in that time of arrival of the elements is not a factor. Instead of being able to retrieve or remove the most recently or least recently added element, priority queues can only retrieve or remove an element that has the highest priority value currently in the queue. In order for the highest value to be determined, the priorities must be of some data type that is ordered.

The specifications of a priority queue are given in Specification 3.4. Note the similarities among priority queues, stacks, and FIFO queues. The latter two could be thought of as priority queues in which arrival times are used as priorities. Priority queues use a user-supplied priority value.

We can think of (abstract) the structure in ways similar to those used for LIFO stacks and FIFO queues. One approach is to consider the structure to be a set (in the mathematical sense) of pairs of values. One member of the pair is the data element value; the other is the associated priority value. Elements being enqueued are paired with their specified priority value, and the pair is added to the set. When serving, an element associated with the highest priority value currently in the set and its priority are copied out. The pair is then removed from the set (see Figure 3.27).

A second approach is to abstract the structure as a list ordered on the elements' priority values. A highest priority element is at the head of the list. The operation *Serve* is simple. The head element and its priority are copied out and deleted from the list; its successor then becomes the new head. The operation *Enqueue* is a bit more complex. Here, an arriving element is placed in the list in any position that allows the list to remain ordered on priority (see Figure 3.28).

Remember that the set and list approaches described above are only abstractions. That is, they are only ways of thinking about priority queues in terms of well-known structures. The problem with this is that the approaches may be suggestive of techniques for implementing the priority queue. The list approach, while perfectly valid, may send strong suggestions to implementors that a list should be chosen for implementation. As we shall see later in this section, such an implementation is likely to exhibit a worse performance than certain nonlinear implementations.

There may be several elements in the priority queue with the same priority value. This raises the question of what ordering we wish to specify within that group of elements. We might specify that within a given priority, the elements will be in LIFO or FIFO order, or specify an ordering by key field values, or specify any of a number of such orderings. However, notice that Specification 3.4 makes no statement at all about such an ordering. What does that imply? It says to the implementor that we are making no assumptions about ordering among elements with equal priority. The implementor is free to choose any ordering that is most advantageous. Since the ordering is not of interest to the user, it should not constrain the implementor in any way. The user is to make no assumptions about such an ordering when using the module.

We now present Specification 3.4 for priority queues and a capsule-like summary in Figure 3.29.

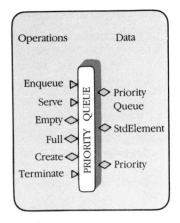

Figure 3.29
Priority queue capsule.

•

TYPE StdElement =
  RECORD
    key: KeyType;
    data: DataType
  END;

Specification 3.4 Priority Queues

DEFINITION MODULE PriorityQueues;

(* **Elements:** Although the elements can be of a variety of types, for concreteness we assume that they are of type StdElement. *)

  FROM StdTypes **IMPORT** StdElement, Priority;

(* **Structure:** Each element of the priority queue is associated with a user-supplied priority value. The priorities must be of an ordered data type. *)

(* **Domain:** The number of elements in a priority queue is bounded. *)

  EXPORT QUALIFIED PriorityQueue, Enqueue, Serve, Length, Full, Create,
                    Terminate;

  TYPE PriorityQueue;   (* *Opaque type to represent a priority queue.* *)

(* **Operations:** There are six operations. Occasionally in the postcondition we must reference the value of the priority queue immediately before execution of the operation. We use PQ-pre as notation for this value. *)

  PROCEDURE Enqueue (**VAR** PQ: PriorityQueue; e: StdElement; p: Priority);
  (* **pre** — The size of PQ is less than the bound.
     post — PQ includes e associated with priority p. *)

continued

Specification 3.4, continued

```
      PROCEDURE Serve(VAR PQ: PriorityQueue; VAR e: StdElement;
                                            VAR p: Priority);
      (* pre  – PQ is not empty.
         post – e is an element associated with the highest priority of PQ-pre;
                p is that priority value; PQ does not contain e. *)

      PROCEDURE Length(PQ: PriorityQueue): CARDINAL;
      (* post – Length is the number of elements in PQ. *)

      PROCEDURE Full(PQ: PriorityQueue): BOOLEAN;
      (* post – If the size of PQ is less than its bound, then Full is false
                else Full is true. *)

      PROCEDURE Create(VAR PQ: PriorityQueue): BOOLEAN;
      (* post – If a priority queue can be created then PQ exists and is empty,
                and Create is true; else Create is false. *)

      PROCEDURE Terminate(VAR PQ: PriorityQueue);
      (* post – PQ-pre does not exist. *)

END PriorityQueues.
```

3.4.1 Implementations

Suppose that we choose to represent the priority queue as a linked list. We can use the same sort of linked list as we used for a FIFO queue—singly linked, with a NIL next value marking the end of the list and a *head* pointer providing access to the list. No *tail* pointer is necessary. The nodes are slightly different since they contain augmented elements. The list node data type is shown in Figure 3.30. The rest of the changes are concentrated on a single operation— *Enqueue*. It must not place the element being added at one end of the list, as was the case for stacks and queues, but in a position so that the list is ordered by priority, with the highest priority at the list head. Figure 3.31 shows such a linked list and the possible points of insertion (enqueuing) of a new element whose priority is 7.

The *Enqueue* procedure must sequentially search for the proper position before actually doing the insertion. Assuming that there are n elements whose priorities are evenly distributed, we can expect to probe approximately $n/2$ nodes before the proper position is found. The insertion is then a matter of rearranging a few pointers. The search is an $O(n)$ operation, whereas the insertion is $O(1)$.

If an array implementation were used, on the average half of the list elements must be moved to make room for the new one. Both the search and the data movement are operations that take $O(n)$ work.

We shall see in Chapter 4 that it is possible to improve the search time considerably by doing a binary search. Without going into the details of binary

```
TYPE NodePointer =
        POINTER TO Node;
     Node =
        RECORD
           el   : StdElement;
           py   : Priority;
           next: NodePointer
        END;
```

Figure 3.30
Data types for a linked list priority queue.

searches, the important consequence is that a binary search takes $O(\log_2 n)$ work, a considerable improvement for large n. However, the $O(n)$ work of moving list elements to do the actual insertion remains. Binary searches on linked lists are less efficient than sequential searches; therefore, they result in no improvement for linked lists.

Priority queues implemented as lists are forms of sorted lists, an abstract type that we will investigate in Section 4.3. Since the details of their implementations and performance are covered there, we will not pursue the subject here. The important point is that enqueuing takes $O(n)$ work for linear implementations, either in data movement for an array representation or in comparisons for a linked list representation.

There is a nonlinear data structure that gives considerably improved performance for large priority queues. It is called a ***heap*** and can be thought of as a form of binary tree. Section 5.8 is about heaps and their use as priority queues. Using heaps, the priority queue operations achieve a performance of $O(\log_2 n)$ for both enqueuing and serving. Understanding heaps is easier after studying binary trees, so we will delay discussion of heap implementation of priority queues until Chapter 5. Figure 3.32 summarizes the performance of the three types of priority queue implementation—sorted lists in arrays, sorted linked lists, and heaps.

	List		Heap
	Array	**Linked**	
Enqueue	$O(n)$	$O(n)$	$O(\log n)$
Serve	$O(1)$	$O(1)$	$O(\log n)$

Figure 3.32 Performance estimates of priority queue implementations.

Exercises 3.4

1. Design, program, and test an array implementation of a priority queue. What are the orders-of-magnitude estimates of the performance expected of the operations?
2. Design, program, and test a linked list implementation of a priority queue. What are the orders-of-magnitude estimates of the performance expected of the operations?
3. Discuss the relative advantages and disadvantages of the array and linked implementations of priority queues.
4. Explain how a FIFO queue can be considered to be a special case of a priority queue.
5. Explain how a stack can be considered to be a special case of a priority queue.
6. Write specifications for the following operations that might also be specified for a priority queue:
   a. Change the priority of an element (identified by its key value).
   b. Delete an element (identified by its key value).
   c. Combine two priority queues into a larger priority queue.
7. Suppose that the priority of a standard element is its key value. Describe how a priority queue might be used to sort a collection of such elements.

As shown below for a priority of 7, enqueuing an element in a priority queue may lead to several possible points of insertion:

Enqueue(e,7)

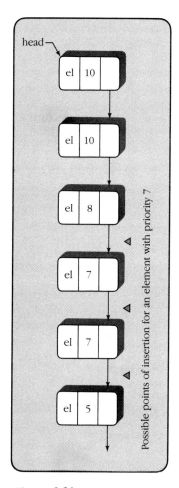

Figure 3.31
Linked list representation of a priority queue.

3.5 Application of Queues: Scheduling I/O Requests on a Magnetic Disk

Interactive time-shared computer systems often encounter a problem in scheduling I/O tasks for a magnetic disk. It is common to find such systems serving many terminals but having only one, or perhaps a few, magnetic disk drives. For example, such a system might service 48 terminals at any one time and have a single magnetic disk of several hundred megabytes capacity. At any time, the users could be running programs, compiling, text editing, and what not. These activities generate a mix of requests for I/O on the magnetic disk. The servicing of these requests can create a bottleneck, which substantially affects system performance. The I/O requests generated by all of the computing activities of the users are intermixed, and at any time the disk can expect to have a group of I/O requests waiting for execution. Disks, however, can do only one thing at a time, so the requests must be put into some order for service. The order chosen—called the **disk-scheduling policy**—is the subject of this section.

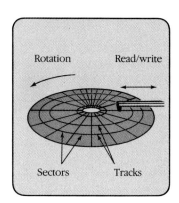

Figure 3.33
Magnetic disk surface.

We can consider the **disk** to be a single platter, or surface, with a **read/write head** that can be moved radially across its surface. Most disks have multiple surfaces, but a single surface is sufficient to illustrate the problems. Figure 3.33 shows the surface of the disk and the arm holding the read/write head. The disk, which is rotating at a constant angular velocity (3600 rpm is typical), is divided into a set of concentric circles called **tracks;** each track is divided into segments called **sectors.** By the time an I/O request arrives at the disk to be executed, the disk sees it as a request to read or write sector S on track T. No matter how complex the I/O request from the user, it is translated by the system software, firmware, and hardware into these two simple operations and a target track and sector.

The time (t) that it takes the disk to satisfy an I/O request is the sum of three component times (see Matick, 1977):

$$t_{I/O} = t_{seek} + t_{rotation} + t_{transmission}$$

$t_{I/O}$	Time to service the I/O request
t_{seek}	Time to move the arm to the target track
$t_{rotation}$	Time to wait until the target sector rotates to the read head
$t_{transmission}$	Time to transmit the data
C_1, C_2	Constants

Let us simplify the expression by an approximation that is adequate for our purposes. We will assume that the rotation and transmission times are constant. We will also assume that the seek time is a linear function of the number of tracks that the head must cross in order to get from its current track $T_{initial}$ to the track T_{target}, which contains the sector it is to read or write. We then have

$$t_{I/O} = t_{seek} + C_2 = C_1 \times (T_{target} - T_{initial}) + C_2$$

At any moment, there might be a group of waiting I/O requests. Request r is to read or write sector S_r on track T_r:

$$r = (read/write, S_r, T_r)$$

It is important to note that the composition of the group changes over time. Requests are being serviced by the disk while new requests continue to arrive, thereby changing the mix of tracks and sectors awaiting service.

3.5.1 Disk Scheduling

What should the disk-scheduling policy be? The first approach might be to argue that the I/O requests should be served on a first-come/first-served basis. The requests, upon arriving for service, should be put into a FIFO queue such as the abstraction that we discussed in Section 3.3. Such a policy seems, in a sense, "fair." When the disk has completed an I/O request, it interrupts the central processing unit (CPU) and the I/O scheduler serves the next queued request and sets the disk to work on it. Arriving I/O requests are enqueued by the I/O scheduler.

Is this "fair" strategy really fair? Why not use a strategy that commands the disk to go to the closest I/O request? It would seem that such a policy would result in a smaller average value for $t_{I/O}$. The disk head will always be moved the shortest distance to the next I/O request and therefore spend less time seeking and more time transmitting data. This strategy is called **shortest seek time first (SSTF).** The FIFO strategy, in attempting to be fair to everyone, may really be unfair to everyone due to a longer average time to satisfy I/O requests. The system would appear to the users to be running more slowly since the disk would spend more of its time in seeks.

What data abstraction can be used to represent the set of I/O requests that is awaiting service under the SSTF disk-scheduling policy? It is, in fact, a priority queue. The priority of an I/O request r is determined by the distance between the target track and the track on which the read head is currently positioned:

$$priority_r = abs(T_r - T_{current})$$

When the disk has completed an I/O request, it interrupts the CPU, and the I/O scheduler serves the next closest (highest priority) request and puts the disk to work on it.

There is an important factor for implementation that is inherent in the scheme. Look at the example in Figure 3.34(a). Initially, the read/write head is positioned at some track, call it the current track T_C. Three I/O requests, X, Y, and Z, located at tracks T_X, T_Y, and T_Z, respectively, are awaiting service. The priorities are the distances *(d)* of the three requests from T_C and are shown with 1 being the highest priority. The head is moved to I/O request X and is served [Figure 3.34(b)]. At that point, notice that the relative priorities of the two remaining requests have changed. Whereas in Figure 3.34(a), request Z was next highest priority and Y was third, in Figure 3.34(b), after X is served, Y assumes a higher priority than Z and is next to be served. In other words, the priorities are not static. Serving the highest priority request may change the priorities of the remaining ones.

The abstraction remains a priority queue but one in which the priorities may shift each time the queue is served. The implementation issues involved are interesting, as you will see when you do Exercises 3.5, 1 and 2.

What sort of improvement over an FIFO strategy do we get using an SSTF strategy? Our metric, or measurement of improvement, is the expected number of tracks that must be passed over in order to satisfy the pending I/O requests or, equivalently, the expected time to satisfy an I/O request. A complete answer

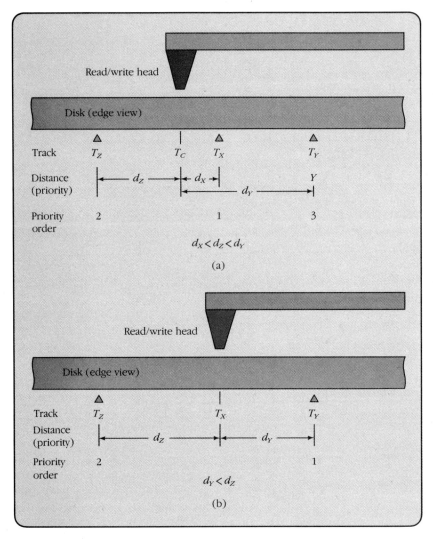

Figure 3.34 I/O requests and shifting priorities. (a) Before serving X. (b) After serving X.

to that question is complex, and you can refer to Hofri (1980) and Coffman and Hofri (1982) for a more complete discussion. The references show that a number of factors can affect the results: the rate of arrivals of new requests, the distribution of requests on the disk surface, and the characteristics of the disk drive.

Hofri (1980) demonstrates that with a uniform random distribution of requests on the disk surface and parameter settings that approximate an IBM 3330 disk, SSTF is superior to FIFO in mean waiting time for service. He obtained similar results for requests distributed nonuniformly on the disk surface, although the superiority of SSTF is less.

Have we in fact chosen the correct factor to reduce? It should be clear that we have chosen a strategy that will keep the disk busier with actual I/O operations and reduce the amount of head movement between requests. But is keeping the disk productively busy the right thing to do? Increasing the amount of productive work the disk does per unit of time should speed up overall system operation and give the users shorter response times at their terminals. Is the expected response time at the terminals the correct thing to optimize? We shall see that although the answer may be yes, there are other considerations.

Consider the situation shown in Figure 3.35. We see the surface of the disk from an edge view. The symbol "$\triangle$" points to the tracks with pending I/O requests. Notice that there is a large cluster of requests near the head T_C and a much smaller group near position T_X. The distribution of requests among the tracks would appear to be nonuniform. We assume that requests are continually arriving and that most will be in the vicinity of T_C. If we use the SSTF strategy, the head might remain in the vicinity of T_C for quite some time. Only if the set of pending requests around T_C is completely served will the head move to the vicinity of T_X and serve the few requests waiting there. The disk is being used efficiently but the users whose I/O requests are clustered about T_X may experience long waits before they get some response at their terminals. Frustration levels and tempers rise, and at least some users might feel that the system is serving them poorly.

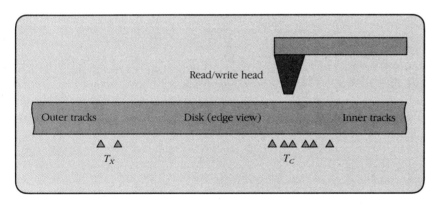

Figure 3.35 I/O requests in two clusters.

The problem is one of human engineering. The system hums along for one group of users but crawls for another. Would it be better for everyone to have a moderately slower average response time, while guaranteeing that no one experiences an unacceptably long wait? We could do this by returning to an FIFO disk-scheduling policy. This way, no one would have to wait an inordinately long time for terminal response.

Or is there a strategy that gives a low expected response time while avoiding abnormally slow response times for any terminal? Consider the following. Suppose that we let the disk arm sweep across the disk from inner to

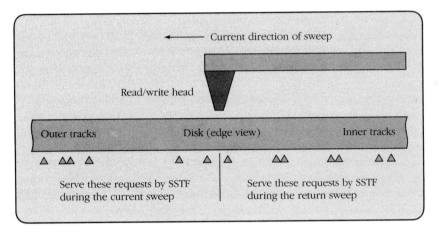

Figure 3.36 Sweep/SSTF disk-scheduling policy.

outer tracks (Figure 3.36). Any requests that are in front of the head in the direction that it is traveling will be served using an SSTF strategy. The head sweeps across the disk in one direction stopping at each track that has an I/O request pending. It ignores any requests that fall behind it. When it has satisfied the last request that it finds in front of it, it turns around and starts a reverse sweep from inner tracks to outer, again serving any requests that it finds in front of it using an SSTF strategy. In this way we can attempt to strike some balance between minimizing average seek time and avoiding inordinately long seek time.

What impact does this strategy have upon the abstract data type chosen to effect it? The set of requests ahead of the read/write head in the direction of the current sweep is a priority queue based upon track number. The set of requests behind the head is also a priority queue, but one that will not be served until the head turns about and begins to sweep in the opposite direction. The priorities of the second queue are inverted on track number. If higher (lower) track numbers were high priority in the inner-to-outer sweep, then lower (higher) track numbers would be given higher priority in the outer-to-inner sweep. Regardless of the details, conceptually we have two separate priority queues.

Remember that the situation is dynamic. As requests are being served, new requests are arriving and are being enqueued. A question arises about the placement of the requests. Those arriving behind the head in its current sweep direction are certainly placed in the queue awaiting the return sweep. However, what about those arrivals that are in front of the head? Should they immediately be placed in the current sweep queue? Or should they be placed in the return sweep queue? What effect does the decision have on the implementation of the queues? We leave these questions for you in Exercises 3.5, 3 and 4.

Coffman and Hofri (1982) discuss the performance of the sweep/SSTF strategy. Again we emphasize that this is a complex problem in which the assumptions made and the parameter values chosen affect the results. Our primary purpose here is to study the data structures involved, not to do an in-depth study of disk-scheduling strategies. (For a review of the literature on the disk-scheduling problem, refer to Wiederhold, 1983, page 341.)

3.5.2 An Abstract Schedule

The topics discussed in Section 3.5.1 are implementation details. They are concerned with techniques for carrying out a scheduling strategy. Programmers using the schedule should be shielded from the details of how the scheduling is done. What data abstraction might we specify to do this?

The essence of a disk schedule lies in two operations: (1) presenting a request to be scheduled and (2) obtaining the next request on the schedule so that it can be executed on the disk. The requests are as defined previously—$r = (R/W, S_r, T_r)$. Thus, we can write Specification 3.5 and summarize the operations in Figure 3.37.

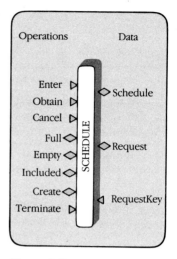

Figure 3.37
Schedule capsule.

Specification 3.5   Schedules

DEFINITION MODULE Schedules;

(* **Elements:** The data elements are disk I/O requests of type Request defined in the TYPE statement below. *)

(* **Structure:** Some mechanism for determining an ordering of the requests in the schedule. *)

(* **Domain:** The number of requests in the schedule is bounded. *)

```
    EXPORT QUALIFIED Request, RequestKey, Enter, Obtain, Cancel, Full, Empty,
                     Included, Create, Terminate;

    TYPE Schedule;
         RequestKey = CARDINAL;
         IO         = (Read, Write);
         Request    = RECORD
                          reqid: RequestKey;          (* Request identifier. *)
                          inout: IO;                  (* I/O action requested. *)
                          s    : [1..20];             (* Target sector. *)
                          t    : [1..200]             (* Target track. *)
                      END;
```

(* **Operations:** *)

```
    PROCEDURE Enter(VAR S: Schedule; r: Request);
    (* pre  — S is not full.
       post — r is in schedule S. *)
```

continued

Specification 3.5, continued

PROCEDURE Obtain(**VAR** S: Schedule; **VAR** r: Request);
(* **pre** — S is not empty.
    post — r is the next scheduled action; S does not contain r. *)

PROCEDURE Cancel(**VAR** S: Schedule; rid: RequestKey);
(* **pre** — Request rid is in S.
    post — A request with reqid = rid is not in S. *)

PROCEDURE Full(S: Schedule);
(* **post** — If the number of requests in S has reached its bound
            then Full is true else Full is false. *)

PROCEDURE Empty(S: Schedule): BOOLEAN;
(* **post** — If there are no requests in schedule S then Empty is true
            else Empty is false. *)

PROCEDURE Included(S: Schedule; rid: RequestKey): BOOLEAN;
(* **post** — If a request with reqid = rid is in schedule S
            then Included is true else Included is false. *)

PROCEDURE Create(**VAR** S: Schedule): BOOLEAN;
(* **post** — Schedule S exists and contains no requests. *)

PROCEDURE Terminate(**VAR** S: Schedule);
(* **post** — Schedule S-pre does not exist. *)

END Schedules.

Someone using the schedule need not know which disk-scheduling strategy is being used by the implementation. Thus, for example, various strategies may be tested and an optimal strategy may be determined with no changes in the programs that use the abstract schedule.

Exercises 3.5

1. Write the specifications for a priority queue to be used in the SSTF disk scheduling. The request to *Enqueue* should contain the identification of the request (key), the request type (read or write), the sector (S_r), and the track (T_r). Assume that the current hard disk head position is stored in a globally available variable *current*. Be sure to account for the shifting priorities caused by the movement of the read/write head to the next request [see Figure 3.34(a) and (b)].
2. Design, program, and test an implementation of the SSTF priority queue described in Exercise 1.
3. Write specifications for the priority queue(s) to be used in the sweep/SSTF disk-scheduling strategy discussed in the text and shown in Figure 3.36.
4. Design, program, and test an implementation of the sweep/SSTF priority queue described in Exercise 3.

3.6 Summary

In Chapter 3 we have looked at a variety of data structures that have the characteristic that retrieval and deletion of elements is restricted to a single element. With stacks, the user only has access to the most recently added element, whereas with queues the user only has access to the least recently added element. It is the implementor's job to keep track of which element is currently the most recent or least recent one. Of course, the user ultimately determines the order by the sequence of insertions and deletions requested, but it is up to the implementor to handle the details.

Different implementations of stacks and queues generally exhibit no differences in overall performance characteristics. Both the linked and array implementations of stacks carry out all of their operations with $O(1)$ work (the exception is clearing a linked stack or queue). We might expect, however, to find some smaller differences due to the use of linked versus array structures.

A larger difference in performance occurs in the case of priority queues. We have deferred the discussion of heap implementations until Section 5.8; there we will find that implementations based on heaps have better performance than those that use lists, at least for large queues.

Table 3.1 gives a rough guide to the complexity of the implementation modules in Chapter 3. We can easily see from the average number of lines of code in Table 3.1 that all of the implementations of stacks and queues that we have presented are quite simple. The array implementation of a stack is especially so.

TABLE 3.1   Implementation modules in Chapter 3.

Implementation module	Data type	Representation	Number of procedures	Lines of code	Lines of code per procedure	
					Average	Maximum
3.1	Stack	Array	6	14	2.3	5
3.2	Stack Pair	Array	6	22	3.7	6
3.3	Stack	Linked list	6	15	2.5	4
3.4	Queue	Array	6	19	3.2	8

Linear Structures

4.1 Introduction

4.2 Lists
    4.2.1 List Specification
    4.2.2 List Array Implementation
    4.2.3 List Linked Implementation
    Exercises 4.2

4.3 Ordered Lists
    4.3.1 Chronologically Ordered Lists
    Exercises 4.3.1
    4.3.2 Sorted Lists
    Exercises 4.3.2
    4.3.3 Frequency-Ordered Lists
    Exercises 4.3.3

4.4 Rings
    Exercises 4.4

4.5 Sequences
    4.5.1 Sequence Specification
    4.5.2 Modula-2 Files
    Exercises 4.5

4.6 An Application: Single-Letter and Digraph Frequencies in English Text
    4.6.1 The Frequency Analysis Program
    4.6.2 Timing Studies

4.7 Summary

4.1 Introduction

Linear Structure

A finite set of elements has linear structure if it is empty or if it contains one element or if

1. There is a unique element called the first, and
2. There is a unique element called the last, and
3. Every element except the last has a unique successor, and
4. Every element except the first has a unique predecessor.

In this chapter we will study several abstract data types that share a common property—they are linear. The data elements may be thought of as being laid out in a straight line or, in the case of a ring, a circle. Progression from one end of the line to the other, or completely around the circle, means encountering all of the elements of the data structure.

We will begin by treating the elements as if they were ordered only by position. We call the abstract data type a list (Section 4.2). Then we will study some variations that have other orderings. For example, chronological lists (Section 4.3.1) require that the elements be ordered by their times of insertion into the list, and sorted lists (Section 4.3.2) require that the elements be ordered by ascending or descending element key values. Frequency-ordered lists (Section 4.3.3) require that their elements be ordered by the frequencies with which they are accessed.

Although we can consider a ring (Section 4.4) to be a list whose two ends are tied together, we will define an abstract ring that is simpler. It has fewer operations than the list we specified. Consequently, it is simpler to implement.

In Section 4.5 we will examine sequences. They are lists that have a very different set of operations from the kind described in Section 4.2. A sequential file is one kind of sequence. Typical operations allow us to open the file and position the file cursor to the first file element. *Read* or *Get* operations move the file cursor from its current position to the next element. The file may also be opened for output, and new elements may be appended to its trailing end. We will look at Modula-2 files as an example.

Linear Structures Discussed in Chapter 4

Lists
Chronologically ordered lists
Sorted lists
Frequency-ordered lists
Rings
Sequences
Files

We will consider each of these data structures as an abstract data type and will discuss their specifications. We will give the complete implementation modules for the array and linked representations of the list (Implementation Modules 4.1 and 4.2) and for the linked representation of the ring (Implementation Module 4.3). The implementations of the other types, with the exception of sequences, are variants of these, and we will restrict our discussion to the parts of the modules that are changed.

We will look closely at the performance characteristics of each implementation module. In Section 4.6, we will use the modules for an application—finding the frequencies of occurrence of single letters and pairs of letters in a sample of English language text. The performance of each module is measured by timing studies. (There are a few surprises in the results.) Section 4.7 is a summary.

Linear structures are important because they occur so often. A line of customers at a bank window, a line of cars at a traffic light, records stored on a magnetic tape, the statements or instructions of a computer program, the characters of a character string, the pages of a book, and the batting order of a baseball team are all linear structures. In each, every element, except possibly the first and last, has a unique preceding and following element.

The essence of linearity lies in this uniqueness of an element's preceding and following elements. An important consequence of linearity is our ability to assign an integer to each element in the list. Starting at the element that has no predecessor (the first element) we assign the integer 1. Moving through the list from each element to the following one, we assign successive integers. The integer assigned to an element is its position in the list.

If you have written programs, you have undoubtedly used a software package that operates on lists. It is a text editor or word processor. The lines of a program form a list. Text editors are packages that have a set of operations that can be performed on such lists. You will find a strong resemblance between the operations of the list data type specified in Specification 4.1 and the operations of an editor. It is only one example of packages that deal with linear structures.

> A text editor performs operations on a list. The data elements are lines of text.

4.2 Lists

What is a **list**? Recall that an abstract data type consists of three parts: (1) the specification, which includes the user's view of the data elements, structure, and operations; (2) the representation of the data and its structure; and (3) the implementation of the operations. (Remember that we often use the word implementation to mean the combination representation and implementation.) Let us first look at a list's specification.

1 Shannon
2 Backus
3 Aitken
4 Babbage
5 Lovelace

Figure 4.1
A list whose component elements are names.

4.2.1 List Specification

Look at the names in Figure 4.1. Each name has one of a consecutive set of integers (starting with 1) associated with it. We will say that these integers are the **positions** of the names in the group. Although the names are shown neatly ordered by position, we could equally as well show them scattered about in a random fashion, as in Figure 4.2. As long as we keep the integers attached to the names, we can keep our notion of position. (Do not worry now about how efficient it might be to do something with the list such as find the position of 'Shannon' or find which name is associated with 5. That is an implementation issue, so just relax and assume that any operation that we define can be done with perfect efficiency.)

A list contains *n* elements, where *n* varies over time as elements are inserted and deleted. We assume that elements of type *StdElement* are stored in the list. We also assume that the key field has the unique identification property. This assumption is not necessary, but it makes the specification a bit simpler (see Exercise 4.2, 6).

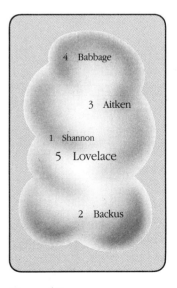

Figure 4.2
Another view of the list.

Specification 4.1   Lists

DEFINITION MODULE Lists;

(* **Elements:** We assume that the elements are of type StdElement. *)

  FROM StdTypes **IMPORT** StdElement, KeyType;

(* **Structure:** The relationship among elements is linear (see Section 1.4.2).
    Essentially this means that there is a first element with a
    unique successor and a last element with a unique predecessor, and
    every other element has both a unique successor and a unique
    predecessor.
      Each element is assigned a unique position. The position of the
    first element is 1. If the position of an element is k, then the
    position of its successor is k + 1. Thus, if the list is not empty,
    its elements are assigned positions 1, 2, 3, ... n, where n is the
    size of the list. *)

(* **Domain:** The number of elements in a list is bounded. *)

  EXPORT QUALIFIED List, FindNext, FindPrior, Findith, FindKey, Retrieve,
              Update, InsertBefore, InsertAfter, Delete, CurPos,
              Full, Size, Create, Terminate;

  TYPE List;   (* *An opaque type used to represent a List.* *)

(* **Operations:** We consider a set of 14 operations. If the list is not
    empty, then one of the list elements is designated as the current
    element (see Figure 4.3). If the list is empty, then the current
    element is not defined. Occasionally, in the postcondition, we need
    to refer to the current element as it was just before executing the
    operation. We use c-pre for this reference. The predecessor and
    successor of c-pre are referred to as c-prior and c-next,
    respectively. The list just before executing an operation is L-pre. *)

  PROCEDURE FindNext(L: List);
  (* **pre** — The current element is not the last element and L is not empty.
     post — The current element is c-next. *)

  PROCEDURE FindPrior(L: List);
  (* **pre** — The current element is not the first element and L is not empty.
     post — The current element is c-prior. *)

  PROCEDURE Findith(L: List; i: CARDINAL);
  (* **pre** — 1 <= i <= Size(L).
     post — The current element is the element in the ith list position. *)

  PROCEDURE FindKey(L: List; tkey: KeyType): BOOLEAN;
  (* **post** — If L contains an element whose key value is tkey
            then that element is the current element and FindKey is true,
            else FindKey is false. *)

continued

Specification 4.1, continued

PROCEDURE Retrieve(L: List; **VAR** e: StdElement);
(* **pre** — L is not empty.
    post — e has the value of the current element. *)

PROCEDURE Update(**VAR** L: List; e: StdElement);
(* **pre** — L is not empty.
    post — The current element has the value of e. *)

PROCEDURE InsertBefore(**VAR** L: List; e: StdElement);
(* **pre** — L is not full.
    post — e is an element of L and is the current
        element; if L-pre was not empty then e is
        the predecessor of c-pre and, if c-prior
        exists, e is the successor of c-prior. *)

PROCEDURE InsertAfter(**VAR** L: List; e: StdElement);
(* **pre** — L is not full.
    post — e is an element of L and is the current element;
        if L-pre was not empty then e is the successor of c-pre and, if
        c-next exists, e is the predecessor of c-next. *)

PROCEDURE Delete(**VAR** L: List);
(* **pre** — L is not empty.
    post — c-pre is not in L;
        if L contains a single element, then that element is current;
        if L contains at least 2 elements, then c-next, if it exists, is
        current, else the first element is current;
        if c-next and c-prior both exist, then c-next is the successor of
        c-prior. *)

PROCEDURE CurPos(L: List): CARDINAL;
(* **pre** — L is not empty.
    post — CurPos is the position of the current element. *)

PROCEDURE Full(L: List): BOOLEAN;
(* **post** — If Size(L) is not less than the bound
        then Full is true, else Full is false. *)

PROCEDURE Size(L: List): CARDINAL;
(* **post** — Size is the number of elements in the list. *)

PROCEDURE Create(**VAR** L: List): BOOLEAN;
(* **post** — If a list can be created then L exists and is empty, and Create
        is true, else Create is false. *)

PROCEDURE Terminate(**VAR** L: List);
(* **post** — List L-pre does not exist. *)

END Lists.

TYPE StdElement =
    RECORD
      key: KeyType;
      data: DataType
    END;
        •

```
               1 Shannon
               2 Backus
               3 Aitken
Current →      4 Babbage
               5 Lovelace
```

Figure 4.3
List with current element.

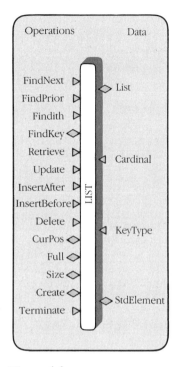

Figure 4.4
List capsule.

The examples below show the results of executing some of the specified operations.

The operations can be (arbitrarily) grouped by function. The first group permits the user to specify which element is current. The operations are *FindNext, FindPrior, Findith,* and *FindKey.* The operations *FindPrior* and *FindNext* make the current element's predecessor and successor respectively, current. The operation *Findith* makes the element in the *i*th position current. The operation *FindKey* makes an element whose key value is equal to a target key value current. If a match to the target key value cannot be found, *FindKey* returns false, and the current element remains unchanged.

The second group of operations performs on the current element. The operations are *Retrieve, Update, InsertBefore, InsertAfter,* and *Delete.* The operations *InsertBefore* and *InsertAfter* insert a new element into the list just before and just after the current element, respectively. They also permit insertions at the ends of the list. Both cause a change of +1 in the positions of all elements following the inserted element.

In deleting a list element, we specify that all of the elements beyond it (at higher positions) retain their positions relative to each other but move up one position in the list. Since the current element is deleted, the question of what to do about the current element arises. We will arbitrarily leave it at the same

FindKey('Shannon')

Before		After
1 Shannon	→	1 Shannon
2 Backus		2 Backus
3 Aitken		3 Aitken
→ 4 Babbage		4 Babbage
5 Lovelace		5 Lovelace

InsertAfter('Hopper')

Before	After
1 Shannon	1 Shannon
→ 2 Backus	2 Backus
3 Aitken	→ 3 Hopper
4 Babbage	4 Aitken
5 Lovelace	5 Babbage
	6 Lovelace

Findith(2)

Before		After
1 Shannon		1 Shannon
2 Backus	→	2 Backus
3 Aitken		3 Aitken
→ 4 Babbage		4 Babbage
5 Lovelace		5 Lovelace

Retrieve(e)

1 Shannon	
2 Backus	
3 Aitken	e :=
→ 4 Babbage	'Babbage'
5 Lovelace	

Delete

Before		After
1 Shannon		1 Shannon
2 Backus		2 Backus
3 Aitken		3 Aitken
→ 4 Babbage	→	4 Lovelace
5 Lovelace		

FindPrior

Before		After
1 Shannon		1 Shannon
2 Backus		2 Backus
3 Aitken	→	3 Aitken
→ 4 Babbage		4 Babbage
5 Lovelace		5 Lovelace

Update('Hopper')

Before		After
1 Shannon		1 Shannon
2 Backus		2 Backus
3 Aitken		3 Aitken
→ 4 Babbage	→	4 Hopper
5 Lovelace		5 Lovelace

Delete

Before		After
1 Shannon	→	1 Shannon
2 Backus		2 Backus
3 Aitken		3 Aitken
4 Babbage		4 Babbage
→ 5 Lovelace		

position as the new element that is assigned to that position as the result of the deletion being the current element. If the tail element is the one deleted, the position is no longer in the list and the first element is made the current element.

The third group permits the user to check the preconditions used for operations in the first two groups and to create and terminate the list. They are *Full, CurPos, Size, Create,* and *Terminate.*

The list abstraction that we have specified is arbitrary. We have chosen to include 14 operations. Other designers who have the same conceptual view of the data may define a different set of operations. A designer may find, for example, that for the application at hand *FindPrior* is never needed. He or she may choose to use an implementation of the original type since the new abstract type is a subset of it. Alternatively, he or she might create a new implementation that is more efficient for the set of operations defined.

We have defined the abstract object. We know what it is supposed to do, and we know how the user is visualizing the structure, the data elements, and the operations. Now let us look into how the structure and operations might be represented and implemented.

4.2.2 List Array Implementation

We will first represent the list using an array. This kind of representation, like any other, has its good and bad points, which we will discuss as we encounter them.

• Representation

The data types and structures that we are going to need are shown in Figures 4.6 and 4.7.

```
CONST MaxSize      = 10;                    (* Set as needed. *)
TYPE List          = POINTER TO ListInstance;
     Position       = [1..MaxSize];
     Count          = [0..MaxSize];
     ListInstance = RECORD
                        current: Count; (* Current element. *)
                        n      : Count;       (* List size. *)
                        list   : ARRAY Position OF StdElement
                     END;
```

Figure 4.7   Array representation for a list.

• Implementation

There are 14 operations that we have to implement. The 10 listed in the margin are simple. Their implementing code is given in Implementation Module 4.1. The four remaining operations—*FindKey, InsertBefore, InsertAfter,* and *Delete*—take a little more thought.

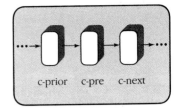

Figure 4.5

```
           [1] Shannon
current→ [2] Backus
           [3] Aitken
           [4] Babbage
      n→ [5] Lovelace
           [6]
            ⋮
        [MaxSize]
```

Figure 4.6
Array representation of the list of names.

Simple Procedures and Functions of Array Implementation

Terminate	*Size*
CurPos	*FindNext*
FindPrior	*Retrieve*
Update	*Findith*
Create	*Full*

The operation *FindKey* tries to make the list element that has a given key value current. If it does not succeed, it leaves the current element indicator unchanged. Remember that as far as our module knows, the key values of elements are arranged randomly, since the positions of insertions are under control of the user. Under these circumstances, a sequential exhaustive search from position 1 is as efficient as any other method for finding an element with the target key value. A sequential search algorithm for *FindKey* is given in Figure 4.8.

```
PROCEDURE FindKey (L: List; tkey: KeyType): BOOLEAN;
VAR k: Position;                    (* Make list element with *)
BEGIN                               (* key = tkey current.     *)
   WITH L↑ DO
      IF n = 0 THEN RETURN FALSE (* The list is empty. *)
         ELSE   k := 1;                    (* Search the list. *)
            LOOP
               IF tkey = list[k].key THEN current := k;
                                           RETURN TRUE
                  ELSIF k = n THEN RETURN FALSE
                  ELSE  INC(k)
               END
            END
      END
   END
END FindKey;
```

Figure 4.8   List array implementation FindKey using a sequential search.

If we assume that each element of the list is equally likely to be the target, then in the case of a successful search, the probability that each list element has the target key value is

$$p_i = \frac{1}{n}, \quad 1 \leq i \leq n$$

The amount of work that can be expected in doing the search is determined by the number of probes, that is, the number of keys in the list against which the target key must be compared before a matching key is found. The expected number of probes can be found as follows:

$$\text{Expected probes} = 1 \times 1/n + 2 \times 1/n + 3 \times 1/n + \cdots + n \times 1/n$$
$$= \sum_{i=1}^{n} i/n = \frac{(n+1)}{2} \sim O(n)$$

On the average, we can expect to search half the list. Notice that each time we loop through the repeat statement, one statement is executed in the body of the loop and two conditions are checked. It is possible to speed up the repeat loop up by the use of a device called a sentinel.

• Sentinels

The idea of a *sentinel* is to put the target key value into the list so that we are certain to find it successfully. If we post it at the first position past the end of the list, temporarily extending the list size by one, we will find it there if our search of the rest of the list has been unsuccessful. A structured English version of the algorithm is given in Figure 4.9. The benefit is that there need be no explicit check for the end of the list. The search will continue until the target key value is found, as it must be eventually.

After the time-consuming search loop is completed, a test is made to see if the key that was found was the sentinel. By removing the explicit test for the end of the list from the loop we produce a faster algorithm.

Translating this strategy into Modula-2, we get the algorithm shown in Figure 4.10. An example of the operation *FindKey* using a sentinel is shown in Figure 4.11.

```
PROCEDURE FindKey (L: List; tkey: KeyType): BOOLEAN;
VAR k: Position;              (* Make list element with *)
                             (* key = tkey current.    *)
BEGIN
    WITH L↑ DO                       (* Uses a sentinel.  *)
        list[n+1].key := tkey;        (* Set sentinel.    *)
        k := 1;
        WHILE list[k].key # tkey DO INC(k) END;
        IF k = n + 1
            THEN RETURN FALSE    (* Sentinel was found.      *)
            ELSE current := k; (* List element was found. *)
                RETURN TRUE
        END
    END
END FindKey;
```

Figure 4.10   List array representation FindKey using a sequential search and a sentinel.

It has been estimated that the average program spends about 90% of its execution time in looping. If a program's performance is to be improved, then the place to begin is in the loops, particularly in the innermost loops if they are nested. By using a sentinel, we have reduced the number of conditions that are checked in the until clause from two to one. Figure 4.12 shows the results of timing studies of both methods. The use of sentinels clearly gives superior performance. We will include this version in the list module.

There is one matter concerning the use of sentinels that we have ignored so far. If the list is full ($n = MaxSize$) when the search begins, the sentinel is going to be dropped beyond the end of the list array (statement {1} of *FindKey*). It happily turns out that the only algorithm of our module that we must change to ensure that this does not happen is the *Full* algorithm. It must consider a full list to be of size *MaxSize* − 1 instead of *MaxSize*.

Place the target key value into position $n + 1$.

Search sequentially from position 1 until the target key value is found.

If   the value found is in position $n + 1$,
then the sentinel was found—
        report a search failure
else search was successful—
        adjust the cursor.

Figure 4.9
Sequential search using a sentinel.

•

Before
1 Shannon
2 Backus
3 Aitken
current → 4 Babbage
n → 5 Lovelace

After
1 Shannon
2 Backus
3 Aitken
current → 4 Babbage
5 Lovelace
$n + 1$ → 6 Hopper
(sentinel)

Figure 4.11
FindKey(L,'Hopper') using a sentinel.

FindKey can also be written using recursion, though in this case the result is a lengthier algorithm. (See Exercise 4.2, 7.)

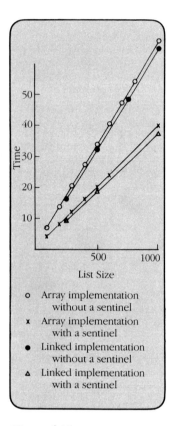

Figure 4.12
Timing studies of sequential searches for array and linked lists with and without sentinels.

Random use of operations *InsertBefore* and *InsertAfter* is a costly operation for the array implementation. In order to make room for a new element, on the average half of the list must be moved to create a gap into which it can be physically placed. The total number of data element moves that can be expected when building the entire list of n elements with random insertions is E_{build}, where

$$E_{build} = \frac{0}{2} + \frac{1}{2} + \frac{2}{2} + \cdots + \frac{(n-1)}{2}$$

$$= \frac{1}{2}\sum_{k=0}^{n-1} k = \frac{1}{2}\frac{n(n-1)}{2}$$

$$= \frac{n(n-1)}{4} \sim O(n^2)$$

Building a list with random insertions then takes $O(n^2)$ work.

The list type allows the user control over which element is current before executing an insertion. The point of insertion could be chosen to minimize the number of moves. If the insertions are always made at the tail of the list, only the elements being inserted would need moving and the list could be built in an amount of time that is $O(n)$.

We have defined the *Delete* operation to delete the current list element. Each list element past the current takes a position that is one less than its original position. As with insertion, if the deleted elements occur in random positions in the list, we find that on the average half of the list must be moved to delete one element—an $O(n)$ amount of work.

An array implementation of *Lists* follows.

Implementation Module 4.1   *Lists*

```
IMPLEMENTATION MODULE Lists;
(* Lists; array implementation; meets Specification 4.1.   *)

FROM StdTypes IMPORT StdElement, KeyType;
FROM Storage  IMPORT ALLOCATE, DEALLOCATE, Available;
FROM SYSTEM   IMPORT TSIZE;

CONST MaxSize     = 10;                                (* Set as needed. *)
TYPE List         = POINTER TO ListInstance;
     Position     = [1..MaxSize];
     Count        = [0..MaxSize];
     ListInstance = RECORD
                        current: Count;                (* Current element. *)
                        n      : Count;                   (* List size. *)
                        list   : ARRAY Position OF StdElement
                    END;
```
                                                                    continued

Legend for Figure 4.12:

o   Array implementation without a sentinel
x   Array implementation with a sentinel
●   Linked implementation without a sentinel
△   Linked implementation with a sentinel

```
PROCEDURE FindNext(L: List);                        (* Move current to its successor. *)
BEGIN
    INC(L↑.current)
END FindNext;

PROCEDURE FindPrior(L: List);                       (* Move current to its predecessor. *)
BEGIN
    DEC(L↑.current)
END FindPrior;

PROCEDURE Findith(L: List; i: CARDINAL);            (* Make ith list element current. *)
BEGIN
    L↑.current := i
END Findith;

PROCEDURE FindKey(L: List; tkey: KeyType): BOOLEAN;
VAR k: Position;                         (* Make list element with key = tkey current. *)
BEGIN
    WITH L↑ DO                                              (* Uses a sentinel. *)
      list[n+1].key := tkey;                                (* Set sentinel. *)
      k := 1;
      WHILE list[k].key # tkey DO INC(k) END;
      IF k = n + 1
          THEN RETURN FALSE                            (* Sentinel was found. *)
          ELSE current := k;                        (* List element was found. *)
                RETURN TRUE
          END
      END
END FindKey;

PROCEDURE Retrieve(L: List; VAR e: StdElement);
BEGIN                                              (* Retrieve the current element. *)
    e = L↑.list[L↑.current]
END Retrieve;

PROCEDURE Update(VAR L: List; e: StdElement);
BEGIN                                         (* Change the current element's value. *)
    L↑.list[L↑.current] := e
END Update;

PROCEDURE InsertAfter(VAR L: List; e: StdElement);
VAR k: Position;                (* Insert new list element e after the current element. *)
BEGIN
    WITH L↑ DO
      IF n # current
          THEN FOR k := n TO current+1 BY -1 DO    (* Move bottom elements         *)
                  list[k+1] := list[k]             (* to make room (Figure 4.13).  *)
              END
      END;
      INC(current);
      list[current] := e;
      INC(n)
    END
END InsertAfter;
```

continued

Implementation Module 4.1, continued

```
PROCEDURE InsertBefore(VAR L: List; e: StdElement);
BEGIN                        (* Insert new list element before the current element. *)
    IF L↑.n # 0 THEN DEC(L↑.current) END;
    InsertAfter(L, e)
END InsertBefore;

PROCEDURE Delete(VAR L: List);                (* Delete the current list element. *)
VAR k: Position;
BEGIN
    WITH L↑ DO
        FOR k := current+1 TO n DO
            list[k-1] := list[k]
        END;
        IF n = 1 THEN current := 0
            ELSIF current = n THEN current := 1
        END;
        DEC(n);
    END
END Delete;

PROCEDURE Full(L: List): BOOLEAN;               (* Has list reached its bound? *)
BEGIN
    RETURN (L↑.n = MaxSize-1)
END Full;

PROCEDURE Size(L: List): CARDINAL;          (* Number of elements in the list. *)
BEGIN
    RETURN L↑.n
END Size;

PROCEDURE CurPos(L: List): CARDINAL;            (* Current element's position. *)
BEGIN
    RETURN L↑.current
END CurPos;

PROCEDURE Create(VAR L: List): BOOLEAN;                 (* Create a new list. *)
BEGIN
    IF Available(TSIZE(ListInstance))
        THEN NEW(L);
            L↑.n := 0; L↑.current := 0;
            RETURN TRUE
        ELSE RETURN FALSE
    END
END Create;

PROCEDURE Terminate(VAR L: List);                      (* Terminate list L. *)
BEGIN
    DISPOSE(L)
END Terminate;

END Lists.
```

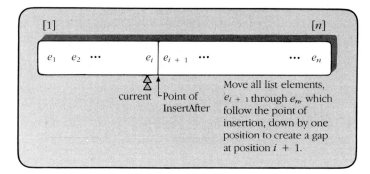

Figure 4.13   Inserting an element in a list.

• Performance

Reviewing the performance characteristics of our implementation, we find that all the operations take an amount of work that is $O(1)$ except for *FindKey, InsertBefore, InsertAfter,* and *Delete.* The operation *FindKey* requires $O(n)$ compares, and the others make $O(n)$ data element moves.

4.2.3 List Linked Implementation

We have seen in Section 4.2.2 that an array implementation of lists is relatively inefficient for inserting, deleting, and finding elements that have a given key value. In addition, storage may be wasted because of the necessity for specifying the size of the array before it is used for the list. Usually the size specified must be the worst, or maximum, list length. If that is far above the average list length, then much allocated space will go unused. Some of these drawbacks can be avoided by representing the structure as a linked list.

Recall the discussion of simple linked structures in Section 2.4. We discussed the use of pointers to form simple linked lists and used the Modula-2 built-in procedures *NEW* and *DISPOSE* to provide dynamically varying list sizes. Nodes of the lists were created and destroyed when inserting and deleting elements. By these means, the amount of memory required by the list at any time was exactly matched to the amount of data in the list at that time. Recall also, however, that the price of such efficient memory use was some overhead in pointer space in each node and some amount of time to execute the allocation and deallocation of nodes.

Let us investigate the application of such linked structures in implementing the abstract list data type.

• Representation

We must first decide on some linked representation of lists. There are a number of design decisions that must be made (see list in margin).

Is the list to be doubly or singly linked? The operations that are required by our list specification dictate this. The critical ones are *FindPrior, Delete,* and

---

Performance of a List Array Implementation

O(1)	O(n)
Findith	*FindKey*
FindNext	*InsertBefore*
FindPrior	*InsertAfter*
Retrieve	*Delete*
Update	
Size	
CurPos	
Terminate	
Create	
Full	

•

Linked List Design Decisions

1. Singly or doubly linked?
2. Which access pointers? Head? Tail? Current?
3. How are the list's ends marked?
4. Is the linked list circular?

•

We choose a doubly linked, circular list with *head* and *current* pointers.

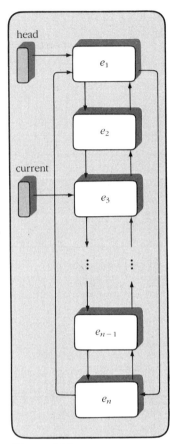

Figure 4.14
List representation: doubly
linked and circular.

InsertBefore. Take *Delete* as an example. Doing this operation with the array, representation was simple. With the linked representation, we keep *current* as a pointer in the Modula-2 sense. If the list is singly linked, then there is no reference in the current node to the preceding node. The only way to locate a node's predecessor is to go to the head of the list and traverse forward using a working pointer until it points to a node whose *next* pointer equals *current*. The node that meets the condition is the desired preceding element. Such an approach is inefficient and argues strongly for each node to point to not only its successor, but also its predecessor. In other words, the list should be doubly linked.

Although it is not apparent before writing the code, a circular linked list results in more compact code that is easier to understand (see Exercise 4.2, 5). Therefore, we choose to make the list doubly linked and circular.

Only two access pointers are needed—*head* and *current*. The tail of the list is readily reached from the head since the list is circular. The presentation looks as shown in Figure 4.14.

The nodes of the list are of data type *Node* as shown in Implementation Module 4.2.

• Implementation

Implementation Module 4.2 implements the list that is represented as shown in Figure 4.14. The module is a good example of the use of doubly linked lists.

Implementation Module 4.2   *Lists*

```
IMPLEMENTATION MODULE Lists;
(* List; linked implementation; meets Specification 4.1. *)

FROM StdTypes IMPORT StdElement, KeyType;
FROM Storage  IMPORT ALLOCATE, DEALLOCATE, Available
FROM SYSTEM   IMPORT TSIZE;

TYPE NodePointer  = POINTER TO Node;
     Node         = RECORD
                        el          : StdElement;
                        next, prior: NodePointer
                    END;
     List         = POINTER TO ListInstance;
     ListInstance = RECORD
                        head, current: NodePointer;
                        n, icurrent  : CARDINAL      (* Current size, position. *)
                    END;
```
                                                                    continued

Implementation Module 4.2, continued

```
PROCEDURE FindNext(L: List);                    (* Make current's successor current. *)
BEGIN
    WITH L↑ DO
        current := current↑.next;
        INC(icurrent)
    END
END FindNext;

PROCEDURE FindPrior(L: List);                   (* Make current's predecessor current. *)
BEGIN
    WITH L↑ DO
        current := current↑.prior;
        DEC(icurrent)
    END
END FindPrior;

PROCEDURE Findith(L: List; i: CARDINAL);        (* Make ith list element current. *)
VAR k: CARDINAL;
BEGIN
    WITH L↑ DO
        current := head;
        IF (i-1) <= (n-1)                       (* Is ith element closer to head or tail? *)
            THEN FOR k := 1 TO i-1 DO            (* Traverse from head forward. *)
                    current := current↑.next
                END
            ELSE FOR k := n TO i BY -1 DO        (* Traverse from tail backward. *)
                    current := current↑.prior
                END
        END;
        icurrent := i
    END
END Findith;

PROCEDURE FindKey(L: List; tkey: KeyType): BOOLEAN;
VAR p: NodePointer;                             (* Make element with key = tkey current. *)
    k: CARDINAL;
BEGIN
    WITH L↑ DO
        IF n = 0 THEN RETURN FALSE END;
        k := 1;  p := head;
        WHILE (p↑.next # head) & (p↑.el.key # tkey) DO          (* Search. *)
            p := p↑.next;  INC(k)
        END;
        IF p↑.el.key = tkey                            (* Matching key value found? *)
            THEN current := p;                              (* Yes. *)
                icurrent := k;
                RETURN TRUE
            ELSE RETURN FALSE                              (* No. *)
        END
    END
END FindKey;
```
continued

Implementation Module 4.2, continued

```
PROCEDURE Retrieve(L: List; VAR e: StdElement);
BEGIN                                    (* Retrieve current element value. *)
    e := L↑.current↑.el
END Retrieve;

PROCEDURE Update(VAR L: List; e: StdElement);
BEGIN                                    (* Change current element value. *)
    L↑.current↑.el := e
END Update;

PROCEDURE InsertAfter(VAR L: List; e: StdElement);
VAR p: NodePointer;                          (* Insert e as the successor *)
BEGIN                                        (* to the current element.    *)
    WITH L↑ DO
        NEW(p); p↑.el := e;
        IF n = 0
            THEN head := p; icurrent := 1;
                 p↑.next := p; p↑.prior := p
            ELSE current↑.next↑.prior := p;        (* Link node p↑ into the *)
                 p↑.next := current↑.next;         (* doubly linked list.   *)
                 p↑.prior := current;
                 current↑.next := p;
                 INC(icurrent)
        END;
        INC(n);
        current := p
    END
END InsertAfter;

PROCEDURE InsertBefore(VAR L: List; e: StdElement);
BEGIN                                        (* Insert e as the predecessor *)
    WITH L↑ DO                               (* to the current element.     *)
        IF n # 0
            THEN current := current↑.prior;
                 DEC(icurrent)
        END;
        InsertAfter(L,e);
        IF current↑.next = head THEN head := current END
    END
END InsertBefore;
```

continued

Implementation Module 4.2, continued

```
PROCEDURE Delete(VAR L: List);                    (* Delete the current list element. *)
VAR precurrent: NodePointer;
BEGIN
    WITH L↑ DO
        precurrent := current;                        (* Relink list to           *)
(*1*)   current↑.prior↑.next := current↑.next;        (* exclude deleted node.     *)
(*2*)   current↑.next↑.prior := current↑.prior;
        IF precurrent↑.next = head                (* Is tail node to be deleted? *)
            THEN icurrent := 1                                    (* Yes. *)
        END;
        current := current↑.next;
        IF n = 1 THEN head := NIL
            ELSIF head = precurrent
                    THEN head := current
        END;
        DEC(n);
        DISPOSE(precurrent)
    END
END Delete;

PROCEDURE CurPos(L: List): CARDINAL;              (* Get current element's position. *)
BEGIN
    RETURN L↑.icurrent
END CurPos;

PROCEDURE Full(L: List): BOOLEAN;                 (* Has the list reached its bound? *)
BEGIN
    RETURN (NOT Available(TSIZE(Node)))
END Full;

PROCEDURE Size(L: List): CARDINAL;
BEGIN                             (* Get the current number of elements in the list. *)
    RETURN L↑.n
END Size;

PROCEDURE Create(VAR L: List): BOOLEAN;                        (* Create list L. *)
BEGIN
    IF Available(TSIZE(ListInstance))
        THEN NEW (L);
            L↑.n := 0; L↑.head := NIL;
            RETURN TRUE
        ELSE RETURN FALSE
    END
END Create;
```

continued

Implementation Module 4.2, continued

```
PROCEDURE Terminate(VAR L: List);                    (* Terminate list L. *)
VAR p, q: NodePointer;
    i    : CARDINAL;
BEGIN
   WITH L↑ DO
      p := head;
      FOR i := 1 TO n DO                              (* Dispose list nodes. *)
         q := p;
         p := p↑.next;
         DISPOSE(q)
      END
   END;
   DISPOSE(L)
END Terminate;

END Lists.
```

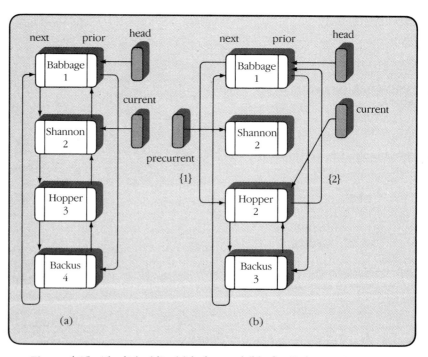

Figure 4.15   The linked list (a) before and (b) after *Delete*.

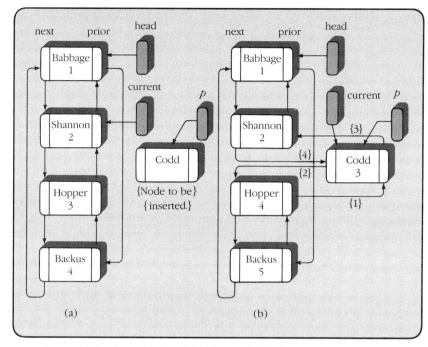

Figure 4.16   The linked list (a) before and (b) after *InsertAfter.*

The *InsertBefore* and *InsertAfter* procedures, although simple in concept, involve some pointer manipulations that must be managed carefully. The procedures are given in Implementation Module 4.2. Figure 4.16 shows the pointer relinkages and references each back to the statement numbers of the *InsertAfter* procedure. The amount of work required is independent of the number of elements in the list (two-to-four pointer manipulations). We can say that the magnitude of the work required is $O(1)$. This is in contrast to the array implementation that required $O(n)$ data moves.

The *Delete* procedure also requires only a few pointer manipulations. Figure 4.15 shows the deletion of a node from the interior of a list. (The numbers in braces ({1}, {2}) refer to similarly marked statements in the *Delete* procedure.) It also requires $O(1)$ work. Again, this is a substantial improvement over the $O(n)$ work required by the array implementation.

The procedure *FindKey*, which locates the element with a given key value, is very similar in concept to the array implementation of the same operation. However, a sentinel is not used. The list is exhaustively searched from position 1 until a matching key is found. The operation requires $O(n)$ work for both successful and unsuccessful searches.

For the operations considered thus far, the linked implementation performs as well as or better than the array implementation. The exception is *Findith(i).* This operation is efficient with an array implementation since *cur-*

rent is an array index and was set as follows by the statement *current := i*. The linked implementation suffers from the lack of random access in a linked list. The *i*th element can only be found by doing a partial list traversal from either the head forward or the tail backward, depending on which is closer to the target position. Being able to proceed from either end reduces the expected number of nodes that must be traversed from $(n + 1)/2$ to $(n + 1)/4$, but the result is still $O(n)$. (We could also traverse from the current element.)

• Performance

Performance of a Linked Implementation of a List

$O(1)$	$O(n)$
FindNext	*Findith*
FindPrior	*FindKey*
Delete	*Terminate*
Retrieve	
Update	
Size	
CurPos	
Create	
InsertBefore	
InsertAfter	
Full	

The underlined operations are those that have changed performance from the array implementation.

The expected performance of the linked implementation is shown in the margin. The underlined operations are those that have changed performance from the array implementation. There is a substantial difference between the linked and array implementations of the procedure *Terminate*. In the array case (Implementation Module 4.1), *Terminate* executed one *DISPOSE* operation to release the storage used for an instance of *ListInstance*. The linked implementation (Implementation Module 4.2) uses dynamic memory allocation not only to create an instance of *ListInstance* when the list is created but also to create an instance of a node every time a new element is inserted into the list. *Terminate* must deallocate not only the instance of *ListInstance* but also all the nodes remaining in the list. Since there are *n* nodes, the linked version of *Terminate* executes in a time that is $O(n)$. The difference in performance of *Terminate* and *Delete* is due to the dynamic nature of the linked list, which uses only as much memory as current list size requires. Insertions cause the allocated memory to increase by one node to accommodate the new data, whereas *Delete* and *Terminate* return unused memory to the operating, or run-time, system. The procedures *NEW* and *DISPOSE* take time to execute, but the time can be assumed to be a constant, independent of the list size. The array implementation *Delete* had to physically move, on the average, half of the list.

The linked implementation, Implementation Module 4.2, is roughly 100% more code than the array implementation, Implementation Module 4.1. We shall see in Section 4.6, however, that it is more efficient in execution.

At this point, before any timing studies are done, we can summarize what we have learned:

1. The array implementation is more concise in code and simpler in concept.
2. Using orders-of-magnitude estimates, the linked implementation performs at least as well as the array except for the *Findith* operation and *Terminate*.
3. The linked implementation makes efficient, dynamic use of memory and is suited for lists that vary greatly in size or whose average sizes are far below the maximum that might occur.

Exercises 4.2

1. Which implementation of a list, Implementation Module 4.1 or 4.2, gives better use of memory space? Explain your answer.
2. The term **associative access** refers to the finding of an element of a data structure based on the value of one or more of its fields. The list operation *FindKey* is an example. In contrast, **positional access** refers to the finding of an element based on its position or relationship to other elements. The list operations *Findith, FindNext,* and *FindPrior* are examples of such operations.
   a. Explain how the use of a sentinel improves performance when doing associative access.
   b. How might a sentinel be used in the linked implementation of *FindKey* given in Implementation Module 4.2?
3. Which operations in Implementation Module 4.2 would need modification if the representation were changed to a singly linked circular list? What would the modifications be?
4. Discuss alternate specifications for the list abstract data type specified in Specification 4.1. What other operations might be defined? How might those that have been defined be changed?
5. We have chosen in Implementation Module 4.2 to represent the linear list as a circular doubly linked list with *head* and *current* pointers. This form tends to make the algorithms simpler. Suppose that instead you had decided to represent the list by a noncircular doubly linked list whose ends are marked by nil pointer values in the *next* and *prior* field of the last and first nodes, respectively. The access pointers are to be *head, tail,* and *current.* You may also use a sentinel if you wish. Write another implementation of the list specifications (Specification 4.1) using this form of representation. Implement and test your module.
6. Suppose that we had relaxed the assumption that the key values of the list elements have unique values. What effect would it have on Specification 4.1? What corresponding effects would it have on the implementations in Implementation Modules 4.1 and 4.2?
7. Figures 4.8 and 4.10 are algorithms for implementing *FindKey.* Write and test a recursive version of *FindKey* for the array representation used in Implementation Module 4.1.

4.3 Ordered Lists

The list that we specified in Specification 4.1 allows the user to insert new elements at any position. The resulting ordering of the elements is under the control of the user. The essential difference between such a list and the three kinds of ordered lists that we shall now study is that the **ordered lists** have some ordering of the elements defined as part of the abstract specifications. To ensure that the correct order of the elements is maintained, control of the point of insertion is taken from the user and placed with the implementor. This guarantees the integrity of the list.

With ordered lists, the place of insertion of new elements is to be under control of the implementor, not the user.

The three orderings that we shall consider are

1. Chronologically ordered lists, in which the elements are placed in the list in the order in which they arrive for insertion. New elements are always placed after the element in the last position.
2. Sorted lists, in which elements are placed in the list according to the values of their key fields.
3. Frequency-ordered lists, in which elements are placed in the list so that the most frequently sought (*FindKey*) element is in position 1, the second most frequently sought in position 2, and so on.

Chronologically ordered lists have a relationship between the elements' positions and their times of arrival in the list. The list may be considered sorted on arrival time, the earliest arrival being in position 1. Such lists have a close relationship to stacks and queues, which are usually implemented as some form of list. These issues are discussed in Section 4.3.1.

Sorted lists have to maintain the following condition:

$$\text{key value}_i \le \text{key value}_{i+1}, 1 \le i < n$$

The fact that the list is sorted on key value allows the *FindKey* operation to be implemented by the very efficient binary search algorithm, which can be used with an array representation. Sorted lists are discussed in Section 4.3.2.

The third kind of ordered list that we will study is a list that is ordered on the frequency with which each element is the target of a *FindKey* operation. This assumes that all elements are not equally likely to be the target (the access probability distribution is nonuniform). Since the *FindKey* operation is implemented by searching the list sequentially from position 1, placing the frequently accessed elements near the head of the list will reduce the average number of compares that must be made during the search.

In addition to frequency-ordered lists, we will discuss self-organizing lists, which "automatically" reorder their elements to approximate the optimal order or to adapt to a frequency distribution that changes with time. Both types of lists are discussed in Section 4.3.3.

Since most of the operations for ordered lists will be the same as those that we have previously defined for simple lists, we will only discuss those operations that are different.

4.3.1 Chronologically Ordered Lists

A ***chronologically ordered list*** is one in which the elements appear in the list in the order in which they arrive for insertion. In effect, insertions can be made only at the end (position $n + 1$) of the list. Deletions do not affect the chronological order. Deletion of an element from the list, followed by reinsertion of the same element, will cause that element to go to the end of the list. Specification 4.2 for chronologically ordered lists follows. Figure 4.17 shows an example of such a list.

1 Shannon
2 Backus
3 Aitken
4 Babbage
$n \rightarrow$ 5 Lovelace

← Insertions

Figure 4.17
Chronological list.

Specification 4.2 ChronLists

DEFINITION MODULE ChronLists;

(* **Elements:** We assume that the elements are of type StdElement. *)

   FROM StdTypes **IMPORT** StdElement, KeyType;

(* **Structure:** The same as the structure of Lists (Specification 4.1), with
      the following additional constraint:
      The time of insertion of the element in position i is earlier than
      the time of insertion of the element in position j for i < j. *)

(* **Domain:** The number of elements in a list is bounded. *)

   EXPORT QUALIFIED ChronList, FindNext, FindPrior, Findith, FindKey,
                   Retrieve, Update, Insert, Delete, CurPos, Full, Size,
                   Create, Terminate;

   TYPE ChronList;   (* *Opaque type used to represent a chronological list.* *)

(* **Operations:** The operations are the same as those of Lists
      (Specification 4.1), except that InsertAfter and InsertBefore are
      replaced by the single operation Insert. *)

         .
         .
         .

PROCEDURE Insert(**VAR** CL: ChronList; e: StdElement);
(* **pre** – CL is not full.
    post – e is the last element of CL and is the current element;
          the size of CL is Size(CL-pre) + 1. *)

         .
         .
         .

END ChronLists.

• Implementation

The only algorithms that are different from those in Implementation Modules
4.1 and 4.2 are the insertion algorithms. For the array implementation, the new
Insert algorithm, which always inserts at the end, is a simple change and is
given in Figure 4.18. The linked implementation can also be easily changed to
always insert at the tail of the list. The resulting algorithm is given in Figure
4.19.

```
PROCEDURE Insert(VAR CL: ChronList; e: StdElement);
BEGIN
    WITH CL↑ DO                                    (* Insert new list element e at *)
        INC(n);                                    (* list tail.                    *)
        list[n] := e;
        current := n
    END
END Insert;
```

Figure 4.18 Chronological list, array implementation, *Insert*.

```
PROCEDURE Insert(VAR CL: ChronList; e: StdElement);
VAR p, tail: NodePointer;                          (* Insert e as the         *)
BEGIN                                              (* successor to the current *)
    WITH CL↑ DO                                    (* tail element.            *)
        NEW(p); p↑.el := e;
        IF n = 0
            THEN head := p;
                p↑.next := p; p↑.prior := p
            ELSE current := head↑.prior;           (* Point current to tail. *)
                head↑.prior := p;                  (* Link node              *)
                p↑next := current↑.next;           (* p↑ into                *)
                p↑.prior := current;               (* the doubly             *)
                current↑.next := p                 (* linked list.           *)
        END;
        INC(n);
        current := p; icurrent := n
    END
END Insert;
```

Figure 4.19 Chronological list, linked implementation, *Insert*.

Chronologically ordered linear lists are closely related to the stacks and queues that we studied in Chapter 3. A stack can be implemented as a chronological list in which deletion and retrieval are constrained to the last element. The last element must always be the current element. No *Find* operations are allowed. For queues, deletion and retrieval are allowed only on the head element, and insertion is allowed only at the end of the list.

Exercises 4.3.1

1. Stacks and queues may be implemented as forms of chronologically ordered lists. The operations of the *Stacks* and *Queues* data types may be written in terms of operations on the chronologically ordered lists data type. Some examples of stack operations follow.

Stack operation	Chronological list operations
Push(e)	*Insert(e)*
Pop(e)	*Findith(Size)*
.	*Retrieve(e)*
.	*Delete*
	.
	.

Write implementations for the *Queues* data type in this way.

2. In implementing stacks and queues as chronological lists in Exercise 1, it becomes clear that some operations would be easier to use if the chronological list specifications were modified. For example, the *Pop* operation given in Exercise 1 requires the operation *Findith*(Size) because *Delete* is specified to move the cursor to the first list element if the last list element is deleted. The operation would be more efficient if the specification were to move the cursor to the new last element if the current last element is deleted. What other modifications of the chronological list specifications can you think of after answering Exercise 1?

3. Can priority queues be implemented by using operations on a chronological list as we did for stacks and queues in Exercise 1? Explain your answer.

4. What is the order-of-magnitude performance estimate for building a chronological list by starting with an empty list and then doing insertions? For example, what amount of work is required to build a list of 50 elements?

5. Construct a table showing the performance of each operation of a chronological list for

   a. An array implementation   **b.** A linked implementation

4.3.2 Sorted Lists

Lists often need to be kept so that the elements are in an order that is determined by the value of some field of the element. For example, the list of names that we considered in Section 4.1 could be kept so that the names are in alphabetical order. This type of **sorted order** can be useful for searching for an element with a given key value (*FindKey*) if the sort field is the key field. The lists are called **sorted lists.** (See Figure 4.20.)

An everyday (and overworked but effective) example is the telephone directory. The elements contain name, address, and telephone number fields. The key field is name, and the entries are sorted by its value. The analog of a *FindKey* operation is to look up the record with a given name. If you are looking for a name that begins with the letter "S", for example, you are likely to open the telephone book from two-thirds to three-fourths of the way into it. You would not begin your search on page 1. What you are doing is casting away a large section of the book that can be ruled out immediately and does not have to be searched. From there the search proceeds more slowly as you turn smaller and smaller groups of pages until you turn single pages. Finally, you arrive at the correct page. You then skip around until you reach the area in which the name you are seeking is located. Only then do you scan sequentially one name at a time.

1 Aitken
2 Babbage
3 Backus
4 Lovelace
5 Shannon

Figure 4.20
Sorted list.

The critical factor in the search technique is the ability to cast aside large sections of the book without searching them in detail. This is made possible by the fact that the book is sorted on the field that is your search key—the person's name. Imagine the same search if the names were randomly arranged in the book. You could only start at the beginning (or any other place) and exhaustively search through the entries until you either found the name you wished or covered the entire book.

One reason for sorting is to make searching, whether by a computer or a person, more efficient. Computers search sorted lists in ways that differ somewhat from the way in which a person would search the list, but each uses the technique of isolating large sections of the list that are known not to contain the target element and casting them aside. We can get a good feel for the effort required for a sequential search versus that required for a search based upon sorted lists from the telephone book example. A ***binary search,*** a technique that takes advantage of the sorted order of the list, takes an amount of work that is $O(\log_2 n)$. A ***sequential search,*** the kind we used for *FindKey* for an unsorted list, takes $O(n)$ work. Whenever you are wondering how much improvement an $O(\log_2 n)$ method is over an $O(n)$ method, think about the telephone book example. (The technique used by the person in the telephone book search is really more like an ***interpolation search***—discussed later— since one is continually trying to estimate how many pages to turn, but the general effect is the same. We will see examples of both a binary search and an interpolation search later in this section.)

In Section 4.3.2, we will concern ourselves with lists that are built starting with an empty list. Insertions are done so that the list remains sorted. There is another approach. It is possible to build the list in any order; then, when the list is required to be sorted, a special sort algorithm is invoked that rearranges the elements into sorted order. The techniques for these sorting algorithms form an important class of methods to which we devote Chapter 6. However, in this section insertions will be controlled by the module to ensure that the list always remains sorted.

Using a sequential search or a binary search, how many probes would it take to search the phone book of the town in which you live?

Specification 4.3   SortedList

DEFINITION MODULE SortedList;

(* **Elements:** We assume that the elements are of type StdElement. *)

   FROM StdTypes **IMPORT** StdElement, KeyType;

(* **Structure:** The same as the structure of Lists (Specification 4.1), with
      the following additional constraint:
      The key value of the element in position i is less than the key
      value of the element in position j for i < j.   *)

(* **Domain:** The number of elements in a sorted list is bounded. *)

continued

Specification 4.3, continued

```
EXPORT QUALIFIED SortedList, FindNext, FindPrior, Findith, FindKey, Retrieve,
            Update, Insert, Delete, CurPos, Full, Size, Create,
            Terminate;

TYPE SortedList;          (* An opaque type used to represent a sorted list.  *)

(* Operations: The operations are the same as those of a list (Specification
      4.1) except for Update, and InsertBefore and InsertAfter are replaced
      by a single Insert operation. *)
                          .
                          .
                          .

PROCEDURE Update(VAR SL: SortedList; e: StdElement);
(* pre  – SL is not empty and the value of e.key is equal to
            the value of the key of the current element.
   post – The current element has the value of e. *)

PROCEDURE Insert(VAR SL: SortedList; e: StdElement);
(* pre  – SL is not full and does not contain an element whose key value is
            equal to e.key.
   post – e is in SL and is the current element; the list size is
            size(SL-pre) + 1. *)
                          .
                          .
                          .

END SortedList.
```

• Array representation and implementation

Maintaining a sorted list pays dividends when the list is searched. The array implementation shows the most improvement, so let us consider it first. We use the same representation as was used in Implementation Module 4.1. In fact, the module for the sorted list will be exactly the same as Implementation Module 4.1 except for three algorithms—*FindKey, Insert,* and *Update.*

The specification of the *FindKey* operation has not changed from that of a list. However, the implementation and performance are quite different. Searches for target key values can take advantage of the fact that the existing list is sorted. We can use a technique that casts out large sections of the list that are known not to contain the target key value.

Suppose that we compare the target key value to the key value of the element that is midway in the list. The midpoint position can be calculated as follows:

$$mid = (1 + n)/2$$

Since the list is sorted, if the target key value is less than the key value at position *mid,* we know for certain that the target element is not in the half of the list from *mid* to *n.*

This action is a ***probe*** and has the following construction:

```
IF tkey < list[mid].key
     THEN the target element is not in [mid..n] range
   ELSIF tkey > list[mid].key
     THEN the target element is not in [1..mid] range
   ELSE the target element is at position mid;
        search successful
END;
```

Casting aside the portion of the list that we know does not contain the target element, we are left with a sublist and exactly the same problem. We can attack it in the same way. Assuming that the lower half *(1 ... mid)* of the list was discarded, we now probe at

$$\text{mid} = [(\text{mid} + 1) + n]/2$$

which is the midpoint of the remaining sublist.

We can continue this approach, always discarding half of the remaining sublist, until the sublist is reduced to one element, which either is our target element or is not. If it is not, we can be certain that no element in the list had a key that matches the target key. In the course of probing, the element at the midpoint may happen to be the target element, in which case we stop the search.

This technique is the binary search we mentioned earlier and is very efficient. An example of the probe sequence of a binary search is shown in Figure 4.21. The amount of work required is determined by the number of probes that must be performed. This is fairly easily determined by noting that each probe results in the list size being halved. The question becomes how many times, say *k,* can a list of size *n* be halved before the size of the remaining sublist is one element. Let *k* be the smallest integer such that

$$\frac{n}{2^k} = 1$$

Solving for *k,* we get

$$k = \text{ceiling}(\log_2 n)$$

where ceiling(*x*) returns the smallest integer that is larger than or equal to *x.*

We have ignored what happens if we come upon the target element at one of the midpoint probes. The answer is that it would not change the basic result. We can show that the upper bound on the number of probes is floor($\log_2 n$) + 1, whereas the average for a successful search is approximately $\log_2 n - 1$ (Knuth, 1973b). We can, therefore, conclude that the binary search requires $O(\log_2 n)$ comparisons, or probes. A general example of a binary search is shown in Figure 4.22.

Probe 1

low →	1	Aitken
	2	Babbage
	3	Backus
(probe) mid →	4	Hopper
	5	Knuth
	6	Lovelace
high →	7	Shannon

Probe 2

low →	5	Knuth
(probe) mid →	6	Lovelace
high →	7	Shannon

Probe 3

(probe) mid →	5	Knuth

Figure 4.21
Probe sequence binary search for *FindKey* ('Knuth'). Note that mid = (low + high) DIV 2.

•

low →	element
	⋮ lower sublist
mid − 1 →	element
(probe) mid →	element midpoint
mid + 1 →	element
	⋮ upper sublist
high →	element

Figure 4.22
Binary search.

Although it is easy to understand how a binary search works, it is somewhat tricky to write a correct algorithm. It is even trickier, and counterintuitive to our first thoughts and even second thoughts, to find the most efficient algorithm. First, let us generalize the notion of probing. We define the sublist to have a lower position of *low* and an upper position of *high*. Originally we start with *low* = 1 and *high* = *n*. We probe at

mid = (low + high) DIV 2

If the target element is not at the probed position, the result of the probe is to allow the sublist for the next probe to be halved by adjusting either *low* or *high*. A structured English version of the *FindKey* algorithm that implements this logic is given in Figure 4.23.

```
low := 1; high := n;
WHILE low < high DO
    mid := (low + high) DIV 2;
    IF tkey < list[mid].key
        THEN discard upper sublist by setting high to mid − 1
    ELSIF tkey > list[mid].key
        THEN discard lower sublist by setting low to mid + 1
    ELSE target element is at position mid; search successful
    END;
END
Target key is not in the sorted list − search unsuccessful.
```

Figure 4.23 Binary search, method 1 (Knuth, 1973b).

The algorithm in Figure 4.23 can be improved. Bentley (1983b) and Standish (1980) discuss several methods for doing so. We will look at one of them.

Notice that two comparisons are done in the algorithm in Figure 4.23 (method 1) to differentiate among three conditions at the position being probed:

1. *tkey < list[mid].key*
2. *tkey = list[mid].key*
3. *tkey > list[mid].key*

The reason for the test for equality is to see if the probe has landed on the target key. The probability of that happening (assuming all elements are equally likely to be the target of the search) is

$$p \leq \frac{1}{(\text{high} - \text{low} + 1)}$$

where p is small until the sublists also become quite small.

If we did not test for the equal condition, we could reduce the number of tests in the search loop from 2 to 1. We could then test for equality once, when the sublist had been reduced to a single element and the search loop is completed. We could avoid wasting the effort of testing for an improbable

Binary searches are usually further complicated by the consideration of where the last probe is to land when the search is unsuccessful.

event, even though the search loop would continue after a midpoint probe had fallen on the target element. The new algorithm [which Knuth (1973b) credits to Bottenbruch (1962)] is given in Figure 4.24.

```
low := 0;  high := n;
WHILE low < high DO
    mid := (low + high + 1) DIV 2;
    IF tkey < list[mid].key
        THEN discard upper sublist by setting high to mid − 1
        ELSE discard lower sublist by setting low to mid
    END
END;

IF (high = 0) OR (tkey # list[mid].key)
    THEN the target key is not in the sorted list;
         search unsuccessful
    ELSE the target element is at position mid;
         search successful
END;
```

Figure 4.24   Binary search, method 2 (Bottenbruch's algorithm).

Notice that the calculation of the midpoint is slightly different from what it was in the previous case. This change is necessary in order to make the search converge to one element. Otherwise, the search may converge to two elements and never reach the condition *low* greater than or equal to *high,* which terminates the while statement. This is the sort of problem that makes the binary search algorithm tricky to write.

In order for this algorithm to be an improvement, the cost of adding 1 in the calculation

```
mid := (low + high + 1) DIV 2
```

plus the cost of not detecting an equality in probing (which results in more probes) must be less than the cost of the second test

```
ELSIF tkey > list[mid].key
```

which was required in method 1.

We conducted timing studies using lists of integers for both successful and unsuccessful searches. Method 1 is more efficient than method 2 for successful searches, and the difference is larger for smaller lists. This is explained by the fact that method 1 sometimes probes at the target element, and the search terminates. The smaller list being searched, the greater the probability of that happening. Method 2, however, always continues probing until the remaining sublist is of size 1. Even if it probes at the target element, it does not detect that fact. The differences in times required by both methods are small, being in all cases less than 15%.

The situation is reversed for unsuccessful searches. Method 1 loses time by testing for an event (probing at the target element) that will never occur.

If one probe takes 1 microsecond, then in 1 second, a sequential search could search a list of

$$n = 2,000,000$$

elements. In the same time, a binary search could search a list of

$$n = 2^{1,000,000}$$
$$\cong 10^{300}$$
$$=$$

1,000,000,000,000,000,
000,000,000,000,000,
000,000,000,000,000,
000,000,000,000,000,
000,000,000,000,000,
000,000,000,000,000,
000,000,000,000,000,
000,000,000,000,000,
000,000,000,000,000,
000,000,000,000,000,
000,000,000,000,000,
000,000,000,000,000,
000,000,000,000,000,
000,000,000,000,000,
000,000,000,000,000,
000,000,000,000,000,
000,000,000,000,000,
000,000,000,000,000,
000,000,000,000,000,
000,000,000,000,000

elements.

Method 2 only tests for the target element outside of the inner loop. Again the time difference is less than 15%.

Notice that what we have done to improve the efficiency of the algorithm is the same kind of thing that we did to introduce a sentinel in the sequential search. We have removed operations from the inner loop in the hope that although there are more lines of code, the resulting algorithm will be faster. The timing studies show that although there are differences in the two methods, they are small. (Bear in mind that the timing studies are for a specific high-level language using a specific compiler and executed on a single computer system.)

Figure 4.25 shows the results of timing studies for searching the same lists with a binary search and with a sequential search. The binary search becomes more efficient at a list size of about 128.

If we assume that the time for the binary search is

$$t_b(n) \sim C_b \log_2 (n)$$

the time for a sequential search is

$$t_s(n) \sim C_s \times n/2$$

and the value of n at which the two methods execute in an equal time is $n = 128$, we get

$$t_b(128) = t_s(128)$$
$$C_b \log_2 128 = C_s \times 64$$

from which we get

$$\frac{C_b}{C_s} = \frac{64}{\log_2 128} = \frac{64}{7} = 9.1$$

where C_b and C_s are the times per probe for binary and sequential searches, respectively. From the above calculation we can conclude that for the system used for the timing tests, the overhead for a binary search is about one order of magnitude greater than that for a sequential search. Lists of less than 128 elements are more efficiently searched by sequential searches.

There is a good chance that we are, like Don Quixote, tilting at windmills. The binary search is fast for large lists and, because of its overhead, it should not be used for small lists. Any attempt at improvement may be misplaced and should be focused on other portions of the program. (A binary search of 2 billion elements takes about 32 probes.) A minor improvement of the binary search algorithm is likely to have a negligible effect on the performance of most programs. The methods used for improving the algorithm, however, are interesting and worth noting. Implementation Module 4.3 shows the algorithms for array implementation of a sorted list.

The *Insert* operation must insert the new element in the correct position in the list. In order to do so, that position must first be found by searching. The binary search algorithm *BinSearch* is designed to produce an index value pointing to a list element if the binary search is unsuccessful. That element has

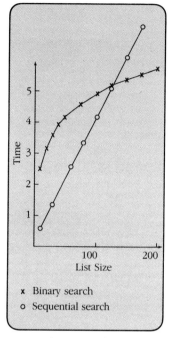

Figure 4.25
Searching a list implemented by using an array to show measured search times for binary and sequential searches.

Recall that these results are for a single compiler and computer system, but they should alert you to take care in drawing conclusions from order-of-magnitude estimates.

Implementation Module 4.3   *SortedList*

```
IMPLEMENTATION MODULE SortedList;
(* SortedList; array implementation; meets Specification 4.3. *)
(* All items are the same as in Implementation Module 4.1 except for
   procedures FindKey, Update, and Insert (which replaces InsertBefore
   and InsertAfter). *)
                          .
                          .
                          .

PROCEDURE BinSearch(VAR SL: SortedList; tkey: KeyType; VAR lo, hi: Count);
(* Binary search of the sublist from positions lo to hi for an element
   with key value = tkey; if success, then hi (= lo) is the position
   of the found element; if not, then hi (= lo) is the position of
   the next smaller key value, or possibly 0. Uses method 2. *)
VAR mid: Count;
BEGIN
    WITH SL↑ DO
        WHILE lo < hi DO
            mid := (lo + hi + 1) DIV 2;
            IF tkey < sortedlist[mid].key
                THEN hi := mid − 1
                ELSE lo := mid
            END
        END
    END
END BinSearch;

PROCEDURE FindKey(SL: SortedList; tkey: KeyType): BOOLEAN;
VAR low, high: Count;
BEGIN
    WITH SL↑ DO
        low := 0; high := n;
        BinSearch(SL, tkey, low, high);
        IF (high # 0) & (tkey = sortedlist[high].key)
            THEN current := high;              (* tkey found in sorted list. *)
                RETURN TRUE
            ELSE RETURN FALSE
        END
    END
END FindKey;

PROCEDURE Update(VAR SL: SortedList; e: StdElement);
BEGIN                                          (* Update current's data value. *)
    SL↑.sortedlist[SL↑.current].data := e.data
END Update;
```

continued

Implementation Module 4.3, continued

```
PROCEDURE Insert(VAR SL: SortedList; e: StdElement);
VAR low, high, k: Count;
BEGIN
    WITH SL↑ DO
        low := 0; high := n;
        BinSearch(SL, e.key, low, high);
        FOR k := n TO (high+1) BY -1 DO
            sortedlist[k+1] := sortedlist[k]
        END;
        current := high + 1;
        sortedlist[current] := e;
        INC(n)
    END
END Insert;
            .
            .
            .

END SortedLists.
```

the next smaller key value than the key of the element being inserted. The new element can be correctly inserted immediately after the indicated position.

The binary search algorithm can be written using recursion. A recursive version of BinSearch is shown in Figure 4.26 below.

```
PROCEDURE BinSearch(VAR SL: SortedList; tkey: KeyType;
                    VAR lo, hi: Count);
(* Recursive binary search of the sublist from positions
   lo to hi for an element with key value = tkey; if
   success, then hi (= lo) is the position of the found
   element; if not, then hi (= lo) is the position of the
   next smaller key value, or possibly 0. Uses method 2. *)
VAR mid: Count;
BEGIN
    IF lo < hi
        THEN mid := (lo + hi + 1) DIV 2;
            IF tkey < SL↑.sortedlist[mid].key
                THEN BinSearch(SL, tkey, lo, mid-1)
                ELSE BinSearch(SL, tkey, mid, hi)
            END
    END
END BinSearch;
```

Figure 4.26 Recursive version of a binary search.

An interpolation search has the same general objective as a binary search—disposing of large sublists that are known not to contain the target. Rather than routinely chopping the list in half, it does this by trying to estimate

An interpolation search tries to estimate the best position at which to probe.

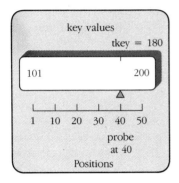

Figure 4.27
Example of an interpolation search.

where the target element should be in the list. For example, if the key value of the first list element is 101, the key value of the last (*n*th) position is 200, *n* = 50, and we are searching for target key = 180, we might estimate that it is 80% of the way through the list as follows (see also Figure 4.27):

$$\frac{180 - 101 + 1}{200 - 101 + 1} \times 100 = 80\%$$

Instead of probing at the midpoint (50% of the list) as we would do with a binary search, we would probe at the 80% point, estimating that the position of the element we are seeking is the same fraction in the range of positions as its key value is in the range of keys:

$$probe = .80 \times 50 = position\ 40$$

Testing the value of *list[40].key* against the target key tells us whether target key may be in the upper (> 40) or lower (< 40) portion. We can ignore the sublist known not to contain the key. The new sublist boundaries are set either to *low* = 1, *high* = 39 or to *low* = 41, *high* = 50, depending on the results of the test, and the interpolation technique is applied again. The general expression for the probe position is

$$fract = \frac{(tkey - list[low].key + 1)}{(list[high].key - list[low].key + 1)}$$

$$probe = [fract \times (high - low + 1)] + 1$$

Fibonacci numbers are defined as follows:

$F(0) = 0, F(1) = 1$
$F(i) = F(i - 1) + F(i - 2),$
$\qquad i > 1$

The development of an algorithm that makes use of this method is left to you (see Exercise 4.3.2, 5).

An interpolation search is somewhat like the telephone book search we used as an example in the beginning of this section. It attempts to estimate the best place to probe within the sublist being searched instead of always probing at the center, as a binary search does. The efficiency of the algorithm is dependent upon the distribution of the keys in the list, but it has been shown (Yao and Yao, 1976) that if the keys are numeric and randomly distributed on the interval between the minimum and maximum keys, then the expected number of probes for the search is $O(\log \log n)$, an excellent result. However, the amount of calculation per probe is quite a bit higher than that required of a binary search. Binary searches are usually preferred for data stored in RAM.

There are several other methods for searching sorted lists. A ***multiplicative search*** (Standish, 1980) avoids the use of division and is therefore suited for processors that do not have that operation. The method is basically a binary search, but it requires an auxiliary array of size *n*.

The first few ***Fibonacci numbers*** are 0, 1, 1, 2, 3, 5, 8, 13, ... Each number is the sum of the two previous numbers. Refer to Figure 4.28 as you read this. If we split a list whose size is a Fibonacci number (e.g., 13) into two parts (8 and 5), each of which equals a Fibonacci number that formed the original size, we can further split each of the two new lists into sizes that are their Fibonacci number components.

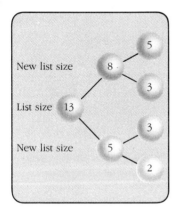

Figure 4.28
Fibonacci numbers.

Such subdividing can form the basis of a probing pattern, called a ***Fibonacci search*** (Knuth, 1973b), similar to that used by a binary search. Since Fibonacci numbers can be calculated by addition and subtraction, such a method can be useful for computers that have no hardware divide.

It is worthwhile noting that hardware processors that do not have a divide instruction often have a right shift operation. Right shifting a register by 1 bit is equivalent to dividing it by 2, exactly the division we need to compute the midpoint of a sublist during a binary search.

• Performance

Keeping a list sorted (assuming an array representation is used) pays great dividends in the efficiency of the *FindKey* operation. Instead of a sequential search, which requires $O(n)$ effort, we are able to use a binary search, which requires $O(\log_2 n)$. However, each insertion requires $O(n)$ data moves, and building the entire list so that the list always remains sorted requires $O(n^2)$ data moves. But this is no different than building an unsorted linear list if insertions are in random positions. If we built an unsorted list by always inserting at the end of the list (i.e., a chronologically ordered list), the total number of data moves to build the list would be $O(n)$. We will find that a good sorting algorithm (Chapter 6) requires $O(n \log n)$ work to sort the list. If we do not have to perform any *FindKey* operations until the list is completely built, then the latter strategy of building the list chronologically and then sorting it all at one time might be more efficient.

• Linked implementation

Keeping the list sorted if a linked representation is used does not pay the same dividends as keeping a list sorted if an array representation is used. A binary search is incompatible with linked lists. The problem lies in probing at the midpoint of the list. Using arrays, we were able to calculate an index, *mid,* and access *list[mid]* using the underlying array mapping function. That is not the case with a linked list. Although we may still calculate the position *mid,* finding the element at that position requires traversing the list from either position *low* or *high,* an operation that takes $O[(high - low + 1)/2]$ pointer manipulations. In fact, a linked list binary search would take a total of n such manipulations in the course of probing. A successful sequential search can be expected to take $(n + 1)/2$ compares, so the binary search is less efficient.

There is a small gain to be had by sorting the linked list. It does not improve the successful sequential search, but the expected effort for an unsuccessful search can be improved by a factor of 2. In the unsorted case, the fact that the search has been unsuccessful is not detected until the end of the list is reached, the entire list having been probed. If the list is sorted, the search can stop when the first list key greater than the target key is reached. At that point, we know that the target key cannot lie any further in the list and the search can be terminated.

The construction of the *FindKey* and *Insert* algorithms is left as an exercise for you (see Exercise 4.3.2, 7).

Exercises 4.3.2

1. The binary search algorithms of Figures 4.23 and 4.24 converge at the same position if the search is unsuccessful. What is that position? What is the position if the target key value is less than that of the element in position 1? Greater than that in position n?

2. What is the maximum number of probes made by a binary search in a list of
   a. 128 elements?
   b. 1024 elements?
   c. 435 elements?

3. Conduct timing studies on a system available to you to compare the performance of the two binary search algorithms. Measure times for various list sizes for both successful and unsuccessful searches. Which performs best for successful searches? Unsuccessful searches? Overall?

4. Conduct timing studies to determine the list size for which binary searches become more efficient than sequential searches. Using your results, find the approximate cost per probe ratio between the two types of searches.

5. Implement and test an interpolation search in place of the binary search in the key-sorted list module (Implementation Module 4.3). Time the performance of each and compare them for various values of n, the list size.

6. Design, implement, and test a Fibonacci search algorithm. Put it in the place of the binary search algorithm in the sorted list module (Implementation Module 4.3). Test the resulting module.

7. Write and test the *FindKey* and *Insert* implementations for the circular doubly linked list representation of sorted lists.

4.3.3 Frequency-Ordered Lists

If a list is to be searched sequentially, it is advantageous to construct it so that the element that is the likeliest to be the target of a *FindKey* operation is placed in the first position, the second likeliest in the second position, and so on. This is called a **frequency-ordered list.** If each element has an associated probability that it will be the one that is the target of a search, then the expected number of probes in doing a successful sequential search is

$$E_s = 1 \times p_1 + 2 \times p_2 + 3 \times p_3 + \cdots + n \times p_n$$

where p_i is the probability that the element in position i is the target of the search. Each term is the probability of an element being the target times the number of probes it will take to get to that element—$i \times p_i$.

E_s can be minimized by arranging the elements so that

$$p_1 \geqslant p_2 \geqslant \cdots \geqslant p_n$$

If the probabilities are all equal ($p_i = 1/n$), then the ordering is immaterial, and E_s reduces to the familiar

$$E_s = 1/n(1 + 2 + 3 + \cdots + n) = (n + 1)/2$$

We are assuming, of course, that the probabilities are known and that the list is built by the user so that the elements are correctly ordered.

Knuth (1973b) analyzed the improvement gained by ordering the lists by frequency given a number of probability distributions. For example, if the distribution is as follows:

$$p_1 = 1/2, p_2 = 1/4, \ldots, p_i = 1/2^i, \ldots, p_{n-1} = 1/2^{n-1}, p_n = 1/2^{n-1}$$

then the expected number of probes for a successful search can be shown to be

$$E_s = 2 - 2^{1-n}$$

which is less than 2 for any size list.

A second and perhaps more realistic distribution follows the so-called 80–20 rule. This distribution is found in a number of real-world situations. For example, a bank may find that 80% of its daily account transactions involve only 20% of the accounts, and 20% of that 20%—the most active 4% of the accounts—account for 80% of the 80%, or 64% of the transactions, and so on. The distribution can be approximated mathematically, and the resulting expected number of probes is

$$E_s = 0.122n$$

which is a factor of 4 improvement over the $n/2$ that would be expected for random permutations of the elements in the list.

Regardless of the distribution, we can always expect an improvement by arranging the list so that the elements are in decreasing order by probability of access.

• Self-organizing lists

If the probabilities are not known in advance or if they vary with time, an implementation package can be designed to make the elements adjust their positions to approximate the optimal arrangement. Such lists are called ***self-organizing lists,*** and there are three methods that we will consider.

The first method uses the recorded frequencies of access as approximations to the unknown or changing probabilities. An additional field, *freq,* is attached to the element. It is an integer that will contain the number of times the element has been the target of a search for a matching key value (*FindKey*). The augmented element type is defined by

```
TYPE AugElement = RECORD
                    el  : StdElement;
                    freq: CARDINAL
                  END;
```

In the array representation, the list becomes

```
VAR list: ARRAY [1..MaxSize] OF AugElement;
```

The structured English version of the *FindKey* algorithm is as follows:

```
IF successful
   THEN Move the element found forward in the list until
        it passes all elements before it that have a
        lower value of freq; make it the current element
END;
```

The only other operation whose implementation must be changed from those of the list (Implementation Modules 4.1 and 4.2) is *Insert*. New elements added to the list start with frequency 1 and are always added at the tail of the list. A slight modification of the chronological list *Insert* procedures (Figures 4.18 and 4.19) will do the job.

The second and third methods are similar in that no extra field need be attached to the element. Both "reward" an element that is the target of a successful search (*FindKey*) by moving it forward in the list.

> Method 2. Move the target element forward one position by exchanging it with its predecessor.

> Method 3. Delete the target element from its current position in the list and insert it at position 1.

In method 2, an element that is frequently accessed will slowly drift toward the head of the list. In method 3, an element that is accessed will leap to the head of the list. If it is infrequently accessed, it will tend to drift slowly toward the tail of the list.

Bentley and McGeoch (1985) give an analysis of the performance of self-organizing lists.

• Representation and implementation

The operation *Insert* is the same as in a chronologically ordered list (Figures 4.18 and 4.19). The operation *FindKey* uses the sequential search of an unsorted list (Implementation Module 4.1) but with the addition of code that "rewards" the found element by moving it forward one position. The algorithm for method 2 using a linked representation is given in Figure 4.29.

Notice that the internal procedure *Swap* accomplishes its job not by relinking the list to move the accessed node forward by one position but simply by swapping the data element contents between the current node and its predecessor. This approach is much simpler than relinking the nodes of the doubly linked list, but it may not be more efficient if the elements are long. (See Exercise 4.3.3, 1.)

```
PROCEDURE FindKey(SOL: SelfOrganizingList; tkey:
                    KeyType): BOOLEAN;

VAR p: NodePointer;
    k: Count;

    PROCEDURE Swap(q: NodePointer);
    VAR temp: StdElement;
    BEGIN
        temp     := q↑.el;
        q↑.el    := q↑.prior↑.el;
        q↑.prior↑.el := temp
    END Swap;

BEGIN
    WITH L↑ DO
        IF n = 0 THEN RETURN FALSE END;
        k := 1; p := head;
        WHILE (p↑.next # head) & (p↑.el.key # tkey) DO      (* Search. *)
            p := p↑.next; INC(k)
        END;
        IF p↑.el.key = tkey                          (* Matching key value found? *)
            THEN IF p # head                                    (* Yes. *)
                    THEN Swap(p);                        (* Swap contents *)
                        current := p↑.prior;             (* of kth and *)
                        icurrent := k-1;                 (* (k-1)th nodes. *)
                    ELSE icurrent := 1;              (* First element found. *)
                        current := head
                END;
                RETURN TRUE
            ELSE RETURN FALSE                                    (* No. *)
        END
    END
END FindKey;
```

Figure 4.29   Self-organizing list using a linked representation.

Exercises 4.3.3

1. We have chosen to implement the *FindKey* algorithm for the self-organizing linear list, which moves the found element forward one position in the list by swapping the element values of the two nodes whose positions are to have been exchanged (Figure 4.29). Another method, which avoids any data movement, is to move the found element forward one position by relinking the list appropriately using only pointer manipulations. For a visceral exercise in pointer manipulation, implement the *FindKey* algorithm using this latter strategy.

2. One method of self-organizing a list is to keep a count stored in the list along with each element. When an element is the target of a *FindKey* operation, its count is increased by 1. Then the element is moved forward in the list past all

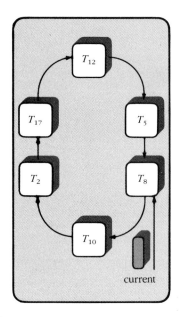

Figure 4.30
A ring.

elements with a lower count. The list is thus kept sorted on the count fields. Design, program, and test such an implementation of self-organizing lists for either an array or a linked representation.

3. Give some examples of applications in which frequency-ordered and self-organizing lists might be used.

4. Construct a table showing the orders of magnitude of the performance estimates for both array and linked implementations of self-organizing lists.

4.4 Rings

Time-sharing computer systems allow a single computer system to be shared among many interactive users. Each user has the impression that he or she is the only one on the system. Assume that each user is sitting at an interactive terminal and that the system has associated a packet of data (which we will call the ***terminal data element***) with that terminal.

Imagine that each terminal data element contains communication data and work space. They can be visualized as a circular structure such as that shown in Figure 4.30. An access pointer *current* points to the terminal currently receiving service (T_8 in Figure 4.30). After some interval of time, *current* is simply moved forward one element, and the terminal associated with the new *current* node is serviced (T_{10}). Service continues endlessly in this circular fashion. However, terminals are constantly logging onto and off of the system. Data elements for newly arrived terminals must be inserted into the circular list, and terminals that log off must be removed from it. Since the only access to the list is through *current,* terminals that log off must wait until they are being serviced before their node can be removed. The nodes of arriving terminals, on the other hand, can be inserted at whatever place in the list *current* is presently indicating. Since the position of *current* when a new terminal arrives is more or less random, the list will be in random order.

This structure is an example of an abstract data type called a ***ring.*** In the case shown, each element has another element that follows it. There is no beginning or end of the list, just an element that is current. Note that though the structure is linear, there need be no concept of position or predecessors. Each element, without exception, has a unique successor; *current* points to one of the ring elements.

We again call your attention to the fact that these specifications are arbitrary. We could as well have specified that each element occupied a position and/or had a predecessor. Such a choice would have made the ring specification very close in structure to that of a list. The essential difference between a ring and a list is that the former has no head or tail. We have chosen to specify no positions or predecessors for the sake of variety and to demonstrate the effect of the reduced specifications on the representation and implementation. The specifications of a ring are given in Specification 4.4 and summarized in Figure 4.31.

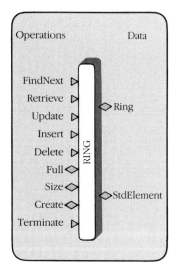

Figure 4.31
ring capsule.

Specification 4.4 Rings

DEFINITION MODULE Rings;

(* **Elements:** For concreteness, we assume that the elements are of type StdElement. *)

   FROM StdTypes **IMPORT** StdElement;

(* **Structure:** Each ring element has a unique successor that is a member of the ring. *)

(* **Domain:** The number of elements in the ring is bounded. *)

   EXPORT QUALIFIED Ring, FindNext, Retrieve, Update, Insert, Delete,
                  Full, Size, Create, Terminate;

TYPE Ring;

(* **Operations:** There are 9 operations. If the ring is not empty, then one element of the ring is designated as the current element. The notation for the ring and the current element just prior to execution of an operation is R-pre and c-pre, respectively. *)

PROCEDURE FindNext(R: Ring);
(* **pre** — R is not empty.
   post — The successor of c-pre is current. *)

PROCEDURE Retrieve(R: Ring; **VAR** e: StdElement);
(* **pre** — R is not empty.
   post — e has the value of the current element. *)

PROCEDURE Update(**VAR** R: Ring; e: StdElement);
(* **pre** — R is not empty.
   post — The value of the current element is e. *)

PROCEDURE Insert(**VAR** R: Ring; e: StdElement);
(* **pre** — R is not full.
   post — The element e is a member of R and is the current element;
           if Size(R-pre) > 0, then c-pre is the predecessor of e. *)

PROCEDURE Delete(**VAR** R: Ring);
(* **pre** — R is not empty.
   post — c-pre is not in R; if Size(R) > 0 then the successor of c-pre
           is current. *)

PROCEDURE Full(R: Ring): BOOLEAN;
(* **post** — If the number of elements in R has reached the bound
           then Full is true; else Full is false. *)

PROCEDURE Size(R: Ring): Cardinal;
(* **post** — Size is the number of elements in R. *)

continued

Specification 4.4, continued

```
PROCEDURE Create(VAR R: Ring): BOOLEAN;
(* post — If a ring can be created then R exists and is empty, and Create
          is true; else Create is false. *)

PROCEDURE Terminate(VAR R: Ring);
(* post — R-pre does not exist. *)

END Rings.
```

Although it is possible to represent the specified ring as an array, such a representation is not very efficient. We suggest a linked representation, which is nearly ideal, and we leave that to you as an exercise.

Exercises 4.4

1. Design, write, and test an implementation module for a ring according to Specification 4.4, using a singly linked list for the representation.
2. Design an array representation of a ring abstract data type, and program and test an implementation. The implementation should be written to Specification 4.4.
3. Give examples of some applications in which a ring data type might be used.

4.5 Sequences

Another common linear type is the type ***sequence.*** Like the ring data type that we specified, sequences usually have no explicit notions of positions or predecessors. Their most outstanding difference from the other linear types is in their set of operations. We will look at these in detail in Section 4.5.1.

Many programming languages include sequences as a native data type. Most often they are included as a form of ***sequential file.*** Some languages include the sequence data type in forms other than files. The language LISP, which is very important in artificial intelligence research and is one of the oldest computer languages still in wide use, is completely based on sequences. (In LISP, the sequences are called lists.)

4.5.1 Sequence Specification

A sequence is an important object in mathematics, in which it is usually defined as a function whose domain is the set of all natural numbers—1, 2, 3, ... (MacLane, 1967, page 43). An important aspect of this definition is that each sequence value contains an infinite number of component elements.

The notion of a sequence that we will use is one in which each sequence value contains a finite number of component elements arranged linearly, with the explicit understanding that an additional element can be appended to any

$< e_1, e_2, e_3, ..., e_n >$

(a) A sequence.

$< e_1, e_2, e_3, ..., e_n >$
 ↑
 current

(b) After *FindFirst.*

$< e_1, e_2, e_3, ..., e_n >$
     ↑
     current

(c) After *FindNext.*

$< e_1, e_2, e_3, ..., e_n, e_{n+1} >$
                    ↑
                    current

(d) After *Append.*

Figure 4.32
Some sequence operations.

sequence. (Figure 4.32 illustrates specifications for sequences.) The effect is that there is no specified upper bound on the size of a sequence. As an abstraction, this causes no problem since we need not concern ourselves with implementation details. The abstraction is useful, and certain variations of it can be used for data types such as strings and files.

However, we must realize that all computer memories are finite. We cannot implement an unbounded data type. Take the example of files. They often have no specification of an upper bound on the number of elements they can contain. However, an attempt to append one more element to the file when the computer system is out of memory space will cause an undefined result.

Specification 4.5 is the specification of a (unbounded) sequence. Note that in contrast to earlier data types, there is no operation *Full* and no precondition to the operation *Append* that the sequence is not full.

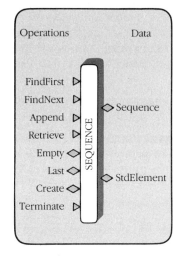

Figure 4.33
Sequence capsule.

Specification 4.5   Sequences

DEFINITION MODULE Sequences;

(* **Elements:** For concreteness, we assume that the elements are of type
    StdElement. *)

FROM StdTypes **IMPORT** StdElement;

(* **Structure:** A sequence is linear. *)

(* **Domain:** The number of elements in a sequence is unbounded. *)

EXPORT QUALIFIED Sequence, FindFirst, FindNext, Append, Retrieve, Empty,
                Last, Create, Terminate;

TYPE Sequence;

(* **Operations:** There are 8 operations. If the sequence is not empty,
    then one element is designated as the current element. The
    current element and its successor immediately before execution
    of an operation are denoted by c-pre and c-next, respectively. *)

PROCEDURE FindFirst(S: Sequence);
(* **pre** − S is not empty.
   post − The first element is the current element. *)

PROCEDURE FindNext(S: Sequence);
(* **pre** − S is not empty and the current element is not the last element.
   post − c-next is the current element. *)

PROCEDURE Append(**VAR** S: Sequence; e: StdElement);
(* **post** − S contains e as the last element and as the current element. *)

continued

Specification 4.5, continued

```
PROCEDURE Retrieve(S: Sequence; VAR e: StdElement);
(* pre  − S is not empty.
   post − The contents of the current element are in e. *)

PROCEDURE Empty(S: Sequence): BOOLEAN;
(* post − If S has no element then Empty is true; else Empty is false. *)

PROCEDURE Last(S: Sequence): BOOLEAN;
(* pre  − S is not empty.
   post − If the last element is the current element then Last is true;
          else Last is false. *)

PROCEDURE Create(VAR S: Sequence): BOOLEAN;
(* post − If a sequence can be created then Sequence S exists and is empty,
          and Create is true; else Create is false. *)

PROCEDURE Terminate(VAR S: Sequence);
(* post − Sequence S-pre does not exist. *)

END Sequences.
```

Notice that the only way to reach an element in the sequence is to execute *FindFirst* and then traverse forward by successive executions of *FindNext*. An essential difference between lists and sequences is in this restriction of the find operations. Elements of a sequence can only be accessed in sequence, hence the name.

A sequence is in many respects a simpler data structure than a list. Because of its simplicity, it is a desirable abstraction upon which to base the specification of other data structures. The list specification, for example, could be based upon a sequence.

Sequences are often found as native data types of programming languages in the form of sequential files. Pascal, for instance, has a native data type *file,* which is patterned after sequences. COBOL, FORTRAN, and C do also. Ada has a generic package (similar to a Modula-2 module) called *SEQUENTIAL_IO.* There are many kinds of file organizations with more or less sequence-like features. Since we are using Modula-2 as a language for this book, let us examine some of the file facilities of that language.

4.5.2 Modula-2 Files

Modula-2 has no file native data type. Rather than providing files as part of the Modula-2 language, its designer decided to use the module facility of Modula-2 to provide for various types of files and their associated operations. The reasoning behind this decision is discussed in Wirth (1983).

Our concern here is with the relationship of certain kinds of files to the abstract notions of sequences and lists. Wirth specifies several kinds of file abstractions. We choose one for study. *InOut* is sequence-like since its operations provide only for sequential movement through the file.

• InOut

Specification 4.6 is taken from Wirth (1983).

Specification 4.6   InOut

DEFINITION MODULE InOut;

EXPORT QUALIFIED
    EOL, Done, termCH,
    OpenInput, OpenOutput, CloseInput, CloseOutput,
    Read, ReadString, ReadInt, ReadCard,
    Write, WriteLn, WriteString, WriteInt, WriteCard, WriteOct, WriteHex;

CONST EOL = 36C;
VAR Done: BOOLEAN;
    termCH: CHAR;

PROCEDURE OpenInput(defext: **ARRAY OF** CHAR);

(* Request a file name and open input file "in".
   Done := "file was successfully opened".
   If open, subsequent input is read from this file.
   If name ends with ".", append extension defext. *)

PROCEDURE OpenOutput(defext: **ARRAY OF** CHAR);
(* Request a file name and open output file "out".
   Done := "file was successfully opened".
   If open, subsequent output is written on this file. *)

PROCEDURE CloseInput:
(* Closes input file; returns input to terminal. *)

PROCEDURE CloseOutput;
(* Closes output file; returns output to terminal. *)

PROCEDURE (Read(**VAR** ch: CHAR);
(* Done := **NOT** in.eof. *)

PROCEDURE ReadString(**VAR** s: **ARRAY OF** CHAR);
(* Read string, i.e., sequence of characters not containing
   blanks nor control characters; leading blanks are ignored.
   Input is terminated by any character <=" ";
   this character is assigned to termCH.
   DEL is used for backspacing when input from terminal. *)

continued

Specification 4.6, continued

PROCEDURE ReadInt(**VAR** x: INTEGER);
(* Read string and convert to integer. Syntax:
   integer = ["+"|"-"]digit{digit}.
   Leading blanks are ignored.
   Done = "integer was read". *)

PROCEDURE ReadCard(**VAR** x: CARDINAL);
(* Read string and convert to cardinal. Syntax:
   cardinal = digit{digit}.
   Leading blanks are ignored.
   Done = "cardinal was read". *)

PROCEDURE Write(ch: CHAR);

PROCEDURE WriteLn;
(* Terminate line. *)

PROCEDURE WriteString(s: **ARRAY OF** CHAR);

PROCEDURE WriteInt(x: INTEGER; n: CARDINAL);
(* Write integer x with (at least) n characters on file "out".
   If n is greater than the number of digits needed,
   blanks are added preceding the number. *)

PROCEDURE WriteCard(x, n: CARDINAL);

PROCEDURE WriteOct(x, n: CARDINAL);

PROCEDURE WriteHex(x, n: CARDINAL);

END InOut.

Module *InOut* is a variation of the sequence abstraction. We show it exactly as written by Wirth. The style of specification he used in definition modules is, as you can see, different from that used in this book. The syntax, which is determined by the rules for constructing definition modules, is the same. The method of specifying semantics differs. We use pre- and postconditions for that purpose. Wirth uses a more informal style. While postconditions are implicit in the comments following each procedure declaration, preconditions are not stated. On careful examination, you will find that instead of explicit preconditions, a flag *Done* is used to signal the success or failure of an execution of operations. We have noted in Chapter 1 that preconditions could always be replaced by such a flag in the postcondition. Thus instead of checking the precondition of an operation and then executing the operation with a guarantee of successful execution, one attempts to execute an operation and then checks the flag to see if the execution was successful.

InOut handles text files—files of characters. It is also an example of a file structure called a ***stream.*** Wirth (1983) defines a stream as follows:

1. All elements of a stream are of the same type, the stream's base type. If it is CHAR, the stream is called a *text stream*.
2. The number of elements of the stream is not known a priori. The stream is therefore (a simple case of) a dynamic structure. The number of elements is called the *length* of the stream, and the stream with length 0 is called the empty stream.
3. A stream can be modified only by appending elements at its end (or by deleting the entire stream). Appending an element is called *writing*.
4. Only a single element of a stream is visible at any one time, namely the element at the stream's current *position*. Accessing this element is called *reading*. A read operation typically advances the stream's position to the next element.
5. A stream has a *mode:* it is either being written or read. Hence every stream has an associated state consisting of length, position, and mode.

InOut is a text stream, and its relationship to a sequence as defined in Specification 4.6 is apparent. There are differences, but the two are the same kind of data type in many respects. Due to practical considerations, *InOut* has a number of *Read* and a number of *Write* operations, one for each of a number of data element types. *InOut* has four operations to set the mode—*OpenInput, OpenOutput, CloseInput,* and *CloseOutput*—whereas *Sequences,* as we defined them, have no notion of mode.

The *Retrieve/FindNext* combination of *Sequences* is equivalent to the *Read*s of *InOut,* and *Append* is equivalent to the *Write*s. Neither has a notion of a bound on the number of elements, and consequently neither has a *Full* operation specified (*Done* is not used for the *Write* operations of *InOut*).

We have seen a number of uses of *InOut* thus far in this book. Section 4.6.1 has another more extensive one.

Exercises 4.5

1. Choose a representation for, and implement the sequence abstraction given in, Specification 4.5. What aspect of Specification 4.5 is it not possible to implement? Why?
2. What file modules have you specified for the implementation of Modula-2 that are available for your use? Which of these is a sequential file structure? How are the others related to the other linear types of this chapter (lists, chronological lists, sorted lists, and rings)?
3. Recast Specification 4.6—*InOut*—into the form used throughout this book, i.e., specify the semantics by means of pre- and postconditions.

4.6 An Application: Single-Letter and Digraph Frequencies in English Text

Now that we have studied a number of linear data types, we will look at an application that allows a comparison among them.

A landmark paper of computer science is one by von Neumann (1946) in which he outlined principles of computer architecture that have served as the

Lines from von Neumann's Paper

Preliminary Discussion of the
Logical Design of an Electronic
Computing Instrument

1. Principal Components of the
Machine.

1.1 Inasmuch as the completed
device will be a general purpose
computing machine, it should
contain . . .

basis for most computers built since that time. We will use the text of that paper as data and perform two analyses used by cryptographers. One is the determination of the frequencies of occurrence of each letter of the alphabet. The second is a similar determination of the frequencies of occurrence of pairs of letters, called ***digraphs.***

4.6.1 The Frequency Analysis Program

The program for analyzing the frequencies of single letters provides a small example of the use of lists and the file module *InOut.* We will use chronological lists (Specification 4.2) as an example. Chronological lists, frequency-ordered lists, self-organizing lists, and sorted lists are all used in the timing studies of Section 4.6.2.

The program that performs the frequency analysis has the following characteristics:

1. It asks the user for the name of the file to be analyzed.
2. It uses procedure *OpenInput* of module *InOut* to open the file in input mode.
3. It uses procedure *Read* of module *InOut* to read the characters of the file one by one until the end of file is encountered.
4. Nonalphabetic characters are ignored. Alphabetic characters are transformed into uppercase.
5. The uppercase letters are searched for in the chronological list. If not there, they are added to the list with a frequency count (their data field) of 1. If already in the list, their frequency count is incremented by 1.
6. At the end of file, the results are printed, the file is closed, and the program terminates.

```
TYPE KeyType  = CHAR;
     DataType = CARDINAL;
     StdElement =
         RECORD
              key : KeyType;
              data: DataType
     END;
```

Type *StdElement* is defined as shown in the margin. Since the program is a simple one, it is presented in Figure 4.34 without further comment.

```
MODULE CharFreq;

    FROM InOut        IMPORT WriteString, WriteLn, Read,
                             OpenInput, CloseInput,
                             ClearScreen, ReadString, Write,
                             WriteCard, Done;
    FROM StdTypes     IMPORT StdElement, KeyType, DataType;
    FROM ChronLists   IMPORT ChronList, Create, Insert,
                             Update, Retrieve, FindKey,
                             Full, Size, Findith, Terminate;
    TYPE Problem      = (none, listFull, noFile, noList);

    VAR L    : ChronList;
        error: Problem;                              continued
```

continued

```
PROCEDURE ProcessChar(VAR L: ChronList; ch: CHAR);
VAR e: StdElement;
BEGIN
    e.key := ch;
    IF FindKey(L,e.key)
        THEN Retrieve(L,e);
             INC(e.data);
             Update(L,e);
        ELSE e.data := 1;
             IF NOT Full(L)
                 THEN Insert(L,e);
                 ELSE error := listFull;
             END
    END
END ProcessChar;

PROCEDURE ProcessText(L: ChronList);
VAR ch: CHAR;
BEGIN
    WriteLn;
    OpenInput("TXT");                          (* Prompts for file name,  *)
                                               (* adds "TXT", and opens. *)
    IF NOT Done THEN error := noFile; RETURN END;
    LOOP
        Read(ch);
        IF (NOT Done) OR (error # none) THEN EXIT
            ELSE CASE ch OF
                    'a'..'z': ch := CAP(ch);
                             ProcessChar(L,ch)        |
                    'A'..'Z': ProcessChar(L,ch)
                   ELSE
                END
        END
    END;
    CloseInput
END ProcessText;

PROCEDURE Display(L: ChronList);
VAR i: CARDINAL;
    e: StdElement;
BEGIN
    FOR i := 1 TO Size(L) DO
        Findith(L,i);
        Retrieve(L,e);
        WriteLn; Write(e.key); WriteCard(e.data,5)
    END;
    WriteLn
END Display;
```

M	17
O	72
D	50
U	21
L	82
E	172

The first six letters output when module CharFreq is used to analyze itself.

continued

```
BEGIN
   error := none;
   ClearScreen; WriteLn;
   WriteString('Frequency analysis of the characters of
                  a file.'); WriteLn;
   IF Create(L)
      THEN ProcessText(L)
      ELSE error := noList
   END;
   CASE error OF
      none    : Display(L);
                Terminate(L)           |
      noFile  : WriteString('Could not open file');
                WriteLn                |
      listFull: WriteString('List filled; program quit');
                WriteLn                |
      noList  : WriteString('Could not create a list');
                WriteLn
   END
END CharFreq.
```

Figure 4.34   Modula-2 program for the frequency analysis of alphabetic characters in a text file.

4.6.2 Timing Studies

In English text, the letter "e" is usually the most frequently occurring single letter, and "th" is the most frequently occurring digraph. We will use four of the linear data types studied in this chapter to store the letters, digraphs, and frequencies with which they occur. The major emphasis will be on the comparative performance of these data types.

The data elements for these studies will contain key and data components. The key will be of type CHAR for single letters and of

TYPE KeyType = **ARRAY** [1..2] **OF CHAR**

in the case of digraphs. The data part will be a count field of type CARDINAL in both cases. As each letter and digraph is encountered in the text it is processed. ***Processing*** a letter means searching to see if it is already in the list. If so, its count field is incremented by 1. If not, it is added to the list with a count of 1. A similar process is done with digraphs.

For each analysis (see Figures 4.36–4.43), timing studies were conducted with different kinds of lists holding the data. The list types and their corresponding symbols are given in Figure 4.35. Each list has both array and linked implementations.

Figures 4.36, 4.37, 4.38, and 4.39 pertain to the frequency analysis of single letters. Figure 4.36 shows the number of distinct letters found as a function of the number of letters processed. (For both individual letters and digraphs,

---

Processing a Single Letter or a Digraph

tkey is a single letter or a digraph.

The list is searched for tkey.
IF   a matching key is found
THEN the count for the element found is increased by 1
ELSE a new data element with a key of tkey and a count of 1 is inserted into the list.

> •

x   Chronological list
•   Frequency-ordered list
▲   Self-organizing list
○   Sorted list, sequential search
□   Sorted list, binary search

Figure 4.35
Legend for symbols used in Figures 4.36–4.43.

uppercase characters are transformed to lowercase before the analysis begins. Thus there are a maximum of 26 distinct letters and a maximum of 676 distinct digraphs.)

Figure 4.36 shows the number of distinct letters rising quickly to 20 and then increasing slowly to 24. Processing 2000 letters results in only 24 insertions. This case is essentially the study of small, static lists with few insertions. The major activities are those of searching and updating.

Figure 4.37 shows the expected number of probes for a search, or expected search length, as a function of the size of the list. We see that the number of probes to locate a letter in the chronological list is about three times the number required using a binary search of a sorted list. If a sequential search is used, then a frequency-ordered list gives the minimum possible search length.

Figures 4.38 and 4.39 show the average time required to process a single letter as a function of the number of letters of text processed. The main difference between them is that Figure 4.38 shows the results for an array representation and Figure 4.39 shows the results for a linked representation. There are several interesting aspects of the results.

First, observe that the binary search of a sorted list (Figure 4.38) requires the longest time, even though its search length is shortest (Figure 4.37). The

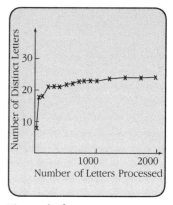

Figure 4.36
Frequency analysis of single letters. Number of distinct letters.

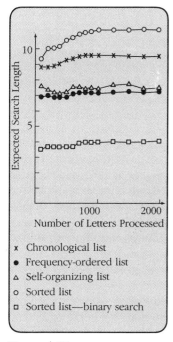

Figure 4.37
Frequency analysis of single letters. Expected search length.

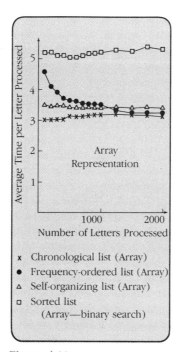

Figure 4.38
Frequency analysis of single letters. Array representations. Average measured time per letter processed.

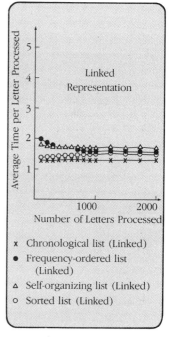

Figure 4.39
Frequency analysis of single letters. Linked representations. Average measured time per letter processed.

explanation for this apparent contradiction is that each binary search probe is more complex than a sequential probe and therefore requires more time. We also see that the organization that has the longest expected search length (a chronological list) requires the shortest processing time. The explanation is that for a chronological list no time is spent organizing the list, and for the example at hand, the time saved by not organizing the list is larger than the time lost by making longer searches.

Compare Figures 4.38 and 4.39 and observe that the linked representation gives substantially smaller processing times. There is no reasonable explanation for these differences in terms of the data structures used. It seems reasonable to explain the differences by the need to compute the array mapping function at each probe, but an examination of the object code showed little difference due to this cause. These observed differences are produced by an idiosyncrasy of the compiler and hardware on which these experiments were run. The user must be wary of such differences when using high-level languages.

The general conclusion to be drawn from the results in Figures 4.36 through 4.39 is that for small static lists with simple keys, any list organization will do well as far as execution time is concerned. Algorithms with a relatively high overhead per operation (such as binary search) should be avoided. The choice of organization can be based on factors other than speed of execution, that is, on factors such as the order in which the elements will be used.

Figure 4.40 shows the number of distinct digraphs encountered as a function of the number of letters processed. At 2000 letters, new digraphs were still being found; a total of 270 were found. The digraph case is a study of moderate-sized dynamic lists. The *Insert* operation continues to be a factor at 2000 letters. The size of the lists is approximately one order of magnitude larger than in the single letter case.

Figure 4.41 shows the expected number of probes, or expected search length, required when searching for a digraph. Observe that the number of probes required for a binary search, $O(\log_2 n)$, is substantially less than the number required by a sequential search of any list, $O(n)$. This emphasizes, again, the large difference between the value of $\log_2 n$ and the value of n. As noted before, a frequency-ordered list gives the minimum possible search length for a sequential search. Comparing the search length of other organizations with the search length of a frequency-ordered list shows how the other organizations compare relative to the organization with the shortest possible search length.

The measured times to process a digraph are given in Figure 4.42 for array representations and in Figure 4.43 for linked representations. Figure 4.42 shows that a binary search of a sorted list requires the least time when the number of digraphs being searched is sufficiently large. When there are only a few digraphs (fewer than about 150), binary search takes longer because of its greater overhead per probe. A chronological list still performs almost as well as any other approach and has the virtue that it is the simplest to implement.

Compare Figures 4.42 and 4.43 and observe that the processing time for the array representations are approximately the same as for the corresponding

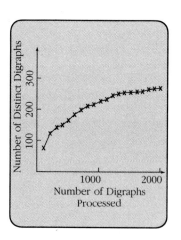

Figure 4.40
Frequency analysis of digraphs. Number of distinct digraphs processed.

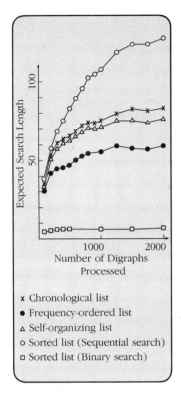

Figure 4.41
Frequency analysis of digraphs.
Expected search length.

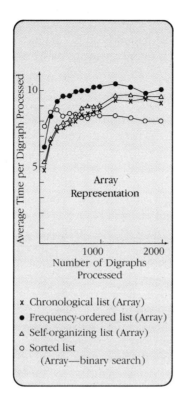

Figure 4.42
Frequency analysis of digraphs.
Array representations. Average
measured time per digraph
processed.

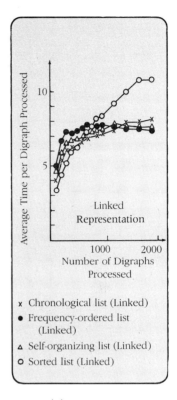

Figure 4.43
Frequency analysis of digraphs.
Linked representations. Average
measured time per digraph
processed.

linked representations but that the linked representations are slightly faster. The explanation of this better performance is probably that the array representation requires an evaluation of an array mapping function (see Chapter 2) each time a probe is made, whereas the linked representation does not.

What conclusions might we draw from these timing studies? They are the result of implementing the abstract data types that we introduced in the text. The timing results are, of course, dependent upon the code generated by the compiler and on the hardware of the computer system used for the timing studies. However, they serve as a reminder that orders-of-magnitude estimates of performance are crude and assume large lists. There are important factors that these estimates do not take into account. Although it is tempting to say that an $O(\log n)$ method is superior to an $O(n)$ method, if the actual expressions are

$$25\log n + 10 \quad \text{and} \quad 0.25n + 1.0$$

then the data structure size will be large before the $O(\log n)$ method begins to pay off. Its overhead is 100 times that of the $O(n)$ method. Take care not to draw too grand a conclusion from order-of-magnitude estimates!

4.7 Summary

The simple list with which we opened Chapter 4 is one of the most general abstract data types that we shall encounter. We have seen rings, chronologically ordered lists, key-sorted lists, frequency-ordered lists, sequences, and files, all of which can be implemented using a list together with an appropriate collection of operations. We could have implemented a chronologically ordered list by using a simple list and requiring that its currency pointer always be moved to the last element before an *Insert* operation. A sorted list could have been implemented using a linear list by allowing the user to do the binary search and position the currency pointer correctly before insertion. A frequency-ordered list could have been implemented by always inserting at the tail of the linear list and by implementing the swapping of elements in a self-organizing list at the user level.

We have seen in Chapter 3 that stacks, queues, and priority queues can be abstracted as lists with constrained access and insertion. Many of the other data structures that we shall see in the remainder of this text will have a set of operations that is a subset of the operations specified for lists.

We have seen the performance characteristics of the implementations of the various versions of lists. Theory aside, the application of lists to the problem of single letter and digraph frequency analysis of English text has provided some useful insights into the use of these data types in programs run on a real computer.

The complexity of the implementation modules presented in this chapter is shown in Table 4.1.

TABLE 4.1 Implementation modules in Chapter 4.

Implementation module	Data type	Representation	Number of procedures	Lines of code	Lines of code per procedure	
					Average	Maximum
4.1	List	Array	14	37	2.6	9
4.2	List	Linked	14	71	5.1	16
Fig. 4.18	Chron. list	Array	13	33	2.5	9
Fig. 4.19	Chron. list	Linked	13	73	5.6	16
4.3	Sorted list	Array	13	45	3.5	10

Trees 5

5.1 Introduction
Exercises 5.1

5.2 Ordered Trees, Oriented Trees, and Terminology
5.2.1 Elements of Trees
5.2.2 Structure of Trees—Hierarchical Relationships
Exercises 5.2

5.3 Abstract Binary Tree
5.3.1 Structure
5.3.2 Specification and Operations
Exercises 5.3.2
5.3.3 Linked Representation and Implementation
5.3.4 Sequential Representation
Exercises 5.3.4
5.3.5 Threaded Trees
Exercises 5.3.5

5.4 Abstract Binary Search Tree
5.4.1 Specification and Operations
5.4.2 Binary Search Tree Representation and Implementation
Exercises 5.4

5.5 Enumeration and Performance
Exercises 5.5

5.6 AVL Trees
5.6.1 AVL Tree Representation and Implementation
Exercises 5.6

5.7 Frequency Analysis Revisited
Exercises 5.7

5.8 Heaps and Priority Queues
5.8.1 Heap Data Structure
5.8.2 Heap Implementation of a Priority Queue
Exercises 5.8

5.9 B-Trees
5.9.1 Insertion and Deletion Illustrated
5.9.2 Algorithmic Descriptions of Insertion and Deletion
5.9.3 Specification
Exercises 5.9

5.10 Summary

5.1 Introduction

. . . trees, the most important nonlinear structure arising in computer algorithms. (Knuth, 1973a)

This chapter introduces data structures that have a ***hierarchical***, or ***nested***, or ***one-to-many relationship*** among their component elements. One reason we are interested in these ***hierarchical data structures*** is that they represent, in a natural way, many of the relationships among elements that surround us in our world: The relationship between parent and child is one to many. ***One to zero*** and ***one to one*** are special cases of one to many. The relationship between a person and the books that person owns is one to many. The relationship between a person and the books that person has read is one to many. The relationship between a basketball team and the players on that team is one to many. The relationship between a car and the people in that car is one to many. The list of examples is endless. In this chapter we will discuss the use of a computer to represent and manipulate such one-to-many structures.

Trees are a species of nonlinear structure of considerable importance in computer science, partly because they provide natural representations for many sorts of nested data that occur in computer applications, and partly because they are useful in solving a wide variety of algorithmic problems. (Standish, 1980)

We will begin with a concrete example of a library card catalog (Figure 5.1), which illustrates several hierarchical relationships. Suppose we want to find a book in a library. One way to proceed is to start with the library's card catalog. The card catalog is usually divided into three sections that organize the books in three ways: by author, by title, and by subject. This is a hierarchical (one-to-three) relationship. To be even more concrete, suppose that we are looking for the book *Data Structure Techniques* by T. A. Standish. We continue our search by (arbitrarily) choosing the section of the card catalog that is organized by author—call it the author catalog.

The author catalog contains a large number of file drawers, and there is a hierarchical relationship between the author catalog and the file drawers it contains. The drawers are arranged in alphabetical order, and each drawer is labeled to show the sequence of authors' names about which it contains information (see Figure 5.1). We search for the drawer containing the name Standish. We could use a sequential search, starting with the first drawer and plodding onward from each drawer to its successor until the proper drawer is found. But we are more likely to use a technique that is essentially an interpolation search (Chapter 4). In any event, we locate the proper drawer. Its label might describe its contents as Stafford, R.–Stanford, R. (In one library this is drawer number 761 in an author index containing 900 drawers. In this case the relationship between the author index and the drawers it contains is 1 to 900.)

Each drawer contains many cards—a third hierarchical relationship. We search through the cards (again using an interpolation search) until we find our target card or until we determine that there is no such card. If there is no such card, it may mean that the library does not have the book we need. If we find the card, it will probably tell us the catalog number of our book. We must now convert that catalog number into a specific location on a library shelf on which the book should be located (if it is not already checked out).

We will leave our book-finding expedition at this point. We have already seen three examples of hierarchical organizations. There are others that you will discover by completing the search for the location of the book. What are they?

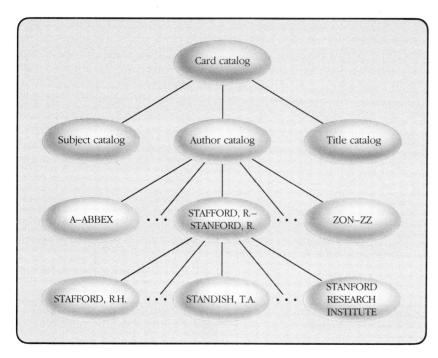

Figure 5.1 The card catalog of a library has a hierarchical structure.

Computer representations of hierarchical structures are often called ***trees.*** In our introduction to the subject we will consider a few of the many possibilities. Treating only a few types of trees permits us to lay a solid foundation for further study.

Most of Chapter 5 (Sections 5.2–5.6) is concerned with binary trees. Binary trees are simple in the sense that the hierarchical relationships are, at most, one to two. They are useful in their own right, but they also exhibit many characteristics of other types of trees. Thus, a study of binary trees prepares you for the study of other hierarchical structures. We will consider several variations of binary trees, including binary search trees, AVL trees, threaded trees, and heaps.

In Section 5.7 we will continue the empirical study begun in Section 4.6. We will report the results of using trees to perform frequency analysis of the letters and digraphs (pairs of letters) in a string of text.

Section 5.8 describes a heap. This data structure is often implemented using an array, but it is best seen as a complete binary tree. A heap is the data structure of choice for, among other things, implementing a priority queue. Implementation Module 5.4 gives that implementation.

Another type of tree, quite different from a binary tree, is a B-tree. We will introduce this important data structure in Section 5.9 in order to indicate some of the variety in the way computers are used to represent trees, as well as because of the importance of this particular structure in computer science. The discussion of B-trees is introductory. It describes a data structure that is

Trees We Will Discuss

Ordered trees
Oriented trees
Binary trees
    Binary search trees
    Full trees
    Complete trees
    Random trees
    Threaded trees
    AVL trees
Heaps
B-trees

frequently used in conjunction with the storage of large data files on direct access storage devices. The name "B-tree" is unfortunate. It is often inferred that B-tree is a synonym for binary tree, or that B-tree refers to a special type of binary tree. A B-tree is, however, quite a different data structure.

In Appendix C we will introduce the problem of printing binary trees. The techniques presented will allow us to print pretty pictures of trees. Such pictures make the study of binary trees more visual and therefore easier. Several of the algorithms for printing trees use an auxiliary data structure—a linked list of linked lists—that is of interest in its own right.

Exercises 5.1

1. Use the card catalog at your school library to locate a copy of this text. Make a list of all the hierarchical relationships you encounter. If your library does not have a copy of this text, request that one be ordered immediately!

2. Think of at least five examples of hierarchical relationships that impinge on your daily life. Be creative—do not restrict yourself to mundane examples such as libraries and basketball teams.

3. Any Modula-2 procedure or function has a nested, or hierarchical, structure. Make a sketch, similar to the one in Figure 5.1 for the card catalog of a library, that shows this structure for procedures *Findith, Insert,* and *Delete* in Implementation Module 4.1.

5.2 Ordered Trees, Oriented Trees, and Terminology

We will begin our discussion of trees with a special type of tree—an ordered tree. ***Ordered trees*** are the special case of trees that are most naturally implemented using digital computers. In many data structures texts, the term "tree" refers to an ordered tree. Ordered trees will provide a perfect jumping off point for our discussion of other trees. We begin by introducing a number of basic notions about trees.

5.2.1 Elements of Trees

A tree can contain any elements we choose. We will assume that the elements are all standard elements as described in Section 1.4.1. That is, each element contains information that describes some object, and that information is divided into two parts: a key part and a data part. The key part has the unique identification property.

When we discuss trees we will rarely refer to their elements but will instead refer to their nodes. Each ***node*** may contain one or more elements. Reference to a node is therefore an implicit reference to the elements that it contains. They will appear as globes, spheres, or capsules in the figures in this chapter.

For the sake of simplifying our discussion, each node in a tree will contain a single element, and that element will be a single integer, a single character, or a single word (see Figure 5.2). Such nodes and the information they contain

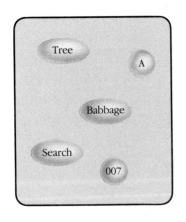

Figure 5.2
Each of these nodes contains a single item—the value of the key for the element in that node.

will be illustrated by printing the element inside the globe or sphere that represents the node. If the element in each node has both a key part and a data part, we will normally print the key part (but not the data part) in the globe or sphere representing the node.

In addition to containing elements, a node may contain information about its relationship with other nodes. Exactly what additional information it contains depends on how the tree is implemented. It is customary to illustrate hierarchical relationships among nodes with arcs connecting pairs of related nodes. These arcs are referred to as edges or branches or links. We will call them **edges.** It should be noted that there are other relationships among nodes besides hierarchical relationships. We will introduce some of them in a later section. In this chapter we will reserve the term "edge" to describe hierarchical relationships. (See Figure 5.3.)

Each edge in an ordered tree (which we have not defined yet) connects two distinct nodes. Each of these edges has an orientation, or direction. In the trees that we will discuss, the direction can always be inferred from its illustration. Even so, it is sometimes helpful to show the direction explicitly, and we will use the traditional arrowhead ($\longrightarrow$) for this purpose.

The components of a tree that we have introduced are nodes and edges. The nodes of a tree have a hierarchical relationship. The edges, from our current perspective, are simply used to illustrate hierarchical relationships among nodes. In Section 5.2.2 we will describe hierarchical relationships and contrast them with linear relationships.

5.2.2 Structure of Trees—Hierarchical Relationships

The essential requirement of a linear structure, you may recall, is that each object, with two exceptions, has a unique successor and a unique predecessor. A logical view of a linear data structure is shown in Figure 5.4. In a more formal

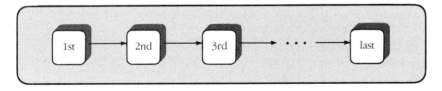

Figure 5.4   A logical view of a linear data structure.

vein, we can characterize a linear structure as being empty, as containing a single element, or as having the relationship among its elements described in Figure 5.5.

The relationship among objects in a linear structure is one to one. Look at the characterization of a linear structure in Figure 5.5 to see that this is the case. The relationship among nodes in a tree is one to many, or hierarchical, or nested, as shown in Figure 5.6. A tree is a natural structure for keeping track of information that has a one-to-many (or hierarchical, or nested) relationship among its elements.

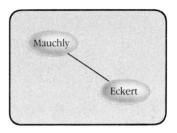

Figure 5.3
Two nodes connected by an edge. Each node contains a single element that contains information about a person. The key value, which is shown, is the person's last name.

•

1. There is a unique first element, which has no predecessors and has a unique successor.
2. There is a unique last element, which has no successors and has a unique predecessor.
3. Each element, other than the first and the last, has a unique predecessor and a unique successor.

Figure 5.5
Relationships among elements in a linear structure.

•

1. There is a unique first node, called the **root node**, that has no predecessors and that may have many successors.
2. There may be many nodes that have no successors. These nodes are called **leaf nodes**, and each of them has a unique predecessor.
3. Each node that is neither the root node nor a leaf node has a unique predecessor and at least one successor.

Figure 5.6
Relationships among nodes in a hierarchical structure.

Another example of the use of trees is the classification of topics that make up a subject. One way that the subjects of computer science might be categorized is presented in *Computing Reviews* (1982). It provides an outline of the way computer science subjects can be organized in order to help you locate books and articles by subject; it is called the "CR Classification Tree." Figure 5.7 is a portion of the tree that shows how data structures and trees fit into the larger scheme of things.

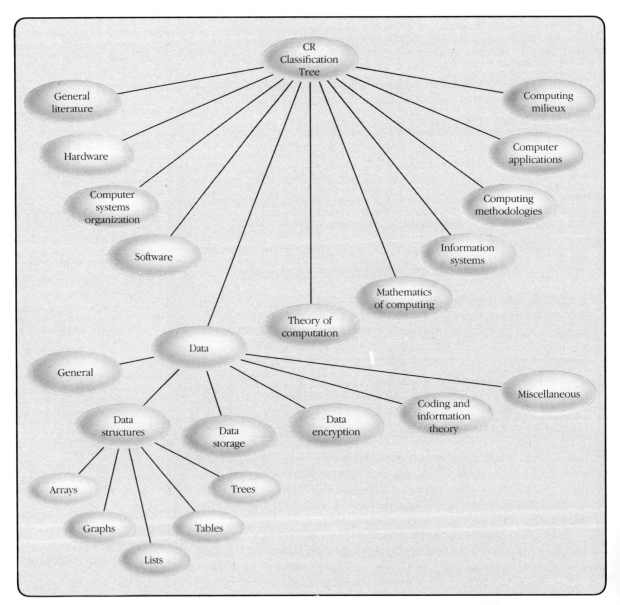

Figure 5.7   A CR Classification Tree of topics in computer science. (*Computing Reviews*, 1982)

We can contrast the basic relationships between nodes in a tree with the corresponding relationships between elements in a linear data structure. Compare Figures 5.5 and 5.6. Observe that besides terminology, the only basic difference between trees and linear data structures is the number of successors that an element (or node) is permitted to have.

The tree described in Figure 5.6 is oriented by its root node. Since it may not be obvious why this is the case, we will discuss the point further. First, we need some terminology.

For each node, let there be an edge between that node and each of its successors. There are no other edges. (There are other relationships among nodes, but we will not represent them with edges.) All of the figures above show both nodes and edges.

A **simple path** is a sequence of nodes—$n1, n2, \ldots, nk$—such that the nodes are all distinct and such that there is an edge between each pair of nodes—$(n1, n2), (n2, n3), \ldots, (n[k-1], nk)$. This simple path is said to be from node $n1$ to node nk. The **path length** of any simple path is equal to the number of nodes it contains, which is one greater than the number of edges. (In some texts the path length is the number of edges.)

Each node in an oriented tree is connected to the root node by a unique simple path. In Figure 5.7, "Trees" is connected to "CR Classification Tree" by the following path: CR Classification Tree, Data, Data structures, Trees. In Figure 5.8, node H is connected to the root node by the path A, D, H (whose path length is three). Node I is connected to the root node by the path A, C, G, I (whose path length is four). Every edge in the tree participates in at least one such path. (See Figure 5.9.)

The direction associated with each edge is the direction that is away from the root and toward the leaf node of any path of which it is a member. If an edge participates in several paths, the direction assigned is the same in every case, so the direction of an edge is well defined. Normally these directions are not explicitly shown, since once the root node is identified they are easy to determine.

Much of the terminology used to describe trees is borrowed from genealogy. Genealogy describes the hierarchical relationships between a person and his or her ancestors and descendants. Because these relationships are hierarchical, the terms used to describe them can be directly applied to trees.

The relationship between a node and its successors is described as a **parent–child relationship.** The predecessor of a node is said to be that node's **parent.** A successor of a node is said to be that node's **child.** In a tree, every node except the root node has a unique parent. A node that has no children is called a **leaf node.** Every node that is not a leaf node has at least one child. Two nodes that have the same parent are said to be **siblings.**

The tree in Figure 5.10 has six leaf nodes; K is the root node; E is the parent of both B and J; and J is the parent of G. The children of S are P and V, and the child of Z is W. Since N and Q have a common parent, they are siblings.

Our next objective is to generalize the terms "parent" and "child" so as to provide definitions of the terms "ancestor" and "descendant". Our intuition

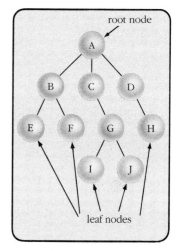

Figure 5.8

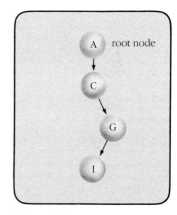

Figure 5.9
The unique simple path from the root node to the node containing I, with directions indicated by arrowheads. (From Figure 5.8.)

In Figure 5.10, the ancestors of J are K and E. The ancestors of M are K, S, P, and N. The root node is the only node that has no ancestors.

The descendants of P are M, N, and Q. The descendants of V are T, W, and Z. The leaf nodes have no descendants.

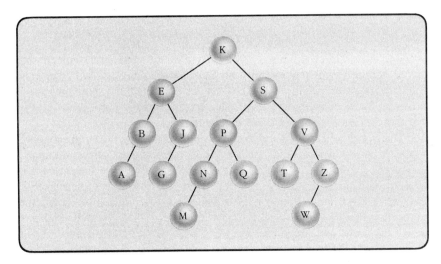

Figure 5.10

tells us that the ancestors of a node consist of its parent, the parent of its parent, and so on. However, "and so on" is not a very satisfactory phrase to include in a definition. There are a number of approaches that we could take to make the definition more precise, and from them we choose a recursive one. This is done because, as will become more apparent, recursion is a very important tool when dealing with trees.

First, we will define ***ancestors.*** Let A be any node in a tree. If A is the root node, then it has no ancestors. Otherwise, the parent of A and all the ancestors of the parent of A are ancestors of A. Node A has no other ancestors. We could also have defined the ancestors of a node as those nodes that lie on the unique simple path between the given node and the root of the tree.

Which are the ***descendants*** of a node? Try to define this term—both intuitively and formally—before reading on.

Let D be any node in a tree. If D is a leaf node then it has no descendants. Otherwise, each child of D and all the descendants of each child of D are descendants of D. Node D has no other descendants.

Given any node in a tree, that node together with all of its descendants turns out to be a particularly important subset of a tree, called a ***subtree.*** If T is any tree, a subtree of T is any node in T, say S, together with all of the descendants of S.

Let S be any node in a tree. To visualize either the descendants of S or the subtree whose root is S, remove the edge of the tree between S and its parent. All the nodes that are still connected to S are S's descendants. Together with S, this set of descendants forms a subtree of the original tree and has the root node S. Figure 5.11 is an illustration of a subtree of Figure 5.10.

We have described trees by using pictures, in terms of the relationships between their nodes, and by using examples. We have yet to specify what we mean by oriented trees and ordered trees. We have deferred doing so because the usual definitions of these terms are recursive. It seems that these definitions are more palatable if the basic idea of a tree has already been introduced.

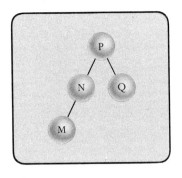

Figure 5.11
A subtree whose root node is P. It is formed from Figure 5.10 by disconnecting P from its parent.

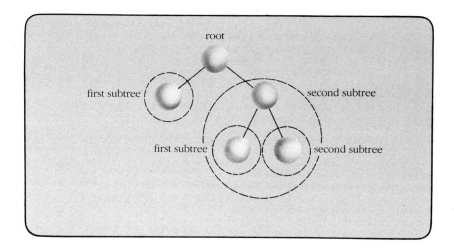

Figure 5.12
Illustration of an ordered tree.
In this simple example the first
subtree is the subtree drawn to
the left of its parent, and the
second subtree is drawn to the
right of its parent.

We will begin with a ***recursive definition*** of an oriented tree (that is, a definition in which oriented tree is defined in terms of itself).

An ***oriented tree*** contains a finite collection of one or more nodes. One of these nodes is called the root node. The remaining nodes, if any, are partitioned into disjoint sets, each of which is an oriented tree.

Recursive definition of an oriented tree.

The selection of a unique root node determines the orientation of each edge in the tree. That is why a tree with a designated root node is called an oriented tree. [See Standish (1980) and Knuth (1973a) for a discussion of the difference between a tree and an oriented tree.]

If we start with an oriented tree and add an ordering among the subtrees of each (and every) node the result is an ordered tree. An ***ordered tree*** contains a finite collection of one or more nodes. One of the nodes is called the root node. The remaining nodes, if any, are partitioned into m disjoint sets, $T_1, T_2, \ldots, T_m$, which are ordered by their subscripts, and each of them is an ordered tree. Figure 5.12 shows an example of an ordered tree.

Recursive definition of an ordered tree.

Observe that each of the sets, $T_1, T_2, \ldots, T_m$, in the above definition is not only an ordered tree in its own right, but it is also a subtree of the original tree. The term "ordered" is appropriate since the subtrees are ordered by their subscript values. That is, $T_j \leq T_k$ if $j \leq k$. An ordered tree is an oriented tree because it has a unique root node.

There are many techniques that can be used to order the subtrees of a node. If a node has k subtrees, then there are k factorial ($k!$) distinct ways of ordering them. In computer science the subtrees of a node are usually ordered (whether you want them to be or not) because of the way nodes are represented. It is this implicit ordering, as a by-product of the way nodes are represented, that makes ordered trees the natural focus of study in computer science.

Now that we have defined ordered and oriented trees, we will introduce a few more terms that will be used throughout Chapter 5.

A major difference between linear structures and trees exists when we talk about ***height.*** Let us define the height of a linear data structure containing n elements to be n. What is the height of a tree? To determine the height it is helpful to introduce the notion of ***level.*** Each node in a tree is at a particular

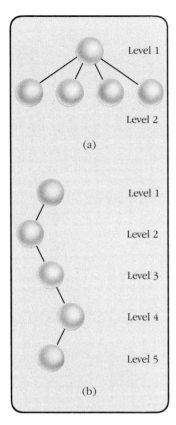

Figure 5.13
Levels of trees: (a) A tree of height 2. (b) A tree of height 5.

level in that tree. The root node is assigned level 1, and each child has a level that is one greater than the level of its parent. Figure 5.13 shows the levels associated with two trees.

The height of a tree is the maximum level associated with any of its nodes. The tree in Figure 5.7 contains many nodes and has a height of 4; the tree in Figure 5.8 contains 10 nodes and has a height of 4; and the tree in Figure 5.10 contains 15 nodes and has a height of 5.

An alternate definition of height can be given in terms of path length. Recall that the length of a path is the number of nodes that it contains. The height of an oriented tree is the path length of the longest simple path that begins at its root node.

The final topic of this section is a philosophical one. If you look back at the illustrations of the trees presented so far you will discover that in each case the root node is at the top of the illustration and the tree "grows" downward. There is certainly no horticultural justification for this (unless you think of a hanging vine); after all, the roots of real trees are at the bottom and the leaves are at the top. Why then do we draw the root at the top? The answer is simple—tradition!

In most texts and articles about trees the illustrations are all oriented so that the root is at the top. We will usually follow this tradition, but there are times when it is uncomfortable to do so. An important case of this occurs when we discuss moving up or down the edges of a tree between a child and its parent. It is contrary to intuition to move up in a tree—toward the root—and have the effect be to decrease the level.

This section of the text mainly introduced new terminology. We defined ordered and oriented trees and contrasted trees with linear data structures. We defined terms including root node, leaf node, parent, child, ancestor, descendant, simple path, path length, height, and level. We also began to make use of recursion in dealing with trees. All of the remaining sections of Chapter 5 will use the ideas and notation you learned in this section.

Exercises 5.2

1. Describe the following terms in your own words:

node	ancestor	siblings	parent
simple path	edge	ordered tree	descendant
child	path length	oriented tree	height

2. What are the similarities between a linear data structure and a hierarchical data structure? What are the differences?

3. Does Figure 5.6 describe an oriented tree? An ordered tree? Explain your answer.

4. Figure 5.14 shows a number of nodes connected by edges. The edges, as shown, have no orientation. Choosing any node as the root node orients the tree in the sense that it implies a direction or orientation for each edge. Since there are six nodes, there are six distinct oriented trees—one for each possible root node. Draw all six of these trees. Include arrowheads to show the orientation of each edge.

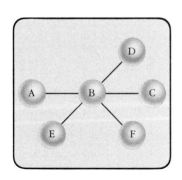

Figure 5.14

5. Figure 5.15 shows an oriented tree. There are 12 distinct ways to order the subtrees of this tree, and hence 12 possible distinct ordered trees. Show all of them.

6. Consider the tree shown in Figure 5.8.
   a. What is its height?
   b. What are its leaf nodes?
   c. What is the unique simple path from the root node to each of the leaf nodes? What is the path length of each of these paths?

7. The following algorithm finds all the ancestors of a node and pushes a pointer to each of them on a stack. The pointer to the node that is the root of the tree is called *treeRoot*. Assume that procedures *Push* and *FindParent* are provided. Replace procedure *Ancestor* with a recursive procedure that does the same thing.

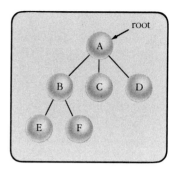

Figure 5.15

```
PROCEDURE Ancestor (p: pointer);
BEGIN
    WHILE p # treeRoot DO
        FindParent(p);
        Push(p)
    END
END Ancestor;
```

8. Each of the following statements is either true or false. If a statement is true, explain why it is true. If it is false, give a specific example that shows that it is false.
   a. Every oriented tree is an ordered tree.
   b. Every ordered tree is an oriented tree.
   c. The root node is the only node in an oriented tree that has no ancestors.
   d. Suppose that an oriented tree contains n nodes and that each node has either two subtrees or zero subtrees. The number of leaf nodes is at least n DIV 2.
   e. Suppose that an oriented tree contains n nodes and that each node has at most two subtrees. The number of leaf nodes is at least n DIV 2.

5.3 Abstract Binary Tree

5.3.1 Structure

A **binary tree,** like an oriented tree or an ordered tree, contains nodes and edges. It has the following important characteristics:

1. Each node can have at most two subtrees—and therefore at most two children.
2. Each subtree is identified as being either the **left subtree** or the **right subtree** of its parent.
3. It may be empty.

We will continue the convention of drawing the root node at the top of each illustration and letting the tree grow downward. Therefore, the direction of each edge, from parent to child, will be downward. Figure 5.16 shows a binary tree.

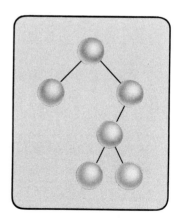

Figure 5.16
A binary tree.

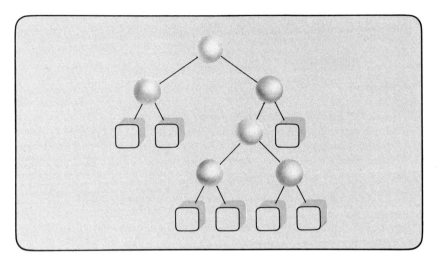

Figure 5.17   The extended binary tree corresponding to the tree in Figure 5.16.

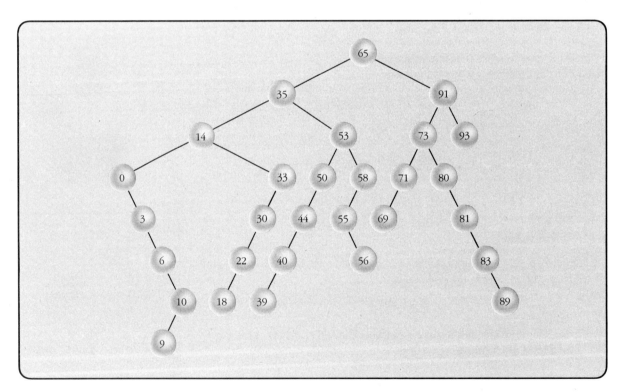

Figure 5.18   A binary tree in which each node contains an integer. This binary tree contains 29 nodes and is of height 8. The longest simple path, which starts at the root, is 65, 35, 14, 0, 3, 6, 10, 9. The length of this path is 8. (This tree was "drawn" by the tree-printing algorithm in Section 5.8.)

Since we will distinguish between the left subtree and the right subtree of each node, our illustrations must place the root of each left subtree to the left of its parent and the root of each right subtree to the right of its parent.

A leaf node in a binary tree has no children, and is therefore the parent of two empty subtrees. A node with one child is also the parent of one empty subtree. It is sometimes helpful to show the empty subtrees and we use the symbol ▢ for that purpose. Figure 5.17 shows the empty subtrees for the tree in Figure 5.16.

Figure 5.18 shows a binary tree in which each node contains a single integer. The tree contains quite a few more nodes than any of the examples presented so far. We want to give you at least some idea about the size and shape of trees that would be big enough to be worth storing in a computer.

Figure 5.19 shows a binary tree each of whose nodes contains a name (or in one case two names), a year, and the title of a presentation. The individuals are all recipients of the ACM Turing Award for distinguished contributions to com-

The empty subtrees that take the place of missing children in a tree are referred to as **external nodes,** and a tree together with its external nodes is called an **extended tree.**

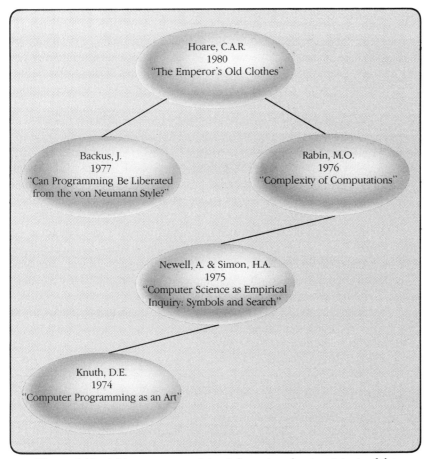

Figure 5.19   A binary tree containing information about recipients of the ACM Turing Award. Note that each element in a node contains three items.

$\{[(a + b) \times c] + 7\}$
$(a + b) \times (c + 7)$

Figure 5.20

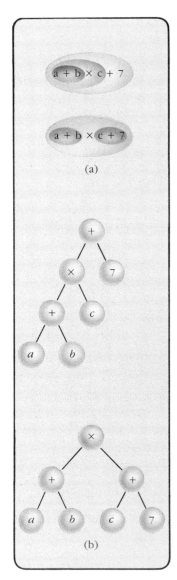

(a)

(b)

Figure 5.21
(a) A nested view of the expressions in Figure 5.20. (b) The expressions of Figure 5.20 in binary trees.

puter science. The year is the year in which the award was presented, and the title is the title of the presentation made by the recipient(s) at the awards ceremony. This example is intended to stress the fact that although the nodes in a binary tree will normally contain a single element, each element frequently contains several items. In Figure 5.19, page 203, each element contains three items.

Now that you have seen an example of a tree in which each node contains several items, we will discuss trees in which each node contains a single item. This will be done for two reasons. First, it is much easier to discuss and present figures for trees whose node content is simple. Second, a tree structure can be illustrated just as well with trees whose nodes contain a single item as it can with trees whose nodes contain many items.

The final example of this section illustrates the use of binary trees to store nested information. Figure 5.20 shows two simple algebraic expressions. Both expressions are completely grouped in the sense that no precedence rules are needed in order to evaluate them unambiguously. The grouping symbols provide nesting, or hierarchical, information. They prescribe the order in which the terms are to be evaluated.

Figure 5.21 shows two alternate ways of presenting the expressions in Figure 5.20. Figure 5.21(a) emphasizes the nesting of operations implied by the expressions. Figure 5.21(b) shows how this nesting can be represented by binary trees. The point is that if we store the components of these expressions in trees, we can use the tree structure to provide the same information supplied by the grouping symbols or the nesting.

The trees shown in Figure 5.21(b) are examples of what we will call **expression trees.** They are closely related to **parse trees,** which are frequently generated by compilers as part of the process of evaluating expressions. The process of converting expressions into parse trees is called (what else!) parsing. This process is an important part of a course about compilers. We will not discuss expression trees in this chapter, but we will explore the subject further in the exercises.

We have discussed the structure of a binary tree. We have seen that not only is each node in a binary tree limited to having at most two subtrees, but each subtree must be labeled as either the left or the right subtree. This label is required even if there is only one subtree. In addition, a binary tree can be empty, whereas an ordered tree cannot be.

To summarize the binary tree structure and to provide a comparison with the earlier recursive definition of an ordered tree, we conclude this section with a recursive definition of a binary tree.

Recursive Definition of a Binary Tree

A binary tree either is empty or is a node, called the root node, together with two binary trees. These two binary trees are disjoint from each other and from the root node and are called the left and right subtrees of the root.

5.3.2 Specification and Operations

We will complete the specification of an abstract binary tree by presenting a collection of operations. Our point of view, once again, is that the set of operations in an abstract data structure is described from a logical point of view. There is no concern for representation and implementation details. All a programmer would need to know in order to use a module that implements an abstract data structure is given in its specification. (The software designer, in order to make informed design decisions, would need to understand representation, implementation, and performance issues.)

Before discussing specific operations, we need to describe the framework of our software module. We will start with a binary tree whose structure has already been described. In order to protect the integrity of the binary tree structure, we will limit the ways in which the user can access it. An input to our binary tree module always consists of an operation and a list of parameters. The operation must be one of the operations supported by our binary tree module. The parameter list, which may be empty, is specified by the selected operation. Specification 5.1 for a binary tree and a capsule summary in Figure 5.22 follow.

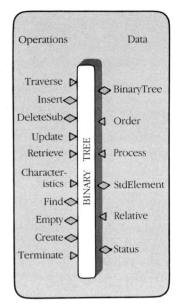

Figure 5.22
A capsule-like view of the binary tree.

Specification 5.1   Binary Trees

DEFINITION MODULE BinaryTrees;

(* **Elements:** The elements of a binary tree are nodes. We will assume that each node contains one standard element. A node may contain other items. *)

FROM StdTypes **IMPORT** StdElement;

(* **Structure:** A binary tree either is empty or is a node, called the root node, together with two binary trees. These two binary trees are disjoint from each other and from the root node and are called the left and right subtrees of the root node.

Note that a binary tree has a hierarchical structure. There is (unless the tree is empty) a unique root node. Each node (except the root) has a unique parent. Each node has zero, one, or two children. A child is designated as either the left or right child of its parent. *)

(* **Domain:** The number of nodes in a binary tree is bounded. *)

EXPORT QUALIFIED BinaryTree, Order, Relative, Status, ProcElt, Traverse,
                 Insert, DeleteSub, Update, Retrieve, Characteristics,
                 Find, Empty, Create, Terminate;

continued

Specification 5.1, continued

```
    TYPE BinaryTree;              (* Opaque data type used to represent a binary tree. *)

        Order    = (preOrder, inOrder, postOrder);
        Relative = (leftChild, rightChild, root, parent);
        Status   = RECORD                          (* Several characteristics of   *)
                        size   : CARDINAL;          (* a binary tree: size, height, *)
                        height : CARDINAL;          (* and average path length.     *)
                        avePath: REAL
                   END;

        ProcElt  = PROCEDURE (StdElement, CARDINAL);
```

(* **Operations**: If the binary tree is not empty then one node is
    designated the current node. We use BT-pre and current-pre in the
    postcondition to refer, respectively, to the binary tree and the
    current node in the binary tree prior to the operation. *)

PROCEDURE Traverse (BT: BinaryTree; ord: Order; proc: ProcElt);
(* **pre** − BT is not empty.
    post − Each element in the tree has been processed exactly once by
            the user-supplied procedure proc. The order in which nodes
            were processed depends on the value of ord as follows:

    case ord of
        preOrder : Each node is processed before any node in either
                   of its subtrees.
        inOrder : Each node is processed after all nodes in its left
                   subtree and before any node in its right subtree.
        postOrder: Each node is processed after all nodes in both of
                   its subtrees. *)

PROCEDURE Insert (**VAR** BT: BinaryTree; e: StdElement; rel: Relative): BOOLEAN;
(* **pre** − Either rel = root and BT is empty or rel # root and BT
            is not empty.
    post − Insert is false if (1) BT-pre has reached its maximum allowable
            size, (2) rel = parent, (3) rel = leftChild and current-pre has
            a left child, or (4) rel = rightChild and current-pre has a
            right child. Otherwise, Insert is true and e is the current
            element in BT as described below.

    case rel of
        root   : Element e is the element in the root of the tree.
        leftChild : Element e is the left child of current-pre.
        rightChild: Element e is the right child of current-pre. *)

PROCEDURE DeleteSub (**VAR** BT: BinaryTree): BOOLEAN;
(* **pre** − BT is not empty.
    post − If this operation fails then DeleteSub is false. Otherwise,
            DeleteSub is true and if current-pre is the root of BT-pre
            then BT is an empty binary tree, else the subtree of current-pre
            is not in BT, and the root node is the current node. *)

continued

```
PROCEDURE Update (VAR BT: BinaryTree; e: StdElement);
(* pre  - BT is not empty.
   post - The current node contains e. *)

PROCEDURE Retrieve (BT: BinaryTree; VAR e: StdElement);
(* pre  - BT is not empty.
   post - Element e is the value of the element in the current node. *)

PROCEDURE Characteristics (BT: BinaryTree; VAR st: Status);
(* post - Record st contains the size, height, and average path
          length of BT. *)

PROCEDURE Find (VAR BT: BinaryTree; rel: Relative): BOOLEAN;
(* pre  - BT is not empty.
   post - The current node of BT is determined by the value of rel as
          follows:

      case rel of
          root:       The root node is the current node.
          leftChild:  If current-pre had a left child then it is the
                      current node and Find is true else Find is false.
          rightChild: If current-pre had a right child then it is the
                      current node and Find is true else Find is false.
          parent:     If current-pre had a parent then it is the current
                      node and Find is true else Find is false. *)

PROCEDURE Empty (BT: BinaryTree): BOOLEAN;
(* post - If BT contains zero nodes then Empty is true else Empty
          is false. *)

PROCEDURE Create (VAR BT: BinaryTree): BOOLEAN;
(* post - If a binary tree can be created then BT is an empty
          binary tree and Create is true else Create is false. *)

PROCEDURE Terminate (VAR BT: BinaryTree);
(* post - BT does not exist. *)

END BinaryTrees.
```

Each of the operations in the specification is described in detail below.

Many of the operations depend on a ***current node,*** which always exists if the tree is not empty (see Figure 5.23). The current node may be set by the operations *Insert, DeleteSub,* and *Find.* The *Find* operation (or at least repeated applications of the *Find* operation) allows the user to set any node as the current node. The element contained in the current node is called the ***current element.***

The *Create* operation creates an empty binary tree. It must be invoked before any other operation in the module. Logically, it is the same as the *Create* operation for any of the modules described in this text.

Operation *Terminate* deletes the binary tree.

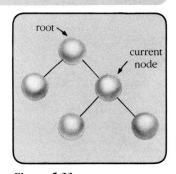

Figure 5.23
Every tree, except the empty tree, has a current node.

IF the list is not empty
   THEN find the first node
      REPEAT
         process the current
         node; find the next
         node
      UNTIL there are no more
      nodes
END

Figure 5.24
A traversal algorithm for a linear list.

• **Tree traversal**

We will begin our study of tree traversal by examining the traversal of a list. For uniformity of terminology let us suppose that the objects that make up the list are called nodes. A list traversal algorithm is shown in Figure 5.24. It performs a relatively high-level operation that is based on these more primitive operations:

1. Find the first node.
2. Find the next node.
3. Determine when there are no more nodes.
4. Process the current node.

To **process** the current node means to perform some simple operation such as printing the content of the node or updating the value of the element it contains. The important point is that processing the current node is not affected by the structure in which that node is placed. It makes no difference whether the node is part of a tree, a graph, or a list. Therefore, we turn our attention to the other primitive operations in which the structure does make a difference.

The operations *find* the first node and *find* the next node have obvious and unambiguous meanings for a list. Similarly, we know that there are no more nodes in a list when we find a node that has no successor.

What is the first node in a tree? Is it the root node? In a tree, what does it mean to *find* the next node? In a tree, how do we determine that there are no more nodes?

Before attempting to answer these specific questions about trees, let us abstract (and thereby simplify) the idea of traversal.

> To **traverse** a finite collection of objects means to process each object in the collection exactly once.

IF the list is not empty
   THEN find the last node
      REPEAT
         process the current
         node; find the prior
         node
      UNTIL there are no more
      nodes
END

Figure 5.25
Another traversal algorithm for a linear list.

We have seen one algorithm for traversing a list. A second one is shown in Figure 5.25. The algorithm in Figure 5.24 processes the nodes in a first-to-last order. The algorithm in Figure 5.25 reverses the order of processing and proceeds last to first. Based on the above definition, they both carry out a genuine traversal of any list.

The two list traversal algorithms are the same in that they both traverse a finite collection of objects. They differ in the order in which the nodes are traversed. An obvious question is this: In how many distinct orders can a collection of n objects be traversed? The answer is n factorial ($n!$); and the answer is the same no matter what structure is used to relate the objects. If a list contains n nodes, then that list can be traversed in n factorial distinct orders. If a tree contains n nodes, then that tree can be traversed in n factorial distinct orders.

There are two natural traversal orders for a list, and we have seen algorithms for both of them. The order in which these algorithms process the nodes depends on the two basic operations, *find* the next node and *find* the prior node.

There are three natural traversal orders for a binary tree. We will now describe them. We will give two descriptions of **binary tree traversal.** One of the descriptions is heuristic and involves an imaginary person called a **tree observer.** Figure 5.26 shows an extended binary tree. The dashed line shows the path of the tree observer as he or she "observes" the tree; the arrowheads indicate the tree observer's direction. Recall that ☐ illustrates an empty subtree.

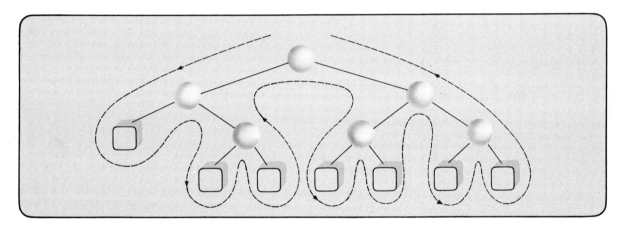

Figure 5.26 Path of the tree observer.

The order of observation for any node, relative to its two subtrees, is as follows:

1. The node is observed.
2. All the nodes in the left subtree of the node are observed.
3. The node is observed for the second time.
4. All the nodes in the right subtree of the node are observed.
5. The node is observed for the third and final time.

The three binary tree traversal algorithms that we describe are called **preorder, inorder,** and **postorder** traversal.

1. During a preorder traversal, each node is processed during step 1. That is, each node is processed the first time it is observed by the tree observer. Stated another way, each node is processed before any node in either of its subtrees.

2. During an inorder traversal, each node is processed during step 3. It is processed the second time it is observed by the tree observer. That is, each node is processed after all the nodes in its left subtree but before any of the nodes in its right subtree.

During a preorder traversal each node is processed before any node in either of its subtrees.

During an inorder traversal each node is processed after all nodes in its left subtree but before any node in its right subtree.

During a postorder traversal each node is processed after all nodes in both of its subtrees.

3. During a postorder traversal, each node is processed during step 5. It is processed the third time it is observed by the tree observer. That is, each node is processed after all nodes in both of its subtrees.

To illustrate the traversal process, Figure 5.27 shows three copies of the same binary tree. Each node contains an integer that shows the processing order for that node. From left to right, the trees illustrate preorder, inorder, postorder traversal.

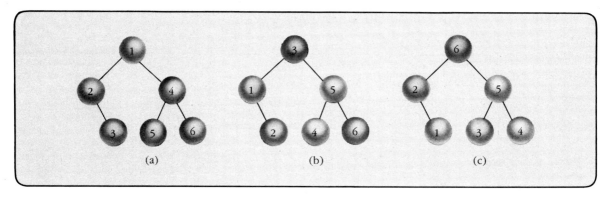

(a)   (b)   (c)

Figure 5.27   Traversal process. Node processing order: (a) preorder; (b) inorder; (c) postorder.

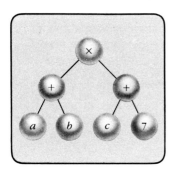

Figure 5.28

As a second example consider the binary tree shown in Figure 5.21(b). It is repeated here as Figure 5.28 for easy reference. The order in which the nodes of that tree are processed during our three traversal processes is

Preorder traversal $\times$, $+$, a, b, $+$, c, 7
Inorder traversal a, $+$, b, $\times$, c, $+$, 7
Postorder traversal a, b, $+$, c, 7, $+$, $\times$

It is noteworthy that a postorder traversal processes the nodes in an order that is particularly conducive to the evaluation of the original expression (see Figure 5.20). Such an algorithm is discussed in Exercise 5.3.2, 4.

We have now completed our introduction to binary tree traversal. Each of the binary tree implementations discussed in this chapter offers all three traversal operations—preorder, inorder, and postorder. Two parameters are required for each of these operations:

1. The name of a procedure that processes each of the nodes during the traversal. Each of the traversal operations passes the tree nodes, in the proper order, to a procedure supplied by the user for processing.
2. The order (preorder, inorder, or postorder) of the traversal.

The discussion of binary tree traversal has been lengthy, and if you are seeing this material for the first time it may seem complex. It would be easy to get the impression that implementation of tree traversal is complicated. It is not. The recursive implementation of tree traversal is very simple and uses algorithms that are among the most elegant in computer science.

• Operations other than traversal

The *Find* operation changes the current node according to the value of an order parameter, which may be root, leftChild, rightChild, or parent. The operation fails if the designated relative does not exist.

The *Retrieve* operation returns the content of the current node, and *Update* replaces the content of the current node with user-specified values.

The *Insert* operation adds an element to the tree in a designated position. The position (*root, leftChild,* or *rightChild*) is given by the user. In this section adding a root node is limited to an empty tree. This is a restricted version of an important operation.

Many people wonder, when encountering it for the first time, about the use of an operation that adds a new root. Its practical importance is considerable. We will use this operation in the construction of B-trees (Section 5.9) and the construction of Huffman codes (Chapter 8). In the abstract data structure we are currently discussing, it is the only operation that will add a node to an empty tree. Without it we cannot get started.

Operation *DeleteSub* causes the current node and all of its descendants to be removed from the tree. This may seem rather drastic since if a node is not a leaf node the only way to get rid of it is to delete the entire subtree of which it is the root. This does make sense in cases in which deletion of a parent implies deletion of all its descendants. Figure 5.29 provides an example of this. Deletion of a subject area requires deletion of all other subjects that represent subdivisions of that area. Operation *DeleteSub* is what is needed for deletions from such a tree.

In a list we can delete a node by connecting its predecessor to its successor. In a binary tree a node may have only one child. If so, that node can be deleted by attaching its parent to that child. However, the node to be deleted may have two children. Attaching both of them to the parent of the node being deleted may cause that node to have three children. Stated another way, deleting a node that has two subtrees from a binary tree leaves one subtree with no place to be attached. This is an inherent problem with deletion from hierarchical structures. We will see one way to work around it in Section 5.4 and another in Section 5.9. In the meantime we will delete entire subtrees, which in some cases is the appropriate thing to do.

Operation *Characteristics* returns three values.

1. The number of nodes in the tree (its size)
2. The height of the tree
3. The average path length between the root node and a node in the tree

We will refer to these three values as the **Status** of the tree. Figure 5.30 shows the status of three example trees.

From Section 4.2.2 we know that the average path length from the head

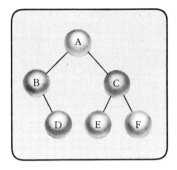

Figure 5.29
Node B is easily deleted by making D the left child of A. The deletion of C, without removing its entire subtree, is more complicated. This complication is inherent in hierarchical structures.

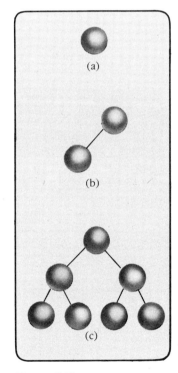

Figure 5.30
The value of status for several example trees. (a) Size = 1, height = 1, average path length = 1. (b) Size = 2, height = 2, average path length = $(1+2)/2$. (c) Size = 7, height = 3, average path length = $17/7$.

of a list to any other element in the list is $(n + 1)/2$. It is interesting to speculate about the corresponding value for binary trees. This question is addressed in Section 5.5. It turns out that, in most cases, the average path length for a binary tree is $O(\log_2 n)$. This is one of the reasons why binary trees are useful data structures.

In summary, the binary tree operations are intended to permit the user to *Insert, Delete, Update,* and *Retrieve* at any point in the tree. They also allow users to *Traverse* the tree and measure its *Characteristics.* We can think of the operations as being divided into four groups. The first group includes the basic operations *Traverse, Insert, DeleteSub, Update, Retrieve,* and *Characteristics.* The second group contains a single operation, *Find,* which permits any node in the tree to be designated as the current node. The third group also contains a single operation, *Empty,* which permits the user to test the preconditions. The final group contains the operations *Create* and *Terminate.*

Exercises 5.3.2

1. Explain the following terms in your own words:

binary tree	traverse
internal node	postorder traversal
inorder traversal	external node
extended tree	preorder traversal

2. Each of the following statements is true or false. If true explain why. If false give an example to demonstrate that it is false.
   a. A binary tree that is not empty is an oriented tree.
   b. A binary tree that is not empty is an ordered tree.
3. Show how a binary tree might be used to represent the relationships between one person and all of that person's ancestors. Sketch the tree for yourself and your ancestors. What person is in the root node of the tree?
4. Consider the expression tree shown in Figure 5.31. Suppose that the tree is traversed in postorder and that processing a node during traversal is as follows:

```
IF  the node contains a variable identifier
    THEN push that identifier's value onto the stack
    ELSE the node contains an operator.  Apply the
         operator to the top two values on the stack
         to produce a new value.   Push the new value
         onto the stack.
END
```

At the conclusion of the traversal, the value of the expression will be on top of the stack. Table 5.1 shows the stack content during the traversal.
   a. Complete Table 5.1.
   b. Construct an expression tree and a table corresponding to the above for the expression $[a + (b \times c \times d)]/x$.

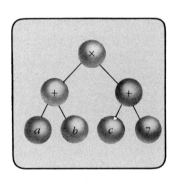

Figure 5.31

TABLE 5.1

After processing the node whose content is	The content of the stack is top ⟵⟶ bottom
a	*a*
b	*b, a*
+	*a* + *b*
c	*c, a* + *b*
7	7, *c, a* + *b*
+	
×	

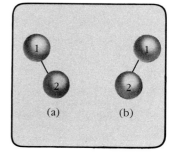

Figure 5.32
(a) Inorder sequence 1, 2.
(b) Inorder sequence 2, 1.

5. Consider a binary tree containing n nodes whose elements are the integers 1, 2, ..., n.
   a. Consider all permutations of the first n integers; in each case attempt to construct a binary tree whose preorder sequence is 1, 2, ..., n and whose inorder sequence is the permutation.

   For $n = 2$ each of the 2 factorial (2!) trees can be constructed and are shown in Figure 5.32. For $n = 3$ you will only be able to construct trees for five of the six permutations.
   b. If the preorder sequence is 1, 2, 3, 4, 5 and the postorder sequence is 4, 2, 1, 3, 5 then (if there is such a tree) its root node must be 1, the left subtree must contain 2 and 4, and the right subtree must contain 3 and 5. (Why?)

   This tree cannot be constructed because 3 precedes 4 in preorder, whereas 4 is in the left subtree of 1 and 3 is in the right subtree of 1.

   Generalize the above discussion. If the preorder sequence is 1, 2, ..., n and the inorder sequence is $i_1, i_2, ..., i_n$, then describe the circumstances under which a tree with these sequences cannot be constructed.
6. Do the following:
   a. Draw the binary tree containing n nodes whose preorder sequence is the same as its inorder sequence.
   b. Draw the binary tree containing n nodes whose inorder sequence is the same as its postorder sequence.
   c. Explain why a binary tree with more than one node cannot have the same preorder and postorder sequence.
7. Each of the following statements is either true or false. If true, explain why. If false, construct an example that shows that it is false.
   a. x is a descendant of y if and only if y precedes x in preorder and x precedes y in postorder.
   b. x is a descendant of y if and only if y precedes x in preorder and x precedes y in inorder.
   c. If x and y are leaf nodes their order is the same in
      i. Preorder and inorder
      ii. Inorder and postorder
      iii. Preorder and postorder
8. There are many other traversal algorithms. Consider the following seven operations:
   a. Process the root.
   b. Process the left child.
   c. Process the right child.

d. Traverse the left subtree of the left child.

e. Traverse the right subtree of the left child.

f. Traverse the left subtree of the right child.

g. Traverse the right subtree of the right child.

These operations can be arranged in 7 factorial (5040) ways. Show how to arrange these seven operations for the three natural traversal orders.

An important traversal order, called level order, processes the nodes as follows:

```
IF the tree is not empty
   THEN current level := 1
        REPEAT
            process all nodes at the current level;
            increment the current level
        UNTIL there are no nodes at the current level
END
```

Is it possible to implement level-order processing using some permutation of the seven operations given above? If so show how. If not, explain why not.

9. Write the specifications for operation

```
FindNext(ord: order);
```

which moves the cursor from its input position to its successor determined by the value of ord.

10. Let p_1 and p_2 be pointers to two binary trees. Write the specifications for an operation that creates a new binary tree with e: StdElement in the root node and with the trees pointed at by p_1 and p_2 as the left and right subtrees.

5.3.3 Linked Representation and Implementation

Figure 5.33 (given below) shows one representation for a binary tree.

Each node contains one element and two pointers (see Figure 5.34). The element is the standard element described in Section 1.4.1 and used through-

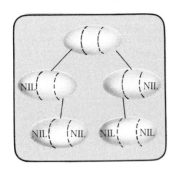

Figure 5.34
Illustration of a linked representation of a binary tree. Edges are represented by storing two pointers in each node. The pointer value NIL indicates an empty subtree.

```
TYPE NodePtr = POINTER TO Node;      (* Pointer to a node *)
                                     (* of a binary tree. *)
     Node     = RECORD               (* Node of a binary tree. *)
                    elt       : StdElement;
                    left,right: NodePtr        (* Pointers *)
                END;                           (* to node's *)
                                               (* children. *)
     BinaryTree = POINTER TO BTtype;  (* Binary tree data *)
                                      (* type. *)
     BTtype   = RECORD
                    treeRoot: NodePtr;  (* Root of tree. *)
                    current : NodePtr   (* Current node. *)
                END;
```

Figure 5.33

out this text. The pointers provide access to the node's children. They are a particular implementation, using the Modula-2 data type POINTER, of the edges of a binary tree.

We will discuss node representations that differ in two respects from that shown in Figure 5.33. Think of the left and right pointers in 5.33 as identifiers that provide access to related nodes. We will consider different ways of representing such identifiers (pointers is one way), and we will consider additional identifiers. However, we will concentrate on the representation in Figure 5.33, which appears to be the most frequently used and the most "natural" approach.

In addition to identifiers for its children, a node may contain identifiers for other nodes such as its parent node, its sibling, its preorder, inorder, and postorder successor, and preorder, inorder, and postorder predecessor. Deciding which identifiers to include involves the classic space–time trade-off. Adding identifiers takes up more storage space but reduces the time required to access the nodes whose identifiers are added. Our binary tree modules will include two identifiers, one for each child. Each identifier will therefore correspond to an edge in the hierarchical structure of the tree. We will discuss adding other identifiers from time to time as appropriate.

Several of the operations in our binary tree module have relatively simple implementations and are not discussed in this section. Procedures for them are included in the binary tree module (Implementation Module 5.1).

Another group of operations is implemented recursively. Because of the importance of recursion in dealing with trees and because of the large number of operations that use recursion, we will discuss these operations first. We will begin with the most important, and perhaps the most interesting—*Traverse*.

The implementation of several operations is straightforward and is not discussed. Procedures for them are shown in Implementation Module 5.1. These operations are

> *Create*
> *Find*
> *Insert*
> *Retrieve*
> *Update*

The operations implemented using recursive traversal are

> *Clear*
> *Traverse*(any order)
> *DeleteSub*
> *Characteristics*

• Traversal procedures

Three recursive traversal procedures are shown in Figure 5.35.

```
PROCEDURE PreOrder(p: NodePtr);
BEGIN
    IF p # NIL
        THEN Process(p);
            PreOrder(p↑.left);
            PreOrder(p↑.right)
    END
END PreOrder;
```

```
PROCEDURE InOrder(p: NodePtr);
BEGIN
    IF p # NIL
        THEN InOrder(p↑.left);
            Process(p);
            InOrder(p↑.right)
    END
END InOrder;
```

```
PROCEDURE PostOrder(p: NodePtr);
BEGIN
    IF p # NIL
        THEN PostOrder(p↑.left);
            PostOrder(p↑.right);
            Process(p)
    END
END PostOrder;
```

Figure 5.35   Recursive traversal procedures.

The similarity and simplicity of these three procedures are striking. The burden of implementing tree traversal has been removed from the programmer and passed on to the compiler, which must translate the recursive calls into the nonrecursive machine language of the host computer. To illustrate this point, as well as to emphasize the importance of a stack in implementing recursion, we will discuss the nonrecursive implementation of both preorder and inorder traversal.

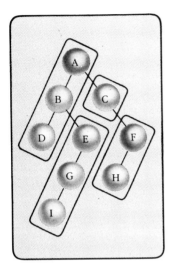

Figure 5.36
A binary tree with the left shells of nodes A, E, C, and F emphasized. Note that each left shell is a linear data structure.

We will assume that we have a *Stack* module that includes the operations *Push* and *Pop*. The operation *Push(Sp)* pushes the pointer variable *p* onto the top of stack *S*, and *Pop(Sp)* pops the pointer variable *p* off the top of stack *S*. (See Specification 3.1).

To help us describe our nonrecursive traversal procedures we will introduce the notion of the left and right shells of a node. Let N be any node in a binary tree. Then, N and the left child of N are members of the **left shell** of N. Any node in the left shell of N's left child is also in the left shell of N. The **right shell** of N is defined in a similar fashion. The left and right shells of a node combine to form its **shell**. Heuristically, the shell of the root of a subtree forms a roof over that subtree. See Figure 5.36 for an illustration.

Depending on the compiler, nonrecursive preorder traversal (Algorithm 5.1) may produce more efficient code than the recursive version. The difference is easy to see in the simple case of a preorder traversal. Execution of a recursive call typically involves pushing the address of the next instruction and the values of all appropriate variables on a stack. Thus, execution of the statement *PreOrder(p ↑ .right)* in Figure 5.35 may result in useless information being pushed onto the stack. The information is useless because there are no additional statements to be executed in that procedure. A smart compiler would recognize the situation and not save the information in such a case. The nonrecursive preorder traversal does not push the corresponding information onto the stack. To pursue this important point further, as well as to illustrate the involvement of a stack in the traversal process, consider the tree shown in Figure 5.37. It is an annotated tree because sequence numbers have been added to each node. The sequence numbers permit us to link the tree diagram with Figures 5.38 and 5.39, which show the content of the stack during traversal of the tree.

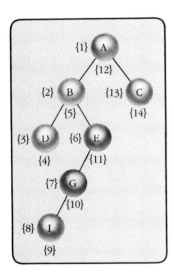

Figure 5.37
Each node has two labels, which are used to show the sequence of stack operations during traversal.

Figure 5.38   Stack content during nonrecursive preorder traversal of the tree in 5.37 using Algorithm 5.1.

Figure 5.39   Items pushed onto the stack as a result of the recursive calls preorder (p ↑ .left), preorder(p ↑ .right) during a recursive *PreOrder* traversal of the tree in Figure 5.37. Items pushed on the stack as a result of calls to procedure Process are, to reduce the clutter, not shown.

```
PROCEDURE PreOrder(p: NodePtr);
BEGIN                                    (* An instance of a stack, Stk,  *)
    WHILE p # NIL DO                     (* is used by this procedure.    *)
        Process(p);                      (* Process the left shell of a node-- *)
        IF p↑.right # NIL                (* saving pointers to any nonempty right *)
            THEN Push(Stk,p↑.right)      (* subtrees on the stack.        *)
        END;
        IF p↑.left # NIL                 (* When the end of a left shell is *)
            THEN  p := p↑.left           (* reached, pop the pointer of the *)
            ELSIF Empty(Stk) THEN RETURN (* most recent right subtree, and  *)
            ELSE  Pop(Stk,p)             (* process the left shell of its   *)
        END                              (* root.                          *)
    END
END PreOrder;
```

Algorithm 5.1   Nonrecursive preorder traversal of a binary tree.

Figures 5.38 and 5.39 are constructed as follows. We start with an empty stack, which is called the **current stack.** Each time a *Push* is executed the specified pointer is added to the top of the current stack, and the label for the node being processed is placed beside the stack. Each time a *Pop* is executed, we replace the current stack by a new stack formed by removing the top element. This new stack becomes the current stack. The purpose of this is to construct a figure that will help us understand the connection between tree traversal and stacks.

Figure 5.38 shows that three pointers were pushed onto the stack. We now repeat the process using the recursive preorder procedure shown in Figure 5.35. A **recursive procedure call** is similar to an ordinary subroutine call, so a return address must be saved. It is usually pushed onto the stack along with the values of all local parameters. Suppose, for illustration, that the address of the instruction following *PreOrder(p ↑ .left)* is *a1,* and the address of the instruction following *PreOrder(p ↑ .right)* is *a2.* Each stack entry will consist of a return address and a pointer value. The result is shown in Figure 5.39. Note that only items pushed onto the stack as a result of recursive calls are shown. We have ignored those stack operations associated with calls to procedure *Process.* Labels appended to the left of the stack correspond to those in Figure 5.37.

Compare Figures 5.38 and 5.39. Do not be discouraged by the apparent complexity of Figure 5.39. There is a regularity to it that permits it to be constructed using a relatively mindless process. Discovering that process is well worth the effort, since it makes it clear how recursion is implemented using a stack.

Observe that the recursive procedure pushes many more items onto the stack than the nonrecursive version does. It is clear that if performance is an issue, recursion should be used with caution.

An introductory discussion of the details of recursive procedure calls is given in Baron and Shapiro (1980), pages 369–379. Appendix B introduces recursion and provides an overview of this important topic.

Figure 5.39 shows an element pushed onto the stack for each of the recursive calls PreOrder (p ↑ .right). These elements are easily recognized because they are precisely those elements with return address a2. Notice (Figure 5.35) that putting these elements on the stack is pointless since PreOrder(p ↑ .right) is the last statement in the procedure. A recursive call that is the last statement in a procedure is called tail recursion, and many compilers omit the stack operation associated with these calls.

The nonrecursive implementation of an inorder traversal is more complex. It is shown in Algorithm 5.2.

```
PROCEDURE InOrder(p: NodePtr);
BEGIN                                    (* An instance of a stack, Stk, *)
   WHILE p # NIL DO                      (* is used by this procedure.   *)

      WHILE p↑.left # NIL DO             (* Traverse a left shell, saving *)
         Push(Stk,p);                    (* a pointer to each node except *)
         p := p↑.left                    (* the last.                     *)
      END;

      LOOP                               (* Traverse a left shell, from leaf *)
         process(p);                     (* to root, processing each node and *)
         IF p↑.right # NIL               (* looking for a node with a right *)
            THEN  p := p↑.right;  EXIT   (* subtree. If a right subtree is  *)
            ELSIF Empty(Stk) THEN RETURN (* found, EXIT to the outer loop and *)
            ELSE  POP(Stk,p)             (* process the left shell of its   *)
         END                             (* root. RETURN when the stack is  *)
      END                                (* empty.                          *)

   END
END InOrder;
```

Algorithm 5.2   Nonrecursive inorder traversal.

Observe that both nonrecursive algorithms (Algorithms 5.1 and 5.2) are based on traversing left shells, which are linear lists and therefore easy to traverse. Figure 5.36 shows the left shells traversed by both nonrecursive procedures in a specific instance. During a preorder traversal each node is processed; and if there is a right child, a pointer to that child is saved on the stack. During an inorder traversal a pointer to each node in the shell is stacked.

Having reached the end of a left shell, a preorder traversal backs up to the right child that is on top of the stack. The process begins again by traversing the left shell of that node. An inorder traversal backs out by considering every node in the left shell. Each node is processed, and if it has a right child, the left shell of that child is traversed.

Procedure *Terminate* uses a postorder traversal (see Figure 5.40). Processing a node means using the DISPOSE statement to deallocate that node's memory. A postorder traversal is necessary because a node cannot be deleted until its two subtrees have been deleted

Deleting a subtree means traversing that subtree and disposing of the memory occupied by its nodes. It is different from *Terminate* in two respects. First, only a subtree is traversed, instead of the entire tree. Second, and most important, the edge between the root of the subtree and its parent must be

```
PROCEDURE Terminate;
BEGIN
      postorder traversal to dis-
      pose of all nodes in the
      tree; dispose of the tree
      node
END Terminate;
```

Figure 5.40

changed. This requires finding the parent node. This is a complex task because in the representation we are using there is no parent identifier. See Figure 5.41.

The *Characteristics* operation reports size, height, and average path length. All three are determined using a traversal. Any traversal will do, and we have used inorder (see Figure 5.42). The traversal procedure must provide the level of the node being processed. This is easy to do, and the details are shown in Implementation Module 5.1. The height of the tree will be the largest value of level encountered, and it is saved in the global variable *h*.

The path length to any node is the same as the level of that node. The average path length (for the tree) is the sum of the path lengths for the individual nodes divided by the number of nodes (size). This sum is accumulated in variable *sum*.

The procedure to find the parent of the current node is trivial if each node contains a parent pointer. In our package there is no such pointer, so a little effort is required. Our strategy is to traverse the tree and process each node as follows:

> **IF** one of the children is the current node
> **THEN** the target parent node is found
> **ELSE** it is not; keep traversing.
> **END**

This operation has a great deal in common with finding the predecessor of the current element in a singly linked list. The strategy is the same, only the terminology is different:

> **IF** the successor is the current element
> **THEN** the target predecessor element is found
> **ELSE** it is not; keep traversing.
> **END**

The major difference between operating on these two data structures is, of course, in the way in which the traversal is implemented. For the tree we could use any of the recursive procedures shown in Figure 5.35. The trouble is that it is difficult to stop such a traversal in the middle; that is, as soon as the target parent is found. (Because you have no way to empty the stack that is used to implement the recursion.) Therefore, we choose to implement the traversal directly. The order makes no difference, so we choose the easiest to implement, a preorder traversal. Figure 5.43 summarizes the technique.

We are now ready to see the complete module for the binary tree; Implementation Module 5.1 follows.

PROCEDURE DeleteSub;
BEGIN
    Find the parent of the current node;
    Eliminate the edge between the current node and its parent;
    Postorder traversal to dispose of all nodes in the subtree whose root is the current node
END DeleteSub;

Figure 5.41

PROCEDURE Characteristics (status);
BEGIN
    Inorder traversal to determine size, height, and the sum of the path lengths to all nodes;
    Compute average path length
END Characteristics;

Figure 5.42

PROCEDURE Find(parent);
BEGIN
    Nonrecursive preorder traversal to find the parent of a specified node;
    Since the traversal is likely to terminate in the middle of the tree, it is necessary to clear the stack used for the traversal
END Find;

Figure 5.43

Implementation Module 5.1   *Binary Trees*

```
IMPLEMENTATION MODULE BinaryTrees;
(* BinaryTrees, linked implementation; meets Specification 5.1. *)

FROM StdTypes IMPORT StdElement;
FROM Storage  IMPORT ALLOCATE, DEALLOCATE, Available;
FROM SYSTEM   IMPORT TSIZE;
IMPORT PtrStks;        (* Module PtrStks meets the specification for a stack   *)
                       (* given in Specification 3.1. The elements stored in   *)
                       (* a PtrStack are of type ADDRESS. That is, for a PtrStk, *)
                       (*                                                       *)
                       (*     StdElement = RECORD                               *)
                       (*                      key: ADDRESS                     *)
                       (*                   END;                                *)

TYPE NodePtr = POINTER TO Node;              (* Pointer to a node of a binary tree. *)
     Node    = RECORD                                 (* Node of a binary tree. *)
                  elt      : StdElement;
                  left,right: NodePtr              (* Pointers to node's children. *)
               END;

  BinaryTree = POINTER TO BTtype;                        (* Binary tree data type. *)
     BTtype   = RECORD
                  treeRoot: NodePtr;                              (* Root of tree. *)
                  current : NodePtr                             (* Current node. *)
               END;

PROCEDURE Traverse (BT: BinaryTree; ord: Order; proc: ProcElt);      (* Traverse *)

   PROCEDURE PreOrd (p: NodePtr; level: CARDINAL);
   BEGIN
      IF p # NIL
         THEN
            proc (p↑.elt,level);
            PreOrd (p↑.left,level+1);
            PreOrd (p↑.right,level+1)
      END
   END PreOrd;

PROCEDURE InOrd (p: NodePtr; level: CARDINAL);
BEGIN
   IF p # NIL
      THEN InOrd (p↑.left,level+1);
           proc (p↑.elt,level);
           InOrd (p↑.right,level+1)
   END
END InOrd;
```

continued

Implementation Module 5.1, continued

```
    PROCEDURE PostOrd (p: NodePtr; level: CARDINAL);
    BEGIN
        IF p # NIL
            THEN PostOrd (p↑.left,level+1);
                 PostOrd (p↑.right,level+1);
                 proc (p↑.elt,level)
        END
    END PostOrd;

BEGIN                                                          (* Traverse *)
    CASE ord OF
        preOrder : PreOrd  (BT↑.treeRoot,1) |
        inOrder  : InOrd   (BT↑.treeRoot,1) |
        postOrder: PostOrd (BT↑.treeRoot,1)
    END
END Traverse;

PROCEDURE Insert (VAR BT: BinaryTree; e: StdElement; rel: Relative): BOOLEAN;
VAR  p: NodePtr;
BEGIN
    IF NOT Available(TSIZE(Node)) OR (rel = parent)
        THEN RETURN FALSE
        ELSIF (rel = leftChild)  AND (BT↑.current↑.left  # NIL)
            THEN RETURN FALSE
        ELSIF (rel = rightChild) AND (BT↑.current↑.right # NIL)
            THEN RETURN FALSE
        ELSE
            NEW(p); p↑.left := NIL; p↑.right := NIL; p↑.elt := e;
            CASE rel OF
                root      : BT↑.treeRoot := p        |
                leftChild : BT↑.current↑.left := p   |
                rightChild: BT↑.current↑.right := p
            END; (* case *)
            BT↑.current := p;
            RETURN TRUE
    END
END Insert;

PROCEDURE DeleteSub (VAR BT: BinaryTree): BOOLEAN;                (* DeleteSub *)
VAR pt: NodePtr;
BEGIN
    WITH BT↑ DO
        IF current = treeRoot
```

continued

Implementation Module 5.1, continued

```
                    THEN TreeDispose(current);
                         treeRoot := NIL;
                         current  := NIL
              ELSIF FindParent(BT,pt)                    (* Find parent of current node. *)
                 THEN IF pt↑.left = current
                         THEN pt↑.left  := NIL           (* Detach subtree from parent. *)
                         ELSE pt↑.right := NIL
                      END;
                      TreeDispose(current);                  (* Dispose of the subtree. *)
                      current := treeRoot
              ELSE RETURN FALSE
        END
    END;
    RETURN TRUE
END DeleteSub;

PROCEDURE Update (VAR BT: BinaryTree; e: StdElement);                    (* Update *)
BEGIN
    BT↑.current↑.elt := e
END Update;

PROCEDURE Retrieve (BT: BinaryTree; VAR e: StdElement);                (* Retrieve *)
BEGIN
    e := BT↑.current↑.elt
END Retrieve;

PROCEDURE Characteristics (BT: BinaryTree; VAR st: Status);     (* Determine      *)
VAR ht,sz : CARDINAL;                                          (* several tree *)
    ap,tpl: REAL;                                    (* characteristics: height, size, *)
                                                     (* and average path length.       *)

    PROCEDURE InOrd (p: NodePtr; level: CARDINAL);          (* Inorder traversal. *)
    BEGIN
        IF p # NIL
           THEN InOrd (p↑.left,level+1);
                INC(sz);
                tpl := tpl + FLOAT(level);
                IF ht < level THEN ht := level END;
                InOrd (p↑.right,level+1)
        END
    END InOrd;

BEGIN                                                       (* Characteristics *)
    sz := 0;  ht := 0;  tpl := 0.0;
    IF NOT Empty(BT)
```

continued

Implementation Module 5.1, continued

```
        THEN InOrd (BT↑.treeRoot,1);
             ap := tpl/FLOAT(sz)
        ELSE ap := 0.0
    END;
    st.size := sz;  st.height := ht;  st.avePath := ap
END Characteristics;

PROCEDURE Find (VAR BT: BinaryTree; rel: Relative): BOOLEAN; (* Find a        *)
VAR p: NodePtr;                                              (* relative of the *)
BEGIN                                                        (* current node.   *)
    WITH BT↑.current↑ DO

        CASE rel OF
            root      : BT↑.current := BT↑.treeRoot |
            leftChild : IF left # NIL
                            THEN BT↑.current := left
                            ELSE RETURN FALSE
                        END |
            rightChild: IF right # NIL
                            THEN BT↑.current := right
                            ELSE RETURN FALSE
                        END |
            parent    : IF (BT↑.current # BT↑.treeRoot) & (FindParent (BT,p))
                            THEN BT↑.current := p
                            ELSE RETURN FALSE
                        END

        END;
        RETURN TRUE
    END
END Find;

PROCEDURE Empty (BT: BinaryTree): BOOLEAN;                            (* Empty *)
BEGIN
    RETURN (BT↑.treeRoot = NIL)
END Empty;

PROCEDURE Create (VAR BT: BinaryTree):BOOLEAN;                       (* Create *)
BEGIN
    IF Available(TSIZE(BTtype))
        THEN NEW(BT); BT↑.treeRoot := NIL;  BT↑.current := NIL;
             RETURN TRUE
        ELSE RETURN FALSE
    END
END Create;
```

continued

Implementation Module 5.1, continued

```
                                        (* TreeDispose and FindParent are not exported. *)
PROCEDURE TreeDispose (p: NodePtr);
(* pre  – NodePtr p is a pointer to a node in a tree of type BinaryTree.
   post – All nodes in the subtree with root p↑ are disposed. *)

BEGIN
    IF p # NIL
        THEN TreeDispose (p↑.left);             (* Postorder traversal that  *)
             TreeDispose (p↑.right);            (* disposes of all nodes in  *)
             DISPOSE (p)                         (* the subtree with root p↑. *)
    END
END TreeDispose;

PROCEDURE FindParent(BT: BinaryTree; VAR p: NodePtr): BOOLEAN;
(* pre  – BT is not empty and p points to a node in BT other than the
            root node.
   post – NodePtr p points to the parent of p-pre and FindParent is true–
            unless a stack cannot be created–in which case FindParent is false. *)

VAR ps: PtrStks.Stack;
BEGIN
    IF PtrStks.Create(ps)            (* Create a stack for nonrecursive traversal. *)
        THEN PtrStks.Push (ps,NIL);
            WITH BT↑ DO
                p := treeRoot;
                WHILE (p # NIL) & (p↑.left # current) & (p↑.right # current) DO
                    IF p↑.right # NIL
                        THEN PtrStks.Push (ps,p↑.right)
                    END;
                    IF p↑.left # NIL
                        THEN p := p↑.left
                        ELSE PtrStks.Pop (ps,p)
                    END
                END
            END;
            PtrStks.Terminate(ps);                       (* Dispose of the stack. *)
            RETURN TRUE
        ELSE RETURN FALSE
    END

END FindParent;

PROCEDURE Terminate(VAR BT: BinaryTree);                              (* Terminate *)
BEGIN
    TreeDispose(BT↑.treeRoot);
    DISPOSE(BT)
END Terminate;

END BinaryTrees.
```

5.3.4 *Sequential Representation*

There are a variety of ways to store the elements of a hierarchical structure in a sequence. We will discuss three possibilities for storing the elements of a binary tree and will use an array representation in each case.

Using an array exacts the usual penalty associated with a static data structure. The memory allocated cannot be adjusted to match that actually required. Deletions can be a problem because a gap is created that is expensive to fill. Similarly, an insertion may require making space by moving other records out of the way. For these reasons the sequential storage of a hierarchical structure is usually applied only to static sets of data. The problems arising from insertions and deletions can be eliminated if enough memory is allocated. The third approach below, which shows how this can be done, is applied to heaps and priority queues in Section 5.8.

Perhaps the most obvious way to represent a binary tree using an array is to use index values instead of pointers to represent edges. This is done as shown in Figure 5.44.

```
CONST TreeSize = 200              (* User supplied *)

TYPE Edge = [0..TreeSize];
     Node = RECORD
                 elt  : StdElement;
                 left : Edge;
                 right: Edge
             END;

VAR binaryTree: ARRAY Edge OF Node;
```

   Figure 5.44

Index	Element	Left	Right
1	A	2	3
2	B	4	6
3	C	0	0
4	D	0	0
5	I	0	0
6	E	7	0
7	G	5	0

Figure 5.45
The tree in Figure 5.37 using array indexes to represent edges.

An *Edge* value of 0 is used to indicate an empty subtree. Location *binaryTree*[1] can be reserved for the root of the tree, or one of the edges in *binaryTree* [0] can be used to give the location of the root. Figure 5.45 shows how the tree in Figure 5.37 might be stored using this representation.

A second approach is to store the elements in one of the natural traversal orders. To illustrate this approach we will use the order given by a preorder traversal. You can then think of a tree being stored as a sequence of left shells (see Figure 5.36). Each node needs only 2 bits of information in addition to its element. One bit indicates if it has a left child (it can also be thought of as marking the last node in a left shell), and the other indicates the presence (or absence) of a right child. This approach economizes on storage, although it would be hard to realize the full savings in Modula-2 since boolean values are apt to be stored in bytes (or words). A possible Modula-2 representation is shown in Figure 5.46.

```
CONST TreeSize =                              (* As needed. *)

TYPE node = RECORD
                  elt  :  StdElement;
                  left :  BOOLEAN;
                  right:  BOOLEAN
            END;

VAR BinaryTree: ARRAY [1..TreeSize] OF node;
```

Figure 5.46   Representing a binary tree by storing nodes in the order in which they would be encountered during a preorder traversal.

Index	Element	Left	Right
1	A	T	T
2	B	T	T
3	D	F	F
4	E	T	F
5	G	T	F
6	I	F	F
7	C	F	F

Figure 5.47
The tree in Figure 5.37 stored sequentially in preorder order.

If *left (right)* is true then the node has a *left (right)* child. Figure 5.47 shows how the tree in Figure 5.37 would be stored using this approach.

In the final approach edges are represented implicitly. Each node has an assigned position and cannot be stored anyplace else. The root of the tree is stored in *tree*[1], and its children are stored in *tree*[2] and *tree*[3]. In general, the left child of *tree*[i] is stored in *tree*[$2i$], and the right child of *tree*[i] is stored in *tree*[$2i + 1$]. The advantage is that edges are not stored at all. The disadvantage is that space must be allocated for every possible node at each level. If a node is not present, the space is wasted. We will use this approach in Section 5.8 to represent heaps and implement priority queues.

Exercises 5.3.4

1. In your own words, summarize the advantages and disadvantages associated with an array representation of a binary tree.
2. Implement procedures that convert a binary tree from its linked representation to each of the three sequential representations described in this section.
3. Implement procedures that convert a binary tree from each of the three sequential representations described in this section to a linked representation.
4. Describe how insertion of a new node might be handled for each of the three sequential representations. How many compares and how many moves would be needed in each case?
5. Describe how deletion of a node might be handled for each of the three sequential representations. How many compares and how many moves would be needed in each case?

5.3.5 Threaded Trees

A binary tree with n nodes has $n + 1$ empty subtrees. A linked representation of a binary tree ordinarily contains $n + 1$ pointers with the value NIL. The idea of a **threaded tree** is to replace all those NIL pointers with pointers that provide access to other nodes in the tree. A common way to do this is to use these pointers to identify preorder, inorder, or postorder predecessors and successors. These pointers permit efficient nonrecursive traversal of a tree in return for a small increase in memory requirements. The procedures that insert

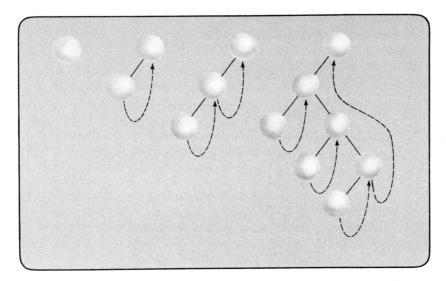

Figure 5.48   Four binary trees in which the pointer to a node's empty right subtree is replaced by a pointer to that node's inorder successor.

and delete nodes in a threaded tree are only slightly more complex than the corresponding procedures for trees that are not threaded.

To illustrate threaded trees we will discuss trees in which a pointer to an empty right subtree is replaced by a pointer to that node's inorder successor. Figure 5.48 shows four such trees. The threads—pointers to a node's inorder successor—are shown with dashed lines.

These illustrations lead to a couple of observations about the inorder successor of a node *that does not have a right child.* The inorder successor of a left child is the child's parent. The inorder successor of a right child is the closest ancestor in whose left subtree it lies. There is always one node that does not have an inorder successor. It is found by starting at the root of the tree and following right pointers until an empty subtree is found.

Operation *FindNext* specified by

FindNext ( ): BOOLEAN;
>   **pre** — The tree is not empty.
>   **post** — If c-pre had an inorder successor then it is the current node, else the operation fails.

is easy to implement for the threaded trees we are discussing. The representation of a node must specify whether the right pointer is a thread or a pointer to a subtree. This can be handled with a boolean variable as shown in Figure 5.49.

If traversing a tree in a particular order is an important operation, then threads are worth considering. They offer two advantages. First, a stack is not needed. Second, a traversal can begin at any node in the tree, without having first to accumulate the information that would be in the stack at that point

NodePtr = **POINTER TO**
                    ThreadedNode;

ThreadedNode =
        RECORD
                elt   : StdElement;
                left   : NodePtr;
                right : NodePtr;
                thread: BOOLEAN
        END;

Figure 5.49
Representation of a node in which one of the pointers may be a thread.

```
PROCEDURE ThreadedInOrder(p: NodePtr);        (* Inorder traversal of a tree with *)
BEGIN                                         (* threads to inorder successors.    *)
    WHILE p # NIL DO

        WHILE p↑.left # NIL DO                         (* Traverse a left shell *)
            p := p↑.left                               (* to find its last node. *)
        END;
        process(p);

        WHILE p↑.thread DO                     (* Process the inorder successors *)
            p := p↑.right;                     (* determined by threads.          *)
            process(p)
        END;
        p := p↑.right                  (* Get the first node in a new left shell. *)

    END
END ThreadedInOrder;
```

Algorithm 5.3

during a recursive traversal. Algorithm 5.3 shows one possibility for the inorder traversal of a tree containing threads for inorder successors.

This section has only introduced the idea of threaded trees. A good introduction with further details is given in Reingold (1986, pages 240–251).

Exercises 5.3.5

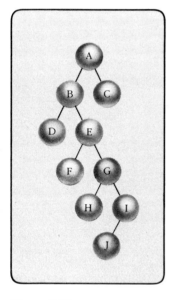

Figure 5.50

1. In the tree shown in Figure 5.50, use dashed lines to show the threads that would be used to point to
   a. Preorder successors
   b. Inorder successors
   c. Postorder successors
2. The text describes the location of the inorder successor of a node based on whether the node is the left or right child of its parent. Is there an analogous description of the location of a node's
   a. Preorder successor?
   b. Postorder successor?
   Explain your answer.
3. Implement a procedure for operation *FindNext* as specified in the text.
4. Implement a procedure that inserts nodes in a binary tree that has threads to identify a node's inorder successor.
5. Implement a procedure that traverses a threaded tree. Compare the time required to traverse a threaded tree with that required for a recursive traversal. Plot the traversal time as a function of the size of the tree.

5.4 Abstract Binary Search Tree

Suppose that each node of a binary tree contains a single element and that each element contains information that describes a particular object. We want to find the node that contains a particular key value. We will call the node we seek the ***target node.*** We will start our search at the root node. If it is the target node, then we are finished. If not, then we face a dilemma. Should we continue our search in the left subtree or in the right subtree? We need a tree such that starting at the root node and proceeding from parent to child, we always know which subtree to search in order to proceed directly to the target node. We would like to follow the unique simple path from the root node to the target node. A ***binary search tree*** is such a tree.

The potential advantage of a binary search tree seems clear. Look again at the tree in Figure 5.18. Its height is 8. If it were a binary search tree (which it is), then searching for any node in the tree would, at the very worst, require examining 8 nodes. If the same set of nodes were in a linear structure, then searching for a node might require examining as many as 29 elements.

A binary search tree is a special binary tree in which each node's location in the tree is determined by the value of some item in that node. We will always use the value of the key, but the value of almost any item will do. The advantage is that searching the tree for the node containing a particular value is usually very efficient—hence the name search tree. Insertions and updates, however, must be restricted in such a way as to guarantee that the binary tree remains a binary search tree.

5.4.1 *Specification and Operations*

Consider a binary search tree, each of whose nodes contains one integer. Suppose that the tree is initially empty and that we add 65 to the tree. (We do not really add 65 of course, we really add a node containing 65.) The resulting tree is shown in Figure 5.51.

Next we add 87 to the tree. Since 87 is greater than 65 it goes in 65's right subtree. Since the right subtree is empty, 87 becomes the root of the right subtree. The result is shown in Figure 5.52.

Next we add 73 to the tree. Since 73 is greater than 65 it goes in the right subtree of 65. This brings us to the node containing 87. Since 73 is less than 87 it goes in the left subtree of 87, which is empty. Therefore, 73 becomes the root of the left subtree of 87. The result is shown in Figure 5.53.

The tree we are constructing can be characterized as follows.

> A binary search tree is a binary tree such that for each node, say N, the following statements are true:
>
> 1. If L is any node in the left subtree of N, then L is less than N.
> 2. If R is any node in the right subtree of N, then R is greater than N.

Figure 5.18 shows a binary search tree. To say that node A is less than node B for that tree means that the integer contained in node A is less than

Figure 5.51
A binary search tree containing one node.

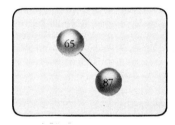

Figure 5.52
The binary search tree after adding 87.

Figure 5.53
The binary search tree after adding 73.

A binary search tree is a special case of a binary tree as shown in the box. This difference between a binary tree and a binary search tree is a constraint that the implementation module for a binary search tree is responsible for imposing.

the integer contained in node B. If each node contained a character string, then we could specify that one node is "less than" another if the character string it contains lexicographically precedes the character string contained in the second node.

What if each node contains several items? Figure 5.19 shows an example of such a binary search tree. That tree is organized according to the recipient's name. The node (Backus, J., 1977, "Can Programming...") is less than the node (Hoare, C.A.R., 1980, "The Emperor's...") because Backus, J. lexicographically precedes Hoare, C.A.R.

In the remainder of this chapter, each node will be restricted to containing a single element. Since each element has a key value that uniquely identifies it, that value also identifies the node that contains it. If the key values are taken from a totally ordered set (Section 1.4.2), then the key values can be used to order the nodes of the tree. The key values can be used to make the notion less than, which is needed to construct a binary search tree, precise.

The essence of searching a binary search tree is captured in Algorithm 5.4.

```
WHILE the target element is not found AND
      there is more tree to search DO
   IF the target element is "less than"
      the current element
      THEN search the left subtree
      ELSE search the right subtree
   END
END
```

Algorithm 5.4

If we apply Algorithm 5.4 to find the node containing 55 in the tree in Figure 5.18, then the search follows the path shown in Figure 5.54. If 51 is added to the tree, it will be added as the left subtree of 55. If 31 is added to the tree, it will be added as the right subtree of 30.

Algorithm 5.4 defines a unique path for every node in a binary search tree. The path is from the root node to any target node and is the *shortest* such path. One of the main attractions of binary search trees is that this path is usually (but not always) very short. Therefore, searching a binary search tree is usually an efficient operation. We will examine the lengths of these paths in Section 5.5.

We have examined the elements and structure of an abstract binary search tree. The elements are the same as the elements in any binary tree except that their key values (or the values of some other item) must be from a totally ordered set so that it makes sense to compare two elements. The structure of a binary search tree is the same as the structure of a binary tree except for one additional constraint: If N is any node in the tree, then all of the nodes in N's left subtree are less than N, and all of the nodes in N's right subtree are greater than N. We will complete the discussion of the specification of our abstract binary search tree by describing its operations.

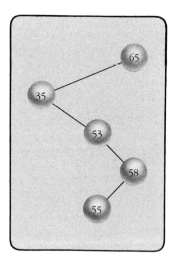

Figure 5.54
The binary search tree path to the node containing 55. (See Figure 5.18.)

• Operations

Many of the operations on a binary tree apply directly to a binary search tree. Two exceptions are *Update* and *Insert.* These operations must be modified to ensure that the binary search tree constraint is always satisfied. Two new operations, which take advantage of the additional structure of a binary search tree, are added. They are *FindKey* and *DeleteKey.*

Specification 5.2 for a binary search tree follows.

Specification 5.2   Binary Search Trees

DEFINITION MODULE BinarySearchTrees;

(* **Elements:** The elements of a binary search tree are nodes. We will
       assume that each node contains one standard element. A node may
       contain other items. *)

  FROM StdTypes **IMPORT** StdElement, KeyType;

(* **Structure:** The structure of a binary search tree is the same as the
       structure of a binary tree except that, in addition, if N is any
       node in the tree, then all nodes in its left subtree are smaller
       than N, and all nodes in its right subtree are larger than N.
       Smaller and larger refers to a comparison of key values, which
       must come from some ordered set. *)

(* **Domain:** The number of nodes in a binary search tree is bounded. *)

  EXPORT QUALIFIED SearchTree, Order, Relative, Status, Process, Insert,
              Delete, FindKey, Update, Traverse, DeleteSub, Retrieve,
              Characteristics, Empty, Full, Create, Terminate;

  TYPE SearchTree;   (* *Opaque type used to implement a binary search tree.* *)
       Order   = (preOrder, inOrder, postOrder);   (* *Traversal order.* *)
       Relative = (leftChild, rightChild, root, parent);

       Status   = **RECORD**   (* *Several characteristics of*   *)
                    size   : CARDINAL;   (* *a binary tree: size, height,* *)
                    height : CARDINAL;   (* *and average path length.*   *)
                    avePath: REAL
                 END;

       ProcElt = **PROCEDURE** (StdElement, CARDINAL);

(* **Operations:** A tree that is not empty always has a current node. We
       use BT-pre and c-pre in the postcondition to refer, respectively,
       to the binary tree and the current node in the binary tree prior to
       the operation. *)

PROCEDURE Insert (**VAR** BST: SearchTree; e: StdElement): BOOLEAN;
(* **pre** – BST has not achieved its maximum allowable size.
    post – If BST-pre did not contain an element with key value e.key,
            then e is in BST and Insert is true, else Insert is false. *)   *continued*

Specification 5.2, continued

PROCEDURE Update (**VAR** BST: SearchTree; e: StdElement);
(* **pre** — BST is not empty.
   post — The element in c-pre is not in BST and the current node
             contains e. *)

PROCEDURE Delete (**VAR** BST: SearchTree; tkey: KeyType): BOOLEAN;
(* **post** — If BST-pre contained an element with key value tkey then
             that element is not in BST and Delete is true, else
             Delete is false. *)

PROCEDURE FindKey (**VAR** BST: SearchTree; tkey: KeyType): BOOLEAN;
(* **post** — If BST contains a node whose key value is tkey then that
             node is the current node and FindKey is true, else the
             current node is the node to which the node containing tkey
             would be attached as a child if it were added to BST, and
             FindKey is false. *)

PROCEDURE Full (BST: SearchTree): BOOLEAN;
(* **post** — If BST has reached its maximum size then Full is
             true, else Full is false. *)

(* *The specification for each of the following operations is identical
    to that given in Specification 5.1--except that BinaryTree is now
    SearchTree and BT is changed to BST.* *)

PROCEDURE Traverse   (BST: SearchTree; ord: Order; proc: ProcElt);
PROCEDURE DeleteSub   (**VAR** BST: SearchTree);
PROCEDURE Retrieve   (BST: SearchTree; **VAR** e : StdElement);
PROCEDURE Characteristics   (BST: SearchTree; **VAR** st: Status);
PROCEDURE Empty   (BST: SearchTree): BOOLEAN;
PROCEDURE Create   (**VAR** BST: SearchTree): BOOLEAN;
PROCEDURE Terminate   (**VAR** BST: SearchTree);

END BinarySearchTrees.

We will discuss the new operations that apply only to a binary search tree [see Figure 5.55(b)]. Three of these operations involve an element specified by its key value. The fourth, *Update,* operates on the current node. Any of these operations may change the relative positions of elements in the tree in order to ensure that the tree continues to be a search tree. This is in contrast with the operations against a binary tree, which (except for *Traverse* and *Characteristics*) apply to either the root node or the current node and never change the relative positions of nodes.

The new operations are more powerful and more restrictive. Given a key value, they determine the location of the node on which to operate. The user is freed from locating these nodes. On the other hand, the user is not permitted to determine these locations since doing so would jeopardize the integrity of the search tree. The binary tree operations differ in that they require (permit)

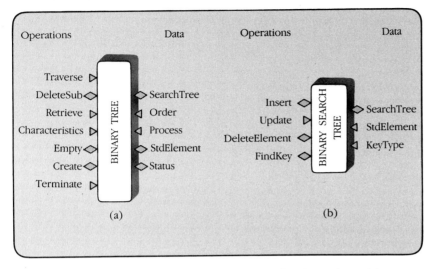

Figure 5.55 Capsules. (a) Binary tree operations that also apply to a binary search tree. (b) Binary tree operations that apply only to a binary search tree.

the user to identify the nodes to be operated on by setting a current node or specifying the root node.

The operation *FindKey* searches the binary tree for a node whose element has a specified key value. We did not include *FindKey* in our abstract binary tree. We could have, but implementing it would have involved traversing the entire tree. This is one of the most important operations for a binary search tree, since the structure of the tree makes this operation efficient.

The operation *DeleteKey* searches for the node whose element contains a specified key value (using *FindKey*) and then removes that element (but not necessarily that node) from the tree. We did not include this operation in our abstract binary tree because deleting a node with two subtrees left us in a quandary about how to structure the tree in order to provide places to reattach both subtrees. The additional structural requirements of a search tree provide us with a conceptually simple way out of this quandary. We shall see what that is when we discuss implementation.

An *Update* operation that simply changes the values in the current node could (in the hands of a careless user) cause the integrity of the binary search tree to be violated. Operation *Update* must protect the integrity of a binary search tree. If the user wants to change the key value of a node, then the proposed new value must be larger than any key value in the left subtree and smaller than any key value in its right subtree. If this is not the case, then either the proposed update must be rejected or the tree must be restructured to accommodate the new key value. One way to accomplish this is to delete the element to be modified and then insert an element with the new values. This is a pessimistic, but conceptually simple approach, and we will adopt it in our implementation module.

Given an element, the *Insert* operation determines the proper location and adds a node containing that element to the tree. The location of an insertion is not specified by the user, who might make an error.

5.4.2 Binary Search Tree Representation and Implementation

• Representation

```
NodePtr = POINTER TO Node;
Node   = RECORD
             elt  : StdElement;
             left : NodePtr;
             right: NodePtr
         END;
```

Figure 5.56

We will use the same linked representation for a node that was used for a binary tree (see Figure 5.56).

• Implementation

Once again, our implementation is a module containing functions and procedures. This module emphasizes operations that differ in implementation from the corresponding operations for a binary tree. Before presenting the module, we will discuss the implementation of three operations, *FindKey, Insert,* and *DeleteKey,* in detail.

The *find* operation follows the unique simple path to the location of the target node. If the target node is not found, the current node is the node to which it would be attached if it were in the tree.

The target node for the operation *FindKey* is the node whose element contains a specified value of its key. A search begins at the root node and follows the unique simple path that leads to the location at which the target node is located or the target node would be if it were in the tree. If the target node is found, it becomes the current node. If not, the leaf node to which it would be attached—if it were added to the tree—becomes the current node. Setting the current node in this way permits operation *FindKey* to be used by operation *Insert.*

Insert uses operation *FindKey* to see if the element to be added is already in the tree. If not, it is attached to the tree's current node, which was set by *FindKey.*

The nodes searched by operation *FindKey* are on a path from the root to the target node or to a leaf node. The nodes on this path form a linear structure whose size is bounded by the height of the tree. This is usually a very efficient operation because the height of a tree is usually much smaller than the size of a tree.

There is a more general find-by-value operation in which the target node is the node whose element contains a value specified for an item that is not necessarily the key. If the search item is not the key, then the search must traverse the entire tree. In this case the user specifies the desired item (not necessarily the key) and its value. The search could use a tree traversal in every case. Alternately, the search could check to see if the specified item was the key and, if so, examine only the simple path from the root to the location of that node. Our module does not implement this more general *find* operation but requires that the target node be specified using a value of the key.

The expected search length using Algorithm 5.4 is $O[\log_2(n)]$. This is the same as the expected search length for a binary search of a sorted list (Chapter 4). It does not seem surprising that these two values for the expected search length are the same, since the two techniques are so similar. However, there is an important performance difference between the two.

In the worst case, a binary search of a sorted list requires $\log_2(n)$ comparisons. In the worst case, searching a binary search tree requires *n* comparisons. As we have emphasized several times before, *n* is much much larger than $\log_2(n)$, even for relatively small values of *n*. The worst case performance for searching a binary search tree occurs when most of the nodes in the tree have only one child. These trees look a lot like lists (draw a few!). They are actually somewhat worse than lists for purposes of searching, since there will be more overhead in the search algorithm.

The question that we are beginning to discuss here is this: What is the shape of an average binary search tree? Are binary search trees short and wide? Or are they tall and narrow? Can we be more precise about the terms "shape" and "average"? The answers to these questions are sufficiently important—and sufficiently interesting—that a separate section (Section 5.5) is devoted to their discussion.

There is only one *Insert* operation in the binary search tree module. The user supplies an element, and the module, based on the value of the key, adds a node containing that element to its proper position in the tree. Any other *Insert* operation—in which the user has a voice in locating the new node— would jeopardize the integrity of the binary search tree.

Our implementation uses procedure *FindKey* to determine if the element to be inserted is already in the tree and, if not, to make the node to which the new node must be attached the current node.

The performance of *Insert* is essentially that of the *FindKey* operation. Once the location of the new node is found it is simply a matter of attaching it to its parent.

The order in which nodes are added to a binary search tree affects the shape of the tree that is produced. To illustrate this point look at Figure 5.57. It shows two binary search trees containing the same elements. (An element contains only a key, and in this case a key is an integer.) The difference between the two trees occurs solely because of the order in which the elements were inserted. The statements used to construct trees (a) and (b) in Figure 5.57, using the binary search tree module, are as follow:

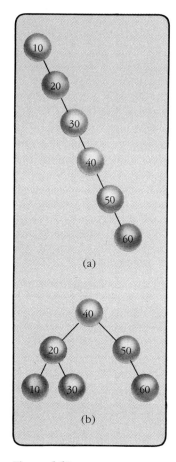

Figure 5.57
Two different trees are constructed using the same elements. (a) One of the tallest trees containing six nodes. (b) One of the shortest trees containing six nodes.

Create(BST);	*Create*(BST);
Insert(BST,10);	*Insert*(BST,40);
Insert(BST,20);	*Insert*(BST,20);
Insert(BST,30);	*Insert*(BST,50);
Insert(BST,40);	*Insert*(BST,10);
Insert(BST,50);	*Insert*(BST,30);
Insert(BST,60);	*Insert*(BST,60);
(a)	(b)

The binary search tree module contains one delete operation, *Delete,* which deletes the element with a specified key from the tree. Assuming the prescribed element is found, it also removes one node from the tree. However, it is important to note that the node removed may not be the node that originally contained the element to be deleted! The reason for this is that it is

The *Delete* operation is the most complex in the binary search tree module. An element may be deleted by removing the node that contains it from the tree. In some cases, however, it is necessary to delete an element by replacing it with an element from another node and removing the other node.

An element is deleted; a node is removed.

difficult to remove a single node from the tree unless it has at least one empty subtree. This is an inherent constraint that affects the removal of a single node from any hierarchical structure. Because of the rearrangement associated with the removal of a single node, the deletion process is a complex one. Therefore, we will give four examples and an English language description of the deletion process. While studying the examples, refer ahead to the description in Algorithm 5.5. This will help you understand the Modula-2 procedures for deletion that are given in Implementation Module 5.2 for the binary search tree.

It is helpful to be clear about two terms used to describe deletion: delete and remove. **_Delete_** refers to eliminating an element from the tree. This may be accomplished without eliminating the node that contains the element to be deleted. **_Remove_** refers to eliminating (by unlinking) a node from the tree. Removing a node has the side effect of deleting the element it contains. The result is that both an element and the node that contained it are no longer part of the tree. The structure of the tree is changed.

In some cases deletion of an element is accomplished by removing the node that contains that element. In other cases the element to be deleted is replaced by the element from a second node, and that second node is then removed from the tree.

Our first example, Figure 5.58, shows the deletion of the content of a node that has two empty subtrees. This is accomplished by removing the node. As illustrated, the left pointer of the parent node is replaced by either the left or the right pointer from the node to be deleted. It does not matter which one is used since they are both nil.

Our second example, Figure 5.59, shows deletion of the content of a node with an empty right subtree. This is accomplished by replacing its parent's pointer (70's right pointer) with its left pointer (110's left pointer). Once again, the deletion is accomplished by removing the node.

Generally speaking, suppose that a node has one empty subtree. That node may be removed by replacing the pointer from its parent node with the pointer to its other (possibly not empty) subtree.

Our third example shows the deletion of the content of a node that does not have an empty subtree. Two different deletion procedures will be illustrated. The first (Figure 5.60) uses the largest element in the left subtree of the element to be deleted. That largest element is contained in the right most node in the left subtree. An alternative is to use the smallest element in the right subtree. It is contained in the left most node in the right subtree.

Our approach is first to replace the element to be deleted by the largest element in its left subtree and then to remove the node that contained that largest element (the right most element in the left subtree) from the tree. It is essential to this process that the right most node in the left subtree have at least one empty subtree. It does—its right subtree is always empty.

We can only replace the element to be deleted with the largest element in its left subtree because we must still have a binary search tree after the deletion is complete. The element that replaces the deleted element must be larger than any element in its left subtree. The only element in the left subtree

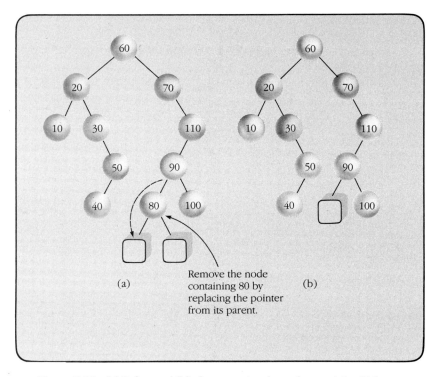

Figure 5.58 (a) Before and (b) after removing the node containing 80 from the binary search tree.

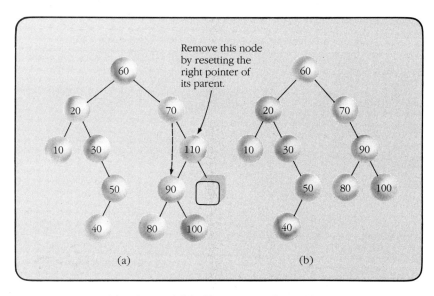

Figure 5.59 (a) Before and (b) after removing the node whose content is 110.

of the element to be deleted that is larger than all the other elements is, of course, the largest element.

Figure 5.61 shows the deletion of 60 based on the left most element in the right subtree.

The logic of the delete operation is given in Algorithm 5.5.

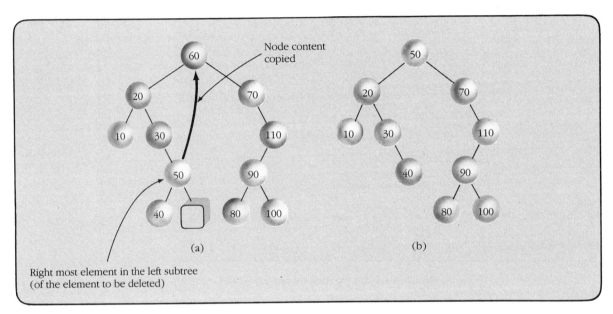

Figure 5.60
(a) Before and (b) after deleting the content of the root node using the right most element in the left subtree.

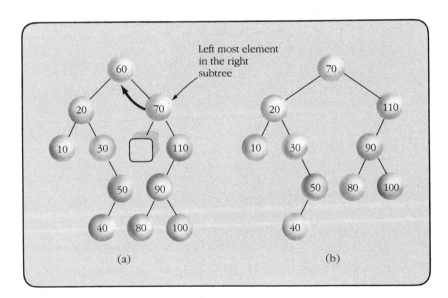

Figure 5.61
(a) Before and (b) after deleting the content of the root node using the left most element in the right subtree. The large arrow indicates the node content that is copied.

```
PROCEDURE Delete;                        (* Delete the element with a given key *)
                                         (* value from a binary search tree.    *)
BEGIN
    Search for the node whose element is to be deleted
    IF not found THEN report failure
        ELSIF either subtree of the node is empty
              THEN remove that node by replacing the pointer from its parent with
                   the pointer to its nonempty subtree. (If both subtrees are empty
                   then either pointer will do.)
        ELSE  find the right most node in the left subtree of the node whose element
              is to be deleted--call this node righty. Move righty's content to the
              node containing the element to be deleted. Replace the pointer from
              righty's parent with the pointer to righty's left subtree.
    END;
    Reclaim the storage used by the node that is removed.
END Delete;
```

Algorithm 5.5

In summary, procedure *Delete* searches for the node that contains the element to be deleted from the tree. If that node has an empty subtree, then it is removed. If not, then the content of that node is replaced by the content of the right most node in its left subtree. The latter node will always have an empty right subtree, and it is removed. In either case a node with at least one empty subtree is actually removed. Implementation Module 5.2, Binary Search Tree, now follows.

Implementation Module 5.2 *Binary Search Trees*

```
IMPLEMENTATION MODULE BinarySearchTrees;
(* BinarySearchTrees; linked implementation; meets Specification 5.2. *)

    FROM InOut     IMPORT WriteLn, WriteString, WriteCard;
    FROM StdTypes  IMPORT StdElement, KeyType;
    FROM Storage   IMPORT ALLOCATE, DEALLOCATE, Available;
    FROM SYSTEM    IMPORT TSIZE;

    TYPE NodePtr    = POINTER TO Node;     (* Pointer to a node of a binary tree. *)
         Node       = RECORD                         (* Node of a binary tree. *)
                         elt      : StdElement;
                         left,right: NodePtr    (* Pointers to node's children. *)
                      END;

         SearchTree = POINTER TO SearchType;    (* Binary search tree data type. *)
         SearchType = RECORD
                         treeRoot: NodePtr;                    (* Root of tree. *)
                         current : NodePtr                     (* Current node. *)
                      END;
```

continued

Implementation Module 5.2, continued

```
PROCEDURE Insert (VAR BST: SearchTree; e: StdElement): BOOLEAN;      (* Insert e. *)
VAR p: NodePtr;
BEGIN
    IF NOT FindKey(BST, e.key)                              (* If e is not found *)
        THEN NEW(p);                                        (* construct a        *)
             p↑.left := NIL; p↑.right := NIL; p↑.elt := e;  (* new tree node.     *)
             WITH BST↑ DO
                IF treeRoot = NIL THEN treeRoot := p        (* Make it the root.  *)
                    ELSIF e.key < current↑.elt.key
                        THEN current↑.left := p             (* Make it a left child.  *)
                        ELSE current↑.right := p            (* Make it a right child. *)
                END;
                current := p                                (* Make it the current node. *)
             END;
             RETURN TRUE
        ELSE RETURN FALSE
    END
END Insert;

PROCEDURE Update (VAR BST: SearchTree; e: StdElement);             (* Update e. *)
VAR b: BOOLEAN;
BEGIN
    b := Delete(BST, BST↑.current↑.elt.key);        (* Delete the current element. *)
    b := Insert(BST, e)                             (* Insert element e. *)
END Update;

PROCEDURE Delete(VAR BST: SearchTree; tkey: KeyType): BOOLEAN;            (* Delete *)
VAR p, remove: NodePtr;

    PROCEDURE SubDel(VAR q: NodePtr);
    BEGIN
        IF q↑.right # NIL                       (* Recursive search for the right  *)
            THEN SubDel(q↑.right)               (* most element in the left subtree. *)
            ELSE remove↑.elt := q↑.elt;         (* Replace element to be deleted. *)
                 remove := q;
                 q := q↑.left                   (* Delete one node from the tree. *)
        END
    END SubDel;

VAR bln: BOOLEAN;

    PROCEDURE Del(tkey: KeyType; VAR p: NodePtr);
    BEGIN
        IF p = NIL
            THEN bln := FALSE; RETURN
        END;
```

continued

Implementation Module 5.2, continued

```
        WITH p↑ DO
            IF tkey < elt.key        THEN Del(tkey,left)       (* Recursive search *)
                ELSIF tkey > elt.key THEN Del(tkey,right)      (* for tkey.        *)
                ELSE remove := p;                              (* Found tkey in p↑. *)
                    IF right = NIL        THEN p := left       (* No right child.  *)
                        ELSIF left = NIL THEN p := right       (* No left child.   *)
                        ELSE SubDel(left)                      (* Both children.   *)
                    END;
                    DISPOSE(remove);
                    bln := TRUE
            END
        END
    END Del;

BEGIN
    Del(tkey, BST↑.treeRoot);
    IF bln
        THEN BST↑.current := BST↑.treeRoot;
            RETURN TRUE
        ELSE RETURN FALSE
    END
END Delete;

PROCEDURE FindKey (VAR BST: SearchTree; tkey: KeyType): BOOLEAN;       (* FindKey *)
VAR p, prior: NodePtr;
BEGIN
    WITH BST↑ DO
        p := treeRoot;

        WHILE p # NIL DO
            prior := p;
            IF tkey = p↑.elt.key
                    THEN current := p;                             (* Found tkey. *)
                        RETURN TRUE
                ELSIF tkey < p↑.elt.key THEN p := p↑.left          (* Search left or *)
                    ELSE p := p↑.right                             (* right subtree. *)
                END
        END;

        current := prior;         (* tkey was not found--make the node to which *)
        RETURN FALSE              (* it would be attached the current node.      *)
    END
END FindKey;
```

continued

Implementation Module 5.2, continued

```
PROCEDURE Full (BST: SearchTree): BOOLEAN;                    (* Is the tree full? *)
BEGIN
    IF NOT Available(TSIZE(Node))
        THEN RETURN TRUE
        ELSE RETURN FALSE
    END
END Full;

(* The implementation of each of the following procedures is identical to    *)
(* that given in Implementation Module 5.1.                                   *)

PROCEDURE Traverse          (    BST: SearchTree; ord: Order; proc: ProcElt);
PROCEDURE DeleteSub         (VAR BST: SearchTree);
PROCEDURE Retrieve          (    BST: SearchTree; VAR e : StdElement);
PROCEDURE Characteristics   (    BST: SearchTree; VAR st: Status);
PROCEDURE Empty             (    BST: SearchTree): BOOLEAN;
PROCEDURE Create            (VAR BST: SearchTree): BOOLEAN;
PROCEDURE Terminate         (VAR BST: SearchTree);

END BinarySearchTrees.
```

Exercises 5.4

1. Describe a binary search tree in your own words.
2. Explain why an associative find may be faster for a binary search tree than for a binary tree.
3. Describe the *Delete* operation.
    a. When is the element that is to be deleted in the node that is removed from the tree? When is this not the case?
    b. What is the significance of the right most node in the left subtree? The left most node in the right subtree?
    c. Write a procedure that implements the following operation:

    ```
    PROCEDURE RightMost (BST: SearchTree);
        pre  – The tree is not empty.
        post – The current node is the right most node in
               the left subtree of c-pre (the current node
               before the operation).
    ```

4. For the binary search tree in Figure 5.62 answer and do the following:
    a. In how many distinct orders could the elements be inserted to produce the result shown?
    b. Show the tree after deleting each of the following nodes. Each deletion operates on the original tree.
        i.   45   iii. 25
        ii. 40   iv.   50

Figure 5.62

5. Write specifications for an *Update* operation that does the following:
   a. Updates the current node if the key value is not changed and fails otherwise
   b. Updates the current node if the new key value satisfies the requirements of a binary search tree without moving the node
6. Implement the operations specified in Exercise 5.
7. Specify and implement a function that tests a binary tree to determine if it is a binary search tree.
8. Specify and implement a procedure that converts a binary tree to a binary search tree containing the same elements.
9. The *Delete* operation in Implementation Module 5.2 is recursive. Write a nonrecursive procedure that meets the same specification.

5.5 Enumeration and Performance

The performance of algorithms for binary trees is complicated by the fact that binary trees can have many different shapes. For example, Figure 5.63 shows two binary trees, each containing seven nodes. In Figure 5.63(a), the height of the tree is 3 and the average path length is 17/7. In Figure 5.63(b) the height is 7 and the average path length is 4. Because the characteristics of trees vary widely, it will simplify matters if we divide all binary trees into subgroups whose members are more nearly alike. We will consider four such groups: degenerate, full, minimum height, and random.

   A tree such as the one shown in Figure 5.63(b), which is similar to a list, is a degenerate binary tree. In a ***degenerate binary tree*** each node, except for its one leaf node, has exactly one child. That child may be either the left or the right, but it is the only one. From a logical point of view, a degenerate binary tree is a linear structure with some unnecessary overhead (the identifier for the empty subtree). It can be characterized as the tallest (greatest height) possible binary tree containing a given number of nodes.

   The other extreme in terms of height is a ***full binary tree,*** such as the one shown in Figure 5.63(a). A tree is full if all of its empty subtrees occur on the same level. In other words, a tree is full if every level that contains any node contains the maximum number of nodes that can occur on that level. Table 5.2 shows how the nodes are distributed in a full binary tree.

TABLE 5.2 Node distribution in a full binary tree.

Level	Number of nodes at each level	Cumulative number of nodes by level
1	1	1
2	$2 = 2^1$	$3 = 2^2 - 1$
3	$4 = 2^2$	$7 = 2^3 - 1$
4	$8 = 2^3$	$15 = 2^4 - 1$
$\vdots$	$\vdots$	$\vdots$
k	$2^{(k-1)}$	$2^k - 1$

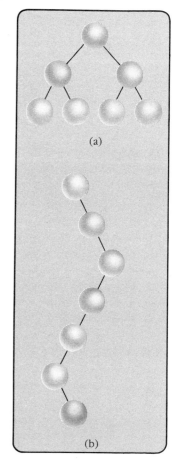

Figure 5.63
(a) A full binary tree. (b) A degenerate binary tree.

The number of nodes in a full binary tree must be $2^k - 1$ for some integer k. Since this condition is quite restrictive, the requirement for a full binary tree is relaxed slightly to specify a ***minimum height binary tree.*** A binary tree is minimum height if there is no other binary tree containing the same number of nodes whose average path length is less. The average path length of a tree is the sum of the path lengths of all nodes divided by the number of nodes (Figure 5.30). Figure 5.64 shows minimum height binary trees of heights 3 and 4.

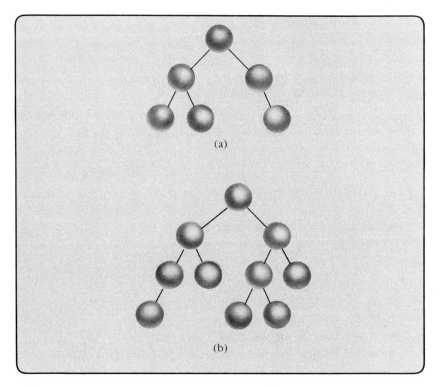

Figure 5.64   (a) A minimum height tree of height 3. (b) A minimum height tree of height 4.

Degenerate and minimum height trees constitute two extremes. For a given number of nodes, a degenerate tree has maximum height whereas a minimum height tree has minimum height.

The height of full trees is easy to derive. From Table 5.2 we can see that if a full tree contains n nodes and is of height h, then

$$n = 2^h - 1$$

Solving for h, we have

$$h = \log_2(n + 1)$$

In a binary search tree the number of nodes that must be examined in order to find a node is the ***search length of that node.*** It is the path length of the simple path from the root to that node. The ***search length of a tree*** is the average of the search lengths for all of its nodes.

The search length of a full tree is approximately one less than its height. The search length of a minimum height tree is approximately the same. Now we know the search lengths for the extreme cases—full and minimum height trees and degenerate trees. What about your average garden variety binary tree?

The final type of tree considered in this section is the ***random binary search tree.*** We will refer to it simply as a ***random tree.*** Its properties are derived from trees that are formed by adding elements, in random order, to a binary search tree.

It is important to understand at the outset that a random tree has properties, but that the tree itself does not really exist. The properties are obtained by computing the average value of the specified property over all possible trees in a particular group. Let us begin by describing the random trees of sizes 3 and 4.

There are six (3 factorial) permutations of the first three integers (see Figure 5.65). For each permutation a binary search tree is formed by inserting the integers, in order, into an initially empty tree. For three nodes the six resulting trees are as shown in Figure 5.66.

Two of the trees are identical. Thus the six permutations lead to only five distinct binary search trees. However, identical trees produced by distinct permutations count as separate entities when computing averages to determine properties of the random tree. The height of *the* random tree containing three nodes is calculated in Figure 5.67.

```
1  2  3
1  3  2
2  1  3
2  3  1
3  1  2
3  2  1
```

Figure 5.65
The six permutations of the first three integers.

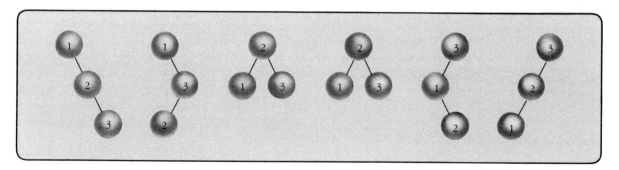

Figure 5.66   Six trees resulting from the permutation of three integers.

Similarly, there are 24 (4 factorial) permutations of the first four integers and hence 24 binary trees that are used to determine the properties of the random tree with four nodes. Of these 24 trees, 14 are distinct and are shown in Figure 5.69. The number in the brackets below each tree is the number of permutations of the first four integers that result in the construction of that tree.

$$\frac{1}{6}(3 + 3 + 2 + 2 + 3 + 3) = \frac{8}{3}$$

Figure 5.67
Height of the random tree with three nodes.

Of the 24 trees, 12 are minimum height. This illustrates an important fact that is generally true: There is a propensity for random trees to be minimum height. Calculation of the height of *the* random tree containing four nodes is shown in Figure 5.68.

In general, there are n factorial permutations of the first n integers, and therefore there are n factorial binary trees in the collection associated with *the* random tree containing n nodes.

Table 5.3 extends the results of Figures 5.66 and 5.69. It shows the number of trees of various classifications as a function of the number of nodes in the tree.

$$\frac{1}{24}(8 \times 4 + 16 \times 3) = 3\frac{1}{3}$$

Figure 5.68
Height of the random tree with four nodes.

TABLE 5.3 Number of distinct trees as a function of tree size.

Number of distinct nodes	Factorial of the number of nodes	Number of distinct binary search trees	Number of distinct minimum height binary search trees
1	1	1	1
2	2	2	2
3	6	5	1
4	24	14	4
5	120	42	6
6	720	132	4

The number of distinct binary search trees that can be constructed from n nodes is given by the nth Catalan number, whose value is

$$\frac{1}{n+1}\binom{2n}{n}$$

This result is derived in Knuth (1973a), pages 388–389, and Standish (1980), pages 54–57.

The second column in Table 5.3 shows the number of trees over which the average is taken in determining the properties of *the* random tree. The third column shows how many of the trees that are produced are actually distinct, and the fourth column shows the number of distinct trees that are minimum height. It is clear, intuitively at least, that the number of distinct trees that are minimum height is quite small. This is misleading because Table 5.3 does not show how many distinct permutations give rise to minimum height trees. In the case of 4 nodes, for example, 12 distinct permutations produce minimum height trees, of which only 4 are distinct binary trees.

Since random trees are binary search trees, the effort of a *Find* operation is determined by the height of the tree rather than its size. The usefulness of random trees will be determined by whether their height is $O(n)$, such as a degenerate tree, or $O(\log_2 n)$, such as a minimum height tree. The paucity of distinct minimum height trees raises the fear that random trees may be close cousins of degenerate trees. Fortunately, for lovers of binary trees, this is not the case. The trees that are minimum height and others of nearly minimum height are generated by many distinct permutations. The height of a random tree is of the same order of magnitude as the height of a minimum height tree. The expected and maximum heights of trees for each of our four categories are shown in Table 5.4.

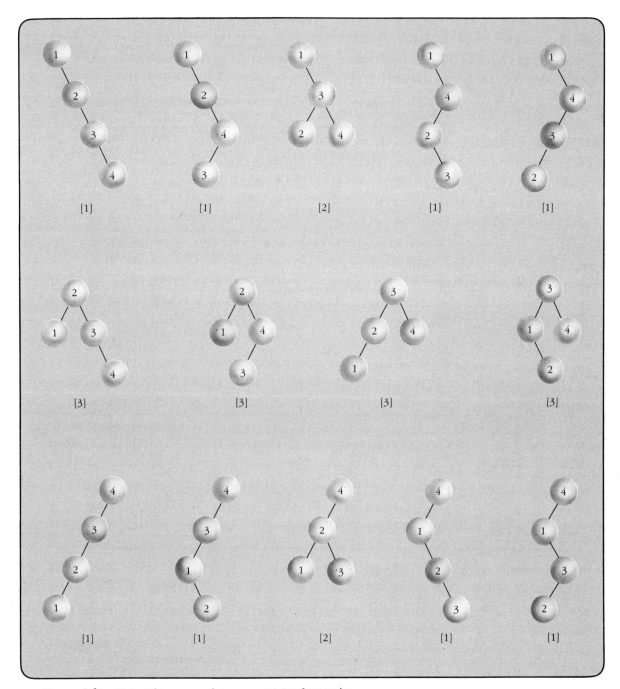

Figure 5.69 Distinct binary search trees containing four nodes.

The results concerning the
search length for a tree are
developed in Wirth (1976),
pages 213–214, Knuth (1973a),
page 427, and Standish (1980),
pages 104–105.

TABLE 5.4 Search length for a binary tree.

Type of tree	Approximate search length for the tree	Maximum search length of any node
Degenerate	$1/2\,(n + 1)$	n
Random	$1.4 \log_2(n + 1)$	n
Minimum height	$\log_2(n + 1)$	$\lceil \log_2(n + 1) \rceil$
Full	$\log_2(n + 1)$	$\log_2(n + 1)$

The results in Table 5.4 are important because they show that the expected
effort of searching a random binary search tree (although 40 percent greater
than for a minimum height tree) is proportional to $\log_2 n$. There is also a note
of caution: In the worst case, searching a randomly generated binary search
tree requires as much effort as a sequential search. Ensuring that this worst
case does not occur is the primary motivation for the AVL trees described in
Section 5.6.

Table 5.5 shows the order of magnitude of effort required for basic operations on a variety of data structures.

TABLE 5.5 Orders of magnitude of effort required to perform basic operations on various data structures.
Insertion and deletion results do not include the effort of a search to find the point of insertion or the element to
be deleted.

Data Structures	List (array)	Sorted list (array)	List (linked)	Linked implementation Binary tree	Binary search tree
Associative access	$O(n)$	$O(\log n)$	$O(n)$	$O(n)$	$O(\log n)$
Insertion	$O(1)$	$O(n)$	$O(1)$	$O(1)$	$O(1)$
Deletion	$O(1)$	$O(n)$	$O(1)$	$O(1)$	$O(1)$
Traversal in sorted order	$O(n \log n)$	$O(n)$	$O(n \log n)$	$O(n \log n)$	$O(n)$
Traversal	$O(n)$	$O(n)$	$O(n)$	$O(n)$	$O(n)$
Access by position	$O(1)$	$O(1)$	$O(n)$	$O(n)$	$O(n)$

Access by value (associative access) in a binary tree requires traversing
the tree until the element with the specified value is found. For a binary search
tree, only the simple path from the root to the location at which the target
element is located, or would be located if it were added to the tree, needs to
be searched. The number of compares needed to search a binary search tree
is comparable to the number required for a binary search of a sorted list.

Insertions and deletions require only $O(1)$ operations for a linked binary search tree and $O(n)$ moves for a sorted list stored in an array. A possible conclusion is that a large collection of data that is to be frequently searched but that is static (few insertions or deletions) should be stored in an array rather than a binary search tree. However, if there are frequent insertions or deletions, a binary search tree is the better structure.

The problem with conclusions such as the one just presented is that it ignores overhead—the constant term in an order-of-magnitude expression. We assume that a binary search of an ordered list (which requires $\log_2 n$ probes) is faster than searching a binary search tree (which requires about 1.4 $\log_2 n$ probes). Each probe in a binary search requires a calculation to determine the location of that probe. No such calculation is needed while searching a linked binary search tree. The address of the next node to be probed need only be read from its parent. Which method is actually faster depends on the programming language software and the hardware that executes the object code. Some timing studies are reported in Section 5.7.

Accessing data in sorted order means either a traversal or sorting the data and then a traversal. For a binary search tree, accessing the data in sorted order is accomplished by an inorder traversal. The data in a list or a binary tree must be sorted before it can be traversed in order. As discussed in Chapter 6, sorting usually requires $O(n \log_2 n)$ operations.

Access by position refers to accessing the kth component of the data structure. For an ordered binary tree, that means conducting an inorder traversal until the kth node is reached. On the average, half of the nodes will need to be traversed, so the effort required is $O(n)$. The effort required can be reduced to $O[\log_2(n)]$ by recording in each node the number of nodes in the left subtree. Finding the kth node then simply requires searching the simple path from the root to the desired node.

Table 5.5 does not take into account the effect that large elements might have on performance. For example, if large elements must be moved, then the number of *move* operations associated with a given data structure must be considered. Similarly, if comparing two elements is complex, then the number of comparisons must be considered separately.

Table 5.5 also does not consider memory requirements. The linked representation of trees emphasized in this chapter requires an overhead of two pointers per element—the same as a doubly linked list. Alternatives to this are discussed in Section 5.3.4, but they involve static data structures and either minimum height trees or more complex algorithms.

One of the reasons that binary trees are important is illustrated in Table 5.5. For each of the basic operations, except *Traverse*, there are one or more data structures that have the worst performance. Among the first three operations listed, a binary search tree is never one of the bad data structures. In that sense, binary search trees are uniformly not bad.

File organization techniques can be compared according to different criteria, such as storage utilization, access time in random and sequential processing, ease of modification, and usability in both one-level and two-level stores. For any one of these criteria one chooses to consider, one can usually find a file organization method which is superior to binary search trees.

However, techniques which are close to optimal in one respect have a tendency to be poor in some other respect.

The importance of binary search trees comes from the fact that they strike a reasonable compromise between the various conflicting requirements that must be considered in designing file structures. (Nievergelt, 1974)

Exercises 5.5

1. Explain the following terms in your own words:

full binary tree   degenerate binary tree
random binary tree   minimum height binary tree

2. Draw all of the distinct minimum height binary trees that contain six nodes. Each of these trees has the same search length. What is it?

3. Write specifications for and then implement a function that determines if a binary tree is a minimum height binary tree.

4. What is the height of the random tree with two nodes? With five nodes?

5. Consider binary search trees whose elements are integers. Use a random number generator to generate a sequence of random integers that are inserted one by one to create a binary search tree. Plot the height of the tree as a function of n, the number of nodes it contains. Plot the value of $1.4 \log_2 n$ on the same graph.

6. Consider Table 5.5:
   a. Describe how the values are obtained for binary trees and binary search trees.
   b. How can the values shown be used to select a data structure for an application when the value of n is small?
   c. What other factors, not shown in the table, are important in the selection of a data structure?

5.6 AVL Trees

We have seen in previous sections that binary trees are likely to have a height that is $O(\log_2 n)$. We have also seen that binary trees may have a height that is $O(n)$. If the operation we wish to perform involves traversing a simple path from the root node to a leaf, then $O(\log_2 n)$ is desirable, whereas $O(n)$ is a relative disaster. A natural question to ask is this: Can we insert and delete elements from a binary tree so that (1) the height of the tree is guaranteed to be $O(\log_2 n)$ and (2) the cost of insertion and deletion is not "outrageous"? There are several approaches that achieve this goal, and we will discuss one of them in sufficient detail to provide the flavor of the process.

We will assume throughout this section that we are working with a binary search tree. The algorithms we will discuss will apply in principle to any binary tree, but some of the details will be different if the tree is not a search tree. Our starting point is Implementation Module 5.2, Binary Search Tree, minus the *Insert* and *Delete* procedures.

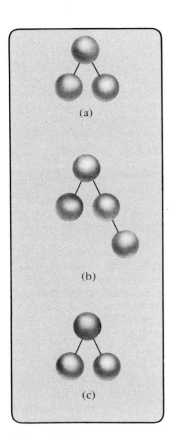

Figure 5.70
(a) A tree that is a height-balanced p-tree for any p. (b) A tree that is a height-balanced p-tree for any $p > 0$. (c) The only AVL tree that contains three nodes.

An ***AVL tree*** is a special case of a ***height-balanced tree.*** A binary tree is a ***height-balanced p-tree*** if for each node in the tree, the difference in height of its two subtrees is at most p. An AVL tree is a height-balanced 1-tree. That is, in an AVL tree, the difference in height of the two subtrees of any node is at most 1. See Figure 5.70.

To introduce and motivate the discussion of AVL trees, let us examine two sequences of trees. The first sequence contains binary search trees formed by inserting the integers 1, 2, ..., n in order. After adding n nodes, the height of the tree is n. Each tree in this sequence appears as shown in Figure 5.71.

The second sequence contains AVL trees formed by inserting the same integers in the same order. Figure 5.72 shows two trees in the sequence.

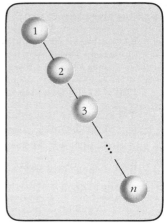

Figure 5.71
A binary search tree after inserting 1, 2, ..., n.

All binary search tree operations, except *Insert* and *Delete*, apply to an AVL tree. In this section we discuss only *Insert*.

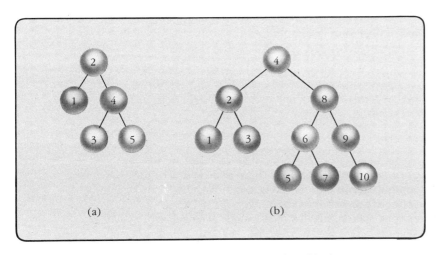

(a)   (b)

Figure 5.72   AVL trees: (a) After inserting 1, 2, 3, 4, 5. (b) After inserting 1, 2, ..., 10.

The remarkable thing about the above AVL trees is that each of them is of minimum height. It can be shown (Knuth, 1973a, page 453) that the height of an AVL tree never exceeds about $1.45 \log_2 n$. Empirical studies suggest that, as indicated by Figure 5.72, the height is approximately $\log_2 n$. This section shows how AVL trees are constructed. We will begin with an AVL tree specification (see also Figure 5.73).

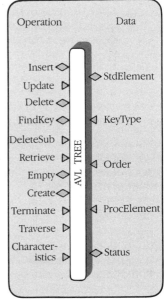

Figure 5.73
AVL tree capsule.

DEFINITION MODULE AVLTrees;

(* **Elements:** The elements of an AVL tree are nodes. We will assume that
    each node contains one standard element. A node may contain
    other items. *)

    FROM StdTypes **IMPORT** StdElement, KeyType;

(* **Structure:** The structure of an AVL tree is the same as the structure
    of a binary search tree except that, in addition, the difference in
    height of the two subtrees of any node is at most one. *)

(* **Domain:** The number of nodes in an AVL tree is bounded. *)

    EXPORT QUALIFIED AVLTree, Order, Relative, Status, Process, Insert,
                    Delete, FindKey, Update, Traverse, DeleteSub, Retrieve,
                    Characteristics, Empty, Create, Terminate;

```
    TYPE AVLTree;                    (* Opaque data type used to implement an AVL tree. *)
         Order    = (preOrder, inOrder, postOrder);
         Relative = (leftChild, rightChild, root, parent);

         Status   = RECORD                        (* Several characteristics of   *)
                      size   : CARDINAL;           (* a binary tree: size, height, *)
                      height : CARDINAL;           (* and average path length.     *)
                      avePath: REAL
                    END;

         ProcElt  = PROCEDURE (StdElement, CARDINAL);
```

(* **Operations:** A tree that is not empty always has a current node.
    Specification of the operations for an AVL tree is the same as the
    specification of the operations for a binary search tree
    (Specification 5.2) except that BST is replaced everywhere by AVL.

    Consider the Insert operation for an AVL tree. Note that it is
    responsible for returning an AVL tree. The insert operation for
    a binary search tree is responsible for returning a binary search
    tree. This illustrates a basic difference between AVL tree
    operations and binary search tree operations. *)

```
PROCEDURE Insert     (VAR AVL: AVLTree; e   : StdElement): BOOLEAN;
PROCEDURE Update     (VAR AVL: AVLTree; e   : StdElement);
PROCEDURE Delete     (VAR AVL: AVLTree; tkey: KeyType)    : BOOLEAN;
PROCEDURE FindKey    (VAR AVL: AVLTree; tkey: KeyType)    : BOOLEAN;
PROCEDURE DeleteSub  (VAR AVL: AVLTree);
PROCEDURE Retrieve   (    AVL: AVLTree; VAR e: StdElement);
PROCEDURE Empty      (    AVL: AVLTree): BOOLEAN;
PROCEDURE Create     (VAR AVL: AVLTree): BOOLEAN;
PROCEDURE Terminate  (VAR AVL: AVLTree);
PROCEDURE Traverse   (    AVL: AVLTree; ord: Order; proc: ProcElt);
PROCEDURE Characteristics (AVL: AVLTree; VAR st: Status);
```

END AVLTrees.

5.6.1 AVL Tree Representation and Implementation

The representation of AVL trees is similar to the representation of binary trees. The implementation of AVL trees is identical to the implementation of binary search trees except for operations *Insert* and *Delete,* which are more complex because they must return an AVL tree.

• **Representation**

We will discuss a linked representation, which is very similar to that used for a binary tree. The only difference is the addition of a balance field that records the relationship in height of each node's two subtrees. Using the enumerated data type,

An AVL tree is just a balanced binary search tree. The problem is how to keep the balance while inserting and deleting.

```
Balance = (tallLeft, equalHt, tallRight);
```

the representation of each node is

```
NodePtr = POINTER TO Node;
Node    = RECORD
              elt  : StdElement;
              left : NodePtr;
              right: NodePtr;
              bal  : Balance
          END;
```

If the value of *bal* for a node is tallLeft then the left subtree of that node has a height one greater than the right subtree. The other values have similar meanings. If *bal* = equalHt, then the node is said to be *balanced.* We will show the values of *bal* in figures using the symbols −, 0, + to stand for tallLeft, equalHt, tallRight, respectively.

• **Implementation**

The *Insert* operation starts out just like insertion for a binary search tree. Starting at the root, the unique simple path to the location that the node would occupy, if it were in the tree, is constructed. We will refer to this path as the **search path.** The new node is added just as it would be in a binary search tree. The tree must then be adjusted to make sure that it is still an AVL tree.

Consider the node on the search path whose balance is either tallLeft or tallRight and is closest to the new node. We will refer to this node as the ***pivot node.*** There are three cases to consider.

Case 1. There is no pivot node. Every node on the search path is balanced. In this case the tree is adjusted simply by assigning new balance values to each node on the search path. Figure 5.74 shows two examples that illustrate Case 1.

The *Insert* Operation

1. Attach the new node as in a binary search tree. The path to this node from the root is the search path.
2. Find the node on the search path that is not balanced and is closest to the new node. Call it the pivot node.
3. Adjust the tree so that the values of balance are correct and it is still an AVL tree. There are three cases to consider:
   a. There is no pivot node.
   b. The new node is added to the subtree of the pivot node, which is *short.*
   c. The new node is added to the subtree of the pivot node, which is *tall.*

Case 2. The pivot node exists and the subtree to which the new node is added has the smaller height. Adjusting the tree simply involves changing the value of *bal* for each node on the search path starting with the pivot node. Figure 5.75 shows two examples.

Symbol	Meaning
+	tallRight
−	tallLeft
0	equalHt

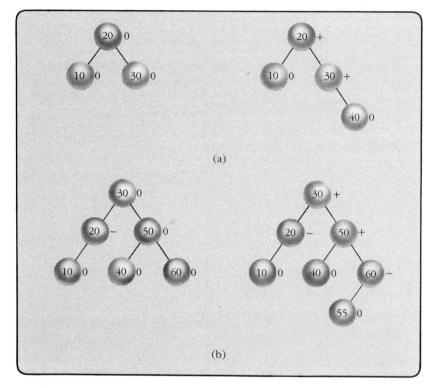

(a)

(b)

Figure 5.74   Two examples illustrating Case 1: Every node on the search path is balanced. (a) Before and after inserting 40. (b) Before and after inserting 55.

Case 3. The pivot exists, and the subtree to which the new node is added has the larger height. Adding the new node creates a tree that is not an AVL tree. The structure of the tree must be adjusted to create an AVL tree. An example of this situation is shown in Figures 5.76–5.79.

Adding a node to the tall subtree of the pivot node requires an adjustment to the tree's structure. There are two cases to consider. We will refer to them as **single rotation** and **double rotation.** With a little new notation, these cases can be described generically.

Single rotation is shown in Figure 5.77. To aid in implementing the rotation later we will assign identifiers to the pivot's parent node, $p1$, the pivot itself, $p2$, and the child of the pivot that is on the search path, $p3$.

Subtrees $T1$, $T2$, and $T3$ are arbitrary except that they all have the same height and all nodes on the search path from node A to the new node are balanced. The *remainder of the tree* is also an arbitrary tree structure subject

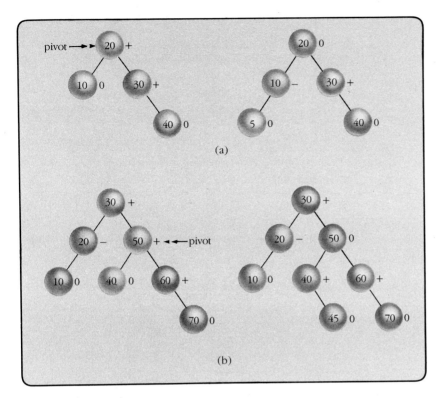

Figure 5.75 Two examples illustrating Case 2: Attaching the new node to the short subtree. (a) Before and after inserting 5. (b) Before and after inserting 45.

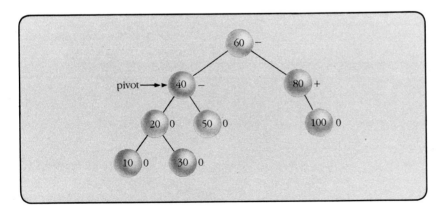

Figure 5.76 Adding 5 to this tree would create a tree that is not an AVL tree.

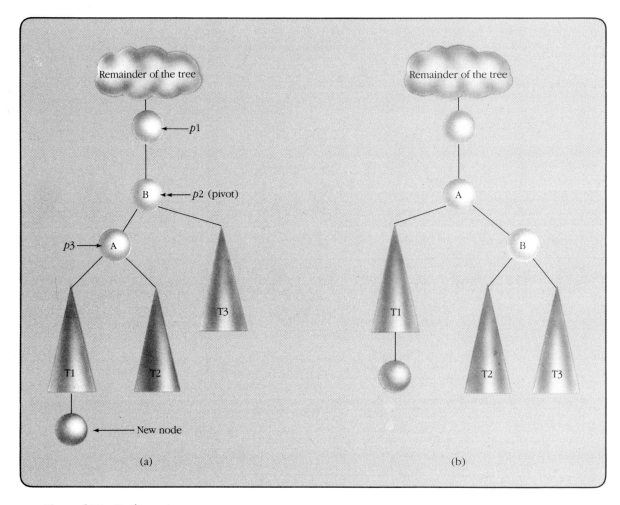

Figure 5.77   Single rotation.

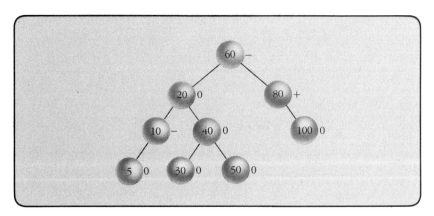

Figure 5.78   The results after adding 5 to the tree in Figure 5.76.

to the constraint, of course, that the tree is an AVL tree. It is important to note that neither the structure of the *remainder of the tree* nor the balance of any of its nodes is affected by the rotation. The reason for this is that the height of the subtree with root pivot is not changed by the insertion. Study Figure 5.77 to make sure that you see this is the case.

If 5 is added to the tree in Figure 5.76, the result of applying the rotation shown in Figure 5.77 is as shown in Figure 5.78.

Single rotation includes the mirror image of the case shown in Figure 5.77. For example, adding 110 to the tree in Figure 5.76 results in Figure 5.79.

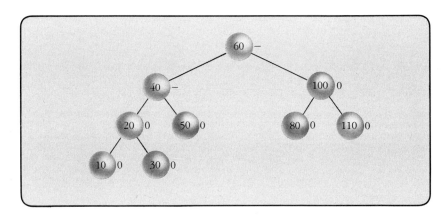

Figure 5.79   After adding 110 to the tree in Figure 5.76.

We will now consider the one remaining case—double rotation. It is generically shown in Figure 5.80.

Subtrees $T1$, $T2$, $T3$, and $T4$ are arbitrary except that $T2$ and $T3$ are of the same height and that height is one less than the height of either $T1$ or $T4$. Subtrees $T1$ and $T4$ have the same height. The portion of the search path from A to the new node contains only balanced nodes. As before, neither the structure nor the balance of any node in the *remainder of the tree* is affected by the rotation. The reason is, once again, that the height of the subtree whose root is the pivot node is not changed by the rotation.

Figure 5.81 illustrates the application of Figure 5.80 to a specific tree. Inserting any value between 20 and 60 has the same effect on the tree structure. The two values chosen for purposes of illustration are 25 and 45. The values of balance shown as ? depend on which of the two nodes is inserted.

We are now ready for Algorithm 5.6, following Figure 5.81.

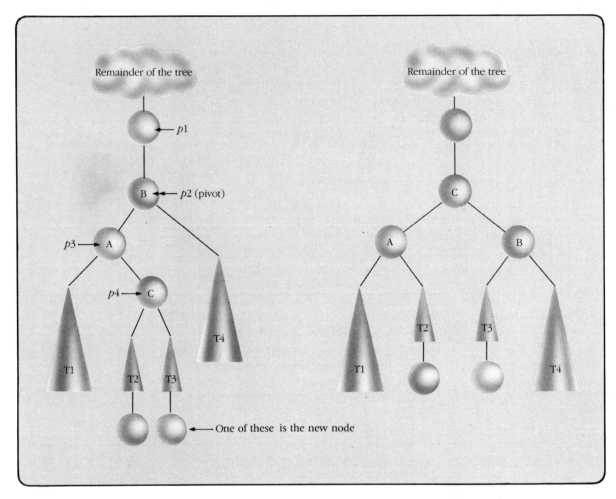

Figure 5.80 Double rotation.

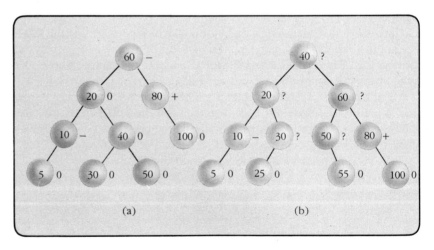

Figure 5.81 (a) Before and (b) after adding either 25 or 55 to the AVL tree.

```
PROCEDURE Insert(VAR AVL: AVLTree; e: StdElement);
BEGIN
    Attach the new element as if this were a binary search tree;
    Search for the pivot node;
    IF there is no pivot node
            THEN reset balances along the entire search path
        ELSIF the subtree is short in the direction of the new node
            THEN reset balances from the pivot node to the new node
        ELSE IF a single rotation is needed
                THEN perform single rotation
                ELSE perform double rotation
            END
    END
END Insert;
```
   Algorithm 5.6

The next step in the process of implementing *Insert* for an AVL tree is shown as Algorithm 5.7. The remainder of the implementation is left for the exercises.

```
PROCEDURE Insert(VAR AVL AVLTree; e: StdElement);
VAR p1,p2,p3,p4: NodePtr;
    PROCEDURE SetPointers();
    (* post — NodePtrs p1, p2, p3, and p4 are set as shown in Figure 5.80.
                If there is no pivot node then p2 is NIL. If p2 points to the root
                of the tree then p1 is NIL. *)

    PROCEDURE Reset(p: NodePtr);
    (* pre  — NodePtr p points to a node in tree AVL that is on the search path
                to the node containing element e.
        post — The balance of each node on the search path from p↑ to the node
                containing e is correct. That is, it recognizes the presence
                of the node containing e. *)

    PROCEDURE Short(): BOOLEAN;
    (* pre  — NodePtr p2 has the value returned by SetPointers.
        post — If e is on the short side of p↑ then Short is true else Short
                is false. *)

    PROCEDURE Single(): BOOLEAN;
    (* pre  — NodePtr p2 has the value returned by SetPointers.
        post — If a single rotation is required to balance the tree then Single
                is true else Single is false. *)

    PROCEDURE SingleRot();
    (* pre  — NodePtrs p1, p2, p3, and p4 have the values returned by SetPointers.
                AVL is not an AVL tree, but one single rotation as shown
                in Figure 5.77 will convert it to an AVL tree.
        post — AVL is a correctly balanced AVL tree. *)                    *continued*
```

PROCEDURE DoubleRot();
(* **pre** – NodePtrs p1, p2, p3, and p4 have the values returned by SetPointers.
          AVL is not an AVL tree, but one double rotation as shown in Figure 5.80
          will convert it to an AVL tree.
    post – AVL is a correctly balanced AVL tree. *)

BEGIN
    Attach the new element as if this were a binary search tree;
    SetPointers();
    IF p2 = NIL   **THEN** Reset(AVL↑.TreeRoot)
       ELSIF Short() **THEN** Reset(p2)
       ELSE IF Single()
               THEN SingleRot()
               ELSE DoubleRot()
            END
    END
END
END Insert;

Algorithm 5.7

The changes required by insertion into or deletion from an AVL tree are limited to a path between the root and a leaf. The work required is therefore at most $O(\log_2 n)$. The resulting data structure performs well when subjected to a mixture of insertions, deletions, and retrievals.

Performance penalties, all $O(n)$, that are avoided by balanced trees include the retrieval costs associated with either a degenerate binary tree or a linked list and the insertion and deletion costs imposed by a list implemented using an array. On the other hand, implementation of an AVL tree is more complex and includes more overhead than any data structure we have studied so far.

If the data set is static, then storage in an array in sorted order has desirable characteristics. Storage overhead is a minimum, and binary search yields a search length as short as can be provided by any binary tree.

For further information about AVL trees see Nievergelt (1974), Wirth (1976), pages 215–226, and Standish (1980), pages 108–118.

If the data set is of moderate size and the insertions and deletions occur in random order, then a binary search tree is preferable because of its lower overhead. To illustrate these points, in Section 5.7 we continue by applying binary search trees and AVL trees to the frequency analysis problems introduced in Chapter 4.

Exercises 5.6

1. Explain the following terms in your own words:

   AVL tree   double rotation
   single rotation   pivot node
   balanced node

2. Figure 5.72 shows an AVL tree after inserting the integers 1, 2, ..., 10. Show the tree after inserting 11, 12, ..., 20.

3. Start with the AVL tree shown in Figure 5.76 and show the tree that results from inserting

a. 15   **b.** 25
c. 45   **d.** 55

Each of these insertions acts on the original tree.

4. Figure 5.75 (b) shows an AVL tree after the integer 45 is added to a given tree. Starting with that tree, show the AVL tree that results after adding
   a. 75 and then 80   **c.** 75, 35, and 47
   b. 75 and then 65   **d.** 75, 35, and 32

5. For $n = 1, 2, ...$, draw an AVL tree containing n nodes such that no other AVL tree has greater height. Compare the height of each such tree with the value of $1.45 \log_2 n$.

6. Write an algorithm, comparable to Algorithm 5.6, for deleting an element from an AVL tree.

7. Write specifications for and then implement a function that tests a binary tree to see if it is an AVL tree.

8. Complete the implementation of the *Insert* operation begun in the text (Algorithm 5.7).

9. Write specifications for and then implement a procedure that converts a given binary tree into an AVL tree.

10. Consider an AVL tree whose elements are integers. Use a random number generator to generate a sequence of integers that are added to an AVL tree. Plot the height of the tree as a function of its size. Also plot the values of $1.45 \log_2 n$ and $\log_2 n$.

5.7 Frequency Analysis Revisited

Section 4.6 reported the results of applying a variety of linear data structures to two frequency analysis problems. This section reports the results of applying binary search trees and AVL trees to those same two problems.

First, let us briefly review the problems. The objective is to perform a frequency analysis on a string of characters. The character string is the first 2000 characters in von Neumann (1946). The basic operation is processing a character (a single letter) or a digraph (a pair of letters). Processing a digraph is described in Algorithm 5.8. The description is given for digraphs; it is the same for characters.

The first analysis is for characters. Only letters are considered, and uppercase letters are treated as if they were lowercase. Thus, a maximum of 26 elements is possible. In fact, only 24 occur among the first 2000 characters of the sample text. This example illustrates the application of a variety of data structures to a small number of elements. The predominant operation is searching the data structure.

The second analysis is for digraphs. There are at most 26^2, or 676, elements. For the sample text, only 270 distinct digraphs occur among the first 2000 characters. The number of elements is still rather small, but it is an order of magnitude larger than in the first case. The elements themselves are still small.

Figures 4.36 and 4.40 show the number of distinct characters and digraphs, respectively, as a function of the number of elements processed. In both cases,

Get the next digraph from von Neumann (1946).

Search to see if that digraph is already an element stored in the data structure.

IF it is
    THEN increment the frequency counter for that digraph
    ELSE insert the digraph with a frequency count of 1
END

Algorithm 5.8
Processing one digraph

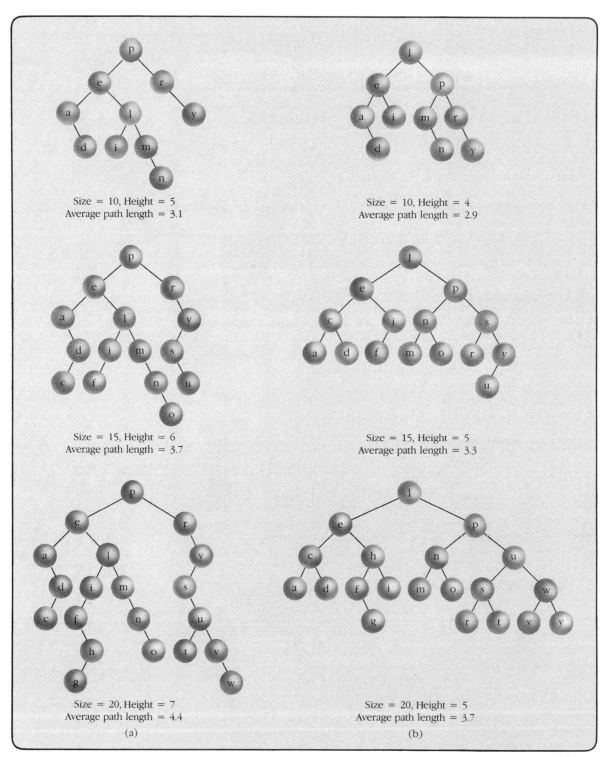

Size = 10, Height = 5
Average path length = 3.1

Size = 10, Height = 4
Average path length = 2.9

Size = 15, Height = 6
Average path length = 3.7

Size = 15, Height = 5
Average path length = 3.3

Size = 20, Height = 7
Average path length = 4.4

Size = 20, Height = 5
Average path length = 3.7

(a)

(b)

Figure 5.82   Comparison of (a) binary search trees and (b) AVL trees used in the frequency analysis of characters.

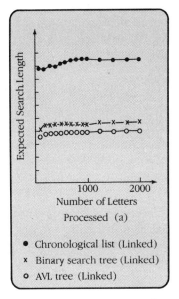

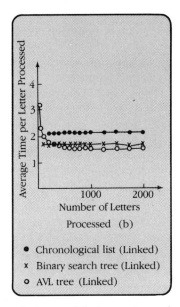

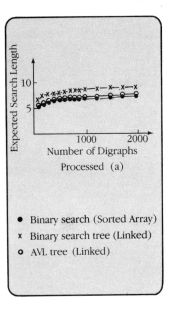

Figure 5.83 Frequency analysis of single letters. (a) Expected search length. (b) Linked representation. Average time per letter processed.

as is expected, the analysis initially involves many insertions but later involves mostly updating existing values.

It is interesting to compare the shape of binary search trees and AVL trees grown under identical circumstances. Figure 5.82 makes this comparison for the insertion of characters. The first few words analyzed are "preliminary discussion of the . . . ." Notice how the first character, "p," has an important impact on the shape of the binary search tree. All of the AVL trees are of minimum height for their size. In order to avoid a bias in their presentation, the trees are shown as printed using *Vprint,* discussed in Appendix C.

Figure 5.83 shows results for the frequency analysis of characters. Figure 5.83(a) plots the expected search length as a function of the number of characters processed. The expected search length for the binary search tree is about 20% more than for the AVL tree. The result for a chronological list is included for comparison.

Figure 5.83(b) plots the average processing time per character versus the number of characters processed. Early in the analysis, the performance of AVL trees is slower because of relatively frequent rotations. Later on, when rotations are rare, shorter expected search length compensates, and the AVL tree approach is faster. After 2000 characters, the difference is about 10%.

The time for a chronological list is included for comparison. Note that the expected search length for a chronological list is about twice that for the trees, yet the time required is nearly the same. The reason is partly the extra time required to construct the trees but mostly the extra overhead (deciding which way to go) associated with searching a tree.

Figure 5.84 shows the results for frequency analysis of digraphs. The

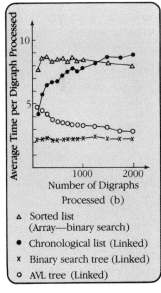

Figure 5.84
Frequency analysis of digraphs. (a) Expected search length. (b) Linked representation. Average time per digraph processed.

expected search length for a binary search of an array has been added for comparison. The result is as expected. The AVL and binary search trees have essentially the same search lengths. A binary search tree has a search length that is about 25% greater.

Figure 5.84(b) compares the times for the frequency analysis of digraphs. A sorted list using binary search and a chronological list are added for comparison. Note that after processing 2000 digraphs, the search length for the chronological list is about nine times that of a binary search tree, whereas the processing time is only about four times greater.

Figure 5.84(b) shows that the time for the analysis using binary search of a sorted array is much greater than for the trees. This is surprising since the expected search length of a binary search is $O(\log_2 n)$, as it is for both types of trees. There are two reasons why use of this data structure is relatively time consuming. First, sorted order must be maintained, so insertions usually require moving many elements in an array but none in a linked structure. Second, each probe of binary search requires calculating the location of that probe. The comparable action that occurs while traversing a search tree is following a pointer. No calculation is necessary.

Exercises 5.7

1. Repeat one or both of the studies reported in this section. Compare your results with those reported above. Explain any differences.
2. Extend the study in this section to a data set in which there are many more distinct elements. For example, do a frequency analysis of the words in some input text.
3. Extend the study in this section to a data set in which the records are much larger. An example is a collection of records about people. Each record contains a key (perhaps an integer or a name) and several hundred characters of additional information.

5.8 Heaps and Priority Queues

A **heap** is (or at least can be thought of as) a constrained binary tree data structure. It can be effectively implemented using a sequential representation based on an array, as described in Section 5.3.4. In this section, we will describe the heap structure and then use it to give an efficient implementation of a priority queue (Section 3.4). Heaps are also applied to the problems of sorting (Section 6.3.3) and graph traversal (Section 9.4).

5.8.1 Heap Data Structure

Suppose that $r[1], r[2], ..., r[n]$ is a sequence of elements. This sequence is a heap if

$$r[i] < r[2i] \text{ and } r[i] < r[2i + 1]$$

for all applicable values of i. These two inequalities will be referred to as the

heap conditions. Figure 5.85 shows three arrangements of a sequence of elements that form a heap. Each element is an integer, and each sequence contains the same set of integers. The arrows in Figure 5.85(b) show the elements that are related by the heap conditions.

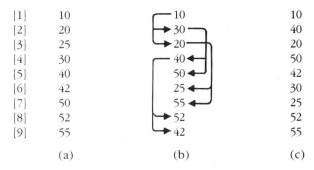

	(a)	(b)	(c)
[1]	10	10	10
[2]	20	30	40
[3]	25	20	20
[4]	30	40	50
[5]	40	50	42
[6]	42	25	30
[7]	50	55	25
[8]	52	52	52
[9]	55	42	55

Figure 5.85 Three distinct heaps formed from the same set of integers.

The data in Figure 5.85(a) are sorted. Sorted data always form a heap; but, as indicated in Figure 5.85, many other arrangements of the same data also form a heap.

In what sense is a heap a constrained binary tree? Consider the heap in Figure 5.85(b). The elements in the heap are to be inserted, in order, into a binary tree. The tree is to be constructed one level at a time, beginning at the root and working down toward the leaves. Within each level, the nodes are to be added from left to right. Applying this construction technique produces the binary tree shown in Figure 5.86. A digit inside square brackets, [ ], has been appended to each integer to show the order in which it was added to the tree. The tree shown in Figure 5.86 is a complete tree. Any minimum height tree with the nodes on the lowest level in their left most positions is a ***complete tree.***

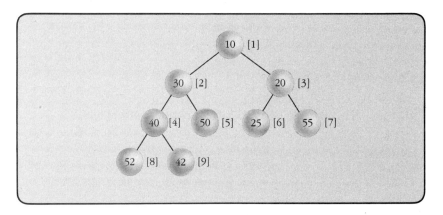

A heap can alternatively be defined as a complete binary tree in which each parent is

(a) greater than, or
(b) greater than or equal to, or
(c) less than, or
(d) less than or equal to

either of its children.

Figure 5.86 The binary tree constructed from the heap shown in Figure 5.85(b).

Look at Figures 5.85 and 5.86. The elements related by the heap conditions are precisely the elements that have a parent–child relationship in the binary tree. That is, the elements connected by arrows in Figure 5.85(b) are precisely the elements connected by the edges of the binary tree. A heap is a complete binary tree in which each parent is less than either of its children. Specification 5.4 for heaps follows.

Specification 5.4   Heaps

DEFINITION MODULE Heaps;

(* **Elements:** Because we will use heaps to implement priority queues, we assume that the elements of a heap are of type PriorityElement as shown below.

```
Priority        = CARDINAL;              (* Or other type as needed. *)
PriorityElement = RECORD
                      elt: StdElement;
                      pty: Priority
                  END; *)
```

FROM StdTypes **IMPORT** PriorityElement;

(* **Structure:** Data type Priority must be an ordered set of values. Comparing two elements from the heap means to compare their two items of type Priority. The elements form a complete binary tree such that each parent is less than either of its children. *)

(* **Domain:** The number of elements in a heap is bounded. *)

EXPORT QUALIFIED HeapCreate, SiftUp, SiftDown;

(* **Operations:** This module contains the following basic operations. *)

PROCEDURE HeapCreate (**VAR** H: **ARRAY OF** PriorityElement; n: CARDINAL);
(* **post** – Elements H[1], H[2], ... , H[n] satisfy the heap
            conditions. H[0] is not in the heap. *)

PROCEDURE SiftUp (**VAR** H: **ARRAY OF** PriorityElement; n: CARDINAL);
(* **pre** – Elements H[1], H[2], ... , H[n-1] satisfy the heap conditions.
   post – Elements H[1], H[2], ... , H[n] satisfy the heap conditions. *)

PROCEDURE SiftDown (**VAR** H: **ARRAY OF** PriorityElement; k,n: CARDINAL);
(* **pre** – Elements H[k+1], H[k+2], ... , H[n] satisfy the heap conditions.
   post – Elements H[k], H[k+1], ... , H[n] satisfy the heap conditions. *)

END Heaps.

Along any path from the root to a leaf, the elements encountered will always form an increasing sequence. Since this is true for any path, we conclude that the root element in the heap is its smallest element.

We could specify a heap in terms of a list using the heap conditions, but we do not choose to do so. We will define a heap as a constrained complete binary tree. This appears to provide a clearer, more logical, view of the heap conditions. The implementation we discuss, however, will be based on a sequential representation of the binary tree. In the heap construction example below we will present both views.

The remainder of this section discusses the construction of a heap from an arbitrary collection of elements. For purposes of illustration, we will continue to use integers as our elements.

Figure 5.87 shows two views of a complete binary tree. Figure 5.87(b) is a traditional view of a binary tree and its edges. Figure 5.87(a) is a sequential representation of the same tree. The heap conditions are not satisfied. Observe, however, that five of the elements have no children and therefore satisfy the heap conditions.

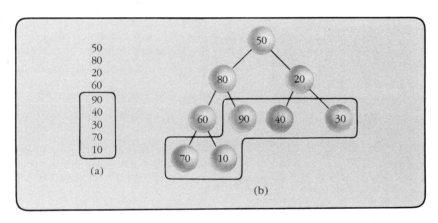

Figure 5.87 Two logical views of the same data. Boxed off elements have no children and therefore satisfy the heap conditions.

Our heap construction process will be to increase, one element at a time, the set of elements that satisfies the heap conditions. The first step, in terms of Figure 5.87(a), is to insert 60 into the sequence below it. Since our objective is to expand the set of elements satisfying the heap conditions to include 60, the technique is easier to visualize in terms of Figure 5.87(b). Since there is only one level of the tree below 60, at most one descendant of 60 will be affected by the insertion. Observe that if 60 is exchanged with its smaller child, 10 in this case, then the last six elements in the sequence will satisfy the heap conditions. This is the fundamental operation in constructing a heap—moving small children up one level in the tree.

The second step is to insert 20 into the sequence of six elements below it. Figure 5.87 is still applicable and shows that there is only one level of the tree below 20. Hence, there is only one element of concern in terms of the heap relationships. This time, since 20 is smaller than its smallest child, no exchange is necessary. The situation at this point is as shown in Figure 5.88.

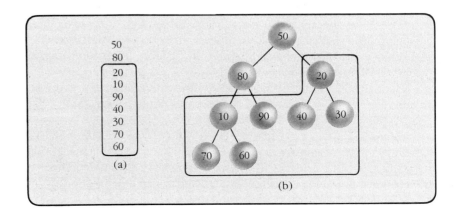

Figure 5.88
The data after 60 and 20 have been inserted. Boxed off elements must, because of the construction, satisfy the heap conditions.

The next step is to insert 80 among the seven elements below it in the sequence. The only elements that will be affected by this insertion are elements in the binary tree that lie on a path from 80 down toward a leaf node. The edges in the path are always between a parent node and its smallest child. The path terminates when a node is found that has no child smaller than the element being inserted. With regard to inserting 80 in Figure 5.88(b), the path is from 80 to 10, and from 10 to 60.

If the path length is not zero, the insertion process is simply to save the element being inserted, move the content of each of the other nodes in the path ahead one position, and insert the original element into the terminal node of the path.

The final step (see Figure 5.89) is to insert 50 into the sequence below it. The insertion path is from 50 to 10 where it terminates because both children

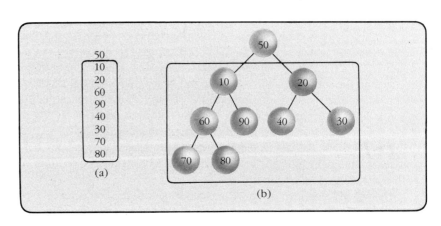

Figure 5.89
The data after 80 has been inserted. Boxed off elements must, because of the construction, satisfy the heap conditions.

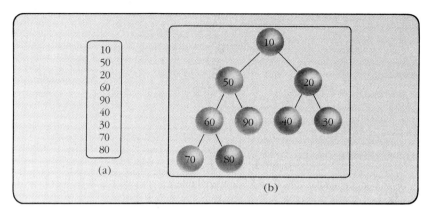

Figure 5.90 A heap.

of 10 are larger than 50. The final action is to exchange 50 and 10. The result is the heap shown in Figure 5.90.

The implementation module for heaps (Implementation Module 5.3) follows. Procedure SiftDown performs the sifting down process described by the example just discussed. It sifts an element down so that it satisfies the heap conditions. Procedure SiftUp is closely related to SiftDown. It sifts an element up so that it satisfies the heap conditions. Procedures SiftUp and SiftDown are imported and used in the priority queue module (Implementation Module 5.4) in the next section. A *PriorityElement* is a *StdElement* with an additional field of type *Priority*.

Implementation Module 5.3 *Heaps*

```
IMPLEMENTATION MODULE Heaps;
(* Heaps; array implementation; meets Specification 5.4. *)

    FROM StdTypes IMPORT Priority, PriorityElement;

PROCEDURE HeapCreate (VAR H: ARRAY OF PriorityElement; n: CARDINAL);
VAR k: CARDINAL;
BEGIN
    k := (n DIV 2) + 1;
    WHILE k > 1 DO
        DEC(k);
        SiftDown(H,k,n)
    END
END HeapCreate;
```

continued

Implementation Module 5.3, continued

```
PROCEDURE SiftUp (VAR H: ARRAY OF PriorityElement; n: CARDINAL);      (* Sift the *)
VAR child, parent : CARDINAL;                                  (* nth element up into its *)
    insertPriority: Priority;                                  (* proper position in the  *)
BEGIN                                                          (* priority queue.         *)
   insertPriority := H[n].pty;
   H[0] := H[n];                                               (* Save nth element and    *)
   child := n; parent := n DIV 2;                              (* establish a sentinel.   *)

   WHILE H[parent].pty > insertPriority DO         (* Find the position at which *)
     H[child] := H[parent];                        (* to insert the element with *)
     child := parent; parent := parent DIV 2       (* priority insertPriority.   *)
   END;

   H[child] := H[0];              (* Move the saved element to its new position. *)
END SiftUp;

PROCEDURE SiftDown (VAR H: ARRAY OF PriorityElement; k,n: CARDINAL);      (* Sift *)
VAR parent,child  : CARDINAL;                         (* the kth element down into its *)
    insertPriority: Priority;                         (* proper position in the heap.  *)
BEGIN
   parent := k; child := 2 * k;
   H[0] := H[k];                                             (* Save the kth element *)
   insertPriority := H[k].pty;                              (* and its priority.     *)

   LOOP
      IF child > n THEN EXIT END;                (* If there are no children exit. *)
      IF child < n                                         (* If there are two    *)
        THEN IF H[child].pty > H[child+1].pty             (* children select the *)
                THEN INC(child)                           (* one with smaller    *)
             END                                          (* priority.           *)
      END;
      IF insertPriority < = H[child].pty                   (* If the insertion point *)
        THEN EXIT                                          (* is found then exit,    *)
        ELSE H[parent] := H[child];                        (* else move the search   *)
             parent := child; child := 2*child            (* down one level.        *)
      END
   END;

   H[parent] := H[0];       (* Insert the saved element into its proper position. *)
END SiftDown;

END Heaps.
```

It is easy to develop an upper bound on the effort required to construct a heap. Procedure *SiftDown* follows a simple path from the root of a binary tree to one of its leaves. It examines, therefore, at most $\log_2 n$ elements. Procedure *HeapCreate* applies *SiftDown* to $n/2$ elements so a bound on the total effort is $n/2 \log_2 n$.

A heap is an excellent choice as the data structure to use in implementing a priority queue. We will now turn to a discussion of why this is the case and to the presentation of a priority queue module.

5.8.2 Heap Implementation of a Priority Queue

The specifications for a priority queue are given in Section 3.4. The discussion there shows that the effort shown in Figure 5.91 is required to implement a priority queue using a list representation.

The representation (as a heap) and implementation are given below in Implementation Module 5.4. The heap representation is chosen so that operations *Enqueue* and *Serve* will both require $O(\log_2 n)$ effort. Notice that the highest priority element is always the first element in the heap. An array representation of a heap makes locating either the child or the parent of an element simple—without the requirement of three pointers per element.

The most complex operations in the priority queue package are *SiftDown* and *SiftUp*. Each of these operations is restricted to a single path between the root of the heap and a leaf node. Because of this they each require at most $O(\log_2 n)$ effort. Each of these operations starts with $k + 1$ elements, of which k satisfy the heap conditions. Elements are rearranged so that all $k + 1$ elements satisfy the heap conditions. Operation *SiftUp* moves an element toward the root, and *SiftDown* moves an element toward a leaf. Details are in Implementation Module 5.3.

	Linked List	Heap
Enqueue	$O(n)$	$O(\log_2 n)$
Serve	$O(1)$	$O(\log_2 n)$

Figure 5.91
Effort required for the basic priority queue operations as a function of the data structure used to implement the priority queue.

Implementation Module 5.4 *Priority Queues*

```
IMPLEMENTATION MODULE PriorityQueues;
(* PriorityQueues; array implementation; meets Specification 3.4. *)

    FROM StdTypes IMPORT StdElement, PriorityElement, Priority;
    FROM Storage  IMPORT ALLOCATE, DEALLOCATE, Available;
    FROM SYSTEM   IMPORT TSIZE;
    FROM Heaps    IMPORT SiftUp, SiftDown;

    CONST MaxSize = 200;                        (* Or other value as needed. *)

    TYPE PriorityQueue = POINTER TO QueueType;
         QueueType     = RECORD
                             queue: ARRAY [0..MaxSize] OF PriorityElement;
                             size : [0..MaxSize]
                         END;

PROCEDURE Enqueue (VAR PQ: PriorityQueue; e: StdElement; py: Priority);
BEGIN
    WITH PQ↑ DO
        INC(size);
        queue[size].elt := e;  queue[size].pty := py;
        SiftUp(queue, size)
    END
END Enqueue;
```

continued

Implementation Module 5.4, continued

```
PROCEDURE Serve (VAR PQ: PriorityQueue; VAR e: StdElement; VAR py: Priority);
BEGIN
    WITH PQ↑ DO
        e := queue[1].elt; py := queue[1].pty;
        queue[1] := queue[size];
        DEC(size);
        SiftDown(queue, 1, size)
    END
END Serve;

PROCEDURE Length (PQ: PriorityQueue): CARDINAL;
BEGIN
    RETURN PQ↑.size
END Length;

PROCEDURE Full (PQ: PriorityQueue): BOOLEAN;
BEGIN
    RETURN (PQ↑.size = MaxSize)
END Full;

PROCEDURE Create (VAR PQ: PriorityQueue): BOOLEAN;
BEGIN
    IF Available(TSIZE(QueueType))
        THEN NEW(PQ); PQ↑.size := 0;
                RETURN TRUE
        ELSE RETURN FALSE
    END
END Create;

PROCEDURE Terminate (VAR PQ: PriorityQueue);
BEGIN
    DISPOSE(PQ)
END Terminate;

END PriorityQueues.
```

Exercises 5.8

1. Explain the following terms in your own words:

complete binary tree
heap

2. Using HeapCreate in Implementation Module 5.4 construct a heap from each of the following sequences of integers:
a. 10, 20, 30, 40, 50, 60, 70, 80
b. 80, 70, 60, 50, 40, 30, 20, 10
c. 80, 10, 70, 20, 60, 30, 50, 40

3. HeapCreate in Implementation Module 5.4 constructs a heap with the smallest element in the root or first position. What changes are required so that the heap will have the largest element in the first position?

4. How many moves and how many compares are required to construct a heap using HeapCreate in Implementation Module 5.4 if the original data is
   a. in sorted order?
   b. already a heap?
   c. in the inverse of sorted order?

5. Which positions might be occupied by the element with the third largest priority in a priority queue of size 32? (Assume that priorities are unique.)

6. What are the minimum and maximum numbers of elements that must be moved during operation *Serve* in Implementation Module 5.4? Show example priority queues of sizes 7, 15, and 31 that achieve these bounds.

7. Use a random number generator to generate priorities for elements to be inserted into a priority queue. Determine the number of moves and the number of compares required for operations *Enqueue* and *Serve* in Implementation Module 5.4. Plot these values as a function of the size of the priority queue. Plot the value of $\log_2(\text{size})$ on the same graph.

8. Replace HeapCreate with an algorithm that uses *SiftUp* (see Implementation Module 5.4) instead of *SiftDown* to construct a heap.

9. Describe the structure of a heap in terms of a list instead of a complete binary tree.

10. Why is a heap a good data structure for implementing a priority queue?

11. Consider the following operation.

```
PROCEDURE MergePQ(VAR PQ1,PQ2: PriorityQueue);
(* pre  — PQ1 and PQ2 are priority queues.
   post — PQ1 is a priority queue that contains all
          the elements of both PQ1-pre and PQ2-pre.
          PQ2 is empty. *)
```

An implementation of MergePQ is said to be efficient if it does not require examining a positive fraction of the elements in the priority queues that are merged.
   a. Implement MergePQ and determine if your implementation is efficient.
   b. One algorithm for MergePQ is to add each of the elements in PQ2 to PQ1. Another algorithm is to add the elements from both PQ1 and PQ2 to a third priority queue, which is returned as PQ1. Which of these two algorithms requires examining the fewest moves and compares of elements of PQ1 and PQ2?
   c. Read Sack (1985) and then repeat (a) and (b).

5.9 B-Trees

A **B-tree** is a special type of tree that has properties that make it useful for storing and retrieving information. Like a binary search tree, finding an element stored in a B-tree requires searching only a single path between the root and a leaf. Like an AVL tree, the insertion and deletion algorithms guarantee that the longest path between the root and a leaf is $O(\log n)$. The insertion and

B-trees are most often used to store data on magnetic or optical disks.

deletion algorithms are, however, quite different from those used for an AVL tree.

Unlike a binary tree, each node may contain many elements and may have many children. Because of this and because it is well balanced (like an AVL tree), a B-tree provides the possibility of very short path lengths for accessing very large collections of elements.

We will begin our presentation of B-trees with an example that illustrates the insertion and deletion processes. We will then give an algorithmic description of these operations and specifications for a B-tree. We will conclude with a discussion of the performance of B-trees.

5.9.1 Insertion and Deletion Illustrated

Each node in a B-tree contains between d and $2d$ elements, where d is the **order of the tree.** The root node is the only exception to this rule, and it may contain between 1 and $2d$ elements. The number of children of a B-tree node either is 0 or is one greater than the number of elements in that node. Let us consider an example of a B-tree of order 2 (see Figure 5.92). Keep in mind that we use a small order so as to make node illustrations feasible. In practice, B-trees of order 100 or more are common.

Each node in our example tree (except the root) contains between 2 and 4 elements. The number of children is 0, 3, 4, or 5. In our example, we assume that each element is an integer. Figure 5.92 shows a B-tree (of order 2) that contains a single node. It contains three elements. Observe that the elements in the node appear in sorted order. This is always true of a B-tree node and is part of the reason that finding an element only requires searching a single path from the root to a leaf node.

If we add 30 to the tree in Figure 5.92 the result is the tree in Figure 5.93. The tree contains one full node. Adding one additional element illustrates the most important aspect of the insertion algorithm: **node split.** Suppose we add 50. Since the only node in the tree is full, 50 cannot be stuffed into it. We then do the following and get the result shown in Figure 5.94.

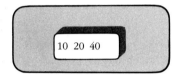

Figure 5.92
A node in a B-tree of order 2.

Figure 5.93
After adding 30 the node is full.

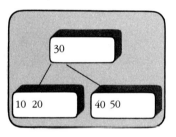

Figure 5.94
Adding 50 causes a node split.

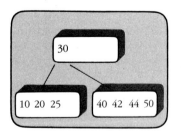

Figure 5.95
Results of adding 25, 42, 44 to the B-tree in Figure 5.94.

1. Split the node into two nodes.
2. Put the smallest two elements in the left node.
3. Put the largest two elements in the right node.
4. Create a new root node.
5. Put the middle element, 30, in the root node.

If we add 25, 42, and 44 to our B-tree, the result is as shown in Figure 5.95. The result is not affected by the order in which these three elements are added.

If any integer less than 30 is inserted in the B-tree, it will simply be added to the left node on the second level. If any integer greater than 30 is added, the insertion process will begin with the right node on the second level. Since that node is full, it must be split. To be specific, suppose that 41 is added. The result is shown in Figure 5.96.

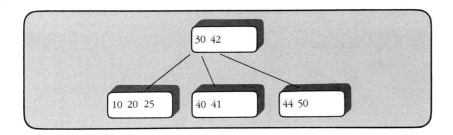

Figure 5.96
Results of adding 41.

A search for any value less than 30 begins at the root and follows 30's left pointer. A search for any value between 30 and 42 follows the pointer between those values. A search for any value greater than 42 follows 42's right pointer. Insertion begins at the leaf node that the element being inserted would be in if it were in the tree. If there is room, it is simply added to that node. If 32, 38, and 56 are added to our example tree in any order, the result is as shown in Figure 5.97.

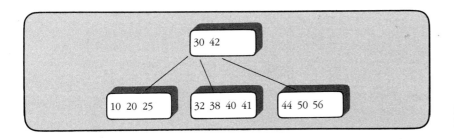

Figure 5.97
Results of adding 32, 38, and 56.

Now, if we insert any value between 30 and 42 the middle node splits. If 34 is added, then 38 is the middle element and is passed up to the level above. The result is shown in Figure 5.98. After adding 58, 60, 52, and 54 (see Figure 5.99) we are at a critical juncture.

If an integer between 42 and 56 is added, then the fourth node on level two splits. An element is therefore passed up to the root node. But the root node is full. The solution is to split the root node and pass the middle value up to a new root node. To illustrate we add 46, and the B-tree that results is shown in Figure 5.100.

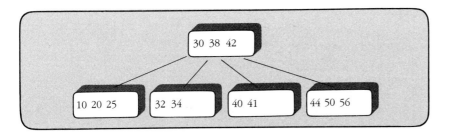

Figure 5.98
Results of adding 34.

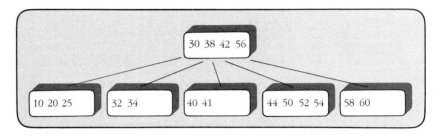

Figure 5.99   Results of adding 58, 60, 52, and 54.

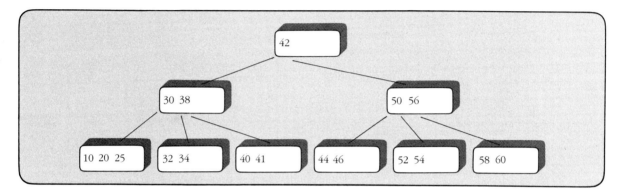

Figure 5.100   Results of adding 46.

5.9.2 Algorithmic Descriptions of Insertion and Deletion

We are now ready for a general description of the insertion algorithm. The first step is always to find the leaf node where the element would be if it were in the tree. After the correct leaf node is found, a sequence of insertion processes begins. Each process adds one element to a level of the tree and, if a node split is required, passes an element to the level above. We call these processes Insert1, Insert2, and Insert3. They act as follows, and Figure 5.101 shows how they are linked together to construct a B-tree insertion algorithm.

Insert1.   The node contains fewer than $2d$ elements and so has room to accommodate an additional element. The element is added so as to maintain sorted order, and the insertion process terminates.

Insert2.   The node is full (it contains $2d$ elements) so a node split is required. A new node is created that receives the largest d elements from the node that is being split. The smallest d elements remain in their original node, and the middle element is passed to the parent of the split node. The insertion process continues.

Insert3.   The root node is split. A new root node is created, and the element passed up becomes its only element. The insertion process terminates.

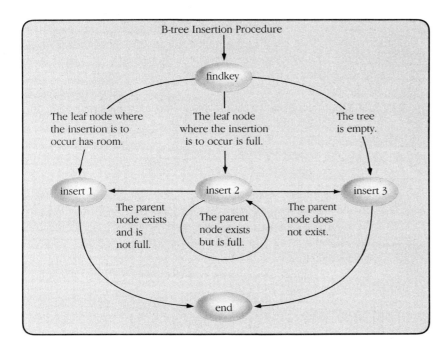

Figure 5.101   Construction of a B-tree-insertion algorithm.

An insertion in a B-tree always begins by adding an element to a leaf node. The B-tree resists increasing its height by examining every node on the path from the root to that leaf node to see if any has room for an extra element. The height of the tree increases only if all of the nodes are full. Since the height of the tree is increased by adding a new root, the tree remains well balanced.

The deletion algorithm, like insertion, begins with a leaf node. If the element to be deleted is not in a leaf node, it is replaced by the smallest element in the left most node in its right subtree (or the largest element in the right most node in its left subtree). This replacement requires removing an element from a leaf node, so we are back to starting with a leaf node. As with insertion, there are three cases to consider. The process begins with a leaf node, but these processes apply to a node at any level. We refer to the node from which the element is being removed as the ***target node.***

Delete1. The target node contains more than d elements. The target element is removed and the process terminates.

Delete2. The target node contains exactly d elements so removing one causes an underflow. If either the right or left sibling of the target node contains more than d elements, then elements are borrowed to prevent the underflow. This causes the element in the parent that separates these two children to change. This is usually done so as to balance the number of elements in the two children. The process then terminates.

If both the right and left siblings contain exactly d elements, then the target node is combined with one of them to form a new node containing $2d$ elements. One of these is the element from the parent node that separated the two nodes that are combined.

If the parent node contained more than d elements, the process terminates. Otherwise, the parent node becomes the target node and the process continues.

Delete3. The target node is the root node. As long as at least one element remains, the height of the tree does not change. If the last element was removed, then the one remaining child becomes the root of the tree.

A couple of examples will illustrate these deletion procedures. If 32 is deleted from the tree shown in Figure 5.98, 25 is borrowed from the left sibling of the node containing 32. Then 25 goes to the parent as the new separator, and 30 replaces 32. The result is shown in Figure 5.102.

If 34 is deleted next, it cannot borrow from an adjacent sibling and therefore must be combined with one. If it is combined with its right sibling the result is as shown in Figure 5.103.

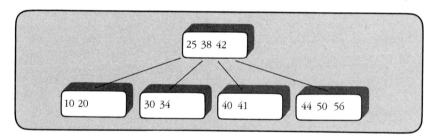

Figure 5.102 Results of deleting 32 from the B-tree shown in Figure 5.98.

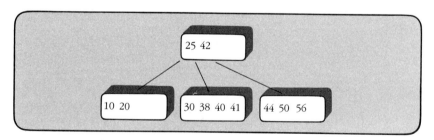

Figure 5.103 Results of deleting 34.

5.9.3 Specification

With an understanding of insertion and deletion, we are ready for the specifications of a B-tree.

Specification 5.5 BTrees

DEFINITION MODULE BTrees;

(* **Elements:** The elements of a B-tree are nodes. Each node contains
between d and 2d standard elements where d is the order of the
B-tree. One exception to this is the root node which contains
between 1 and 2d elements. *)

   FROM StdTypes **IMPORT** StdElement, KeyType;

(* **Structure:** A B-tree is an oriented tree. Each node, except the
root, has a unique parent. Each node, except the leaf nodes,
has one more child than the number of elements it contains. A
leaf node has no children. *)

(* **Domain:** The number of nodes in a B-tree is bounded. *)

   EXPORT QUALIFIED BTree, Order, Status, Process, Traverse, Insert,
                  Delete, Update, Retrieve, Characteristics, FindKey,
                  Empty, Full, Create, Terminate;

   TYPE BTree;   (* *Opaque data type used to implement a B-tree.* *)
       Order = (preOrder, postOrder);

       Status = **RECORD**   (* *Several characteristics of* *)
                   size   : CARDINAL;   (* *a B-tree: size, height,* *)
                   height : CARDINAL;   (* *and average path length.* *)
                   avePath: REAL
               END;

       ProcElt = **PROCEDURE** (StdElement, CARDINAL);

(* **Operations:** A B-tree that is not empty has a current node. We use
B-pre in the postcondition to refer to the B-tree prior to
the operation. *)

PROCEDURE Traverse (B: BTree; ord: Order; proc: ProcElt);
(* **pre** — B is not empty.
   post — Each node in the tree has been processed exactly once. The
          order in which nodes were processed depends on the value of
          ord as follows:

          CASE ord **OF**
              preOrder : Each node is processed before any node in
                         any of its subtrees.
              postOrder: Each node is processed after all nodes in all
                         of its subtrees.
          END *)

continued

Specification 5.5, continued

PROCEDURE Insert (**VAR** B: BTree; e: StdElement): BOOLEAN;
(* **pre** — B has not achieved its maximum allowable size.
    post — If B-pre did not contain an element with key value e.key,
          then e is in B and Insert is true, else Insert is false. *)

PROCEDURE Delete (**VAR** B: BTree; tkey: KeyType): BOOLEAN;
(* **post** — If B-pre contained an element with key value tkey then that
          element is not in B and Delete is true, else Delete is false. *)

PROCEDURE Update (**VAR** B: BTree; e1, e2: StdElement);
(* **pre** — B contains an element with key e1.key, but does not contain
    an element with key e2.key.
    post — B does not contain an element with key e1.key, but does
          contain e2 and e2 is in the current node. *)

PROCEDURE Retrieve (B: BTree; tkey: KeyType; **VAR** e: StdElement);
(* **pre** — B contains an element with key value tkey.
    post — Element e is the element in B with key value tkey. *)

PROCEDURE FindKey (**VAR** B: BTree; tkey: KeyType): BOOLEAN;
(* **post** — If B contains an element whose key value is tkey then the node
          that contains that element is the current node and FindKey is
          true, else the current node is the node in which an element
          containing tkey would be inserted if it were added to B, and
          FindKey is false. *)

PROCEDURE Characteristics (B: BTree; **VAR** st: Status);
(* **post** — Record st contains the size, height, and average path length
          of B. *)

PROCEDURE Empty (B: BTree): BOOLEAN;
(* **post** — If B contains zero nodes then Empty is true, else Empty
          is false. *)

PROCEDURE Full (B: ScarchTree): BOOLEAN;
(* **post** — If B has reached its maximum allowable size then Full is
          true, else Full is false. *)

PROCEDURE Create (**VAR** B: BTree): BOOLEAN;
(* **post** — If a B-tree can be created then B is an empty B-tree and
          Create is true, else Create is false. *)

PROCEDURE Terminate (**VAR** B: BTree);
(* **post** — B does not exist. *)

END BTrees.

Compare the specification for a B-tree (Specification 5.5) with the specification for a binary search tree (Specification 5.2). You will see many similarities. Some of the similarities and differences are the following.

Specifications for the following operations are identical: *Insert, Delete, Empty, Create, Terminate,* and *Characteristics.* Differences involve operations *Update, Retrieve, FindKey,* and *Traverse.*

Update modifies the element in the current node in a binary search tree. In a B-tree, since each node contains several elements, a specific element to update within a node must be identified.

Retrieve returns the element in the current node in a binary search tree. In a B-tree a specific element to retrieve within a node must be identified.

Both *FindKey* operations search for a target element. Their specifications differ in the descriptions of the node returned in the event the target element is not found. Both operations return the last node encountered during their search. For a binary search tree this is the node to which the target element would be attached if it were added to the tree. For the B-tree this is the node that would contain the target element if it were added to the tree—and the node was not full.

The traverse operation for a binary search tree includes three orders: preorder, inorder, and postorder. For a B-tree the traverse orders offered are either preorder or postorder, but not inorder, because inorder traversal—as defined for a binary tree—does not make sense for a B-tree.

• Representation

If the B-tree is of order $d,$ then each node needs to allow space for its children to store up to $2d$ elements and as many as $2d + 1$ pointers. In addition, it is convenient to have a parent pointer (to assist in processing node splits and consolidations) and a count of the number of elements actually in the node. A suitable linked representation is given in Figure 5.104.

```
CONST order    = 2;                         (* Order of the B-tree. *)
      nodeSize = 2*order;            (* Maximum elements per node. *)

TYPE NodePtr = POINTER TO Node; (* Pointer to a node of a B-tree. *)
     Node    = RECORD                       (* Node of a B-tree. *)
                 parent: NodePtr;
                 data  : ARRAY [1..nodeSize] OF StdElement;
                 ptrs  : ARRAY [0..nodeSize] OF NodePtr;
                 noElt : CARDINAL
               END;

     BTree   = POINTER TO BType;            (* B-tree data type. *)
     BType   = RECORD
                 treeRoot: NodePtr;             (* Root of tree. *)
                 current : NodePtr           (* Current node. *)
               END;
```

Figure 5.104

• Performance

The operations on a B-tree, with the exception of those involving traversal, require visiting a single node or, at most, the nodes on a path from the root to a leaf. It is important, therefore, to determine the height of B-trees in order to see how long such a path may become. We begin by constructing Table 5.6, which shows the maximum and minimum number of nodes and elements that can occur on each level of a B-tree of order d.

TABLE 5.6

Level	Minimum number of nodes	Minimum number of elements	Maximum number of nodes	Maximum number of elements
1	1	1	1	$2d$
2	2	$2d$	$2d + 1$	$2d(2d + 1)$
3	$2(d + 1)$	$2d(d + 1)$	$(2d + 1)^2$	$2d(2d + 1)^2$
4	$2(d + 1)^2$	$2d(d + 1)^2$	$(2d + 1)^3$	$2d(2d + 1)^3$
$\vdots$	$\vdots$	$\vdots$	$\vdots$	$\vdots$
k	$2(d + 1)^{k-2}$	$2d(d + 1)^{k-2}$	$(2d + 1)^{k-1}$	$2d(2d + 1)^{k-1}$

It can be seen that, in the worst case, the height of the B-tree containing n nodes is $O(\log_{d+1}n)$. To emphasize an important point, let us substitute $d = 100$ into Table 5.6. The result is shown in Table 5.7.

TABLE 5.7

Level	Minimum number of nodes	Minimum number of elements	Maximum number of nodes	Maximum number of elements
1	1	1	1	200
2	2	200	201	40,200
3	202	20,200	40,401	8,080,200
4	20,402	2,040,200	8,120,601	1,624,000,000

TABLE 5.8

Number of elements	Height of B-tree of order 100
1,000	2
10,000	2
100,000	3
1,000,000	3
10,000,000	4

Now we will translate the results in Table 5.7 into some information about the height of a B-tree of order 100 of various sizes. Table 5.8 shows the results. Table 5.8 shows how effectively a B-tree structure controls the height of a tree over a wide range of tree sizes. This makes it a valuable tool for storing a variety of large data sets. A more complete introduction to B-trees is given in Comer (1979). Implementations of B-trees are found in Bayer and McCreight (1972) and Wirth (1976). The insert operation is implemented in Appendix C.

Exercises 5.9

1. Write a structured English description of insertion and deletion operations for a B-tree of order d.

2. Show the B-tree of Figure 5.98 after
   a. inserting 26 and 27
   b. inserting 57, 58, 59, 60, and 61
   c. deleting 50
   d. deleting 25 and 30
3. Show the B-tree of Figure 5.100 after inserting 61, 62, 63, . . ., until the tree is of height 4.
4. Show the tree of Figure 5.100 after
   a. deleting 25
   b. deleting 41
5. Construct the equivalent of Table 5.8 for a B-tree of order 200.
6. Find the relationship between the height h of a B-tree of order d and its size n.
   a. Assume the tree is of maximum height.
   b. Assume the tree is of minimum height.
   c. Assume each node in the tree is exactly ⅔ full. (Empirical results suggest that in practice the expected number of elements in a B-tree node is ⅔ of its capacity.)
7. A B-tree of order 1 is often called a 2–3 tree since each node contains at most 2 elements and has at most 3 children. Construct Table 5.7 for a 2–3 tree. Construct a similar table for a binary tree. Discuss the advantages and disadvantages of a 2–3 tree relative to binary search trees and AVL trees.

It can be shown that the height of a B-tree of order d is between

$$\log_{(2d+1)}(n+1) \quad \text{and} \quad 1 + \log_{(d+1)}((n+1)/2)$$

and that the expected number of node splits during an insertion is at most $1/d$. Wright (1985) shows, assuming the root node is half full, that the average height of a B-tree is

$$1 + \log_{(1.38d+1)}(n/(d+1))$$

and that the average number of node splits during an insertion is $1/(1.38d)$.

5.10 Summary

Chapter 5 introduced trees. Despite its length, many types of trees and many applications were not mentioned. We introduced the basic notation and terminology of trees and explored binary trees in some depth.

Four binary tree modules are included, among them Implementation Module 5.1 for binary trees and Implementation Module 5.2 for binary search trees. Several attributes of the four modules are given in Table 5.9. These attributes can be compared with the same attributes for stacks, queues, and lists given in Tables 3.1 and 4.1.

We have observed the hierarchical structure of trees, seen the basic tree operations (such as *Insert, Delete,* and *Traverse*), observed the important relationship among stacks, recursion, and trees, and briefly considered several alternative sequential representations of trees. One of these, the heap, provides a particularly effective representation for another important data struc-

TABLE 5.9

Implementation Module	Data structure	Representation	Number of procedures	Total lines	Average lines	Maximum lines
5.1	Binary tree	Linked	13	124	9.5	37
5.2	Binary search tree	Linked	4	56	14.0	28
5.3	Heaps	Array	3	44	14.7	22
5.4	Priority queues	Array	6	37	6.2	9

ture—the priority queue. A specification for the priority queue is given in Chapter 3 (Specification 3.4), and Implementation Module 5.4 provides an implementation.

We discussed applying both binary search trees and AVL trees to the frequency analysis of single characters and digraphs. This example supports the contention that binary search trees perform well when subjected to a mix of operations including *Insert, Delete,* and *FindKey.*

The introduction to B-trees was brief, but it gives us a glimpse of one of the variety of tree structures available. Specification 5.5 describes the B-tree data structure and emphasizes its similarity to binary trees and binary search trees.

Internal Sorting 6

6.1 Introduction
  6.1.1 The Sorting Problem
  6.1.2 Specification of Sorting Algorithms
  Exercises 6.1

6.2 Simple Sort Techniques
  6.2.1 Selection Sort
  6.2.2 Exchange Sort
  6.2.3 Insertion Sort
  *6.2.4 Insertion Sort—Implemented for a
        Linked List*
  6.2.5 Performance of Simple Sorts
  Exercises 6.2

6.3 Advanced Sort Techniques
  6.3.1 Quicksort
  6.3.2 Treesort
  6.3.3 Heapsort
  6.3.4 Mergesort
  Exercises 6.3

6.4 Radix Sort
  6.4.1 Example of a Radix Sort
  6.4.2 General Process for a Radix Sort
  6.4.3 Drawbacks of a Radix Sort
  Exercises 6.4

6.5 Summary

Many different sorting algorithms have been invented, and we will be discussing about 25 of them in this book. This rather alarming number of methods is actually only a fraction of the algorithms that have been devised so far.

Why are there so many sorting methods? . . . the answer is that each method has its own advantages and disadvantages so that it outperforms the others on some configurations of data and hardware.

. . . there are many best methods, depending on what is to be sorted on what machine for what purpose. (Knuth, 1973b)

6.1 Introduction

A good deal of the effort in computing is related to putting data available to users in some particular order. For example, lists of names are frequently printed in alphabetical order, mailing labels are often printed in zip code order, and delinquent accounts are often in order according to the length of time the account has been delinquent.

Ordering data has an important impact on searching. Data that are not ordered must normally be searched using a sequential scan of all the data. Ordered data lend themselves to simple search techniques, such as a binary search, which have superior performance characteristics. (See Section 4.3.2 for a discussion of binary search.)

In this chapter we are concerned with rearranging the data so that it is in **sorted order.** There are two important and largely disjoint categories related to sorting data—**internal sorting** and **external sorting.** They are illustrated in Figure 6.1.

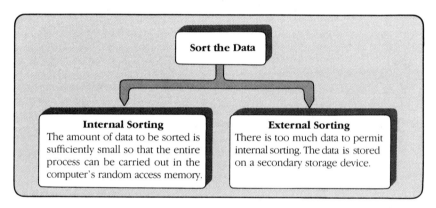

Figure 6.1   Sorting data.

Much of the discussion in this chapter assumes that the elements to be sorted are stored in an array. Most of the algorithms can easily be converted to sort elements in a doubly linked list. Only a few of the algorithms work well for singly linked lists since scanning a list in both directions becomes very expensive. At least one algorithm, radix sort, works well for linked lists, but it does not work for arrays. We will discuss the issues involved in applying sorting algorithms to various list implementations as we proceed.

In this chapter we will only be concerned with internal sorting. There are a large number of internal sorting techniques, and the determination of the best one for a particular problem requires careful analysis of many alternatives.

We will introduce the fundamental principles of internal sorting and suggest references for those of you who want to know more. There is one internal sort algorithm that is widely regarded as the best general-purpose algorithm available. This algorithm, quicksort, is described in detail in Section 6.3.1.

Internal sorting algorithms are often classified according to the amount of work required to sort a sequence of elements. The amount of work refers to the two basic operations of sorting: comparing two elements and moving an element from one place to another. The major internal sorting techniques fall into one of three categories with respect to the work required to sort a sequence of n elements—simple sort, advanced sort, and radix sort. These categories are shown in Figure 6.2.

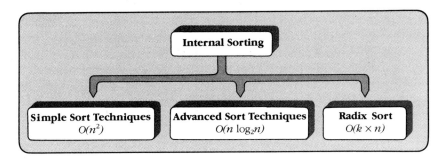

Figure 6.2 Internal sorting.

The performance of an algorithm for various representations of the list data structure is important because the user of a sort algorithm will not want to convert the data from one representation to another, sort it, and then convert it back. If the data are in a linked list, the user will want an algorithm that sorts linked lists.

Simple sort techniques, discussed in Section 6.2, can be expected to require on the order of n^2 compares and/or moves to sort a list of n elements. Advanced sort techniques, discussed in Section 6.3, can be expected to require on the order of $n \log_2 n$ compares and/or moves to sort a list of n elements. Radix sort, discussed in Section 6.4, requires on the order of $k \times n$ pointer manipulations to sort a linked list of n elements. (k is the number of characters in the item upon which the sort is based.)

6.1.1 The Sorting Problem

Table 6.1 shows a list of elements containing information about employees. The information for each employee, contained in one ***element,*** is shown on one line. The collection of all such elements is called an employee list. In this example, the employee list contains nine elements and for purposes of internal sorting would probably be stored using either an array or a linked representation.

TABLE 6.1 Employee file sorted into ascending order by employee number.

Element position	Employee number	Name	Department	Salary
1	007	Eckert, John	Hardware	72
2	015	Mauchly, John	Hardware	40
3	021	Backus, John	Language	46
4	036	Turing, Alan	Cryptography	74
5	042	Good, I.J.	Cryptography	40
6	049	von Neumann, John	Language	69
7	077	Hopper, Grace	Language	37
8	098	Babbage, Charles	Hardware	74
9	103	Lovelace, Ada	Language	64

Each element contains a number of ***fields.*** In our example, each element has four fields and one element position. ***Element position*** refers to the location of the element within the list and is not stored as part of the element.

If the list is stored using an array, position is also the ***index,*** or ***subscript,*** value of an element.

Any particular copy of a list can be sorted with respect to at most one of its fields (or perhaps a concatenation of several fields). We will call that field the ***sort field,*** or ***sort item.*** Sorting a list thus refers to placing the elements in the list in order with respect to the values in the sort item. The sort item can be any item, or combination of items, as long as the values in that item, or combination of items, can be ordered.

For example, if we sort the list in Table 6.1 using salary as the sort item, we get the list shown in Table 6.2.

In Table 6.2 the data in each element have been moved to a new position relative to the other elements. (Note the new values of element position.) If each element contains a lot of data in addition to the value in the sort item, it may be prudent to sort only the sort item without involving the other data in the element. This can result in a substantial performance improvement if the sort technique requires numerous moves of the elements being sorted, as illustrated in Table 6.3.

TABLE 6.2 Employee file sorted into ascending order by salary.

Element position	Employee number	Name	Department	Salary
1	077	Hopper, Grace	Language	37
2	015	Mauchly, John	Hardware	40
3	042	Good, I.J.	Cryptography	40
4	021	Backus, John	Language	46
5	103	Lovelace, Ada	Language	64
6	049	von Neumann, John	Language	69
7	007	Eckert, John	Hardware	72
8	036	Turing, Alan	Cryptography	74
9	098	Babbage, Charles	Hardware	74

TABLE 6.3 Employee list sorted into ascending order by salary. Element position points to the element as stored in Table 6.1.

Salary	Element position
37	7
40	2
40	5
46	3
64	9
69	6
72	1
74	4
74	8

Table 6.3 shows an alternative to Table 6.2. It is obtained by sorting the salary field (the sort item) of each element, together with the element's position in the list. This permits the list to be sorted without the expense of moving all the data in each element. The element position serves as a pointer to the complete element as it is actually stored (see Table 6.1). The abbreviated list is often called an ***index array*** or ***index list.***

Section 6.1.1 establishes an understanding about the basic nature of internal sorting algorithms. To summarize, lists are generally sorted on the value of a particular field. The sort process may involve moving entire elements, or the elements of an index list, or not moving elements at all. The basic sort mechanisms, however, are not affected by how much of each element participates in the sorting operation. With this in mind, we will describe sorting algorithms in terms of lists that contain simple elements—elements that consist of a single integer. This is done so as to make the description of the underlying algorithms as clear as possible.

Converting an algorithm that sorts a list of integers to an algorithm that sorts a list of elements, each containing many fields, is a straightforward matter. The algorithms presented in Chapter 6 should be viewed from this perspective. Several of the exercises ask you to make such conversions.

In several of the algorithms in Chapter 6 it will become necessary to exchange two elements. For example, suppose x and y are two elements. Instead of inserting a code segment each time an exchange of x and y is needed, we will use procedure *Swap,* shown in Figure 6.3.

```
PROCEDURE Swap (VAR x,y:
                      StdElement);
VAR t: StdElement;
BEGIN
    t := x;
    x := y;
    y := t
END Swap;
```

Figure 6.3
Procedure *Swap.*

6.1.2 Specification of Sorting Algorithms

A Modula-2 definition module for the sorting algorithms described in this chapter is given in Specification 6.1. The sorting algorithms are all shown in one definition module in order to emphasize the uniformity of the interface. The implementations are not collected together in one implementation module, but are distributed over the entire chapter.

Note that in each case the data to be sorted is passed to the sort procedure using an open array parameter.

Specification 6.1   Sorting

```
DEFINITION MODULE Sorting;

(* Each of the procedures in this module, except HeapSort, sorts an
   array of standard elements into ascending order. HeapSort sorts into
   descending order.

   The sorting procedure implementations are scattered throughout
   Chapter 6. The definition module provides an overview of the
   procedures given and emphasizes the uniformity of the interfaces. *)

FROM StdTypes IMPORT StdElement;

EXPORT QUALIFIED SelectSort, ExchangeSort, InsertSort, QS2, QS3,
                 MergeSort, HeapSort;

PROCEDURE SelectSort   (VAR r: ARRAY OF StdElement);
PROCEDURE ExchangeSort (VAR r: ARRAY OF StdElement);
PROCEDURE InsertSort   (VAR r: ARRAY OF StdElement);
PROCEDURE QS2          (VAR r: ARRAY OF StdElement);          (* QuickSort *)
PROCEDURE QS3          (VAR r: ARRAY OF StdElement);  (* Improved QuickSort *)
PROCEDURE MergeSort    (VAR r: ARRAY OF StdElement);
PROCEDURE HeapSort     (VAR r: ARRAY OF StdElement);

END Sorting.
```

Exercises 6.1

1. Write procedure *Swap* for the case in which x and y are pointers to nodes in a doubly linked list.
2. Replace Specification 6.1 with a Modula-2 definition module to sort data stored using a doubly linked list.
3. In Specification 6.1 each procedure accepts an array of records as input, rearranges the array elements, and returns the array with the records in sorted order. Write a definition module so that each procedure has the array r of elements to be sorted as input and an array, say t, of type CARDINAL as output. The elements of array r are not moved by the sort process. Instead, the output array provides access to the elements of r in sorted order. That is, the identifiers $r[t[1]], r[t[2]], r[t[3]], \ldots$ access the elements of r in sorted order.

6.2 Simple Sort Techniques

6.2.1 Selection Sort

The basic operation in a **selection sort** is the selection of the smallest (or largest) element from a sequence of elements. Figure 6.4 illustrates the process for a sequence of five integers.

Figure 6.4(a) shows the five integers that constitute the input to the selection sort. The smallest integer, 45, is selected and exchanged with the first integer, 390. This produces a sorted list of length one, as shown in Figure 6.4(b). Integers that are sorted are shown in boldface throughout this chapter.

Next, the smallest integer among the second through the last integers is selected and then exchanged with the second integer in the list. This produces a sorted list of length two, as shown in Figure 6.4(c).

The transition from Figure 6.4(c) to Figure 6.4(d) is accomplished by selecting the smallest integer among the third through the last integers in the list. This element is then exchanged with the third integer in the sequence. The result, shown in Figure 6.4(d), is a sorted list of length three.

The final step is to select the smallest integer from among the fourth and fifth integers and to exchange that integer with the fourth integer. This is done, and, as shown in Figure 6.4(e), the entire list is now sorted.

Algorithm 6.1 implements selection sort as we just described it.

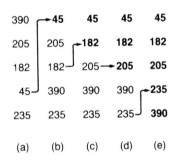

Figure 6.4
Selection sort. The integers that are known to be sorted at the beginning of each step are shown in boldface.

```
PROCEDURE SelectSort (VAR r: ARRAY OF StdElement);
VAR j,k,small: CARDINAL;                    (* Selection sort. *)
BEGIN
    IF HIGH(r) > 0
    THEN FOR k := 0 TO HIGH(r)-1 DO
            small := k;
            FOR j := k+1 TO HIGH(r) DO       (* Find smallest   *)
                IF r[j].key < r[small].key   (* element of      *)
                    THEN small := j          (* r[k]..r[HIGH(r)] *)
                END                          (* & exchange      *)
            END;                             (* with r[k].      *)
            Swap(r[k],r[small])
        END
    END
END SelectSort;
```

Algorithm 6.1   Selection sort.

The logic of procedure *SelectSort* is typical of the logic of simple sort algorithms. It consists of an ***outer loop*** and an ***inner loop.*** In procedure *SelectSort* each of these is implemented using a FOR construct. The inner loop is executed the following number of times:

$$(n - 1) + (n - 2) + \cdots + 1 = \frac{1}{2}n(n - 1) = O(n^2)$$

The outer loop is executed $n - 1$ times. Each execution of the inner loop requires one comparison and an unknown number of assignments. Each execution of the outer loop requires one exchange. The total effort is summarized in Figure 6.5.

It is noteworthy that the effort required, as measured by the number of comparisons and exchanges, is independent of the arrangement of the data being sorted. On the negative side, *SelectSort* requires $O(n^2)$ compares no matter how the data are initially ordered. On the positive side, it never requires more than $O(n)$ moves. This makes *SelectSort* a good method for large elements (that are expensive to move) with short sort items (that are easy to compare). Other methods become competitive in this case if only the sort item along with a pointer to the data are actually sorted or if the data are in a doubly linked list.

Exchanges $= n - 1$
Compares $= 1/2\,n(n - 1)$

Figure 6.5
Execution of *SelectSort*.

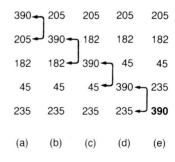

(a)   (b)   (c)   (d)   (e)

Figure 6.6
Exchange sort. The first pass of an exchange sort.

6.2.2 Exchange Sort

The basic operation in an ***exchange sort*** is the exchange of an adjacent pair of elements. The overall sort process consists of a number of passes over the data. Each pass starts at one end of the array and works toward the other end. Each pair of elements that is out of order is exchanged. Figure 6.6 illustrates the process of sorting into ascending order.

In Figure 6.6, the first pass is made over the data given in Figure 6.2(a).

First, 390 is compared with 205; then they are exchanged since 205 is smaller. The result is shown in Figure 6.6(b). Next, 390 is compared with 182, and they are exchanged. The result is shown in Figure 6.6(c). Then, 390 is compared with 45, and they are exchanged, giving Figure 6.6(d). Finally, 390 is compared with 235, and they are exchanged. The final result is seen in Figure 6.6(e).

The first pass moves the largest element to the nth position, forming a sorted list of length one. The second pass only has to consider $n - 1$ elements. The second pass moves the second largest element to the $n - 1$ position. Therefore the third pass only needs to consider $n - 2$ elements. In general, after i passes the i largest elements will be in the last i positions, so pass $i + 1$ need only consider $i - 1$ elements.

In the meantime the small elements are moving slowly, or bubbling, toward the top. Therefore this sort technique is frequently referred to as a **bubble sort.**

If no exchanges are made during one pass over the data, the data are sorted and the process terminates. We check to see if an exchange is made in a given pass by using the boolean variable *sorted*. At the beginning of each pass *sorted* is set to *true*. If an exchange is made, then *sorted* is set to *false*. (In fact, *sorted* is set to *false* every time an exchange is made, not just the first time. This is a small performance penalty.)

Algorithm 6.2 now shows the procedure that implements an exchange, or bubble, sort.

```
PROCEDURE ExchangeSort (VAR r: ARRAY OF StdElement);
VAR j,k,small: CARDINAL;                    (* Exchange sort *)
    sorted    : BOOLEAN;
BEGIN
   k := HIGH(r); sorted := FALSE;
   WHILE (k > 0) AND (NOT sorted) DO
      sorted :- TRUE;
      FOR j := 0 TO k-1 DO
         IF r[j].key > r[j+1].key
            THEN Swap (r[j],r[j+1]); (* Reorder adjacent *
               sorted := FALSE      (* elements so that *
            END                      (* smaller is first. *
      END;
      k := k - 1
   END
END ExchangeSort;
```

Algorithm 6.2   Exchange, or bubble, sort.

In procedure *ExchangeSort* the outer loop is implemented with a WHILE statement and the inner loop with a FOR statement. The inner loop is executed the following number of times:

$$(n - 1) + (n - 2) + \cdots + (n - k_{\text{sorted}}) = \frac{1}{2}(2n - k_{\text{sorted}} - 1)(k_{\text{sorted}})$$

where k_{sorted} is the number of executions of the outer loop before there is a pass during which there are no exchanges. The inner loop contains one comparison and sometimes an exchange.

The best performance occurs when k_{sorted} is 1. This means that no exchanges occur because the original data were sorted. The number of comparisons used by procedure *ExchangeSort* to determine this is

$$\frac{1}{2}(2n - 2)(1) = n - 1 = O(n)$$

The worst performance occurs when k_{sorted} is $n - 1$. The inner loop is then executed the following number of times:

$$\frac{1}{2}n(n - 1) = O(n^2)$$

When we translate loop executions into exchanges and compares, we obtain the results shown in Figure 6.7.

An *ExchangeSort* has two major drawbacks. First, its inner loop contains an exchange that requires three moves. Notice that in *SelectSort* there are no moves in the inner loop. Second, when an element is moved, it is always moved to an adjacent position. In *SelectSort,* an element may move a long distance, and it always moves to its sorted position. All in all, *ExchangeSort* is one of the slowest sorting algorithms known. Its popularity seems to stem from its catchy alias—bubble sort.

6.2.3 Insertion Sort

The basic operation in an ***insertion sort*** is the insertion of a single element into a sequence of sorted elements so that the resulting sequence is still sorted. Figure 6.8 illustrates the process for five elements, each of which is an integer.

The input data, an array of five integers, are shown in Figure 6.8(a). When the fifth element, 235, is considered by itself, it is a sorted list of length one.

The transition from Figure 6.8(a) to Figure 6.8(b) consists of inserting 45 into the list of elements that is already sorted. Since 45 is less than 235, the insertion of 45 is at the top of the list. As shown in Figure 6.8(b), the sorted segment of the list now has a length of two.

The transition from Figure 6.8(b) to Figure 6.8(c) is accomplished by inserting 182 into the list of elements that is already sorted. Since 182 is between 45 and 235, it is inserted between them by moving 45 up to make room. The sorted subset of the list has now grown to a length of three.

Figure 6.8(d) is obtained by inserting 205 into the list of elements that is already sorted. This is accomplished by moving 45 and 182 up to make room. Finally, Figure 6.8(e) is obtained by inserting 390 into the list of elements (of length four) that is already sorted.

Figure 6.8 illustrates the procedure in Algorithm 6.3, which follows. The algorithm performs an insertion by scanning the elements below the element to be inserted. Each element that is small compared to the element to be

Exchanges = $1/2n(n - 1)$
Compares = $1/2n(n - 1)$

(a)

Exchanges = 0
Compares = $n - 1$

(b)

Figure 6.7
Execution of *ExchangeSort.*
(a) Worst case. (b) Sorted data.

•

. . . in fact, the Bubblesort has hardly anything to recommend it except its catchy name. (Wirth, 1976)

•

390	390	390	390	45
205	205	205	45	182
182	182	45	182	205
45	45	182	205	235
235	235	235	235	390

(a) (b) (c) (d) (e)

Figure 6.8
Insertion sort. The integers that are known to be sorted at the beginning of each step are boldface.

•

Moves   = $1/2n(n - 1)$
Compares = $1/2n(n - 1)$

(a)

Moves   = $1/4n(n - 1)$
Compares = $1/4n(n - 1)$

(b)

Moves   = $2(n - 1)$
Compares = $n - 1$

(c)

Figure 6.9
Execution of *InsertSort.* (a) Worst case. (b) Average. (c) Sorted data.

inserted is moved up one position. As soon as an element is found that is large compared to the element to be inserted, the scan terminates and insertion occurs ahead of the large element.

```
PROCEDURE InsertSort (VAR r: ARRAY OF StdElement);
VAR j,k : CARDINAL;                    (* Insertion sort *)
    save: StdElement;
BEGIN
   IF HIGH(r) > 0
      THEN FOR k := HIGH(r)-1 TO 0 BY -1 DO
              j := k + 1; save := r[k];

              WHILE (j <= HIGH(r)) AND
                    (save.key > r[j].key) DO
                 r[j-1] := r[j];    (* Insert r[k] into *)
                 j := j + 1         (* its sorted       *)
              END;                  (* position among   *)
                                    (* r[k+1]..r[n].    *)
              r[j-1] := save
           END
   END
END InsertSort;
```

Algorithm 6.3 Insertion sort.

The outer loop of procedure *InsertSort* is always executed $n - 1$ times. The number of executions of the inner loop depends both on the value of k and the order of the data. In the case of sorted data, the inner loop is never executed. In the worst case it is executed the following number of times:

$$1 + 2 + \cdots + n - 1 = \frac{1}{2}n(n - 1) = O(n^2)$$

Given all possible initial orderings of data, on the average, the inner loop is executed half as many times as in the worst case. This is because the inner loop of procedure *InsertSort* is probing a sorted list looking for the first element that is larger than the one being inserted. On the average, this requires probing half the list.

The inner loop of *InsertSort* requires more effort than the inner loop of *SelectSort*—one move versus none. It requires less effort than *ExchangeSort*. For short elements, the move in the inner loop is more than balanced by only executing the inner loop half as often, and *InsertSort* gives better performance.

Because of its low overhead and favorable performance for nearly sorted data, *InsertSort* will be combined with quicksort (in Section 6.3.1) to produce the best general-purpose internal sorting algorithm known at this time.

So far, we have ignored sorting data that are stored in a doubly linked list. Section 6.2.4 moves in that direction by considering an implementation of an insertion sort for linked lists.

6.2.4 *Insertion Sort—Implemented for a Linked List*

This section uses the same insertion sort algorithm (Algorithm 6.3) as Section 6.2.3. The difference is that here we use a linked list rather than an array. The performance implications of this change may be considerable. With an array a substantial number of element moves may be required. **With a linked list the number of element moves is zero!**

  Figure 6.10 provides a logical view of the doubly linked data structure used in this section. The list is accessed by two pointers, *head* and *tail,* which identify the ends of the list. This is similar to the doubly linked list discussed in Section 4.2. Algorithm 6.4 presents a Modula-2 procedure, *SortLink,* for an insertion sort for a doubly linked list.

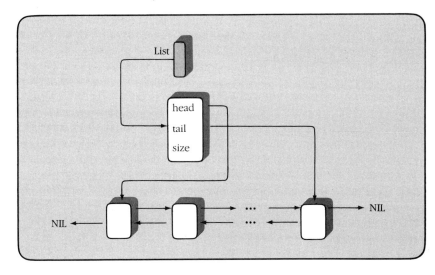

Figure 6.10
Logical view of a doubly linked data structure.

```
PROCEDURE SortLink(VAR L: List);      (* Insertion sort for a doubly linked list. *)
VAR p, psave, pinsert: Pointer;                      (* See Figure 6.10. *)
BEGIN
    IF (L↑.size # 0) AND (L↑.head # L↑.tail)
       THEN p := L↑.tail↑.prior;

          WHILE p # NIL DO                (* Use psave to save the location of *)
              psave   := p↑.prior;        (* the next element to be inserted.   *)
              pinsert := Locate(p);       (* Procedure Locate finds the node    *)
              IF pinsert # p↑.next        (* such that p↑ is its predecessor.   *)
                 THEN Remove(L,p);                    (* Remove p↑ from the list. *)
                      InsertBefore(L,p,pinsert)         (* Insert p↑ as the pre- *)
              END;                                     (* decessor of pinsert↑.  *)
              p := psave
          END

                                          (* Procedures Locate and Remove *)
       END                                (* are left as exercises.       *)
END SortLink;
```

Algorithm 6.4   Insertion sort for sorting a doubly linked list into ascending order.

Procedures *Locate, Remove,* and *InsertBefore* are special cases of the procedures given in Chapter 4. The number of executions of the inner and outer loops for the linked implementation is the same for the array implementation. The main differences between a linked and an array implementation lie in the complexity of the procedures, the addressing mechanism, the number of moves of data elements, and the overhead.

The linked list version is longer than the array version, and for that reason alone it is undoubtedly more complex. Long does not necessarily mean difficult, however, and each piece of the linked implementation performs a simple task.

The array implementation uses positioning and calculation (the array mapping function) to access elements. The array mapping function may slow this approach down, which is one reason why better performance is expected from the linked implementation. More important, however, is how the linked list version handles element moves.

The array implementation of an insertion sort contains a move in the inner loop and a move in the outer loop. The inner loop moves are of the worst variety; an element is moved to an adjacent position. These moves are eliminated in the linked list version. The move in the outer loop may be over longer distances. In the linked version it is replaced by pointer manipulations.

The selection and exchange sorts could easily be converted to implementations for doubly linked lists. The linked implementation of a selection sort would be little different from its array counterpart. The main difference is that procedure *Swap* would not have to move any data but would only have to manipulate pointers.

A linked implementation of a selection sort will be less complex than the linked implementation of an insertion sort. The inner loop in both cases is simply a search. The insertion sort has a performance advantage because, on the average, its inner loop search will be half as long as for a selection sort. It is the logic required to implement this advantage that explains its increased complexity.

The advantage of linked sorts over array sorts is that data are not moved. The price for this is the storage needed for pointers and the slightly more complex implementations.

A user who needs to sort large data elements that are stored in an array has three basic choices: (1) Sort the array and accept the performance penalty associated with moving the large elements. (2) Move the data to a linked list, sort them, and if necessary move them back to an array for further processing. This simple approach would probably improve performance, but requires enough extra memory to store the linked list. (3) Create an index array. This only makes sense if it is the data, and not the sort items, that make the elements large. The index array is sorted, and its indexes provide access to the original data in sorted order (see Table 6.3). Once again, the price for improved performance is the requirement for extra memory. The approach selected necessarily depends on many factors: the availability of extra memory, the size of the elements to be sorted, and the importance of sort performance.

6.2.5 Performance of Simple Sorts

Figure 6.11 shows the measured times required to sort an array of integers. Three different initial orders are sorted—random, sorted, inverse—using each of the four procedures presented in this section. The time required for one of the advanced sort techniques, quicksort, is included to provide perspective (and to entice you to study the following section).

The graphs in Figure 6.11 provide useful comparisons, but you must remember that they refer to simple elements, a particular implementation of the algorithms, and a particular language and computer system. The comparison is among three array implementations and one linked implementation. The linked implementation of an insertion sort shows a substantial performance improvement, about 30%, when compared with its array counterpart.

Table 6.4 provides more perspective. It shows order-of-magnitude expressions for the number of element moves and the number of keys that must be compared by each of the four simple sort procedures. The results are presented for three different initial orderings of n elements—sorted, random, and inverse.

The word "random" means that the value shown is the average for all n factorial ($n!$) possible initial orderings. Inverted order gives the worst per-

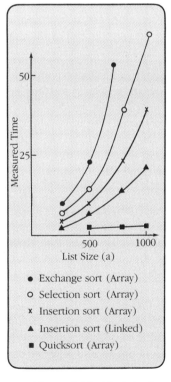

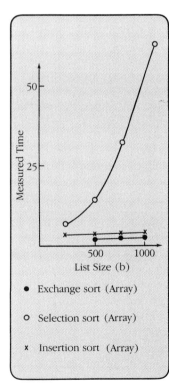

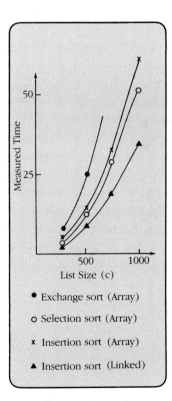

Figure 6.11   Time that is needed to sort a list of integers. (a) Integers are initially in random order. (b) Integers are initially in sorted order. (c) Integers are initially in inverse order.

TABLE 6.4 Order-of-magnitude expressions for the number of moves and compares required by simple sort algorithms.

		Initial order of data		
Algorithm		**Sorted**	**Random**	**Inverse**
Selection	Moves	$O(n)$	$O(n)$	$O(n)$
	Compares	$O(n^2)$	$O(n^2)$	$O(n^2)$
Exchange	Moves	0	$O(n^2)$	$O(n^2)$
	Compares	$O(n)$	$O(n^2)$	$O(n^2)$
Insertion—array	Moves	$O(n)$	$O(n^2)$	$O(n^2)$
	Compares	$O(n)$	$O(n^2)$	$O(n^2)$
Insertion—linked list	Moves	0	0	0
	Compares	$O(n)$	$O(n^2)$	$O(n^2)$

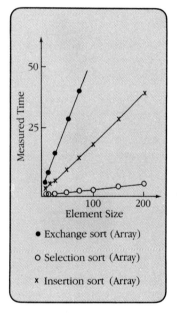

Figure 6.12
Time to sort an array of 100 elements, initially in random order, as a function of the element size. The key, or sort item, is an integer, and the data are an array of characters.

formance for each of the four procedures. Observe that the results shown in Table 6.4 predict the performance reported in Figure 6.11. Computations leading to these results are described in Wirth (1976).

Figure 6.11 only reports the results of sorting integers. This can be misleading since element size has an important impact on how some algorithms perform. In Figure 6.12 the number of elements being sorted is fixed at 100, and element size is the variable. Selection sort, which does not move elements in its inner loop, is seen to perform best for large elements stored in an array.

• Comparison of sort algorithms

A comparison of sort algorithms should include performance, memory requirements, complexity, and stability.

Performance is determined by the number of moves, the number of compares, the complexity of the inner loop, the size and nature of the sort item, and the size and initial order of the elements being sorted. It is impossible to consider the interaction of all these variables, but some rules of thumb can be provided.

1. Forget about the exchange sort. Since its inner loop requires an exchange, it is expensive in most cases. The one case in which it is fast—sorted data—is unlikely to occur and can be handled well by other algorithms.
2. If random data are in an array that is to be sorted, the following is true:
   a. A selection sort will give the best performance for large elements with small sort items. A selection sort requires fewer moves than an insertion sort, and comparing sort items is not the dominant activity.
   b. An insertion sort will give the best performance for small elements or for elements with sort items that are time consuming to compare. The reason for this is that the expected search length (and hence the number of compares) is twice as long for a selection sort as for an insertion sort.

3. If random data are in a doubly linked list that is to be sorted, then use an insertion sort. There are no data to be moved and an insertion sort minimizes the number of comparisons.
4. The above rules do not take into account advanced sorting techniques, radix sort, or unusual initial orderings of the data.

None of the algorithms discussed in this section requires any extra memory. They are all **in-place sorts.** Of course, if the data are moved to a new structure for sorting, for example, by extracting the sort item and an index from an array, then extra memory is needed.

None of these algorithms is very complex. However, *SelectSort* is undoubtedly the simplest. *InsertSort* uses a sentinel that complicates its inner loop. *ExchangeSort* uses a boolean variable to stop processing after a pass in which no exchanges are made. Complexity is of more consequence for the linked implementations.

A sort algorithm is **stable** if it preserves the order of elements with equal sort items. This is desirable if data are already sorted on another item. For example, if student elements were in order by city and a second sort on students' majors were executed, then a stable sort would retain the city order within each major. In the exercises, you are asked to investigate the stability of the algorithms used in this section.

Exercises 6.2

1. Apply the three algorithms in Section 6.2 to sort the following sequence of eight integers:

56, 27, 22, 95, 79, 45, 45, 96

In each case, keep track of the number of moves and compares required. Discuss your results in view of the results in Table 6.4.

2. Generate a sequence of n random integers using the expression

$$r[k + 1] := (29 * r[k] + 217) \bmod 1024$$

a. Modify each of the algorithms in Section 6.2 so that they keep track of the number of moves and compares required to sort a list. Plot these values as a function of n. Discuss these results in comparison with the results found in Table 6.4.

b. Modify the algorithms in Section 6.2 so that each time an element is moved they keep track of how far that element is moved. Plot a histogram of frequency versus distance moved for each of the algorithms of this section.

3. A sorting algorithm is stable if it preserves the order of elements with equal keys. Which of the algorithms in Section 6.2 are stable?

4. A sequence of elements is formed by starting with a sorted sequence and then exchanging one pair. For example, starting with the sequence

1, 2, 3, 4, 5, 6, 7, 8, 9, 10

and exchanging the second and fifth elements yields the sequence

1, 5, 3, 4, 2, 6, 7, 8, 9, 10

Discuss the effectiveness of the algorithms in Section 6.2 for sorting such a list. Consider both the size of the list and the specific pair of elements exchanged.

5. A sequence of *n* sorted elements has *k* randomly selected elements appended to its end. Discuss the effectiveness of the algorithms in Section 6.2 for sorting such a list.

6. Procedure *ExchangeSort* (see Algorithm 6.2) can be thought of as moving the largest remaining element to the end of a sequence each time it makes a pass over the data. It is therefore relatively effective for moving large elements to the end of the list. It would, for example, sort the following sequence in two passes:

10, 1, 2, 3, 4, 5, 6, 7, 8, 9

The first pass would move 10 to the end of the list, and the second pass would make no exchanges and thus leave *sorted* with the value *true*. On the other hand, small elements move, or bubble, to the top slowly. For example, the sequence

2, 3, 4, 5, 6, 7, 8, 9, 10, 1

would require the maximum number of passes, nine, to sort the data.

An alternative procedure to *ExchangeSort,* called shaker sort (see Wirth, 1976), overcomes this problem. Alternate passes start at alternate ends of the list. Apply shaker sort to the sequence in Exercise 1. Compare its performance with the performance of *ExchangeSort.*

7. Discuss the use of each of the algorithms in Section 6.2 to sort a singly linked list.

8. The inner loop of procedure *InsertSort* (Algorithm 6.3) uses a sequential search to find the location at which insertion is to occur. In Algorithm 6.3, but not in Algorithm 6.4, this can be replaced by a binary search. Discuss the advantages and disadvantages of doing this.
   a. How is the performance for small lists affected?
   b. Is any additional memory required?
   c. How is the number of compares affected?
   d. How is the number of moves affected?

9. When an element is moved by a sort algorithm we would like it to be moved to its sorted position. Define the effectiveness of a move as

$$1 - \frac{\text{Distance after}}{\text{Distance before}}$$

where distance after is the distance of the element from its sorted position after it is moved, and distance before is its distance from its sorted position before it is moved.

Modify the algorithms in Section 6.2 to compute the average of the effectiveness of its moves for sorting a permutation of the integers 1, 2, 3, . . . , 100.

6.3 Advanced Sort Techniques

6.3.1 Quicksort

Quicksort consists of a series of steps, each of which takes a list of elements to be sorted as input. The output from each step is a rearrangement of the elements so that one element is in its sorted position and there are two sublists that remain to be sorted.

If the elements to be sorted are

$$r[1], r[2], \ldots, r[n]$$

then one step of the quicksort process would rearrange the elements so as to produce the ordering shown in Figure 6.13.

$$r[1], r[2], \ldots, r[j-1] \qquad r[j] \qquad r[j+1], r[j+2], \ldots, r[n]$$

$$\text{(a)} \qquad\qquad\qquad \text{(b)} \qquad\qquad \text{(c)}$$

Figure 6.13 Result of applying one step of the quicksort process to the list of elements $r[1], r[2], \ldots, r[n]$. (a) Sequence that remains to be sorted. Each of these elements is smaller than $r[j]$. (b) Element is in its sorted position. (c) Sequence that remains to be sorted. Each of these elements is larger than $r[j]$.

In other words, each step of quicksort partitions a given list into three disjoint sublists. One of these sublists is a single element that is in its sorted position (Figure 6.13b). The other two sublists share a common property. Each of them contains elements that are all either larger than (Figure 6.13c) or smaller than (Figure 6.13a) the element that is in its sorted position. This permits each of these two sublists to be sorted without reference to any element in the other sublists. That is, each step of quicksort replaces the problem of sorting one long list by the problem of sorting two short lists. The sorting problem is said to have been **partitioned.**

Consider the list of integers shown in Figure 6.14. Each integer is considered to be an element in terms of our discussion above. One way to rearrange these integers so that 53 is in its sorted position is shown in Figure 6.15.

There are many other suitable rearrangements. In fact, any arrangement in which the integers smaller than 53 (51 and 52) are to the left of 53 and the integers larger than 53 (54, 55, . . . , 59) are to the right of 53 will suffice. (It is interesting to note, although it is not important for our purposes, that in this case there are 1440 suitable rearrangements.)

We will describe the algorithmic process used to rearrange the elements later. At this point we can ignore it and concentrate on the overall structure of quicksort. Initially, we select the first, or left most, element as the one to move to its sorted position. Later, we will modify this selection process in order to obtain improved performance.

. . . if the file fits into the memory of the computer, there is one algorithm, called Quicksort, which has been shown to perform well in a variety of situations. Not only is this algorithm simpler than many other sorting algorithms, but empirical and analytic studies show that Quicksort can be expected to be up to twice as fast as its nearest competitors. The method is simple enough to be learned by programmers who have no previous experience with sorting, and those who do know other sorting methods should also find it profitable to learn about Quicksort. (Sedgewick, 1978)

53 59 56 52 55 58 51 57 54

Figure 6.14
A sequence of integers.

52 51 **53** 56 55 58 59 57 54

Smaller than 53   Larger than 53

Figure 6.15
The integers in Figure 6.14 rearranged so that 53 is in its sorted position. Sorted integers are shown in boldface in this and following figures.

Repeated application of the quicksort process to the unsorted sublists that are successively generated ultimately produces a sorted list. The entire process is succinctly described by the recursive algorithm given in Algorithm 6.5. Assume that the elements to be sorted are stored in a global array named r. The indexes of the first and last elements in the sequence to be sorted are *left* and *right*, respectively.

```
PROCEDURE QS1 (left,right: CARDINAL);        (* Quicksort *)
VAR j,k: CARDINAL;
BEGIN
    IF left < right
        THEN
            Rearrange the elements in the sequence
                    r[left], ... , r[right]
            in order to produce a new sequence that
            is partitioned as follows:

            r[left], ... , r[j-1] are all smaller than r[j],
            r[j] is in its sorted position, and
            r[j+1], ... , r[right] are all larger than r[j]

            QS1 (left,k-1);              (* Sort left sublist. *)
            QS1 (k+1,right)             (* Sort right sublist. *)
    END
END QS1;
```

Algorithm 6.5   The first of three versions of quicksort.

73 79 76 72 75 78 71 77 74

Figure 6.16
A sequence of integers.

72 71 **73** 76 75 78 79 77 74

Figure 6.17
The integers in Figure 6.16 rearranged so that 73 is in its sorted position.

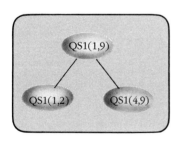

Figure 6.18
The initial call and the first two recursive calls to *QS*1 for the sequence in Figure 6.16.

Suppose that procedure *QS*1 in Algorithm 6.5 is applied to the list of integers shown in Figure 6.16. Input to *QS*1 are *left* = 1 and *right* = 9. The first step puts 73 into its sorted position. One such rearrangement (which we will describe how to construct later) is shown in Figure 6.17.

The last two statements in *QS*1 are recursive calls to *QS*1. In our example, the first pair of calls will be *QS*1(1,2) and *QS*1(4,9). The first of these is executed immediately, and the second is pushed onto the stack for later processing.

In order to illustrate the process, we will construct a binary tree. Each node in the tree represents a call to *QS*1; the root of the left subtree is the first recursive call, and the root of the right subtree is the second recursive call. The process discussed so far for our example is shown in Figure 6.18.

The procedure call *QS*1(1,2) causes 72 to be placed in its sorted position among 71 and 72. The resulting list is shown in Figure 6.19. In terms of calls to *QS*1 the entire process for our example is shown in Figure 6.20.

For the next two recursive calls, *QS*1(1,1) and *QS*1(3,2), the *left* index is greater than or equal to the *right* index. This means that the sublist to be sorted is empty. Thus, *QS*1(4,9) is now popped off the stack and processing continues.

Figure 6.21 shows the order of the integers after *QS*1(4,9), and Figure 6.22 shows the order after *QS*1(7,8). The list is sorted!

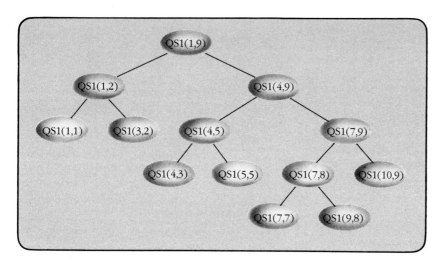

Figure 6.19
The sequence after $QS1(1,2)$.

Figure 6.20 The initial call and all the recursive calls to $QS1$ required to sort the sequence in Figure 6.16.

The order in which rearrangement of the integers occurs is given by a preorder traversal of the tree in Figure 6.20. Since leaf nodes do not induce a rearrangement, the above example requires six applications of the quicksort rearrangement process to sort the list.

Leaving our example list, we turn to the following question: How do we implement the rearrangement step? First, we will write Algorithm 6.6, which is a complete quicksort. Note that to provide the interface prescribed in Specification 6.1 the basic quicksort procedure is embedded within $QS2$.

Our discussion of Algorithm 6.6 will focus on the repeat–until statement that contains statements (* 1 *), (* 2 *), and (* 3 *). This statement houses the inner loop of the algorithm and is the heart of the rearrangement process. Our discussion of the inner loop in Algorithm 6.6 is illustrated with the sequence of integers shown in Figure 6.23.

71 **72 73** 74 75 **76** 79 77 78

Figure 6.21
The sequence after $QS1(4,9)$.

71 **72 73** 74 75 76 77 **78** 79

Figure 6.22
The sequence after $QS1(10,9)$.
The recursive calls $QS1(7,7)$ and $QS1(9,8)$ complete the sort.

40   15   30   25   60   10   75   45   65   35   50   20   70   55

Figure 6.23 A sequence of integers.

```
PROCEDURE QS2 (VAR r: ARRAY OF StdElement);                          (* Quicksort *)

    PROCEDURE Quick2 (left,right: INTEGER);
    (* post — Element r[left]-pre is in its sorted position, say k,
             with r[left] ... r[k-1] less than r[k] and r[k+1] ...
             r[right] larger than r[k]. *)
    VAR j,k: INTEGER;
    BEGIN
        IF left < right
            THEN j := left; k := right;
                IF r[left].key > r[right].key                (* Place a sentinel in *)
                    THEN Swap (r[left],r[right])             (* position r[right].   *)
                END;

                REPEAT
                    REPEAT j := j + 1 UNTIL r[j].key >= r[left].key;        (* 1 *)
                    REPEAT k := k - 1 UNTIL r[k].key <= r[left].key;        (* 2 *)
                    IF j < k THEN Swap (r[j],r[k]) END                      (* 3 *)
                UNTIL j > k;

                Swap (r[left],r[k]);              (* Put r[left] in sorted position. *)

                Quick2 (left,k-1);                   (* Sort left subinterval.   *)
                Quick2 (k+1,right)                   (* Sort right subinterval.  *)
        END
    END Quick2;

BEGIN   (* QS2 *)
    Quick2 (0,HIGH(r))
END QS2;
```

Algorithm 6.6 A second version of quicksort, which is a refinement of Algorithm 6.5.

The first time statement (* 1 *) is executed it scans to the right along the sequence of integers, beginning with the element whose index is *left* + 1. The scan continues until an element is found that is larger than *r[left]*. In our example, the scan starts at 15 and ends at 60, as illustrated in Figure 6.24.

40   15   30   25   60   10   75   45   65   35   50   20   70   55

Figure 6.24 Statement (* 1 *) scans to the right until it finds a value larger than 40.

The first call to Quick2 for the example in Figure 6.24 is Quick2(0,13).

Similarly, statement (* 2 *) scans to the left, starting with the right most element in the sequence. This scan ends when an element smaller than *r[left]* is found, as illustrated in Figure 6.25.

40   15   30   25   60   10   75   45   65   35   50   20   70   55

Figure 6.25 Statement (* 2 *) scans to the left until it finds a value smaller than 40.

If the two scans did not overlap, that is, $j < k$, then statement (* 3 *) exchanges the two elements at which the scans terminated. In our example, 60 and 20 are exchanged. Figure 6.26 shows the result of this exchange.

40 15 30 25 20 10 75 45 65 35 50 60 70 55

Figure 6.26 Sequence of elements after statement (* 3 *) has exchanged 60 and 20.

Now, since $j < k$, statements (* 1 *), (* 2 *), and (* 3 *) are repeated. Statement (* 1 *) begins scanning at the element on the right of where it left off. Once again the scan terminates when a value larger than $r[left]$ is found. Similarly, statement (* 2 *) scans to the left. The result for our example is shown in Figure 6.27.

40 15 30 25 20 10 75 45 65 35 50 60 70 55

Figure 6.27 Statements (* 1 *) and (* 2 *) continue to scan to the right and left, respectively.

Since $j < k$, 75 and 35 are exchanged by statement (* 3 *). Statements (* 1 *) and (* 2 *) are executed again, and the scans are illustrated in Figure 6.28.

40 15 30 25 20 10 35 45 65 75 50 60 70 55

Figure 6.28 Here 75 and 35 are swapped, and statements (* 1 *) and (* 2 *) continue their scans. We now have $j > k$.

Observe that this time the scans have crossed. That is, after statements (* 1 *) and (* 2 *) are executed we have $j > k$. Therefore, $r[j]$ and $r[k]$ are not exchanged, and we drop through the repeat–until loop. Then $r[left]$, 40 in this case, is exchanged with $r[k]$, which is 35. The result is the sequence shown in Figure 6.29.

35 15 30 25 20 10 **40** 45 65 75 50 60 70 55

Smaller than 40   Sorted   Larger than 40

Figure 6.29 35 and 40 are swapped, and the first step of quicksort is complete.

The pair of recursive calls is then Quick2(1,6) and Quick2(8,14). In general, observe that when statement (* 3 *) is executed, a large element (larger than

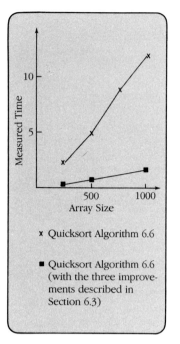

Figure 6.30
Measured times to sort an array
of integers initially in random
order.

Median of Three Modification

The element to be moved to
its sorted position is chosen
as the median of r[left],
r[right], and r[(left + right)
DIV 2]. The elements are
distributed as follows;

r[left] ⟵⟶ median value
r[left + 1] ⟵ smallest value
r[middle] ⟵⟶r[left + 1]
r[right] ⟵⟶ largest value

Arranging the values in this
way saves two comparisons
for each subsequence
processed.

---

r[*left*]) is exchanged with a small element (smaller than r[*left*]). The effect of this is to move small elements to the front of the sequence and large elements to the rear of the sequence. Observe also that it is possible for elements to move long distances as a result of a single exchange. This is one of the heuristic explanations for the good performance of quicksort. Having collected all elements smaller than r[*left*] at the front of the sequence and all elements larger than r[*left*] at the rear of the sequence, it only remains to place r[*left*] in the middle to complete one step of the quicksort process.

• Improvements in quicksort

We will now discuss three improvements for procedure QS2. A procedure that implements the first two improvements is given in Algorithm 6.7. The effect on performance is shown in Figure 6.30 and is discussed below.

An important aspect of quicksort is the way that it partitions lists to, in effect, form a binary tree of subproblems (see Figure 6.18). The problem is that this partitioning process has a large overhead as compared with a simple technique such as an insertion sort. It is a reasonable conjecture that there is a sublist length below which a simple sort procedure should be used in place of quicksort. A study of this issue shows that small sublists, length about 10 or less, should be ignored until the end when one pass of insertion sort is used to complete the sort. Performance improvements of 12% (for large lists) to more than 20% (for small lists) are obtained. (See Sedgewick, 1978.)

A second improvement involves the selection of the element to be moved to its sorted position. The procedure in Algorithm 6.6 simply selects the left element in the string to be sorted. This can be disastrous if the list to be sorted is already either sorted or nearly sorted. In this case quicksort becomes "slow-sort"! Our improved algorithm selects the element to be inserted into its sorted position as the median of the three elements, as illustrated in the box in the margin.

If the list to be sorted consists, for example, of the nine integers 31, 32, . . . , 39, we will select the element to be inserted as the median element among 31, 35, and 39. We will refer to this process as ***median of three modification.***

Median of three modification is ideal for a sorted list since partitioning will always be into two equal parts. Thus, quicksort will give its best performance for sorted lists. The time required to sort a sorted sequence with quicksort is shown in Figure 6.36(b).

Algorithm 6.7 shows an implementation of the two improvements just described.

There are two nuances of the median of three modification, as implemented in Algorithm 6.7, that are worthy of mention. A little study will show that the median of three modification process rearranges as many as four elements in the list that is to be sorted. These elements are r[*left*], r[*left* + 1], r[*middle*], and r[*right*], where middle is *(left + right) DIV 2*.

Since the median value is moved to r[*left*], inserting r[*left*] into its sorted position has the effect of inserting the median value into its sorted position. Since r[*right*] now contains a large value, at least as large as r[*left*], this value will act as a sentinel. Note that a sentinel was provided in procedure QS2 by

```
PROCEDURE QS3 (VAR r: ARRAY OF StdElement);                    (* Quicksort *)

    PROCEDURE Quick3 (left,right: CARDINAL);
    VAR j,k: CARDINAL;
    BEGIN
        IF left < right
            THEN Swap (r[(left+right) DIV 2],r[left+1]);   (* Median of 3:         *)
                 IF r[left+1].key > r[right].key           (* r[left] = median,    *)
                     THEN Swap(r[left+1],r[right]) END;     (* r[left+1] = small,   *)
                 IF r[left].key > r[right].key              (* r[right] = large     *)
                     THEN Swap(r[left],r[right])    END;    (* of r[left],          *)
                 IF r[left+1].key > r[left].key             (* r[right], and        *)
                     THEN Swap(r[left+1],r[left])   END;    (* r[left+right DIV 2 *)

                 j := left + 1;   k := right;

                 REPEAT
                     REPEAT j := j + 1 UNTIL r[j].key >= r[left].key;
                     REPEAT k := k - 1 UNTIL r[k].key <= r[left].key;
                     IF j < k THEN Swap(r[j],r[k]) END
                 UNTIL j > k;

                 Swap(r[left],r[k]);

                 IF (k-left)  > 10 THEN Quick3(left,k-1)   END;   (* Ignore small *)
                 IF (right-k) > 10 THEN Quick3(k+1,right)  END    (* sublists.    *)
        END
    END Quick3;

BEGIN   (* QS3 *)
    Quick3(0,HIGH(r));                    (* Sort r into sublists of 10 or less. *)
    InsertSort (r)                        (* Sort remaining sublists.            *)
END QS3;
```

Algorithm 6.7   A third version of quicksort, which is a refinement of Algorithm 6.6.

swapping *r[left]* and *r[right]* if necessary in order to prevent the scan to the right, statement (* 1 *), from continuing past the right end of the array. In addition, the variable that scans to the left, *k* in statement (* 2 *), is initialized as *k := right* instead of *k := right* + 1. This saves one comparison for each step. Similarly, since *r[left* + 1] is now small, the variable that scans to the right, *j* in statement (* 3 *), is initialized as *j := left* + 1 instead of *j := left*. This saves another comparison during each step.

Another improvement to the quicksort implementation is to implement recursion directly rather than "expose ourselves to the whims of compilers." There are two reasons for this: First, the depth of the stack required for recursive calls can be limited to a maximum of $\log_2 n$ if the shorter sublist is always sorted first (see Hoare, 1962). Otherwise, in the worst case the depth of the stack might be as large as *n*. Second, the last recursive call can be treated more efficiently.

Figure 6.31 shows the time required to sort an array of integers in random order using several algorithms. Three versions of quicksort are included—two

Median of three modification, in effect, samples the list to be sorted and selects the median based on that sample. A technique that samples all the elements in the list is called **meansort**. It is described in Motzkin (1983) and is discussed further in Exercise 6.3, 9.

•

Recursion is implemented directly. This allows us always to process the short sequence and save the longer sequence to process later. Another advantage is that the second recursive call, which is not really recursive, can be treated more efficiently.

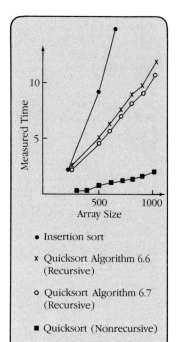

Figure 6.31
The time to sort an array of integers initially in random order is shown to compare recursive and nonrecursive implementations of quicksort.

recursive and one nonrecursive. The major difference in performance is a warning about the potentially poor performance associated with recursion. Other compilers and other machines may handle recursion more efficiently, but recursion should always be applied carefully if performance is a concern.

Both the expected and the minimum number of compares required by quicksort are $O(n \log_2 n)$. In the worst case, quicksort requires $O(n^2)$ compares. Without the median of three modification quicksort exhibits its worst performance for sorted data. With the median of three modification, it is at its fastest for sorted data. Wainwright (1985) empirically compares seven versions of quicksort and discusses in detail a variation designed to work well for data that are nearly sorted or that are in reverse order.

As Figure 6.31 indicates, quicksort is very fast. We will extend our comparison to heapsort, mergesort, and radix sort in Sections 6.3.3, 6.3.4, and 6.4 and will see that quicksort remains, in general, the fastest internal sort algorithm.

6.3.2 Treesort

Treesort is a two-step process. First, the elements are inserted into a binary search tree. Second, the elements are retrieved, in sorted order, using an inorder traversal. Figure 5.35 and the inorder traversal procedure in Implementation Module 5.1 perform these two steps.

A binary search tree is not an attractive approach to sorting because a heap does the same job with less effort. Instead of starting out by putting the elements in a binary search tree, we begin by forming a heap. If, however, the elements are in a binary search tree, then an inorder traversal accesses them in sorted order with $O(n)$ effort.

6.3.3 Heapsort

As is the case for a treesort, **heapsort** is a two-step process. First, the data are put into a heap, and, second, the data are extracted from the heap in sorted order. A heapsort is a cousin of a selection sort because both algorithms select and then swap into sorted order successively larger elements. A heapsort uses a more efficient data structure than a selection sort. But a selection sort will be faster for a small set of elements.

We can construct a heap by using Implementation Module 5.3. Recall that in a heap organization the smallest element is on top. That is, if the elements forming the heap are stored as the array elements

$$r[1], r[2], \ldots, r[n]$$

then the element with the smallest key will be stored as $r[1]$. The trick is to find the element with the second largest key. We will proceed as follows.

The first pass over the data exchanges $r[1]$ and $r[n]$ and then sifts down $r[1]$ in the sequence $r[1], \ldots, r[n-1]$ so that $r[1], \ldots, r[n-1]$ forms a heap. The result is that $r[n]$ is a sorted list of length one and the second smallest element is $r[1]$. Figure 6.32 summarizes this process.

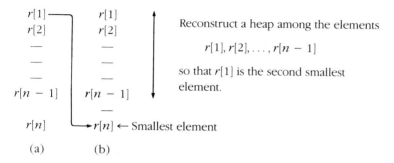

Reconstruct a heap among the elements

$$r[1], r[2], \ldots, r[n-1]$$

so that $r[1]$ is the second smallest element.

Figure 6.32   The first step of heapsort.

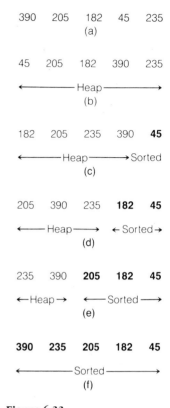

Figure 6.33
An illustration of a heapsort. During each step, the smallest element is taken from the top of the heap and moved to the sorted list. A heap is formed among the remaining elements using procedure *SiftDown*. The process then repeats. (a) Data to be sorted. (b) Construction of a heap.

The second step exchanges $r[1]$ with $r[n-1]$ and then sifts down $r[1]$ in the sequence $r[1], \ldots, r[n-2]$, creating a heap with $n-2$ elements. Now, $r[n-1]$ and $r[n]$ form a sorted list of length two, and $r[1]$ is the third largest element.

The ith step exchanges $r[1]$ with $r[n-(i-1)]$ and sifts down $r[1]$ in the sequence $r[1], \ldots, r[n-i]$ creating a heap with $n-i$ elements. The sequence $r[n-(i-1)], \ldots, r[n]$ is sorted, and $r[1]$ is the ith largest element.

The key process in all this is the procedure to insert one element into the bottom of a heap so that a new heap is formed that contains all the old elements plus the one inserted. The procedure that accomplishes this is *Sift-Down*. Using *SiftDown* as a basic tool, Algorithm 6.8, page 310, implements procedure *HeapSort*.

The first step of procedure *HeapSort* is the construction of a heap (see Figure 6.33b). This requires applying *SiftDown* to half the elements. The maximum number of compares (or moves) needed by *SiftDown* is $\log_2 n$. Construction of the initial heap thus requires at most $(n/2)\log_2 n$ compares or moves.

Sorting the data after a heap is formed requires applying *SiftDown* to $n-1$ elements. An upper bound for moves and compares is therefore $(n-1)\log_2 n$. Combining the results for heap construction and subsequent sorting assures us that at most $(3/2)n \log_2 n$ moves or compares will be required. This must be a very conservative bound on the effort required because *Sift-Down* is often applied to a heap with fewer than n elements. Suggestions for an improved implementation of *HeapSort* are given in Bentley (1985).

```
PROCEDURE SiftDown (VAR r: ARRAY OF StdElement; pos,end: CARDINAL);
VAR i,j    : CARDINAL;
    save   : StdElement;
    finished: BOOLEAN;
BEGIN
    i := pos; j := 2 * pos + 1; save := r[pos];
    finished := FALSE;

    WHILE (j <= end) AND NOT finished DO
        IF j < end                              (* If there are two children, *)
            THEN IF r[j].key > r[j + 1].key     (* select the smaller.         *)
                    THEN j := j + 1
                 END
        END;

        IF save.key <= r[j].key                 (* If the proper position is *)
            THEN finished := TRUE               (* found then finished, else *)
            ELSE r[i] := r[j];                  (* move everything up one     *)
                 i := j; j := 2 * j + 1         (* level and start over.      *)
        END
    END;

    r[i] := save
END SiftDown;

PROCEDURE HeapSort (VAR r: ARRAY OF StdElement);          (* Heap sort *)
VAR j,k: CARDINAL;
BEGIN
    j := (HIGH(r)+1) DIV 2;                    (* Construct the  *)
    WHILE j > 0 DO                             (* initial heap.  *)
        j := j - 1;
        SiftDown(r,j,HIGH(r))
    END;
    k := HIGH(r);                              (* Extract the elements *)
    WHILE k > 0 DO                             (* in sorted order.     *)
        Swap(r[0],r[k]);
        k := k - 1;
        SiftDown(r,0,k)
    END
END HeapSort;
```

Algorithm 6.8 SiftDown and HeapSort.

Algorithm 6.8 sorts into descending order. To sort into ascending order, change *SiftDown* so that the largest element is in the first position.

6.3.4 Mergesort

Two sublists, each already sorted, can be merged together to form one aggregate list that is also sorted. A simple and effective procedure for doing this, called **mergesort,** begins by comparing pairs of elements—one from each sublist. The smallest element is appended to a sorted list and is replaced by the next element from its sublist. This continues until there are no more elements in one of the sublists. The remaining elements in the other sublist are then appended to the sorted list, and the sort is complete.

This sounds good when there are two sorted sublists with which to begin (Figure 6.34). If there are not, the problem is to decide how to get started. There are several possibilities.

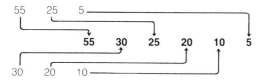

Figure 6.34   An illustration of merging two sorted lists.

One approach is to consider individual elements as sorted sublists of length one. Pairs of these sublists are merged to produce sorted lists of length two. Pairs of these lists are then merged to produce sorted lists of length four. This process continues until only one sorted list remains. This process is illustrated in Figure 6.35 and implemented in Algorithms 6.9 and 6.10.

Notice that *MergeSort* requires two arrays—r, which originally holds the data to be sorted, and t, an array of the same type. The merges are in pairs—first from r to t, then from t to r. Thus *MergeSort* requires space for $2 \times n$ elements.

The procedure *Merge*, page 312, makes a pass over the entire array each time it is called. This occurs approximately $\log_2 n$ times in sorting a list of length n. The procedure *Merge* moves all n of the elements during each pass. Thus it requires $n \log_2 n$ moves no matter how the data are initially ordered. It will therefore perform better for a linked list than for an array.

The number of compares during a pass depends on the order of the data. If sublists of length one are being merged, then there will be $n/2$ compares. If

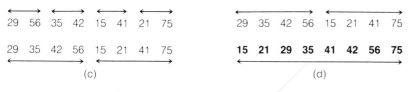

Lists of length 1 are merged to form sorted lists of length 2.

Lists of length 2 are merged to
form sorted lists of length 4.

Lists of length 4 are merged to
form a sorted list of length 8.

Figure 6.35   Illustration of procedure *MergeSort.*

```
PROCEDURE Merge (L: CARDINAL; VAR r,t: ARRAY OF StdElement);
(* pre  – Array r contains sorted sublists of length L.
   post – Array t contains sorted sublists of length 2L. *)
VAR q,k,k1,k2,end1,end2: CARDINAL;
BEGIN
   k1 := 0;   k2 := L;  q := 0;                      (* k1 and k2 are indexes for  *)
   REPEAT                                            (* the sublists to be merged. *)
   end1 := k1 + L;
       IF end1 > HIGH(r)                             (* Mark the ends of the    *)
           THEN end1 := HIGH(r) + 1                  (* sublists to be merged.  *)
           ELSE end2 := k2 + L;
               IF end2 > HIGH(r)
                   THEN end2 := HIGH(r) + 1;
               END;

               REPEAT                                (* Merge the       *)
                   IF r[k1].key <= r[k2].key         (* sublists        *)
                       THEN t[q] := r[k1];  k1 := k1 + 1    (* until one of *)
                       ELSE t[q] := r[k2];  k2 := k2 + 1    (* them is ex-  *)
                   END;                              (* hausted.        *)
                   q := q + 1
               UNTIL (k1 = end1) OR (k2 = end2)
       END;

       IF k1 < end1                                  (* Tack on elements from *)
           THEN REPEAT                               (* the sublist with more *)
                   t[q] := r[k1];                    (* elements.             *)
                   q := q + 1; k1 := k1 + 1
               UNTIL k1 = end1
           ELSE REPEAT
                   t[q] := r[k2];
                   q := q + 1; k2 := k2 + 1
               UNTIL k2 = end2
       END;
                                                     (* Set indexes for the    *)
       k1 := k2;  k2 := k2 + L                       (* next pair of sublists. *)
   UNTIL k1 >= HIGH(r)
END Merge;
```

Algorithm 6.9 Merge.

```
PROCEDURE MergeSort (VAR r: ARRAY OF StdElement);                    (* Merge sort *)

    PROCEDURE MSort (VAR r: ARRAY OF StdElement; t: ARRAY OF StdElement);
    VAR k,L: CARDINAL;
    BEGIN
        L := 1;
        IF (HIGH(r) >= 2)
            THEN REPEAT                            (* Merge sublists of length *)
                    Merge(L,r,t); L := 2 * L;      (* L until at most one       *)
                    Merge(L,t,r); L := 2 * L;      (* merge is needed to        *)
                UNTIL L >= ((HIGH(r) + 1) DIV 2)   (* complete the sort.        *)
        END;
        IF L < (HIGH(r) +1)
            THEN Merge(L,r,t);                            (* If necessary, a *)
                FOR k := 0 TO HIGH(r) DO                  (* final merge.    *)
                    r[k] := t[k]
                END
        END
    END MSort;

BEGIN
    MSort (r,r);
END MergeSort;
```

Algorithm 6.10 Mergesort.

sublists of length greater than $n/2$ are being merged, then as many as $n - 1$ compares may be required. The procedure *MergeSort* therefore requires approximately $n \log_2 n$ moves (or pointer manipulations) and somewhere between $n/2 \log_2 n$ and $n \log_2 n$ compares. It is a very consistent performer since the effort required to use it is not affected much by the initial order of the data. It is also fast since it, like *HeapSort*, requires $O(n \log_2 n)$ effort, even in the worst case.

Figure 6.36 compares sort times for four algorithms: *MergeSort, HeapSort, QuickSort,* and *InsertSort.* Note that *MergeSort* requires approximately the same time for all three initial orderings of the data.

InsertSort is fastest for sorted data because it requires only $n - 1$ compares and no moves. *QuickSort* is fastest for random data because of its simple inner loop, its ability to move elements through long distances, and its use of *InsertSort* (and its relatively low overhead) to finish up after the data are nearly sorted.

For data in inverted order *MergeSort* is best, not because its performance improves in this case, but because its performance changes very little, whereas the other algorithms' performances deteriorate. *InsertSort* requires $O(n^2)$ effort, and *QuickSort* requires many more moves than is normally the case.

A drawback to *MergeSort* for arrays is its requirement for twice as much memory as any of the other algorithms. *QuickSort* needs a stack, but its height is at most $\log_2 n$.

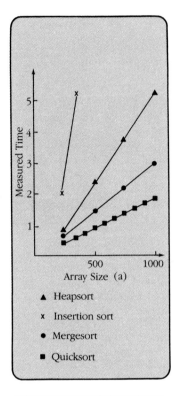

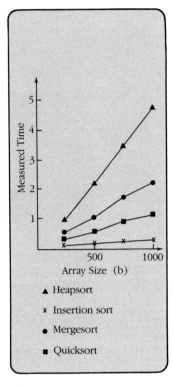

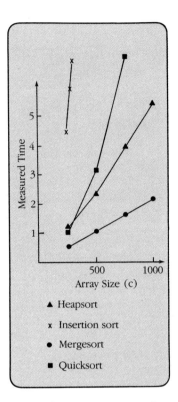

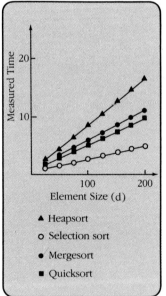

Figure 6.36   Comparison of the time it takes to sort an array of integers or elements for *MergeSort, HeapSort, QuickSort,* and *InsertSort.* (a) Integers initially in random order. (b) Integers initially in sorted order. (c) Integers initially in inverse order.

Comparison of the time to sort an array of elements as a function of the element size.

Section 6.4 presents our final sort algorithm, *RadixSort.* Following that is a Chapter 6 summary and our rules of thumb for choosing an internal sorting algorithm.

Exercises 6.3

1. Use Algorithm 6.7 to sort the following list of 15 integers. Ignore sublists of length four or less.

   482, 231, 928, 204, 145, 428, 659, 379, 235, 47, 577, 992, 66, 131, 22

   a. How many compares and how many moves (assume one exchange requires three moves) are required?
   b. Using Figure 6.28 as a model, draw the scans used to place the first integer in its sorted position.
   c. Draw the diagram that corresponds to Figure 6.20.
2. Implement a version of Algorithm 6.7 that keeps track of the number of compares and moves during a sort. Use this implementation to plot the moves and

compares required to sort a list of random integers. Compare your results with those in Exercise 6.2, 2.

3. Implement both recursive and nonrecursive versions of *QuickSort* and compare their execution times.

    a. Let the size of a subfile below which an *InsertSort* is used be a variable and plot execution time as a function of this variable.

    b. Replace the *InsertSort* with another elementary sorting technique and determine the effect on performance. Explain why the performance is affected as it is.

    c. Replace the inner loop of *QuickSort* with embedded assembly language code (see Sedgewick, 1978). Determine how this affects performance.

4. Apply Algorithm 6.6 to a list of elements that is already sorted.

    a. Draw the first four levels of the binary tree corresponding to Figure 6.20.

    b. Describe in English what happens when $QS2(j,k)$ is executed in this case.

    c. How many compares and how many moves are required by $QS2(j,k)$ in this case?

    d. Combine the results from Exercises (a) and (c) to determine the total number of compares and moves needed to "sort" a sorted list.

5. Repeat Exercise 4 using Algorithm 6.7 instead of Algorithm 6.6.

6. Repeat Exercise 4 for the case in which all elements to be sorted have the same sort item value.

7. A nonrecursive implementation of *QuickSort* can be implemented using a stack to keep track of unsorted sublists. Consider using a queue for this purpose. Will the sort algorithm still work? If so, will it be as efficient? Explain your answers.

8. The speed of *QuickSort* is attributed to three aspects of the algorithm:

    a. The simplicity of its inner loop

    b. Its ability to move elements long distances

    c. Its use of insertion sort to mop up short sublists

    Both *InsertSort* and *ExchangeSort* are particularly deficient with respect to item (b). They both plod along, moving elements from one position to an adjacent position. An approach that can be used to modify either of these algorithms is often called **ShellSort.** *ShellSort* attempts to move elements through long distances. It does this by breaking the sort process into a sequence of subsorts, which we will call *k*-sorts. For example, if there are the following 10 array components to sort:

$$r[1], r[2], r[3], \ldots, r[10]$$

then a 3-sort would be to sort the following three sublists:

$$r[1], r[4], r[7], r[10]$$
$$r[2], r[5], r[8]$$
$$r[3], r[6], r[9]$$

Any technique can be applied to sort the sublists. *ShellSort* consists of a sequence of *k*-sorts such that the last value of *k* is 1. The hope is that by the time *k* is 1 all elements will be near their sorted position. A sequence of *k* values that seems to work well is

$$\ldots, 364, 121, 40, 13, 4, 1$$

It is a fairly simple matter to modify the insertion sort algorithm so that it becomes a *ShellSort* algorithm. Do this. Compare the resulting algorithm with the others we have already studied; see Exercise 6.2, 2.

Further information about shellsort can be found in Knuth (1973b).

9. An alternative to the median of three modification is described in Motzkin (1983). This approach, called *MeanSort,* uses the mean value of those elements being partitioned. The mean value for use during partitioning step k is determined during the scan of a previous step. The first partitioning step simply uses the left element.

   Median of three modification is expensive to apply to a doubly linked list because finding the middle element requires traversing half the list. Using the approach and *MeanSort,* the *QuickSort* algorithm can be efficiently applied to a doubly linked list.

   a. Implement *MeanSort* for an array, and compare its performance with Algorithm 6.7.

   b. Implement *MeanSort* for a doubly linked list and compare its performance with Algorithm 6.7.

10. Sort the list of integers given in Exercise 1 using
    a. *HeapSort*   **b.** *MergeSort*

    Keep track of the number of moves and compares required for each technique, and compare with the answers obtained in Exercise 1.

11. Repeat Exercise 2 for *HeapSort* and *MergeSort*.

12. Which of these algorithms—*QuickSort, HeapSort,* or *MergeSort*—are stable? (See Exercise 6.2, 3.)

13. Answer Exercise 6.2, 5 for *QuickSort, HeapSort,* and *MergeSort*.

14. Modify algorithms for *QuickSort, HeapSort,* and *MergeSort* to compute the effectiveness of a move as defined in Exercise 6.2, 9. Implement these algorithms, apply them to a sequence of random integers, and determine the average value of the effectiveness of all moves for each of the algorithms.

15. What are the similarities and the differences between *SelectSort* and *HeapSort?*

16. The algorithm for *HeapSort* given in the text places elements in descending order. What changes are needed so that the result will be in ascending order?

17. It is noted in the text that $(3/2)n \log_2 n$ is a conservative bound for the number of moves and of compares required for *HeapSort*. Run tests on random sequences of integers to determine the number of moves and compares actually required. Plot the experimental results along with the value of $(3/2)n \log_2 n$. Do the same thing for *MergeSort.*

6.4 Radix Sort

All of the sort techniques we discussed so far have been based on comparing and moving (or relinking) the elements to be sorted. A ***radix sort*** makes no comparisons and, assuming a linked data structure, no moves. The basic operation of a radix sort is to take an element from one linked list and add it to another. If the sort item in each element has at most k characters, then each element is relinked k times. The effort is therefore $k \times n$ relink operations. This is a promising approach because no algorithm that is based on comparing pairs of elements can require fewer than $O(n \log_2 n)$ comparisons for random data (see Knuth, 1973b).

6.4.1 Example of a Radix Sort

We will begin our description of radix sort with an example. A sequence of integers, shown in Figure 6.37, is to be sorted. Each integer in our example contains three digits; therefore, $k = 3$. The first step is to add each integer to one of several lists, called **character lists,** based on the value of the integer's least significant digit. There must be one character list for each possible character value. In this case the possible values are 0, 1, . . . , 9. The result is shown in Figure 6.38, where [0], . . . , [9] identify the character lists.

The integers are now sorted according to the values of their least significant digits. It is an easy matter, although not necessary, to concatenate the character lists to produce the list shown in Figure 6.39. This list must reflect the order of the character lists used to construct it.

The second step takes the elements, as ordered in Figure 6.39, and adds each of them to a character list based on the value of the 10's digit. The result is shown in Figure 6.40. Concatenation of these lists, preserving their order, produces the list shown in Figure 6.41.

The third step in a radix sort of the list in Figure 6.37 places each integer into a character list based on the value of the most significant digit. The process is shown in Figure 6.42. The sort is completed by concatenating, in order, the character lists as shown in Figure 6.43.

6.4.2 General Process for a Radix Sort

The process we just described is easily generalized. The result is shown in Algorithm 6.11. In this algorithm we assume that the sort item in each element contains k characters and that the data type for these characters has a linear structure. The linear structure permits us to associate each character value with

362 → 745 → 885 → 957 → 054 → 786 → 080 → 543 → 012 → 565

Figure 6.37
List of integers to be sorted.

[0] → 080
[1] →
[2] → 362 → 012
[3] → 543
[4] → 054
[5] → 745 → 885 → 565
[6] → 786
[7] → 957
[8] →
[9] →

Figure 6.38
Each integer is added to a character list based on the value of its 1's digit.

080 → 362 → 012 → 543 → 054 → 745 → 885 → 565 → 786 → 957

Figure 6.39
The lists in Figure 6.38 are concatenated to form a new list.

```
PROCEDURE RadixSort(FirstColumn, LastColumn: CARDINAL);
VAR j, k:   CARDINAL        (* Radix sort of a list of   *)
BEGIN                       (* elements whose sort item  *)
    j := LastColumn;        (* is a string of characters *)
    REPEAT                  (* between firstcolumn        *)
                            (* and lastcolumn.           *)

        Traverse the list to be sorted. Add each element
        to a character list based on the value of its jth
        character.

        Form a new version of the list to be sorted by
        concatenating the character lists, in order, from
        the first list to the last list.

        j := j - 1
    UNTIL j < FirstColumn
END RadixSort;
```
    Algorithm 6.11   Radix sort.

[0] →
[1] → 012
[2] →
[3] →
[4] → 543 → 745
[5] → 054 → 957
[6] → 362 → 565
[7] →
[8] → 080 → 885 → 786
[9] →

Figure 6.40
Each integer is added to a character list based on the value of its 10's digit.

012 → 543 → 745 → 054 → 957 → 362 → 565 → 080 → 885 → 786

Figure 6.41
The lists in Figure 6.40 are concatenated to form a new list.

[0] → 012 → 054 → 080
[1] →
[2] →
[3] → 362
[4] →
[5] → 543 → 565
[6] →
[7] → 745 → 786
[8] → 885
[9] → 957

Figure 6.42
Each integer is added to a character list based on the value of its 100's digit.

012 → 054 → 080 → 362 → 543 → 565 → 745 → 786 → 885 → 957

Figure 6.43
The list formed by concatenating the lists in Figure 6.42 is sorted.

a character list based on the ordinal number of that value. The data type of the characters is almost always either CHAR or 0. .9, so this is not normally a concern.

Radix sort is of historical significance since it can be implemented on a mechanical card sorter in a natural way. **Mechanical card sorters** take a stack of cards piled in a bin and place each of the cards in an output slot determined by the value in the column selected by the operator.

Since we are not constrained by having to move cards around physically, we can improve Algorithm 6.11. We do not have to collect the character lists into a single list before distributing the elements, once again, into the character lists. Instead we can distribute from one set of character lists into another and save the overhead of combining them. This improvement is not possible on a mechanical sorter, since someone (perhaps a robot) must collect the short stacks, combine them into one big stack, and pile the result into the input hopper.

Radix sort appears to be the best technique we have discussed, since it requires only $O(n)$ pointer manipulations to sort a linked list.

6.4.3 Drawbacks of a Radix Sort

The first drawback of a radix sort has already been implied. The list must be a linked list. A radix sort of an array is complicated in two ways. The first is that a move is required instead of pointer manipulations. This is serious if the elements are large. Worse yet, each of the character lists must be capable of accommodating the entire list that is to be sorted. Thus, if there are m possible values for each character, then the extra memory requirement for a radix sort will be m times the size of the original list.

Another potential drawback is the overhead required to convert a character value into the index for the appropriate character list. For example, if the sort item is a three-digit integer, say k, then stripping out individual digits requires high-level language statements such as the following:

```
d3 := k MOD 10;                (* Least significant digit. *)
d2 := (k DIV 10) MOD 10;              (* Ten's digit. *)
d1 := k DIV 100            (* Most significant digit. *)
```

High-level languages are not good for implementing radix sort because they usually prevent the programmer from accessing machine instructions for efficiently stripping off bits and characters. See Sedgewick (1983), pages 115–117, for an introduction to this problem.

Finally, saying that radix sort is $O(n)$ suppresses a constant—the number of characters in the sort item. Radix sort will be less efficient if the sort item contains many characters or digits.

On the other hand, for fixed k and sufficiently large n, radix sort must be faster than any of the other sort algorithms we have discussed thus far. The problem is that the value of n for which radix sort surpasses methods that require $O(n \log_2 n)$ compares or moves may be very large. How large will depend on factors such as language, compiler, computer, and programmer.

Figure 6.44 compares the sort times of *InsertSort, RadixSort,* and *QS*3. Keep in mind that the results are for a simple case—a random set of integers. Also keep in mind that *RadixSort* is not well represented in Figure 6.42 since MOD and DIV were used to strip off individual digits.

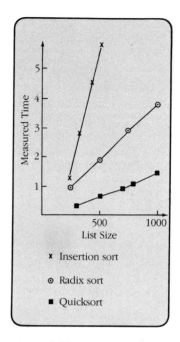

Exercises 6.4

1. Apply *RadixSort* to the list of integers in Exercise 6.3, 1:

> 482, 231, 928, 204, 145, 428, 659, 379, 235, 47, 577, 992, 66, 131, 22

Determine the number of pointer manipulations needed to sort a linked list containing these integers.
2. Does it matter if a linked list to be sorted using *RadixSort* is singly linked or doubly linked? Does it matter for our other sorting algorithms: *SelectSort, InsertSort, QuickSort, HeapSort,* and *MergeSort*? Why?
3. Implement a version of *RadixSort* for the case in which the sort item is
  a. An integer that contains at most maxdigit digits.
  b. **ARRAY**[1..maxchar] **OF** CHAR;
4. Another sort technique that is $O(n)$ is called **distribution sort.** The key values of the items to be sorted must all come from a relatively small domain. For example, suppose that we wanted to sort an array of employee elements based on the value of *empNo* where

Figure 6.44
Comparison of *RadixSort, QS*3, and *InsertSort* for a random set of integers.

```
CONST MaxEmp    =                    (* Maximum number of employees-at most 999. *)

TYPE   Employee = RECORD
                      empNo:  [1..999];
                      data  :                   (* Other information.  *)
                  END;

VAR  noEmp      : [0..MaxEmp];                   (* Actual number of employees. *)
     empList    : ARRAY [1..MaxEmp] OF Employee;
     sortedList: ARRAY [0..999] OF CARDINAL;
```

The simple loop

```
FOR k := 1 TO noEmp DO
   sortedList[empList[k].empNo] := k
END
```

loads sortedList with the index values of the employee elements in empList. The order in which they appear in sortedList is in ascending order by empNo. The number of operations is clearly $O(n)$. How many operations are required to rearrange the elements in empList so that they are in the order specified by sortedList?

Further information about distribution sort is given in Bentley (1983a) and Sedgewick (1983), pages 99–100.

5. Consider a sort key that is a binary number. As in quicksort, scan the list to be sorted from left to right until a key with a leading bit 1 is found. Then scan from right to left until a key with leading bit 0 is found. Exchange these elements and continue until the scans meet. The result will be a list in which all elements with leading bit 0 precede all those with leading bit 1. Applying this technique recursively using bits of successively less significance produces an algorithm (very much like quicksort) that is referred to as a ***radix exchange sort.***

The basic operations of the radix exchange sort described above are: extracting one bit, comparing the extracted bit with 0, and swapping a pair of elements. How many of each of these operations is required if the list begins in sorted order? In the worst case?

6.5 Summary

We will summarize the sort algorithms discussed in this chapter by presenting, in graphical form, some rules of thumb. Figure 6.45 shows these rules for elements in random order stored in an array. If the list is small, use insertion sort for small elements and selection sort for large elements. Both techniques are $O(n^2)$, but for small lists their low overheads make them attractive. Selection sort makes the least moves so it is faster for large elements. Insertion sort makes fewer compares, so it is faster for small elements.

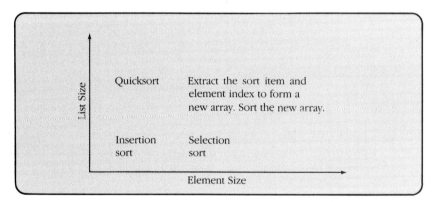

Figure 6.45 Rules of thumb for selecting a sort technique for elements stored in an array. The sort item is assumed to be small.

As the number of elements increases, the $O(n \log_2 n)$ effort of quicksort, along with its simple inner loop, makes it a better choice. Finally, as the elements become large, quicksort spends much of its time moving data from one place to another. We suggest that you form a new array in which the data are replaced by the array index of the array component that contains it. The new array, whose components are small, is now sorted using quicksort. The indexes in this sorted array prescribe the sorted order of the original array. If you wish, the original array can be placed in sorted order with $O(n)$ moves.

Figure 6.46 suggests techniques for sorting elements stored in a doubly linked list. Observe that the horizontal axes in Figures 6.45 and 6.46 have different labels. For arrays it is element size; for linked lists it is sort item size. For a linked list, element size is of little concern since elements are never moved. Sort item size is of interest because if it is small, and the list is large, radix sort is attractive.

These rules of thumb only apply to the special cases cited, and even then the figures shown do not prescribe in any quantitative way the location of the boundaries between methods. We can only repeat, "there are many best methods, depending on what is to be sorted on what machine for what purpose" (Knuth, 1973b).

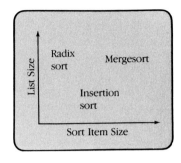

Figure 6.46
Suggestions for selecting a sort technique for elements stored in a doubly linked list. Quicksort may be used in place of merge-sort: see Exercise 6.3, 9.

7.1 Introduction

7.2 Sets of Atomic Types
   7.2.1 Set Specification
   7.2.2 Implementation Using Bit Maps
   Exercises 7.2

7.3 Sets of Structured Objects
   7.3.1 Set Specification
   Exercises 7.3

7.4 Hashed Implementations
   7.4.1 Hashing Functions
   7.4.2 Collision-Resolution Strategies
   7.4.3 Perfect Hashing Functions
   Exercises 7.4

7.5 Hashing Performance
   7.5.1 Performance
   7.5.2 Memory Requirements
   7.5.3 Deletion

7.6 Frequency Analysis of Digraphs
   7.6.1 Hash Function
   7.6.2 Frequency Analysis Summary

7.7 Summary

$S = \{$apple, spoon, leaf, privacy$\}$

(a)

$C = \{$Paul, Mary, Steve, Susan, Bill, Helen$\}$

(b)

Figure 7.1

Sets. (a) Members of set S have no attributes in common. (b) Members of set C have in common that they are all enrolled in the same class.

TYPE Day = (sun, mon, tue, wed, thu, fri, sat);

VAR x, y : **SET OF** Day;
    l, m : **SET OF** [0..9];

```
x := {sat, sun};
x := x  +{wed};
y := x − {sun};
IF y <= x . . .
        ⋮

l := {1..4};
ReadCard(d);
INCL(l,d);
ReadCard(d);
IF d IN l DO . . .
        ⋮
```

Figure 7.2

Examples of Modula-2 sets.

7.1 Introduction

In Chapter 7 we will study data types that share the characteristic that their structure is setlike. Recall from mathematics that a ***set*** is a collection of objects. The objects need not have attributes in common, although they do more often than not. In Figure 7.1(a) the members of collection S have no obvious traits in common except that they are each a member of the set S. We are more likely to find sets such as the one in Figure 7.1(b), in which the members of C are all enrolled in a given class, as well as all being humans.

We are interested in ***sets of data objects.*** The members (elements) of such sets normally share the characteristic that they are all of the same data type. The study of sets of data objects naturally divides into two areas. The first is the study of sets whose members are atomic ordinal data types. (An ***ordinal data type*** has a finite number of values that can be associated one to one with the integers. The ordinal types of Modula-2 are CHAR, INTEGER, CARDINAL, BOOLEAN, any enumerated type, and any subrange type.) Modula-2 has a native data type SET whose elements must be of an enumerated or subrange type. We can declare sets x, y, l, and m as shown in Figure 7.2. In Section 7.2 we will answer these questions: What set operations are provided by Modula-2? How are such sets represented? How are their operations implemented?

In Section 7.3 we will discuss another kind of set, which usually has a quite different group of operations specified. These sets are typified by the types of their data elements, which are structured types. We will assume that they are of type *StdElement,* which we have often used in the preceding chapters. The elements are records, with one portion, the key field(s), having the unique identification property. Typically, an element is placed into the set and is later searched for and found by its key value. The data fields are then used for updating or retrieval.

Sets of structured elements are often implemented by a technique known as hashing, which has a number of interesting variations. Set implementations that use hashing usually exhibit excellent performance. In Section 7.4 we will discuss hashing techniques and in Section 7.5 we will discuss hashing performance.

In Section 7.6, we return to an application that we have used in previous chapters. It is the determination of the frequencies of occurrence of single letters and digraphs in a piece of English prose. This time we will use a set implemented by hashing to store the letters and digraphs and their frequency counts. We will compare the performance of hashed sets to that of binary trees and lists.

Section 7.7 is a summary.

7.2 Sets of Atomic Types

Suppose that we wish to have a data type whose structure is that of a set and whose members (elements) are atomic and enumerable or a subrange of an ordinal type. ***Set structure*** implies that the elements of the structure are related only by their membership in the set. Each element has no prior, next, parent, child, or other related element. There is no first, last, or root element to the structure. An element either is in the set or is not.

Atomic types have no components to their values. In contrast to structured types, their values are treated as single, nondecomposable entities. In effect, their value is both their key and their data value. Referring to the Modula-2 set x in Figure 7.2, we might ask if *tue* is in the set x. If it is, there is no need to retrieve data because *tue* is its data.

7.2.1 Set Specification

Data type *SET* is native to Modula-2. Its specifications are integrated into the specifications of the language itself. Operations include symbols that are used in an integral way instead of the procedure calls we have been using in most of the data types we have specified. For instance, if one wishes to find the intersection of two sets, instead of saying

```
Intersection(S1, S2, S3)
```

we can say

```
S3 := S1 * S2.
```

Specification 7.1 specifies Modula-2 sets. Its form is somewhat different from most other specifications in the book because type *SET* is native to Modula-2.

Specification 7.1   Modula-2 Sets

Note: We write the specifications of type SET in a different manner from that of other specifications since SET is a native data type of Modula-2 and its specifications are built into the language.

Elements: The elements are of some enumerated or subrange type, which we shall call BaseType.

Structure: The data type of the set is declared as SET OF BaseType. The elements are members of a set:
S = {e1, e2, ..., en}.

Domain: The number of elements in a set (its cardinality) is less than or equal to some bound N, where N is usually determined by the wordsize of the host computer system (see Section 7.2.2).

Operations: S1, S2, and S are sets of BaseType, and e is an element whose type is BaseType.

continued

Specification 7.1, continued

```
S1 := S2
post — S1 = S2.

e IN S
post — True if e is a member of S; else false.

S1 * S2
post — Result is the intersection of S1 and S2.

S1 + S2
post — Result is the union of S1 and S2.

S1 - S2
post — Result is the set difference of S2 from S1.

S1 / S2
post — Result is the symmetric difference of S1 and S2.

INCL(S,e)
post — Element e is a member of set S.

EXCL(S,e)
post — Element e is not a member of set S.

{e1, e2, ..., en}
post — Result is a set with members e1, e2, ..., en.

S1 = S2
post — True only if S1 and S2 have exactly the same members.

S1 # S2
post — Not (S1 = S2).

S1 <= S2
post — True only if S1 is a subset (including improper) of S2.

S1 >= S2
post — True only if S2 is a subset (including improper) of S1.
```

Figure 7.2 has some examples of Modula-2 sets and some sample operations. A specific set type must be declared over some ***base type.*** The base types of the sets in Figure 7.2 are *Day* and a subrange of CARDINAL.

There are three restrictions to sets in Modula-2:

1. The members of a set must be constants.
2. The base type of a set must be an enumerated or subrange type.
3. The maximum number of members a set can hold is determined by the Modula-2 implementation.

Restriction 1 allows sets to be written only with members that are constants of the base type.

```
TYPE BaseType = [1..9];
     SampleSet = SET OF BaseType;

VAR e, f, g: BaseType;
    S        : SampleSet;
```

Given these declarations, S := {3,4,7} is allowed, whereas

```
e := 3; f := 4; g := 7;
S := {e, f, g};
```

is not. In order to allow the value of a variable to be included in a set, two standard procedures are provided in Modula-2:

```
INCL(S,e) results in S = S' + {e}

EXCL(S,e) results in S = S' - {e}.
```

S′ is set S prior to execution of the operation; + is set union, and − is set difference.

IN is an operation that allows a test for inclusion of an element in a set. e IN S is true if and only if the value of e is a member of set S. We can also test for set equality and to see if one set is a subset of another.

The restrictions on type SET in Modula-2 sharply limit their usefulness. Restriction 3 says that the maximum cardinality of a set is determined by the Modula-2 implementation. This number is often equal to the number of bits in a word of the host computer. Maximums of 16 and 32 are common.

There is another restriction that is not obvious. To illustrate it, suppose that the maximum cardinality of a set were 32. It would seem that

```
TYPE LowerCase = SET OF ['a'..'z'];
```

would be allowable since there are 26 letters, and thus at most 26 members in sets of this type. However, the not-so-obvious restriction is that the ordinal values of the members of the set must also be less than 32. Since, for example, ORD('a') is 97 in the ASCII character set, Modula-2 compilers would reject the above TYPE statement. As a second example,

```
TYPE Set1 = SET OF [1..20]
```

is allowed, whereas

```
TYPE Day = (sun, mon, tue,
wed, thu, fri, sat);

VAR x, y: SET OF Day;
    l, m: SET OF [0..9];

x := {sat, sun};
x := x +{wed};
y := x − {sun};
IF y <= x ...
    ⋮

l := {1..4};
ReadCard(d);
INCL(l,d);
ReadCard(d);
IF d IN l DO ...
    ⋮
```

Figure 7.2 (repeated)
Examples of Modula-2 sets.

•

=	Set equality
#	Set inequality
<=	Subset
>=	Superset

S1 = S2, S1 # S2, S1 <= S2, and S1 >= S2 are examples.

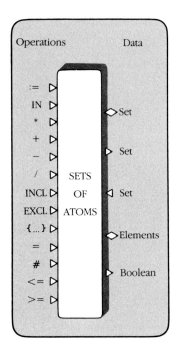

Figure 7.3
Capsule for Modula-2 sets.

•

M = L	True if M and L have exactly the same members
M # L	True if M = L is not true
M <= L	True if every member of M is also a member of L
M >= L	True if every member of L is also a member of M

Figure 7.4
Modula-2 set relational operators.

•

TYPE
    Day = (sun, mon, tue, wed, thu, fri, sat);
    SmallSet = **SET OF** Day;
            (* *Allowed.* *)
    LargeSet = **SET OF** [1..20];
            (* *Too large.* *)

Figure 7.5

TYPE Set2 = **SET OF** [40..50]

is not, even though Set2 sets can have at most 11 members.

The use of sets can make algorithms succinct and efficient.

7.2.2 Implementation Using Bit Maps

Sets of ordinal elements can have a particularly compact and efficient implementation if the implementor has access to the bits of the computer words. For the discussion that follows, let us suppose that the word length on the computer system we are using is 16 bits. Let us also suppose that the sets with which we are dealing are restricted to having no more than 16 possible elements. In Figure 7.5 the set type *SmallSet* is allowed, but the set type *LargeSet* is not. (Modula-2 implementations often have such a restriction, although the maximum is sometimes greater than 16.)

The fact that the element type is ordinal means that the *ORD* function is defined for its values. If we label the 16 bits of the word from right to left as bits 0 through 15, then each bit of the word can be made to correspond to a value of the element type as follows:

| Bits | 0 0 0 0 0 0 0 0 0 0 0 0 0 0 0 0 |
| Positions | 15 14 13 12 11 10 9 8 7 6 5 4 3 2 1 0 |

In Figure 7.5 type *Day* has only seven values; therefore, in the set *D* we use bits 0 through 6 for the values *sun* through *sat*, respectively. A 1 in a bit indicates that the element whose ordinal value is that bit number is in the set. The ordinal of the value *tue* for type *Day* is 2. The statement

    D := {tue};

results in

| Bit map | 0 0 0 0 0 0 0 0 0 0 0 0 0 1 0 0 |
| Positions | 15 14 13 12 11 10 9 8 7 6 5 4 3 2 1 0 |

The statement

    D := {tue, sat, mon};

results in

| Bit map | 0 0 0 0 0 0 0 0 0 1 0 0 0 1 1 0 |
| Positions | 15 14 13 12 11 10 9 8 7 6 5 4 3 2 1 0 |

Digital computers have certain logical and shift operations as part of their machine language. Some typical ones are

OR   Logical or
AND   Logical and
XOR   Exclusive or
NOT   Complement
SHL *n*   Shift word left *n* bits, zero fill
SHR *n*   Shift word right *n* bits, zero fill

The rules governing these operations are shown in Figure 7.6.

Set operations can be performed using these machine-level operations. For example, two values of the sets *D* and *E* are shown in Table 7.1.

TABLE 7.1 Values of sets *D* and *E*.

Operation	Bit map
D := {sun,wed,thu}	*D* is 0000000000011001
E := {wed,fri}	*E* is 0000000000101000

Some operations on the original values of *D* and *E* can be implemented as follows:

$$
\begin{array}{llll}
D := D * E & D & & 0000000000011001 \\
& & AND & \\
& E & & \underline{0000000000101000} \\
& D & & 0000000000001000
\end{array}
$$

$$
\begin{array}{llll}
D := D + E & D & & 0000000000011001 \\
& & OR & \\
& E & & \underline{0000000000101000} \\
& D & & 0000000000111001
\end{array}
$$

$$
\begin{array}{llll}
D := D - E & D & & 0000000000011001 \\
& & XOR & \\
& E & & \underline{0000000000101000} \\
& & & 0000000000110001 \\
& & AND & \\
& D & & \underline{0000000000011001} \\
& D & & 0000000000010001
\end{array}
$$

The other operations are done in a similar fashion.

Finding the bit map for a single element can be accomplished with the *ORD* function. Suppose that the following Modula-2 statement is executed:

```
D := {tue};
```

We can find the bit map as follows:

AND

0 AND 0 = 0
0 AND 1 = 0
1 AND 1 = 1

OR

0 OR 0 = 0
0 OR 1 = 1
1 OR 1 = 1

XOR

0 XOR 0 = 0
0 XOR 1 = 1
1 XOR 1 = 0

NOT

NOT 0 = 1
NOT 1 = 0

SHL 5

Before
1111111111111111

After
1111111111100000

SHR 5

Before
1111111111111111

After
0000011111111111

Figure 7.6
Rules for logical and shift operations.

Operation	Result	
n = **ORD**(tue)		(* n is 2. *)
LOAD 1	0000000000000001	(* Put the bit pattern shown *)
		(* into the computer's register. *)
SHL *n*	0000000000000100	
STORE *D*	*D* = 0000000000000100	(* D is the set with *)
		(* only tue in it. *)

The bit map that results from the SHL operation is stored in the value of *D*.

These examples show us how a bit map representation can be manipulated in an efficient manner by most digital computers. The implementations give us a flavor of the technique.

Exercises 7.2

1. If you are familiar with the assembly language of some computer, write code segments in that language that implement the set operations shown below assuming a bit map representation with the word size native to your computer:
   a. Set intersection
   b. Set union
   c. Test for element inclusion (in)
   d. The subset test (<=)
2. Why can the kind of set described in this section not have real numbers as elements?
3. Suppose that you have a computer that has a 16-bit word. Discuss how you would implement sets that can have more than 16 members.
4. Design, specify, and implement in Modula-2 a set type *LargeSets* in which sets hold atomic objects just as Modula-2 SETs do, but which can have up to 255 member elements.

7.3 Sets of Structured Objects

In Section 7.2 we studied a set data type. We specified a group of operations that were natural for data of that type and structure. We will now study another data type that has a set structure among its elements but whose elements are not atomic.

7.3.1 Set Specification

Suppose that we had elements of type *StdElement,* which we often used in previous chapters. Again we will assume that the key values have the unique identification property. We will also assume that the elements are not associated in any way that interests us except for their membership in the set. What operations might there be for such elements and structure?

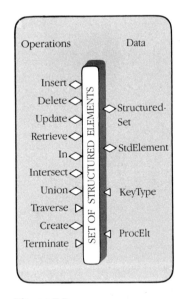

Figure 7.7
Capsule for set of structured elements.

Since elements are not related to each other, operations such as *FindNext, FindPrior, FindParent,* and *FindRoot* do not apply. The basic operations, as usual, are *Insert, Delete, Update,* and *Retrieve.* Since there is no notion of position the target of these operations is specified using key values. *Delete,* for example, attempts to delete an element with a specified key value. *Retrieve* attempts to return an element with a specified key value.

Basic set operations are *In, Intersect,* and *Union.* Others, such as *SymmetricDifference,* could be added. Including operation *Traverse* gives the user the opportunity to observe or process all elements in the set. Without *Traverse* it would be difficult, or impossible, to retrieve all elements in the set since there is no operation analogous to the *FindNext* operation for a list.

Most data structures in this text include a current element, which is the element acted on by the operations *Insert, Delete, Update,* and *Retrieve.* Other operations such as *FindNext, FindParent,* and *FindKey* permit the user to specify the current element. The operations in the structured set module select elements based on their key value, so a current element is not used. The specification for a set of structured elements (Specification 7.2) follows.

```
TYPE StdElement =
    RECORD
        key : KeyType
        data: DataType
    END;
```

Specification 7.2   Structured Sets

DEFINITION MODULE StructuredSets;

(* **Elements:** The elements are of type StdElement. The key field has the
      unique identification property. *)

FROM StdTypes **IMPORT** KeyType, StdElement;

(* **Structure:** The elements form a set. *)

(* **Domain:** The number of elements in the set is bounded. *)

EXPORT QUALIFIED StructuredSet, Insert, Delete, Update, Retrieve,
                    Traverse, Create, Terminate, ProcElt, In, Intersect, Union;

TYPE StructuredSet;   (* *Opaque data type used to represent a set.* *)

       ProcElt = **PROCEDURE** (StdElement);

(* **Operations:** If SS is a structured set then reference to SS-pre in a
      postcondition is a reference to the value of SS just prior to
      the operation. *)

PROCEDURE Insert(**VAR** SS: StructuredSet; e: StdElement): BOOLEAN;
(* **post** — If SS-pre is not full, and does not contain an element whose
          key value is e.key, then SS contains element e and Insert is
          true, else Insert is false. *)

PROCEDURE Delete(**VAR** SS: StructuredSet; tkey: KeyType): BOOLEAN;
(* **post** — If SS-pre contains an element with key value tkey then that
          element is not in SS and Delete is true, else Delete is false. *)

continued

Specification 7.2, continued

PROCEDURE Update(**VAR** SS: StructuredSet; e: StdElement): BOOLEAN;
(* **post** — If SS-pre contains an element with key value e.key then the
            data field of that element is equal to e.data and Update is true,
            else Update is false. *)

PROCEDURE Retrieve(SS:StructuredSet; tkey:KeyType; **VAR** e: StdElement): BOOLEAN;
(* **post** — If SS-pre contains an element with key value tkey then e is
            that element and Retrieve is true, else Retrieve is false. *)

PROCEDURE In(SS: StructuredSet; tkey: KeyType): BOOLEAN;
(* **post** — If SS contains an element with key value tkey then In is true,
            else In is false. *)

PROCEDURE Intersect(**VAR** SS: StructuredSet; SS1,SS2: StructuredSet): BOOLEAN;
(* **post** — If Intersect is true then SS is the set intersection of SS1
            and SS2. *)

PROCEDURE Union(**VAR** SS: StructuredSet; SS1,SS2: StructuredSet): BOOLEAN;
(* **post** — If Union is true then SS is the set union of SS1 and SS2. *)

PROCEDURE Traverse(SS: StructuredSet; PElt: ProcElt);
(* **post** — Each element in SS has been processed by procedure PElt. *)

PROCEDURE Create(**VAR** SS: StructuredSet): BOOLEAN;
(* **post** — If a structured set can be created then SS is an empty structured
            set and Create is true, else Create is false. *)

PROCEDURE Terminate(**VAR** SS: StructuredSet);
(* **post** — Structured set SS does not exist. *)

END StructuredSets.

A set such as the one we are discussing can be implemented by using one of the data types that we specified earlier. Any of the list data types discussed in Chapter 4 could be used. A binary search tree could be used. However, we will use a hash table approach, which is discussed in Section 7.4.

Exercises 7.3

1. Rewrite the set specification assuming a current element as we have for previous data types.
2. How would you implement the kind of set that we specified as a chronologically ordered list? In other words, implement the operations of the set in terms of the operations of the chronologically ordered list. What about using other list types?
3. Give several examples of applications in which a set data type might be useful. Would it be useful for an English language dictionary that is stored on a mass storage device and is accessible through an interactive terminal? Why or why not?

7.4 Hashed Implementations

We have studied several methods for the storage and later retrieval of keyed records. Arrays, linked lists, and several kinds of trees provide structures that allow these operations. In each of these structures, the find operation is necessarily implemented by some form of search. The key values of records in the structure are compared with the desired, or target, key until either a matching value is found or the data structure is exhausted. The pattern of probes is dependent upon the methods of organizing and relating the records of the structure. A sorted list implemented as an array can be probed by a binary search. The same list in linked form can only be searched sequentially.

We might ask if it is possible to create a data structure that does not require a search to implement the find operation. Is it possible, for example, to compute the location of the record that has a given key value,

memory address of record $= f(\text{key})$

where f is a function that maps each distinct key value into the memory address of the record identified by that key? We shall see that the answer is a qualified yes. Such functions can be found, but they are difficult to determine and can only be constructed if all of the keys in the data set are known in advance. They are called **perfect hashing functions** and are further examined in Section 7.4.3.

Normally, there has to be a compromise from a strictly calculated access scheme to a hybrid scheme that involves a calculation followed by some limited searching. The function does not necessarily give the exact memory address of the target record but only gives a **home address** that may contain the desired record:

home address $= H(\text{key})$

Functions such as H are known as **hashing functions.** In contrast to perfect hashing functions, these are usually easy to determine and can give excellent performance. The home address may not contain the record being sought. In that case, a search of other addresses is required, and this is known as **rehashing.** In Section 7.4.1, we introduce a number of hashing functions, and in Section 7.4.2 we examine several rehashing strategies. In Section 7.5 we summarize the performance of hashed implementations, and in Section 7.6 we compare its operation and performance with that of lists and trees for the frequency analysis of digraphs.

The fundamental idea behind **hashing** is the antithesis of sorting. A sort arranges the records in a regular pattern that makes the relatively efficient binary search possible. Hashing takes the diametrically opposite approach. The basic idea is to scatter the records completely randomly throughout some memory or storage space—the so-called **hash table.** The hash function can be thought of as a pseudo-random-number generator that uses the value of the key as a seed and that outputs the home address of the element containing that key.

One of the drawbacks of hashing is the random locations of stored elements. There is no notion of first, next, root, parent, or child or anything analogous. Thus, hashing is appropriate for implementing a set relationship among elements but not for implementing structures that involve relationships among constituent elements. It is for that reason that hashing is discussed in this chapter on sets. There are, however, other appropriate contexts for a discussion of hashing.

One of the virtues of hashing is that it allows us to find records with $O(1)$ probes. The *FindKey* operation has required a number of probes that depend on n in every implementation of every data structure discussed so far: $O(n)$ for a linked implementation of a list, $O(\log_2 n)$ for an array implementation of a sorted list, and $O(\log_2 n)$ for a binary search tree. Since hashing requires the fewest probes to find something, it is frequently considered to be a particularly effective search technique. Also, since hashing stores elements in a table, the hash table, it is sometimes considered to be a technique for operating on tables. All of these views of hashing are correct. We choose to view hashing as a technique for implementing sets. Its other advantages and disadvantages are not changed by this point of view.

It is convenient to consider the hash table to be an array of records and to let the hash function calculate the index value of the home address rather than to calculate its memory address directly. Once the appropriate index value is computed, the array mapping function can complete the transformation into an actual memory address. The hash table is then represented as shown in Figure 7.8.

Suppose we have a hash table defined with TableSize = 7 so that the table entries are table[0], table[1], ..., table[6]. Further suppose that the key of a standard element is of type CARDINAL. For illustration we choose the hash function H as

$$H(\text{key}) = \text{key MOD } 7$$

Notice that the value produced by this function is always a CARDINAL between 0 and 6, which is within the range of indexes of the table.

Operation *Create* will produce the empty table shown in Figure 7.9. If the first record we store has a key value of 374, then the hash function

$$H(374) = 374 \text{ MOD } 7 = 3$$

places the record at table [3]. This is shown in Figure 7.10. If the next record has a key value of 1091, we get

$$H(1091) = 1091 \text{ MOD } 7 = 6$$

and the table becomes that shown in Figure 7.11. A third record with key = 911 gives

---

Hashing is well suited to data types whose structure is setlike.

```
CONST TableSize = 7;
        (* Or other value *)
        (* as needed.     *)
TYPE
   Position = [0..TableSize-1];
   TableType = ARRAY Position
              OF StdElement;

VAR  table: TableType;
```

Figure 7.8
Array representation of a hash table.

Table address	Table contents
[0]	empty
[1]	empty
[2]	empty
[3]	empty
[4]	empty
[5]	empty
[6]	empty

Figure 7.9
Empty table.

$$H(911) = 911 \text{ MOD } 7 = 1$$

and the resulting table is shown in Figure 7.12.

Retrieval of any of the records already in the table is a simple matter. The target key is presented to the hash function that reproduces the same table position as it did when the record was stored. If the target key were 740, a value not in the table, the hashing function would produce

$$H(740) = 740 \text{ MOD } 7 = 5$$

Interrogating table[5], we find that it is empty, and we conclude that a record with key = 740 is not in the table.

The example that we have just seen was constructed to conceal a serious problem. So far, keys with different values have hashed to different locations in the table. That is not generally so and is only the case in our current example because the key values were carefully chosen. Suppose that insertion of a record with a key value of 227 is attempted. Then,

$$H(227) = 227 \text{ MOD } 7 = 3$$

but table[3] is already filled with another record. This is called a **collision**—two different key values hashing to the same location. Why this happens and what to do about it are important because collisions are a fact of life when hashing.

Suppose that employee records are hashed based on Social Security number. If a firm has 500 employees it will not want to reserve a hash table with 1 billion entries (the number of possible Social Security numbers) to guarantee that each of its employee records hashes to a unique location. Even if the firm allocates 1000 slots in its hash table and uses a hash function that is a "perfect" randomizer, the probability that there will be no collisions is essentially zero. This is the **birthday paradox** (Feller, 1950), which says that hash functions with no collisions are so rare that it is worth looking for them only in very special circumstances. These special circumstances are discussed in Section 7.4.3. In the meantime, we need to consider what to do when a collision does occur.

With careful design, strategies for handling collisions are simple. They are commonly called **rehashing** or **collision-resolution strategies**, and we will discuss them in Section 7.4.2.

We selected the hashing function

$$H(\text{key}) = \text{key MOD } n$$

in the example we just completed. We will now see why that was a reasonable thing to do and will also look at a number of other hashing functions.

7.4.1 Hashing Functions

There is a large and diverse group of hashing functions that have been proposed since the advent of the hashing technique. Some are simple and

Table address	Table contents
[0]	empty
[1]	empty
[2]	empty
[3]	374, . . . data
[4]	empty
[5]	empty
[6]	empty

Figure 7.10
First record stored at table[3].

Table address	Table contents
[0]	empty
[1]	empty
[2]	empty
[3]	374, . . . data
[4]	empty
[5]	empty
[6]	1091, . . . data

Figure 7.11
Second record stored at table[6].

Table address	Table contents
[0]	empty
[1]	911, . . . data
[2]	empty
[3]	374, . . . data
[4]	empty
[5]	empty
[6]	1091, . . . data

Figure 7.12
Third record stored at table[1].

Good hashing functions have two desirable properties:

1. They compute rapidly.
2. They produce a nearly random distribution of index values.

straightforward; others are complex. Almost all are computationally simple since the speed of the computation of such functions is an important factor in their use. Lum, Yuen, and Dodd (1971) have a good review of many, including some of the more exotic ones. We will confine our attention to simple but effective methods.

We will now consider several hashing functions.

• Digit selection

The first hashing function we will discuss is ***digit selection.*** Suppose that the keys of the set of data that we are dealing with are strings of digits such as Social Security numbers (nine-digit numbers):

$$\text{key} = d_1 d_2 d_3 d_4 d_5 d_6 d_7 d_8 d_9$$

If the population comprising the data is randomly chosen, then the choice of the last three digits, $d_7 d_8 d_9$, will give a good random distribution of values. A possible implementation is the following:

```
VAR table: ARRAY[0..999] OF Person;
```

where *Person* is a record type for the key and information that we wish to keep. Notice that the hashing function in this case is

$$H(\text{key}) = \text{key MOD 1000}$$

which simply strips off the last three digits of the key.

Care must be taken in deciding which digits to select. If the population with which we are dealing is students at a university, for example, the last three digits, $d_7 d_8 d_9$, are probably a good choice, whereas the first three digits, $d_1 d_2 d_3$, are probably not. State universities tend to draw their student bodies from a single state or geographical region. The first three digits of the Social Security number are based on the geographical region in which the number was originally issued. Most students from California, for example, have a first digit of 5 and clustered second and third digits, indicating various subregions of the state; 567, for example, is very common. If the data were for a California university, almost all of the students' records would map into the 500–599 range of the hash table, and a large subgroup would map into position 567. The output of the function would not be uniform and random but would be loaded on certain positions of the table causing an inordinately high number of collisions. It would not be a good hashing function for that reason.

If the key population is known in advance, it is possible to analyze the distribution of values taken by each digit of the key. The digits participating in the hash address are then easy to select. Such an analysis is called ***digit analysis.*** Instead of choosing the last three digits, we would choose the three digits of the key whose digit analyses showed the most uniform distribution. If d_4, d_7, and d_9 gave the flattest distributions, the hashing function might strip out those digits from a key and put them together to form a number in the range 0–999:

$$H(d_1d_2d_3d_4d_5d_6d_7d_8d_9) = d_4d_7d_9$$

Caution is advised, since although the digits are apparently random and uniform in value, they might have dependencies among themselves. For example, certain combinations of d_7 and d_9 might tend to occur together. Then if d_9 were always 8 when d_7 is 3, d_438 would be the only table position mapped to in the range d_430–d_439, effectively lowering the table size and increasing the chances of collision. Analysis for interdigit correlations might be necessary to bring such a situation to light.

• Division

One of the most effective hashing methods is ***division,*** which works as follows:

$$H(\text{key}) = \text{key MOD } m = h \qquad 0 <= h <= m - 1$$

The bit pattern of the key, regardless of its data type, is treated as an integer, divided in the integer sense by m, and the remainder of the division is used as the table address. h is in the range from 0 to $m - 1$. Such a function is fast on computer systems that have an integer divide, since most generate the quotient in one hardware register and the remainder in another. The content of the remainder register need only be copied into the variable h, and the hash is completed.

In practice, functions of this type give very good results. Lum, Yuen, and Dodd (1971) have an empirical study showing this to be the case. Division can, however, perform poorly in a number of cases. For example, if m were 25, then all keys that were divisible by 5 would map into positions 0, 5, 10, 15, and 20 of the table. A subset of the keys maps into a subset of the table, something that we in general wish to avoid. Of course, using the function $H = \text{key MOD } m$ maps all keys for which key MOD $m = 0$ into table[0], all keys for which key MOD $m = 1$ into table[1], etc., but that bias is unavoidable. What we do not want to do is to introduce any further ones.

The problem underlying the choice of 25 as the table size is that it has a factor of 5. All keys with 5 as a factor will map into a table position that also has that factor. The cure is to make sure that the key and m have no common factors, and the easiest way to ensure that is to choose m so that it has no factors other than 1 and itself—a prime number. For this reason, most of the time that the division function is used the table size will be a prime number. However, Lum, Yuen, and Dodd (1971) show that any divisor with no small factors, say less than 20, is suitable.

• Multiplication

A simple method that is based on ***multiplication*** is sometimes used. Suppose that the keys in question are five digits in length:

$$\text{key} = d_1d_2d_3d_4d_5$$

key = 54321

(a)

```
      54321
  ×   54321
      54321
     108642
     162963
     217284
     271605
  2950771041
```

(b)

h = 077

(c)

Figure 7.13
(a) Key. (b) Results of squaring the key value. (c) Digit selection of the middle digits gives the table position of the record.

The key is squared by

$$\begin{array}{r} d_1d_2d_3d_4d_5 \\ \times\ d_1d_2d_3d_4d_5 \\ \hline r_1\,r_2\,r_3\,r_4\,r_5\,r_6\,r_7\,r_8\,r_9\,r_{10} \end{array}$$

The result is a 10-digit product. The function is completed by doing digit selection on the product. In most cases, the middle digits are chosen, for example, $r_4r_5r_6$. An example is shown in Figure 7.13.

It is important to choose the middle digits. Consider, for example, choosing the right most two digits of the product in the example—41. That value comes only from the product of 1×21 and 2×21; that is, only from the right most two digits of the original key value. All keys ending in 21 will produce the same table location—41. This is the kind of bias that we try to avoid introducing. The middle digits, on the other hand, are formed from products involving the left, middle, and right portions of the key. Changing any one digit in the key is likely to change the hash result. Information from all portions of the key is amalgamated in the calculation of the hash table subscript.

• Folding

The next hash function we will discuss is *folding.* Suppose that we have a five-digit key as we had in the multiplication method:

$$\text{key} = d_1d_2d_3d_4d_5$$

and the programs are running on a simple microcomputer system that has no hardware divide or multiply but that does have an arithmetic add. One way to form a hash function is simply to add the individual digits of the key:

$$H(\text{key}) = d_1 + d_2 + d_3 + d_4 + d_5$$

The result would be in the range

$$0 <= b <= 45$$

and could be used as the index in the hash table. If a larger table were needed (there were more than 46 records), the result could be enlarged by adding the numbers as pairs of digits:

$$H(\text{key}) = 0d_1 + d_2d_3 + d_4d_5$$

The result would then be between 000 and 207 (09 + 99 + 99). Folding is the name given to a class of methods that involves combining portions of the key to form a smaller result. The methods for combining are usually either arithmetic addition or exclusive or's.

Folding is often used in conjunction with other methods. If the key were a Social Security number of nine digits and the program were implemented on a minicomputer that has 16 bit registers and consequently has a maximum positive integer size of 65535, then the key is intractable as it stands. It must somehow be reduced to an integer less than 65535 before it can be used.

Folding can be used to do this. Suppose the key in question has a value

key = 987654321

We can break the key into four-digit groups and then add them:

$$
\begin{array}{r}
0009 \\
8765 \\
\underline{4321} \\
\text{fold(key)} = 13095
\end{array}
$$

This result would be between 0 and 20007. Now apply a second hashing function, say division, to produce a table position within the range $0 \ldots (m - 1)$. If the hash table has m positions, the composite function is

$H(\text{key}) = \text{fold(key) MOD } m$

• Character-valued keys

All of the examples in our discussion of hashing functions assumed that the keys were some form of integer. Quite often, however, the keys are character strings, or **character-valued keys.** How are these handled?

Remember that all data stored in a computer memory are simply strings of bits. The ASCII code for the character 'y', for example, is

1111001_2

which can also be interpreted as the integer value 121. The *ORD* function of Modula-2 reinterprets characters as integers in this fashion:

$\text{ORD}('y') = 121_{10}$

This provides one basis for using characters in hashing functions. If the key values are single characters, division can be applied as follows:

$H(\text{key}) = \text{ORD(key) MOD } m$

In the case key = 'y' and $m = 7$,

$H('y') = \text{ORD}('y') \text{ MOD } 7 = 2$

If the key is a character string of length 2, such as

key = 'jy'

the bit pattern for the string would be

11010101111001_2

The corresponding integer is

$\text{ORD}('j') * 128 + \text{ORD}('y') = 13689$

Since $128 = 2^7$, the multiplication by 128 effectively shifts the bit pattern for 'j' 7 bits to the left. The addition effectively concatenates the 2-bit strings. For the three-character string 'djy', we get

$$\text{ORD('d')} * 16384 + \text{ORD('j')} * 128 + \text{ORD('y')} = 1,652,089$$

16384 is 2^{14}, providing a left shift of 14 bits for 'd'. Notice that the result is beyond the capacity of a 16-bit register, the size register available on most mini- and microcomputer systems. Algorithm 7.1 folds a 21-character string in groups of 3.

```
TYPE String = ARRAY [1..21] OF CHAR;

PROCEDURE Fold(S: String): CARDINAL; (* Folds a string    *)
VAR k, sum: CARDINAL;                (* of 21 characters  *)
BEGIN                                (* in groups of 3.   *)
    k := 1; sum := 0;
      REPEAT
        sum := sum + ORD(S[k])*16384 (* 24 bit            *)
                   + ORD(S[k+1])*128 (* CARDINAL values   *)
                   + ORD(S[k+2]);    (* are required      *)
          k := k+3                   (* for the result.   *)
        UNTIL k > 21;
      RETURN sum
END Fold;
```

Algorithm 7.1   Folding a character string.

Algorithm 7.1 could be written more generally, but doing so would obscure the simple process. Division hashing can be applied to the result of function *Fold*.

7.4.2 *Collision-Resolution Strategies*

A collision-resolution strategy, or rehashing, determines what happens when two or more elements have a collision, or hash to the same address. We will begin by defining some parameters that will be used to help describe these strategies.

We will call the number of different values that a key can assume R. A nine-digit integer (for example, a Social Security number) has

$$R = 1,000,000,000$$

The size of the hash table, **TableSize**, is a second important parameter. It must be large enough to hold the number of elements we wish to store.

The number of records that is actually stored in the table varies with time and is denoted $n = n(t)$. One of the most important parameters is the fraction of the table that contains records at any time. This is called the **load factor** and is written

$$\alpha = \alpha(t) = n / \text{tablesize}$$

In Figure 7.12, $\alpha = 3/7$.

```
CONST BucketSize =
      (* User supplied. *)
      TableSize   =
      (* User supplied. *)

TYPE Bucket = ARRAY
     [1..bucketsize] OF StdEle-
     ment;

VAR Table = ARRAY
    [0..(tablesize − 1)] OF Bucket;
```

In summary, the keys of our data elements are chosen from R different values, and n elements are stored in the hash table that is of size *TableSize* and is $\alpha \times 100$ percent full.

A more general form of hash table is obtained by allowing each hash table position to hold more than a single record. Each of these multirecord cells is called a **bucket** and can hold b records. An array representation of such a hash table is shown in Figure 7.14.

The concept of hash tables as collections of buckets is important for tables that are stored on direct access devices such as magnetic disks. For those devices, each bucket can be tied to a physical cell of the device, such as a track or sector. The hashing function produces a bucket number that results in the transfer of the physically related block into the random access memory (RAM). Once there, the bucket can be searched or modified at high speed.

Buckets of size greater than one are of limited use in hash tables stored in RAM. They tend to slow the average access time to records when searching. We will only discuss buckets of size one in this chapter. Bear in mind, however, that the hash table we discuss is a table of buckets of size one.

The strategies for resolving collisions will be grouped into three approaches. The first approach, **open address methods,** attempts to place a second and subsequent keys that hash to the one table location into some other position in the table that is unoccupied (open). The second approach, **external chaining,** has a linked list associated with each hash table address. Each element is added to the linked list at its home address. The third approach uses pointers to link together different buckets in the hash table. We will discuss **coalesced chaining,** since it is one of the better strategies that use this technique.

• Open address methods

For all the open address methods and their algorithms we will use the hash table represented in Figure 7.8. There are several open address methods using varying degrees of sophistication and a variety of techniques. All seek to find an open table position after a collision. Let us return to Figure 7.12, which is repeated for reference as Figure 7.15, and attempt to add the key whose value is 227. Recall that the example hashing function applied to 227 gives

$$H(227) = 227 \bmod 7 = 3$$

so that 227 collides with 374.

• Linear rehashing

A simple resolution to the collision called **linear rehashing** is to start a sequential search through the hash table at the position at which the collision occurred. The search continues until an open position is found or until the table is exhausted. A probe at position 4 reveals an open address, and the new record is stored there. The result is shown in Figure 7.16. A request to find the record with key = 227 generates the same search path used to store it.

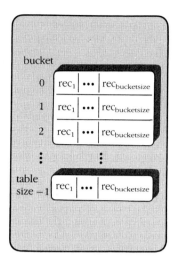

Figure 7.14
Hash table of buckets.

Table address	Table contents
[0]	empty
[1]	911, ... data ...
[2]	empty
[3]	374, ... data ...
[4]	empty
[5]	empty
[6]	1091, ... data ..

Figure 7.15
Three records stored at table[1], table[3], and table[6].

Table address	Table contents
[0]	empty
[1]	911
[2]	empty
[3]	374
[4]	227
[5]	empty
[6]	1091

Figure 7.16
Linear rehashing.

To insert an element we search, beginning at the home address, until an empty address is found or until the table is exhausted. For example, inserting an element whose key is 421 in Figure 7.16 leads to the Figure 7.17. We have added a column to our illustration of hash tables—the number of probes required to find each element stored therein. In the case of linear rehashing, it is easy to determine an element's home address from this added information.

We will add a status field to each position in the hash table. Its values are *empty, occupied,* and *deleted.* The use of *empty* is clear. Let us see how we use the values *occupied* and *deleted.*

TYPE status = (empty,
           occupied,
           deleted);

A status field is added to each position in the hash table.

Table address	Table contents	Probes
[0]	empty	
[1]	911 ⌐	1
[2]	421 ←	2
[3]	374	1
[4]	227	2
[5]	empty	
[6]	1091	1

Figure 7.17
Hash table and the number of probes required to find an element in the table.

Table address	Table contents	Probes
[0]	empty	
[1]	911 ⌐	1
[2]	421 ⌐	2
[3]	374 ⌐	1
[4]	227 ⌐	2
[5]	624 ←	5
[6]	1091	1

Figure 7.18
The probe sequence when searching for 624 (or any other key value whose home address is 1).

Figure 7.18 shows the result of adding 624, whose home address is 1, to the hash table in Figure 7.17. The probes needed to find an empty space for 624 are also shown. A subsequent search using linear rehashing to find 624 will retrace that same path. If any of the three elements, 421, 374, or 227, were deleted and replaced by the value *empty,* subsequent searches for 624 would not work. Upon encountering a location marked *empty* the search would terminate unsuccessfully. A solution to this problem is to mark positions from which elements have been deleted with a special value.

The drawback to the use of the value *deleted* is that it can clutter up the hash table thereby increasing the number of probes required to find an element. A partial solution is to reenter all legitimate elements periodically and to mark the remaining locations *empty.*

Implementation Module 7.1   *Structured Sets*

```
IMPLEMENTATION MODULE StructuredSets;
(* StructuredSets; array implementation; meets Specification 7.2. *)

FROM StdTypes IMPORT KeyType, StdElement;
FROM Storage  IMPORT ALLOCATE, DEALLOCATE, Available;
FROM SYSTEM   IMPORT TSIZE;

CONST TableSize = 13;                            (* Set this value as needed. *)

TYPE  Bucket = RECORD
                    status: (empty, occupied, deleted);
                    elt   : StdElement
               END;

      Position     = [0..TableSize-1];
      HashTable    = POINTER TO TableType;
      TableType    = ARRAY Position OF Bucket;
      StructuredSet = HashTable;              (* A HashTable is used to     *)
                                              (* implement a StructuredSet. *)
                        (*                                                  *)
                        (* Procedures Hash, ReHash and FindPosn are not exported *)
                        (* by Module StructuredSets.                        *)
                        (*                                                  *)

PROCEDURE Hash(k: KeyType): Position;                    (* Division hashing. *)
BEGIN
      RETURN (k MOD TableSize)
END Hash;

PROCEDURE ReHash(p: Position): Position;                  (* Linear rehash. *)
BEGIN
      RETURN ((p+1) MOD TableSize)
END ReHash;
```

continued

```
PROCEDURE Insert(VAR HT: HashTable; e: StdElement): BOOLEAN;              (* Insert *)
VAR home      : Position;                        (* Home position for element e.  *)
    posn      : Position;                        (* Position currently being probed. *)
    firstDelete: [-1..TableSize-1];      (* The first position marked deleted    *)
BEGIN                                    (* found during the search for a place *)
    home := Hash(e.key);                 (* to insert element e.                *)
    posn := home;
    firstDelete := -1;
    LOOP
        IF (HT↑[posn].status = occupied) AND (HT↑[posn].elt.key = e.key)
            THEN RETURN FALSE                        (* The table contains e.key. *)
          ELSIF (HT↑[posn].status = empty)
            THEN EXIT                               (* An empty bucket is found. *)
          ELSIF (HT↑[posn].status = deleted) AND (firstDelete = -1)
            THEN firstDelete := posn                  (* Save the first position *)
        END;                                          (* marked deleted.         *)
        posn := ReHash(posn);                    (* Get the next position to probe. *)
        IF posn = home
            THEN EXIT                    (* The entire table has been searched. *)
        END
    END;
    IF (HT↑[posn].status # empty) AND (firstDelete = -1)
        THEN RETURN FALSE                                 (* The table is full. *)
      ELSIF firstDelete # -1
        THEN posn := firstDelete               (* Insert at a deleted position. *)
    END;
    HT↑[posn].status := occupied;                         (* Finally--the        *)
    HT↑[posn].elt := e;                                   (* actual insertion.   *)
    RETURN TRUE
END Insert;

PROCEDURE FindPosn(HT: HashTable; tkey: KeyType): Position;
(* post — If HT contains an element with key value tkey then FindPosn is that
           element's position. Otherwise, FindPosn is the location of the first
           empty bucket encountered while searching for tkey. If HT does not
           contain either tkey or an empty bucket then FindPosn is the
           home position of tkey. *)

VAR home, posn: Position;
BEGIN
    home := Hash(tkey); posn := home;
    LOOP
        IF ((HT↑[posn].elt.key = tkey) AND (HT↑[posn].status = occupied))
            OR (HT↑[posn].status = empty)
          THEN EXIT
        END;
        posn := ReHash(posn);
        IF posn = home THEN EXIT
        END
    END;
    RETURN posn
END FindPosn;                                                         continued
```

Implementation Module 7.1, continued

```
PROCEDURE Delete(VAR HT: HashTable; tkey: KeyType): BOOLEAN;          (* Delete *)
VAR   posn: Position;
BEGIN
    posn := FindPosn(HT, tkey);
    IF (tkey = HT↑[posn].elt.key) AND (HT↑[posn].status = occupied)
       THEN HT↑[posn].status := deleted;
            RETURN TRUE
       ELSE RETURN FALSE
    END
END Delete;

PROCEDURE Update(VAR HT: HashTable; e: StdElement): BOOLEAN;          (* Update *)
VAR   posn: Position;
BEGIN
    posn := FindPosn(HT, e.key);
    IF (e.key = HT↑[posn].elt.key) AND (HT↑[posn].status = occupied)
       THEN HT↑[posn].elt := e;
            RETURN TRUE
       ELSE RETURN FALSE
    END
END Update;

PROCEDURE Retrieve(HT: HashTable; tkey: KeyType; VAR e: StdElement): BOOLEAN;
VAR   posn: Position;
BEGIN
    posn := FindPosn(HT, tkey);
    IF (tkey = HT↑[posn].elt.key) AND (HT↑[posn].status = occupied)
       THEN e := HT↑[posn].elt;
            RETURN TRUE
       ELSE RETURN FALSE
    END
END Retrieve;

PROCEDURE Traverse(HT: HashTable; PElt: ProcElt);
VAR   k: CARDINAL;
BEGIN
    FOR k := 0 TO TableSize-1 DO
        IF HT↑[k].status = occupied
            THEN PElt(HT↑[k].elt)
        END
    END
END Traverse;
```

continued

Implementation Module 7.1, continued

```
PROCEDURE Create(VAR HT: HashTable): BOOLEAN;
VAR   k: CARDINAL;
BEGIN
    IF Available(TSIZE(TableType))
        THEN NEW(HT);
            FOR k := 0 TO TableSize-1 DO
                HT↑[k].status := empty
            END;
            RETURN TRUE
        ELSE RETURN FALSE
    END
END Create;

PROCEDURE Terminate(VAR HT: HashTable);
BEGIN
    DISPOSE(HT)
END Terminate;

        (*                                                              *)
        (* Implementation of In, Intersect, and Union is left for the exercises.  *)
        (*                                                              *)

PROCEDURE In(SS: StructuredSet; tkey: KeyType): BOOLEAN;

PROCEDURE Intersect(VAR SS: StructuredSet; SS1,SS2: StructuredSet): BOOLEAN;

PROCEDURE Union(VAR SS: StructuredSet; SS1,SS2: StructuredSet): BOOLEAN;

END StructuredSets.
```

The performance of a combined hashing/rehashing strategy is measured by the number of probes it makes in searching for target key values. We will examine the performance of linear rehashing in more detail in Section 7.5, but we can get a feel for the fact that it may not perform very well by looking at the probe sequence that results when a search of Figure 7.18 is undertaken for a key value of 624. Since 624 MOD 7 = 1, the search begins at position 1 in the table. The subsequent search is shown. Five probes are required to find 624. There are two problems underlying the linear probe method.

Problem 1. Any key that hashes to a position, say b, will follow the same rehashing pattern as all other keys that hash to b. Any key that hashes to position 1 in Figure 7.18 will follow the probe sequence shown. This guarantees that any key that hashes to 1 will have to collide with all of the keys that previously hashed to 1 before it is found or before an empty position is found. We will call this phenomenon ***primary clustering***.

Problem 2. Note in Figure 7.18 that the probe pattern for a rehash from position 1 merged with the probe pattern for a rehash from position 3. The two rehash patterns have merged together, a phenomenon called **secondary clustering.**

Consider Figure 7.19 (which is a copy of Figure 7.17). There is a substantial difference in the probabilities of positions 0 and 5 receiving the next new key. Only new keys hashing into positions 6 and 0 will rehash (if necessary) to position 0. Keys hashing into any other position will eventually arrive at position 5.

The expected number of probes for any random key not yet in the table can be calculated as shown in Figure 7.20.

Table address	Table contents	Probes
[0]	empty	
[1]	911 ⌐	1
[2]	421 ⌐	2
[3]	374	1
[4]	227	2
[5]	empty	
[6]	1091	1

Figure 7.19

Original hash position	Number of probes	Empty position found at
0	1	0
1	5	5
2	4	5
3	3	5
4	2	5
5	1	5
6	2	0
Total	18	

Figure 7.20 Expected number of probes for an unsuccessful search in the hash table shown in Figure 7.19. Expected number of probes = 18/7 = 2.57.

The expected number of probes for both **successful** (target key in table) and **unsuccessful** (target key not in table) **searches** will be our measures of performance of rehashing strategies, and we will examine them in a more general way in Section 7.5. We will confine our attention here simply to noting that the performance can be improved by eliminating the problems that we noted—primary and secondary clustering.

You may be tempted to resolve the difficulties by introducing a step size other than 1 for linear rehash. Stepping to a new table position in procedure *ReHash* would become

RETURN (p + c) MOD *TableSize*

where $1 <= c <= (TableSize - 1)$. If *TableSize* is prime, or at least if c and *TableSize* are relatively prime (have no common factors), then the search pattern will cover the entire table, probing at each position exactly once without repetition. This kind of coverage, **nonrepetitious complete coverage,** is highly desirable. Obviously, if a table position that was previously probed were again probed during the same rehashing sequence, the duplicate probe would be wasted and would affect performance. If the probe pattern did not cover the entire table, empty spaces that are not included in the pattern would not be discovered.

Although a value of c that is relatively prime to the table size does give a rehash technique that has these properties of nonrepetition and complete coverage, it does not solve or, in fact, even improve the problems of primary and secondary clustering. An approach that does solve one of these problems is described next.

• **Quadratic rehashing**

One method of improving the performance of rehashing is to probe at

$$k = (\text{home address} \pm j^2) \text{ MOD } TableSize$$

where j takes on the values 1, 2, 3, . . . until either the target key or an empty position is found or until the table is completely searched. This method, called ***quadratic rehashing***, is better than linear rehashing because it solves the problem of secondary clustering (it does not solve the problem of primary clustering). Details of this method are given in Radke (1970), where it is shown that rehashing visits all table locations without repetition provided that *TableSize* is a prime number of the form $4k + 3$.

• **Random rehashing**

Envision a rehashing strategy that, when a collision occurs, simply jumps randomly to a new table position. This method is called ***random rehashing***, and the rehash can be considered to be a jump of a random distance from the original hash position or to be a second hash function applied to the same key. If second and subsequent collisions occur, the process is repeated until the target key or an empty position is found or until the table is determined to be full and not to contain the target key. Since each key would have its own random pattern, there would be no fixed rehashing patterns. (The random sequence would have to be determined by the key value since subsequent accesses with the same key value must follow the same pattern as the original.) Since there would be no common patterns, there would be no primary or secondary clustering. Although this approach is theoretically appealing, it appears difficult to implement. Thus we turn to schemes that are simpler and whose performances are almost as good.

• **Double hashing**

Several methods exist that attempt to approximate the random rehashing strategy without the large overhead of calculation required by it. One of these, ***double hashing***, is computationally efficient and simple to apply.

We have seen that the general pattern for linear probing is to probe at

$$(i + c) \quad \text{MOD } TableSize$$
$$(i + 2 * c) \text{ MOD } TableSize$$
$$(i + 3 * c) \text{ MOD } TableSize$$

where c is a constant ($c = 1$ in our original discussion of linear rehashing). The fact that c is a constant is at the root of the inefficiency of linear rehashing, since it causes fixed probe patterns and clustering. Ideally we would like c to be random but subject to constraints on repetition. Although this is possible, such an approach leads to a computational overhead that is too high.

One solution is to compute a random jump size, c, for each key that has collided at position h and needs rehashing. Thus, c would be a function of the key value so that different keys hashing to the same location are given different values of c. For example, starting with the hashing function

H(key) = key MOD *TableSize*

we define a related step size function

c(key) = [key MOD (*TableSize* $-$ 2)] + 1

Suppose that 421 is to be stored in Figure 7.21. Then, 421 collides with 911 at position 1. When the collision occurs, c is computed as

c(421) = 421 MOD 5 + 1 = 2

so the table is probed at

(1 + 2)   MOD 7 = 3   *(* Collision. *)*
(1 + 2 * 2) MOD 7 = 5   *(* Empty. *)*

If 624 had been the key, it would have also collided with 911 at position 1. However, its rehash pattern would have been different, that is,

c(624) = 624 MOD 5 + 1 = 5

and the probes would have been at

(1 + 5)   MOD 7 = 6   *(* Collision. *)*
(1 + 2 * 5) MOD 7 = 4   *(* Collision. *)*
(1 + 3 * 5) MOD 7 = 2   *(* Empty. *)*

Table address	Table contents
[0]	empty
[1]	911
[2]	empty
[3]	374
[4]	227
[5]	empty
[6]	1091

Figure 7.21

The rehash pattern for the two keys, both of which hashed to the same position originally, is different. Although we can find pairs (or groups) of keys that hash to the same position and produce the same step size c, the probability of such an event is low for hash tables of reasonable size and a good randomizing step size generator. In fact, the performance of double hashing in terms of the expected number of probes for both successful and unsuccessful accesses is quite close to that of random rehashing. Since it has essentially the same performance in numbers of probes and a lower overhead in computation per probe, it has a greater overall efficiency. A rehashing algorithm for double hashing is given as Algorithm. 7.2. It shows the changes that must be made to Implementation Module 7.1, given earlier.

```
PROCEDURE ReHash(p,c: Position): Position;    (* Double   *)
BEGIN                                         (* rehash.  *)
        RETURN ((p+c) MOD TableSize)
END ReHash;

PROCEDURE Insert(VAR HT: HashTable;                (* Insert. *)
                     e: StdElement): BOOLEAN;
VAR
   c : CARDINAL;

BEGIN

   c := (e.key MOD (TableSize-2)) + 1;

   LOOP

      posn := ReHash(posn,c);     (* Get the next      *)
                                  (* position to probe. *)
   END;
END Insert;

PROCEDURE FindPosn(HT: HashTable;
                   tkey: KeyType): Position;
VAR
   c : CARDINAL;

BEGIN

   c := (tkey MOD (TableSize-2)) + 1;

   LOOP

      posn := ReHash(posn,c);

   END;
END FindPosn;
```

Algorithm 7.2   Rehashing algorithm for double hashing.

Algorithm 7.2 shows only one method for computing a random step size. Any randomizing function that produces a step size that is less than *TableSize* − 1 and is not based on the position of the original collision will do. However, the division algorithm that is shown is efficient and simple. In order to avoid introducing biases, *TableSize* should be a prime number. If we use this method of computing c in conjunction with the division method for the original hash, the choice of the two divisors as ***twin primes*** assures an exhaustive search of the table without repetition. If *TableSize* is prime, and k = *TableSize* − 2 is also prime, then an exhaustive search of the table is assured.

• **External chaining**

A second approach to the problem of collisions, called ***external chaining,*** is to let the table position "absorb" all of the records that hash to it. Since we do not usually know how many keys will hash into any table position, a linked

```
TYPE BPtr =
        POINTER TO Bucket;
   Bucket =
        RECORD
            elt  : StdElement;
            next: BPtr
        END;
   Position = [0..TableSize-1];
   HashTable =
        POINTER TO TableType;
   TableType =
        ARRAY Position OF BPtr;
```

Figure 7.22
Representation of a hash table for external chaining.

list is a good data structure to collect the records. A representation based on an array of pointers is shown in Figure 7.22.

As an example, let *TableSize* = 7 and suppose that operation *Create* has initialized the hash table as shown in Figure 7.23.

If a division hash function is chosen, say,

$H(\text{key}) = \text{key MOD } 7$

then insertion of the keys

key = 374	374 MOD 7 = 3
key = 1091	1091 MOD 7 = 6
key = 911	911 MOD 7 = 1

produces the hash table shown in Figure 7.24. Insertion of 227 and 421 produces two collisions (the collisions are not shown in the text):

| key = 227 | 227 MOD 7 = 3 |
| key = 421 | 421 MOD 7 = 1 |

and results in Figure 7.25. Subsequent insertion of 624

| key = 624 | 624 MOD 7 = 1 |

produces the result shown in Figure 7.26.

Table address	Table contents
[0]	NIL
[1]	NIL
[2]	NIL
[3]	NIL
[4]	NIL
[5]	NIL
[6]	NIL

Figure 7.23
Initialized hash table for external chaining.

Table address	Table contents
[0]	NIL
[1]	→ 911
[2]	NIL
[3]	→ 374
[4]	NIL
[5]	NIL
[6]	→ 1091

Figure 7.24
Hash table after insertion of keys 374, 1091, 911.

Table address	Table contents
[0]	NIL
[1]	→ 911 → 421
[2]	NIL
[3]	→ 374 → 227
[4]	NIL
[5]	NIL
[6]	→ 1091

Figure 7.25
Hash table after insertion of keys 227 and 421.

Table address	Table contents
[0]	NIL
[1]	→ 911 → 421 → 624
[2]	NIL
[3]	→ 374 → 227
[4]	NIL
[5]	NIL
[6]	→ 1091

Figure 7.26
Hash table after insertion of key 624.

Each list is a linked list. The designer has all of the choices of list characteristics as he or she has for any linked list—method of termination, single or double linkage, other access pointers, and ordering of the list. If the frequencies with which the various records are accessed are quite different, it may be effective to make each list self-organizing.

Observe that the operations in this case are similar to those on lists discussed in Chapter 4. The only differences are that there are many lists instead of one and that the list in which we are interested is determined by the hash function.

External chaining has three advantages over open address methods:

1. Deletions are possible with no resulting problems.
2. The number of elements in the table can be greater than the table size; α can be greater than 1.0. Storage for the elements is dynamically allocated as the lists grow larger.
3. We shall see in Section 7.5 that the performance of external chaining in executing a *Retrieve* operation is better than that of open address methods and continues to be excellent as α grows beyond 1.0.

In the next technique collisions are resolved, as they are in external chaining, by adding the element to be inserted to the end of a list. The difference is in how the list is constructed.

• Coalesced chaining

To illustrate coalesced chaining consider the hash table with seven buckets shown in Figure 7.27. The hash table is divided into two parts: the **address region** and the **cellar.** In our example, the first five addresses make up the address region, and the last two make up the cellar.

The hash function must map each record into the address region. The cellar is only used to store records that collided with another record at their home addresses. For our example, we will use the division hash function

$$H(\text{key}) = \text{key MOD } 5$$

assuming that each key is an integer.

After inserting key values 27 and 29 we have Figure 7.28. If 32 is inserted next, it collides with 27 and is stored in the empty position with the largest address. In addition, it is added to a list that begins at its home address. The result is shown in Figure 7.29. To assist in visualizing the process, the empty position with the largest address, **epla**, is shown in the figures.

If key value 34 is added, it collides with 29 and is placed in address 5 (the empty position with the largest address) and is added to a list beginning at location 4. The result is shown in Figure 7.30.

Table address	Table contents	
[0]	empty	
[1]	empty	
[2]	empty	address
[3]	empty	region
[4]	empty	
[5]	empty	cellar
[6]	empty	

Figure 7.27
Hash table with seven buckets initialized for coalesced chaining.

Table address	Table contents
[0]	empty
[1]	empty
[2]	27
[3]	empty
[4]	29
[5]	empty
[6]	**epla**

Figure 7.28
Hash table after inserting keys 27 and 29. **epla** is the empty position with the largest address.

Table address	Table contents
[0]	empty
[1]	empty
[2]	27
[3]	empty
[4]	29
[5]	**epla**
[6]	32

Figure 7.29
Results after inserting key 32.

Table address	Table contents
[0]	empty
[1]	empty
[2]	27
[3]	**epla**
[4]	29
[5]	34
[6]	32

Figure 7.30
Results after inserting key 34.

Up to this point coalesced chaining has behaved exactly like external chaining—each new record is added to the end of a list that begins at its home address. The next insertion illustrates how a collision is resolved after the cellar is full.

If 37 is added it collides with 27, so it is placed in location [3] and added to the end of the list that begins at address [2]. The result is shown in Figure 7.31. The point to be made here is that once again the record being inserted was, since its home address was already occupied, placed in the empty position with the largest address. Adding 47 produces the result shown in Figure 7.32.

The term "coalesced" is used to describe this technique because, for example, if 53 were added to the hash table in Figure 7.32, it would cause the list that begins at [2] to coalesce with the list that begins at [3]. Note, however, that lists cannot coalesce until after the cellar is full.

The effectiveness of coalesced chaining depends on the choice of cellar size. Selection of cellar size is discussed in Vitter (1982, 1983) where it is shown that a cellar that contains 14% of the hash table works well under a variety of circumstances.

Because overflow records form lists, the deletion problems of open addressing schemes can be solved without resorting to marking records deleted. Any such approach is, however, more complicated than for the external chaining approach since the lists can coalesce. Details of such a deletion scheme, which essentially relinks elements in a list past the element to be deleted, are given in Vitter (1982).

This concludes our introduction to collision-resolution techniques. In Sections 7.5 and 7.6 we will compare these techniques from the point of view of performance. Before we do so, however, in Section 7.4.3 we will introduce hash functions that guarantee that collisions will not occur—perfect hashing functions.

7.4.3 Perfect Hashing Functions

A perfect hashing function is one that causes no collisions. A ***minimal perfect hashing function*** is a perfect hashing function that operates on a hash table having a load factor of 1.0. Since perfect hashing functions cause no collisions, we are assured that exactly one probe is needed to locate an element that has a given key value. This is, of course, very desirable. The problem is that such functions are not easy to construct.

Perfect hashing functions may only be found under certain conditions. One such condition is that all of the key values are known in advance. Certain applications have this quality; for example, the reserved, or key, words of a programming language. In Modula-2 there are 40 reserved words: AND, ARRAY, BEGIN, ... When a compiler is translating a program, as it scans the program's statements it must determine whether it has encountered a reserved word. Suppose the reserved words are stored in a hash table accessible by a perfect hashing function. Determining if a word encountered in the scan

Table address	Table contents
[0]	empty
[1]	**epla**
[2]	27
[3]	37
[4]	29
[5]	34
[6]	32

Figure 7.31
Results after inserting key 37.

Table address	Table contents
[0]	**epla**
[1]	47
[2]	27
[3]	37
[4]	29
[5]	34
[6]	32

Figure 7.32
Results after inserting key 47.

Modula-2 Reserved Words

AND	**LOOP**
ARRAY	**MOD**
BEGIN	**MODULE**
BY	**NOT**
CASE	**OF**
CONST	**OR**
DEFINITION	**POINTER**
DIV	**PROCEDURE**
DO	**QUALIFIED**
ELSE	**RECORD**
ELSIF	**REPEAT**
END	**RETURN**
EXIT	**SET**
EXPORT	**THEN**
FOR	**TO**
FROM	**TYPE**
IF	**UNTIL**
IMPLEMEN-	**VAR**
TATION	**WHILE**
IMPORT	**WITH**
IN	

is a reserved word requires only one probe. The word is hashed, and the content of the specified table is compared with the word from the scan. If they are the same, a reserved word was found. If not, we can be certain that the word is not a reserved word.

Another condition for perfect hashing functions is a practical one. It concerns the amount of computation necessary to find a perfect hashing function, which can be enormous. The total amount of computation (and therefore time) increases exponentially with the number of keys in the data. The number of possible functions that map the 31 most frequently occurring English words into a hash table of size 41 is approximately 10^{50}, whereas the number of such functions that give unique (perfect) mappings is approximately 10^{43} (Knuth, 1973b). Thus, only one of each 10 million functions is suitable. In practice, if the number of keys is greater than a few dozen, the amount of time to find a perfect hashing function is unacceptably long on most computers.

There are several proposals for perfect hashing functions. Sprugnoli (1977) has proposed functions that are perfect but not minimal. Cichelli (1980) has suggested some simple minimal perfect functions and has given examples and the times to compute them. Jaeschke (1981) has proposed other minimal perfect functions that avoid some problems that might arise with Cichelli's method.

Let us look briefly at Cichelli's method. The functions that he proposed are for keys that are character strings. Take, for example, the 36 reserved words of Pascal. The hashing function is

$$H(\text{key}) = L + g(\text{key}[1]) + g(\text{key}[L])$$

where

$$L = \text{length of the key}$$

The function $g(x)$ associates an integer with each character x; thus, $g(\text{key}[1])$ is the integer associated with the first letter of the key, and $g(\text{key}[L])$ is the integer associated with the last letter of the key.

Cichelli's technique will not work for Modula-2 because there are pairs of reserved words—EXIT and TYPE, for example—that have the same length and the same pair of first and last characters. Sebesta (1986) developed a perfect hashing function for Modula-2 by using Cichelli's approach and adding the alphabetic position of the next to last character. This is a modification of a technique proposed in Wolverton (1984). The hashing function that results is

$$H(\text{key}) = L + g(\text{key}[1]) + g(\text{key}[L]) + Alphabetic$$

where L is the length of the reserved word and *Alphabetic* is the alphabetic position of its next to last character.

Figure 7.33 shows the value of $g(x)$ for a perfect hashing function for Modula-2. Applying those values to EXIT gives

$$H(\text{EXIT}) = 4 + g(E) + g(T) + 8 = 1$$

Figure 7.34 shows the home addresses of all the Modula-2 reserved words.

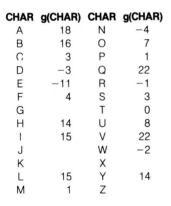

CHAR	g(CHAR)	CHAR	g(CHAR)
A	18	N	−4
B	16	O	7
C	3	P	1
D	−3	Q	22
E	−11	R	−1
F	4	S	3
G		T	0
H	14	U	8
I	15	V	22
J		W	−2
K		X	
L	15	Y	14
M	1	Z	

Figure 7.33
Sebesta's table for hashing Modula-2's reserved words.

The hashing function is simple, as it should be. There are several problems, however. The first is that of looking up the integer associated with the two or more letters, but that can be done with reasonable efficiency. A second and more serious problem is that of determining which integer should be associated with each character. The integers are found by trial and error using a ***backtracking algorithm.*** (Of course, the associated integer table, see Figure 7.33, need built only once.) Cichelli (1980) has a good discussion of the backtracking algorithm used for this problem.

In summary, perfect hashing functions are feasible when the keys are known in advance and the number of records is small. In that case, a perfect hashing function is determined in advance of the use of the hash table. Although its determination may be costly, it need only be done once. The resulting access to the records of the hash table requires only one probe.

[0]	**ELSE**	[20]	**FOR**
[1]	**EXIT**	[21]	**IN**
[2]	**END**	[22]	**OR**
[3]	**WHILE**	[23]	**FROM**
[4]	**THEN**	[24]	**VAR**
[5]	**REPEAT**	[25]	**BEGIN**
[6]	**ELSIF**	[26]	**CONST**
[7]	**MODULE**	[27]	**OF**
[8]	**TYPE**	[28]	**TO**
[9]	**DO**	[29]	**IF**
[10]	**SET**	[30]	**DIV**
[11]	**POINTER**	[31]	**AND**
[12]	**EXPORT**	[32]	**QUALI- FIED**
[13]	**NOT**	[33]	**BY**
[14]	**CASE**	[34]	**LOOP**
[15]	**MOD**	[35]	**WITH**
[16]	**PROCE- DURE**	[36]	**UNTIL**
[17]	**DEFINI- TION**	[37]	**ARRAY**
[18]	**RETURN**	[38]	**IMPORT**
[19]	**RECORD**	[39]	**IMPLE- MENTATION**

Figure 7.34
The hash table for Modula-2 reserved words.

Exercises 7.4

1. Explain the following terms in your own words:

hash function	home address	perfect hashing function
collision	collision resolution	double hashing
load factor	linear rehash	
external chaining	coalesced chaining	

2. The division hash function

$$H(\text{key}) = \text{key MOD } m$$

is usually a good hash function if m has no small divisors. Explain why this restriction is placed on m.

3. Develop a hash function to convert nine-digit integers (Social Security numbers) into integers in the range $0 \ldots 999$. Test your hash function by applying it to 800 randomly generated keys. Determine how many of the addresses received $0, 1, 2, \ldots$ of the hashed keys.

Compare your experimental results with the results that would be obtained using a "perfect randomizer." The number of addresses receiving exactly k hashed values if the hash function is a perfect randomizer is approximated by

$$e^{-\alpha} \frac{\alpha^k}{k!}$$

where α is the load factor.

4. Develop a hash function to convert keys of the type

```
KeyType = ARRAY[1..15] OF CHAR;
```

into integers in the range 0..999. Implement your hash function and determine its execution time. Do the same for the hash function in Exercise 3 and compare their execution times.

An algorithm for constructing perfect hashing functions that is relatively simple, but requires more overhead for retrieval, is discussed in Cormack (1985).

5. Implement the perfect hashing function described in Section 7.4.3. Determine its execution time and compare it with the results obtained in Exercise 4.

6. Use the hash function $H(\text{key}) = \text{key MOD } 11$ to store the sequence of integers

$$82, 31, 28, 4, 45, 27, 59, 79, 35$$

in the hash table

```
VAR table: ARRAY[0..10] OF INTEGER;
```

a. Use linear rehashing
b. Use double hashing
c. Use external chaining
d. Use coalesced chaining with a cellar size of four and the hash function

$$H(\text{key}) = \text{key MOD } 7$$

For each of the above collision-handling strategies determine (after all values have been placed in the table) the following:
e. The load factor
f. The average number of probes needed to find a value that is in the table
g. The average number of probes needed to find a value that is not in the table

7. Implement a collection of procedures that forms a hashing package according to Specification 7.2. Use
a. Linear rehashing
b. Double hashing
c. External chaining
d. Coalesced chaining with a cellar size of 70.
Define a hash function by $H(\text{key}) = \text{key MOD } 501$. [The hash function for coalesced chaining will be $H(\text{key}) = \text{key MOD } 431$.] Use a random number generator to produce a sequence of integers to store in the hash table. Determine, as a function of the load factor, the average number of probes needed to find an integer in the table.

8. Complete the implementation of Specification 7.2 by supplying code for operations *In, Intersect,* and *Union.*

9. Implement Specification 7.2 using (instead of a hash table)
a. A list (Chapter 4), or
b. A binary tree (Chapter 5).

7.5 Hashing Performance

For this discussion, the operations in Specification 7.2 are divided into two groups. The first group includes operations that do not involve searching the hash table: *Create, Terminate,* and *Traverse.* The effort to execute these operations does not depend on which collision-resolution strategy is used. Operation *Create* requires $O(TableSize)$ effort since each table position must be initialized to empty. Operation *Traverse* also requires $O(TableSize)$ effort, whereas *Terminate* requires $O(1)$ effort.

Each operation in the second group requires searching the hash table for the key value of an element. These associative searches are either successful (an element for which the target key value is found) or unsuccessful (an element for which the target key value is found) or unsuccessful. The operations in this group are *Insert, Delete,* and *Retrieve.* The performance of all these operations is determined primarily by the associated search. We will therefore discuss the number of compares required for successful and unsuccessful searches. We will single out the *Delete* operation for discussion later.

7.5.1 Performance

Explicit expressions that give the expected number of compares required for successful and unsuccessful searches can be developed. Results for three different collision-resolution policies are shown in Figures 7.35 and 7.36. Figure 7.35 shows the algebraic expressions [see Knuth (1973b) for their development], and Figure 7.36 shows the results of graphing the algebraic expressions.

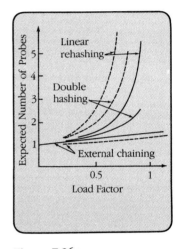

Figure 7.36
Number of probes required for successful and unsuccessful searches in a hash table. —, successful; -------, unsuccessful.

Collision-resolution strategy	Unsuccessful	Successful
Linear rehashing	$\frac{1}{2}\left(1 + \frac{1}{(1-\alpha)^2}\right)$	$\frac{1}{2}\left(1 + \frac{1}{(1-\alpha)}\right)$
Double hashing	$\frac{1}{1-\alpha}$	$-\left(\frac{1}{\alpha}\right) \times \log(1-\alpha)$
External chaining	$\alpha + e^{\alpha}$	$1 + \frac{1}{2}\alpha$

Figure 7.35 Algebraic expressions for the number of probes expected for successful and unsuccessful searches in a hash table.

Expressions for coalesced chaining are given in Vitter (1982). Note that if the cellar is not full, the result for coalesced chaining is the same as for external chaining. In general, the search effort of coalesced chaining is approximately the same as that of external chaining. See Vitter (1982) in which the performance of coalesced chaining is compared with all the hashing techniques discussed in this chapter. Coalesced chaining is shown to give the best performance for the circumstances we considered.

Notice in Figures 7.35 and 7.36 that the performance curves for hashing methods are monotonically increasing functions of α, the load factor. The performance curves for lists and trees are monotonically increasing functions of n, the number of elements in the data structure. The number of elements, n, is not under the implementor's control. However, for hashing, the load factor, α, may be made arbitrarily small by increasing the table size. For a given value of n, we can reduce the load factor and improve the performance of hashing. The price is more memory.

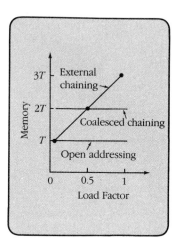

Figure 7.37
Memory requirements when an element occupies the same amount of memory as a pointer.

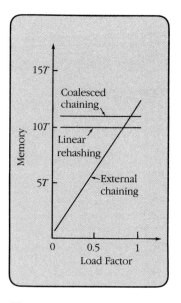

Figure 7.38
Memory requirements when an element occupies 10 times the amount of memory as a pointer.

7.5.2 *Memory Requirements*

In addition to performance, it is important to compare the memory requirements of various hashing techniques. Let T be the number of buckets in the hash table; assume that a pointer occupies one word of memory and that an element occupies w words of memory. The memory requirements for a hash table containing n elements are then

$T \times w$ for any open addressing method

$T \times (w + 1)$ for coalesced chaining

$T + n(w + 1)$ for external chaining

These expressions are based on the following assumptions. Each position in a hash table for open addressing contains room for one element. For coalesced chaining the hash table contains one pointer and one element in each position. For external chaining the hash table contains one pointer in each position and one pointer and one element for each element in the table. We will now use the expressions to consider two cases.

If w is 1 (perhaps we store a pointer to an element rather than the element itself), then the memory required as a function of load factor is that shown in Figure 7.37. Open addressing always requires the least memory. When the table is nearly full, open addressing requires only one-third as much memory as external chaining. Of course, when the table is nearly full (see Figure 7.36), the performance of open addressing is poor. In this case, coalesced chaining provides good performance with a substantial saving in memory requirements.

If w is 10, then the memory requirements are as shown in Figure 7.38. External chaining is attractive over a wider range of load factors and extracts less of a penalty when the table is nearly full. This analysis leads to the following rules of thumb for constructing hash tables to be stored in RAM: For small elements and load factors, open addressing provides competitive performance and saves memory. For small elements and large load factors, coalesced chaining provides good performance with reasonable memory requirements. If elements are large, external chaining provides good performance with minimum, or nearly minimum, memory requirements.

These rules are based on the assumption that the maximum number of elements in the table can be estimated. Often that is not the case. Take, for example, the symbol table of a compiler that is used to store data about the user-defined identifiers in programs. The compiler must be able to process both large and small programs with a wide range in the numbers of identifiers. It may be possible for the table to overfill; that is, have a load factor greater than 1.0. The compiler should continue to operate smoothly. Such situations are often handled by the use of external chaining, which continues to function for load factors greater than 1.0.

7.5.3 *Deletion*

We will conclude this section with a few comments about deletion. As discussed earlier, hash tables that are constructed using open addressing techniques pose problems when subjected to frequent deletions. The space previously occupied by a deleted record cannot simply be marked *empty* but must be marked *deleted*. This clutters up the hash table and hurts performance. No such problem arises if external chaining is used for collision resolution. Deletion is handled just as it is for any linked list. For coalesced chaining deletion is no problem as long as the cellar has never been full, since deletion can be handled essentially as it is for external chaining. Once the cellar is full and the possibility of coalesced lists exists, then deletion must be handled carefully. An algorithm is given in Vitter (1982). It is (slightly) more complicated and would extract a small performance penalty. When designing a hashing strategy, the frequency of deletion must be considered along with performance and memory requirements.

In Section 7.6 we will apply several hashing methods to the frequency analysis of digraphs. We will see how the theoretical results apply in a specific case.

7.6 **Frequency Analysis of Digraphs**

We have discussed frequency analysis of digraphs before. In Section 4.6 we used lists for the analysis, and in Section 5.7 we used binary search trees and AVL trees. In this section we will compare four hashing strategies. All four use a division hashing function, but they differ in the collision-resolution strategy: linear rehashing, double hashing, coalesced chaining, and external chaining. We will conclude with a summary of results involving all of the data structures we have used to analyze digraphs.

7.6.1 *Hash Function*

The hash table will be of the form shown in Figure 7.39. The hash function must map each digraph (pair of letters) into the integers between 0 and *TableSize*. We accomplish this as follows. Let d_1 and d_2 be the first and second characters of digraph d:

$$d = d_1 d_2$$

Let i_1 and i_2 be computed as follows:

$$i_1 = \text{ORD}(d_1) - \text{ORD}(\text{`a'})$$

$$i_2 = \text{ORD}(d_2) - \text{ORD}(\text{`a'})$$

HashTable = **ARRAY** [0..TableSize] **OF** Bucket;

Figure 7.39
Hash table.

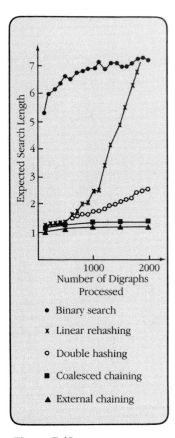

Figure 7.42
Frequency analysis of digraphs.
Expected search length.

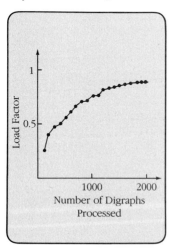

Figure 7.43
Frequency analysis of digraphs.
Load factor.

where i_1 and i_2 are CARDINALS between 0 and 25. Finally, let $I(d)$ be computed by

$$I(d) = 26\, i_1 + i_2$$

where $I(d)$ has values between 0 and 675. Sample values of I are shown in Figure 7.40.

The hash function for digraph analysis is

$$H(d) = I(d) \ MOD \ (TableSize + 1)$$

where *TableSize* is to be selected so that *TableSize* + 1 has no small divisors. The frequency analysis results reported in this section are based on *TableSize* = 300. Figure 7.41 shows the values of H(digraph) for the first few digraphs from von Neumann (1946).

Digraph	I
aa	0
ab	1
ac	2
⋮	⋮
zz	675

Figure 7.40
Values of I for digraph analysis.

Digraph	H(digraph)
pr	206
re	145
el	115
li	294
im	220
mi	19

Figure 7.41
Home address of the first few digraphs from von Neumann (1946). The table size = 300.

Figure 7.42 shows the expected search lengths for the four hashing strategies and, for comparison, a binary search of a sorted array. The results are as predicted in Section 7.5.

Recall (see Figure 4.40) that processing 2000 digraphs causes 270 distinct values to be entered into the hash table. The relationship between load factor and the number of digraphs processed, with *TableSize* = 300, is shown in Figure 7.43.

Figure 7.44 shows the average time required to process a digraph for the four hashing techniques and, for comparison, a binary search tree. Also included for comparison is the time required for a ***direct addressing*** scheme. Direct addressing is implemented just like hashing with, in this case, $H(d) = I(d)$. Direct addressing is possible in this case because we can assign a distinct address to each of the 676 possible digraphs. This eliminates collisions, simplifies the algorithms, and ensures that the number of probes to find a digraph is one. The price for this is the requirement for more memory. Direct addressing should not be confused with hashing. A hash function randomizes the elements stored in the hash table. Our direct addressing scheme places the digraphs in the table in alphabetical order.

The results shown in Figure 7.44 are those expected. Direct addressing, with one probe per digraph, gives the best performance. External chaining and coalesced chaining give essentially the same performance. Using a binary search tree gives better performance than either linear or double hashing, despite requiring more probes during a search. This is because searching a hash table requires more overhead: evaluating the hash function and the array mapping function. If the data structure were bigger, the difference in number of probes required would be larger and the hash techniques would provide better performance than would a binary search tree.

Note that initially, linear probing is faster than double hashing. This is because clusters have little effect on performance, whereas collisions require an extra computation (the step size) for double hashing. As the hash table fills and clusters form, the performance of linear probing deteriorates.

Another consideration for hashing is worst-case performance. Table 7.2 shows the maximum number of probes required to find a digraph as a function of the number of digraphs processed.

Observe that for coalesced and external chaining the maximum number of probes is little different from the average. For linear rehashing and, to a lesser extent, double hashing the maximum number of probes becomes quite large as the table fills. In the worst case, every element hashes to the same home address, and the performance can be disastrous. A general discussion of the worst-case performance of hash files, which compares linear searching, random hashing, and external chaining, is given in Larson (1982).

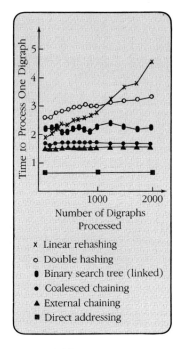

Figure 7.44
Frequency analyses of digraphs. Hashed representations. Average measured time per digraph processed.

TABLE 7.2 Comparison of hashing techniques, including the maximum number of probes for a successful search. The table size = 300 and the cellar size for coalesced chaining is 43.

Digraphs processed	Distinct digraphs	Load factor	Linear search Avg probes	Linear search Max probes	Double hashing Avg probes	Double hashing Max probes	Coalesced chaining Avg probes	Coalesced chaining Max probes	External chaining Avg probes	External chaining Max probes
500	165	0.55	1.33	6	1.41	7	1.15	2	1.15	2
1000	225	0.75	2.44	57	1.72	7	1.27	3	1.22	3
1500	256	0.85	5.44	103	2.12	23	1.30	3	1.23	3

7.6.2 *Frequency Analysis Summary*

Let us now review and compare all the approaches we have used for our frequency analysis problem. We have used three data structures: lists, binary trees, and sets. The analysis with lists involved two representations—array and linked—and four different orders—chronological, sorted, frequency ordered, and self-organizing. The analysis with binary trees used linked representations of both binary search trees and AVL trees. The analysis using sets was based

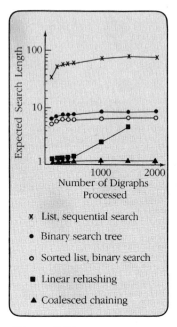

Figure 7.45
Frequency analysis of digraphs. Comparison of methods—log plot. Expected search length.

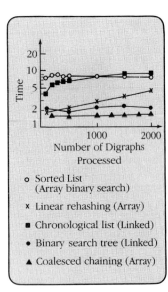

Figure 7.46
Frequency analysis of digraphs. Comparison of methods—log plot. Average measured time per digraph processed.

on an array representation of a hash table and considered four collision-resolution policies—linear rehashing, double hashing, coalesced chaining, and external chaining.

Figure 7.45 shows the expected search lengths for five representative data structures—sequential search of a list in chronological order, binary search of a sorted list, binary search tree, hashing with linear rehashing, and hashing with coalesced chaining. A semilog plot is used because of the range of search lengths.

Figure 7.46 compares the performance of the data structures considered in Figure 7.45. A semilog plot is used so that differences can be clearly seen. A comparative analysis of data structures includes performance (both average and worst case), memory requirements, algorithm complexity, and particular strengths and weaknesses. Figures 7.45 and 7.46 show the results of empirical studies of performance. Memory requirements are discussed in the chapters in which we introduced the data structures. All of the data structures in this text are (relatively) simple. We can, however, see one impact of complexity by comparing Figures 7.45 and 7.46. Sequential search of a list requires many more probes than does binary search of a sorted list. However, because one probe during a binary search is more complex than one probe during a sequential search, the number of elements must be large before a binary search pays off. The meaning of "large" varies with the processor and software used, and for our example it appears that large means 150 or more elements.

An example of a data structure weakness is the order of hashed data. Since the elements are stored in random order, it would be difficult to find all elements whose key values are in a given interval. It would be easy to do this for data in a sorted list, and that is an advantage of that data structure. As we suggest here, selection of a data structure involves matching application requirements with data structure strengths. We have seen in the case of a simple problem, frequency analysis of digraphs, that there are many trade-offs to consider.

7.7 Summary

In this chapter we have studied data structures whose structure is setlike. The only relationship of interest among the elements is that they are members of the set. We have distinguished between two kinds of sets—those whose elements are atomic and those whose elements are structured.

We have seen that a particularly important implementation technique for sets of structured elements is hashing. We studied several hashing functions and several collision-resolution (or rehashing) strategies. The rehashing strategies upon which we concentrated were linear rehashing and double hashing (both open address methods) and external and coalesced chaining. Performance analyses and comparisons were made in Sections 7.5 and 7.6. They clearly showed that hashing is an excellent method in terms of the execution times of its algorithms.

One question that we have not yet addressed is a comparison of the complexity of hashing algorithms with those of lists and trees. In previous chapters we closed by giving tables containing at least crude measures of the complexity of the various modules presented in the chapter. As a substitute here, Table 7.3 compares the complexity of a single operation—*FindKey*—for various data structures and their implementations. We see that in terms of the simple measure we are using, complexity of the hashed (open address) implementations of *FindKey* are comparable with those of the other data structures. (In the hashed implementation the corresponding operation is called *Find-Posn.*)

TABLE 7.3 Complexity of *FindKey* for various data structures.

Data type	Representation	Lines of code for *FindKey*
List	Array	9
List	Linked	14
Sorted list	Array (binary search)	17
Binary search tree	Linked	18
Set	Hashed	15

Strings 8

8.1 Introduction

8.2 Characters

    8.2.1 Fixed-Length Representations

    8.2.2 Embedded Shift Instructions

    8.2.3 Embedded Mode Shift
       Instructions—An Application

    8.2.4 Representing Characters with a
       Variable Number of Bits

  Exercises 8.2

8.3 Strings

    8.3.1 Specification of a String Data Type

    8.3.2 Representation of Strings

    8.3.3 Array Implementation of Strings

    8.3.4 Linked Implementation of Strings

    8.3.5 Comparison of Array and Linked
       Implementations

  Exercises 8.3

8.4 Summary

8.1 Introduction

Much of the information in the world is stored as ***strings of characters***. A book can be thought of as a string of characters. A program can be viewed as a string of characters. A record describing a person's tax return (stored on a disk or tape by the IRS) can be thought of as a string of characters. Since computers are frequently used to store, edit, extract information from, and ultimately, output character strings, it is important to have data structures that can be used to carry out these tasks efficiently and effectively.

A number of questions come to mind. What data structures can be used to store character strings? What operations on character strings are useful? How can they be implemented? What are the performance considerations relating operations to string data structures? In this chapter we will consider these questions and some answers to them.

Section 8.2 describes individual characters, or character strings of length one. This is a natural beginning since character strings are sequences of individual characters. The atomic data type *character* is supported by many programming languages and forms an important data type in its own right.

Section 8.3 begins with the specification of an abstract string and continues with a discussion of two possible implementations: one based on arrays and one based on a linked list of substrings or chunks of the string being represented. String operations are discussed with emphasis on the *Find* or pattern-matching operation. Finally, the array and linked list implementations are compared in Section 8.3.5.

8.2 Characters

We will present an informal description of the ***character data type.*** The domain of atomic data type character normally contains Latin letters, numerals, special characters such as [,], {, +, −, $, and nonprintable control characters. Three popular sets of characters are CDC Scientific, American Standard Code for Information Interchange (ASCII), and Extended Binary Coded Decimal Interchange Code (EBCDIC).

The values of type character have a linear relationship that preserves the natural ordering of letters of the alphabet and of the numerals. Other relationships, however, are seemingly arbitrary. In ASCII, numerals precede capital letters, which precede lowercase letters. In the EBCDIC system, lowercase letters precede uppercase letters, which precede the numerals. In CDC, uppercase letters precede numerals, and lowercase letters are not represented.

8.2.1 Fixed-Length Representations

The usual technique for representing characters is simple: Each character is stored using a fixed number of bits in the computer's memory. Each of the schemes we mentioned uses a different number of bits for this purpose—see Table 8.1. Keep in mind that the maximum number of distinct patterns that

TABLE 8.1

Technique	Number of bits to store each character	Maximum number of distinct bit patterns generated
CDC	6	64
ASCII	7	128
EBCDIC	8	256

can be generated with n bits is 2^n. For convenience, this value is also included in the table.

In order to represent the 26 Latin letters in both lower- and uppercase, we need 52 distinct bit patterns. Adding the numerals 0 through 9 brings the required number of bit patterns to 62. Adding other essential characters, such as a space ( ), a comma (,), and a period (.), brings the total past 64.

Since the CDC technique has only 64 patterns it cannot store a reasonable character set containing both lower- and uppercase Latin letters. In fact, the CDC technique is used to represent only uppercase letters. The specific characters represented are shown in Figure 8.1.

```
:   A   B   C   D   E   F   G   H   I
J   K   L   M   N   O   P   Q   R   S
T   U   V   W   X   Y   Z   0   1   2
3   4   5   6   7   8   9   +   −   *
/   (   )   $   =       ,   .   ≡   [
]   %   ≠   ⌐   ∨   ∧   ↑   ↓   <   >
≤   ≥   ¬   ;
```

Figure 8.1
The printable CDC scientific characters.

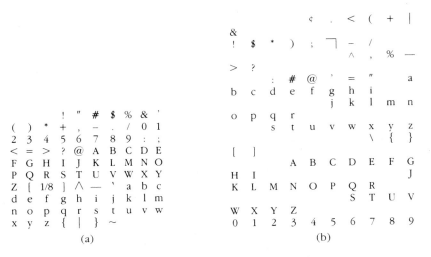

(a)

Figure 8.2
(a) The printable ASCII characters. They have a linear structure with space the first character (the predecessor of !), ~ the last, and the successor of each character listed immediately following it. There are 95 characters in the set. The ASCII character set also includes 33 special control characters that are not printable. (b) The EBCDIC character set contains 70 nonprintable control characters and 94 printable characters. Thus, 164 out of the 256 bit patterns are used. The printable characters are shown. Codes 00–63 and 250–255 represent nonprintable control characters. Other nonprintable characters are indicated by blanks.

The ASCII scheme has 128 distinct bit patterns and can therefore easily accommodate both upper- and lowercase Latin letters. ASCII is the standard representation technique for most micro- and minicomputers and is used on many larger machines.

A common technique for storing characters in a computer's memory is to store each character in 1 byte. A ***byte*** is (usually) a sequence of 8 bits. In many digital computers it is the smallest unit of information that can be addressed directly. Such machines operate efficiently on individual characters.

• Parity

Consider storing each ASCII character in seven bits and using an extra bit as a ***parity bit***. For ***even parity***, the extra bit is set so that each byte contains an even number of ones and, therefore, an even number of zeros. For ***odd parity***, the extra bit is set so that each byte contains an odd number of ones. Table 8.2 shows the ASCII bit pattern and the value of the parity bit for several example characters.

TABLE 8.2 ASCII representation of several characters showing the value of a parity bit for even parity.

Character	Parity bit	ASCII bit pattern	Number of bits set
A	0	100 0001	2
B	0	100 0010	2
C	1	100 0011	4
D	0	100 0100	2
0	0	011 0000	2
1	1	011 0001	4
2	1	011 0010	4
3	0	011 0011	4

There are multiple bit error detection schemes, some of which allow not only detection but also correction of the error.

Observe that if one of the bits representing a character is incorrect, then the error will be detected by a single parity bit. If two bits are incorrect, however, a single parity bit will not detect the error. More generally, use of a single parity bit will detect an error that involves an odd number of bits, but it will not detect an error that affects an even number of bits. Fortunately, in most cases, single-bit errors are much more likely than multiple-bit errors. A single parity bit does not give enough information to allow correction of a detected error.

• Representing numbers

Before leaving this section we will emphasize a point that seems to trouble people who have not previously studied how numbers, as opposed to characters, are represented in the memory of a digital computer.

There are separate considerations, and therefore separate techniques, for storing characters, integers, and real numbers. Many micro- and minicomputers store each integer in 16 bits, each real in 32–48 bits, and each character using 8 bits. The IBM S/370 and 3000 series computers store each character in 8 bits but use 32 bits (4 bytes) to store an integer or a real number. Computers intended primarily for scientific applications use even more bits to store inte-

TABLE 8.3

Value	Stored as a character in 8 bits using ASCII with even parity	Stored as an integer in 16 bits using a two's complement representation	Stored as a real number in 16 bits: sign bit, 7-bit exponent (excess 64), 8-bit mantissa
1	1011 0001	0000 0000 0000 0001	0100 0001 1000 0000
2	1011 0010	0000 0000 0000 0010	0100 0010 1000 0000
3	0011 0011	0000 0000 0000 0011	0100 0010 1100 0000
−5	0010 1101 0011 0101	1111 1111 1111 1011	1100 0100 1010 0000

gers and real numbers; 60 or 64 bits are not unusual. Table 8.3 shows typical bit patterns used to represent the integers 1, 2, 3, and −5 in character, integer, and real number form.

The point of Table 8.3 is not to introduce a discussion of how to represent integers and real numbers; you can read Section 1.5.3 and *Signum* (1979) for this information. The point is that integers and real numbers are represented in quite distinct ways. The issues involved, especially in the case of real numbers, are complex.

Observe that the representation of −5, a negative value, requires the same number of bits as the representation of a positive value that is treated as an integer or as a real number. However, if a negative value is to be represented in character mode, it must be stored as two characters—a character string of length two.

We will now return to our study of storing characters using a fixed number of bits. Section 8.2.2 examines a technique, first suggested by Karlgren (1963), for representing more than 2^n distinct characters with n bit patterns.

8.2.2 Embedded Shift Instructions

Karlgren's (1963) idea for representing more than 2^n distinct characters with n bit patterns closely parallels the use of a shift key, which is used to switch from lowercase to uppercase letters on a standard typewriter or computer terminal. In terms of stored data, the shift key is a bit pattern that is not data but that signals a shift from lowercase to uppercase. A second bit pattern could be used to signal a shift from uppercase to lowercase.

Suppose, for example, that we wish to store the pair of words

DATA STRUCTURES

with the first letter of each word uppercase and the remainder of the letters lowercase. One way to accomplish this, called **embedded shift instructions**, would be to embed the special shift patterns into the character string in four places as follows:

#D&ATA #S&TRUCTURES

where & signals a shift from uppercase to lowercase, and **#** signals a shift from lowercase to uppercase.

The use of some bit patterns to signal a shift in print mode significantly extends the number of distinct objects that can be represented by n bits. For example, 6 bits can be used to form 64 distinct patterns. If two of those patterns are used to signal a shift to and from a second print mode, such as lowercase, then the number of objects represented is increased to 124. If two other bit patterns were used to signal a shift to and from a third print mode, such as italics, then the number of objects represented becomes

$$4 \times (64 - 4) = 240$$

In this case each character may "appear" in one of four different ways:

Uppercase normal
Uppercase italics
Lowercase normal
Lowercase italics

A problem with this technique is the necessity to store the signals that specify mode shifts. These signals take up storage space so that a character string that contains many mode shifts will require more storage than a string that does not. On the other hand, each character can be represented by fewer bits. The combined effect on storage requirements depends on the frequency of mode shifts and the number of distinct modes. An interesting analysis of the combined effect of these two considerations is given in Standish (1980), pages 291–295.

8.2.3 Embedded Mode Shift Instructions—An Application

This section describes an example of how embedded signals are used to control a specific printer. The printer is an Epson MX-80. Input to this printer is bit patterns of length eight. These patterns are interpreted either as ASCII characters to be printed or as signals to change the mode of the printer. Since the printer has a large number of print modes, signals to change mode may occupy more than one character. Table 8.4 shows some of the command sequences and the effect each sequence has on the printer.

The shift mode instructions are one, two, or a variable number of bytes in length. All shift instructions that are longer than 1 byte begin with the same signal byte. This is an interesting generalization of the idea discussed in Section 8.2.2. It permits one pattern to be interpreted both as a character to be printed and, when preceded by a specified pattern, as a mode shift instruction.

The tab set sequence is another interesting generalization of the approach in Section 8.2.2. It consists of a byte that signals the start of a sequence of special commands and a byte that signals the end of the sequence. The number of bytes in between is not specified, but each is interpreted in a special way (in this case as a tab position). Figure 8.3 shows an example of a tab set sequence.

Some shift mode instructions use a single bit pattern. That pattern acts as a switch that turns a mode on, if it is off, and off, if it is on. This will work as long as the affected mode is independent of all other modes. Likely candidates for such switches include the following:

UPPER- and lowercase
Italics and any other mode
Boldface and not boldface

0001 1011
0100 0100
0000 1111
0001 1110
0010 0011
0011 1110
0000 0000

Figure 8.3
The sequence that sets tabs for the Epson MX-80 as 15, 30, 35, and 62.

TABLE 8.4 Examples of signals for print modes on Epson MX-80.

Command sequence		Effect on the printer
	0000 1110	Subsequent characters printed double width
	0001 0100	Cancels double width mode
	0000 1111	Subsequent characters printed in condensed size
	0001 0010	Cancels condensed size mode
0001 1011	0100 0101	Subsequent characters printed in emphasized mode
0001 1011	0100 0110	Cancels emphasized mode
0001 1011	0100 0111	Subsequent characters printed with overstrike
0001 1011	0100 1000	Cancels overstrike mode
0001 1011	0011 0000	Sets line spacing to 1/8 inch
0001 1011	0011 0001	Sets line spacing to 7/72 inch
0001 1011	0011 0010	Sets line spacing to 1/6 inch
0001 1011	0100 0100	Initiates reading of horizontal tab positions
	0000 0000	Terminates reading horizontal tabs

If the Epson MX-80 printer includes the graphics option, then there are many other modes that may be selected. Among them are italics, subscript, superscript, underline, and strikeout.

8.2.4 Representing Characters with a Variable Number of Bits

Suppose we have eight characters with which to construct messages. A sequence of 3 bits provides eight distinct bit patterns, so we can record messages using 3 bits for each character. For concreteness suppose that our eight characters are a, b, c, d, e, f, g, and h and that we know typical values for the frequency with which each character occurs in our messages. Table 8.5 shows example values.

We are interested in finding representations for our characters that will permit messages to be stored in the least amount of space. Table 8.6 shows a scheme that uses fewer bits for frequently occurring characters and more bits for less frequently occurring characters. Does this scheme require less storage for typical messages?

If we use 3 bits to store each character and if a message contains n characters, then $3n$ bits of storage are required. Using the scheme of Table 8.6 and the frequencies of Table 8.5, the storage requirement for an n character message is

$$\frac{1}{100}(40 \times 1 + 20 \times 3 + 10 \times 3 + 8 \times 4 + 8 \times 4 + 5 \times 4 + 5 \times 5 + 4 \times 5)n$$
$$= 2.59n$$

The scheme of Table 8.6 requires about 14% less space to store a message.

In addition to reducing storage space, the scheme in Table 8.6 has another

TABLE 8.5

Character	Number of occurrences per 100 characters of text
a	40
b	20
c	10
d	8
e	8
f	5
g	5
h	4

TABLE 8.6 A variable length character code for the characters in Table 8.5.

Character	Binary representation
a	1
b	001
c	011
d	0001
e	0101
f	0100
g	00001
h	00000

essential property. No character has a representation that is the prefix of the representation for any other character. Therefore, messages stored using this scheme can be unambiguously converted back to the original character set. A representation for which this is true is said to have the ***prefix property***.

We would like to know if there is another scheme that uses even less storage than that proposed in Table 8.6. There is not. The representation in Table 8.6 is a ***Huffman code*** for the frequencies in Table 8.5. It is known that for a given set of frequencies, a Huffman code representation will require the smallest possible average number of bits to represent each character.

A Huffman code can be constructed whenever there is a finite character set for which the frequencies of occurrence are known. It can be shown that a Huffman code minimizes, for the specified frequencies, the average number of bits required to represent each character. A proof of this result is in Hu (1981), pages 164–170.

Let us see how a Huffman code representation is constructed. We begin with a binary tree representation of the result shown in Table 8.6. The tree is shown in Figure 8.4.

Each branch of the tree is associated with a binary digit. Each leaf node contains one of the characters for which we seek a representation. The Huffman code for any character is the sequence of binary digits encountered on the simple path from the root to that character.

Construction of such a binary tree is conceptually simple. We begin by forming a forest of one-node binary trees. There is one node for each entry in

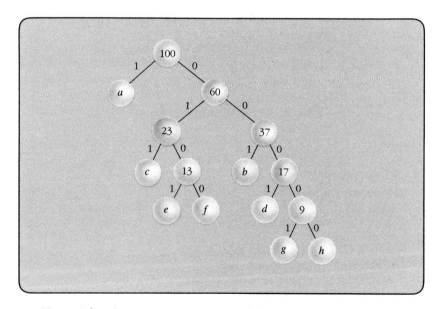

Figure 8.4   A binary tree representation of the result in Table 8.6.

the frequency table, and that node contains the frequency. For the data in Table 8.5 the result is as shown in Figure 8.5.

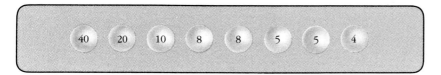

Figure 8.5   One node for each character in Table 8.5.

It is convenient, but not necessary, to order the nodes by their frequency values. We combine the two nodes of lowest frequency to form a new binary tree. This tree has a new node as its root and the two input nodes as leaf nodes. The positions of the leaf nodes do not matter—Huffman codes are not unique. For our example we have Figure 8.6, which is a collection, or **forest**, of seven binary trees:

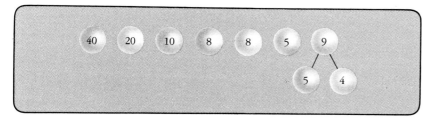

9 is added to the forest.

Figure 8.6   After adding a root node containing 9.

The process repeats. We take the two root nodes of lowest frequency and form a new tree as before. The result is as shown in Figure 8.7.

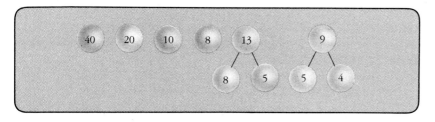

13 is added as the root of a tree in the forest.

Figure 8.7   After adding a root node containing 13.

Once again we combine the root nodes of lowest frequency to form a new tree. The result is shown in Figure 8.8:

17 is added as the root of a tree in the forest.

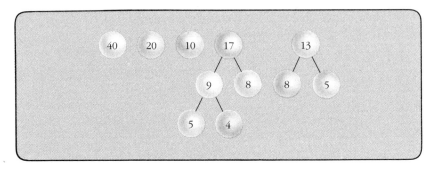

Figure 8.8   After adding a root node containing 17.

Remember that the order in which the nodes are placed does not matter. Any order produces an optimal (but not unique) Huffman code. After combining two more root nodes we have the results shown in Figure 8.9:

37 and 23 are added as root nodes of trees in the forest.

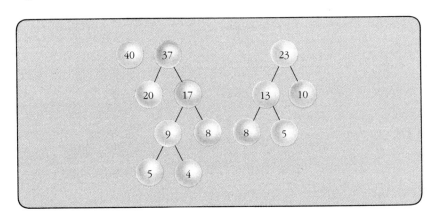

Figure 8.9   After adding root nodes containing 37 and 23.

The final tree is obtained by adding two more root nodes, replacing each of the original frequencies by the letter corresponding to that frequency, and assigning 0 or 1 to each edge. When two frequencies are the same, it does not matter how the letters are assigned. It does not matter how the 0's and 1's are assigned as long as the two edges that share a common parent have distinct values. Compare this tree in Figure 8.10 with the tree in Figure 8.4. They are almost the same. Both give valid Huffman codes.

To implement a Huffman code module we need a data structure that is efficient for insertion and for searching for smallest frequencies. For small problems, storing the frequencies in a sorted list would work as well as any data structure and would be conceptually simple. Linked implementation is indicated by the frequent rearrangement of nodes.

For large problems, a priority queue of root pointers would reduce the effort required for the insertions and deletions associated with building the binary tree. Details of such an implementation are given in Sedgewick (1983), pages 286–293.

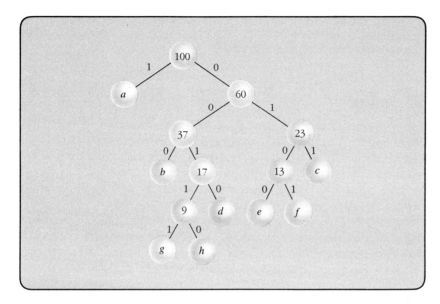

60 and 100 are added as root nodes of trees in the forest.

Figure 8.10 After adding root nodes containing 60 and 100 and replacing leaf node frequencies by the corresponding character.

Exercises 8.2

1. Write a program to print the character set for your Modula-2 implementation. Is it the same as shown in Figure 8.2(a)?
2. Explain why the maximum number of bit patterns that can be represented with n bits is 2^n.
3. Give some of the advantages and disadvantages of embedded shift instructions.
4. Suppose that the text of a message contains 1000 characters. Printing this message requires upper- and lowercase in both ordinary print and italics. Also needed is the ability to underline any letter. There are 10 special characters in addition to the letters of the alphabet. The text is to be stored as a sequence of bits using fixed-length representations and embedded shift patterns.

   How many bits should be used for each character? What special patterns should be used? Assume that there are 100 changes between lower- and uppercase, 40 changes between italics and nonitalics, and 25 changes between underlined and not underlined letters.
5. Find a Huffman code representation corresponding to each of the following frequency tables. In each case determine the average number of bits required to store a message.

a.

Character	Frequency
a	60
b	20
c	20

b.

Character	Frequency
a	25
b	25
c	25
d	25

c.

Character	Frequency
a	25
b	30
c	10
d	25
e	10

6. Using a list module (Chapter 4) or a priority queue module (Chapter 5), implement a procedure to construct the Huffman code representations of an input list of characters and frequencies.

8.3 Strings

The first sentence in this paragraph, including spaces and the period at the end, is a string. This paragraph, including this sentence, is a string. A ***string*** is a list, or sequence, of characters. The subject of this chapter is strings, which is a special case of the list data structure discussed in Chapter 4. Why should we spend an entire chapter discussing a special case of a topic previously covered? There are two main reasons.

First, since most information related to computing can be viewed as a character string, it is worth discussing in more detail. Second, the basic operations for strings are different from the basic operations for lists discussed in Chapter 4. Since both lists and strings have a linear relationship among their components, it is true that the operations for lists apply to strings and that the operations for strings can be applied to lists. From a pragmatic point of view, however, the operations that have been found useful for strings are different from the basic operations for lists. Because the operations are different, the abstract data types are different. The question we must now answer is why are the operations different.

The lists in Chapter 4 had components that were elements. Each element had a key part and a data part and was thought of as the computer representation of some (possibly complex) object. The operations on lists in Chapter 4 referred to individual elements. Data structures of type *String* have individual characters as their components. Operations on strings usually refer to an entire sequence of components instead of just one. For example, the operation *Find-Key* on a list of elements searches for the specific element with a specified value of its key. The corresponding operation for a string searches for a sequence of characters that is itself a string. Searching for a single component is a different operation from searching for a sequence of contiguous components. In fact, searching for a single component (as in Chapter 4) can be thought of as a special case of searching for a sequence of components. In general, operations on strings involve a sequence of components, whereas operations on lists involve individual components.

We can refer to the characters of a string in terms of their position in the string. If S is a string, then $S[1]$ is its first character, $S[2]$ (the successor of $S[1]$) is second character, and $S[k]$ (the successor of $S[k - 1]$) is its kth character. For $S[k]$, k is the position of the character in the string S. If S contains n characters, then it will be said to have length n. If S is a string of length n, and if $1 <= i <= j <= n$ then the sequence of characters

$$S[i], S[i + 1], \ldots, S[j]$$

is a ***substring*** of S. A string that contains no characters is called the ***empty string*** and has length 0.

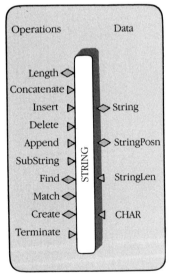

Figure 8.11
Capsule form of the *String* data type.

8.3.1 Specification of a String Data Type

We will begin this section with Specification 8.1 for the string data type and will then give a short tutorial on the operations for a string.

Specification 8.1 Strings

DEFINITION MODULE Strings;

(* **Elements:** The elements of a string are characters. *)

(* **Structure:** There is a linear relationship among the elements. Each character has a unique position in a string. The first character is in position 1. The successor of the character in position k is in position k+1. *)

(* **Domain:** A string's length is between 0 and MaxLength characters. *)

EXPORT QUALIFIED String, MaxLength, StringPosn, StringLen, Insert, Delete, Length, Concatenate, SubString, Create, Match, Terminate, Find, Append;

CONST MaxLength = 100;

TYPE String;
　　　　StringPosn = [1..MaxLength];　　　(* *Position of a character in a string.* *)
　　　　StringLen = [0..MaxLength];　　　　　　(* *Length of a string.* *)

(* **Operations:** If S is a string then reference to S-pre in a post-condition is a reference to the value of S just prior to the operation. *)

PROCEDURE Length(S: String): StringLen;
(* **post** – Length is the number of characters in S. *)

PROCEDURE Concatenate(**VAR** S1: String; S2: String);
(* **pre** – Length(S1) + Length(S2) is at most MaxLength.
　post – S1 is the following string:

　S1-pre[1], ... , S1-pre[Length(S1-pre)], S2[1], ... , S2[Length(S2)] *)

PROCEDURE Insert(**VAR** S1: String; S2: String; pos: StringPosn);
(* **pre** – Length(S1) + Length(S2) is at most MaxLength.
　post – S1 is the string obtained by inserting S2 between
　　　　　　S1-pre[pos-1] and S1-pre[pos]. *)

PROCEDURE Delete(**VAR** S: String; pos: StringPosn; len: StringLen);
(* **pre** – The value of (pos + len - 1) is at most Length(S).
　post – S is S-pre with the following characters deleted.

　　　　　　S-pre[pos], S-pre[pos + 1], ... , S-pre[pos + len - 1]. *)

PROCEDURE Append(**VAR** S: String; c: CHAR);
(* **pre** – Length(S) < MaxLength.
　post – S is S-pre with character c appended as its last character. *)

continued

Specification 8.1, continued

PROCEDURE SubString(S1:String; **VAR** S2:String; pos: StringPosn; len: StringLen);
(* **pre** — The value of pos + len - 1 is at most Length(S1).
    post — S2 is the string whose characters are:

            S1[pos], S1[pos + 1], ... , S1[pos + len - 1]. *)

PROCEDURE Find(S1, S2: String; pos: StringPosn): StringLen;
(* **pre** — The value of pos is at most Length(S1).
    post — Find is the smallest integer greater than or equal to pos
            such that S2 is the same as the string

            S1[Find], S1[Find + 1], ... , S1[Find + Length(S2) - 1]

            provided S1 contains such a substring. If not, Find is 0. *)

PROCEDURE Match(S1, S2: String; pos: StringPosn): BOOLEAN;
(* **pre** — Length(S2) + pos - 1 is at most Length(S1).
    post — If S2 is the same string as S1[pos], ... , S1[Length(S1)+pos-1]
            then return true else return false. *)

PROCEDURE Create(**VAR** S: String): BOOLEAN;
(* **pre** — None.
    post — If a string can be created then S is an empty string and
            Create is true, else Create is false. *)

PROCEDURE Terminate(**VAR** S: String);
(* **post** — S does not exist. *)

END Strings.

The function *Length* simply returns the length of *S*. The length of a string may be zero or a positive integer. Our specification of an abstract string may include an upper bound on the length of a string (as it does in Specification 8.1) or it may not. We discuss this issue later.

With the operation *Concatenate,* S2 is appended to the end of S1—immediately after its last character. The result is a string, $S1$, whose length is increased by the length of $S2$. If $S2$ is the empty string, then concatenate makes no changes. If $S1$ is the empty string, then concatenate makes $S1$ a copy of $S2$.

With the operation *Insert,* S2 is inserted into S1 beginning at position $S1[pos]$. If we specify two new strings, $WS1$ and $WS2$, in terms of $S1$ as it exists before the *Insert* operation, by

$$WS1 = S1[1], S1[2], ... , S1[pos - 1]$$

and

$$WS2 = S1[pos], S1[pos + 1], ... , S1[length(S1)]$$

str1 = 'com'
Length(str1) = 3
str2 = ' science'
Concatenate(str1,str2)
str1 = 'com science'
str2 = ' science'

str3 = 'puter'
Insert(str1,4,str3)
str1 = 'computer science'
str3 = 'puter'

then *Insert* constructs in $S1$ the same string that is placed in $WS1$ by the pair of concatenate operations

```
Concatenate(WS1, S2);
Concatenate(WS1, WS2);
```

If $S2$ is empty, then $S1$ is not changed. If $pos = 0$, then the effect of *Insert* is to concatenate $S1$ onto the end of $S2$.

Delete(str1,4,5)
str1 = 'com science'

The effect of *Delete* is to remove a substring from S. The first character of the substring is $S[pos]$, and it contains *len* characters. $Delete(S,1,1)$ removes the first character from S, whereas $Delete(S,Length(S),1)$ removes the last. $Delete(S,1,Length(S))$ deletes all of S.

The operation *Substring* copies a substring from S. The substring contains the characters

str1 = 'com science'
substring(str1, str4, 5,7)
str4 = 'science'
str1 = 'com science'

```
S[pos], S[pos + 1] ... , S[pos + len - 1]
```

The operation *Create* allows us to bring a string S into existence—provided an instance of a string can be created. The operation *Append* allows us to append single characters to the end of a string, making S one character longer. These two operations allow a string to be created and then built up character by character.

The operation *Find* searches $S1$, starting at $S1[pos]$, in an attempt to find an occurrence of $S2$. $S2$ is often called a **pattern,** and operation *Find* is referred to as **pattern matching.** Note that even if we consider a string to be a linear list of characters, what we are doing with this operation is quite different from what is accomplished by the traditional find operation for a list. The traditional find operation searches for patterns of length one. This operation searches for a sequence containing one or more characters. Searching for a pattern of length one is implemented in the usual way—a sequential search. Searching for a pattern of length greater than one is, from an implementation point of view, a fascinating topic because several ingenious techniques have been developed. We shall study some of them shortly.

str5 = 'Fast pattern matching in strings'
str6 = 'Fast'
k := Find(str5,str6,1)
k = 1
str7 = 'string'
k := Find(str5,str7,1)
k = 26

Figure 8.12 lists the operations provided by four different string modules. It is clear that except for naming conventions the basic operations are similar in all four modules. The major difference lies in the ability of a module to create and terminate strings dynamically. The operations *Create* and *Terminate* in column (a) provide this capability, as do operations *createnull, define,* and *destroy* in column (d). Operation *define* dynamically creates an empty string—although it does not check to see if there is enough available memory before beginning—so the user may be at the mercy of the operating system. Operation *createnull* converts an existing string into an empty string.

The operations in columns (c) and (d) provide conversion options not offered by the other two modules. Operation *convertarray* takes a specified number of characters from an array of characters and puts them into a string. Operation *convertliteral* takes all the characters in an array of characters and puts them into a string. Operations *readstring* and *writestring* provide for the transfer of characters between a string and a file.

Insert	Insert	insert	insert
Delete	Delete	delete	delete
Append			
Concatenate	Concat	concatenate	concatenate
Substring	Copy	extract	extract
	Assign	copy	copy
Match	CompareStr	equal	equal
		lessthan	lessthan
Find	Pos	search	search
Create			createnull
			define
Terminate			destroy
		convertarray	convertarray
		convertliteral	convertliteral
		readstring	readstring
		writestring	writestring
(a)	(b)	(c)	(d)

Figure 8.12   Operations listed in four Modula-2 definition modules. Those in column (a) are from Specification 8.1, operations in (b) are from Gleaves (1984), page 114, and those in (c) and (d) are from Ford (1985), pages 216 and 259, respectively.

Modula-2 provides for string constants and the assignment of string constants to arrays. A Modula-2 string constant begins and ends with either ' or ". Examples are shown in Figure 8.13.

'ABCDEFG'

"ABCDEFG"

"We can't go."

'He said, "Come here quick." '

Figure 8.13.   Four Modula-2 string constants. A string that contains ' must begin and end with ". A string that contains " must begin and end with '. A string cannot contain both ' and ".

A Modula-2 string is assignment compatible with an array whose first index value is 0. If str is given by

VAR   str: **ARRAY** [0..5] **OF CHAR**;

then str := '012345' fills str with the constant string as shown. The assignment str := '01234567' results in truncation on the right so that str contains '012345'. Finally, str := '0123' causes str to be padded on the right with two null characters. The *WriteString* operation in module *InOut,* for example, recognizes the null character as a string terminator. Padding on the right with null characters is an implicit way to specify string length.

8.3.2 Representation of Strings

There are two basic approaches for representing strings. The first is an **array representation**, which places each string in a segment of memory of specified size. This can be accomplished in Modula-2 as shown in Figure 8.14.

```
CONST MaxLength =                    (* User specified. *)

TYPE  StringPosn = [1..MaxLength];
      StringLen  = [0..MaxLength];
      String     = POINTER TO RECORD
                            slen: StringLen;
                            data: ARRAY StringPosn
                                            OF CHAR
              END;
```

Figure 8.14   One possibility for using arrays to represent strings.

There are many variations on this approach, but they all share the same characteristics. This approach is simple and handles many simple applications quite nicely.

An obvious drawback is the usual one associated with static arrays. If a string varies in length, then memory must be allocated to accommodate its maximum length. Another drawback is the precondition for *Concatenate* and *Insert* that limits the sum of the lengths of the strings. Many current implementations execute those operations, if that precondition is violated, by truncating the result.

It would be nice if there were no upper limit on string length, and we could certainly specify such a string data type. A discussion of strings, the abstraction of strings as sequences, and their implementation using the Pascal data type file are given in Sale (1979).

The second basic approach uses a **linked list of chunks** to store pieces of a string. There are many variations on this approach, and we have used a variation of the one described in Bishop (1979). The representation is shown in Figure 8.15.

Data type *String* is represented using a record that stores the length of the string, a *Pointer* to a singly linked list of *Chunks,* and a *Pointer* to the last *Chunk* in the list. An illustration of a string stored in a linked list of *Chunks* is shown in Figure 8.16. The chunk size is 10.

To store messages of statistically varying length, it has been shown (Sipala, 1981) that the *ChunkSize* that minimizes wasted space for several distributions of string length L is

$$\sqrt{2bL}$$

where b is the overhead in each chunk.

```
CONST ChunkSize =                        (* User specified. *)
TYPE   Pointer = POINTER TO Chunk
       Chunk   = RECORD
                     next: Pointer;
                     data: ARRAY [1..ChunkSize] OF CHAR
                 END;

       String  = POINTER TO RECORD
                              head: Pointer;
                              tail: Pointer;
                              slen: CARDINAL
                          END;
```

Figure 8.15   One possibility for using dynamically allocated chunks to represent strings.

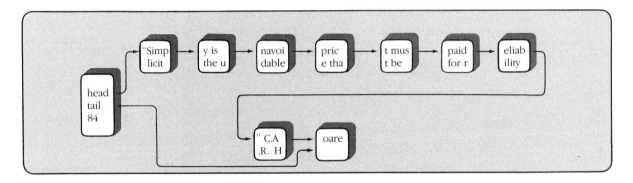

Figure 8.16   A string stored in a linked list of chunks. The chunk size is 10.

In Section 2.4.3 we discussed linked list design parameters. The parameters chosen in this case are as follows:

1. There are *Head* and *Tail* pointers to mark the ends of the list. The *Tail* pointer makes the *Concatenate* operation more efficient.
2. A single pointer links each chunk to its successor. A pointer to a chunk's predecessor is not as useful as it was in Chapters 2 and 4. This is because both *Insert* and *Delete* for strings operate primarily on characters rather than on the chunks that contain them. The insertion or deletion point is found by searching forward from the head of the string. Once that point is found, there is no need to locate the predecessor chunk. Prior chunk pointers might be useful in implementing the *Find* operation. This is discussed in Section 8.3.5.
3. No access pointers, besides *Head* and *Tail,* are used. The string operations apply to entire strings, so there is little advantage to maintaining pointers to positions in the middle of the string.

Another possibility for representing strings is given in a definition module in Gleaves (1984), page 114. The module is named Strings and the data type used is given in Figure 8.17.

```
TYPE String = ARRAY [0..80] OF CHAR;
```

Figure 8.17   Another possibility for using arrays to represent strings (refer also to Figure 8.14).

Compare the string representations given in Figures 8.14 and 8.17. In both cases the characters in a string value are stored in an array. In Figure 8.14 a *String* is a pointer to a record that contains the array. In 8.17 a *String* is an array. Let us examine some of the differences between these two approaches.

The representation in Figure 8.17 has no explicit representation for length. If the string does not fill the array then an implicit indication of length, such as padding on the right with the null character, is necessary. This approach makes it relatively expensive to determine string length.

If data type *String* is a pointer then it can be declared in the definition module as an opaque data type and all details of its representation are hidden from the user. This is done in Specification 8.1. In addition, instances of the data type can be created and terminated dynamically by the implementation module.

If data type *String* is an array then full representation details must be presented in the definition module so that they are visible to users of that module. In addition, instances of type String must be declared in the user's program at the time it is written. Note also that a formal parameter of type String will, in this case, almost certainly be an open array type.

8.3.3 *Array Implementation of Strings*

An implementation of the string abstraction based on an array representation is given in Implementation Module 8.1 at the end of this section. We begin with a comment about operations that may produce strings that are too long to fit in the array in which they are to be stored. This is followed by a discussion of algorithms for the *find* operation.

Several operations—*Concatenate* and *Insert,* for example—combine two strings to produce a longer string. If the string that results is too long to fit in the array that contains it, the implementor may have a problem. In Specification 8.1 preconditions have been given that warn the user to check the length of the resultant string before using the operation. In this case the implementor is not responsible for taking any special action if the result is too long to be stored.

In some implementations a result that is too long is simply truncated—usually on the right end—and the user is not given any warning about what has happened. For an example of this see Ford (1985), page 218.

If a string is represented as a dynamic list of substrings (Figure 8.15, for example), combining strings to produce a longer string is not a problem as long as memory is available for creating storage for new substrings.

Implementing the *Find* operation:

```
Find(S1, S2: String; pos: StringPosn): CARDINAL;
```

requires some discussion. Recall that *S1* is searched, beginning with *S1*[*pos*], for the first occurrence of *S2*. Its position is returned as the value of the function. If *S2* is not found, then the value returned is zero. *S2* is often referred to as a pattern, and the search operation is then referred to as pattern matching. If the operation is carried out with dispatch, we might even refer to "fast" pattern matching.

In keeping with what appears to be more mnemonic terminology, the discussion below references operation *Find* specified as

```
Find(text,pattern: String; pos: StringPosn): StringLen;
```

To aid in the discussion we will assign specific meanings to the terms match, hit, and miss. A ***match*** occurs when a substring of *text* is found that is the same as *pattern*. A ***hit*** occurs when a single character of *pattern* is the same as a corresponding character of *text*. A ***miss*** occurs when a character of *pattern* is different from a corresponding character of *text*. Match and hit have the same meaning only if *pattern* is of length one.

• Obvious algorithm

There are three basic approaches to implementation of the *Find* operation. Each of them is conceptually simple; the performance of the third one is, in many cases, substantially better than the first two. The first approach, called the ***obvious algorithm***, is the one that most people would initially think of if confronted with the problem of pattern matching. Consider the text and pattern shown in Figure 8.18. (This example is taken from Knuth et al. 1977.) In all our examples we will assume that *pos* = 1; that is, the search begins at the left end of the text to be searched.

B A B C B A B C A B C A A B C A B C A B C A C A B C
A B C A B C A C A B

Figure 8.18

B A B C **B** A B C A B C A A B C A B C A B C A C A B C
 A B C **A** B C A C A B

Figure 8.19

B A **B** C B A B C A B C A A B C A B C A B C A C A B C
  A B C A B C A C A B

Figure 8.20

B A B C B A B C A B C A A B C A B C A B C A C A B C
           A B C A B C A C A B

Figure 8.21
A match is found at positions 16–25 after 32 hits and 15 misses, or a total of 47 comparisons.

The pattern is placed beneath the left end of the text. Since the first character of the pattern, A, does not hit the first character of the text, B, we move the pattern one position to the right. The two characters in bold-face in the figures are the characters that cause the miss that requires the pattern to be moved.

After we move the pattern one position to the right, we find three hits before a miss, as shown in Figure 8.19.

Once again the pattern is advanced one position to the right. Failure to hit occurs at the first pattern character (Figure 8.20), so the pattern is shifted, once again, one position to the right. This process continues until the text is exhausted or until a match (not just a hit) is found. In our example a match is found after 47 comparisons, as shown in Figure 8.21.

This obvious algorithm can be succinctly described as shown in Algorithm 8.1.

```
Place pattern at text[pos];
WHILE pattern NOT matched AND text NOT exhausted DO
    WHILE pattern character differs from text character DO
        shift pattern one character to the right;
        start search at the left end of the pattern
    END;
    advance to next character of both text and pattern
END
```

Algorithm 8.1   Obvious algorithm.

If the text contains n characters and the pattern m, then the worst that can happen with the obvious algorithm is that $O(m \times n)$ compares will be required to find the pattern. An example of such a text–pattern pair is shown in Figure 8.22.

```
Text     →   a a a a a ... a a a b
Pattern  →   a a ... a b
```

Figure 8.22
$O(m \times n)$ compares needed to find a match using the obvious algorithm.

• Knuth–Morris–Pratt algorithm

In Knuth, Morris, and Pratt (1977) an algorithm is described that is shown to require at most $m + n$ compares. Since it is a conceptually simple modification of the obvious algorithm, we will describe it next. To see how the algorithms differ, return to the example shown in Figure 8.18 and consider the following situation.

The pattern is positioned beneath the second through eleventh characters of the text. There have been three hits, and on the fourth comparison there is a miss (see Figure 8.23). Instead of sliding the pattern one position to the right, as the obvious algorithm does, consider the possibility of sliding it further. Refer to Figure 8.24. Because of the three hits and one miss, we have information about four characters in the text.

To illustrate this, let us replace text characters we do not know yet with a ?, those we no longer care about with a #, and those whose values we know with themselves. Finally, let the symbol [A] signify a character known, because of a miss, *not* to be an A.

How far can we shift the pattern to the right based on the above information? The answer is the essence of the ***Knuth–Morris–Pratt (KMP) algorithm***. It is important, and is summarized in the margin.

Let us apply this heuristic to the information shown in Figure 8.24. The information was obtained from one miss and three hits. We know that the first character in the pattern, an A, must hit the corresponding character in the text. We can see that sliding the pattern one, two, or three positions to the right will

```
B A B C B A B C A B C A A B C A B C A B C A C A B C
A B C A B C A C A B
```

Figure 8.23

```
# A B C [A] ? ? ? ... ? ?
A B C A # # # # # #
```

Figure 8.24

Basis of the KMP Algorithm

Using the information from one miss and zero or more hits, move the pattern as far as possible.

lead to a miss for the leading A. Therefore, we can slide the pattern at least four positions without passing any possible matches. We cannot slide the pattern further, because the next text character is not known; it may be an A. If a miss occurs in the first pattern position (one miss and zero hits), then the best we can do is slide the pattern one place to the right.

B A B C B A B C A B C A **A** B C A B C A B C A C A B C
    A B C A B C A **C** A B

Figure 8.25

. . . # # A B C A B C A **[C]** ? ? ? . . .
    A B C A B C A **C** # #

Figure 8.26
The information from seven hits and a miss.

. . . # # A B C A B C A [C] ? ? ? . . .
      A B C A B C A C A B

Figure 8.27
After sliding the pattern three positions—four definite hits and the possibility of a fifth, we must consider the possibility of a match.

B A B C B A B C A B C A **A** B C A B C A B C A C A B C
    A B C A **B** C A C A B

Figure 8.28
The search continues here—the first four characters are known to yield hits.

B A B C B A B C A B C A A B C A B C A B C A C A B C
    A B C A B C A C A B

Figure 8.29
The KMP algorithm finds a match after 23 hits and 5 misses, or a total of 28 comparisons.

Continuing with our example, suppose that the pattern is aligned with the sixth text character, as shown in Figure 8.25. In this position, there are seven hits before the first miss. Based on the seven hits and the miss, we have the information shown in Figure 8.26.

How far forward can we slide the pattern without ignoring any possible matches? There is a hit for the first pattern character after sliding three places. We must also check that pattern characters two through five hit the corresponding text characters. This can be visually checked by actually sliding the pattern three positions.

If the pattern is slid three positions, we see that all required matches occur. Thus, moving the pattern three positions is the best that can be accomplished. Note that B is compared with [C]. Since [C] may be a B, the possibility of a match here must be considered.

After sliding the pattern three positions, as shown in Figure 8.27, comparison with the text continues with the fifth pattern character. We know that the first four characters hit, so there is no need to check them again. In general the KMP algorithm never ***backs up***; that is, it never returns to consider a text character previously considered. On the other hand, the obvious algorithm clearly does back up, and this could slow it down considerably if backing up caused it to fetch a page, for the second time, from secondary storage.

An important question is this: Why is the KMP algorithm based on values that a text character does not have? Why not act based on the actual text values? In our example above, Figure 8.27, [C] is actually an A. Since this does not hit B in the pattern, we could have done better than sliding the pattern three positions. Using the fact that [C] is an A in this case allows us to slide the pattern seven positions. The reason is that the KMP algorithm preprocesses the pattern and constructs a table showing how far to move the pattern after each possible miss. This table depends only on the pattern and must work for any text encountered. The most you can say about the text character where the miss occurs is what it is *not*.

The KMP algorithm could be modified to act on the actual value of the text character when a miss occurs, but the overhead could be considerable since the text character may have many possible values.

Figure 8.30 shows three sample patterns. The digit below each character shows how far the pattern is moved if the first miss occurs at that character. Procedures that compute these values are given in Knuth, Morris, and Pratt (1977) and Smit (1982). You should be able to determine the values based on the heuristics discussed above, but writing the algorithms is difficult and should not be attempted without consulting the references.

An algorithm for Knuth–Morris–Pratt is shown in Algorithm 8.2. It is designed to be comparable with the obvious algorithm (Algorithm 8.1) given earlier.

Empirical studies (Smit, 1982) show that the performance of the KMP algorithm is not much different from the performance of the obvious algorithm. The reason is that these algorithms normally spend much of their effort looking for a hit for the first character in the pattern. A variation of the above approaches, suggested by Horsepool (1980), is to select the character in the pattern that occurs least frequently in the text being searched. Pattern matching then begins with a scan of the text looking for the (rare) occurrences of that character.

```
A P P L E
1 1 2 3 4

P R E P A R E D
1 1 2 4 3 5 6 7

A B C A B C B
1 1 2 4 4 5 3
```

Figure 8.30
Sample patterns and associated tables for the KMP algorithm. The value recorded beneath each character is the distance the pattern can be moved to the right based on a miss at that position. The obvious algorithm is the special case in which each of the values is 1.

```
Place pattern at text[pos];
WHILE pattern NOT fully matched AND text NOT exhausted DO

    WHILE pattern character differs from text character DO
        shift pattern as far to the right as possible;
        start search at the text character where the miss
            occurred
    END;

    advance to the next character of both text and pattern
END
```

Obtain this distance from a table calculated by preprocessing the pattern.

Algorithm 8.2   Knuth–Morris–Pratt algorithm.

When one is found, a check for a complete match is undertaken. As an example, searching English prose for the word "snooze" would begin by looking for instances of the letter "z."

• **Boyer–Moore algorithm**

The third approach to pattern matching is described in Boyer and Moore (1977). We will refer to it as the **Boyer–Moore algorithm**. It is based on the ingenious observation that it is more efficient to compare characters starting at the right end of the pattern and working to the left.

Consider the text–pattern pair shown in Figure 8.31. (This example is taken from Boyer and Moore, 1977.)

The first comparison is between F and T. Since there is a miss we must decide how far the pattern can be moved to the right. The Boyer–Moore algorithm

```
WHICH_FINALLY_HALTS._AT_THAT
AT_THAT

?????? F??...          ?????? [T]??...
AT_THAT               AT_THA T
    (a)                    (b)
```

Figure 8.31

WHICH_FINALLY_HALTS._AT_THAT
                AT_TH**A**T

#????? _??...   #??????[**T**]??...
AT_THA **T**   AT_THA **T**
        (a)   (b)

Figure 8.32

WHICH_FINALLY_HA**L**TS._AT_THAT
                AT_TH**A**T

#?????L??..   #?????[A]T??..
   AT_THAT   AT_TH AT
        (a)   (b)

Figure 8.33

          * A P P L E
(2a) →   5 4   2 1
(2b) →   5 5 5 5 1

          * P R E P A R E D
(2a) →   8   4 3 2 1
(2b) →   8 8 8 8 8 8 1

          * A B C A B C B
(2a) →   7   3 2 1
(2b) →   7 7 7 7 7 2 1

Figure 8.34
Three examples that show the
result of preprocessing for the
Boyer–Moore algorithm. The
(2a) and (2b) refer to the list in
the text. Row (2a) contains an
entry for each character in the
alphabet. An * represents all
characters not in the pattern.
The value for each character is
its distance from the right end of
the pattern. Row (2b) shows the
distance the pattern can be
moved based on a miss in the
indicated location. Implementation details for all three algorithms are given in Smit (1982).
Variations and simplifications for
the Boyer–Moore algorithm are
given in Horsepool (1980).

uses two independent analyses to decide how far to shift the pattern. In our example—Figure 8.31—they are labeled (a) and (b).

From Figure 8.31(a), since the pattern does not contain the character F, we can slide the pattern seven positions to the right. Using Figure 8.31(b), we can slide the pattern only one position since [T] might be a hit with A. The pattern is moved the maximum of these two values—seven positions. The result is shown in Figure 8.32.

The first comparison in this position, between _ and T, is again a miss. The decision about how far to slide the pattern is based on the information shown in Figures 8.32(a) and (b).

From Figure 8.32(a), sliding the pattern four positions results in a possible match. Figure 8.32(b), once again, permits moving the pattern only one place. The four-place move leads to Figure 8.33.

This time the T's hit, and a miss occurs when L and A are compared. Note that the Boyer-Moore algorithm backs up. The decision about advancing the pattern is now based on the information shown in Figures 8.33(a) and (b).

From Figure 8.33(a) since the pattern does not contain an L, a slide of six positions is indicated. From Figure 8.33(b), since the pair [A] T might match _ T, a three-plane move is permitted. The pattern slides six positions.

From this example we can see that the essential features of the Boyer–Moore algorithm are as follows:

1. Character comparisons are made starting at the right end of the pattern and working toward the left. The important effect of this is that some text characters are never considered. In both the obvious and the KMP algorithms, each text character is checked at least once.
2. After a miss, the decision about how far to advance the pattern is based on two independent considerations:
   a. The value of the text character at which the miss occurs and the distance to the left at which that value first occurs in the pattern.
   b. The values of all text characters that have been hit together with the value that is known not to occur because of a miss. Note that this is the same information used by the KMP algorithm.
3. The pattern is moved the distance given by the larger of 2(a) and 2(b) above.

The Boyer–Moore algorithm preprocesses the pattern and constructs two tables. The first table records the distance from the right end of the pattern to the first occurrence of each letter of the alphabet for the application at hand. This table is particularly easy to construct and provides the distance needed in item 2(a). The second table contains one value for each character in the pattern. Several examples are shown in Figure 8.34.

A description of the Boyer–Moore algorithm, which is comparable to the previous descriptions of the obvious and KMP algorithms, is given in Algorithm 8.3.

```
Place pattern at text[pos];

WHILE pattern NOT matched AND text NOT exhausted DO

    WHILE pattern character differs from text character DO
        shift pattern as far to the right as possible;
        start search at the right end of pattern
    END;

    back up to the prior character of both text and pattern
END
```

Obtain this distance from two tables determined by preprocessing the pattern.

Algorithm 8.3   Boyer–Moore algorithm.

• Comparison of algorithms

We will now compare the performances of the three algorithms we just discussed.

Figure 8.35 plots the number of characters examined divided by the number of characters passed for each of the three algorithms. This figure is based on data in Smit (1982), which is considerably more detailed than our data here. The point is clear. Neither the obvious nor the KMP algorithm can do better than one character examined per character passed. The performance of these algorithms is approximately the same since it is rare, for the data considered, to find several hits before a miss. Most of the time is spent looking for the first hit.

The Boyer–Moore algorithm, because it starts on the right of the pattern, has the ability to pass many more characters than it examines. For the data considered in Smit (1982) and for sufficiently long patterns, this is clearly the case. Other implementation issues, such as using fast machine-level scan instructions, are discussed in Horsepool (1980). The conclusion is the same as indicated by Figure 8.35—the Boyer–Moore algorithm may be much faster if the pattern length is sufficiently large.

This section concludes with a module (Implementation Module 8.1) that uses an array representation to implement the string abstract data type.

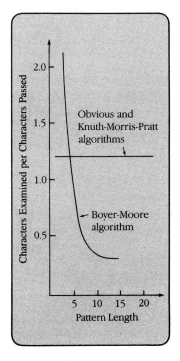

Figure 8.35
Characters examined per character passed for the three algorithms we discussed. (See Smit, 1982.)

Implementation Module 8.1 *Strings*

```
IMPLEMENTATION MODULE Strings;
(* Strings; array implementation; meets Specification 8.1. *)

FROM Storage IMPORT ALLOCATE, DEALLOCATE, Available;
FROM SYSTEM  IMPORT TSIZE;

TYPE String  = POINTER TO StrType;

     StrType = RECORD
                   strLen: StringLen;
                   data  : ARRAY StringPosn OF CHAR
               END;

PROCEDURE Length(S: String): StringLen;              (* Return the length of S. *)
BEGIN
    RETURN S↑.strLen
END Length;

PROCEDURE Concatenate(VAR S1: String; S2: String);   (* Concatenate S1 and      *)
VAR  k: StringLen;                                   (* S2 placing the result *)
BEGIN                                                (* in S1.                *)
    WITH S1↑ DO
       FOR k := 1 TO Length(S2) DO
          data[strLen+k] := S2↑.data[k]
       END;
       strLen := strLen + Length(S2)
    END
END Concatenate;

PROCEDURE Insert(VAR S1: String; S2: String; pos: StringPosn);   (* Insert S2 *)
VAR  len1, len2, k: StringLen;                       (* into S1 beginning at *)
BEGIN                                                (* position pos.        *)
    len1 := S1↑.strLen; len2 := S2↑.strLen;

    IF len2 > 0
       THEN WITH S1↑ DO
               FOR k := 0 TO len1-pos DO             (* Move characters in *)
                  data[len1+len2-k] := data[len1-k]  (* S1 out of the way. *)
               END;
               FOR k := 0 TO len2-1 DO               (* Insert characters *)
                  data[pos+k] := S2↑.data[k+1]       (* from S2.          *)
               END;
               strLen := strLen + Length(S2)
            END
    END
END Insert;
```

continued

Implementation Module 8.1, continued

```
PROCEDURE Delete(VAR S: String; pos: StringPosn; len: StringLen);
VAR  k, mov: StringLen;                          (* Delete a substring from S. *)
BEGIN
    WITH S↑ DO
        IF Length(S) >= (pos+len)                (* Any characters past the *)
            THEN mov := Length(S) - (pos+len);   (* end of the deleted sub- *)
                FOR k := 0 TO mov DO             (* string must be moved.   *)
                    data[pos+k] := data[pos+len+k]
                END
        END;
        strLen := strLen - len                   (* Adjust the length of S. *)
    END
END Delete;

PROCEDURE Append(VAR S: String; c: CHAR);                  (* Append c to S. *)
BEGIN
    WITH S↑ DO
        data[strLen+1] := c;
        strLen := strLen + 1
    END
END Append;

PROCEDURE SubString(S1: String; VAR S2: String; pos: StringPosn; len: StringLen);
VAR  k: StringLen;                               (* S2 is assigned a   *)
BEGIN                                            (* substring from S1. *)
    FOR k := 1 TO len DO
        S2↑.data[k] := S1↑.data[pos+k-1]
    END;
    S2↑.strLen := len
END SubString;

PROCEDURE Match(S1, S2: String; k: StringPosn): BOOLEAN;    (* Does S2 match *)
VAR  kpat, last: StringPosn;                               (* the substring *)
BEGIN                                            (* of S1 beginning at k ? *)
    kpat := 1; last := Length(S2);               (* If it does return true *)
    WHILE S2↑.data[kpat] = S1↑.data[k] DO        (* else return false.     *)
        IF kpat = last
            THEN RETURN TRUE
            ELSE INC(kpat); INC(k)
        END
    END;
    RETURN FALSE
END Match;

(*                                                                           *)
(*            Two different implementations of Find are supplied.            *)
(*                                                                           *)
```

continued

Implementation Module 8.1, continued

```
PROCEDURE Find(text, pat: String; pos: StringPosn): StringLen;       (* Find the *)
VAR kbegin, kend: StringPosn;                    (* first instance of pat in text starting *)
BEGIN                                            (* at pos. Return the position if found, *)
    IF Length(Pat) > Length(Text)                (* and 0 otherwise.                       *)
        THEN RETURN 0                            (* The obvious algorithm.                 *)
    END;
    kbegin := pos;
    kend := Length(Text)-Length(Pat)+1;
    WHILE kbegin <= kend DO
        IF Match(Text, Pat, kbegin)
            THEN RETURN kbegin
            ELSE kbegin := kbegin + 1
        END
    END;
    RETURN 0
END Find;

PROCEDURE Find(text, pat: String; pos: StringPosn): StringLen;       (* Find the *)
                                                 (* first instance of pat  *)
    PROCEDURE PreProcess(length: StringLen);     (* in text. Return its     *)
    VAR ch: CHAR;                                 (* position if found and *)
        k:  StringPosn;                           (* 0 otherwise.           *)
    BEGIN
        FOR ch := ' ' TO '}' DO
            D[ch] := length
        END;
        FOR k := 1 TO (length-1) DO              (* Simplified version of *)
            D[pat↑.data[k]] := length - k        (* Algorithm 8.3.         *)
        END;
    END PreProcess;

VAR D:  ARRAY [' '..'}'] OF StringPosn;
    patLen, textLen, kBegin: StringLen;

BEGIN
    IF Length(pat) > Length(text)
        THEN RETURN 0
    END;
    patLen := Length(pat); textLen := Length(text);
    PreProcess(patLen);
    kBegin := pos + patLen - 1;

    WHILE kBegin <= textLen DO
        IF Match(text, pat, kBegin-patLen+1)
            THEN RETURN (kBegin-patLen+1)
            ELSE kBegin := kBegin + D[text↑.data[kBegin]]
        END
    END;

    RETURN 0
END Find;
```

continued

Implementation Module 8.1, continued

```
PROCEDURE Create(VAR S: String): BOOLEAN;        (* If possible, create one *)
BEGIN                                            (* instance of a String.   *)
    IF Available(TSIZE(StrType))
        THEN NEW(S);
             S↑.strLen := 0;
             RETURN TRUE
        ELSE RETURN FALSE
    END
END Create;

PROCEDURE Terminate(VAR S: String);      (* Dispose of one instance of a String. *)
BEGIN
    DISPOSE(S)
END Terminate;

END Strings.
```

8.3.4 Linked Implementation of Strings

We will begin this section by discussing implementation issues for the *Concatenate* operation. They are conceptually simple, but we must choose between two possibilities. Suppose that we are to concatenate *S2* onto the end of *S1*, illustrated in Figure 8.36. Character positions available, but not used in the last *Chunk,* are indicated with an *. The operation is as follows:

```
Concatenate (VAR S1: String; S2: String);
```

If we simply append the chunks in *S2* to the chunks in *S1*, without considering the unused positions at the end of *S1*, the result is as shown in Figure 8.37. The *Concatenate* operation will be very efficient (if *ChunkSize* is large and we can copy chunks efficiently) and can operate as follows:

```
FOR each chunk in S2 DO
    create a new chunk;
    append the new chunk to the end of S1;
    copy the data in the S2 chunk to the S1 chunk
END
```

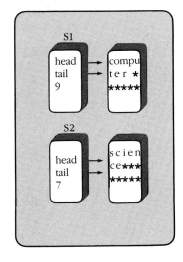

Figure 8.36
Example strings; *ChunkSize* = 15.

The problem with this approach is that we will be introducing unused positions into the middle of the string, which will do the following:

1. Complicate almost every other string operation
2. Waste memory

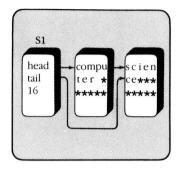

Figure 8.37
Concatenation without removing the gap at the end of *S*1.

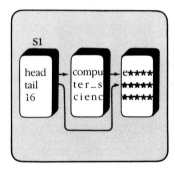

Figure 8.38
Concatenation with the gap at the end of *S*1 removed. The result is cleaner, but more effort may be required.

For these reasons we choose to remove any gaps that exist at the end of *S*1. Figure 8.38 illustrates this approach. The algorithm to accomplish this is as follows:

```
FOR each character IN S2 DO
    IF there is NOT room IN the last chunk of S1
        THEN append a new chunk to S1
    END;
    copy the character from S2 to S1
END
```

Since characters, instead of chunks, are being copied, this later approach requires an effort that is greater by a factor of *ChunkSize* (assuming that copying an entire chunk can be accomplished in one operation). We could check to see if the last chunk of *S*1 is full, and if so append chunks instead of individual characters. We do not consider this since the probability of this is low for reasonably sized chunks.

We can handle empty strings as special cases. Possible logic is as follows:

```
IF S2 is empty THEN there is nothing to do
    ELSIF S1 is empty THEN S1 is simply a copy of S2
    ELSE  append S2 character by character as above
END
```

If *L* is the expected size of a string and *ch* is the size of a *Chunk,* then the *Concatenate* operation requires moving $O(L)$ characters and creating $O(L/ch)$ chunks.

The operation *Delete* is very much like *Concatenate.* We start with one string, take a piece out of the middle creating two strings, and then append the second onto the end of the first. See Figure 8.39 for an example. The logic is as follows:

```
Find the beginning and end of the substring to be
deleted;
(* Let S1 be the substring that precedes the sub- *)
(* string to be deleted, and S2 the substring      *)
(* that follows it.                                 *)
Append S2 onto the end of S1;
Dispose of any chunks that are no longer in use
```

The effort required for *Find* depends on *ChunkSize.* The larger the chunk size the better. The ordinal number of the first character to be deleted is divided by the chunk size, yielding the relative position of its chunk, call it *Ichunk.* A pointer to *Ichunk* is set by scanning forward from the head of the list. The relative position of the chunk containing the end of the string, call it *Jchunk,* is calculated and is located by scanning forward from *Ichunk.* The effort to locate these two characters is therefore $O(L/ch)$. Appending the tail end onto the front end requires *O(L)* character moves. Finally, disposing of unused chunks requires disposing of *O(L/cb)* chunks.

The *Insert* operation uses the same basic machinery as both *Concatenate* and *Delete*. The insertion point in *S*1 divides it into two strings, say *S*1*a* and *S*1*b*. Insertion involves appending *S*2 onto *S*1*a* and then *S*1*b* onto that result. Locating the insertion point requires traversing *O(L/cb)* chunks. Appending the string to be inserted requires moving *O(L)* characters, and appending the tail end of the original string requires moving another *O(L)* characters. In addition we need to create *O(L/cb)* new chunks.

The *SubString* operation copies a piece out of the middle of one string and makes it the content of a target string. We must prepare by finding the beginning of the substring to be extracted. This is done in the same way as for *Delete* and requires *O(L/cb)* effort. Characters are transferred, one at a time, to the target string. This requires copying *O(L)* characters. If there are extra chunks because the target string existed before issuing the *SubString* command, they must be disposed of. If not, it may be necessary to create new chunks in order to accommodate the extracted substring. The worst that can happen is *O(L/cb)* operations to create or dispose of chunks.

Implementation of the *Find* operation is simple for the KMP algorithm in the sense that this algorithm does not back up. The obvious algorithm backs up but never further than the character matched with the beginning of the pattern. By maintaining a pointer for the chunk that contains this text character, backing up is logically simple and efficient.

The Boyer–Moore algorithm backs up every time there is a hit. To do this efficiently we would doubly link the list of chunks. The alternatives are either complex or inefficient. The easiest approach of all is the one taken here—no implementation is given. (We have, of course, suggested that *you* do it in an exercise.)

8.3.5 Comparison of Array and Linked Implementations

The array implementation of strings is the simplest and most widely used method to implement the data type *String*. Unfortunately, fixed length arrays may not make efficient use of memory and cause restrictions to be placed on, or incorrect results to result from, operations such as *Concatenate* and *Insert*.

Linked implementations make efficient use of memory in that only the minimum number of chunks required for a string is allocated. On the other hand, extra memory is required for pointers and for the unused portion of the last chunk. There is the potential for the *Concatenate* or *Insert* operation's failing because no memory is left for allocation of additional chunks.

A difficult question for the linked representation is the following: If the chunks are all the same size, what should that size be? If *ChunkSize* is small, then a high proportion of memory will be used for pointers, and operations requiring *O(L/cb)* effort will be inefficient. If chunks are large, then there may be many wasted spaces in the last chunk. (See margin note, page 381.)

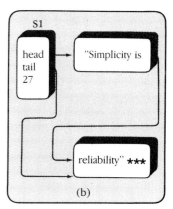

Figure 8.39
In (a), note that *ChunkSize* = 15. The operations

Delete(S1,15,44)
Delete(S1,28,length(S1) − 27)

result in (b).

Operation counts based on a linked implementation are summarized in Table 8.7.

TABLE 8.7 Operation counts based on linked implementation.

Operation	Searching	Character moves	Creating or deleting chunks
Concatenate	—	$O(L)$	$O(L/cb)$
Delete	$O(L/cb)$	$O(L)$	$O(L/cb)$
Insert	$O(L/cb)$	$O(L)$	$O(L/cb)$
SubString	$O(L/cb)$	$O(L)$	$O(L/cb)$

For a reasonably large chunk size the impediment to performance is clearly character-by-character transfer. To improve the performance of these operations, we need to move characters on a chunk-by-chunk basis rather than one character at a time. If the target processor permits us to make chunk-by-chunk moves efficiently, then we have to deal either with empty spaces in the middle of a string or with variable size chunks.

If we permit empty space in the middle of a string, then finding characters by position becomes $O(L)$. This can be reduced to $O(L/cb)$ by adding an integer to each chunk that records the number of real characters stored therein. Search overhead is increased and, of course, we have purchased performance in return for using more memory. An additional operation is desirable. It is a **garbage collection** operation that takes a string, removes the wasted character positions, and disposes of unneeded chunks. It will require a character-by-character transfer and thus will expend $O(L)$ effort.

Suppose that variable sized chunks are used to store the string. Each chunk contains an integer that records its size. Finding a character by position requires $O(L/cb)$ effort, and we have eliminated the problem of wasted character positions. The price we pay is the overhead for managing variable sized chunks.

Exercises 8.3

1. Give the specification of an abstract string. Use your own words to describe each of the operations.
2. Describe each of the following:

    string length

    substring

    empty string

3. Let three strings have the following values:

    $S1$ = 'hot'

    $S2$ = ' fudge'

    $S3$ = ' sundae'

    Find the value of each of the strings after each of the following operations.

The effect of the operations is cumulative.

> *Concatenate*(*S*1,*S*2);
> *Concatenate*(*S*1,*S*3);
> *Delete*(*S*1,1,4);
> *Insert*(*S*1,*S*2,6);
> *Concatenate*(*S*1,*S*1)
> *k* := *Find*(*S*1,*S*3,1);

4. What are the advantages and disadvantages of the two representation techniques for strings discussed in this chapter?
5. Implement a module for the array representation of strings using the obvious algorithm for the *Find* operation.
6. Determine the number of character comparisons required to find the pattern 'compare' in this sentence.
   a. Use the obvious algorithm.
   b. Use the Knuth–Morris–Pratt algorithm.
   c. Use the Boyer–Moore algorithm.
7. Write a Modula-2 procedure that uses operation *Find* to locate all occurrences of a pattern in a string of text. Put the positions at which the occurrences are found in a queue. Use the queue operations in Chapter 3.
8. Explain why the Knuth–Morris–Pratt algorithm does not back up, whereas the obvious and the Boyer–Moore algorithms do.
9. Both the Knuth–Morris–Pratt and the obvious algorithms normally examine approximately one character for each text character that they pass. Explain why.
10. Determine the values corresponding to those in Figure 8.30 for the patterns
    a. orange
    b. cancan
11. Repeat Exercise 10 for the values in Figure 8.35.
12. Implement the Boyer–Moore and obvious algorithms. Using a sample text of your choosing, construct a graph similar to that shown in Figure 8.35.
13. Implement a string package using a linked representation.
14. Survey several different implementations of Modula-2. Indicate at least three that include a module for data type *String*.
    a. Construct a table that shows which implementations support which operations.
    b. Compare the syntax used to call the string operations among the various implementations with that given in the text. Discuss advantages and disadvantages of the different approaches.
15. A palindrome is a character string that reads the same backwards as forwards: A man, a plan, a canal—Panama.
    a. Write the specification for a string operation that determines if a string is a palindrome.
    b. What representation (array or linked) would you recommend for implementing the "palindrome" operation?
    c. Implement this operation for the representation you recommend in part b.
16. A node in a computer network receives messages. Each message is of unknown length and arrives in packets. Each packet contains *lp* characters, a message identifier, a relative packet number, and an indication of whether that packet

is the last one in the message. Packets do not always arrive in the order they are sent.

a. Write the specifications for a module that is to receive the packets, assemble the packets in the proper order, and report whether the message is complete or not. (This module is only sent packets from a single message at any one time.)

b. What representation would you recommend for this application?

c. Discuss the performance of the operations in your module.

8.4 Summary

In this chapter we discussed characters and strings. We considered a variety of ways to represent characters: three based on using the same number of bits to represent each character, and one (Huffman codes) that used a variable number of bits to represent a character. Using a fixed number of bits to represent a character is simple and is probably the most frequently used technique. Using a variable number of bits to represent a character is more complex but has the advantage that less memory may be required to store a set of characters.

In Section 8.3 the *String* data type is discussed in some detail. Six common string operations are discussed: *Length, Concatenate, Delete, Insert, SubString,* and *Find.* Three different algorithms for operation *Find* are described and compared, and it is shown that the Boyer–Moore algorithm is the most effective.

Two techniques for implementing strings are considered. Implementation details for an array approach are discussed in Section 8.3.3 and for a linked approach in Section 8.3.4. These two approaches are compared in Section 8.3.5. The array approach is simple, but it may use memory inefficiently and it places restrictions on the operations that may increase the length of a string. The linked approach is more flexible, but it requires a more complex implementation and raises the question of how many characters to store in each chunk.

The usual rough indication of complexity, in this case for the array implementation of a string, is given in Table 8.8.

TABLE 8.8 Complexity of the array implementation of a string.

Implementation module	Data structure	Representation	Number of procedures	Total lines	Average lines	Maximum lines
8.1	String	Array	11	115	10.5	29

Graphs 9

9.1 Introduction

9.2 Terminology
Exercises 9.2

9.3 Graph Data Structure
9.3.1 Specification
9.3.2 Representation
9.3.3 Implementation
Exercises 9.3

9.4 Traversal
9.4.1 Graph Traversal Algorithms
9.4.2 Implementation
Exercises 9.4

9.5 Applications
9.5.1 Abstract Solutions
9.5.2 Implementation
Exercises 9.5

9.6 Directed Graphs
9.6.1 Transitive Closure
9.6.2 Topological Sorting
Exercises 9.6

9.7 Summary

9.1 Introduction

The structure of a graph is the most general structure considered in this text. A graph structure is a generalization of a hierarchical structure which, in turn, is a generalization of a linear structure.

Recall that the essence of a linear structure is that each of its components, with two exceptions, has a unique predecessor and a unique successor. The essence of a hierarchical structure is that each of its components, with a few exceptions, has a unique predecessor and a bounded number of successors. In a graph, each component may be related to any other component. We will see shortly how to restrict a graph so that it is a hierarchy.

As an example, consider 14 states in the United States as components of a graph. Let us say that we wish to divide the 14 states into three groups—large, medium, and small—by area, as shown in Figure 9.1. In Figure 9.2, the states are listed according to the three groups. Note that each state has a relationship to the largest state in its group. We can illustrate these relationships by artistically arranging the states on a page and then drawing an arc between each related pair of states. Note that no state is related to itself. The graph for our 14 states is shown in Figure 9.3.

A second example of a graph, which is used throughout this chapter, involves states that are related if they have a common boundary. Figure 9.4 shows 14 states related in this way.

Graph structures are important to us because they describe so many relationships of interest. It is easy to think of examples of graphs in which the components are chips on a printed circuit board, departments in a corporation, and switching stations in a power network. What other graphs can you describe?

In Section 9.2, which follows, we will introduce the basic terminology associated with graphs.

In Section 9.3 we will discuss the specification (Section 9.3.1), representation (Section 9.3.2), and implementation (Section 9.3.3) of a graph data struc-

Group	Area (square miles)
Large	25,000→
Medium	10,000 – 25,000
Small	0 – 10,000

Figure 9.1
The 14 states are divided by area into the three groups shown.

Group	State	Area (square miles)
Large	N.Y.	49,576
	Pa.	45,333
	Ohio	41,222
	Va.	40,817
	Maine	33,215
Medium	W. Va.	24,181
	Md.	10,577
Small	Vt.	9,609
	N.H.	9,304
	Mass.	8,257
	N.J.	7,836
	Conn.	5,009
	Del.	2,057
	R.I.	1,214

Figure 9.2
Each state is related to the largest state in its group.

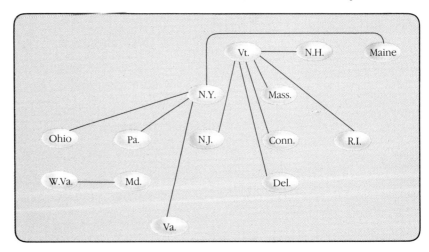

Figure 9.3 Example of a graph in which 14 states are related by area.

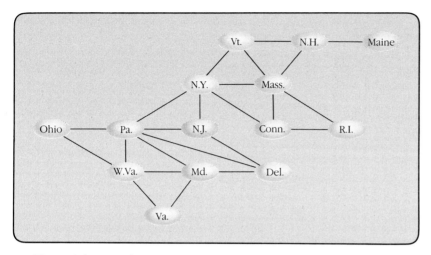

Figure 9.4 Example of a graph showing states related if they share a common boundary.

ture. This will serve as a jumping off point for discussing several basic operations and applications involving graphs. Section 9.4 discusses three variations of traversal—a basic graph operation. Traversal of a graph has several parallels with traversal of a tree. In particular, we will see that graph traversal relies on the same underlying data structures—stacks, queues, and priority queues.

In Section 9.5 we will apply our graph traversal knowledge to three problems, all of which are special cases of the problem of connectivity. The problems are as follows:

1. Given a graph, determine if two nodes are connected; or, more generally, determine which nodes form connected subgraphs.
2. Given a weighted graph, determine the shortest path between one node and each of the other nodes.
3. Given a connected graph, determine a minimum connected subgraph; i.e., a spanning tree. If the graph is weighted, do this so that the sum of the weights in the spanning tree is a minimum.

In Section 9.6, we will consider corresponding issues for a directed graph. Section 9.7 is a summary.

9.2 Terminology

A **graph** consists of nodes and edges. A **node** is a basic component, which usually contains some information. An **edge** connects two nodes. We will illustrate nodes by drawing an ellipse or circle around a node identifier. We will illustrate edges by using arcs or line segments. Figures 9.3 and 9.4 show examples in which the information in each node is the name of a state. We will use parts of those figures to illustrate the terminology we are introducing.

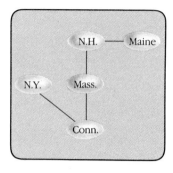

Figure 9.5
A subgraph of the graph in Figure 9.4. Also a simple path from Maine to N.Y.

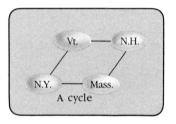

Figure 9.6
A cycle.

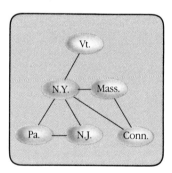

Figure 9.7
N.Y. and its neighbors.

A **subgraph** is a graph that contains a subset of a graph's nodes and edges (see Figure 9.5). A **path** is a sequence of nodes such that each successive pair is connected by an edge. A path is a **simple path** if each of its nodes occurs once in the sequence. A simple path from Maine to N.Y. in Figure 9.4, for example, is Maine, N.H., Mass., Conn., N.Y. (see Figure 9.5).

A graph is a **connected graph** if there is a path between every pair of its nodes. The graph in Figure 9.3 is not connected, whereas the graph in Figure 9.4 is.

A **cycle** is a path that is simple except that the first and last nodes are the same. In Figure 9.4 a cycle is N.H., Mass., N.Y., Vt., N.H. (see Figure 9.6).

Two nodes are **adjacent nodes** if there is an edge that connects them. The **neighbors of a node** are all nodes that are adjacent to it. Figure 9.7 shows N.Y. and its neighbors.

Let us note some of the differences between graphs and linear and hierarchical structures. A graph has no notion of either a first or root node. Given a node, there is no notion of a prior or parent node and no notion of a next or child node. There is no notion of last or leaf node. **The basic relationship in a graph is simply that any node can be related to any other node.**

A **tree** is the special case of a graph that

1. Is connected
2. Has no cycles

It turns out that if a connected graph has n nodes and $n - 1$ edges, it cannot have any cycles and is therefore a tree. Starting with any connected graph, we can remove edges (in order to eliminate cycles) until we get a tree. Such a tree is called a **spanning tree** for the original graph. Figure 9.8 shows a spanning tree for the graph of Figure 9.4.

An **oriented tree** is a tree in which one node has been designated the root node (see Section 5.2). Choosing any node as the root node in Figure 9.8 makes that graph an oriented tree.

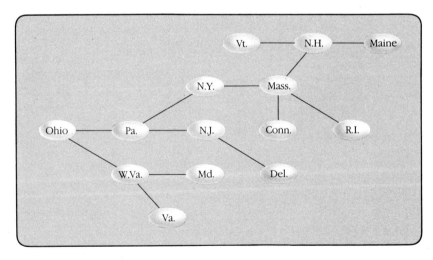

Figure 9.8
A spanning tree for the graph in Figure 9.4.

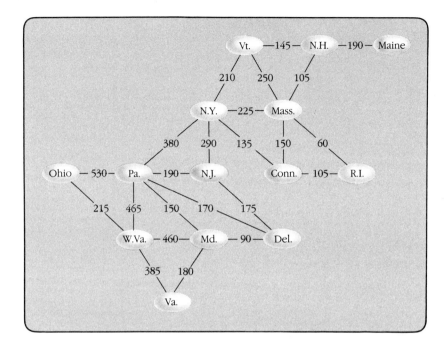

Figure 9.9
A weighted graph. The weight is the distance between capital cities of adjacent states.

A **directed graph** (or **digraph**) is a graph in which each edge has an associated direction. A **weighted graph** is a graph in which each edge has an associated value. Figure 9.9 shows the graph in Figure 9.4 weighted with the distances, in kilometers, between the capital cities of adjacent states. We now have all the terminology we will need for an introduction to graphs.

Exercises 9.2

1. Define each of the following terms in your own words:

graph	connected graph	spanning tree
path	cycle	directed graph
simple path	neighbor	weighted graph

2. How many distinct paths are there from Maine to Ohio in Figure 9.4?
3. Add the following states to Figure 9.4: Ky., Tenn., Miss., and Ga.
4. What is the minimum number of edges that need to be added to the graph in Figure 9.3 so that it will be connected?
5. In how many distinct ways can edges be removed from the graph in Figure 9.4 in order to create a spanning tree? Having created such a spanning tree, how many distinct oriented trees can be specified? Combining the two previous results, how many distinct oriented trees can be specified starting with the graph in Figure 9.4 and proceeding as outlined above?
6. What is the relationship between components in a graph? Give an example of entities and a relationship between them so that the result is a graph but not a tree.

9.3 Graph Data Structure

9.3.1 Specification

Specification 9.1 Graphs

DEFINITION MODULE Graphs;

(* **Elements:** A graph consists of nodes and edges. Although, in general each node may contain many elements, in Chapter 9 each node will contain exactly one element of type StdElement. Since an element is assumed to have a unique key, each node is uniquely identified by the key value of the element it contains. *)

    FROM StdTypes **IMPORT** KeyType, StdElement;

(* **Structure:** An edge is a one-to-one relationship between a pair of distinct nodes. A pair of nodes can be connected by at most one edge, but any node can be connected to any collection of other nodes. *)

(* **Domain:** The number of elements in a graph is bounded. *)

    EXPORT QUALIFIED Graph, InsertNode, InsertEdge, DeleteNode, DeleteEdge,
                         Update, Retrieve, Create, Terminate;

    TYPE Graph;

(* **Operations:** If G is a graph then reference to G-pre in a postcondition is a reference to the value of G just prior to the operation.

    Note that the traverse operations for a graph are discussed, and implementations given, later in this chapter. *)

PROCEDURE InsertNode(**VAR** G: Graph; e: StdElement): BOOLEAN;
(* **post** — If G-pre is not full and does not contain an element whose key value is e.key, then G contains e and InsertNode is true, else InsertNode is false. *)

PROCEDURE InsertEdge(**VAR** G: Graph; key1, key2: KeyType): BOOLEAN;
(* **post** — If key1 # key2, and G-pre is not full, contains nodes n1 and n2 with elements whose key values are key1 and key2, and does not contain an edge connecting those nodes, then G contains an edge connecting n1 and n2 and InsertEdge is true, else InsertEdge is false. *)

PROCEDURE DeleteNode(**VAR** G: Graph; key1: KeyType): BOOLEAN;
(* **post** — If G-pre contains node n1, whose element has key value key1, then G does not contain n1 or any of the edges that connected n1 to other nodes in G-pre, and DeleteNode is true, else DeleteNode is false. *)

continued

Specification 9.1, continued

PROCEDURE DeleteEdge(**VAR** G: Graph; key1,key2: KeyType): BOOLEAN;
(* **post** − If G-pre contains an edge connecting nodes whose elements have
         key values key1 and key2 then G does not contain that edge and
         DeleteEdge is true, else DeleteEdge is false. *)

PROCEDURE Update(**VAR** G: Graph; e: StdElement): BOOLEAN;
(* **post** − If G-pre contains element e-pre with key value e.key then G
         contains e, but not e-pre, and Update is true, else Update
         is false. *)

PROCEDURE Retrieve(G: Graph; key1: KeyType; **VAR** e: StdElement): BOOLEAN;
(* **post** − If G-pre contains element e-pre with key value key1, then e is
         e-pre and Retrieve is true, else Retrieve is false. *)

PROCEDURE Create(**VAR** G: Graph): BOOLEAN;
(* **post** − If a Graph can be created then G is an empty graph and Create
         is true, else Create is false. *)

PROCEDURE Terminate(**VAR** G: Graph);
(* **post** − Graph G does not exist. *)

END Graphs.

9.3.2 Representation

We will consider two basic approaches to representing graphs: adjacency matrixes and adjacency lists.

• Defining adjacency matrixes and lists

In an ***adjacency matrix*** we use a two-dimensional array whose component type is boolean and whose index values are, or at least correspond to, the nodes. Figure 9.11 shows an adjacency matrix representation for states. Two states are related if they have a common boundary. The graph for this example is a subgraph of the one shown in Figure 9.4.

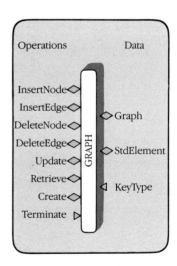

Figure 9.10
Capsulelike representation of operations for the graph data structure.

	N.Y.	Vt.	N.H.	Mass.	N.J.	Conn.
N.Y.	0	1	0	1	1	1
Vt.	1	0	1	1	0	0
N.H.	0	1	0	1	0	0
Mass.	1	1	1	0	0	1
N.J.	1	0	0	0	0	0
Conn.	1	0	0	1	0	0

Figure 9.11 Adjacency matrix representation. States are related if they have a common boundary.

Node list	Edge lists			
N.Y.	Vt.	Mass.	N.J.	Conn.
Vt.	N.Y.	N.H.	Mass.	
N.H.	Vt.	Mass.		
Mass.	N.Y.	Vt.	N.H.	Conn.
N.J.	N.Y.			
Conn.	N.Y.	Mass.		

Figure 9.12
Adjacency list representation. States are related if they have a common boundary.

In Figure 9.11, a "1" indicates a boolean value of true, and a "0" indicates a value of false. Actually, fewer than half the entries are needed, since each edge is recorded twice and the diagonal contains all zeros. Therefore, using a lower triangular matrix is possible, but it is not convenient in Modula-2. In a directed graph the full matrix, except for the diagonal, is needed.

An adjacency matrix representation makes sense if many components are related so that the matrix of boolean values is "dense." Otherwise, a large amount of memory is used to store the boolean value false.

For a weighted graph we can use a component type of cardinal, or integer, or real to record the weight that relates two components.

The second approach to representing graphs, ***adjacency lists,*** can be conceptually viewed as a list of lists. The basic list contains one entry for each node and will be called the ***node list.*** For each node in the node list there is a list, call it an ***edge list,*** of the neighbors of that node. The graph of Figure 9.11 is shown as an adjacency list in Figure 9.12.

• Representing adjacency matrixes in Modula-2

The ideas behind adjacency matrixes and adjacency lists are simple. Carrying them out in Modula-2 is a bit sticky. For an adjacency matrix we might proceed as illustrated by the following example.

For the graph in Figure 9.11, let us define a new atomic data type as

TYPE Nodes = [NY, Vt, NH, Mass, NJ, Conn];

and the graph as

VAR Graph = **ARRAY** Nodes, Nodes **OF** BOOLEAN;

The chief drawback to this approach is that it is impossible to insert or delete nodes. Storing descriptive information about a node is also difficult, as is traversing the set of nodes. An alternative approach, which is more in line with that used in previous chapters, is shown in Figure 9.13.

The array nodes are used to store information associated with each node. This approach permits nodes to be deleted and inserted (up to *GraphSize*), but it requires that elements be shifted around in array nodes in order to corre-

```
CONST MaxSize  = 20;          (* Or other value as needed. *)

TYPE GraphSize = [0..MaxSize];
     Index     = [1..MaxSize];
     Graph     = POINTER TO GraphType;
     GraphType = RECORD
                    nodes: ARRAY Index OF StdElement;
                    edges: ARRAY Index, Index OF BOOLEAN;
                    size : GraphSize
                 END;
```

Figure 9.13 Adjacency matrix representation of a graph.

spond to the index value in an array graph. If the graph contains many of its possible edges [computed by $(\frac{1}{2}) \times GraphSize \times (GraphSize - 1)$], this may be a good approach since it will be efficient in its use of memory, allow most operations to be implemented simply, and provide good performance.

• **Representing adjacency lists in Modula-2**

Let us now consider representing an adjacency list in Modula-2. The node list need not be a list—it could just as well be a tree or a hash table. For concreteness, we will choose a linked list that is singly linked, has both head and tail pointers, and has a sentinel.

Each graph node must contain the pointers needed to link it to its edge nodes. There are a variety of ways to do this.

One approach is for each edge in the graph to be represented by two edge nodes—one on each of the lists of the graph nodes it connects. This makes determining the neighbors of a node easy, although at the expense of storing twice as many edge nodes as necessary.

Another approach, which we will use, is to represent each edge in the graph by a single edge node. Adding an edge node to only one graph node list minimizes the pointer overhead, but it makes it difficult and expensive to determine the neighbors of a graph node. We will attach each edge node to two lists—one for each of the graph nodes it connects. An illustration of the approach we will implement, for the graph in Figure 9.12, is shown in Figure 9.14.

Each edge node contains two key values and thereby identifies the two nodes it connects. Each node is linked to two edge lists. In the first of these, the node's key value is the first of the pair of values in each edge node. In the second, the node's key value is the second of the pair of values. This approach, and variations of it, work well if the number of edges is small. Details of the representation shown in Figure 9.13 will be given in Section 9.3.3.

9.3.3 Implementation

We present implementations using both adjacency list (Implementation Module 9.1) and adjacency matrix (Implementation Module 9.2) approaches. The discussion here focuses on the adjacency list approach; the reader is encouraged to prepare a parallel discussion for the adjacency matrix approach.

In previous chapters we learned three basic structures for implementing node lists and edge lists—linear, hierarchical, and hashed. In particular, we will now consider linear lists, binary search trees, and hash tables.

Let n be the number of nodes in the graph and e be the number of edges. The maximum number of edges is $\frac{1}{2}n(n - 1)$. We shall assume that the expected number of edges associated with any node is e/n. If the number of edges approaches the maximum, then an adjacency list is not the best representation—an adjacency matrix is better. For the sake of discussion, we will assume that the number of edges is $e = O(n \log n)$ and that the expected number of edges per node is $e/n = O(\log n)$.

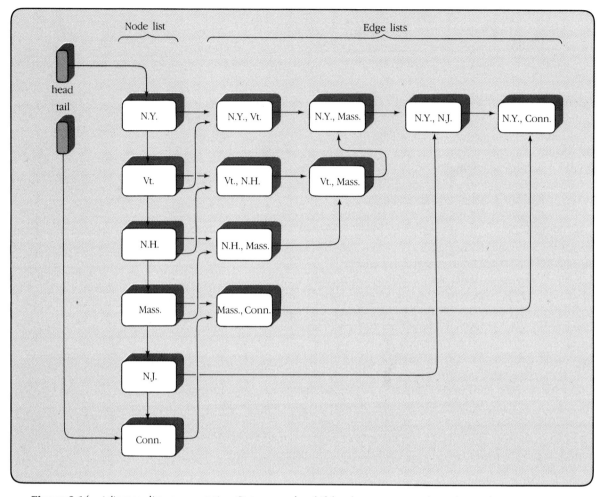

Figure 9.14 Adjacency list representation. States are related if they have a common boundary. Nil pointers are not shown.

We want to examine the effort required to perform the basic operations on a graph. The operations *InsertNode, InsertEdge, DeleteNode, DeleteEdge, Update,* and *Retrieve* are implemented using two operations that are not exported by Implementation Module 9.1. The first of those operations, *FindNode,* searches the graph for an element with a prescribed key value. The second operation, *FindEdge,* searches a given edge list for an edge node that connects a particular pair of graph nodes.

We will consider list, binary search tree, and hashed structures for storing the graph nodes. We will assume that the edge nodes are stored in a singly linked list (as illustrated in Figure 9.14) in every case.

Table 9.1 summarizes the effort required for the basic operations, depending on which technique is used to store the graph nodes. A discussion follows the table.

TABLE 9.1 Expected effort required for several graph operations as a function of the data structure used to implement the graph nodes. Assumes an adjacency list representation.

	n	$=$ number of nodes
	e	$=$ number of edges
	$\frac{1}{2}n(n-1)$	$=$ maximum number of edges in the graph
	e/n	$=$ expected number of edges per node
	Assume e	$= O(n \log n)$

	Data structure for the node list		
Graph operations	**Linked list**	**Binary search tree**	**Hash table**
FindNode	$O(n)$	$O(\log n)$	$O(1)$
FindEdge	$O(n)$	$O(\log n)$	$O(\log n)$
InsertNode	$O(n)$	$O(\log n)$	$O(1)$
InsertEdge	$O(n)$	$O(\log n)$	$O(\log n)$
DeleteNode	$O(n \log n)$	$O((\log n)^2)$	$O((\log n)^2)$
DeleteEdge	$O(n)$	$O(\log n)$	$O(\log n)$

The effort to insert a node is essentially that required to search for that node to make sure it is not already in the graph. The results for *InsertNode* and *FindNode* are the same.

Operation *InsertEdge* requires checking to make sure that the edge to be inserted is not already in the graph. If it is not in the graph, the new edge node is added as the first edge node on two edge lists. The effort required is essentially that of searching for an edge. Thus *FindEdge* and *InsertEdge* have the same values in Table 9.1.

To delete an edge node we begin by searching for the graph nodes it connects. We then search for the edge node in order to verify that it is in the graph and also to find its predecessor in the singly linked list of edge nodes. Deletion then requires resetting a few pointers and disposing of the edge node.

Deleting a node is rather complicated. The node must be found, and then all the edges that connect it to other nodes must be deleted. Finally, the graph node itself is deleted. Recall (Figure 9.14) that each graph node has two edge node lists. We assume there are $O(\log n)$ edge nodes to delete. Deleting one edge node requires searching for a graph node and then searching an edge list. The total effort is $O(\log n)$ times the effort to find a graph node plus the effort to search one edge list.

Figure 9.15 is a copy of Figure 9.14 except that the only pointers shown are those that would be changed if Vt. were deleted.

We can now write Implementation Modules 9.1 and 9.2 for a graph module. They give adjacency list and adjacency matrix representations for a graph.

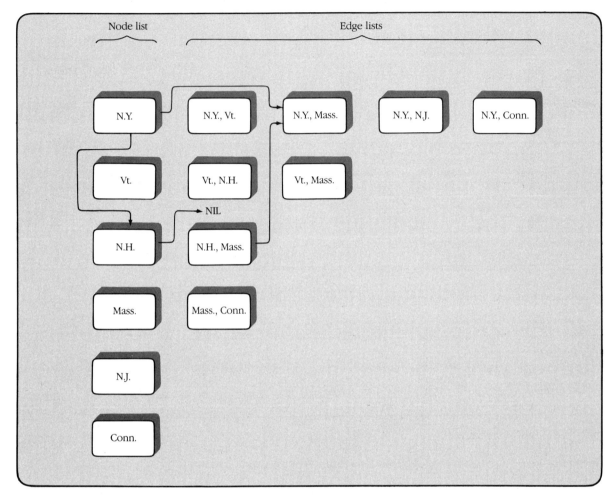

Figure 9.15   The pointers that would be changed if Vt. were deleted.

Implementation Module 9.1   *Graphs*

```
IMPLEMENTATION MODULE Graphs;
(* Graphs; adjacency list implementation; meets Specification 9.1. *)

   FROM StdTypes IMPORT KeyType, StdElement;
   FROM Storage  IMPORT ALLOCATE, DEALLOCATE, Available;
   FROM SYSTEM   IMPORT TSIZE;
```

continued

Implementation Module 9.1, continued

```
TYPE NodePtr   = POINTER TO GraphNode;
     EdgePtr   = POINTER TO EdgeNode;
     List      = [1..2];                             (* Edge list index. *)

     GraphNode = RECORD
                     elt      : StdElement;
                     nextGraph: NodePtr;                (* Next graph node. *)
                     edgeHead : ARRAY List OF EdgePtr;  (* Two edge lists. *)
                 END;

     EdgeNode  = RECORD                            (* The keys of the elements *)
                     key1,key2: KeyType;           (* connected by this edge. *)
                     nextEdge : ARRAY List OF EdgePtr  (* Two edge lists. *)
                 END;

     Graph     = POINTER TO GraphType;
     GraphType = RECORD
                     head, tail: NodePtr;        (* Implement Graph as a list. *)
                     sentinel  : NodePtr         (* For sequential searches. *)
                 END;

PROCEDURE InsertNode(VAR G: Graph; e: StdElement): BOOLEAN;    (* Insert a    *)
                                                               (* graph node. *)
   PROCEDURE CreateNode(VAR p: NodePtr);              (* Create a graph node. *)
   BEGIN
       NEW(p);
       WITH p↑ DO
          elt := e; nextGraph := NIL;
          edgeHead[1] := NIL; edgeHead[2] := NIL
       END
   END CreateNode;

VAR gp: NodePtr;
BEGIN
   IF Available(TSIZE(GraphNode)) & (FindNode(G,e.key) = NIL)    (* If a graph *)
       THEN CreateNode(gp);                       (* node can be created, and G   *)
            WITH G↑ DO                             (* does not contain e.key, then *)
               IF head = NIL                       (* create a new node and attach *)
               THEN head := gp                     (* it to the end of the list of *)
                  ELSE tail↑.nextGraph := gp       (* graph nodes.                 *)
               END;
               tail := gp;
               RETURN TRUE
            END
       ELSE RETURN FALSE                           (* Insufficient memory, or e.key *)
   END                                             (* is already in the list.       *)
END InsertNode;
```

continued

Implementation Module 9.1, continued

```
PROCEDURE Sort(VAR k1,k2: KeyType);              (* Put two key values in sorted order. *)
VAR t: KeyType;
BEGIN
    IF k1 > k2
        THEN t  := k1;                           (* Not exported by module Graphs. *)
             k1 := k2;
             k2 := t
    END
END Sort;

PROCEDURE InsertEdge(VAR G: Graph; k1, k2: KeyType): BOOLEAN;    (* Insert an   *)
VAR gp1, gp2: NodePtr;                                           (* edge node.  *)

    PROCEDURE AttachEdge();
    VAR ep: EdgePtr;
    BEGIN
        NEW(ep);                                          (* Create an edge node. *)
        WITH ep↑ DO
            key1 := k1; key2 := k2;                       (* Insert key values. *)
            nextEdge[1] := gp1↑.edgeHead[1];              (* Link to successor *)
            nextEdge[2] := gp2↑.edgeHead[2];              (* edge nodes.       *)
            gp1↑.edgeHead[1] := ep;                          (* Link to prior *)
            gp2↑.edgeHead[2] := ep;                          (* graph nodes.  *)
        END
    END AttachEdge;

VAR ep1,ep2,ep3,ep4: EdgePtr;
BEGIN
    IF k1 # k2
        THEN
            Sort(k1,k2);
            IF Available(TSIZE(EdgeNode))       (* If an edge node can be created,  *)
                THEN gp1 := FindNode(G, k1);    (* then search for the graph nodes. *)
                     gp2 := FindNode(G, k2);
                    IF (gp1 # NIL) & (gp2 # NIL)            (* If both nodes are found,   *)
                        THEN ep2 := gp1↑.edgeHead[1];       (* then search for the edge.  *)
                             ep4 := gp1↑.edgeHead[2];
                            IF (NOT FindEdge(1,k1,k2,ep1,ep2))         (* If the edge   *)
                             & (NOT FindEdge(2,k1,k2,ep3,ep4))         (* is not found *)
                                THEN AttachEdge();             (* then attach the edge. *)
                                     RETURN TRUE
                            END
                    END
            END
        END;
    RETURN FALSE                  (* Insufficient memory, or one of the nodes missing, *)
END InsertEdge;                   (* or the edge was already in the graph.             *)
```

continued

```
PROCEDURE DeleteNode(VAR G: Graph; tkey: KeyType): BOOLEAN;          (* Delete a    *)
VAR target1,target2,search: NodePtr;                                 (* graph node. *)
     ep,ep1,ep2    : EdgePtr;
BEGIN
    target1 := FindNode(G,tkey);
    IF target1 # NIL
        THEN WITH target1↑ DO
                WHILE edgeHead[1] # NIL DO              (* Delete the edge nodes *)
                    ep := edgeHead[1];                  (* on the first list.    *)
                    edgeHead[1] := edgeHead[1]↑.nextEdge[1];
                    target2 := FindNode(G,ep↑.key2);
                    ep2 := target2↑.edgeHead[2];
                    IF FindEdge(2,tkey,ep↑.key2,ep1,ep2)
                        THEN RemoveEdge(2,target2,ep1,ep2)
                    END;
                    DISPOSE(ep)
                END;
                WHILE edgeHead[2] # NIL DO              (* Delete the edge nodes *)
                    ep := edgeHead[2];                  (* on the second list.   *)
                    edgeHead[2] := edgeHead[2]↑.nextEdge[2];
                    target2 := FindNode(G,ep↑.key1);
                    ep2 := target2↑.edgeHead[1];
                    IF FindEdge(1,ep↑.key1,tkey,ep1,ep2)
                        THEN RemoveEdge(1,target2,ep1,ep2)
                    END;
                    DISPOSE(ep)
                END;
            END;
                                                         (* Delete the target node. *)
            IF G↑.head # target1          (* Is target at the head of the list? *)
                THEN search := G↑.head;                        (* No, find the *)
                    WHILE search↑.nextGraph # target1 DO       (* predecessor  *)
                        search := search↑.nextGraph            (* of target.   *)
                    END;
                    IF G↑.tail = target1               (* If target is at the    *)
                        THEN G↑.tail := search;        (* end of the list reset  *)
                            G↑.tail↑.nextGraph := NIL  (* two pointers.          *)
                    END;
                    search↑.nextGraph := target1↑.nextGraph;   (* Set nextGraph *)
                                                  (* so target is not in the list. *)
                ELSE G↑.head := target1↑.nextGraph;        (* Yes, delete the first *)
                    IF G↑.tail = target1                   (* node and adjust tail  *)
                        THEN G↑.tail := NIL                (* if necessary.         *)
                    END
            END;
            DISPOSE(target1);
            RETURN TRUE
        ELSE RETURN FALSE              (* The target node was not in the graph. *)
    END
END DeleteNode;                                                        continued
```

Implementation Module 9.1, continued

```
PROCEDURE FindEdge(k: List; tk1,tk2: KeyType; VAR ep1,ep2: EdgePtr): BOOLEAN;
BEGIN
    ep1 := NIL;                              (* Search the kth edge list,       *)
    WHILE (ep2 # NIL) & ((tk1 # ep2↑.key1)   (* pointed at by ep2, for an edge  *)
          OR (tk2 # ep2↑.key2)) DO           (* containing key values tk1 and   *)
        ep1 := ep2;                          (* tk2. If found, ep2 points at    *)
        ep2 := ep2↑.nextEdge[k]              (* the edge node and ep1 points    *)
    END;                                     (* at its predecessor, or is NIL   *)
    IF ep2 # NIL                             (* if ep2 points at the first      *)
        THEN RETURN TRUE                     (* node in the edge list.          *)
        ELSE RETURN FALSE
    END                                      (* Not exported by module Graphs. *)
END FindEdge;

PROCEDURE RemoveEdge(k: List; tn: NodePtr; ep1,ep2: EdgePtr);       (* Remove the *)
BEGIN                                             (* edge node pointed at by *)
    IF ep1 # NIL                                  (* ep2 from the kth edge    *)
        THEN ep1↑.nextEdge[k] := ep2↑.nextEdge[k] (* list of graph node tn↑. *)
        ELSE tn↑.edgeHead[k]   := ep2↑.nextEdge[k] (* ep1 points to the pre-  *)
    END                                           (* decessor of ep2↑.       *)
END RemoveEdge;                               (* Not exported by module Graphs. *)
```

continued

Implementation Module 9.1, continued

```
PROCEDURE DeleteEdge(VAR G: Graph; tk1,tk2: KeyType): BOOLEAN;      (* Delete an   *)
VAR tn1,tn2        : NodePtr;                                       (* edge node. *)
    ep1,ep2,ep3,ep4: EdgePtr;
BEGIN
    Sort(tk1,tk2);
    tn1 := FindNode(G,tk1);                               (* Search for the nodes that  *)
    tn2 := FindNode(G,tk2);                               (* connect the edge to delete. *)
    IF (tn1 # NIL) & (tn2 # NIL)                       (* If they are both in the graph, *)
        THEN ep2 := tn1↑.edgeHead[1];                 (* then search for the edge.      *)
             ep4 := tn1↑.edgeHead[2];
          IF FindEdge(1,tk1,tk2,ep1,ep2)                 (* If the edge is on the    *)
              THEN RemoveEdge(1,tn1,ep1,ep2);            (* first edge list remove   *)
                   ep2 := tn2↑.edgeHead[2];              (* it, get the other graph  *)
                   IF FindEdge(2,tk1,tk2,ep1,ep2)        (* node, find the edge       *)
                       THEN RemoveEdge(2,tn2,ep1,ep2);   (* node on its second        *)
                            DISPOSE(ep2);                (* edge list, and            *)
                            RETURN TRUE                  (* remove it.                *)
                   END
          ELSIF FindEdge(2,tk1,tk2,ep3,ep4)             (* If the edge is on the    *)
              THEN RemoveEdge(2,tn1,ep3,ep4);            (* second edge list ...     *)
                   ep4 := tn2↑.edgeHead[1];
                   IF FindEdge(1,tk1,tk2,ep3,ep4)
                       THEN RemoveEdge(1,tn2,ep3,ep4);
                            DISPOSE(ep4);
                            RETURN TRUE
                   END
          END
    END;
    RETURN FALSE             (* The graph did not contain the edge to be deleted. *)
END DeleteEdge;

PROCEDURE Retrieve(G: Graph; tkey: KeyType; VAR e: StdElement): BOOLEAN;
VAR target: NodePtr;
BEGIN
    target := FindNode(G,tkey);                               (* Search for tkey.  *)
    IF target # NIL                                  (* If tkey is found, assign the *)
        THEN e := target↑.elt;                       (* corresponding element to e.  *)
             RETURN TRUE
        ELSE RETURN FALSE                            (* Key value tkey was not found. *)
    END
END Retrieve;
```

continued

Implementation Module 9.1, continued

```
PROCEDURE Update(VAR G: Graph; e: StdElement): BOOLEAN;                (* Update. *)
VAR target: NodePtr;
BEGIN
    target := FindNode(G, e.key);                  (* Search for the key value of e. *)
    IF target # NIL                                    (* If found, replace the cor- *)
        THEN target↑.elt := e;                         (* responding element with e.  *)
            RETURN TRUE
        ELSE RETURN FALSE                      (* Key value e.key was not found. *)
    END
END Update;

PROCEDURE FindNode(VAR G: Graph; tkey: KeyType): NodePtr;          (* Find a      *)
VAR gp: NodePtr;                                                   (* graph node. *)
BEGIN
    WITH G↑ DO
        IF head # NIL
            THEN sentinel↑.elt.key := tkey;            (* Attach a sentinel node. *)
                tail↑.nextGraph := sentinel;
                gp := head;
                WHILE tkey # gp↑.elt.key DO            (* Sequential search of      *)
                    gp := gp↑.nextGraph               (* the list of graph nodes.  *)
                END;
                tail↑.nextGraph := NIL;
                IF gp # sentinel
                    THEN RETURN gp                         (* Search successful. *)
                END
        END;
        RETURN NIL                          (* Either the graph is empty or the *)
    END                                     (* search was not successful.        *)
END FindNode;

PROCEDURE Create(VAR G: Graph): BOOLEAN;                           (* Create a graph. *)
BEGIN
    IF Available(TSIZE(GraphType))
        THEN NEW(G);
            WITH G↑ DO
                head := NIL; tail := NIL;
                IF Available(TSIZE(GraphNode))
                    THEN NEW(sentinel);
                        RETURN TRUE
                END
            END
    END;
    RETURN FALSE
END Create;
```

continued

Implementation Module 9.1, continued

```
PROCEDURE Terminate(VAR G: Graph);                    (* Terminate a graph. *)
VAR bl: BOOLEAN;
BEGIN
    WHILE G↑.head # NIL DO
        bl := DeleteNode(G,G↑.head↑.elt.key)
    END
END Terminate;

END Graphs.
```

Implementation Module 9.2   *Graphs*

```
IMPLEMENTATION MODULE Graphs;
(* Graphs; adjacency matrix representation; meets Specification 9.1. *)

    FROM StdTypes IMPORT KeyType, StdElement;
    FROM Storage  IMPORT ALLOCATE, DEALLOCATE, Available;
    FROM SYSTEM   IMPORT TSIZE;

    CONST MaxSize  = 20;

    TYPE GraphSize = [0..MaxSize];
         Index     = [1..MaxSize];
         Graph     = POINTER TO GraphType;
         GraphType = RECORD
                        nodes: ARRAY Index OF StdElement;
                        edges: ARRAY Index,Index OF BOOLEAN;
                        size : GraphSize
                     END;

PROCEDURE InsertNode(VAR G: Graph; e: StdElement): BOOLEAN;    (* Insert a node. *)
VAR loc: GraphSize;
BEGIN
    WITH G↑ DO
        loc := FindNode(G,e.key);                         (* Search for e.key. *)
        IF (loc = 0) & (size < MaxSize)                (* If e.key is not found,    *)
            THEN INC(size);                            (* and the graph is not full,*)
                 nodes[size] := e;                     (* then add e to the graph.  *)
                 RETURN TRUE
            ELSE RETURN FALSE                          (* The graph was full, or it *)
        END                                            (* already contained e.key.  *)
    END
END InsertNode;
```

continued

Implementation Module 9.2, continued

```
PROCEDURE InsertEdge(VAR G: Graph; key1,key2: KeyType): BOOLEAN;     (* Insert    *)
VAR loc1,loc2: GraphSize;                                            (* an edge. *)
BEGIN
    loc1 := FindNode(G,key1);  loc2 := FindNode(G,key2);     (* Search for the    *)
    IF loc1 > loc2 THEN Swap(loc1,loc2) END;                 (* nodes to connect. *)
    IF (loc1 > 0)                                     (* If they are both found,  *)
        THEN IF G↑.edges[loc1,loc2] # TRUE            (* and they are not connected, *)
                THEN G↑.edges[loc1,loc2] := TRUE;     (* then connect them.        *)
                    RETURN TRUE
            END
    END;
    RETURN FALSE                              (* The graph already contained that edge. *)
END InsertEdge;

PROCEDURE DeleteNode(VAR G: Graph; key: KeyType): BOOLEAN;     (* Delete a node. *)
VAR loc,k1,k2: GraphSize;
BEGIN
    WITH G↑ DO
        loc := FindNode(G,key);                   (* Search for the node to delete. *)
        IF loc > 0                                     (* If it is found, move      *)
            THEN FOR k1 := 1 TO loc-1 DO               (* some edge indicators      *)
                    FOR k2 := loc TO size-1 DO         (* one position to the       *)
                        edges[k1,k2] := edges[k1,k2+1] (* left.                     *)
                    END
                END;
                FOR k1 := loc TO size-1 DO             (* And move some edge        *)
                    nodes[k1] := nodes[k1+1];          (* indicators one            *)
                    FOR k2 := loc TO size-1 DO         (* position to the left      *)
                        edges[k1,k2] := edges[k1+1,k2+1] (* and one position up.    *)
                    END
                END;
                DEC(size);                             (* Decrement graph size.     *)
                RETURN TRUE
            ELSE RETURN FALSE                          (* The graph did not contain *)
        END                                            (* the edge to be deleted.   *)
    END
END DeleteNode;
```

continued

Implementation Module 9.2, continued

```
PROCEDURE DeleteEdge(VAR G: Graph; key1,key2: KeyType): BOOLEAN;      (* Delete   *)
VAR loc1,loc2: GraphSize;                                            (* an edge. *)
BEGIN
    loc1 := FindNode(G,key1);  loc2 := FindNode(G,key2);       (* Find the nodes    *)
    IF loc1 > loc2 THEN Swap(loc1,loc2) END;                  (* connected by the  *)
    IF (loc1 > 0)                                             (* target edge.      *)
        THEN IF G↑.edges[loc1,loc2]                  (* If the edge already    *)
                THEN G↑.edges[loc1,loc2] := FALSE;   (* exists, then delete it. *)
                    RETURN TRUE
             END
    END;
    RETURN FALSE                              (* The graph did not contain *)
END DeleteEdge;                               (* the edge to be deleted.   *)

PROCEDURE Update(VAR G: Graph; e: StdElement): BOOLEAN;           (* Update an *)
VAR loc: GraphSize;                                              (* element.  *)
BEGIN
    loc := FindNode(G,e.key);             (* Search for the element to update. *)
    IF loc > 0                                          (* If found,  *)
        THEN G↑.nodes[loc] := e;                        (* update it. *)
            RETURN TRUE
        ELSE RETURN FALSE                   (* The graph does not contain         *)
    END                                     (* an element with key value e.key.   *)
END Update;

PROCEDURE Retrieve(G: Graph; tkey: KeyType; VAR e: StdElement): BOOLEAN;
VAR loc: GraphSize;                                   (* Retrieve an element. *)
BEGIN
    loc := FindNode(G,tkey);              (* Search for the element to retrieve. *)
    IF loc > 0                                          (* If found,   *)
        THEN e := G↑.nodes[loc];                        (* retrieve it. *)
            RETURN TRUE
        ELSE RETURN FALSE                   (* The graph does not contain         *)
    END                                     (* an element with key value tkey.    *)
END Retrieve;
```

continued

Implementation Module 9.2, continued

```
PROCEDURE Create (VAR G: Graph): BOOLEAN;                    (* Create a graph. *)
VAR k1,k2: Index;
BEGIN
    IF Available(TSIZE(GraphType))              (* If there is sufficient memory, *)
        THEN NEW(G);                            (* then create a graph and        *)
            WITH G↑ DO                          (* initialize its parameters.     *)
                size := 0;
                FOR k1 := 1 TO MaxSize DO
                    FOR k2 := 1 TO MaxSize DO
                        edges[k1,k2] := FALSE
                    END
                END;
                RETURN TRUE
            END
        ELSE RETURN FALSE               (* Not enough memory to create a graph. *)
    END
END Create;

PROCEDURE Terminate (VAR G: Graph);                      (* Terminate a graph. *)
BEGIN
    DISPOSE(G)
END Terminate;

PROCEDURE FindNode(VAR G: Graph; tkey: KeyType): GraphSize;      (* Find a node. *)
VAR k: Index;
BEGIN                   (* This procedure is not exported by module Graphs. *)
    WITH G↑ DO
        k := 1;
        WHILE k <= size DO                  (* Search for a node containing an  *)
            IF tkey = nodes[k].key          (* element whose key value is tkey. *)
                THEN RETURN k               (* If found return its position.    *)
            END;
            INC(k)
        END;
        RETURN 0                            (* The graph does not contain       *)
    END                                     (* an element with key value tkey.  *)
END FindNode;

PROCEDURE Swap(VAR g1,g2: GraphSize);                    (* Swap two values. *)
VAR t: GraphSize;
BEGIN                   (* This procedure is not exported by module Graphs. *)
    t  := g1;
    g1 := g2;
    g2 := t
END Swap;

END Graphs.
```

Exercises 9.3

1. Write specifications for the following operations on a graph:
   a. You are given two key values. Determine if the nodes that contain them are connected.
   b. You are given two key values. If they are connected, return a simple path between them.
   c. You are given two key values. If they are connected, return the shortest simple path between them.
   d. Return the key values of all nodes that are connected to the current node.
2. **a.** Describe the results returned by the four operations in Exercise 1 if the graph is connected and linear.
   b. Describe the results returned by the four operations in Exercise 1 if the graph is connected and a tree.
3. Describe the adjacency matrix representation of a graph. What are its advantages and disadvantages?
4. Describe the adjacency list representation of a graph. What are its advantages and disadvantages?
5. Extend Table 9.1 to include operations *Create* and *Retrieve*.
6. Replace Table 9.1 by the table that results if we remove the restriction that the expected value of e is $n \log n$. Continue to assume that the expected number of edges per node is e/n.
7. How would Table 9.1 be changed if the second edge list for each node were doubly linked?
8. Complete Table 9.1 for the adjacency matrix implementation of a graph.
9. **a.** Implement a graph package for an adjacency list representation that uses a binary search tree to store the nodes.
   b. Implement a graph package for an adjacency list representation that uses a hash table to store the nodes.

9.4 Traversal

An important graph operation, ***traversal,*** is actually a generalization of the traversal of lists and binary trees discussed in Section 5.3.2. The idea is simple. We want to process each node in a graph exactly once. For trees, this permitted us to conduct associative searches and to answer questions about global tree characteristics. These same questions can be answered for graphs. In addition, there is a class of graph traversals that permits us to answer connectivity questions such as the following: Are two nodes connected? What is the shortest path between them?

9.4.1 Graph Traversal Algorithms

The two basic graph traversal algorithms are breadth first search and depth first search. We will discuss these first and will then show that they are special cases of priority first search.

To help describe our algorithms, we will introduce the notion of ***status.*** Each node is assigned a status of ***waiting, ready,*** or ***processed.*** This is

status = (Waiting,Ready,
                    Processed)

Figure 9.16
Each graph node contains a status field.

implemented as the enumerated data type shown in Figure 9.16. To start a traversal, each node is assigned a status of waiting by procedure *SetWaiting.*

• Breadth first search

Breadth first search requires a queue as an auxiliary data structure; we will call it the ***ready queue.*** The search is described by Algorithm 9.1.

```
PROCEDURE BreadthFirstSearch();

    PROCEDURE Visit(n: Node);
    BEGIN
        Add n to the ready queue;
        WHILE the ready queue is not empty DO
            Get a node from the queue, process it, add any
            of its neighbors with status waiting to the
            ready queue, and change their status to ready.
        END
    END Visit;

BEGIN
    SetWaiting();              (* Set the status of   *)
                              (* each node to waiting. *)
    FOR each node, say n, in the graph DO
        IF the status of n is Waiting
            THEN Visit(n)
        END
    END
END BreadthFirstSearch;
```

Algorithm 9.1

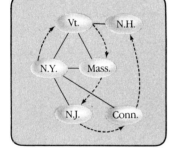

Figure 9.17
Order in which nodes are processed during a breadth first search of the graph shown in Figure 9.12.

The effect of breadth first search is that one node is processed first, followed by all of its neighbors, followed by the neighbors of all its neighbors, and so on. Figure 9.17 shows the order in which nodes are processed during a breadth first traversal of the graph in Figure 9.12. Note that the order in which the edges appear on the edge lists affects the traversal order. The order of breadth first search depends not only on the graph being traversed but also on how the graph is represented.

• Depth first search

Depth first search can be described in a manner analogous to breadth first search. The main difference is the use of a stack instead of a queue. We will refer to the stack as the ***ready stack.*** Compare Algorithm 9.2 with Algorithm 9.1.

```
PROCEDURE DepthFirstSearch;

    PROCEDURE Visit(n: Node);
    BEGIN
        Add n to the ready stack;
        WHILE the ready stack is not empty DO
            Get a node from the ready stack, process it,
            and add any neighbor that has not been
            processed to the ready stack. If a node appears
            twice in the stack, then only the most recently
            arrived entry is retained. (In order to produce
            the same results as Algorithm 9.5, a recursive
            implementation of depth first search, nodes must
            be added to the ready stack in the inverse of
            the order in which they appear in the adjacency
            list representation.)
        END
    END Visit;

BEGIN
    SetWaiting();              (* Set the status of      *)
                               (* each node to waiting.  *)
    FOR each node, say n, in the graph DO
        IF the status of n is Waiting
            THEN Visit(n)
        END
    END
END DepthFirstSearch;
```

Algorithm 9.2

It is noteworthy that procedure *Visit* of Algorithm 9.2 could be described using recursion in the following simple way:

```
PROCEDURE Visit(n: Node);
BEGIN
    Process node n;
    Recursively Visit all neighbors of n
END Visit;
```

In a depth first search, after one node is processed, one of its neighbors is processed, and the rest are placed on the ready stack. If the node just processed has any neighbors, one of them is processed next. Figure 9.18 shows the order in which nodes are processed during a depth first search of the graph shown in Figure 9.12. In a breadth first search, after one node is processed, all of its neighbors are processed before any other node.

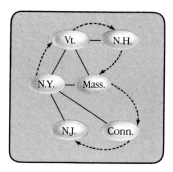

Figure 9.18
Order in which nodes are processed during a depth first search of the graph shown in Figure 9.12.

• **Priority first search**

Finally, we will consider a ***priority first search.*** For this search we use a ***priority queue*** instead of a stack or an ordinary queue. A priority first search is described in Algorithm 9.3. Compare it to Algorithms 9.1 and 9.2.

```
PROCEDURE PriorityFirstSearch;

    PROCEDURE Visit(n: Node);
    BEGIN
        Add n to the priority queue;
        WHILE the priority queue is not empty DO
            Get a node from the priority queue, process it,
            add any of its neighbors with status waiting to
            the priority queue, and change their status to
            ready. Any neighbors that are ready are
            assigned a new priority, and if the new
            priority is higher than the old, then the node
            receives the higher priority.
        END
    END Visit;

BEGIN
    SetWaiting();                   (* Set the status of    *)
                                    (* each node to waiting. *)
    FOR each node, say n, in the graph DO
        IF the status of n is Waiting
            THEN Visit(n)
        END
    END
END PriorityFirstSearch;
```

Algorithm 9.3

If the priority of each node added to the queue is less than the priority of the last node added, then ***the priority queue functions like an ordinary queue, and a priority first search is the same as a breadth first search.*** If the priority of each node added to the queue is greater than the priority of the last node added, then ***the priority queue functions like a stack, and a priority first search is the same as a depth first search.*** We will see other applications of priority first search in Section 9.5. In the meantime, we turn to the Modula-2 implementation of these search operations.

9.4.2 Implementation

To implement the searches we have been discussing, we will add a status field to a graph node as described in Implementation Module 9.1. The ***status field*** records whether a node is waiting, ready, or processed. The graph node that

```
NodePtr    = POINTER TO GraphNode;
EdgePtr    = POINTER TO EdgeNode;
List       = [1..2];

GraphNode = RECORD
                elt        : StdElement;
                nextGraph: NodePtr;
                edgeHead: ARRAY List OF EdgePtr;
                status     : (Waiting, Ready, Processed)
            END;
```

Figure 9.19 Graph node used to implement breadth first
and depth first searches.

```
EdgeNode = RECORD
                key1,key2   : KeyType;
                nextEdge    : ARRAY List OF EdgePtr;
                node1,node2: NodePtr;
            END;
```

Figure 9.20 Edge node used to implement breadth first
and depth first searches.

results is shown in Figure 9.19. (Note that the nodes of the graph are referred
to as ***graph nodes*** to distinguish them from the edge nodes that we use to
record information about edges.)

We will also add two pointers to each edge node. These pointers give us
direct access to the nodes connected by that edge. This allows us to determine
the status of these nodes without having to search for them. The resulting edge
node is shown in Figure 9.20.

Both depth first and breadth first procedures probe each graph node at
least once and each edge node twice. The effort is thus $O(e + n)$. The effort
required for a priority first search is bounded by $O((e + n)\log n)$, assuming a
heap is used for the priority queue. Algorithm 9.4 for breadth first search and
Algorithm 9.5 for depth first search follow on pages 426 and 427.

The breadth first search procedure imports a queue module with the
statement

IMPORT PtrQues

instead of the statement

FROM PtrQues **IMPORT** Queue, Enqueue, Serve, Empty, Full,
                        Create, Terminate;

that is frequently used in modules in this text. There are two differences to
note. First, the statement

IMPORT PtrQues

imports all objects exported by *PtrQues,* not just the ones explicitly named.
Second, reference to an object imported from *PtrQues* must be of the form
PtrQues.xxx, where *xxx* is the referenced object. To call procedure *Enqueue,*
for example, the syntax is *PtrQues.Enqueue(Q,p)*. Further examples are contained in Algorithm 9.4.

Module *PtrQues* exports exactly the objects described in Specification 3.3.
The difference is that the elements stored in a queue from module *PtrQues* are
of type ADDRESS. Thus, any Modula-2 object of type POINTER may be stored
in a queue from *PtrQues*.

```
PROCEDURE BreadthFirstSearch(G: Graph; proc: ProcNode);

VAR Q: PtrQues.Queue;

    PROCEDURE Visit(p: NodePtr);                          (* Visit a graph node. *)
    VAR ep: EdgePtr;
    BEGIN
        PtrQues.Enqueue(Q,p);
        WHILE NOT PtrQues.Empty(Q) DO
            PtrQues.Serve(Q,p);
            proc(p↑.elt);
            p↑.status := Processed;

            ep := p↑.edgeHead[1];
            WHILE ep # NIL DO                              (* Consider all neighbors. *)
                IF ep↑.node2↑.status = Waiting            (* Enqueue each neighbor *)
                    THEN PtrQues.Enqueue(Q,ep↑.node2);    (* with status waiting.  *)
                        ep↑.node2↑.status := Ready
                END;
                ep := ep↑.nextEdge[1]
            END;
            ep := p↑.edgeHead[2];
            WHILE ep # NIL DO                              (* Repeat the process for *)
                IF ep↑.node1↑.status = Waiting            (* the second edge list.  *)
                    THEN PtrQues.Enqueue(Q,ep↑.node1);
                        ep↑.node1↑.status := Ready
                END;
                ep := ep↑.nextEdge[2]
            END
        END
    END Visit;

VAR gp: NodePtr;

BEGIN
    IF PtrQues.Create(Q)
        THEN SetWaiting(G);                               (* Set the status of each node to waiting. *)
            WITH G↑ DO
                gp := head;
                WHILE gp # NIL DO                         (* Traverse the graph nodes *)
                    IF gp↑.status = Waiting               (* and Visit each one that  *)
                        THEN Visit(gp)                    (* that has not already     *)
                        ELSE gp := gp↑.nextGraph          (* been visited.            *)
                    END
                END
            END
        ELSE WriteString('Could not create a queue')
    END
END BreadthFirstSearch;
```

Algorithm 9.4   Breadth first search.

```
PROCEDURE DepthFirstSearch(G: Graph; proc: ProcNode);

    PROCEDURE Visit(p: NodePtr);                        (* Visit a graph node. *)
    VAR ep: EdgePtr;
    BEGIN
        proc(p↑.elt);                                   (* Process the node. *)
        p↑.status := Processed;
        ep := p↑.edgeHead[1];
        WHILE ep # NIL DO                        (* Recursively consider all neighbors. *)
            IF ep↑.node2↑.status = Waiting       (* Visit each neighbor with status *)
                THEN Visit(ep↑.node2)            (* waiting. Since there are two   *)
            END;                                 (* edge lists this requires two   *)
            ep := ep↑.nextEdge[1]                (* essentially identical loops.   *)
        END;
        ep := p↑.edgeHead[2];
        WHILE ep # NIL DO
            IF ep↑.node1↑.status = Waiting
                THEN Visit(ep↑.node1)
            END;
            ep := ep↑.nextEdge[2]
        END;
    END Visit;

VAR gp: NodePtr;

BEGIN
    SetWaiting(G);                       (* Set the status of each node to waiting. *)
    WITH G↑ DO
    gp := head;
        WHILE gp # NIL DO                        (* Traverse the graph nodes *)
            IF gp↑.status = Waiting              (* and Visit each one that   *)
                THEN Visit(gp)                   (* has not already           *)
                ELSE gp := gp↑.nextGraph         (* been visited.             *)
            END
        END
    END
END DepthFirstSearch;
```

Algorithm 9.5 Depth first search.

Exercises 9.4

1. In Algorithm 9.1 every node in the graph is processed, even if the graph is not connected. Simplify Algorithm 9.1 so that only a specified node and nodes connected to it are processed.
2. Change Algorithm 9.2 to a recursive description of depth first search.

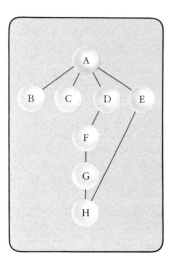

Figure 9.21

3. Consider the graph shown in Figure 9.21.
   a. Show five possible orders in which the nodes might be processed during a breadth first search.
   b. Show five possible orders in which the nodes might be processed during a depth first search.
4. Consider a graph in which the relationships among the nodes is linear. Describe the order in which the nodes will be processed during (a) breadth first and (b) depth first searches that start at one of the nodes with only one neighbor. **What** happens if the search starts at one of the nodes with two neighbors?
5. Consider a graph that is actually an oriented tree. Describe the order in which nodes will be processed during (a) breadth first and (b) depth first searches beginning at the root node.
6. Consider a graph that is actually a binary tree. Describe how to modify a depth first search so that it will process nodes in the same order as a preorder traversal.
7. Write a program that creates a graph containing n nodes with node identifiers $1, 2, \ldots, n$. Use a random number generator to add k edges to the graph. Plot a graph that shows the time required for (a) breadth first and (b) depth first searches of the tree as a function of k and n.
8. Implement (a) breadth first and (b) depth first traversal procedures for the adjacency matrix representation of a graph.
9. Implementation Module 9.1 and Algorithms 9.4 and 9.5 use a list to store graph nodes and start each traversal at the head of the list. Modify these routines to use a ring to store the graph nodes and to begin a traversal with a specified node.

9.5 Applications

In Section 9.5 we will modify our graphs by assigning a positive integer or **weight** to each edge. The weight can be thought of as a cost or a distance, and graphs with such weights are called **networks** (see Figure 9.22). We are interested in finding a subgraph of a given connected graph that is connected and that minimizes the sum of the weights of its edges. Such a subgraph is called a **minimum spanning tree (MST)** (see Figure 9.23). We will use priority first search to solve two problems: finding the minimum spanning tree and finding the shortest path between two nodes. Throughout this section we will assume that the graph is connected.

9.5.1 Abstract Solutions

An abstract solution to each of these problems is easily described. To construct an MST, we start with MST empty and add any graph node to it. We then repeatedly add to MST the graph node that is closest, in the sense of having least weight, to MST. This continues until all the nodes have been added.

To find the shortest path between two given nodes, we begin by generalizing the problem slightly. We will find the shortest path between one of the nodes and every other node in the graph. We start with a tree containing one

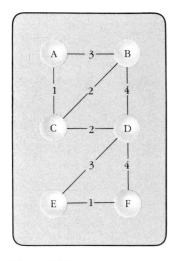

Figure 9.22
A network.

of the nodes and then repeatedly add that node, not in the tree, that is closest to the original node. This continues until all the graph nodes have been added.

In both cases a priority queue is used to store information about all nodes that are neighbors of nodes in the tree being constructed. In the first case, a node's priority is the smallest weight of any edge that connects it to a node in the tree. In the second case, the priority is the sum of weights along a path from the original node. That path, except for the last edge, must lie entirely within the tree constructed so far, and it must minimize the sum of the weights for such paths. In both cases a priority first search does the job.

Algorithm 9.6 examines the construction of a minimum spanning tree in more detail.

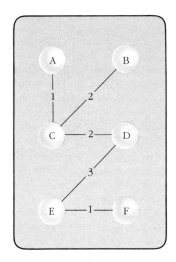

Figure 9.23
A minimum spanning tree for the network in Figure 9.22.

```
Create an empty graph. Call it MST.
Add any node to MST, and add its neighbors to a priority
queue. The priority of a node is the weight of the edge
that connects it to MST. High priority corresponds to
low weight.

WHILE the priority queue is not empty DO
    remove a node from the priority queue
    IF the node is not in MST
        THEN add it to MST, and its neighbors not
            in MST, to the priority queue
    END
END
```

Algorithm 9.6   Construction of a minimum spanning tree.

There are two observations that should be made about Algorithm 9.6. First, the priority queue may contain several distinct entries for the same graph node. This is because one node may be connected to MST by several different edges. Clearly only one edge—the one with the highest priority (lowest weight)—is needed. At the level of abstraction of Algorithm 9.6 it is easy to specify that before adding a node to the priority queue we will check to see if it is already there. If so, we need only retain the one with lowest weight. To do this we need to be able to find and change the priority of any node in the priority queue. Finding the node requires searching the priority queue (a performance penalty) or providing direct access to priority queue entries based on the value of node identifiers. Deleting such a node or adjusting its priority is possible, but it is not one of the operations in the priority queue module in Chapter 5.

The second observation is that the MST may be complete long before the priority queue is empty. It may pay to count the number of nodes added to the MST and terminate the algorithm when this count equals the number of nodes in the original connected graph.

Algorithm 9.6 is called a **_greedy algorithm_** because each node is added on the basis of a locally optimal, or greedy, decision. It must be shown that a sequence of such actions produces the correct end result. In this regard see Exercise 9.5, 8. See Graham (1985) for a history of the minimum spanning tree problem, as well as several other algorithms for its solution.

9.5.2 Implementation

• Minimum spanning tree

To implement construction of an MST in Modula-2, we modify the content of edge nodes by adding a status field and a weight field as shown in Figure 9.24. We also need a priority queue, and the content of a priority queue node is also given in Figure 9.24. Graph nodes remain as given in Figure 9.19.

```
List      = [1..2];                                           (* Edge list index. *)
StatType  = (Waiting, Ready, Processed);

NodePtr   = POINTER TO GraphNode;
EdgePtr   = POINTER TO EdgeNode;
EdgeNode  = RECORD                               (* The keys of the elements *)
              key1,key2  : KeyType;              (* connected by this edge.   *)
              nextEdge   : ARRAY List OF EdgePtr;       (* Two edge lists.  *)
              node1,node2: NodePtr;           (* Nodes connected by this edge. *)
              status     : StatType;
              weight     : CARDINAL
            END;

PQNodePtr = POINTER TO PQnode;
PQnode    = RECORD
              priority: CARDINAL;                 (* Weight of edge PQedge↑.  *)
              PQgraph : NodePtr;                 (* Pointer to a graph node.  *)
              PQedge  : EdgePtr;           (* Pointer to the edge that      *)
              PQnext  : PQNodePtr          (* attaches PQgraph↑ to the MST. *)
            END;
```

Figure 9.24   Representation of a node in the priority queue and an EdgeNode.

The four priority queue operations needed—*PQCreate, PQEmpty, PQEnqueue,* and *PQServe*—are given in Implementation Module 5.3. Algorithm 9.7 shows a Modula-2 implementation of Algorithm 9.6.

```
PROCEDURE MST(G: Graph);                    (* Minimum spanning tree. *)
VAR PQhead: PQNodePtr;

    PROCEDURE EnqNeighbors(p: NodePtr);              (* Add neighbors to   *)
    VAR ep: EdgePtr;                                 (* the priority queue. *)
    BEGIN
        ep := p↑.edgeHead[1];
        WHILE ep # NIL DO
            IF ep↑.node2↑.status = Waiting
                THEN Enqueue(ep↑.node2, ep, ep↑.weight)
            END;
            ep := ep↑.nextEdge[1]
        END;
        ep := p↑.edgeHead[2];
        WHILE ep # NIL DO
            IF ep↑.node1↑.status = Waiting
                THEN Enqueue(ep↑.node1, ep, ep↑.weight)
            END;
            ep := ep↑.nextEdge[2]
        END
    END EnqNeighbors;

VAR gp: NodePtr;
    ep: EdgePtr;

BEGIN
    PQCreate();
    SetWaiting(G);              (* Set the status of each node and edge to waiting. *)
    gp := G↑.head;
    IF gp # NIL
        THEN gp↑.status := Processed        (* Add the first graph node to MST. *)
    END;
    EnqNeighbors(gp);          (* Add all neighbors of gp to the priority queue. *)

    WHILE NOT PQEmpty() DO
        PQServe(gp, ep);                         (* Get graph and edge pointers *)
        IF gp↑.status = Waiting                  (* from the priority queue.     *)
            THEN gp↑.status := Processed;        (* Add a graph node to MST.     *)
                 ep↑.status := Processed;        (* Add an edge node to MST.     *)
                 EnqNeighbors(gp)                (* Enqueue the neighbors of gp↑. *)
        END
    END
END MST;
```

Algorithm 9.7 Construction of a minimum spanning tree.

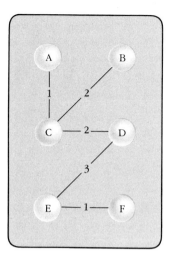

Figure 9.25
An SPL tree for the network
shown in Figure 9.22. Distances
are measured from (A).

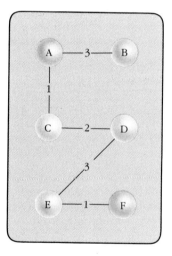

Figure 9.26
Another SPL tree for the network
shown in Figure 9.22. Distances
are measured from (A).

• Shortest path

Modification of Algorithms 9.6 and 9.7 to find a tree, call it **shortest path length (SPL),** that contains only shortest paths beginning at some designated node is simple. It is only a matter of changing the way in which priority is determined. Instead of using the edge weight of the edge that connects a node to MST, we use the sum of weights along a path from the designated node to the node in the priority queue. All but the last edge of the path is a previously determined shortest path.

   Algorithm 9.6 is modified by changing MST everywhere to SPL and by changing the description of the priority of a node.

   We need only two modifications to Algorithm 9.7 to make it compute an SPL. First we add a field to each graph node to record path length, call it pathLength. Each time a node is added to SPL the length of a shortest path to that node is inserted into the pathLength field. Second, we change the computation of priority from $ep \uparrow .wt$ to $ep \uparrow .wt + ep \uparrow .Node1 \uparrow .pathLength$ in the first instance and $ep \uparrow .wt + ep \uparrow .Node2 \uparrow .pathLength$ in the second. (These priority values are computed in the calls to *Enqueue* within procedure *EnqNeighbors* in Algorithm 9.7.) Figures 9.25 and 9.26 show SPL trees for the network given in Figure 9.22.

   Consider execution of Algorithm 9.7 if the graph has $e = n - 1$ edges (and is connected) so that the graph is its own MST. The WHILE loop will be executed $n - 1$ times, an edge will have its status examined $2(n - 1)$ times (resulting in $n - 1$ *Enqueue* operations), and the maximum queue size will be 1. The effort required is $O(n)$, so Algorithm 9.7 appears efficient in this case.

   Next consider execution of Algorithm 9.7 if the graph has every possible edge so that $e = 1/2n(n - 1)$. The WHILE loop is executed once for each edge and each pass through the loop calls *EnqNeighbors,* which in turn examines the status of $n - 1$ graph nodes. Thus the status of a graph node is examined on $e(n - 1) = O(n^3)$ occasions. The kth call of *EnqNeighbors* will result in at least $n - k$ additions to the priority queue, which will reach a maximum size of $O(n^2)$. We see therefore that if the graph is sparse the approach in Algorithm 9.7 is efficient, but if it is not sparse Algorithm 9.7 is very inefficient.

   Implementations that compute an MST with $O(e \log n)$ effort are common (Graham, 1985).

Exercises 9.5

1. Consider the complete graph shown in Figure 9.27.
   a. If the weight of each edge is 1, find all distinct minimum spanning trees.
   b. If the weight of each edge is 1, find all distinct spanning trees that contain only shortest paths and that begin at (A).
   c. If the edge weights are as follows:

$$AB - x, \ AC - 2, \ AD - 3, \ BC - 3, \ BD - 2, \ CD - 3$$

   for what values of x is edge AB in some minimum spanning tree? In some spanning tree that contains only shortest paths and begins at (A)?

2. Consider the graph shown in Figure 9.28 with edge weights as follows:

AB − 3, AC − 1, AD − 3, BC − 2, BD − 4, CD − 2, CE − 3, CF − 2, DE − 3, DF − 4, EF − 1

   a. Find all distinct minimum spanning trees.
   b. Find all spanning trees that contain only shortest paths and that begin at (A).

3. Implement a procedure that finds a minimum spanning tree for a graph that is represented using an adjacency matrix.

4. Implement a procedure that finds a spanning tree containing only shortest paths for a graph represented using an adjacency matrix.

5. Construct a graph containing nodes whose identifiers are 1, 2, ..., n. Use a random number generator to add k edges to the graph. Plot the time required to determine a minimum spanning tree for the graph as a function of k and n.

   Using the graph described above, plot the time required to determine a minimum spanning tree that contains only shortest paths as a function of k and n.

6. Specify an operation that returns the number of nodes connected to the current node in a graph.

7. Specify and implement the following operations for a priority queue:
   a. Searches the priority queue for a node based on the value of a node identifier
   b. Changes the priority of a node in the priority queue
   Using these operations, modify Algorithm 9.7 so that no node appears more than once, at any one time, in the priority queue.

8. Prove that Algorithm 9.6 always produces a minimum spanning tree. (See Sedgewick, 1983, pages 408–411.)

9. Write an algorithm, similar to that in Algorithm 9.1, for finding a maximal spanning tree; that is, a spanning tree such that the sum of edge weights is a maximum.

10. A *fragment* of a graph is a subgraph that is a tree. A fragment consisting of a single node and no edges is a *trivial fragment*. The *distance* between two fragments in a network (weighted graph) is the shortest distance between a node in the first fragment and a node in the second fragment. Each of the following algorithms begins with the set of all graph nodes (trivial fragments) and selectively adds edges until a minimum spanning tree is formed.

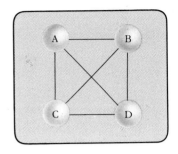

Figure 9.27

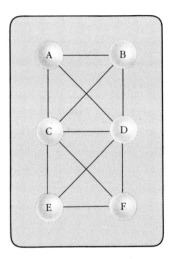

Figure 9.28

Algorithm 1 (Two Nearest Fragments)
Add the shortest remaining edge that joins distinct fragments.

Algorithm 2 (Nearest Neighbor)
Choose a node, say n. Add a shortest edge that joins the fragment containing n to another distinct fragment.

Algorithm 3 (All Nearest Fragments)
For every fragment add the shortest edge that joins it to another fragment. This algorithm assumes that all edge weights are distinct.

Express each of these three algorithms in a form comparable to Algorithm 9.6. Implement Algorithm 1 and discuss the effort required to execute your implementation if **(a)** $e = n − 1$ and **(b)** $e = 1/2n(n − 1)$.

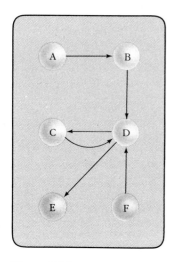

Figure 9.29

	A	B	C	D	E	F
A	0	1	0	0	0	0
B	0	0	0	1	0	0
C	0	0	0	1	0	0
D	0	0	1	0	1	0
E	0	0	0	0	0	0
F	0	0	0	1	0	0

Figure 9.30
Adjacency matrix for the digraph
in Figure 9.29.

Node list		Edge list		
A	$\rightarrow$	B		
B	$\rightarrow$	D		
C	$\rightarrow$	D		
D	$\rightarrow$	C	$\rightarrow$	E
E				
F	$\rightarrow$	D		

Figure 9.31
Adjacency list for the digraph in
Figure 9.29.

9.6 Directed Graphs

As defined in Section 9.2, "Terminology," a directed graph, often called a digraph, is a graph whose edges have direction. Thus an edge not only relates two nodes, it also specifies a predecessor–successor relationship. A graph can be represented as a directed graph with two edges, one in each direction, between each pair of related nodes.

A directed graph is easy to illustrate by using arrow heads to show the direction of each edge. An example is shown in Figure 9.29. A ***directed path*** is a sequence of nodes $d_1, d_2, \ldots, d_k$ such that there is a directed edge from d_i to d_{i+1} for all appropriate i. In this section a directed path will simply be called a ***path,*** since all paths in a directed graph are directed paths. In Figure 9.29, ABDE is a path in the digraph.

The representation of a directed graph has similarities to and differences from the representation of an ordinary graph. Let A be the adjacency matrix representation of a directed graph. If A[i,j] is true, then there is a directed edge from node i to node j. In a directed graph, A, in general, is not symmetric as it would be if A were in an ordinary graph. Therefore, the full matrix is needed to represent a directed graph. Figure 9.30 shows the adjacency matrix representation of the digraph in Figure 9.29.

An entry in an adjacency list specifies not just an edge, but a directed edge from the node given in the node list to the node given in the edge list. Figure 9.31 shows an adjacency list representation of the digraph in Figure 9.29.

The basic operations on a graph—*InsertNode, InsertEdge, DeleteNode,* and *DeleteEdge*—are simpler for a digraph. This is because each edge produces only one entry in an adjacency matrix and appears on only one edge list in an adjacency list. Exercise 9.6, 3 asks you to modify the algorithms in Implementation Module 9.1 so that they apply to a directed graph.

Traversal of directed graphs is also similar to traversal of graphs. Performance is marginally better. Depth or breadth first search of a graph requires visiting each node once and each edge twice. For a digraph, each edge node is only visited once.

A digraph is more complicated with respect to connectedness. If G is a graph with nodes g_1 and g_2, then the existence of a path from g_1 to g_2 assures us that there is a path from g_2 to g_1. This is not true if G is a directed graph.

If G is a graph and S_G is a connected subgraph of G, then there is a path between every pair of its nodes. There is no analogous statement for a directed graph. Let d be a node in a directed graph D. Let $S_D(d)$ be the subgraph of D that includes d and all nodes connected to it. If d_1 and d_2 are nodes in $S_D(d)$, it is certainly not true, in general, that there is a path from d_1 to d_2. This failure motivates a digraph generated by D called the transitive closure of D.

9.6.1 Transitive Closure

Let D be a directed graph and let T_D be the directed graph formed by adding an edge from d_1 to d_2 whenever d_1 and d_2 are nodes in D and there is a path from d_1 to d_2. T_D is the ***transitive closure*** of D.

An obvious approach to computing the transitive closure of a digraph is to perform a depth first search starting at each node of the digraph. For each node visited during a search, add a directed edge to the graph used to store the transitive closure. This could be expensive. If the digraph contains all possible edges, then a single depth first search processes them all and requires $O(n^2)$ effort. This is done n times for a total effort of $O(n^3)$.

S. Warshall gives us an elegant algorithm that computes the transitive closure of the adjacency matrix representation of a digraph. It is shown in Algorithm 9.8.

Let us now see how Warshall's algorithm works. The basic idea is simple: If there is a path from j to i and another from i to k, then there is one from j to k. The clever part of Warshall's algorithm is how this simple idea is used to compute the transitive closure with a single pass over the adjacency matrix.

We will use the digraph in Figure 9.32 to illustrate our discussion. It will also be helpful to have the idea of an interior node of a (directed) path. If d_1, $d_2, \ldots, d_k$ is a path, then all nodes except d_1 and d_k are ***interior nodes*** of that path.

When i is 1, Warshall's algorithm looks for pairs $A[j,1]$, $A[1,k]$, which are both true. When this occurs there is a path $(j, 1, k)$ from j to k so $A[j,k]$ is set to true. The effect is to mark all paths that contain 1 as an interior node. For the digraph in Figure 9.32, $A[3,2]$ is set to true because of the path 3, 1, 2.

When i is 2, Warshall's algorithm adds paths that contain 2 as an interior node. Since paths containing 1 as an interior node are already marked, the result is that all paths between nodes involving 1, or 2, or both as interior nodes are marked. For the digraph in Figure 9.32, $A[1,4]$ is set true because of the path 1, 2, 4, and $A[3,4]$ is set true because of the path 3, 1, 2, 4.

When i is 3, Warshall's algorithm adds 3 to the list of possible interior nodes. For the digraph in Figure 9.32, $A[4,1]$ is set true because of the path 4, 3, 1; $A[4,2]$ is set true because of the path 4, 3, 1, 2; and $A[4,4]$ is set true because of the path 4, 3, 1, 2, 4.

In general, processing $i = k$ produces an adjacency matrix that includes all paths between nodes p and q that contain nodes $1, 2, \ldots, k$ as interior nodes. Figure 9.33 shows an adjacency matrix for the transitive closure of the digraph shown in Figure 9.32. Induction establishes the validity of Warshall's algorithm.

One application of directed graphs is to let nodes represent operations and edges represent precedence relationships among the nodes. An example is a construction project in which some activities, such as electrical work and plumbing, must precede others, such as finishing interior walls. Sorting such events into an order in which these precedence relations are preserved is called topological sorting.

```
FOR i := 1 TO n DO
  FOR j := 1 TO n DO
    IF A[j,i] = 1
    THEN
      FOR k := 1 TO n DO
        IF A[i,k] = 1 THEN
          A[j,k] := 1
        END
      END
    END
  END
END
```

Algorithm 9.8
Warshall's algorithm for computing the transitive closure of a digraph.

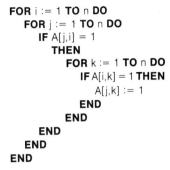

Figure 9.32

	1	2	3	4
1	1	1	1	1
2	1	1	1	1
3	1	1	1	1
4	1	1	1	1

Figure 9.33
Adjacency matrix for the transitive closure of the digraph shown in Figure 9.32.

9.6.2 Topological Sorting

In order to understand the concept of topological order, let us consider the directed graph in Figure 9.34. A ***topological order*** for its five nodes is a linear relationship among the nodes such that each directed edge goes from

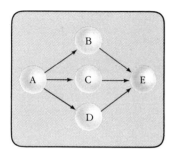

Figure 9.34
Digraph.

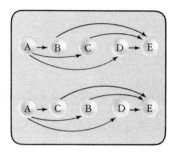

Figure 9.35
Two of six possible topological
orders for the digraph in Figure
9.34.

Node list		Edge list
A	→	B → C → D
B	→	F
C	→	E
D	→	E
E		

Figure 9.36
Adjacency list for the graph in
Figure 9.34.

a node to one of its successors. Figure 9.35 shows two of six possible topological orders.

As an example of what topological orders can show us, consider the following. If each node represents a course and each directed edge represents a prerequisite relationship, then topological order shows how the courses can be taken in a sequence that does not violate any prerequisite.

Since a digraph that contains a cycle does not have a topological order, we can only topologically sort directed acyclic graphs. Such structures are often called ***dags.*** An operation that determines the topological order of a dag is ***topological sorting.*** There are several approaches to topological sorting, and we will describe two that are closely related.

The basic idea of the first approach to topological sorting is to find a node with no successor, remove it from the graph, and add it to a list. Repeating this process until the graph is empty produces a list that is the reverse of some topological order. A simple algorithm that describes this process is given in Algorithm 9.9.

WHILE the graph has a node with no successors **DO**
　　remove one such node from the graph and
　　add it to the end of a list.
END;

IF the above loop terminates with the graph empty
　　THEN the list shows the reverse of some
　　　　topological order
　　ELSE the graph contains a cycle
END

Algorithm 9.9

The second approach to topological sorting is to perform a depth first search (Algorithm 9.5) and to add a node to the list of those topologically sorted each time it is necessary to take a node off the stack in order to continue. The stack is popped when a node has no successors, so this approach is closely related to that described in Algorithm 9.9. An adjacency list for the graph in Figure 9.34 is given in Figure 9.36. Starting at A, the algorithm just described retrieves nodes in the following order: E, B, C, D, A. A nonrecursive implementation of this approach is shown in Algorithm 9.10.

```
PROCEDURE TSort(G: Graph);                              (* Topological sort *)

VAR S:  PtrStks.Stack;          (* Stack type with elements of type ADDRESS  *)
                                (* and operations described in Specification 3.1. *)

   PROCEDURE Visit(p: NodePtr);
   VAR ep: EdgePtr;
   BEGIN
      ep := p↑.edgeHead;

      LOOP
         WHILE ep # NIL DO                  (* Search for a graph node with no    *)
            PtrStks.Push(S, ep);            (* successors or with only successors *)
            p := ep↑.node2;                 (* that have already been processed.  *)
            ep := p↑.edgeHead
         END;

         IF p↑.Order = 0                    (* A graph node with no successors *)
            THEN count := count + 1;        (* has been found. If it has not   *)
                 p↑.order := count          (* been ordered then order it.     *)
         END;

         IF NOT PtrStks.Empty(S)
            THEN PtrStks.Pop(S, ep);        (* Get a previously processed edge. *)
                 p := ep↑.node1;                 (* Get its parent graph node. *)
                 ep := ep↑.nextEdge    (* Get the next edge on the edge list. *)
            ELSE EXIT
         END
      END
   END Visit;

VAR gp    : NodePtr;
    count: CARDINAL;

BEGIN
   PtrStks.Create(S);
   InitOrder(G);                            (* Set the order of each node to 0. *)
   count := 0;
   gp := G↑.head;
   WHILE gp # NIL DO
      IF gp↑.order = 0
         THEN Visit(gp)
      END;
      gp := gp↑.nextGraph
   END
   PtrStks.Terminate(S)
END TSort;
```

Algorithm 9.10 Nonrecursive topological sort.

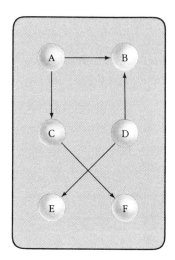

Figure 9.37

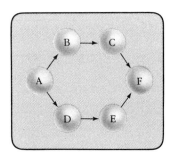

Figure 9.38

Exercises 9.6

1. Explain the following terms in your own words:

   directed graph   directed path   transitive closure
   interior node   topological order   topological sort

2. Consider the digraph shown in Figure 9.37.
   a. Show its adjacency matrix representation.
   b. Show its adjacency list representation.
   c. Find its transitive closure.
3. Modify Implementation Module 9.1 so that it applies to a directed graph.
4. Modify Algorithms 9.4 and 9.5 so that they apply to a directed graph.
5. Suppose that the statement

   FOR i := 1 TO n DO

   in Algorithm 9.8 were changed to

   FOR i := n TO 1 BY -1 DO

   Would the resulting algorithm compute the transitive closure? If so, describe how the algorithm works. If not, explain why not.
6. Characterize the following with as few conditions as possible:
   a. Directed graphs whose transitive closure contains every possible edge
   b. Directed graphs whose transitive closure is equal to the original digraph
7. List all possible orders that might be produced by a topological sort of the directed graph shown in Figure 9.38.
8. Characterize, as simply as possible, directed acyclic graphs that have a unique topological order.
9. Implement a recursive procedure that determines the reverse of topological order.
10. Modify Algorithm 9.10 to produce topological order instead of its reverse.

9.7 Summary

In Chapter 9 we have looked at a few of the many operations on graphs. Basic operations for constructing a graph, such as *InsertNode* and *InsertEdge,* require between $O(1)$ and $O(n)$ operations where the graph contains n nodes.

Traversal operations, breadth first and depth first, require $O(n + e)$ operations for an adjacency list representation and $O(e)$ for an adjacency matrix representation. If the matrix is dense, then $O(e) = O(n^2)$, and the matrix representation is preferred. Otherwise the adjacency list representation is preferred since it conserves storage and requires less effort for traversal.

A priority first search generalizes the notions of breadth first and depth first searches and is most efficiently implemented using a heap as an auxiliary data structure. The effort required is bounded by $O[(n + e)\log n]$ for an adjacency list and $O(e \log n)$ for an adjacency matrix. These bounds are conservative since $\log n$ is a conservative bound for the effort required for one heap operation. Priority first searches are used to find minimum spanning trees and the shortest paths between nodes in weighted trees.

We looked at two problems associated with directed graphs: finding the transitive closure and topological sorting. Finding the transitive closure requires a search (e.g., depth first) for each node in the graph. It is therefore expensive. A topological sort can be accomplished by a single depth first search, and therefore requires $O(n + e)$ or $O(e)$, depending on the representation.

We introduced three basic search tools for working with graphs. The surface of this subject has, however, only been scratched. A good source of additional graph problems is Sedgewick (1983), Chapters 24 through 34.

Table 9.2 compares the complexity of the two implementations of basic graph algorithms.

TABLE 9.2

Implementation module	Data structure	Representation	Number of procedures	Total lines	Average lines	Maximum lines
9.1	Graph	Adjacency list	12	227	18.9	48
9.2	Graph	Adjacency matrix	10	124	12.4	23

Abstract Data Types Revisited 10

10.1 Introduction

10.2 Generic Data Types
Exercises 10.2

10.3 Data Typing Facilities of Ada

10.4 Problem-Level Objects and Data Abstractions

10.5 Formal Specifications of Abstract Data Types
10.5.1 Abstract Model Method
10.5.2 First-Order Predicate Calculus
10.5.3 Formal Specifications
10.5.4 Correctness Proofs
Exercises 10.5

10.6 Summary

10.1 Introduction

In Chapter 1 we discussed the following advantages of abstract data types:

Precise specifications
Modularity
Information hiding
Simplicity
Integrity
Implementation independence

Throughout this text we have used the notion of abstract data types. It has provided us with a unified approach to the study of traditional data structures and has given us a means of systematically approaching the problem of creating data structures and has encouraged precise specifications. It leads naturally to the use of modules.

Now that you are familiar with the concept and have practiced creating and implementing abstract data types, we will present a more advanced treatment and tie up some loose ends.

The notion of abstract data typing resulted from research that had as its objective the production of error-free programs. Researchers felt that the application of techniques for mathematical proofs could allow programmers to prove their programs correct. Current practice relies more heavily on testing (debugging) than on reasoning to produce correct programs.

There are, however, a few informal techniques that involve reasoning. The most useful method appears to be walk-throughs, or design and code reviews. This involves one or more people, other than the designer or coder, reading ("walking through") the design or code, trying to follow the logic flow and details, and pointing out errors. This informal technique, if systematically applied throughout the design and development phases of a project, has proven to be reasonably effective at reducing errors in delivered products.

There is no one cure-all method that we can apply to produce error-free programs. Walk-throughs used in combination with structured top-down methods, high-level languages, and development tools such as editors, formatters, cross-reference generators, debuggers, program library tools, and tools for improved documentation have dramatically improved the quality of modern software. The goal, however, is 100% error-free code, and we have not attained that objective.

Abstract data typing and its resulting modularity promise to be important additions to the set of tools and techniques available to designers and programmers. It has been estimated that the only foreseeable technique that can provide a quantum leap in productivity and quality is the use of well-specified library modules and packages that are known to be correct (Jones, 1981). Abstract data typing provides a systematic approach to producing such modules.

In the late 1960s, researchers investigating techniques for proving program correctness gained insights that had a dramatic impact on how we construct programs. In attempting to prove programs correct, they realized that the use of uncontrolled transfer (*go to*) statements was a major impediment to their task. If only a few types of control statements were allowed, the proofs were greatly simplified. Thus we find that today the recommended control statements are sequential statements, decision (*if . . . then . . . else, case*), looping (*while, for, repeat, loop*), and procedure calls. Unconditional transfers are to be used only within very narrow limits. It is possible, and often desirable, to write programs of any complexity without using them.

Few programs are proven correct using the mathematical proof techniques that were the original aims of the researchers. Most programmers today, however, use the structured programming techniques that are a direct result of that research.

Abstract data typing appears to be following a similar path. Its roots are in proof-of-correctness research. It can, however, be applied with great benefit without carrying out proofs. It is likely to be used by practicing programmers to define and specify modules tightly in a formal or semiformal way, without carrying out the proofs. Libraries of correct implementations of modules specified in this way are being produced.

The result is a software equivalent of the handbooks used by hardware designers. Those contain the specifications of chips that have well-defined inputs, outputs, and functions. The hardware designer is not concerned with the details of the module's innards but only with the functions it performs and its interface specifications. The chips allow the designer to think at a high level and to avoid distracting detail. A precisely specified off-the-shelf software module has the same attributes.

In this chapter we will look at several advanced aspects of abstract data types and modules. Section 10.2 discusses the notion of a ***generic data type.***

Section 10.3 looks at another modular language that is becoming widely used—Ada. It appears that Ada and Modula-2 are going to be the two most popular languages that have significant abstract data typing and module facilities.

Section 10.4 provides an example of the abstract data type process applied to real-world objects. In this text, we have applied abstract data types to rather general structures such as linear structures, trees, and sets. Another area of application of this concept is to user objects. In Section 10.4 we will look at an example of a port that is handling cargo and ships. We shall see that there are three interrelated data types—port, cargo, and ship. Each has a set of operations natural to it. This approach leads to a very natural style of programming when using the abstract objects.

Section 10.5 is concerned with formal methods for writing specifications. Such formality is a necessity if we are going to prove the representation and implementation of a data type to be correct. Even if a proof is not carried out, well-known formal techniques for stating specifications provide far more precision than the structured English that we have used up to this point.

Section 10.6 is a summary.

10.2 Generic Data Types

Suppose that we had two stacks that differed in that their data elements were of different types. Otherwise the two abstractions were exactly the same. We say that two abstractions that only differ in their component element types are of the same ***generic type.*** It seems wasteful to have two stack modules that are exactly the same except for the type specification of their component elements. Is there a way to create a generic module and use it for all stacks, regardless of their data element types? If so, is there a way to do so in Modula-2?

Multiple instances of the same generic data types are more difficult to implement efficiently in Modula-2 than are the multiple instances of the same data type that we have seen throughout this book. Suppose that we had two stacks, one a stack of integers and the other a stack of reals. Could we use a single copy of a stack module to operate both stacks? Unfortunately, it is not possible in Modula-2. We must provide two separate stack modules, one for each stack type.

Specifications 10.1 and 10.2 show the definition modules for stacks of integers and stacks of reals, respectively. They are exactly the same as Specification 3.1, *Stacks,* but with the comments removed and integers and reals being stacked instead of standard elements. They are equivalent to each other except for the data type of the elements being stacked. Thus we can say that they are both of the same generic data type.

It would seem reasonable to have a single generic data type and then, at the time of creating an instance of the generic stack, to inform the implementation module what type of elements are to be stacked. One can envision calling a version of *Create* that is specified in a generic stack definition module to create instances of generic stacks:

```
Create(IS, 'INTEGER');
Create(RS, 'REAL');
```

There is no facility for doing so easily in Modula-2. The existing features of Modula-2 have been used to approximate generic data types (Wiener and Sincovec, 1985, and Beidler and Jackowitz, 1986). It is not clear that the benefits are worth the resulting increase in complexity.

Specification 10.1   Integer Stacks

```
DEFINITION MODULE IntegerStacks;

    EXPORT QUALIFIED IntegerStack, Push, Pop, Empty, Full, Create, Terminate;
    TYPE IntegerStack;

    PROCEDURE Push(VAR IS: IntegerStack; e: INTEGER);
    PROCEDURE Pop(VAR IS: IntegerStack; VAR e: INTEGER);
    PROCEDURE Empty(IS: IntegerStack): BOOLEAN;
    PROCEDURE Full(IS: IntegerStack): BOOLEAN;
    PROCEDURE Create(VAR IS: IntegerStack): BOOLEAN;
    PROCEDURE Terminate(VAR IS: IntegerStack);

END IntegerStacks.
```

Specification 10.2   Real Stacks

DEFINITION MODULE RealStacks;

    EXPORT QUALIFIED RealStack, Push, Pop, Empty, Full, Create, Terminate;
    TYPE RealStack;

    PROCEDURE Push(**VAR** RS: RealStack; e: REAL);
    PROCEDURE Pop(**VAR** RS: RealStack; **VAR** e: REAL);
    PROCEDURE Empty(RS: RealStack): BOOLEAN;
    PROCEDURE Full(RS: RealStack): BOOLEAN;
    PROCEDURE Create(**VAR** RS: RealStack): BOOLEAN;
    PROCEDURE Terminate(**VAR** RS: RealStack);

END RealStacks.

Specifications 10.1 and 10.2 are Modula-2 definition modules that at least allow multiple instances of each of two stack types. Note that they both have the same operation names. We can no longer say simply *Push* to add an element to a stack because the name *Push* is ambiguous. In order to resolve the ambiguity, Modula-2 has a facility for ***qualified reference*** to objects exported from modules. An integer stack push is written

```
IntegerStacks.Push(IS, i);
```

whereas a real stack push is

```
RealStacks.Push(RS, x).
```

The module name qualifies the operation name, thereby providing an unambiguous reference. The same technique is used to qualify other objects, such as exported types, constants, and variables.

    Thus although Modula-2 does not provide true generic data typing facilities, the approach just shown can be used effectively to attain the same end. Ada (U.S. Department of Defense, 1983) has a generic data typing facility, which is discussed in Section 10.3.

Exercises 10.2

1. Describe in your own words the notion of a generic data type.
2. Design and implement a scheme for approximating generic data types in Modula-2. Test your scheme by using it for one of the data types covered in this book.

10.3 Data Typing Facilities of Ada

The concept of abstract data types is having a substantial effect on the design of programming languages. Many recently designed languages have some facilities for modules and other features that directly support the specification and implementation of abstract data types. Mesa (Mitchell, Maybury, and Sweet, 1979), Alphard (Wulf, London, and Shaw, 1976), CLU (Liskov et al., 1977), Ada (U.S. Department of Defense, 1983), and Modula-2 (Wirth, 1980) are examples. Shaw (1980) presents a good review of the subject.

We will review some details of Ada. Alphard and CLU are research languages. Mesa, which was developed by Xerox, has not yet gained wide acceptance.

Ada is a programming language developed by the U.S. Department of Defense. Its design is the result of a multinational collaboration among industry, government, and academic institutions. It is intended to be a common language for programming large-scale and real-time systems.

We do not have the space for a full review of Ada. What we are interested in is its data typing facilities, which we will cover briefly.

Ada's primary feature for abstract data typing is the **package.** Packages are analogous to Modula-2's modules. They are groups of related entities such as types, constants, variables, procedures, and functions that can be separately compiled. Thus packages are a means of supporting both separate compilation and information hiding.

We have seen that Modula-2's modules exist in matched pairs—an implementation unit and a definition module. Ada takes a slightly different approach. There is a single unit—the package—which consists of two subunits. They are the declaration portion and the package body. The **declaration portion** includes those objects that are visible to a user. The **package body** contains the hidden objects and code.

Figure 10.1 is the Ada version of the Modula-2 IntegerStacks module given in Specification 10.1.

Simple Ada Package for Integer Stacks

```
package IntegerStacks is
    type IntegerStack is private;

    procedure Push(IS: in out IntegerStack; e: in integer);
    procedure Pop (IS: in out IntegerStack; e: out integer)
    function Empty(IS: in IntegerStack) return boolean;
    function Full (IS: in IntegerStack) return boolean;

private
    MaxSize : constant: integer := 100;
    type IntegerStack is
        record
            Top  : integer range 0..MaxSize;
            Space: array(1..MaxSize) of integer;
        end record;
end;
```

continued

```
package body IntegerStacks is

    procedure Push(IS: in out IntegerStack; e: in integer) is
    begin
        Top := Top + 1;
        Space(Top) := e;
    end Push;

    procedure Pop (IS: in out IntegerStack; e: out integer) is
                        .
                        .
                        .

    function Full (IS: in IntegerStack) return boolean is
                        .
                        .
                        .

    function Full (IS: in IntegerStack) return boolean is
                        .
                        .
                        .

end IntegerStacks;
```

Figure 10.1

Package IntegerStacks can be used to create as many integer stacks as desired. Figure 10.2 shows the code in a user package that uses IntegerStacks to create two integer stacks, IS1 and IS2.

```
                .
                .
                .

package IS1 is new IntegerStacks;     -- Create a new integer stack
package IS2 is new IntegerStacks;  -- Create a second integer stack
                .
                .
                .

IS1.Push(21);
                .
                .
                .

IS2.Push(5);
                .
                .
                .

IS1.Pop(i);
                .
                .
                .
```

Figure 10.2   Creation and use of two integer stacks—IS1 and IS2.

IntegerStacks allows the creation of stacks of integers. If we wished to create stacks of real numbers or of some other element type, we could write similar packages that differ in their data element types. However, recall that all stacks with the same specifications except for their element types are of the same generic type. Ada provides a ***generic package facility*** for such generic types.

Figure 10.3 shows a generic package for the generic type stack. Figure 10.4 shows how the user package can create and manipulate instances of several types of stacks. IS1 and IS2 are integer stacks. RS1 is a real stack, and CS1 is a stack of characters. Note that the type of data element to be stacked is an argument to GenericStacks. In this way the same package can be used for stacks of many data element types.

Ada packages allow the programmer to have control of the visibility of objects created within a package. Generic packages provide the use of common code to implement several abstract data types, as long as those types differ only in their data element types (i.e., the abstract types are of the same generic type).

```
generic
    type element is private;

package GenericStacks is
    type GenericStack is private;

    procedure Push(IS: in out GenericStack; e: in element);
    procedure Pop (IS: in out GenericStack; e: out element);
    function Empty(IS: in GenericStack) return boolean;
    function Full (IS: in GenericStack) return boolean;

private
    MaxSize : constant: integer := 100;
    type GenericStack is
        record
            Top  : integer range 0..MaxSize;
            Space: array(1..MaxSize) of element;
        end record;
end;

package body GenericStacks is

    procedure Push(IS: in out GenericStack; e: in element) is
    begin
        Top := Top + 1;
        Space(Top) := e;
    end Push;

    procedure Pop (IS: in out GenericStack; e: out element) is
                                    .
                                    .
                                    .

    function Empty(IS: in GenericStack) return boolean is
                                    .
                                    .
                                    .

    function Full (IS: in GenericStack) return boolean is
                                    .
                                    .
                                    .

end GenericStack;
```

Figure 10.3 Generic Ada package for stacks.

```
                                 -- Create an integer stack
package IS1 is new GenericStack(integer);
                               -- Create a second integer stack
package IS2 is new GenericStack(integer);
                                        -- Create a real stack
package RS1 is new GenericStack(real);
                                    -- Create a character stack
package CS1 is new GenericStack(char);
```

Figure 10.4   Creating instances of different stack types.

Ada is a more complex language than Modula-2 and has more features defined as part of the language. A study of Pascal, then Modula-2, and finally Ada provides a solid basis for understanding the languages and a fascinating study in programming language design.

10.4 Problem-Level Objects and Data Abstractions

Throughout this text we have developed many abstract data types of a general nature. For example, in Chapter 3 we specified a priority queue. We have not, however, specified a specific real-world priority queue such as the patients waiting for treatment in the emergency room of a hospital or the requests awaiting service on a magnetic disk.

In applying the abstract data type approach, we can define data abstractions that are identified with the real-world objects we are modeling. In a hospital, for example, people are being treated, and we can define a data abstraction person, the abstractions ward, service, and so on. These words—person, ward, service—we call ***problem-level objects,*** and their data abstractions we call ***problem-level data abstractions.***

We will now look at a simple problem in order to illustrate the process of creating data abstraction for real-world or problem-level objects. Consider the operation of a small water port. Ships arrive, load and unload cargo, and then sail on. Suppose for simplicity that there is only one dock, which can berth only one ship at a time. At any time, there may be a queue (FIFO) of ships waiting for access to the dock. There may be either no ships or a single ship at the dock. If there is a ship at the dock, it may be unloading, loading, or both. Cargo removed from the ship is placed on the dock for further shipment by land-based transport. Cargo arrives on the dock from land-based transport to be loaded onto an appropriate ship.

The port can be considered to be a queue of waiting ships, a ship being serviced (loaded and unloaded), and a dock holding cargo. For simplicity, we will ignore the land-based transport portion.

A ship can be viewed as a set of cargo. Similarly, the dock can be viewed as a set of cargo.

Let us suppose that we are writing a system that will record and control the port operations. We will now look at the data abstractions associated with the problem.

```
Cargo = RECORD
           ID;
           Info: RECORD
                   weight;
                   dimensions;
                   destination;
                       ⋮
                 END
        END;
```

• **Cargo**

A piece of ***cargo*** is recorded as a collection of data such as a unique identifying number (ID), weight, dimensions, destination, and consignee. Cargo is the structured type *record* that exists as a native type in many languages; thus we will not discuss it further.

• **Ship**

A ***ship*** consists of two portions. The first is identifying information such as the ship's name, registration number, gross tonnage, and destination. The second is information about the cargo on the ship. This information is called its ***manifest.*** We assume that although the placement of each piece of cargo is recorded

---

Specification 10.3   Ship Abstraction

Elements: Cargo.

Structure: Ship information plus a set of cargo.

Domain: The maximum number of pieces of cargo on a ship is unknown to the port.

Visible Items: Type ship and 6 operations.

Operations:

PROCEDURE CreateShip(**VAR** S: Ship; M: Manifest);
(* **post** – Ship S exists with S.IDInfo = M.IDInfo and
                S.CargoSet = M.CargoSet. *)

PROCEDURE LoadShip(**VAR** S: Ship; C: Cargo);
(* **pre** – Ship S does not contain cargo C.
    post – Ship S contains cargo C. *)

PROCEDURE UnloadShip(**VAR** S: Ship; CID: CargoID;
                VAR C: Cargo);
(* **pre** – Ship S contains cargo C with ID = CID.
    post – Ship S does not contain cargo C. *)

PROCEDURE Onboard(S: Ship; CID: CargoID): BOOLEAN;
(* **post** – If cargo with ID = CID is a member of the cargo
                set of S then Onboard is true,
                else Onboard is false. *)

PROCEDURE Tally(S: Ship; **VAR** M: Manifest);
(* **post** – M is a manifest of ship S. *)

PROCEDURE SailShip(**VAR** S: Ship);
(* **post** – Ship S-pre does not exist. *)

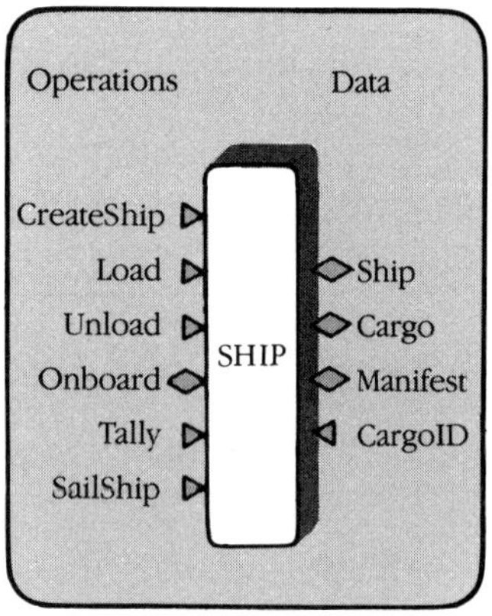

Figure 10.5
Capsulelike representation for ship.

on the manifest, from the port's point of view, the structure of the cargo on the ship is that of a set. Cargo either is a member of the set of ship's cargo or it is not. We have no interest in its relationship to other cargo on board. See Specification 10.3, the Ship Abstraction.

```
Ship = RECORD
         ID;
         Info = RECORD
                  name;
                  tonnage;
                    ⋮
                END
         CargoSet
       END;
```

• **Dock**

The **dock** is very similar to a ship. There is only one dock and it cannot sail away. It can be viewed, however, as a set of cargo. Specification 10.4, Dock Abstraction, and Figure 10.6, a capsulelike representation for dock, follow.

Specification 10.4   Dock Abstraction

Elements: Cargo.

Structure: Set of Cargo.

Domain: The maximum number of pieces of cargo on the dock is unknown.

Visible Items: 4 Operations.

Operations:

PROCEDURE Receive(C: Cargo);
(* **pre** – The dock does not contain cargo C.
   post – The dock contains cargo C. *)

PROCEDURE Remove(CID: CargoID; **VAR** C: Cargo);
(* **pre** – The dock contains cargo C with ID = CID.
   post – The dock does not contain cargo C. *)

PROCEDURE Ondock(CID: CargoID): BOOLEAN;
(* **post** – If cargo C with ID = C.ID is on the dock
              then Ondock is true, else Ondock is false. *)

PROCEDURE Tally(**VAR** I: Inventory);
(* **post** – I is the set of cargo currently on the dock. *)

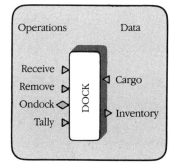

Figure 10.6
Capsulelike representation for dock.

Inventory is a set of Cargo.

• **Port queue**

The **port queue** is a FIFO queue of ships waiting for access to the dock. There is only one, and we assume that it always exists, even though it may be empty. Specification 10.5, Port Abstraction, and Figure 10.7, a capsulelike representation for port, follow.

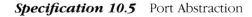

Specification 10.5   Port Abstraction

Elements: Ships.

Structure: FIFO Queue.

Domain: The number of ships in the port queue is bounded.

Visible Items: 4 operations.

Operations:

PROCEDURE Enqueue(S: Ship);
(* **pre** – The port queue is not full.
     post – S is in the queue and is the most recently
     arrived ship. *)

PROCEDURE Serve(**VAR** S: Ship);
(* **pre** – The port queue is not empty.
     post – S is the earliest arrival in port queue-pre;
     the port queue does not contain S. *)

PROCEDURE PortFull: BOOLEAN;
(* **post** – If the number of ships in the port queue has
     reached its bound then PortFull is true, else
     PortFull is false. *)

PROCEDURE Length: CARDINAL;
(* **post** – Length is the number of ships in the port
     queue. *)

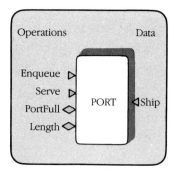

Figure 10.7
Capsulelike representation for
port.

The operations *GetManifest* and
GetCargo are not part of *Port*,
Ship, or *Dock*.

Programming the operation of the port is greatly simplified once these abstractions are identified and specified. For example, suppose that we could process the transactions that occur as the port operates as follows:

```
          ⋮

CASE transaction OF

    ShipArrival: IF NOT PortFull
                    THEN GetManifest(M);   (* External  *)
                         CreateShip(S,M);  (* procedure. *)
                         Enqueue(S)
                    ELSE deny arrival - no room in port
                 END          |
    DockShip   : IF Length > 0              (* Take next *)
                    THEN Serve(DockedShip)  (* ship from  *)
                 END          |             (* port queue *)
                                            (* and dock it. *)
```

```
UnLoadCargo:
    GetCargoID(CID);                    (* External procedure. *)
    IF OnBoard(DockedShip,CID)
        THEN Unload(DockedShip,CID,C);      (* Take Cargo C *)
            IF NOT Ondock(CID)          (* from docked ship. *)
                THEN Receive(C)              (* Put C on dock. *)
                ELSE Error - Cargo C already on dock
        ELSE Error - Cargo with ID = CID not on
                                    docked ship
                                        .
                                        .
                                        .
```

Several details have been ignored in order to reduce the clutter in this example, but it should be clear that programming flows smoothly and naturally when the appropriate data abstractions have been identified and specified.

10.5 Formal Specifications of Abstract Data Types

There are a number of methods used to specify data abstractions. Several of them are listed in Figure 10.8. Liskov and Zilles (1975) have a review of some of them. We will concentrate on one—the abstract model method.

10.5.1 Abstract Model Method

In specifying abstract types in previous chapters, we have used an approach based on an abstract model method that we will explain shortly. Our aim has been to strike a balance among formality, precision, and understandability. When a conflict arose, we chose to emphasize the latter. This had two major effects on the way in which the specifications were written:

1. In many cases, no specific model was used to state a data type's structure. For example, the structure of an FIFO queue was specified as shown in Figure 10.9.

    We shall see that a formal use of abstract models requires that we state some definite "mechanism" by using as a model some other data type that was previously specified.

2. We have stated the pre- and postconditions of a data type's operations in English. For example, the *Enqueue* operation of an FIFO *Queue* was specified as shown in Figure 10.10.

    Notice that both the pre- and postconditions are declarative statements that are either true or false. "Maybe" or "sometimes" are not allowable results. There are formal mathematical notations and methods that are used to make such statements precise.

In Section 10.5.2, we will review the basics of the first-order predicate calculus, a mathematical method for formally making statements and reasoning with them. In Section 10.5.3, we will apply these methods to the writing of specifications. Thus, in Chapter 10 we make the transition from an informal (although systematic) method of writing specifications to a precise, formal method.

Structured English
Programming language code
Axiomatic methods
Algebraic methods
Abstract model methods

Figure 10.8
Methods for specifying abstract data types.

Each element of the priority queue is associated with a user-supplied priority value. The priorities must be of a single ordered data type.

Figure 10.9
Structure of an FIFO Queue.

Enqueue (**VAR** Q: Queue;
            e: StdElement);
pre — The queue is not full.
post — The queue includes e as the most recently added element.

Figure 10.10
Enqueue operation specification for an FIFO Queue.

10.5.2 First-Order Predicate Calculus

Predicates

The sky is blue.

If a creature is a mammal, then it breathes air.

Every person has (had) a mother.

At the heart of the first-order predicate calculus is a language for writing statements that are either true or false—that is, **predicates.** The predicate calculus is a way of symbolizing and formalizing ordinary speech. It is a restricted form of a natural language (e.g., English) that has concise notation applied to it. For example, the term "such that" is allowed; its notation is "|".

Computer programmers are familiar with the use of restricted subsets of natural languages to write programs. Modula-2 is a restricted subset of English with some notation added. The Modula-2 statement

```
x := y
```

for example, is shorthand for "the value in y is to be copied into x."

The statements of a Modula-2 program are **imperative.** That is, they command the Modula-2 virtual processor to do something. Statements of the predicate calculus are predicates. They are either true or false. They do not command.

A complete treatment of the first-order predicate calculus is outside the scope of this text. What we will do is look briefly at some of its key features. Although they are not difficult to grasp, writing statements accurately using the predicate calculus takes some practice. The situation is analogous to lay people learning to write structured programs. They may be able to read programs without undue difficulty, although the programs may seem strange and somewhat stilted. Writing programs of significant size, however, takes a lot of practice.

We will now review the language of the predicate calculus and give a summary of the notation.

• Boolean operators

We assume the **boolean operators** and, or, and not.

• Sets and set operators

There is no notion of ordering or multiple occurrences in a set. Thus $\{a,b\} = \{a,b,a\} = \{b,a\}$.

We assume that you are familiar with the mathematical notion of **sets.** A set is indicated by curly brackets, or braces, {} surrounding its members. Set operations are union ($+$), intersection ($*$), difference ($-$), and inclusion (in). The empty set is indicated by {}.

• Ordered *n*-tuples

$<p,q,r>$ is a 3-tuple. It is not equal to either $<r,p,q>$ or $<p,r,q>$. A single value can appear in more than one position. Thus $<a,b,a>$ is allowed.

An ***n*-tuple** is made up of n values, each occupying a unique position in the n-tuple. The notation is $<a,b,c, ...>$, where the positions are 1 to n from left to right, and the values are $a, b, c, ...$

• Implication

We need notation for **implication;** that is for saying "if a is true then b is true," or, equivalently, "a being true implies that b is true." We use $a \rightarrow b$

to denote this. Notice that the entire statement is either true or false. For example,

being a mammal → four legs

is false (whales, porpoises).

We must also be able to say "*b* is true if and only if *a* is true." This is called **equivalence** and is denoted by $a \longleftrightarrow b$.

• Such that

We must have a way of saying **"such that"** or "where" or "," . The notation for these phrases is "|". Examples of its use are given in the discussions of the existential and universal quantifiers below.

• Existential quantifier

We need a notation for an **existential quantifier;** that is, for saying "there is," "there exists," "there is at least one," or "there is some." The symbol that we shall use is ∃. For example, if C is a set of students enrolled in a class, then one way of saying that the class has at least one member is to say that the value of the following statement is "true":

∃ x | x in C

This statement reads as follows: "There exists at least one x where x is a member of the class."

Suppose that we wished to say "there are some black cats." If C is the set of all cats and B is the set of all black entities, then we say that the following is true:

∃ x | x in C and x in B

If we are making a definitive statement that there are some black cats, then we require that the predicate be true. If, however, we are inquiring whether there are any black cats, we can evaluate the predicate to see if it is true or false. The predicate calculus is the basis of some query languages for database management systems.

• Universal quantifier

We must be able to say "for all," "for each," and "for every." The notation for the **universal quantifier** is ∀. Suppose that we wish to state that every student in a class C must be enrolled in the university. Let C be the set of students in the class and S be the set of people enrolled in the university. Then we say that

∀ x | x in C → x in S

must be true. This statement reads as follows: "For all x's, if x is a member of the class, then x is enrolled in the university."

- **Equality**

The notation for ***equality*** is " = ".

A summary of the notation used in the language of the predicate calculus is given in Figure 10.11.

$\{a,b,c, \ldots\}$	A set with members a, b, c, $\ldots$
$<a,b>$	An ordered pair of members with a in the first position and b in the second
$<a,b,c,d, \ldots>$	An ordered n-tuple of members with a in the first position, b in the second, c in the third, and so on
and	Logical and operator
or	Logical or operator
not	Logical not
in or $\in$	Set inclusion: "a in $\{a,b,c\}$" is true; "r in $\{a,b,c\}$" is false
$\rightarrow$	Implication: $x \rightarrow y$ if x and y are true or if x is false
$\longleftrightarrow$	Equivalence: $x \longleftrightarrow y$ if x and y are true or if x and y are false
$\vert$	"such that" or "where" or ","
$\exists$	Existential quantifier: "there exists" or "there is"
$\forall$	Universal quantifier: "for all" or "for each"
=	Equals, has a value of

Figure 10.11   Summary of notation for the predicate calculus.

Formal statements in the predicate calculus allow us to draw conclusions by following formal rules of inference. This process is the basis of reasoning. It is extremely important to many areas of computer science, especially artificial intelligence.

We have given a very brief coverage of the predicate calculus, but there are many good references on the subject. We especially recommend the book by Stoll (1961).

10.5.3 Formal Specifications

We can now formally write the specifications of a data type using the predicate calculus. Let us take as an example the specifications of a *PriorityQueue* given in Specification 3.3. We show the informal specification on the left and the corresponding formal specification on the right. We will take each aspect of the specification and discuss it.

Priority Queue
Informal Specifications

DEFINITION MODULE PriorityQueues;
(* Informal specification. *)

(* **Elements:** Although the elements can
be of a variety of types, for
concreteness we assume that they
are of type StdElement. *)

FROM StdTypes **IMPORT** StdElement,
Priority;

(* **Structure:** Each element of the
priority queue is associated with
a user-supplied priority value.
The priorities must be of a
single ordered data type. *)

(* **Domain:** The number of elements in a
priority queue is bounded. *)

EXPORT QUALIFIED
        PriorityQueue,
        Enqueue, Serve, Length, Full,
        Create, Terminate;

TYPE PriorityQueue;

(* **Operations:** There are six
operations. Occasionally in the
postcondition we must reference
the value of the priority queue
immediately before execution of
the operation. We use PQ-pre as
notation for this value. *)

   PROCEDURE Enqueue(**VAR** PQ: Priority-
                            Queue;
                      e: StdElement;
                      p: Priority);
   (* **pre** – PQ has not reached its
              maximum allowable size.
       post – PQ includes e associated
              with priority p. *)

continued

Priority Queue
Formal Specifications

DEFINITION MODULE PriorityQueues;
(* Formal specification. *)

(* **Elements:** e of type StdElement *)

FROM StdTypes **IMPORT** StdElement,
Priority;

(* **Structure:** Priority is an ordered
                type. A priority queue PQ
                is
        PQ = {<e1,py1>,<e2,py2>, ...} |
          ei in Domain(StdElement) and
          pyi in Domain(Priority). *)

(* **Domain:** Cardinality(PQ) bounded. *)

EXPORT QUALIFIED
        PriorityQueue,
        Enqueue, Serve, Length, Full,
        Create, Terminate;

TYPE PriorityQueue;

(* **Operations:** *)

   PROCEDURE Enqueue(**VAR** PQ: Priority-
                            Queue;
                      e: StdElement;
                      p: Priority);
   (* **pre** – not (Cardinality(PQ) >=
              MaxSize).
       post – PQ = PQ' + {<e,py>}. *)

continued

Priority Queue
Informal Specifications

PROCEDURE Serve(**VAR** PQ: Priority-
                             Queue;
               VAR e: StdElement;
               VAR py: Priority);
(* **pre** – PQ is not empty.
   post – e is an element associated
             with the highest priority
             of PQ-pre; p is that
             priority value; PQ does
             not contain e. *)

PROCEDURE Length(PQ: PriorityQueue)
                    : CARDINAL;
(* **post** – Length is the number of
              elements in PQ. *)

PROCEDURE Full(PQ: PriorityQueue):
              BOOLEAN;
(* **post** – If PQ has reached its
              maximum allowable size
              then Full is true, else
              Full is false. *)

PROCEDURE Create(**VAR** PQ:
              PriorityQueue)
                    : BOOLEAN;
(* **post** – If a priority queue can be
              created then PQ exists and
              is empty, and Create is
              true; else Create is
              false. *)

PROCEDURE Terminate(**VAR** PQ:
              PriorityQueue);
(* **post** – PQ-pre does not exist. *)

END PriorityQueues.

Priority Queue
Formal Specifications

PROCEDURE Serve(**VAR** PQ: Priority-
                             Queue;
               VAR e: StdElement;
               VAR py: Priority);
(* **pre** – not Cardinality(PQ) = 0.
   post – e = a and py = b and PQ = PQ'
             - {<a,b>} | <a,b> in PQ' and
             $\forall$ <c,d> in PQ', b >= d. *)

PROCEDURE Length(PQ: PriorityQueue)
                    : CARDINAL;
(* **post** – Length = Cardinality(PQ). *)

PROCEDURE Full(PQ: PriorityQueue):
              BOOLEAN;
(* **post** – Full = Cardinality(PQ) =
              Bound. *)

PROCEDURE Create(**VAR** PQ: PriorityQueue)
                    : BOOLEAN;
(* **post** – $\exists$ PQ and Cardinality(PQ) = 0. *)

PROCEDURE Terminate(**VAR** PQ: Priority-
                                   Queue);
(* **post** – not $\exists$ PQ'. *)

END PriorityQueues.

The element type is quite straightforward. The element values must be chosen from the set of allowable values of the type *StdElement*. This set of allowable values is the domain of *StdElement*.

There is a considerable difference in the way in which the structure is specified. The informal version simply states that there must be some "mechanism" for determining the order of arrival of the elements into the priority queue. The formal specification explicitly states what the mechanism is. Each element is associated with its priority by putting both in an ordered pair with the element value in the first position and the priority value in the second position. The value of the priority queue is then a set of such ordered pairs.

It is very important to realize that although the specification of the formal structure is quite definite, it is only an abstraction. The implementor remains free to choose any representation that makes this structure as seen through its defined operations seem to exist.

We have seen in Section 3.4 that a priority queue can be represented as a heap—a form of binary tree—yet that representation and its accompanying implementation meet the formal specifications whose abstract model is a set, not a tree.

The method of writing formal abstract specifications that we are discussing is called the **abstract model method.** That name comes from the technique of stating the structure in terms of known, perhaps simpler, structures. A set of ordered pairs is a well-known type and has formally specified operations. Thus we can specify the values of the priority queue as values of a set of ordered pairs. We shall see below that the operations can be formally specified by using set operations. In this way, we can progress formally from one well-known data type to another.

In writing the operations, both informal and formal methods retain the notion of pre- and postconditions. The general rule is

> If the precondition is true at the beginning of execution
>
> then the postcondition will be true upon completion
>
> else the result is undefined.

The difference between formal and informal specifications is merely in the formality of the statements. They both attempt to state the same thing. It is easier to be precise with the predicate calculus (formal) than with English (informal). However, the meaning (semantics) may be easier to grasp from the English version.

Note the formal postcondition on *Enqueue*. It says that the resulting value of the priority queue, or more specifically the set of ordered pairs with which we are modeling the priority queue, is the value of PQ when execution started (we have chosen the notation PQ´; it corresponds to PQ-pre in the informal specifications) with a single new ordered pair $<e,py>$ added. We show this "addition" by taking the union of PQ´ and a set with a single member—$\{<e,py>\}$.

The postcondition of *Serve* is more complex and more interesting. Its paraphrase in English, while following the form of the predicate calculus, is as follows:

The argument *e* has a value *a,* the argument *py* has a value *b,* and the resulting value of PQ is the starting value of PQ with the single ordered pair <*a,b*> removed

where

<*a,b*> was a member of the starting value of PQ, and for all members <*c,d*> of the starting value of PQ, none had a higher priority value than <*a,b*>.

This is a stilted way of stating something that is true, but then a structured program is a stilted way of describing a process. Both structured programs and the predicate calculus tightly control the constructs that are used to make statements. Both use notation that is confusing to the uninitiated. However, the use of each results in more precise statements.

Formal and informal specifications are complementary. It is often desirable to have both.

Gaining facility with the predicate calculus is worthwhile. After some practice you will begin to appreciate the precision with which you can write specifications. In addition, the specification will be stated in a way that allows a proof of correctness of any implementation. If correctness proofs should become automated, writing specifications formally will be an essential step in the use of such a tool.

10.5.4 Correctness Proofs

Proving the correctness of an implementation is a complex process. The proof for even the simplest data type is more lengthy and complex than the specification and implementation. There is also the likelihood that errors will be made in the proof. If correctness proofs were automated, they could be of great value in producing error-free code. You can read Stanat and McAllister (1977), page 57, for more information on this topic.

Exercises 10.5

1. Write predicate calculus forms of the following statements:
   a. If the product of several integer values is 0, then one of the integer values is 0.
   b. All students must have a major.
   c. Christmas is in December.
   d. All professors are people.
   e. Every student has a student ID number, and only students have student ID numbers.
2. Write the formal specifications for any three of the modules specified in this text.
3. Rewrite the formal specifications given in Section 10.5.3 so that the *Serve* operation will not just give any highest priority element but give the one with highest priority and lowest key value.

4. What changes must be made in both the formal and informal forms of the specifications given in Section 10.5.3 to make the *Serve* operation return elements in FIFO order within a given priority value?

5. Write the formal specifications of a priority queue to include the operations suggested in Exercise 3.4, 6.

10.6 Summary

Approaching problems through the use of abstract data types is a relatively new concept but one that is having a considerable effect in at least four areas:

1. It is influencing the way we think about and solve computing problems. The idea of orienting programs around the data abstractions that are natural to the problem at hand is a powerful one. Once the abstractions are specified, the resulting modules with well-defined interfaces provide a natural way of decomposing the problem and the programming effort. Programs that use the data abstractions flow more easily. We appear to be programming at a higher level with operations that do things directly with the objects of the problem. As we have seen in Section 10.4, the abstractions dock, ship, and port make programming the operation of a port much simpler.

2. It is influencing the design of programming languages. We have referenced several recently developed languages that have abstract data typing facilities (Shaw, 1980).

3. It is influencing the design of computer architectures. The Intel iAPX 432 is a good example (Tyner, 1981). Myers (1982) reviews such architectures.

4. It is changing the way in which we verify the correctness of programs. Defining data abstractions and formally specifying them allows at least the possibility of proving implementations to be correct. Although it is questionable that this will be done routinely until an automated correctness prover is developed, formally specified abstract data types lead to improved precision and give insights not previously recognized.

Abstract data types have a strong relationship to objects. An object has at least the following properties:

1. It is a collection of information. Typically there are data, types, code, state information, and others.
2. The internal details of the object are not visible from the outside.
3. The parts of the object have the same lifetimes. They are created and destroyed together.

There are object-oriented programming languages and object-oriented computer architectures. However, these are the subject of more advanced study.

Comparison of Pascal and Modula-2

A.1 Program/Program Module Structure

A.2 Identifiers

A.3 Comments

A.4 Block Structure

A.5 Declarations

A.6 Label Declaration

A.7 Constant Declaration

A.8 Type Declaration

A.9 Variable Declaration

A.10 Procedure Declaration

A.11 Internal Module Declaration

A.12 Definition Module

A.13 Implementation Module

A.14 Statements

This appendix introduces differences between Modula-2 and Pascal. It is not intended as a detailed or exhaustive treatment of either language or of their differences. It is intended to show, in the most graphic way we could find, some of the differences that a Pascal programmer should know about in order to understand Modula-2. The Modula-2 syntax diagrams closely follow the syntax of Modula-2 in Wirth (1983), which can be consulted for details.

We suggest that you skim Appendix A to obtain an overview of its content and then use it as a reference. To aid in its use as a reference, please refer to the outline on the previous page.

A major difference is that Modula-2 supports separately compiled modules, whereas Pascal does not. To accomplish this, Modula-2 uses three types of modules: program modules, definition modules, and implementation modules. We begin by comparing Pascal programs with Modula-2 program modules.

> "Modules are the most important feature distinguishing Modula-2 from its ancestor, Pascal." (Wirth, 1985)

A.1 Program/Program Module Structure

We defer discussion of definition and implementation modules until Sections A.12 and A.13. Figure A.1 compares the structure of a Pascal program with the structure of a Modula-2 program module. Appendix C contains several examples of Modula-2 program modules.

Figure A.1 introduces several conventions for the syntax diagrams that will be used throughout this appendix. Boldface terms are required keywords. Paths shown with light dashed lines drawn to appear perpendicular to the plane of the page are paths that may be traversed repeatedly. A Modula-2 program module, for example, may have more than one import.

> A Pascal program is similar to a Modula-2 program module except that a Modula-2 program module may include any number of imports and ends with the module identifier followed by a period.

Look at Figure A.1 and observe two differences. First, a Modula-2 program module ends with the module identifier followed by a period. The two identifi-

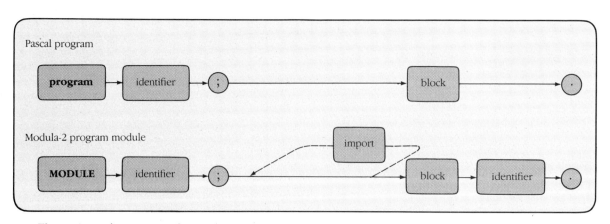

Figure A.1   The structure of a Pascal program compared with the structure of a Modula-2 program module. The structure of definition modules and implementation modules in Modula-2 is not shown.

ers shown for Modula-2 must be identical. Second, a Modula-2 program module permits any number of imports. We discuss imports later. In the meantime think of an import as naming another module and making its constants, data types, variables, and procedures available to the module into which it is imported. Every Implementation Module in this text has several imports.

A.2 Identifiers

Figure A.2 summarizes the differences between identifiers. The only difference is that Modula-2 identifiers are case sensitive while Pascal identifiers are not.

Language	First character	Subsequent characters	Length	Case sensitive
Pascal	Letter	Letter or digit	No limit	No
Modula-2	Letter	Letter or digit	No limit	Yes

Figure A.2   Identifiers in Pascal and Modula-2.

Modula-2 identifiers are case sensitive but Pascal identifiers are not. *DataStructures* and *datastructures* are distinct in Modula-2 but the same in Pascal.

A.3 Comments

Figure A.3 summarizes construction of comments. A major difference is that Modula-2 comments can be nested. This permits, for example, using comments to temporarily remove a section of code that contains comments. Use of {. . .} specifies set membership in Modula-2 and cannot be used to present a comment.

Language	Comment begin	Comment end	Nested
Pascal	(* or {	*) or }	No
Modula-2	(*	*)	Yes

Figure A.3   Comments in Pascal and Modula-2.

Modula-2 comments may be nested, whereas Pascal comments may not.

{Valid comment in Pascal—but not in Modula-2}

(* A Modula-2 comment *)

(* Modula-2 comments (* may be nested *) *)

A.4 Block Structure

Block syntax is compared in Figure A.4. The difference is that Pascal requires **begin** and a statement sequence, whereas Modula-2 does not. Remember that a Modula-2 program may reference many modules. In an implementation module the statement sequence portion of a block is used to initialize variables specified in that module. Since initialization may not be desirable, the inclusion of an initialization section is optional. Further discussion of initialization is given in Section A.11.

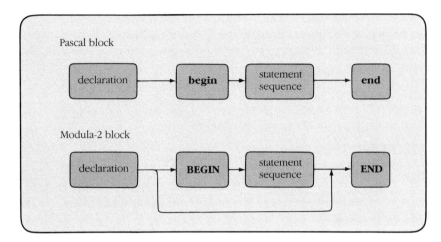

The statement sequence required in a Pascal block is not required in a Modula-2 block. Elaboration on this difference is given in Section A.11.

Figure A.4   The syntax of Pascal and Modula-2 blocks.

A.5 Declarations

The five classes of Modula-2 declarations may occur any number of times and in any order. Each of the five classes of Pascal declarations may appear at most once, and they must appear in the prescribed order. Figure A.5 (a) shows the only order permitted in Pascal and (b), one of the endless possible orders in Modula-2.

In contrast with Pascal, a Modula-2 declaration permits any number of occurrences of constant, type, and variable declarations, and these declarations may appear in any order. A major advantage for Modula-2 is that declarations can be placed near their intended use as an aid to documentation.

Note that a module may be declared in a Modula-2 declaration. More about this in Section A.11, where we shall see that the inclusion of a module within a module allows considerable flexibility in controlling the scope of variables. Figure A.6 compares Pascal and Modula-2 syntax for a declaration.

There are no label declarations in Modula-2, and there are no module declarations in Pascal.

```
Program Example;                MODULE ModExample;

    label ...                       TYPE         ...
    const ...                       PROCEDURES ...
    type  ...                       CONST        ...
    var   ...                       VAR          ...
    procedures and                  TYPE         ...
        functions ...               PROCEDURES ...

begin
    ...                         BEGIN
end.                                ...
                                END ModExample.

        (a)                             (b)
```

Figure A.5   In Pascal (a) only one order of declarations is permitted. In Modula-2 (b) declarations may occur in any order and may be repeated.

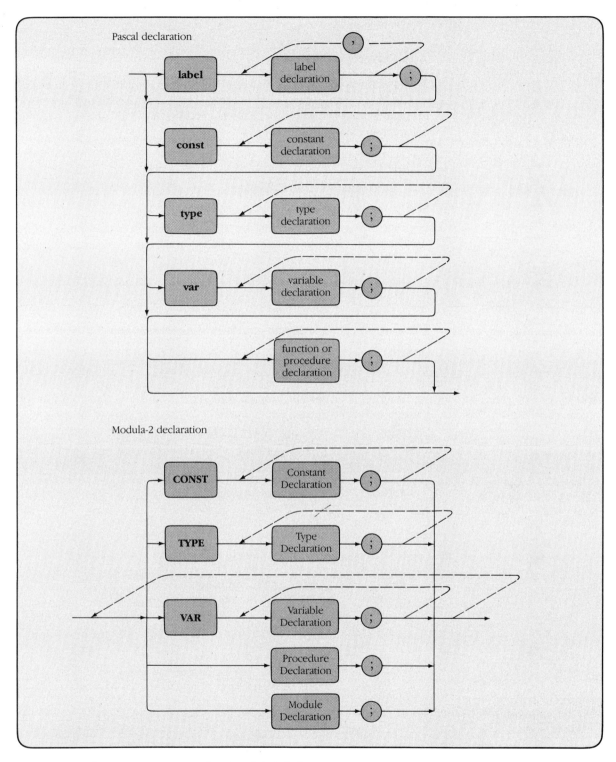

Figure A.6 Comparison of Pascal and Modula-2 declarations.

A.6 Label Declaration

Modula-2 has no label declaration. But Modula-2 has a RETURN statement and an EXIT statement (Section A.14) not shared by Pascal. The RETURN statement terminates the enclosing procedure or module. The EXIT statement terminates the enclosing LOOP statement.

A.7 Constant Declaration

The syntax for constant declarations is shown in Figure A.7. Modula-2 permits constant expressions instead of the constant terms permitted by Pascal. A constant term includes constant identifiers, literal identifiers, and the unary operators + and −. Modula-2, in addition, permits sets and expressions.

Modula-2 permits constant expressions everywhere it permits constants. The following constant declaration is permitted in Modula-2 but not in Pascal.

CONST Order = 3;
        MaxSize = 2*Order;

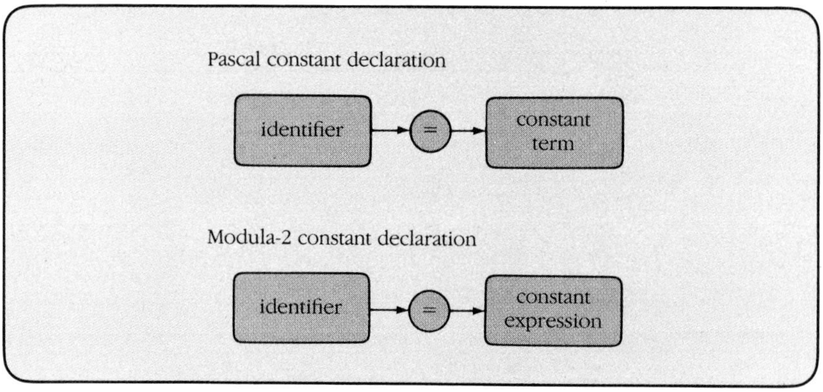

Figure A.7 Syntax diagrams for constant declarations.

Figure A.8 shows examples of constant terms and constant expressions.

```
const                      CONST
    Max     = 1000;            Max     = 1000;
    pi      = 3.14159;         Pi      = 3.14159;
    MinusPi = - pi;            MinusPi = - Pi;
                               TwoPi   = 2.0*Pi;
(* Modula-2 permits *)
(* expressions.     *)
                               Letter = 'A';
    Letter = 'A';              Name   = 'N. Wirth';
    Name   = 'N. Wirth';       Prime  = [2,3,5,7];
(* Modula-2 permits *)         Square = [1,4,9];
(* sets and set     *)         SAndP  = Prime*Square;
(* expressions.     *)
```

                (a)   (b)

Figure A.8 Examples of constant declarations in (a) Pascal and (b) Modula-2.

A.8 Type Declaration

This section surveys differences in syntax for type declarations. The data types supported are shown in Figure A.9. Pascal supports a file type and Modula-2 does not, but Modula-2 supports a procedure type and Pascal does not. Data type file is normally imported in Modula-2 from modules supplied by the implementor. Figure A.9 lists, for each type, the section in which declaration differences are discussed in more detail.

Section	Pascal types	Modula-2 types
A.8.1	Standard	Standard
A.8.2	Simple	Simple
A.8.3	Pointer	POINTER
A.8.4	Array	ARRAY
A.8.5	Record	RECORD
A.8.6	Set	SET
A.8.7	File	
A.8.8		PROCEDURE

Figure A.9   Data types in Pascal and Modula-2.

The data type procedure is included in Modula-2 but not in Pascal.

The syntax of a type declaration, exclusive of details for a specific data type, is shown in Figure A.10.

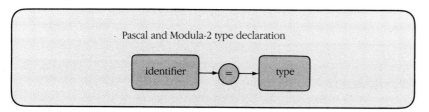

Pascal and Modula-2 type declaration

identifier → = → type

Figure A.10   Type declaration syntax. The syntax is the same in Pascal and Modula-2.

Modula-2 must import its file data type—it is not a standard part of the language as it is in Pascal. Module *InOut* (Appendix E) provides some primitive file operations. Most implementations supply Module *FileSystem*, which provides extensive file handling capabilities.

A.8.1 Standard Types

The standard types for Pascal and Modula-2 are shown in Figure A.11. Four additional types—BYTE, WORD, ADDRESS, and PROCESS—can be imported from module SYSTEM in Modula-2.

Pascal	Modula-2
	BITSET
Boolean	BOOLEAN
Character	CHARACTER
	CARDINAL
	LONGCARD
Integer	INTEGER
	LONGINT
Real	REAL
	LONGREAL

Figure A.11   Standard types in Pascal and Modula-2.

Modula-2 includes five standard types—BITSET, CARDINAL, LONGCARD, LONGINT, and LONGREAL—that are not standard types in Pascal.

Integer variables can be assigned to cardinal variables, and vice versa. But integer and cardinal variables cannot be intermixed in expressions.

If i is of type integer then ORD(i) returns a cardinal value. If c is of type cardinal then VAL(INTEGER,c) returns an integer value.

A.8.2 Simple Types

Status = (wait,ready,done)

Figure A.12
Example declaration of an enumerated data type in both Pascal and Modula-2.

The simple types are enumerated and subrange. The syntax for enumerated types is the same in Pascal and Modula-2, and an example declaration is shown in Figure A.12.

Declarations of subrange types have a number of differences. Modula-2 requires brackets to delimit a subrange type, whereas Pascal does not. An example is shown in Figure A.13. The constants that specify the bounds of a subrange must be constant terms in Pascal, but may be constant expressions in Modula-2. Refer to Figure A.8 for examples of constant terms and constant expressions.

Modula-2 has a predefined type CARDINAL not available in Pascal. Its values are the integers from 0 to MaxCard. The base type of a subrange of the integers in Modula-2 is determined by the lower bound of the subrange. If the lower bound is negative then the base type is INTEGER; otherwise the base type is CARDINAL. To override this convention you must specify the type as shown in the fourth row of Figure A.13(b). In Pascal the base type of a subrange of the integers is always integer.

```
(* Base type CARDINAL *)
(* Base type INTEGER  *)
(* Base type CARDINAL *)
(* Base type INTEGER  *)
```

```
type                      TYPE
   Natural = 1..5000;        Natural = [1..5000];
   SubInt  = -10..10;        SubInt  = [-10..10];
   FiveMax = 0..5000         FiveMax = [0..5*Max]
                             Nat2 = INTEGER[1..5000]
```

(a)   (b)

Figure A.13 Example subrange declarations in (a) Pascal and (b) Modula-2. The Modula-2 base type is given in the margin. Identifier Max is defined in Figure A.7.

The declaration of a subrange type is enclosed in brackets in Modula-2, but not in Pascal. The base type of a subrange of the integers is always integer in Pascal. In Modula-2 a subrange of the integers whose lower limit is 0 or greater has base type CARDINAL—unless overridden as shown in Figure A.13.

An ordinal type is a data type such that each value of the type has a unique position relative to all values of that type. The standard function procedure ORD can be used to extract the position of any value of an ordinal type. The ordinal types in Pascal are boolean, character, enumerated, integer, and a subrange of any ordinal type. The ordinal types in Modula-2 are BOOLEAN, CARDINAL, CHARACTER, enumerated, INTEGER, and a subrange of any ordinal type.

A.8.3 Pointer Types

There are two changes to note with respect to pointer declaration. A major syntactic change is that Pascal's ↑ is replaced by Modula-2's POINTER TO. A minor difference is that the object pointed at in Pascal must be a type identifier, whereas in Modula-2 it may be any type. The syntax diagrams are shown in Figure A.14.

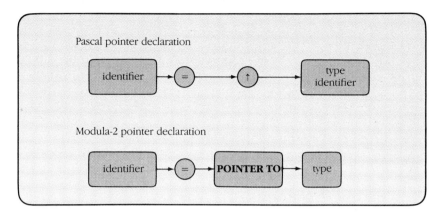

Figure A.14   Pointer declarations in Pascal and Modula-2.

In Pascal a pointer type is declared by

↑ referenced type

but in Modula-2 this same pointer declaration is given by

POINTER TO referenced type

A.8.4 Array Types

Figure A.15 shows the syntax of array type declarations. The term packed does not occur in Modula-2 and the syntax for designating index types is different. Figure A.16 shows examples of array declarations.

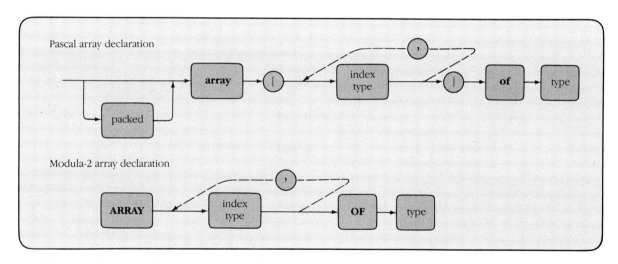

Figure A.15   Syntax diagrams for array declarations.

Packed data types do not occur in most implementations of Modula-2.

In the declaration of an array type in Pascal the index type list is enclosed in brackets. In Modula-2 the brackets are part of each index type.

type
```
  Natural    = 1..1000;
  A1 = array [Natural] of integer;
  A2 = array [0..10,Natural] of real;
  A3 = Array [0..5,1..100] of real;

  Day = (Mon,Tues,Wed);
  A4  = array [Day] of real;
```
(a)

TYPE
```
  Natural = [1..1000];
  A1 = ARRAY Natural OF INTEGER;
  A2 = ARRAY [0..10],Natural OF REAL;
  A3 = ARRAY [0..5],[1..10] OF REAL;

  Day = (Mon,Tues,Wed);
  A4  = ARRAY Day OF REAL;
```
(b)

Figure A.16   Example array declarations in (a) Pascal and (b) Modula-2.

A.8.5 Record Declaration

A record declaration in both Pascal and Modula-2 can be described as a sequence of field lists as shown in Figure A.17.

The declaration of a Modula-2 record type is a considerable extension of the declaration of a Pascal record type. Study the example in Figure A.18 and the syntax diagrams in Figure A.19 to see the differences.

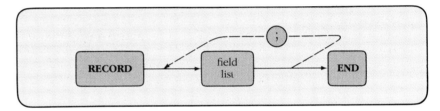

Figure A.17   A record declaration is a sequence of field lists.

To aid in the comparison, Figure A.18 shows an example of a Modula-2 record declaration.

```
RECORD
    x1,x2,x3: CARDINAL;              (* See Figure A.19(a). *)
    CASE value OF                    (* See Figure A.19(c). *)
            0     : small. CARDINAL |
            1..10 : med1 : CARDINAL;
                    med2 : REAL |
            11..99: big1 : INTEGER;
                    big2 : ARRAY [1..10] OF REAL;
                    big3 : CARDINAL
         ELSE
    END;
    CASE ch OF                       (* See Figure A.19(c). *)
          'A','a': alpha: CARDINAL |
          'B','b': beta : CARDINAL
          ELSE     gamma: CHAR;
                   delta: CHAR
       END
END;
```

Figure A.18   Example declaration of a Modula-2 record following the syntax diagram in Figure A.19.

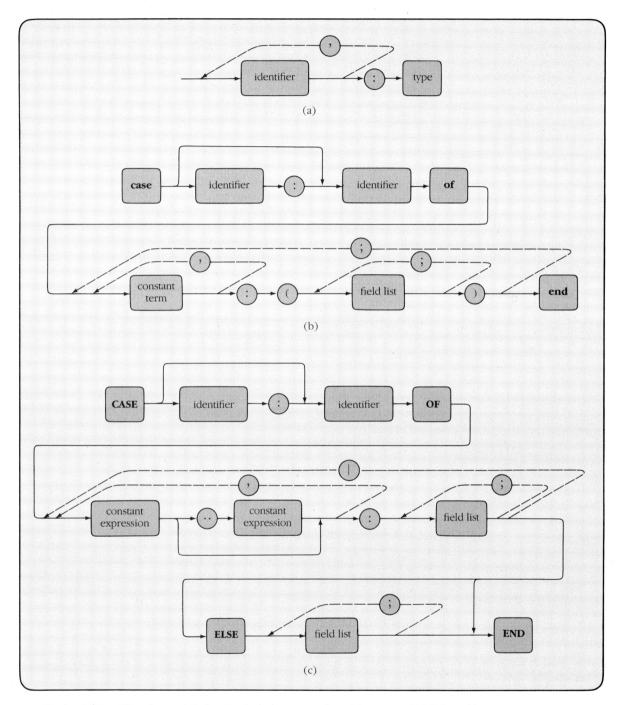

Figure A.19 A Pascal record declaration includes any number of instances of (a) followed by at most one instance of (b). A Modula-2 record declaration includes any interleaving of instances of (a) with instances of (c).

In Figure A.19 we compare the syntax for field list construction in Modula-2 with the syntax used to construct a field list in Pascal. A Pascal record is constructed using any number of instances of (a) followed by at most one instance of (b). A record in Modula-2 is constructed using any interleaving of instances of (a) with instances of (c). The syntax shown in Figure A.19(a) generates what is referred to as the ***fixed part*** of either a Pascal or Modula-2 record. The syntax shown in (b) generates the ***variant part*** of a Pascal record, and the syntax shown in (c) generates the variant part of a Modula-2 record.

A significant difference between Pascal and Modula-2 is that the variant part of a Pascal record contains only one instance of A.19(b), whereas the variant part of a Modula-2 record may contain many instances of A.19(c). Figure A.18 shows an example with two instances of A.19(c).

A.8.6 Set Type Declaration

If *Sample* is declared in Modula-2 as

TYPE Sample = SET OF [0..10];

and s1 is the variable given by

VAR s1: Sample;

then a statement that assigns a value to s1 is

s1 := Sample{2,4,5}

The set constant {2,4,5}, without a preceding identifier, is, by default, of type BITSET.

Except for the case sensitivity of Modula-2, both Pascal and Modula-2 have the syntax for set type declaration shown in Figure A.20. Modula-2 has the predefined set type, called BITSET, whose values are all possible subsets of the set $\{0,1,..., w - 1\}$, where w is the number of bits in a word of the host computer system.

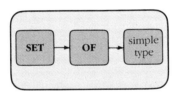

Figure A.20   Set type declaration in Pascal and Modula-2.

A.8.7 File Type Declaration

Modula-2 does not have a file type, but each implementation is expected to include modules which support this type.

A.8.8 Procedure Type Declaration

Pascal does not support a procedure type. Specification 5.1 and Implementation Module 5.1 show a typical use of a procedure type to provide users the ability to process the elements of an opaque data type.

Pascal does not have a procedure type. The syntax for declaring a Modula-2 procedure type is shown in Figure A.21. Be sure to note that a procedure type declaration is distinct from a procedure declaration. The syntax for procedure declarations in Modula-2 is shown in Section A.10 of this appendix.

Several examples of procedure type declarations are shown in Figure A.22. Examples showing the use of procedure type declarations are given in Section A.9.

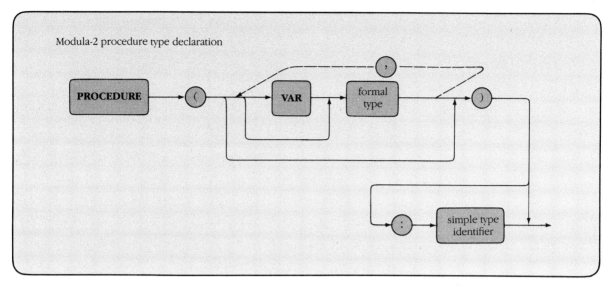

Figure A.21   Syntax of a procedure type declaration in Modula-2.

```
TYPE Proc1 = PROCEDURE ();            (* Same as built-in type PROC. *)
     Proc2 = PROCEDURE ( REAL );
     Proc3 = PROCEDURE ( VAR CARDINAL, INTEGER, INTEGER, INTEGER );
     Proc4 = PROCEDURE ( REAL ): BOOLEAN;
     Proc5 = PROCEDURE ( ARRAY OF REAL );
```

Figure A.22   Example procedure type declarations in Modula-2.

A.9 Variable Declaration

The syntax of variable declaration is shown for both Pascal and Modula-2 in Figure A.23.

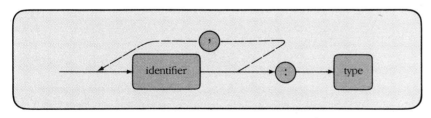

Figure A.23   Variable declaration in either Pascal or Modula-2.

If, for example, procedure types are declared as shown in Figure A.22, then in Modula-2 we might have the variable declaration shown in Figure A.24.

VAR f: Proc1;
g1, g2: Proc4;

Figure A.24
Example variable declaration in Modula-2.

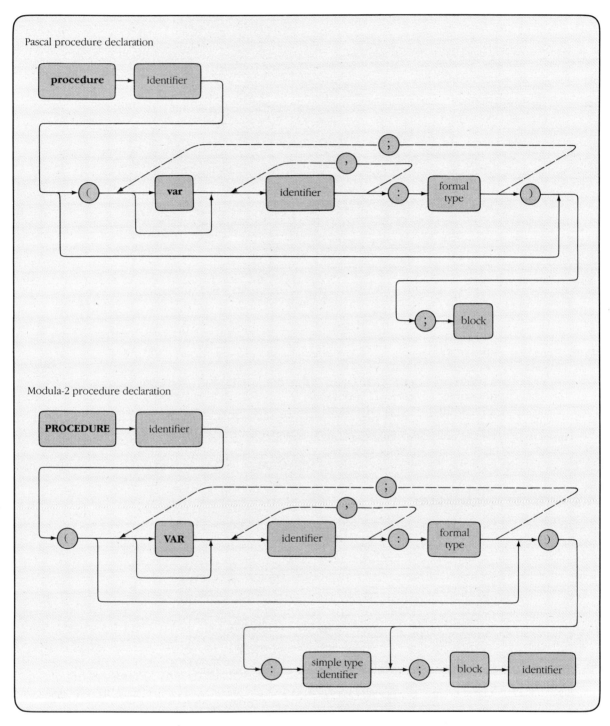

Figure A.25   Procedure declaration syntax for Pascal and Modula-2.

A.10 Procedure Declaration

Pascal has a separate syntax for procedure and function declaration. Modula-2 has a single syntax for both. The comparison shown in Figure A.25 does not give the syntax for a Pascal function.

Note that each Modula-2 procedure declaration ends with the procedure identifier.

Both syntax diagrams in Figure A.25 refer to a formal type. There is a significant difference between a Pascal formal type and a Modula-2 formal type. In Pascal only a type identifier is permitted. In Modula-2 a type identifier may be preceded by ARRAY OF, which creates what is referred to as an open array parameter. An open array parameter permits an array to be passed to a procedure without specifying its index type—the index type is left open. Figure A.27 summarizes the syntax of a formal type, and Figure A.26 shows two example procedure declarations in Modula-2. The first has no formal parameters, and the second has an open array parameter.

The major difference between Pascal and Modula-2 procedure declarations is that Modula-2 permits a formal type that is an array of unspecified size. The result is that Modula-2 procedures may be written to apply to array(s) of any size. A Pascal procedure can be passed only an array whose size is determined at compile time. This makes it difficult to create a library of Pascal routines for doing general-purpose operations like sorting.

PROCEDURE Ex1 ( );	PROCEDURE Ex2 (A: ARRAY OF REAL);
BEGIN	BEGIN
END Ex1;	END Ex2;
(a)	(b)

Figure A.26   Examples of Modula-2 procedure declarations.

Array A in Figure A.26(b) is assumed to contain components A[0], A[1], A[2], . . . , A[HIGH(A)], where HIGH is a built-in operation in Modula-2. Refer to Specification 6.1 for another example of the use of open array parameters. Algorithms 6.1, 6.2, and 6.3 illustrate the use of operation HIGH.

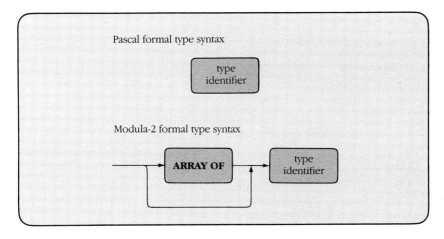

Figure A.27   Syntax for formal type in Pascal and Modula-2.

A.11 Internal Module Declaration

Pascal is a block structured language. Each Pascal program contains a program block as shown in Figure A.28. A program block may, in turn, contain procedure and/or function blocks (Figures A.4 and A.5). A procedure or function block may, in turn, contain procedure and/or function blocks, and so on.

Pascal controls, in one specific way, how objects declared in one block are shared with other blocks, limits the scope of variables declared in a procedure or function block, and provides no mechanism for initializing variables except declaring and initializing them in the program block.

". . . if a Pascal function or procedure intends to remember a value from one call to another, the variable used must be external to the function or procedure. Thus it must be visible to other procedures, and its name must be unique in the larger scope.

". . . there is no way for two [Pascal] routines to share a variable unless it is declared at or above their least common ancestor.

". . . a Pascal program must contain explicit assignment statements to initialize variables. The result is that any variable that is to be initialized has global scope." (Kernighan, 1982)

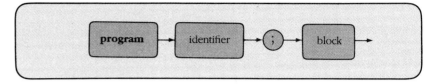

Figure A.28   Structure of a Pascal program.

Each block may declare constants, types, variables, procedures, and functions. The scope of any of these declared objects is the block in which it is declared and all blocks nested within that block. Figure A.29 shows a graphic representation of a program block and five procedure blocks nested within it.

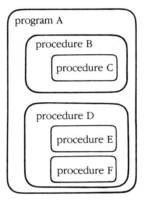

Figure A.29   A graphic representation of the nested relationship of a Pascal program and 5 procedures.

There are restrictions imposed by the block structuring of Pascal.

1. An object declared in a block is not accessible in any block that contains it, but that object is accessible in all blocks nested within the block that declares it. In Figure A.29 an object declared in procedure D is not accessible in program A or procedures B and C, but it is accessible in procedures E and F.

2. A variable declared in a procedure or function block loses its existence and value when that block is not active. In Figure A.29 a variable declared in procedure B exists only during execution of either procedure B or C.

3. The only way to initialize a variable is to make it a global variable and then assign it a value in the program block. In Figure A.29 a variable assigned an initial value in procedure D loses that value (and its existence) when control returns to program A.

Local modules in Modula-2 give the programmer control over how objects are shared, their scope, and provide a mechanism for initializing variables that are not declared in the program module block.

These three restrictions also apply to Modula-2 procedures. But Modula-2 permits a local module to be declared as part of a block (Figure A.5) and thereby allows a programmer to eliminate all three of the restrictions listed above. To illustrate how this can be accomplished, Figure A.30 shows an example of a module, *InternalExample,* that contains a local internal module, *Mod1.*

Module *Mod1* declares two variables, *a* and *b*, and one procedure, *Sum.*

```
MODULE InternalExample;                              (* Internal module example *)

FROM InOut IMPORT Write, WriteString, WriteLn, WriteCard;

VAR a,b: CARDINAL;

    PROCEDURE Spaces(n: CARDINAL);
    VAR k: CARDINAL;                         (* Variable k exists only       *)
    BEGIN                                    (* during execution of Spaces.  *)
        FOR k := 1 TO n DO Write(' ') END
    END Spaces;

    MODULE Mod1;
    IMPORT WriteLn, WriteCard,
        WriteString, Spaces;
    EXPORT QUALIFIED a, Sum;            (* Variable a is exported, but b is hidden. *)
    VAR a,b: CARDINAL;                        (* Variables a and b retain their *)
                                              (* values as long as module       *)
        PROCEDURE Sum(): CARDINAL;            (* InternalExample is alive.      *)
        BEGIN
            RETURN (a+b)
        END Sum;

    BEGIN                                (* Initialization code for local    *)
        Spaces(3);                       (* modules is executed in the order *)
        WriteString('Module Mod1');      (* in which those modules appear,   *)
        WriteLn; a := 2; b := 5;         (* and before the "main" program.   *)
        Spaces(3); WriteCard(a,4);
        WriteCard(b,4); WriteLn
    END Mod1;

BEGIN
    WriteString('Module Internal'); WriteLn;
    WriteCard(Mod1.a,4); WriteCard(Mod1.Sum(),4); WriteLn;
    a:= 10; b:= 15;
    WriteCard(a,4); WriteCard(b,4); WriteLn
END InternalExample.
```

Figure A.30   Example of a Modula-2 module that contains a local module.

Since *a* and *Sum* are declared external they are accessible in the module that contains *Mod1*—as long as they are referenced using the qualified identifiers *Mod1.a* and *Mod1.Sum*. If *Mod1* contained nested modules the only variables accessible to them would be those specifically imported.

Module *Internal* declares variables *a* and *b* as well as procedure *Spaces*. Neither *a* nor *b* is accessible in *Mod1* since neither of them is imported. *Spaces* is imported and is therefore accessible in *Mod1*.

Observe that module *Mod1* contains BEGIN and a statement sequence, which are optional (Figure A.4). These statements are essentially initialization statements and are executed once, in the order that the local modules appear, before the statement sequence of the program module is executed.

Study Figure A.30 to see that the output it produces is as shown in Figure A.31.

```
Module Mod1
   2   5
Module Internal
   2   7
  10  15
```

Figure A.31
Output produced by the program given in Figure A.30.

A variable declared in a module, say *M1*, exists and retains its value as long as that module is active.

Figure A.32 gives the syntax for a local module. Compare it with the syntax for a program module given in Figure A.1.

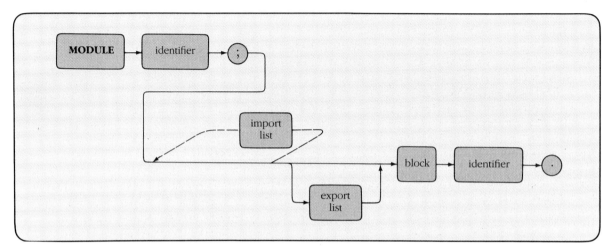

Figure A.32   Syntax for a Modula-2 module.

A.12 Definition Module

A Modula-2 definition module exports constants, types, variables, and procedure headings that form the user interface to an abstract data type. The user need not be concerned with lower levels of detail.

A type definition in a definition module may omit specifying the type. The details of the type are then not visible to the user and the type is referred to as opaque. Many of the specifications in the text use opaque data types. For some examples see Specifications 3.1, 4.1, and 5.1.

This book contains many examples of definition modules, including one for the specification of each data structure.

If a program is thought of as a hierarchy of abstractions, then, in Modula-2, each abstraction may be divided into a definition module and a corresponding implementation module. The definition module declares the essentials of the abstraction—but may hide the details that are then provided in the implementation module. Thus the details do not clutter up the user's view of the abstraction, they cannot be tampered with by the user, and they can be changed by the implementor as long as they meet the specifications provided by the definition module.

The syntax for a definition module is given in Figure A.33.

The syntax for a definition declaration is shown in Figure A.34. It is similar to a Modula-2 declaration, Figure A.6, except that type declaration is changed to type definition, procedure declaration is replaced by procedure heading, and module declaration is eliminated.

The difference between a type declaration and a type definition is important. The difference in syntax is shown in Figure A.35.

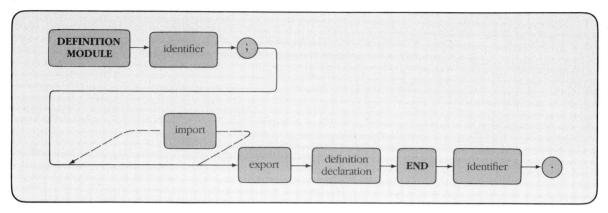

Figure A.33 Syntax for a Modula-2 definition module.

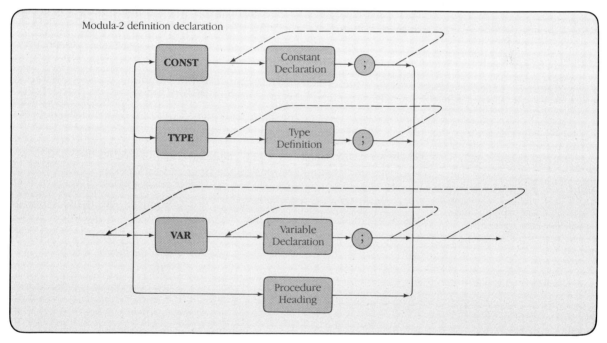

Figure A.34 Modula-2 definition declaration.

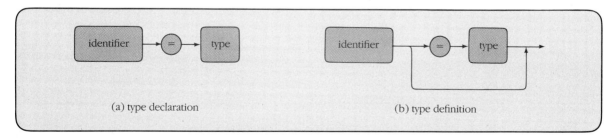

Figure A.35 The syntactic difference between a type declaration and a type definition.

Figure A.35 shows that a type definition need not specify the type to be associated with a type identifier. For example, the definition module in Specification 5.1 contains the type definition

TYPE BinaryTree;

A type definition that omits the type is called an opaque type. The user, who sees only the definition module, cannot see the details of how an opaque type is implemented. An opaque type is usually a pointer to a record (whose details are hidden). An opaque type must be a pointer or a subrange of a standard type. If the type is given in a type definition then that type is referred to as a transparent type—the user does see the implementation details.

It is a major advantage to be able to omit the type portion of a type definition because (1) the user need not absorb unnecessary details, (2) the user is prevented from tampering with the details of the type—and hence the implementation need not protect itself from such tampering, and (3) the way an opaque type is implemented may be changed without affecting any user.

A Modula-2 procedure heading is the same as a procedure declaration (Figure A.25) minus the block and the final identifier.

A.13 Implementation Module

A Modula-2 implementation module provides the details not given in the definition module. An implementation module is independent of the corresponding definition module in the sense that changing the implementation module does not require changing the definition module.

There are many examples of implementation modules in this book—one for each implementation listed inside the front and back covers.

As suggested in Section A.12, think of a program as a hierarchy of abstractions. Each abstraction is implemented, using Modula-2, as a definition module–implementation module pair. The definition module is described in Section A.12. The implementation module provides the details for the definitions given in the definition module. Its syntax is shown in Figure A.36.

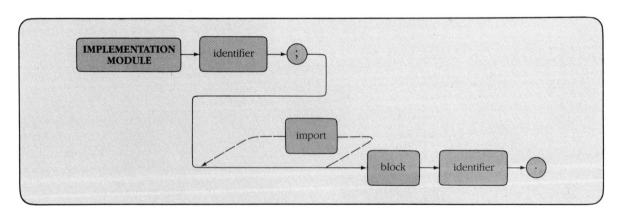

Figure A.36 Syntax for a Modula-2 implementation module. This syntax is the same as the syntax of a program module prefaced with the keyword IMPLEMENTATION.

A.14 Statements

The statements available in Pascal and Modula-2 are summarized in Figure A.37 along with the section in which each statement is discussed.

Section	Pascal	Modula-2
A.14.1	Assignment	Assignment
A.14.2	Compound statement	
A.14.3	Statement sequence	Statement sequence
A.14.4	If	IF
A.14.5	Case	CASE
A.14.6	While	WHILE
A.14.7	Repeat	REPEAT
A.14.8		LOOP and EXIT
A.14.9	For	FOR
A.14.10	With	WITH
A.14.11		RETURN
A.14.12	Procedure or function call	Procedure call

Figure A.37 Pascal and Modula-2 statements.

A.14.1 Assignment

The syntax for assignment is shown in Figure A.38.

A.14.2 Compound Statement

Pascal programs usually contain many compound statements. Modula-2 programs contain almost none—because of the judicious use of keywords in Modula-2 to eliminate the need to bracket a sequence of statements with BEGIN and END (Figure A.39).

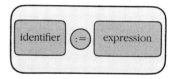

Figure A.38
The syntax for assignment in Pascal and Modula-2.

Modula-2 adds RETURN, LOOP, and EXIT statements to those available in Pascal.

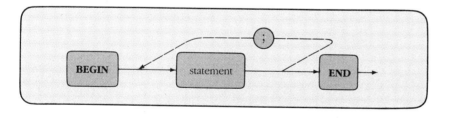

Figure A.39
The syntax of a compound statement.

A.14.3 Statement Sequence

The syntax of a statement sequence is shown in Figure A.40.

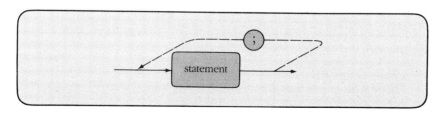

Figure A.40
The syntax of a statement sequence.

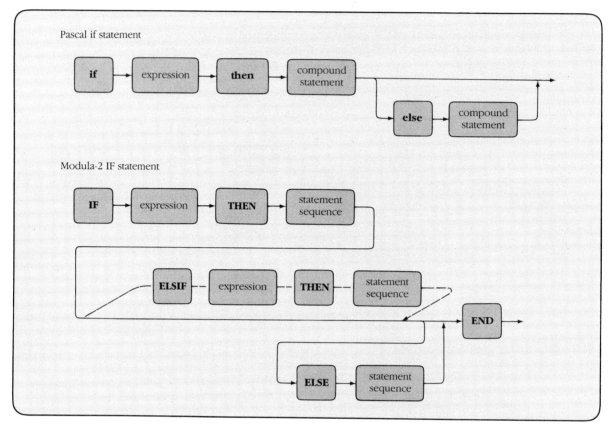

Figure A.41   The syntax of Pascal and Modula-2 if statements.

A.14.4 If Statement

The Pascal if statement syntax is extended, in Modula-2, to include any number of ELSIF clauses and to terminate with END.

The syntax is compared in Figure A.41.

The code segments in Figure A.42 illustrate the difference in logic between Pascal and Modula-2 if statements.

```
if salt in list
    then if pepper in list
       then writeln('Salt and
          pepper')

    else writeln('Salt but not
       pepper')

                (a)
```

```
IF salt in list
    THEN IF pepper in list
       THEN WriteString('Salt and
          pepper')
       END
    ELSE WriteString('No Salt')
END

                (b)
```

Figure A.42   An example to emphasize the difference between the logic of a Pascal if statement (a) and a Modula-2 IF statement (b). In Pascal an else is associated with the closest if that precedes it.

A.14.5 Case Statement

The Modula-2 CASE statement extends the Pascal case statement in two respects. First, the Modula-2 CASE statement contains an ELSE clause that is not present in Pascal. Second, where Pascal cases are identified using one or a sequence of constant terms, Modula-2 cases are labeled using one or more constant expressions or ranges of values whose endpoints are given by constant expressions. The syntax diagrams are shown in Figure A.43.

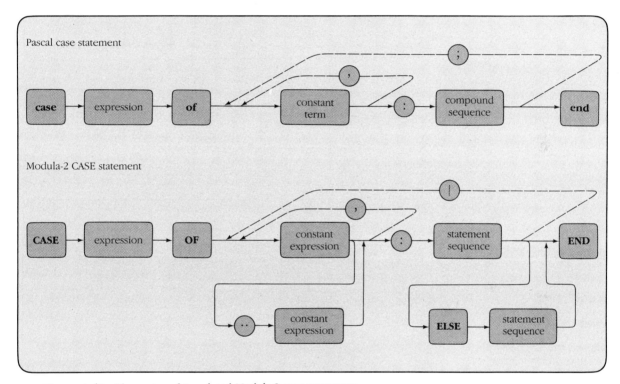

Figure A.43   The syntax of Pascal and Modula-2 case statements.

Implementation Module 5.1 contains several examples of CASE statements. Note the use of "|" to separate a statement sequence from a constant expression.

A.14.6 While Statement

The syntax of Pascal and Modula-2 while statements is nearly identical. The while statement syntax diagrams are shown in Figure A.44.

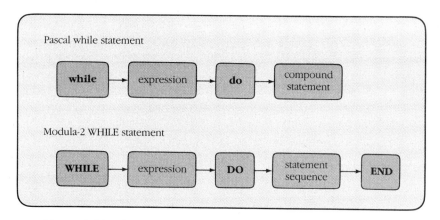

Figure A.44   The syntax of Pascal and Modula-2 while statements.

A.14.7 Repeat Statement

The syntax of Pascal and Modula-2 repeat statements, shown in Figure A.45, is essentially the same.

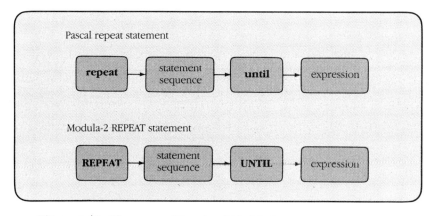

Figure A.45   The syntax of Pascal and Modula-2 repeat statements.

A.14.8 Loop and Exit Statements

A LOOP statement provides for the endless execution of the statements it contains. The statement

```
LOOP
    k := 1
END
```

assigns 1 to k endlessly. The EXIT statement terminates execution of the LOOP statement that contains it, and may occur at several places in the LOOP. For example, the following LOOP has two exit points.

```
LOOP
    x := x*x;
    IF x = y THEN EXIT
    END;
    INC(k,3);
    IF k > 55 THEN EXIT
    END
END
```

Pascal has neither a LOOP statement nor an EXIT statement. The Modula-2 LOOP statement is used in conjunction with the EXIT statement. The LOOP statement, by itself, is an infinite loop. The EXIT statement is the usual tool used to drop out of a loop. Use of the LOOP statement is illustrated in the margin. The syntax for LOOP and EXIT statements is shown in Figure A.46.

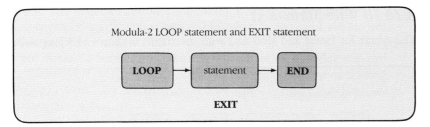

Figure A.46 The syntax of Modula-2 LOOP and EXIT statements.

A.14.9 For Statement

The Modula-2 FOR statement extends the Pascal for statement by permitting an increment, determined by an expression, of size other than one. A comparison of syntax diagrams is given in Figure A.47.

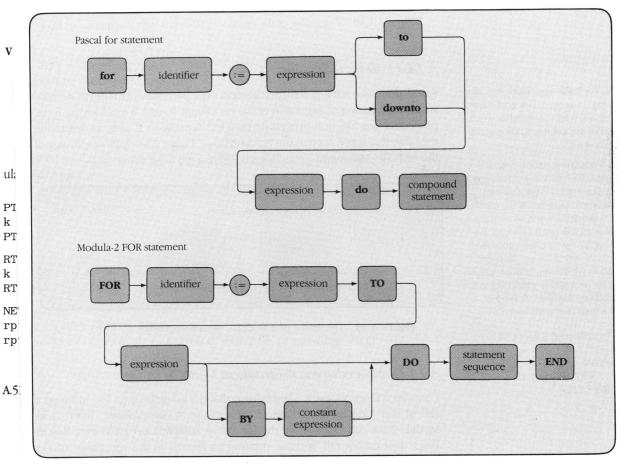

Figure A.47 The syntax of the Pascal and Modula-2 for statements.

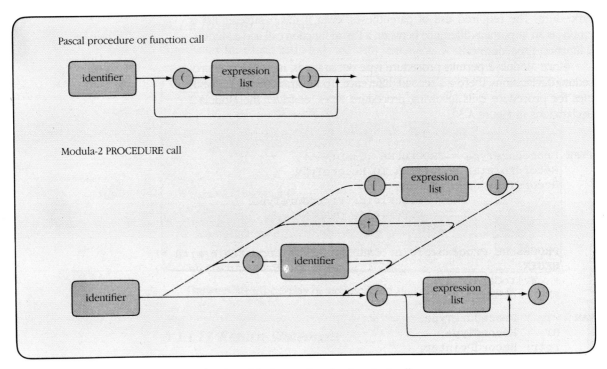

Figure A.51   The syntax of Pascal and Modula-2 procedure (or function) calls.

An example of a Modula-2
procedure call is

A[3] ↑ .B ↑ [5].C

where A is an array of
pointers, B is a pointer to an
array of records, and C is a
field identifier.

Recursion B

B.1 Recursive Functions

B.2 Some Sample Recursive Functions

B.3 How Recursion Is Implemented

B.4 Performance Issues

B.5 Alternatives to Recursion

B.1 Recursive Functions

Recursion is often used to define functions. Simply stated, a function is defined recursively if its value is defined for one or more special cases; for all other cases, it is defined in terms of itself. Consider the definition of the function that is the sum of the integers from 1 to n, where $n > 0$.

$$\text{Sum}(n) = n + (n - 1) + \ldots + 2 + 1$$

We can define the function recursively:

    $\text{Sum}(1) = 1$ (The special case.)
    $\text{Sum}(n) = n + \text{Sum}(n - 1)$

Suppose that we choose n to be 4. We can write

    $\text{Sum}(4) = 4 + \text{Sum}(3)$
    $\text{Sum}(3) = 3 + \text{Sum}(2)$
    $\text{Sum}(2) = 2 + \text{Sum}(1)$
    $\text{Sum}(1) = 1$

Substituting in reverse order, we have

    $\text{Sum}(1) = 1$
    $\text{Sum}(2) = 2 + \text{Sum}(1) = 3$
    $\text{Sum}(3) = 3 + \text{Sum}(2) = 6$
    $\text{Sum}(4) = 4 + \text{Sum}(3) = 10$

Figure B.1   Recursive evaluation of *Sum*(4).

When one first encounters this method, it seems a convoluted way to do something quite simple. What is the benefit? Though it may not be apparent yet, defining functions recursively, or implementing them on a computer with a ***recursive algorithm,*** is often quite natural, economical in terms of the function definition and code, and likely to give insights into the function being defined or coded. Let us look at an algorithm (Algorithm B.1) for the *Sum* function defined above.

```
PROCEDURE Sum(n: CARDINAL): CARDINAL;
BEGIN
    IF n = 1
        THEN RETURN 1
        ELSE RETURN (n + Sum(n-1))
    END
END Sum;
```

Algorithm B.1   Recursive implementation of *Sum.*

Use the function to evaluate *Sum*(4) as we did above. The evaluation path is exactly as shown in Figure B.1. Notice that in the ELSE clause procedure *Sum* calls itself before it exits from a previous call. If we call *Sum*(4), the algorithm attempts to execute the statement

RETURN (4 + Sum(4-1))

In order to do so, *Sum*(3) is called and the addition is suspended until *Sum*(3) is evaluated. But in attempting to evaluate *Sum*(3), the algorithm attempts to execute the statement

RETURN (3 + Sum(3-1))

Similarly, this addition is suspended until *Sum*(2) is evaluated:

RETURN (2 + Sum(2-1))

Again the addition is suspended until *Sum*(1) is evaluated. But in evaluating *Sum*(1), the special case is encountered, the THEN clause is executed, and 1 is returned. The suspended sums are completed in reverse order and the final result is computed.

An important metric associated with recursion and its implementation using computers is the ***maximum depth of the recursion.*** It is the maximum number of pending suspensions that occur at any time in executing the algorithm. In the case of *Sum*(4), the maximum depth of recursion is 3. We will discuss shortly why this measure is important.

B.2 Some Sample Recursive Functions

Let us look at some recursive functions and algorithms for evaluating them.

B.2.1 Factorials

The factorial function of an integer (cardinal) is the product of the integers from n to 1. It is usually written as $n!$.

$$n! = n \times (n - 1) \times \ldots \times 2 \times 1$$

We can define the factorial function recursively:

fact(1) = 1
fact(n) = $n \times$ fact($n - 1$).

The algorithm for implementing it is exactly analogous to Algorithm B.1.

B.2.2 Fibonacci Numbers

Fibonacci numbers are defined recursively. Each Fibonacci number is the sum of the two previous Fibonacci numbers. The first two are 1.

Fib(0) = 1
Fib(1) = 1
Fib(n) = Fib($n - 1$) + Fib($n - 2$)

Thus

$$\text{Fib}(3) = \text{Fib}(2) + \text{Fib}(1) = [\text{Fib}(1) + \text{Fib}(0)] + \text{Fib}(1) = [1 + 1] + 1 = 3$$
$$\text{Fib}(4) = \text{Fib}(3) + \text{Fib}(2) = 3 + 2 = 5$$

Algorithm B.2 is an implementation.

```
PROCEDURE Fib(n: CARDINAL): CARDINAL;
BEGIN
    IF (n = 0) OR (n = 1)
        THEN RETURN 1
        ELSE RETURN (Fib(n-1) + Fib(n-2))
    END
END Fib;
```

Algorithm B.2   Recursive implementation of *Fib*.

B.2.3 A Recursive Search Procedure

Suppose that we have an array of integer values, and we wish to write an algorithm to search the array for a particular value. If the target value is found, we return the index value of its position in the array; if it is not found, we return the index value 0.

Let us define a global array:

```
CONST Max = 100;

TYPE Index = [0..Max];

VAR a: ARRAY [1..Max] OF INTEGER;
```

Procedure *Find* (Algorithm B.3) searches sequentially through the array *a*, from *n* down to 1, to find a value in *a* that matches some given value *target*.

```
PROCEDURE Find(VAR a: ARRAY OF INTEGER; target: INTEGER;
                    n: CARDINAL; VAR position: CARDINAL);
VAR i: Index;      (* Search a[1] through a[n] for an     *)
                   (* element whose value equals target. *)
BEGIN
    IF n = 0 THEN position := 0
        ELSIF a[i] = target THEN position := i
        ELSE Find(a, target, (n-1), position)
    END
END Find;
```

Algorithm B.3   Recursive search of an array.

B.2.4 A Recursive Sort

Chapter 6 covers a variety of sorting algorithms. We will preview one in order to show how recursion is used. A ***selection sort*** sorts an array of elements by finding the element with the largest key value and placing it last in the list. It then does the same thing to the subarray of all elements but the last, then the same to the subarray of all elements but the last two, and so on until the subarray is of size 1. It could alternatively find the smallest element and place it in position 1, the second smallest and place it in position 2, and so on (Chapter 6 uses this second approach). Figure B.2 shows the process using the first approach.

```
[0] 85      [0] 85      [0] 53      [0] 53
[1] 12      [1] 12      [1] 12      [1] 12
[2] 42      [2] 42      [2] 42      [2] 42
[3] 26      [3] 26      [3] 26      [3] 26      . . .
[4] 91      [4] 62      [4] 62      [4] 62
[5] 53      [5] 53      [5] 85      [5] 85
[6] 62      [6] 91      [6] 91      [6] 91
```

Figure B.2 Progress of a selection sort. The arrows show the pending exchanges, and the underline marks the bottom of the subarray of elements not yet sorted.

A pseudocode version of the recursive algorithm is as follows:

```
IF the subarray is of size 1 THEN RETURN
   ELSE swap the maximum element in the subarray with
           the last element in the subarray;
           reduce the subarray size by 1 and repeat this
           process
END
```

The recursive code follows easily and is given in Algorithm B.4.

```
PROCEDURE SelectSort(VAR a: ARRAY OF StdElement);
(* post – a[0] through a[HIGH(a)] are sorted by key values. *)

   PROCEDURE RecursiveSort(VAR a: ARRAY OF StdElement; n: CARDINAL);
   (* post – a[0] through a[n] are sorted by key values. *)
   BEGIN
      IF n = 0 THEN RETURN
         ELSE Swap(a,n,Max(a,n));
              RecursiveSort(a, n-1)
      END
   END RecursiveSort;

BEGIN
   RecursiveSort(a,HIGH(a))
END SelectSort;                                        continued
```

where *Swap* and *Max* are specified as follows:

```
PROCEDURE Swap(VAR a: ARRAY OF StdElement;
                    i,j: CARDINAL);
(* post - The values of the elements of a at indexes
          i and j are exchanged. *)


PROCEDURE Max(VAR a: ARRAY OF StdElement; k:
              CARDINAL): CARDINAL;
(* post - Max is the index of the greatest key
          value in a[0] through a[k]. *)
```

Algorithm B.4   A recursive selection sort.

Implementations of *Swap* and *Max* are left to the reader.

In each of the four examples above, the depth of the recursions is $O(n)$. From the implementation viewpoint, none is a particularly advantageous application of recursion. Each could be replaced by a simple and more efficient iterative procedure.

B.2.5 Passing Through a Maze

Everyone is familiar with the ubiquitous maze puzzle. An example of a small one is shown in Figure B.3.

What is a maze abstraction? A maze is a connected set of intersections. Each intersection can be considered to be three pointers (each possibly NIL) to other intersections—left, straight, and right. Intersections with three NIL pointers are cul-de-sacs. A pointer in one intersection points to the treasure. We can write the *Maze* abstraction as shown in Specification B.1. Figure B.4 is a conceptual view.

Specification B.1   Maze

DEFINITION MODULE Maze;

(* **Elements:** Intersections. See TYPE Intersection below. *)

(* **Structure:** The maze is a set of connected intersections. Each intersection is connected to at most three other intersections, and cycles are not permitted. *)

(* **Domain:** The maze may contain up to MaxIntersects intersections. *)

continued

Specification B.1, continued

    EXPORT QUALIFIED IntersectPtr, Intersection, Search, BuildMaze;

    CONST MaxIntersects = 30;   *(* Set as needed. *)*
    TYPE IntersectPtr = [0..MaxIntersects];
          Intersection = **RECORD**
                        left, straight, right: IntersectPtr
               END;

(* **Operations:** *)

PROCEDURE BuildMaze(**VAR** start: IntersectPtr);
(* **post** — A maze exists with a starting intersection at start. *)

PROCEDURE Search(I: IntersectPtr): BOOLEAN;
(* **post** — If the intersection pointed to by I is on the path to the treasure
           then I is printed and Search is true, else Search is false. *)

END Maze.

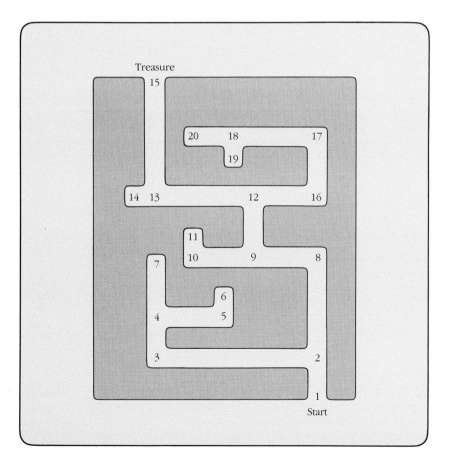

Figure B.3
A maze with labels on the intersections to identify them.

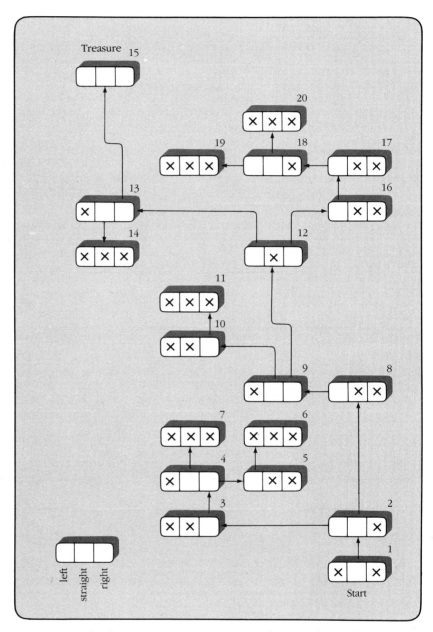

Figure B.4   The maze in Figure B.3 as a set of connected intersections.

1	0	2	0
2	3	8	0
3	0	0	4
4	0	7	5
5	6	0	0
6	0	0	0
7	0	0	0
8	9	0	0
9	0	10	12
10	0	0	11
11	0	0	0
12	13	0	16
13	0	14	15
14	0	0	0
16	17	0	0
17	18	0	0
18	19	20	0
19	0	0	0
20	0	0	0
15	Treasure		

Figure B.5
Data for the maze in Figure B.3.

We are concerned here with the use of recursion to write procedure *Search*. *Search* must return false if *I* is pointing to NIL, or true if it is at the treasure. Otherwise it must branch left, straight, or right, execute *Search* again, and wait for the results of those branchings before deciding whether the intersection it is operating on is on a path to the treasure. We can write *Search* in this way, and the algorithm is given in Implementation Module B.1. (A representation of the maze and an implementation of *BuildMaze* are also shown.)

Implementation Module B.1   *Maze*

```
IMPLEMENTATION MODULE Maze;
(* Maze; array implementation; meets Specification B.1. *)

FROM InOut IMPORT WriteCard, Read, ReadCard, OpenInput, CloseInput,
                  WriteLn, Done;
CONST NIL = 0;                              (* NIL intersection pointer. *)

VAR maze    : ARRAY [1..MaxIntersects] OF Intersection;
    treasure: IntersectPtr;

PROCEDURE Search(I: IntersectPtr): BOOLEAN;
BEGIN
    IF I = NIL                      THEN RETURN FALSE          (* NIL = 0. *)
       ELSIF I = treasure           THEN WriteCard(I,4); RETURN TRUE
       ELSIF Search(maze[I].left)   THEN WriteCard(I,4); RETURN TRUE
       ELSIF Search(maze[I].straight) THEN WriteCard(I,4); RETURN TRUE
       ELSIF Search(maze[I].right)  THEN WriteCard(I,4); RETURN TRUE
       ELSE RETURN FALSE
    END
END Search;

PROCEDURE BuildMaze(VAR start: IntersectPtr);         (* The maze data is in a *)
VAR I : IntersectPtr;         (* file whose name will be requested by OpenInput. *)
    ch: CHAR;            (* Data for the maze in Figure B.3 is shown in Figure B.5. *)
BEGIN                     (* The treasure intersection must be the last in the file. *)
    OpenInput('DATA');
    LOOP
        ReadCard(I); WriteCard(I,3);                    (* Intersection label. *)
        ReadCard(maze[I].left);
        IF Done
            THEN WriteCard(maze[I].left,3)
            ELSE treasure := I; EXIT
        END;
        ReadCard(maze[I].straight); WriteCard(maze[I].straight,3);
        ReadCard(maze[I].right);  WriteCard(maze[I].right,3);
        WriteLn
    END;
    start := 1;
    CloseInput
END BuildMaze;

END Intersections.
```

Using this module with a main module as shown in Figure B.6 gives the result shown in Figure B.7. Figure B.8 is the sequence of values of *Search*'s argument as *Search* recursively executed.

```
MODULE FindMazePath;
(* Find a path to the treasure through a maze. *)

FROM Maze   IMPORT IntersectPtr, Search, BuildMaze;
FROM InOut IMPORT ClearScreen, WriteString, WriteLn, Read;

VAR ch   : CHAR;
    start: IntersectPtr;

BEGIN
   ClearScreen; WriteLn; WriteLn;
   BuildMaze(start);
   IF NOT Search(start)
      THEN WriteString('There is no path to the treasure.')
   END;
   Read(ch)                      (* Delay until any key pressed. *)
END FindMazePath.
```

Figure B.6   Module for finding path to treasure.

15 13 12   9   8   2   1

Figure B.7
Path to the treasure output by *Search* for the maze in Figure B.3. (Read right to left.)

1	0	2	3	0	0	4	0	7	0
0	0	5	6	0	0	0	0	0	8
9	0	10	0	0	11	0	0	0	12
13	0	14	0	0	0	15

Figure B.8
The arguments of *Search* for each call during the execution of *FindMazePath*. Refer to Figure B.3.

(*Search* is a primitive version of a depth first search of a graph, a data type that you will study in Chapter 9.)

You will see many examples of the use of recursion in the body of this book. Most often, both recursive and nonrecursive implementations are given. To gain a better appreciation of the benefits of recursion, look at recursive procedures *PreOrder* and *InOrder* in Figure 5.35. The algorithms are for traversing all the elements stored in a binary tree. Then look at Algorithms 5.2 and 5.3 which are nonrecursive implementations of the same procedures. You do not need to understand the details yet to note the differences in both length and complexity between the recursive and nonrecursive implementations of the same procedure.

Recursion is an important tool in artificial intelligence languages such as LISP and PROLOG. Many expressions in these languages are most concisely stated recursively.

B.3 How Recursion Is Implemented

When it is first encountered, recursion seems somewhat magical. How is it possible for a procedure to call itself? In this section, we will give a simplified example of the mechanism for recursion.

When a procedure is called, it needs space for several objects:

- the address in the calling procedure to which it returns when finished execution
- the arguments in its argument list
- variables local to the procedure.

This collection of objects is called an ***activation record.*** Each time a procedure is called, it must create an activation record for its associated objects; when the procedure terminates execution and exits, it releases its activation record, whose space is then returned to a pool of available space.

The activation record for Algorithm B.3, assuming this simple scheme, is given in Figure B.9.

```
TYPE ActivationPointer = POINTER TO ActivationRecord;
     ActivationRecord  = RECORD
                    return address in the calling procedure: ...;
                    address of array a: ...;
                    copy of n: ...;
                    copy of target: ...;
                    address of position: ...;
                    i: ...
              END;
VAR AP: ActivationPointer;
```

Figure B.9 Activation record for procedure *Find* (Algorithm B.3).

The ***run-time system,*** which handles the execution of Modula-2 programs, has a set of operations that it performs when a procedure is called. These operations are collectively called the procedure's ***prologue.*** Among its duties, the prologue must allocate memory for the activation record by a call to NEW(AP).

It then loads the appropriate values into AP↑, the activation record pointed to by AP: the return address, the base address of *a*, the value of *n*, and so on. At that point, the current execution of *Find* can begin. *Find* uses AP (transparent to the programmer) to locate its variables. Thus the statement

```
position := 0
```

written by the programmer is translated internally into

```
AP↑.position := 0.
```

When *Find* has completed its work, a set of operations called the ***epilogue*** is executed. It must, for example, return the value of *position* to the calling procedure since *position* is a VAR type argument. It retrieves the return address and then releases the activation record using DISPOSE(AP).

The epilogue's last act is to transfer instruction execution to the return address. At that point, execution of that call of *Find* is complete and we are back to the statement succeeding the call to *Find* in the calling procedure.

Figure B.10 summarizes these actions for a call from a program (*Main*) to a nonrecursive procedure (*A*).

Memory	Memory	Memory
Main's activation record	*Main*'s activation record	*Main*'s activation record
	A's activation record	
Code for procedure *A*	Code for procedure *A*	Code for procedure *A*
Code for *Main*	Code for *Main*	Code for *Main*
Main executing before a call to *A*.	*A* executing after a call from *Main*.	*Main* executing after *A* has completed.
(a)	(b)	(c)

Figure B.10   Memory dynamics for a procedure call.

Note that activation records are released in the inverse order of their creation. If procedure *A* calls procedure *B*, which subsequently calls procedure *C*, then when *C* is executing, three activation records—*A*'s, *B*'s, and *C*'s—exist. *C*'s was the latest one to be created and will be the first to be released, since execution of *C* must end before *B* can resume execution. The same is true with *B* and *A*. In fact, the activation records form a **stack,** a data structure covered in Chapter 3.

Although there is an activation record for each suspended procedure and for the active one, there is only one copy of the code for a procedure. It remains in the memory even when the procedure is not active. Thus when a procedure is called, the code is applied to the current activation record. The code at any time "sees" only the latest activation record, the one on top of the stack. All others are hidden from it. We now have the mechanism for recursion.

Let us consider the evaluation of *Sum*(3) as implemented by Algorithm B.1. Assume that there is a module *Main* that originally calls *Sum*. Figure B.11 shows the code and the activation record stack during the evaluation of *Sum*(3).

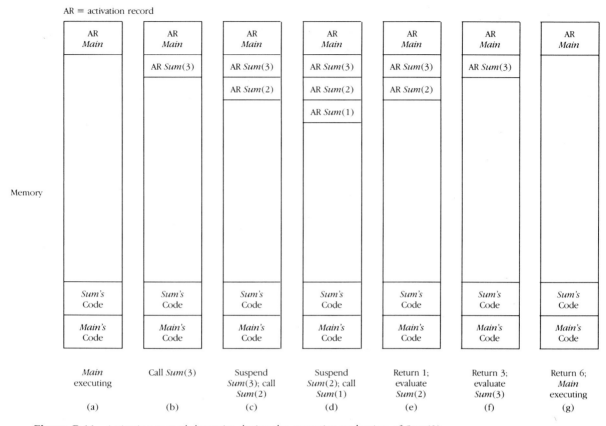

Figure B.11   Activation record dynamics during the recursive evaluation of *Sum*(3).

B.4 Performance Issues

Recursion is often costly in both memory space and execution time. Computer architectures are being designed and built that minimize the procedure call overhead. RISC architectures, for example, have large numbers of fast registers (512 is typical) and the activation records, each composed of 16 registers, are kept in a stack in these registers. However, for most computer architectures, recursion is costly to implement.

Suppose that the activation records defined in Figure B.9 are of length l_{AP} bytes, and that d_{Find} is the maximum depth of the recursion of procedure *Find* for some call to *Find*. The amount of memory being used by *Find* when it is at its maximum depth of recursion is

$$\text{Maximum Memory Used} = (d_{Find} + 1) \times l_{AP}$$

In practice, recursion can use memory quite rapidly as a procedure suspends and recursively calls itself.

The prologue and epilogue of procedure calls each take time to execute and are executed once for each call of the procedure. These times are added

```
PROCEDURE Sum(n:
      CARDINAL): CARDINAL;
BEGIN
  IF n = 1
    THEN RETURN 1
    ELSE RETURN
          (n + Sum(n-1))
  END
END Sum;
```

(a) Recursive implementation of
Sum

```
PROCEDURE Sum(n:
      CARDINAL): CARDINAL;
VAR i, s: CARDINAL;
BEGIN
  s := 1;
  FOR i := 2 TO n DO
    s := s + i
  END;
  RETURN s
END Sum;
```

(b) Iterative implementation of
Sum

```
PROCEDURE Sum(n:
      CARDINAL): CARDINAL;
BEGIN
  RETURN
      ((n * (n+1)) DIV 2)
END Sum;
```

(c) Clever implementation of
Sum

Figure B.12
Implementations of *Sum*.

overhead to the execution of a recursive procedure. Nonrecursive implementations of a procedure need only one execution of the epilogue and prologue and one activation record.

B.5 Alternatives to Recursion

There are alternatives to recursive implementation of procedures. The alternatives fall into two categories, iteration and the use of stacks.

B.5.1 Iteration

In some cases, recursion may be replaced by an iteration. Figure B.12(a) is a recursive implementation of *Sum,* whereas B.12(b) is an iterative implementation. [Of course, the smart thing to do in this case is to use the well-known expression for the sum of the integers from 1 to *n*, as shown in B.12(c).]

B.5.2 Stacking

There are cases when recursion is used not only to process a sequence of objects as the recursion proceeds but also to recall and use those objects as the recursion bottoms out and begins to recede. The recursion stacks the objects as recursive calls are made. They are retrieved as the recursive calls return. The stacking can be supplied directly by the programmer through the use of a stack module rather than relying on the recursive mechanism.

Instead of looking at examples here, you are referred to the material of Chapter 5 on trees. The problem of traversing a binary tree to which we have previously referred—Figure 5.35 and Algorithms 5.2 and 5.3—is a good example of the use of stacks to replace recursion. At that time, you will have also covered Chapter 3, which deals with stacks. Chapter 6, on sorting, and the variations of *QuickSort* given in Section 6.3.1, provide another good example.

Selected Applications

C

C.1 Finding Patterns in Files

C.2 A Random Number Generator

C.3 Insertion Algorithm for a B-Tree

C.4 Printing a B-Tree

C.5 Printing Binary Trees

C.1 Finding Patterns in Files

In this section we consider a sequence of programs that find the number of occurrences of a string (or pattern) in a file. From a user's point of view, here is how it works.

1. The user supplies two file names. The first file contains one or more strings (patterns) that are the target patterns for the search. The second file contains the text to be searched.
2. The file is searched and the number of instances of each of the target patterns that it contains is reported. The programs can be modified (rather easily) to report also where the patterns are found.

We will consider several different techniques for searching for patterns in files and will report the results of a few simple timing studies. We begin with a program that searches for a single pattern. All the subsequent programs search for all the patterns in a file provided by the user. Figure C.1 gives a structured prose description of one way we can solve the problem.

```
IF memory is available to create two strings, and if the
   target pattern can be extracted from its file, and if
   the file containing text to be searched can be opened
   THEN

      REPEAT
         get a line of text to be searched;
         search the line of text for the target pattern;
         clear the line of text
      UNTIL there is no more text to search;

      report the results;
      close any open files
   ELSE report that the analysis is not possible
END
```

Figure C.1 An algorithm to find the number of occurrences of a target pattern in a file.

The string operations we need can be imported from module *Strings* in Chapter 7. The file operations we will use are taken from module *InOut*. The import statements needed are shown in Figure C.2.

```
FROM Strings IMPORT String, Append, Delete, Find, Length,
                    Create, Display;
FROM InOut   IMPORT EOL, Done, OpenInput, CloseInput;
```

Figure C.2 Operations imported from modules *Strings* and *InOut*.

The heart of the algorithm in Figure C.1 is the REPEAT statement. We begin by discussing its implementation, and the first operation to perform is to

```
PROCEDURE OpenFile(): BOOLEAN; (* Open a prescribed file. *)
BEGIN
   WriteLn;
   WriteString('File to be searched ');
   OpenInput('   ');               (* Imported from InOut. *)
   IF Done
      THEN RETURN TRUE
      ELSE RETURN FALSE       (* Return false if the file *)
   END                        (* cannot be opened.         *)
END OpenFile;
```

Figure C.3 Procedure that asks the user for a file to search, attempts to open the file, and reports the success or failure of that attempt.

get a line of text. Getting a line of text implies that a file is already open for reading, so first we need a procedure to open a file. Figure C.3 shows such a procedure.

It is worthwhile to recall that *OpenInput* prompts you for the name of a file to open. A common prompt is in>. You respond with the name of a file. If the file name includes an extension, then *OpenInput* attempts to open the named file. If the file name does not include an extension, then *OpenInput* attaches as an extension the character string passed as a parameter. In Figure C.3 this default extension is ' '. The value of *Done,* also imported from module *InOut,* reports the success or failure of *OpenInput.*

Assuming that *OpenFile* has successfully opened a file to search, we turn to a procedure to read the open file—one line at a time. It is shown in Figure C.4.

```
PROCEDURE GetNextLine(VAR line: String);  (* Get a line of text *)
VAR ch: CHAR;                             (* from the open file. *)
BEGIN
   Read(ch);                           (* EOL and Done are     *)
   WHILE (ch # EOL) & Done DO           (* imported from InOut. *)
      Append(line,ch);                  (* Imported from Strings. *)
      Read(ch)
   END
END GetNextLine;
```

Figure C.4 A procedure to read a line of text from an open file. *EOL* and *Done* are global variables imported from *InOut. String* is an opaque type imported from *Strings.*

Using *GetNextLine* we transfer one line from the open file to a string. The next step is to search the string for the target pattern. We have not discussed actually loading the target pattern, but that process is similar to that shown in *GetNextLine,* so we defer its discussion until later, when we will load an arbitrary number of patterns from a file. In the meantime, assume that *pat* is a variable of type *String* that contains the target pattern. Figure C.5 shows a procedure for searching the string, named *line,* for the pattern stored in *pat.*

```
PROCEDURE SearchLine(line,pat: String; VAR count: CARDINAL);
VAR posn: CARDINAL;
BEGIN
   posn := 0;
   LOOP
      posn := Find(line,pat,posn+1); (* Is pat in line? *)
      IF posn = 0 THEN EXIT END;        (* No, exit loop.  *)
      INC(count)                 (* Yes, increment count and *)
   END;                          (* continue the search.      *)
END SearchLine;
```

Figure C.5   Procedure to search *String line* for the target pattern *pat* and return the number of occurrences found as the value of *count.*

Procedure *SearchLine* depends on procedure *Find* to do most of its work. Procedure *Find* is imported from module *Strings.* Let us review how *Find* operates. *Find* is a function procedure that searches for the first occurrence of *pat* in *line.* The search begins at the location in *line* given by the value of *posn* + 1. Since *posn* is initially 0, the first time *Find* is called it begins its search at location 1 in *line.* The value returned by *Find* is the location of the first occurrence of *pat,* or 0 if *pat* is not found. Since we are counting all occurrences of *pat* the search must continue until *Find* returns the value 0. The location at which to continue the search is one position to the right of the last occurrence of *pat, posn* + 1.

At this point we have retrieved a line of text and searched it for all occurrences of *pat.* It remains only to clear the string used to store a line of the file and begin again. Module *Strings* exports a delete operation that can be used to clear the string named *line* as follows:

```
Delete(line,1,Length(line))
```

Length is also exported by *Strings.*

This completes everything we need for the REPEAT statement in Figure C.1. To summarize, Figure C.6 shows the REPEAT statement from Figure C.1 with the English prose replaced by specific procedure calls.

```
REPEAT
   GetNextLine(line);
   SearchLine(line,pat,count);
   Delete(line,1,Length(line))
UNTIL NOT Done;              (* Done is set by GetNextLine. *)
```

Figure C.6   The REPEAT statement from Figure C.1 with specific procedure calls.

If you look back at Figure C.1 you will see that we still need to create strings for *line* and *pat,* load *pat* from a file, keep track of the number of occurrences of *pat,* report the results, and close the file that was opened for searching. One way to do all these things is shown in Figure C.7—a complete implementation of the algorithm in Figure C.1.

```
VAR line : String;          (* Contains the string to be searched. *)
    pat  : String;                        (* The target pattern. *)
    count: CARDINAL;       (* Count the number of occurrences of pat. *)
BEGIN
    WriteLn;
    WriteString('Find the number of occurrences of a pattern in a file ');
    IF Create(pat) & Create(line) & GetPattern(pat) & OpenFile()
        THEN count := 0;
            REPEAT
                GetNextLine(line);
                SearchLine(line,pat,count);
                Delete(line,1,Length(line))
            UNTIL NOT Done;            (* Done is set by GetNextLine. *)
            Report(pat,count);
            CloseInput()
        ELSE WriteString('Analysis aborted')
    END
END
```

Figure C.7 An implementation of the algorithm in Figure C.1.

A few comments about Figure C.7 are needed. Procedure *Create* attempts to initialize a variable of type *String,* and returns true if it succeeds. *Report* is a procedure supplied by the user to write the values of *pat* and *count.* One possibility, when there is a list of patterns to report, is given later. Finally, *CloseInput* is imported from *InOut* and closes the open file.

Recall that procedure *SearchLine,* Figure C.5, uses operation *Find* in module *Strings* to search for occurrences of *pat* in *line.* Since module *Strings* contains two distinct implementations of *Find,* it is tempting to compare them to see which is faster. To keep things simple we decided to use the implementation module for binary trees, Implementation Module 5.1, as the file to search, and the strings END, WHILE, and PROCEDURE as the target patterns. Figure C.8 compares the search rates, in characters searched per millisecond.

Pattern	Obvious search algorithm	Boyer–Moore search algorithm
END	2.7	3.2
WHILE	2.5	2.4
PROCEDURE	3.3	3.9

Figure C.8 Search rate in characters per millisecond to search Implementation Module 5.1. Chapter 8 discusses the Obvious and Boyer–Moore algorithms, and Implementation Module 8.1 gives the implementations used to obtain the results reported here.

It is disappointing to find that both search algorithms give essentially the same search rate, even for a reasonably long pattern like PROCEDURE. However, if you examine the implementation of the Boyer–Moore algorithm in Implementation Module 8.1 you will see the reason for the less-than-sparkling performance shown in Figure C.8. Every time the Boyer–Moore version of

Find is called, it preprocesses the pattern. The way *Find* is used in the algorithm in Figure C.7 means that the pattern is preprocessed at least once for every line of text, and Implementation Module 5.1 contains 258 lines.

To be fair to the Boyer–Moore algorithm we need to preprocess the pattern once, and then use those results for the entire search. To do this we make simple modifications to both the definition and implementation modules for strings. Specification 8.1 must be modified to export a procedure to preprocess a string. Implementation Module 8.1 needs to move procedure *PreProcess* from its position internal to procedure *Find* to a position as an independent procedure that can be exported. The only change needed in Figure C.7 is to add a call to *PreProcess* just prior to entering the repeat loop. The search rates using this "process once" version of Boyer–Moore are given in Figure C.9. As we expect, the search rates are increased substantially.

Pattern	*PreProcess* once Boyer–Moore search algorithm
END	5.5
WHILE	8.2
PROCEDURE	27.4

Figure C.9   Search rate in characters per millisecond to search Implementation Module 5.1. These rates should be compared with the rates in Figure C.8.

Figure C.9 concludes the first phase of this application: finding the number of occurrences of a pattern in a file. We turn now to the problem of searching a file for a sequence of target patterns. The user puts the target patterns in a file, one per line, and the program reads all the patterns and reports the number of occurrences of each of them in any specified file.

We will consider three approaches to this new problem. The first is a simple generalization of the approach just discussed. Each line of text will be loaded as before, and then searched, once for each target pattern. Having to search the text file once for each target pattern will, as we shall see, decrease the search rate markedly. The other two approaches search the text file only once, so it will be interesting to see the increase in search rate.

The first thing we need for our new problem is a procedure that reads a sequence of patterns from a specified file. The data types used to store the patterns are shown in Figure C.10, and a procedure to load them, *GetPatterns*, is given in Figure C.11.

```
CONST MaxPats = 40;          (* Or other value as needed. *)

TYPE   Element  = RECORD
                    str : String;  (* The pattern - and *)
                    freq: CARDINAL (* its frequency      *)
                  END;             (* of occurrence.     *)
       PatArray = ARRAY [1..MaxPats] OF Element;
```

Figure C.10   Data types used to store a sequence of patterns.

```
PROCEDURE GetPatterns (VAR pats: PatArray; VAR n: CARDINAL): BOOLEAN;
VAR ch: CHAR;                               (* Read strings, one per line, *)
BEGIN                                       (* from a prescribed file.      *)
    WriteLn;
    WriteString ('File that contains the patterns ');
    OpenInput ('   ');
    IF NOT Done THEN RETURN FALSE END;      (* Return false if the file *)
                                            (* cannot be opened.         *)
    n := 0;
    REPEAT
        INC (n);
        IF NOT Create (pats [n].str)        (* Return false if a string *)
            THEN RETURN FALSE               (* cannot be created.        *)
        END;
        pats [n].freq := 0;
        Read (ch);
        WHILE (ch # EOL) & Done DO
            Append (pats [n].str, ch);
            Read (ch)
        END
    UNTIL (NOT Done) OR (n > MaxPats);
    DEC (n);                                (* The number of patterns. *)
    CloseInput ();
    RETURN TRUE
END GetPatterns;
```

Figure C.11 Procedure to load a sequence of patterns from a file.

With the patterns loaded, all that is needed is to modify the repeat loop in Figure C.6 so that each text line is searched for every pattern. Figure C.12 shows how that can be done. The number of patterns to search for is *noPats*.

```
REPEAT
    GetNextLine (line);                 (* Sets Done FALSE if this is the last line. *)
    FOR k := 1 TO noPats DO
        posn := 0;
        LOOP                                        (* Search line for *)
            posn := Find (line, pats [k].str, posn+1);  (* all occurrences *)
            IF posn = 0 THEN EXIT END;              (* of the kth       *)
            INC (pats [k].freq)                     (* pattern.         *)
        END
    END;
    Delete (line, 1, Length (line))
UNTIL NOT Done;
```

Figure C.12 The REPEAT statement from Figure C.1, modified to count the number of occurrences of any number of patterns.

We applied the program of Figure C.12 to the task of finding the frequency of occurrence of Modula-2 reserved words (Appendix D) in Implementation Module 5.1. We started with the first five reserved words in alphabetical order—AND, ARRAY, BEGIN, BY, and CASE—and determined the search rate. Then we added the next five reserved words, in alphabetical order, and again determined the search rate. We repeated this process, adding five reserved words each time, until thirty words were in the file. The search rates, again in characters searched per millisecond, are shown in Figure C.13.

Number of patterns to search for	Search rate
5	0.51
10	0.26
15	0.17
20	0.13
25	0.10
30	0.08

Figure C.13   Search rate, characters per millisecond, while searching for Modula-2 reserved words. The group of n target patterns is the first n, in alphabetical order, Modula-2 reserved words.

Comparing Figure C.13 with Figures C.8 and C.9 confirms that scanning a line of text repeatedly, once for each target pattern, is a slow process. Note also that the Boyer–Moore algorithm is not useful here since there is no reasonable way to avoid preprocessing each pattern for each line of text. In an attempt to increase the search rate we will now consider two approaches to this problem that require scanning the text file only once.

We want to scan a file once and, during that scan, search for any number of patterns. We will accomplish this by identifying, during the scan, substrings that are "of interest." A substring that is "of interest" will be called a ***token.*** The first requirement of a token is that it not contain any spaces. In addition, a token must be surrounded by spaces, or it must begin a line and be followed by a space, or it must end a line and be preceded by a space.

Look at the preceding paragraph. The tokens in it are, almost, the words it contains. Certainly "We", "want", and "to" are tokens according to our definition. Alas, notice that "once," (including the comma) and "interest."" (including the period and one quotation mark character) are also tokens. We could refine our definition of a token so that the tokens would be exactly the words in a paragraph, or the identifiers in a program, but our search algorithms would not be changed, so, in the interest of simplicity, we won't.

Extracting tokens from a string requires access to the individual characters that make up the string, so it is a job that needs to be done by module *Strings*. We will add the following new operation to the definition module.

```
PROCEDURE GetNextToken(S: String;
                       VAR posn,len: CARDINAL): BOOLEAN;
(* pre  - 1 <= posn <= Length(S).
   post - If there is a token in the substring

            S[posn], ... , S[Length(S)]

         then posn is the position of the first such
         token, len is its length, and GetNextToken is
         true, else GetNextToken is false. *)
```

Observe that the specification of *GetNextToken* says nothing about exactly what constitutes a token. It could, but it does not. The implementation of *GetNextToken* is relatively straightforward, but you may need to refer back to Implementation Module 8.1 to see how a string is represented. A possible implementation is provided in Figure C.14.

```
PROCEDURE GetNextToken(S: String; VAR posn,len: CARDINAL): BOOLEAN;
VAR k: CARDINAL;
BEGIN
    WITH S↑ DO
        data[Length(S)+1] := 'A';              (* Install a sentinel. *)
        WHILE data[posn] = ' ' DO            (* Search for a character *)
            INC(posn)                         (* other than a space.    *)
        END;
        IF posn > Length(S)
            THEN RETURN FALSE         (* The end of the string has been reached. *)
        END;
        k := posn + 1;
        data[Length(S)+1] := ' ';              (* Another sentinel. *)
        WHILE data[k] # ' ' DO                (* Search for a space. *)
            INC(k)
        END;
        len := k - posn;                      (* The length of the token. *)
        RETURN TRUE
    END
END GetNextToken;
```

Figure C.14 Procedure to find the next token in a string.

Once a token is located we need to see if it matches any of our target patterns. We will compare the token with each of our patterns in two steps. First we will see if the token and the pattern are the same length. If so, we will use operation *Match,* exported by module *Strings,* to see if they are identical. If so, we increment the frequency counter of the pattern. If not, we go on to the next pattern.

To see how we can use *FindNextToken,* Figure C.15 shows a modification of the REPEAT statement that appears in Figures C.6 and C.12.

```
REPEAT
   GetNextLine(line);
   posn := 1;
   WHILE GetNextToken(line,posn,len) DO
         CheckToken(posn,len);
         INC(posn,len)
   END;
   Delete(line,1,Length(line))
UNTIL NOT Done;
```

Figure C.15   Use of *GetNextToken* in the frequency analysis of a sequence of patterns.

The problem with Figure C.15 is that we haven't discussed procedure *CheckToken*. We can infer what it must do. It must check each pattern to see if that pattern is the same as the token that begins at position *posn* and contains *len* characters. Figure C.16 shows the array that contains the target patterns, and an implementation of *CheckToken*. You might need to refer to Figure C.10 to see the data type of *patArray*.

```
VAR pats  : PatArray; (* The array of target patterns.  *)
    noPats: CARDINAL;    (* Number of target patterns.  *)
    line  : String;         (* Line of text to search.  *)

PROCEDURE CheckToken(posn: StringPosn; len: CARDINAL);
VAR k: CARDINAL;
BEGIN
   FOR k := 1 TO noPats DO
      IF (len = Length(pats[k].str)) &
         (Match(line,pats[k].str,posn))
         THEN INC(pats[k].freq)
      END
   END
END CheckToken;
```

Figure C.16   Procedure to compare a token with all the target patterns in array pats.

Note that *CheckToken* takes advantage of the way that Modula-2 evaluates the condition for the IF statement. That is, Modula-2 short-circuits the evaluation in the sense that

```
IF len # Length(pats[k].str)
```

then the call to *Match* is not made. This is a performance advantage.

The components of our latest search algorithm are now in place, so we turn our attention to performance. Figure C.17 shows the search rates that result if we use our latest search technique to do the same searches reported in Figure C.13. We refer to the technique described in the last few paragraphs as "one pass tokens." The term "one pass" refers to scanning the file once, or

Number of patterns to search for	Search rate from Figure C.13	Search rate, one pass tokens
5	0.51	3.3
10	0.26	2.3
15	0.17	1.8
20	0.13	1.5
25	0.10	1.2
30	0.08	1.1

Figure C.17   Search rate, characters per millisecond, while searching for Modula-2 reserved words. The group of n target patterns is the first n, in alphabetical order, Modula-2 reserved words.

making one pass over that file. The term "tokens" refers to extracting tokens from the file as an important part of the search algorithm.

Figure C.17 shows that our latest approach is at least an order of magnitude faster than the approach used to generate results in Figure C.13. Its relative advantage, of course, increases as the number of patterns increases.

You might think, or at least hope, that we have exhausted the search algorithms to be reported here. If so, you have forgotten that Section 7.4.3 discusses perfect hashing functions and that it includes a perfect hashing function for the reserved words of Modula-2. Our final technique will be to extract a token, using *FindNextToken,* hash the token using the perfect hashing function described in Section 7.4.3, and, if the hash function returns a reasonable address, to compare the token with the content of the hash table at that location.

We begin with the assumption that we have a hash table loaded with the Modula-2 reserved words. In the module used for the timing study we typed the reserved words into a file and then used a procedure similar to *GetPatterns* (Figure C.11) to load the reserved words into the hash table. The key difference between *GetPatterns* and the procedure needed in this case is that the perfect hashing function must be used to determine where each reserved word is stored in the hash table. More about that later. In the meantime, Figure C.18 shows the representation used for the hash table.

```
TYPE Element = RECORD
                 str : String;    (* A reserved word — *)
                 freq: CARDINAL;  (* and its frequency *)
               END;               (* of occurrence.    *)
     Table   = ARRAY [0..39] OF Element;

VAR HT: Table;                              (* The hash table. *)
```

Figure C.18   Representation of the hash table.

The REPEAT statement used this time is essentially the same as used the preceding three times, in Figures C.6, C.12, and C.15, and is shown in Figure C.19.

```
REPEAT
    GetNextLine(line);                    (* Sets Done FALSE if *)
    posn := 1;                            (* this is last line. *)
    WHILE GetNextToken(line,posn,len) DO
        HashAndCompare(line,posn,len);
        INC(posn,len)
    END;
    Delete(line,1,Length(line))
UNTIL NOT Done;
```

Figure C.19 The REPEAT statement from Figure C.1 for finding the frequency of occurrence of the Modula-2 reserved words using a perfect hashing function.

The only procedure in Figure C.19 that has not been discussed is *HashAndCompare*. This procedure considers the substring of line that starts at position *posn* and has length *len*. Each such substring is hashed to produce a home address and then compared with the reserved word found at that home address. The advantage of this approach is that each substring, or token, is compared with at most one reserved word. In the previous approaches each token is compared with every pattern. Figure C.20 presents procedure *HashAndCompare*.

```
PROCEDURE HashAndCompare(line: String; pos: StringPosn; len: CARDINAL);
VAR L,index : INTEGER;
BEGIN
    L := VAL(INTEGER,len);
    index := L + g(SubChar(line,pos)) + g(SubChar(line,pos+len-1)) +
                  VAL(INTEGER,(ORD(SubChar(line,pos+len-2)))) -
                  VAL(INTEGER,ORD('A'));
    IF (0 <= index) AND (index <= 39)
        THEN IF Match(line,HT[index].str,pos)
                THEN INC(HT[index].freq)
            END
    END
END HashAndCompare;
```

Figure C.20 Procedure to compare a substring of *line* with the content of a hash table at the home address of the substring.

The computation of *index* using the perfect hash function looks rather complex. Some of the complexity comes from using VAL, a standard Modula-2 operation, to convert CARDINAL values to INTEGER values. This is necessary because Modula-2 does not permit mixing CARDINAL and INTEGER values in the same expression. In addition, procedure *SubChar* is used to extract individual characters from the string named *line*. Module *Strings,* Specification 8.1, does not include operation *SubChar* and this simple operation had to be added. Finally, computing *index* requires evaluating the function g. One way to implement g is shown in Figure C.21.

```
PROCEDURE g(ch: CHAR): INTEGER;
BEGIN
    CASE ch OF
        'A': RETURN 18 |
        'B': RETURN 16 |
        'C': RETURN  3 |
        'D': RETURN -3 |
        'E': RETURN -11|
        'F': RETURN  4 |
        'H': RETURN 14 |
        'I': RETURN 15 |
        'L': RETURN 15 |
        'M': RETURN  1 |
        'N': RETURN -4 |
        'O': RETURN  7 |
        'P': RETURN  1 |
        'Q': RETURN 22 |
        'R': RETURN -1 |
        'S': RETURN  3 |
        'T': RETURN  0 |
        'U': RETURN  8 |
        'V': RETURN 22 |
        'W': RETURN -2 |
        'Y': RETURN 14
        ELSE RETURN 100
    END
END g;
```

Figure C.21   Implementation of function *g* in Figure C.20.

The final question is: How does the search rate using this hashed technique compare with previous search rates? Look back at Figure C.17 and observe that the search rates when searching for 30 of the 40 reserved words of Modula-2 were 0.08 and 1.1 characters per millisecond. The search rate for the hashed technique, looking for all 40 reserved words, is about 4.3 characters per millisecond—more than four times as fast!

C.2 A Random Number Generator

This section presents a pseudo-random number generator, not an application. We have found that a random number generator is a good thing to have while testing and experimenting with data structures. We have also found that it is very convenient to have a reasonably good random number generator available to assign for student use. The random number generator given on page 518 works on computers with 16-bit integers, and according to chi-square tests produces good results. It is included on the software diskette available from the publisher of this text. Refer to Sedgewick (1983), pages 33–43, for an introduction to random number generators.

Specification C.1   Random Number Generator

```
DEFINITION MODULE Random;                 (* Number generator for a 16-bit machine. *)

EXPORT QUALIFIED Rand1, RandInit;

PROCEDURE Rand1(): CARDINAL;
(* pre  — Must be preceded by a call to procedure RandInit.
   post — Generates a sequence of pseudo-random integers in the range
          0..999. That is, the code segment

              x =                                (* User supplied value. *)
              RandInit(x);
              FOR k := 1 TO N DO
                  pr := Rand1()
              END;

          generates N pseudo-random integers. *)

PROCEDURE RandInit(seed: CARDINAL);
(* pre  — None.
   post — Initialization step for procedure Rand1. *)

END Random.
```

Implementation Module C.1   *Random Number Generator*

```
IMPLEMENTATION MODULE Random;             (* Number generator for a 16-bit machine. *)
(* Random; array implementation; meets Specification C.1. *)

CONST m = 10000; m1 = 100; b = 31;

VAR rIndex: CARDINAL;
    A       : ARRAY[0..54] OF CARDINAL;

PROCEDURE Rand1(): CARDINAL;
BEGIN
   rIndex := (rIndex + 1) MOD 55;
   A[rIndex] := (A[(rIndex+23) MOD 55] + A[(rIndex+54) MOD 55]) MOD m;
   RETURN (A[rIndex] DIV 10)
END Rand1;

PROCEDURE RandInit(seed: CARDINAL);
VAR j: CARDINAL;
BEGIN
   A[0] := seed;
   FOR j := 1 TO 54 DO
      A[j] := (Mult(b,A[j-1])+1) MOD m
   END
END RandInit;
```

Implementation Module C.1, continued

```
PROCEDURE Mult(p,q: CARDINAL): CARDINAL;
VAR   p1,p0,q1,q0: CARDINAL;
BEGIN
    p1 := p DIV m1;  p0 := p MOD m1;
    q1 := q DIV m1;  q0 := q MOD m1;
    RETURN ((((p0*q1 + p1*q0) MOD m1)  * m1 + p0*q0) MOD m)
END Mult;

END Random.
```

C.3 Insertion Algorithm for a B-Tree

This section of Appendix C develops a procedure to insert an element into a B-tree. A prerequisite to this discussion is the material in Section 5.9 of the text.

Every B-tree has an associated value called its **_order,_** which determines the size of its nodes. Each node of a B-tree, except the root, contains between order and 2 * order elements. The root of a B-tree contains between 1 and 2 * order elements. Each node in a B-tree either is a leaf node, and has no children, or has exactly one more child than it has elements. Figures 5.92 through 5.100 show illustrations of B-trees of order 2. Figure 5.99 is repeated below, as Figure C.22, for ease of reference and to provide some feel for how a B-tree looks.

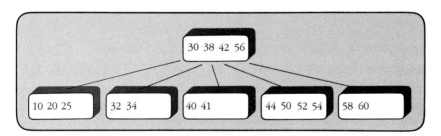

Figure C.22   An example of a B-tree of order 2. Each node, except the root, contains between 2 and 4 elements. The root contains between 1 and 4 elements.

The insertion process for a B-tree is conceptually simple. Following the discussion in Section 5.9 we begin with the following structured prose description of how it is done (Figure C.23).

```
Search the B-tree for the element to be inserted.
IF the element is NOT found
    THEN start at the node, call it the current node, that
        would contain the element if it were in the tree.

        WHILE a node split is needed to add the element
            to be inserted to the current node DO

            Split the current node, and make the parent
            of the previous current node the new
            current node. Make the median element
            remaining from the node split the new
            element to be inserted.
        END

        IF there is a current node
            THEN insert the element into the current node
            ELSE create a new root node, and insert the
                element into it.
        END
    ELSE the insert fails.
```

Figure C.23 Structured prose description of an insertion algorithm for a B-tree.

We now begin the process of successively refining the algorithm in Figure C.23 until we have a working procedure. The resulting collection of eight procedures contains about 125 lines of code, so, as you can imagine, we will encounter some intricacies along the way.

We can use a procedure that searches a B-tree for a target element. This is procedure *FindKey*

PROCEDURE FindKey (**VAR** B: BTree; tkey: KeyType): BOOLEAN;

and it is described in Specification 5.5. What we need to recall about *FindKey* is that if it does not find an element with key value *tkey*, then it makes the node that would contain an element with key value *tkey* the current node, and returns false. If it does find an element with key value *tkey* then it returns true.

A second handy procedure is procedure *SplitNeeded*

PROCEDURE SplitNeeded(p: NodePtr): BOOLEAN;

which is passed a pointer to a B-tree node and returns true if that node must be split to accommodate an additional element and false otherwise.

On the basis of the two procedures just described, we can recast the algorithm in Figure C.23 as shown in Figure C.24.

Figure C.24 shows that there are three basic insertion types to consider: insertion into a node that is not full, insertion into a node that is full and must be split, and insertion into a new root node. Figure 5.101 shows how these basic insertion types fit together to make up a total insertion algorithm. The next step is to specify procedures for these three operations and then see how they fit into the algorithm in Figure C.24. Figure C.25 gives the specifications

```
VAR B : BTree;                    (* A particular B-tree. *)
    e : StdElement;               (* The element to insert. *)
    pi: Nodeptr;                  (* Pointer to the node where *)
                                  (* insertion is to occur.    *)
BEGIN
    IF NOT FindKey(B, e.key);
       THEN pi := B↑.current;     (* Start at the leaf      *)
                                  (* node set by FindKey. *)
            WHILE SplitNeeded(pi) DO
                Split the current node, and make the parent
                of the previous current node the new current
                node. Make the median element remaining from
                the node split the new element to be
                inserted.
            END

            IF there is a current node
               THEN insert the element into the current node
               ELSE create a new root node and insert the
                    element into it.
            END
       ELSE the insert fails because e is already in the
            tree.
END
```

Figure C.24 First refinement of the structured prose description of an insertion algorithm for a B-tree.

```
PROCEDURE Insert1 (e: StdElement; VAR pi,pRight: NodePtr);
(* pre  – The B-tree node pointed at by pi is not full, and pRight
          points to the node that is the right child of element e.
   post – B-tree node pi↑ contains e and pRight. Elements in each
          B-tree node are kept in sorted order. *)

PROCEDURE Insert2 (VAR e: StdElement; VAR pi,pRight: NodePtr);
(* pre  – The B-tree node pointed at by pi is full, and pRight points
          at the node that is the right child of element e.
   post – Node pi↑-pre has been split. Node pi↑ is the parent of
          pi↑-pre, element e is the element that is to be inserted
          into pi↑, and pRight↑ is the node that is the right child of
          e. If the node that was created during the split has
          children, those children point to it as their parent. *)

PROCEDURE Insert3 (e: StdElement; pLeft,pRight: NodePtr);
(* pre  – Nodes pLeft↑ and pRight↑ are the result of the split of node
          that had no parent. Element e is the element passed up
          as a result of that split.
   post – Element e is the only element in the root of the B-tree;
          pLeft↑ is the root of its left subtree and pRight↑ is the
          root of its right subtree. *)
```

Figure C.25 Specification of three insert primitives for a B-tree. These operations inherit, from *Insert,* the precondition that the tree is not full.

and Figure C.26 shows how they can be used to refine the algorithm in Figure C.24. Keep in mind that these three procedures are internal to the *Insert* procedure that has been passed a specific B-tree on which to operate.

```
VAR B     : BTree;                                         (* A particular B-tree.  *)
    e     : StdElement;                                    (* The element to insert. *)
    pi    : Nodeptr;          (* Pointer to the node where insertion is to occur. *)
    pSave: NodePtr;          (* Save a pointer to a node that is about to be split. *)
    pNew  : NodePtr;          (* Pointer to the node created during the last split. *)
BEGIN
    IF NOT FindKey(B, e.key);
        THEN pi := B↑.current;             (* Start at the leaf node set by FindKey. *)
             pSave := NIL; pNew := NIL;

             WHILE SplitNeeded(pi) DO
                 pSave := pi;
                 Insert2(e,pi,pnew)                          (* Split a node. *)
             END

             IF pi # NIL
                 THEN Insert1(e,pi,pNew)      (* Insert into a node that has room. *)
                 ELSE Insert3(e,pSave,pNew)         (* Insert into a new root node. *)
             END;
             RETURN TRUE
        ELSE RETURN FALSE
    END
END
```

Figure C.26   Second refinement of the structured prose description of an insertion algorithm for a B-tree given in Figure C.23.

The insertion is essentially complete. It remains to write *Insert1*, *Insert2*, and *Insert3*. Both *Insert1* and *Insert3* require only a few lines of code and are given in the completed procedure that appears at the end of this section (and is included on the software disk available from the publisher). *Insert2* is not so simple and we proceed, once again by the process of refinement, to work out its details. Figure C.27 gives the structured prose version of *Insert2*.

```
PROCEDURE Insert2 (VAR e: StdElement; VAR pi,pRight: NodePtr);
BEGIN
   Create and initialize a new node;
   Find the position of e in pi↑;
   Move elements (and their pointers), larger than the
   median element, to the new node.
   Select the median element as the new element, e, to be
   inserted (at the next higher level).
   IF e and pRight belong in pi↑
      THEN insert them
   END;
   IF the new node has children
      THEN make the new node their parent
   END;
   Set final values for e, pi, and pRight
END
```

Figure C.27   Structured prose version of *Insert2*.

As usual, the first task is to specify a few basic operations that will be useful in implementing the procedure at hand. In the case of *Insert2* we will use the four shown in Figure C.28.

```
PROCEDURE CreateNode (VAR p: NodePtr): BOOLEAN;
(* post – If a B-tree node can be created then p↑ is an empty node and
          CreateNode is true, else CreateNode is false. *)

PROCEDURE InsertPosition (p: NodePtr; tkey: KeyType; n: CARDINAL): CARDINAL;
(* post – Return the position at which an element with key value tkey
          should be inserted in node p↑, or n+1, whichever is smaller. *)

PROCEDURE InsertElemente (p,pTo: NodePtr; e: StdElement; VAR j2: CARDINAL);
(* pre  – j2 is a valid position in a B-tree node.
   post – Element e and pointer p occupy position j2 in node pTo↑. *)

PROCEDURE MoveElement (pFrom,pTo: NodePtr; VAR j1,j2: CARDINAL);
(* pre  – j1 and j2 are valid positions in a B-tree node.
   post – The element and pointer at position j1-1 in pFrom↑ have been
          copied into position j2 in pTo↑. *)
```

Figure C.28   Several operations that will be used to construct *Insert1, Insert2,* and *Insert3*.

If we use the operations from Figure C.28, and add some control logic, we produce the finished *Insert2* procedure shown in Figure C.29.

```
PROCEDURE Insert2 (VAR e: StdElement; VAR pi,pRight: NodePtr);
VAR pNew : NodePtr;                          (* Pointer to the new node. *)
    posn : CARDINAL;                      (* Position at which to insert e. *)
    eUp  : StdElement;           (* Stores the element to be passed up a level. *)
    j1,j2: CARDINAL;
BEGIN
    CreateNode (pNew);
    pNew↑.noElt  := order;                        (* Initialize the new node. *)
    pNew↑.parent := pi↑.parent;
    posn := InsertPosition(pi,e.key,nodeSize);        (* Find the position *)
                                                      (* of e in pi↑.      *)
(*                                                                         *)
(* We have a new node, and know where e belongs relative to the elements in  *)
(* node pi↑. Fill the new node with elements from pi↑, and perhaps e.       *)
(*                                                                         *)
    j1 := nodeSize+1;                  (* Take elements from slot j1-1 in pi↑. *)
    j2 := order;                       (* Put elements in slot j2 in pNew↑.   *)
    WHILE j2 > 0 DO                     (* While there is room in pNew↑.       *)
        IF j1 = posn                       (* Is this where e goes? *)
            THEN InsertElemente (pRight,pNew,e,j2);          (* Yes, insert e. *)
                 posn := posn + nodeSize
            ELSE MoveElement (pi,pNew,j1,j2)      (* No, move an element from *)
        END                                      (* pi↑ to pNew↑ and          *)
    END;                                         (* decrement j1 and j2.      *)
(*                                                                         *)
(* The new node has all its elements and pointers except its first pointer.  *)
(* Select the element to be passed up and insert the final pointer in pNew↑.  *)
(*                                                                         *)
    IF j1 = posn                          (* Does e get passed up a level? *)
        THEN eUp := e;                                        (* Yes. *)
             pNew↑.ptrs[0] := pRight
        ELSE eUp := pi↑.data[j1-1];               (* No, pass up an    *)
             pNew↑.ptrs[0] := pi↑.ptrs[j1-1];     (* element from pi↑. *)
             DEC(j1)
    END;
(*                                                                         *)
(* pNew↑ has all its elements and pointers, and the element to pass up a     *)
(* level is selected. If e hasn't been placed, insert it in pi↑.            *)
(*                                                                         *)
    IF posn <= order                              (* Does e belong in pi↑? *)
        THEN j2 := order;                                      (* Yes. *)
             WHILE j1 > posn DO                  (* Move elements to make room. *)
                 MoveElement (pi,pi,j1,j2)
             END;
             InsertElemente (pRight,pi,e,j2)                   (* Insert e. *)
    END;
(*                                                                         *)
(* Element e has certainly been inserted. Now, if pNew↑ has any children,   *)
(* they must point to pNew↑ as their parent.                               *)
(*                                                                         *)
```

continued

```
IF pNew↑.ptrs[0] # NIL                (* Does pNew have any children? *)
    THEN FOR j1 := 0 TO order DO            (* Yes, set the          *)
            pNew↑.ptrs[j1]↑.parent := pNew  (* parent of each        *)
        END                                 (* child as pNew↑.       *)
END;
pi↑.noElt := order                    (* Oops, almost forgot this. *)

e := eUp;                          (* Finally, set the values *)
pi := pi↑.parent;                  (* returned by Insert2.     *)
pRight := pNew
END Insert2;
```

Figure C.29   Final version of *Insert2.*

We have finished *Insert2,* and therefore the discussion of the insertion operation for a B-tree. The complete operation, along with other procedures needed to construct and display a B-tree, is included on the diskette available from the publisher, to be used in conjunction with this text.

The insert procedure given here is intended to clearly show the steps followed during insertion into a B-tree. As with many other tree operations, a shorter and more elegant insert procedure can be developed recursively, and you are encouraged to undertake this as an exercise. If you are willing to miss the fun of doing it yourself, recursive insert and delete procedures are given in Wirth (1986), pages 248–253.

C.4 Printing a B-Tree

This section of Appendix C provides code for printing a B-tree. Specification of a B-tree is given in Section 5.9 of the text, and an implementation of several operations, including *Insert,* is given in Section C.3 of this appendix.

The routine that follows is essentially a recursive traversal of a B-tree, printing nodes as the traversal unfolds. It is noteworthy that recursion makes such a traversal both simple and elegant. This particular routine is of note because it centrally locates each node with half its children written on one side and the other half written on the other side. The idea of the traversal is shown in Figure C.30.

To implement the algorithm in Figure C.30, we want to position the nodes attractively on the page, so we include the level of each node as a parameter of the traversal procedure and embed it in another procedure. The

```
Traverse (node);
IF node exists
    THEN
        recursively traverse half the children of node;
        write the content of node;
        recursively traverse the remaining children of node
END
```

Figure C.30   Recursive algorithm to print the contents of a tree.

result, procedure *Display,* is shown in Figure C.31. (You may want to refer to the representation of a B-tree, which is given in Chapter 5.)

```
PROCEDURE Display(B: BTree);                                (* Display a BTree. *)

   PROCEDURE Traverse(p: NodePtr; level: CARDINAL);       (* Traverse a BTree. *)
   VAR k,m: CARDINAL;
   BEGIN
      IF p # NIL
         THEN m := p↑.noElt DIV 2;             (* m is half the elements in p↑. *)
            FOR k := 0 TO m DO
               Traverse(p↑.ptrs[k], level+1)       (* Traverse half the children. *)
            END;
            WriteNode(p,level);                        (* Write node content. *)
            FOR k := m+1 TO p↑.noElt DO
               Traverse(p↑.ptrs[k], level+1);        (* Traverse the other half. *)
            END
      END
   END Traverse;

BEGIN
   Traverse(B↑.treeRoot, 0)
END Display;
```

Figure C.31   Recursive procedure to print a B-tree.

The procedure in Figure C.31 calls another procedure, *WriteNode,* to write the content of a node. Such a procedure, designed for a B-tree of order 2, is given in Figure C.32.

```
PROCEDURE WriteNode(p: NodePtr; level: CARDINAL);       (* Write one BTree node. *)
VAR k: CARDINAL;
BEGIN
   WriteLn;
   FOR k := 1 TO level DO                            (* Position the printer       *)
      WriteString('                 ')             (* horizontally on the page. *)
   END;
   WriteString('[');
   WITH p↑ DO                                        (* Write the key value of     *)
      FOR k := 1 TO noElt DO                         (* each element in the node. *)
         WriteCard(data[k].key,3)
      END
   END;
   WriteString(' ]');
END WriteNode;
```

Figure C.32   Procedure to write the content of a node in a B-tree. The horizontal positioning is intended for a tree of order 2.

The procedures just described were used to display a B-tree of order 2 constructed using cardinal values generated at random. The way the nodes are positioned on the page is shown in Figure C.33.

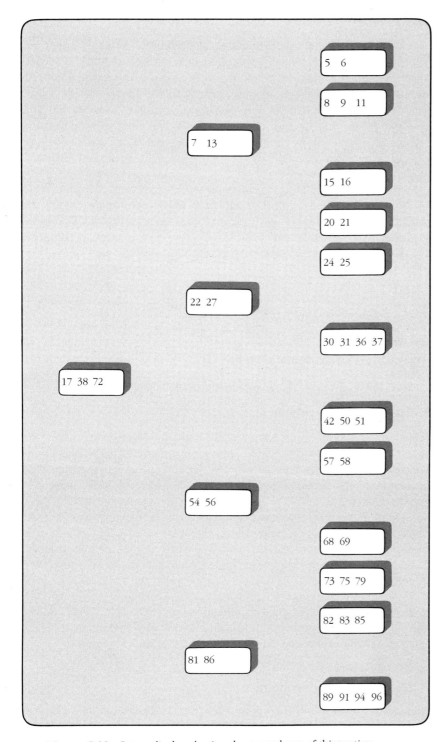

Figure C.33   B-tree displayed using the procedures of this section.

The Basic Tree-Printing Issues

1. The orientation problem
2. The positioning problem
3. The compaction problem
4. The overflow problem

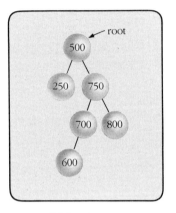

Figure C.34
Placing the nodes as shown
solves both the orientation and
the local positioning problems.

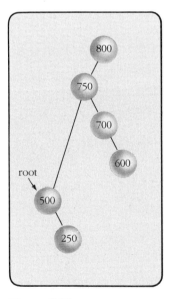

Figure C.35
Placing the nodes as shown does
not solve either the orientation
or the local positioning problem.

C.5 Printing Binary Trees

This section of Appendix C discusses two algorithms for printing binary trees. The first, *Wprint,* is essentially that given in Wirth (1976), and the second, *Vprint,* is similar to that described in Vaucher (1980). The result is not only useful algorithms but also an interesting application of several data structures.

A basic assumption about **line printers** is that they print one line at a time and cannot back up and reprint a previous line. Another assumption is that characters can only be printed in an upright position, not upside down or lying on their sides. In other words, we are assuming a standard, ordinary, garden variety line printer.

The two algorithms represent extremes of complexity. The first (Wirth, 1976) is simple, uses a minimal amount of memory, requires no auxiliary data structure, and produces results that leave something to be desired. The second (Vaucher, 1980) is moderately complex, requires both an auxiliary data structure and its attendant extra memory, and produces pretty trees.

C.5.1 Tree-Printing Issues

We will begin this section by describing four basic issues that must be addressed by an algorithm that is to be used to print trees using an ordinary line printer.

• The orientation problem

If the root of a tree is at the top of a figure and if the tree grows downward, then we would like the content of each node to be printed left to right across the page. Since the orientation of the tree is then consistent with the orientation of each node, the **orientation problem** is considered solved. Figure C.34 shows such a tree.

Figure C.35 shows a tree with the root at the left that grows to the right. The content of each node is printed left to right across the page. The orientation of the node content is inconsistent with the orientation of the tree. In order to be consistent, the display of each node's content would have to be rotated counterclockwise through 90 degrees. (To see this, rotate this page 90 degrees clockwise and look at Figure C.35.)

Since we are assuming that printers print only left to right, algorithms that solve the orientation problem must print trees either with the root at the top growing downward or with the root at the bottom growing upward.

• The positioning problem

We will divide the **positioning problem** into two parts and deal with only one of the parts. The **local positioning problem** is the problem of positioning a node on the page relative to the location of its children. We will consider the local positioning problem solved if a parent node is always located midway between its two children—whenever it has two children. In Figure C.34, parent nodes are all located midway between their children. In Figure C.35 this is not the case. Given any parent node, the local positioning problem deals with the location of its children. The **global positioning problem** deals with the positions of its subtrees. We leave the global positioning problem to the ingenious reader.

• **The compaction problem**

Section 5.4 tells us that most trees are a great deal wider than they are tall. Printing a tree with the root at the top therefore requires a page that is very wide but not too long. Unfortunately, ordinary printers present us with paper that has infinite height but relatively narrow width.

The **compaction problem** is that of making a given tree as narrow as possible so that the widest possible tree will fit on one page. Figure C.34 shows a relatively compact version of the tree in Figure C.36. Solving the compaction problem may well interfere with solving the positioning problem. Narrow trees may tend to be ugly. In any event, compaction may not be a concern if our tree printer solves the last problem—overflow.

• **The overflow problem**

Suppose we print our tree with the root at the top growing downward. This permits us to solve the orientation problem; but no matter how wide our paper or how narrow our printed characters, we will eventually encounter a tree that is too wide to fit on one width of paper. In fact, because of the basically wide but short nature of binary trees, this will occur with surprisingly small trees.

A tree-printing algorithm that solves the **overflow problem** can print trees that are too wide to fit on one page. The basic way to do this is to print any tree that is too wide for one page in strips. The strips are then "pasted" together in order to show the entire tree.

To conclude this introduction we present Table C.1, which shows those of the four problems just described that can be solved by the algorithms we will present. A "yes" in the column means that the problem is solved by the specified algorithm. The remainder of this section discusses the two algorithms—*Wprint* and *Vprint*.

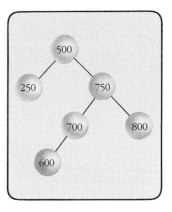

Figure C.36
Wide version of tree in Figure C.34.

TABLE C.1

| | Problem | | | |
Algorithm	Orientation	Positioning (local)	Compaction	Overflow
Wprint	No	No	No	Partially
Vprint	Yes	Yes	Yes	Yes

PROCEDURE
PrintNode(p: pointer);
```
(* Print the content *)
(* of the node       *)
(* pointed at by p.  *)
```

PROCEDURE PrintBlank;
```
(* There is no node  *)
(* to print in this  *)
(* print position.   *)
(* Space over to the *)
(* next print        *)
(* position on       *)
(* this level.       *)
```

PROCEDURE NewLevel;
```
(* A level has been  *)
(* printed, advance  *)
(* the printer to the *)
(* line that will    *)
(* contain the       *)
(* next level.       *)
```

PROCEDURE NewPage;
```
(* Advance the       *)
(* printer to the top *)
(* of a new page.    *)
```

Figure C.37
Common operations in tree-printing algorithms *Wprint* and *Vprint*.

C.5.2 Basic Operations

The two tree-printing algorithms that we present have a few operations in common. These operations do very simple things and provide the interface between our tree-printing algorithms and a particular printer. They are described in Figure C.37. We suggest that you glance at them before reading Sections C.5.3 and C.5.4.

C.5.3 Wprint

Procedure *Wprint* has two major advantages. It is simple, and (unlike *Vprint*) it does not require an auxiliary data structure in order to print the tree. It does not solve the orientation problem (node contents are printed on edge!); it does not solve the positioning problem (node locations can be erratic); it does not compact the tree; and it trades the problem of having the tree too wide for the problem of having the tree too tall. This trade means that a much larger tree can be printed before the width of a page becomes a limiting factor. Eventually, however, that limit is reached, and the only option available to users of *Wprint* is to buy a printer that accepts wider paper—or prints narrower characters.

Procedure *Wprint* makes an inorder traversal of the tree to be printed. As given in Wirth (1976), page 203, the left subtree of each node is traversed before the right subtree. Algorithm C.1 reverses this order so the tree, rather than its mirror image, is printed.

```
PROCEDURE Wprint(BT: BinaryTree);

    PROCEDURE Wp (p: NodePtr; level: CARDINAL);
    VAR k: CARDINAL;
    BEGIN
        IF p # NIL
            THEN
                Wp (p↑.right,level+1);
                FOR k := 1 TO level-1 DO PrintBlank() END;
                PrintNode(p);
                NewLevel();
                Wp (p↑.left,level+1)
        END
    END Wp;

BEGIN
    Wp (BT↑.treeRoot,1)
END Wprint;
```

Algorithm C.1

Figure C.38 shows a binary tree printed by *Wprint*. The tree was formed by inserting words from von Neumann (1946). The first 16 words of 4–7 characters in length were inserted. The insertion order was the same as the order of occurrence of words in the text, with the tree formed as a binary search tree. Uppercase characters were converted to lowercase before insertion.

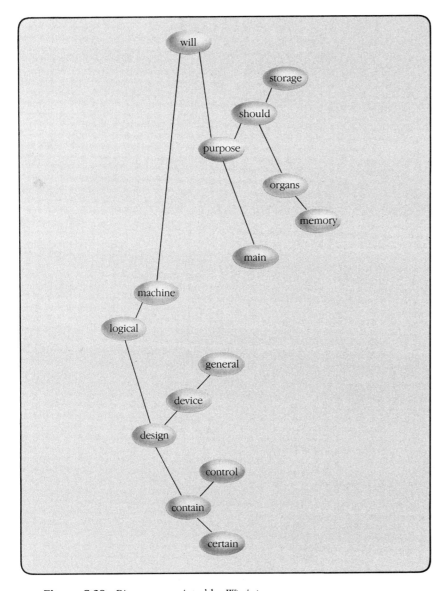

Compare the tree in Figure C.38 with the characterization of *Wprint* given in Table C.1. Explain each of the four shortcomings of *Wprint* in terms of the specific example shown in Figure C.38.

Figure C.38 Binary tree printed by *Wprint*.

C.5.4 Vprint

We begin our discussion of *Vprint* with an example, which is shown in Figure C.39. The example shows the tree to be printed, along with the auxiliary data structure used by *Vprint*.

In Figure C.39 there are six nodes in the tree and therefore six list nodes. There are three levels in the tree and therefore three level nodes. There is a head pointer, called entry, that provides access to the auxiliary data structure.

The structure of the ***auxiliary data structure*** is a list of level nodes each of which contains a head pointer for a list of list nodes. Since the number of levels in the tree and the number of nodes in any level are variables, the auxiliary data structure is a prime candidate for linked implementation.

Figure C.40 shows the result of using *Vprint* to print the tree shown in Figure C.38. These figures allow a direct comparison between the results obtained using *Vprint* and the results obtained using *Wprint*. Examine Figure C.40 to see that *Vprint* does indeed solve the problems of orientation, local positioning, and compaction.

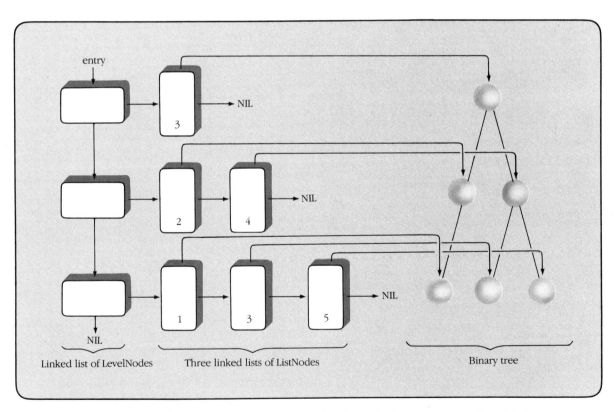

Figure C.39   Example of an auxiliary data structure required by *Vprint* before a tree can be printed.

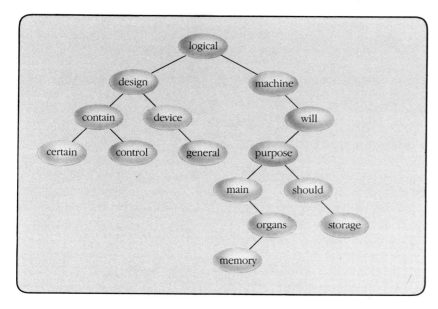

Figure C.40   Binary tree printed by *Vprint*.

• Representation

Although the nodes of the tree could be represented in any way desired, we assume that they are represented as described in Section 5.3. That is, we assume a linked representation for the nodes of the tree. This representation is repeated in Figure C.41 for reference.

The auxiliary data structure also uses a linked representation (see Figure C.42). The *LevelNodes* form a singly linked list whose header is a pointer to the head of the list and whose tail is indicated by a NIL pointer. There are two operations on the list of *LevelNodes*—adding a new node at the tail of the list and deleting (or clearing) the entire list.

Each *LevelNode* contains a head pointer for a singly linked list of list nodes—one for each level in the tree being printed. Each such list is terminated by a NIL pointer. There are two basic operations on these lists: *Insert* a new node at the head of the list and *Delete* a node from the head of the list. The process of inserting a *ListNode* includes linking it to a node in the tree and determining the print position of that tree node.

What is a ***print position?*** Each node must be positioned both vertically and horizontally. The tree is printed with root at the top growing downward. Therefore, the vertical position is determined by the level of the node in the tree. The auxiliary data structure records a node's level by attaching its *ListNode* to the appropriate *LevelNode*. The horizontal position within a level is determined by function *Position,* which is described shortly.

```
TYPE
  NodePtr = POINTER TO node;
  node    = RECORD
                elt: StdElement;
                left,right: NodePtr
            END;
```

Figure C.41
Assumed representation of a node in the tree to be printed.

```
TYPE ListPtr =
        POINTER TO ListNode;
     LevelPtr =
        POINTER TO LevelNode;

     LevelNode =
        RECORD
            first: ListPtr;
            next: LevelPtr
        END;

     ListNode =
        RECORD
            pnode: NodePtr;
            next:  ListPtr;
            pos:   INTEGER
        END;
```

Figure C.42
Representation of *ListNodes* and *LevelNodes* for the auxiliary data structure.

• Implementation

Vprint is implemented using the following two principal operations:

```
Position(p: NodePtr; VAR lp: LevelPtr; pos: INTEGER): INTEGER;
```

and

```
llprint(pagewidth: INTEGER);
```

The function *Position* takes as input a pointer, *p*, to the root of the tree to be printed; a levelpointer, *lp*, which points to the appropriate *LevelNode;* and a tentative horizontal position, say 0, for the root of the tree. It recursively traverses the tree and produces the complete auxiliary data structure, including the horizontal positions of each of the nodes in the tree.

Procedure *Llprint* prints the tree, in strips if the tree is too wide to fit on one page, and disposes of the auxiliary data structure.

We will now describe how *Position* works. The description contains statement numbers that are keyed to procedure *Vprint,* which follows shortly.

Procedures *InsertLevel* and *InsertList* handle the creation of *ListNodes* and *LevelNodes* except for determining the horizontal positions at which to print the tree nodes. These positions are determined by statements (* p1 *) through (* p4 *). Statement (* p4 *) simply inserts the computed position in its *ListNode,* and (* p3 *) updates the global variables *minpos* and *maxpos. Minpos* is the least, or left most, position of any node in the tree. Similarly, *maxpos* records the largest or right most position of any node to be printed. These values are needed by the print procedure *Llprint.*

Since (* p3 *) and (* p4 *) play only bookkeeping roles, statements (* p1 *) and (* p2 *) are the statements that actually determine the horizontal positions of nodes in the tree.

The input to *Position* includes the value of *pos,* which is a tentative horizontal position for the tree node being considered. This tentative position is adjusted by statements (* p1 *) and (* p2 *). The input tentative position for the root of the tree can be any integer. It makes no difference what value is used since the horizontal print positions are all relative. It is set as 0 in *Vprint.* The tentative horizontal position of any right child is one greater than the tentative horizontal position of its parent. The tentative horizontal position of any left child is one less than the tentative horizontal position of its parent.

The order in which the horizontal position of a node is finalized is determined by a traversal of the tree. If N is any node in the tree, then the order in which horizontal positions are determined is the following:

1. All the nodes in the right subtree of N have their horizontal positions determined.
2. All the nodes in the left subtree of N have their horizontal positions determined.
3. Finally, the position of N is determined.

In other words, the print positions are finalized during a postorder traversal in which the right subtree is processed before the left subtree. There are two important consequences of this ordering.

First, the final position of each node is determined after the final position has been determined for its neighbor to the right on the same level. This order is essential for statement (* p1 *), which moves a node to the left (reduces its print position), if it is necessary to ensure that it is at least two positions to the left of its neighbor on the right.

Second, the final position of each node is determined after positions have been determined for all of its children. Statement (* p2 *) depends on this order since it determines the position of each node in terms of the position of its children. In particular, statement (* p2 *) positions each parent as shown in Algorithm C.2.

Let us recap the process used to determine the horizontal print position of a node. It is a four-step process:

1. Each node is given a tentative print position. For the root node this position is supplied by the tree print package. For all other nodes this tentative position is either one greater or one less than the tentative position of the parent.
2. If the node is not the right most node on its level, then statement (* p1 *) applies and moves the node to the left, if necessary, to assure that it is at least two positions to the left of its neighbor on the right. Note that at this point the final position of the right neighbor will have already been determined.
3. The final positions of all nodes in both subtrees are determined. This is implemented by recursive calls to function *Position* in statement (* p2 *).
4. The final position of the node is determined by statement (* p2 *). If a node has two children, then it is placed midway between those children. If a node has one child, then it is placed one position to the right or to the left of that child. If a node has no children, then statement (* p2 *) does not affect its position.

Procedure *Vprint*, which prints binary trees, now follows.

```
IF   there are two
     children
   THEN the parent is
        placed midway
        between them
 ELSIF there is exactly
        one child
   THEN the parent is
        placed one
        position to the
        right of a left
        child and one
        position to the
        left of a right
        child
   ELSE (* there are   *)
        (* no children *)
        the tentative
        position of the
        parent becomes
        its final
        position
```

Algorithm C.2
Placement of a parent relative to its two children.

```
PROCEDURE Vprint(BST: SearchTree; PageWidth: CARDINAL);

   TYPE ListPtr    = POINTER TO ListNode;
        LevelPtr   = POINTER TO LevelNode;
        LevelNode  = RECORD
                        first: ListPtr;             (* Points to a list of ListNodes. *)
                        next: LevelPtr                      (* The next LevelNode. *)
                     END;
        ListNode   = RECORD
                        pnode: NodePtr;             (* Points to a binary tree node. *)
                        pos  : INTEGER          (* Position of the binary tree node. *)
                        next : ListPtr                     (* The next ListNode. *)
                     END;

   PROCEDURE PrintNode(p: NodePtr);   ,            (* Print the content of a node. *)
   BEGIN
      WriteCard(p↑.elt.key,2)
   END PrintNode;

   PROCEDURE PrintBlank();                             (* Print an empty node. *)
   BEGIN
      WriteString('  ')
   END PrintBlank;

   PROCEDURE NewLevel();                (* Move the printer to the next level. *)
   BEGIN
      WriteLn; WriteLn
   END NewLevel;

VAR k, minpos, maxpos: INTEGER;

PROCEDURE Position(p: NodePtr; VAR lp: LevelPtr; pos: INTEGER): INTEGER;
VAR list: ListPtr;

   PROCEDURE InsertLevel(VAR lp: LevelPtr);           (* Create a level node and  *)
   BEGIN                                              (* add it to the end of     *)
      NEW(lp);                                        (* the list of level nodes. *)
      lp↑.next  := NIL; lp↑.first := NIL
   END InsertLevel;

   PROCEDURE InsertList(lp: LevelPtr);            (* Create a list node, link it to *)
   BEGIN                                          (* the binary tree, and attach it *)
      NEW(list);                                  (* as the first node on its level. *)
      list↑.pnode := p; list↑.pos := 0;
      list↑.next  := lp↑.first; lp↑.first := list
   END InsertList;
```

continued

Procedure Vprint, continued

```
BEGIN
    IF p = NIL
        THEN RETURN pos
    END;

    IF lp = NIL THEN InsertLevel(lp)
        ELSIF (pos+2) > lp↑.first↑.pos                          (* p1 *)
            THEN pos := lp↑.first↑.pos - 2
    END;

    InsertList(lp);

    IF p↑.right = NIL                                            (* p2 *)
            THEN  pos :=  Position(p↑.left ,lp↑.next,pos-1) + 1
        ELSIF p↑.left = NIL
            THEN  pos :=  Position(p↑.right,lp↑.next,pos+1) - 1
        ELSE      pos := (Position(p↑.right,lp↑.next,pos+1) +
                          Position(p↑.left ,lp↑.next,pos-1)) DIV 2
    END;

    IF pos > maxpos THEN maxpos := pos END;                     (* p3 *)
    IF pos < minpos THEN minpos := pos END;
    list↑.pos := pos;                                           (* p4 *)
    RETURN pos
END Position;

PROCEDURE Llprint(pw: INTEGER);              (* Print the tree vertically. *)
VAR startpos,center: INTEGER;
    k,k1            : INTEGER;
    lp              : ListPtr;
    level,l2        : LevelPtr;
```

continued

Procedure Vprint, continued

```
BEGIN
    startpos := minpos;
    WHILE startpos <= maxpos DO
        level := entry;                              (* Get first level node. *)
        IF (maxpos - startpos) < pw
            THEN center := ( pw - (maxpos - minpos + 1)) DIV 2
            ELSE center := 0
        END;

        WHILE level # NIL DO                         (* While there is another level. *)
            k   := startpos; lp := level↑.first;
            FOR k1 := 1 TO center DO PrintBlank() END;         (* Center the tree. *)

            WHILE (k < startpos+pw) AND (lp # NIL) DO
                IF lp↑.pos = k
                    THEN PrintNode(lp↑.pnode);
                        level↑.first := lp↑.next;
                        DISPOSE(lp);
                        lp := level↑.first
                    ELSE PrintBlank()
                END;
                k := k + 1
            END;
            NewLevel();
            level := level↑.next                     (* Bump down to next row of nodes. *)
        END;
        startpos := startpos + pw
    END;
    level := entry;
    WHILE level # NIL DO                             (* Dispose of the level nodes. *)
        l2 := level;
        level := level↑.next;
        DISPOSE(l2)
    END
END Llprint;

VAR entry: LevelPtr;

BEGIN (* Vprint *)
    IF BST↑.treeRoot # NIL
        THEN entry := NIL; minpos := 0; maxpos := 0;
            k := Position(BST↑.treeRoot, entry, 0);
            Llprint(INTEGER(PageWidth))
        ELSE WriteString('Tree is empty')
    END;
END Vprint;
```

Modula-2 Reserved Words, Symbols, Identifiers, and Modules

D.1 Reserved Words

D.2 Special Symbols

D.3 Standard Identifiers

D.4 Standard Modules

D.1 Reserved Words

Modula-2 has 40 reserved words, all in uppercase.

AND	ELSIF	LOOP	REPEAT
ARRAY	END	MOD	RETURN
BEGIN	EXIT	MODULE	SET
BY	EXPORT	NOT	THEN
CASE	FOR	OF	TO
CONST	FROM	OR	TYPE
DEFINITION	IF	POINTER	UNTIL
DIV	IMPLEMENTATION	PROCEDURE	VAR
DO	IMPORT	QUALIFIED	WHILE
ELSE	IN	RECORD	WITH

D.2 Special Symbols

+	addition	<=	less than or equal to
−	subtraction	>=	greater than or equal to
*	multiplication	( )	parentheses
/	division	[]	array element brackets
:=	assignment	{}	set brackets
&	logical AND	(**)	comment brackets
=	equality	↑	pointer reference
# <>	inequality	..	ellipsis
<	less than	, . ; : |	punctuation
>	greater than		

D.3 Standard Identifiers

ABS	CHR	FLOAT	INTEGER	PROC
BITSET	DEC	HALT	NEW	REAL
BOOLEAN	DISPOSE	HIGH	NIL	TRUE
CAP	EXCL	INC	ODD	TRUNC
CARDINAL	FALSE	INCL	ORD	VAL
CHAR				

D.4 Standard Modules

The three modules specified in this appendix are standard modules provided with Modula-2 implementations. They differ somewhat from implementation to implementation but are relatively stable. They are used many times in this book. Consult your local Modula-2 implementation documentation.

Specification D.1   SYSTEM

DEFINITION MODULE SYSTEM;
(Fundamental system-level objects and operations. *)*

EXPORT QUALIFIED WORD, SIZE, TSIZE, ADDRESS, ADR,
                   PROCESS, NEWPROCESS, TRANSFER;

TYPE WORD;   *(* Opaque type representing a memory word. *)*
      ADDRESS = **POINTER TO** WORD;   *(* Memory address. *)*
      PROCESS;   *(* Opaque type representing a process. *)*

PROCEDURE SIZE(variable identifier): CARDINAL;
(**post** — SIZE is the number of memory words occupied by the variable. *)*

PROCEDURE TSIZE(type identifier): CARDINAL;
(**post** — TSIZE is the number of memory words occupied by an instance of the
          type, including the different variants of a variant record type. *)*

PROCEDURE ADR(variable identifier): ADDRESS;
(**post** — The memory address at which the variable is stored. *)*

PROCEDURE NEWPROCESS(subprogram: PROC; addr: ADDRESS; workspace: CARDINAL;
                   VAR coroutine: PROCESS);
(**pre** — subprogram is a parameterless procedure and addr is the address at
          which to establish a work space of size workspace.
    post — coroutine is a suspended coroutine whose work space is workspace
          words starting in memory at addr. *)*

PROCEDURE TRANSFER(**VAR** process1, process2: PROCESS);
(**post** — Control has been transferred from process1 to its coroutine
          process2. *)*

END SYSTEM.

Specification D.2   Storage

DEFINITION MODULE Storage;
(This module manages the dynamic allocation of memory. The two operations
    ALLOCATE and DEALLOCATE must be imported by any module using the built-in
    operations NEW and DISPOSE. *)*

(**Elements**: Memory words. *)*

    FROM SYSTEM **IMPORT** ADDRESS;

(**Structure**: Storage (the memory heap) is linear. *)*

(**Domain**: The number of words in storage is bounded. *)*

continued

Specification D.2, continued

    EXPORT QUALIFIED ALLOCATE, DEALLOCATE, Available;

(* **Operations:** *)

PROCEDURE ALLOCATE(**VAR** a: ADDRESS; size: CARDINAL);
(* **pre** – Available(size) is true and ALLOCATE is called from the main
           coroutine.
   post – A space of size words starting at address a is reserved in the
           memory heap. *)

PROCEDURE DEALLOCATE(**VAR** a: ADDRESS; size: CARDINAL);
(* **pre** – a must be a memory address previously generated by a call to
           ALLOCATE and size must be the same number used in that call;
           DEALLOCATE must be called from the main coroutine.
   post – size words of memory starting at memory address a-pre have been
           returned to the memory heap; a's value is undefined. *)

PROCEDURE Available(size: CARDINAL): BOOLEAN;
(* **post** – Available is true if ALLOCATE(p,size) would succeed, false
           otherwise. *)

END Storage.

Specification D.3 InOut

DEFINITION MODULE InOut;
(* A useful module for handling files of characters or words. It is also
   useful for I/O to the interactive terminal. *)

(* **Elements:** Characters (or, equivalently, characters). *)

   FROM SYSTEM **IMPORT** WORD;
   FROM FileSystem **IMPORT** File;

(* **Structure:** Linear. The elements are stored sequentially on a mass storage
               device, interactive terminal, or other external device separate
               from the random access memory of the system. *)

(* **Domain:** Bounded. *)

   EXPORT QUALIFIED EOL, Done, termCH, OpenInput, OpenOutput, CloseInput,
                  CloseOutput, Read, ReadString, ReadInt, ReadCard, ReadWrd,
                  Write, WriteLn, ClearScreen, WriteString, WriteInt,
                  WriteCard, WriteOct, WriteHex, WriteWrd;

   CONST EOL = 15C;   (* *End of line character.* *)
   VAR Done : BOOLEAN;   (* *Operation success flag.* *)
      termCH: CHAR;   (* *Terminating character in ReadString,* *)
                                    (* *ReadInt, and ReadCard.* *)

continued

Specification D.3, continued

(* Operations: *)

PROCEDURE OpenInput (extent: **ARRAY OF** CHAR);
(* **post** — A file name was requested from the terminal; if the file name
ended with a ".", then the suffix extent was appended to the file
name. An attempt was made to open the file. If it was not
successful, then Done is false, else Done is true and the file
is open for input with its cursor at the first element. *)

PROCEDURE OpenOutput (extent: **ARRAY OF** CHAR);
(* **post** — A file name was requested from the terminal; if the file name
ended with a ".", then the suffix extent was appended to the file
name. An attempt was made to open the file. If it was not
successful, then Done is false, else Done is true and the file
is open for output. *)

PROCEDURE CloseInput;
(* **post** — Closes the open input file, if any. Subsequent input will be
from the keyboard of the interactive terminal. *)

PROCEDURE CloseOutput;
(* **post** — Closes the open output file, if any. Subsequent output
will be to the interactive terminal screen. *)

PROCEDURE Read (**VAR** ch: CHAR);
(* **post** — If the end of input file is encountered then Done is false,
else Done is true and ch is the next character waiting for
input in the input file currently open. *)

PROCEDURE ReadString (**VAR** s: **ARRAY OF** CHAR);
(* **post** — If a non-null string was read then Done is true and the string
(not including the terminating character) is in s and the file
cursor is at the first character past the terminating character;
else Done is false. A string is a sequence of characters not
including blanks or any control character; leading blanks are
ignored. The string is terminated by a space, return character,
or any control character; this character is assigned to termCH. *)

PROCEDURE ReadInt (**VAR** x: INTEGER);
(* **post** — If a string was read and converted to an integer then Done is
true and x is the integer's value, else Done is false. The
syntax of an integer is [+|-] digit {digit}; leading blanks are
ignored. The string is terminated by the first character not
of the integer syntax. *)

PROCEDURE ReadCard (**VAR** x: CARDINAL);
(* **post** — If a string was read and converted to a cardinal then Done is
true and x is the cardinal's value, else Done is false. The
syntax of a cardinal is digit {digit}; leading blanks are
ignored. The string is terminated by the first character not
of the cardinal syntax. *)

continued

Specification D.3, continued

PROCEDURE ReadWrd(**VAR** w: WORD);
(* **post** — If the file is not at the end of file, the next word in the file
           was read, Done is true, and w has the value of the word, else
           Done is false. *)

PROCEDURE Write(ch: CHAR);
(* **post** — ch is appended to the current output file. *)

PROCEDURE WriteLn;
(* **post** — An EOL character is appended to the end of the output file. *)

PROCEDURE ClearScreen;
(* **post** — If the interactive terminal screen is open for output then it
           is clear. *)

PROCEDURE WriteString(s: **ARRAY OF** CHAR);
(* **post** — s is appended to the output file. *)

PROCEDURE WriteInt(x: INTEGER; n: CARDINAL);
(* **post** — x is converted to an integer string of at least n characters,
           which are appended to the output file. If n was greater than
           the number of characters needed, then leading blanks were
           padded. *)

PROCEDURE WriteCard(x: CARDINAL; n: CARDINAL);
(* **post** — x is converted to a cardinal string of at least n characters,
           which are appended to the output file. If n was greater than
           the number of characters needed, then leading blanks were
           padded. *)

PROCEDURE WriteOct(x: CARDINAL; n: CARDINAL);
(* **post** — x is converted to an octal string of at least n characters,
           which are appended to the output file. If n was greater than
           the number of characters needed, then leading blanks were
           padded. *)

PROCEDURE WriteHex(x: CARDINAL; n: CARDINAL);
(* **post** — x is converted to a hex string of at least n characters,
           which are appended to the output file. If n was greater than
           the number of characters needed, then leading blanks were
           padded. *)

PROCEDURE WriteWrd(w: WORD);
(* **post** — Word w is appended to the output file. *)

END InOut.

Notes on Checking Preconditions

Throughout this book we have specified procedures by stating pre- and post-conditions. The question arises whether a procedure should check the validity of its own precondition before executing. We have not done so in any of the procedures in this book. At first glance it may seem that the failure of a procedure to check its own preconditions is a serious breach of software engineering principles. Is that so? The following are some thoughts on the subject.

First let us review some aspects of preconditions.

1. We have made the global assumption (really a global precondition) that all arguments being passed contain valid values of their type. For example, in procedure *Findith* of *Lists,* we specify

```
PROCEDURE Findith(L: List; i: CARDINAL)
(* pre  – 1 <= i <= Size(L).
   post – The current element is the one in the
          ith position. *)
```

Specification A

We assume and do not check (perhaps cannot check) that *L* is a valid *List.* We assume also that *i* is a valid value from type CARDINAL. There are ways in which these parameter values can be corrupted; for example, by placing a real value into *i*'s memory cells.

Most procedure code written today assumes valid values in arguments being passed. The burden of assuring valid arguments is placed on the user. The point to note is that having valid argument values is a precondition that is typically not verified by implementations.

2. Procedure arguments must meet any further restrictions indicated by preconditions. In the example above, we specify not only that *i* is a valid value from type CARDINAL but also that it satisfies the additional constraint of the precondition. The question is whether an implementation of *Findith* should assure itself that the precondition is met before executing. We will discuss that shortly.

3. Are there any other conditions that will cause failure of execution of a procedure? If so, then they should either (a) be made part of the precondition or (b) be made part of a return flag or status variable that indicates successful execution, or failure and/or reasons for failure.

As an example of (a), let us respecify *Findith* above as follows:

```
PROCEDURE Findith(L: List; i: CARDINAL): BOOLEAN;
(* post — If 1 <= i <= Size(L) then the current element
           is the one in the ith position and Findith
           is true, else Findith is false. *)
```

Specification B

As an example of (b), suppose that we wanted to differentiate between a failure due to the list's being empty and a failure due to the list's being not empty but $i >$ Size(L) or $i = 0$. The user may want to know this in order to take different actions. We might specify a status variable to be returned.

```
PROCEDURE Findith(L: List; i: CARDINAL; status: CARDINAL);
(* post — If 1 <= i <= Size(L) then the current element
           is the one in the ith position and status = 0,
           else if size(L) = 0 then status = 1, else
           status = 2. *)
```

Specification C

Any foreseeable error conditions should be addressed in the specifications. If one can write code to test for the existence of an error condition, then one can foresee it. If one can't foresee it, then one can't write testing code.

In Specification A, if the implementation does not check the truth value of its precondition, a serious error can occur (the cursor may be moved beyond the tail of the list) and the data structure can become corrupted. It appears at first glance that it is a serious mistake not to check. However, think about what happens next.

If such a situation occurred and the implementation of *Findith* were programmed to detect the condition, then it could do one of several things: (a) print a message, do something unspecified with the cursor, and return, (b) print a message and abort execution or (c) some other action. Choice (a) is fine, but according to the specifications there is no way to inform the calling program (the printed message informs the user, not the program), so the program would smash along unaware of the error. Choice (b) seems a good one. The HALT statement of Modula-2 aborts execution of the program, and the printed message would inform the user of the reason for the termination. Valuable computations and results might be lost, and not all programs can be aborted safely.

Is a solution then to use Specification B? In that case, the user becomes aware that there has been a failure by testing after execution and can take action accordingly. But it is true that in either case we are totally dependent upon the user's testing. With Specification A, it is an a priori test of the precondition:

```
IF i <= Size(L)
  THEN Findith(L,i)
  ELSE Error action
```

With Specification B, it is an a posteriori test of the postcondition:

```
IF NOT Findith(L,i)
  THEN Error action
```

(Specification C provides only a refinement of the concept in B.)

If the user tests as he or she should, then all is OK in both cases. If the user fails to test, then the program will do undefined things in both cases; the only gain from the implementation's being self-aware of the error condition is that it outputs an error message for later reconstruction of the impending disaster.

The solution to the problem is a clear assignment of the error-checking responsibility at various levels. All procedures below a level assume that the errors screened above do not exist and do not check for them. The only logical alternative is for procedures at all levels to check all error conditions that might affect them. This can prove to have a large negative impact on development time and performance. Just as we routinely assume without checking in a procedure that argument values passed to the procedure are valid values of the argument's type, so we can routinely assume conformance with other nonglobal preconditions.

We have generally chosen in the book not to have implementations check the truth value of their preconditions. We have assigned precondition checking to the user level.

There is another approach, which is not provided for by the facilities of Modula-2. That is the notion of an ***exception.*** The concept is too involved to discuss here. The programming language Ada has such a facility, and you are referred to United States Department of Defense, 1983, or to any good Ada textbook for a discussion.

References

Aho, Alfred V., and Ullman, Jeffrey D., *Principles of Compiler Design,* Addison-Wesley, Reading, MA, 1977.

Baron, R. D., and Shapiro, L. G., *Data Structures and Their Implementation*, Van Nostrand Reinhold, NY, 1980.

Bayer, R., and McCreight, C., "Organization and Maintenance of Large Ordered Indexes," *Acta Informatica,* Vol. 1, No. 3, 1972, pp. 173–189.

Beidler, J., and Jackowitz, P., "Consistent Generics in Modula-2," *ACM SIGPLAN Notices,* Vol. 21, No. 4, April 1986.

Bell Labs, *Bell System Technical Journal,* Vol. 57, No. 6 (Issue devoted to UNIX), July–August 1978.

Bentley, J., "Programming Pearls: Thanks Heaps," *Communications of the ACM,* March 1985, pp. 245–250.

Bentley, J. L., and McGeoch, C. C., *Communications of the ACM,* April 1985, pp. 404–411.

Bentley, Jon, "An Introduction to Algorithm Design," *IEEE Computer,* Vol. 12, No. 2, February 1979.

Bentley, Jon, *Writing Efficient Programs,* Prentice-Hall, Englewood Cliffs, NJ, 1982.

Bentley, Jon, "Programming Pearls," *Communications of the ACM,* Vol. 26, No. 8, August 1983a,b, and No. 12, December 1983c.

Bishop, J. M., "Implementing Strings in Pascal," *Software–Practice and Experience,* Vol. 9, 1979, pp. 779–788.

Boswell, F. D., Carmody, F. J., and Grove, T. R., "A String Extension for Pascal," Computer Systems Group University of Waterloo, *WATNEWS,* September–October 1982, pp. 22–24.

Bottenbruch, H., "Structure and Use of ALGOL 60," *Journal of the ACM,* Vol. 9, No. 2, 1962, p. 214.

Boyer, R. S., and Moore, J. S., "A Fast String Searching Algorithm," *Communications of the ACM,* October 1977, pp. 762–772.

Burke, R. W., Goldstine, H. H., and von Neumann, J., "Preliminary Discussion of the Logical Design of an Electronic Computing Instrument," Report prepared for the U.S. Army Ordinance Department, 1946. Reprinted in Bell, C.G., and Newell, A., *Computer Structures: Readings and Examples,* McGraw-Hill, NY, 1971.

Cichelli, R. J., "Minimal Perfect Hash Functions Made Simple," *Communications of the ACM,* Vol. 23, No. 1, January 1980.

Clark, R., and Koehler, S., *The UCSD Pascal Handbook,* Prentice-Hall, Englewood Cliffs, NJ, 1982.

Coffman, E. G., and Hofri, M., "On Scanning Disks and the Analysis of Their Steady State Behavior," *Proceedings of the Conference on Measuring, Modelling and Evaluating Computer Systems,* North Holland, NY, October 1982.

Comer, D., "The Ubiquitous B-Tree," *ACM Computing Surveys,* June 1979, pp. 121–137.

Computing Reviews, *ACM Computing Reviews,* January 1982.

Cooper, D., *Standard Pascal: User Reference Manual.* W.W. Norton, NY, 1983.

Digital Research, (DRI), *CPM 3 User's Guide,* Pacific Grove, CA, 1982.

Feller, W., *An Introduction to Probability Theory and Its Applications,* Wiley, NY, 1950.

Ford, G. A., and Wiener, R. S., *Modula-2: A Software Development Approach,* Wiley, NY, 1985.

Forsythe, G. E., Malcolm, M. A., and Moler, C. B., *Computer Methods for Mathematical Computations,* Prentice-Hall, Englewood Cliffs, NJ, 1977.

Gleaves, R., *Modula-2 for Pascal Programmers,* Springer-Verlag, NY, 1984.

Graham, R. L., and Pavol, H., "On the History of the Minimum Spanning Tree Problem," *Annals of the History of Computing,* January 1985, pp. 43–57.

Gries, D., "Current Ideas in Programming Methodology," in *Research Directions in Software Technology,* P. Wegener (Ed.), MIT Press, Cambridge, MA, 1979, pp. 254–275.

Guttag, J. V., "Abstract Data Types and the Development of Data Structures," *Communications of the ACM,* Vol. 20, No. 6, June 1977.

Hall, A. V. P., and Dowling, G. P., "Approximate String Matching," *Computing Surveys,* December 1980, pp. 381–402.

Halstead, M., *Elements of Software Science,* Elsevier–North Holland, NY, 1977.

Hill, Fredrick J., and Peterson, Gerald R., *Introduction to Switching Theory and Logical Design,* Wiley, NY, 1968.

Hoare, C. A. R., "Quicksort," *Computer Journal,* April 1962, pp. 10–15.

Hofri, Micha, "Disk Scheduling: FCFS vs. SSTF Revisited," *Communications of the ACM,* Vol. 23, No. 11, November 1980.

Horsepool, R. N., "Practical Fast Searching in Strings," *Software—Practice and Experience,* Vol. 10, 1980, pp. 501–506.

Hu, T. C., *Combinatorial Algorithms,* Addison-Wesley, Reading, MA, 1981.

IBM (PL/I), International Business Machines Corporation, *System 360 OS, PL/I Language Reference Manual.*

IEEE, Standard Pascal Computer Programming Language, ANSI/IEEE 770 X3.97-1983, The Institute of Electrical and Electronic Engineers, 1983.

Jaeschke, G., "Reciprocal Hashing—A Method for Generating Minimal Perfect Hashing Functions," *Communications of the ACM,* Vol. 24, No. 12, December 1981.

Jensen, K., and Wirth, N., *PASCAL User Manual and Report,* Springer-Verlag, NY, 1974.

Jones, T. Capers, "Programming Quality and Productivity: An Overview of the State of the Art," ITT Programming Technology Center, Stratford, CT, 1981.

Karlgren, H., "Representation of Text Strings in Binary Computers," *BIT,* 1963, pp. 52–59.

Kernighan, B. W. "Why Pascal Is Not My Favorite Programming Language." In *Comparing and Assessing Programming Languages,* edited by Alan Feuer & Narain Gehani. Prentice-Hall, Englewood Cliffs, NJ, 1984.

Kingston, J. H., "Analysis of Tree Algorithms for the Simulation Event List," *Acta Informatica,* April 1985, pp. 15–33.

Knuth, D. E., *The Art of Computer Programming: Fundamental Algorithms,* Vol. 1, 2nd Edition, Addison-Wesley, Reading, MA, 1973a.

Knuth, D. E., *The Art of Computer Programming: Sorting and Searching,* Vol. 3, Addison-Wesley, Reading, MA, 1973b.

Knuth, D. E., "Dynamic Huffman Coding," *Journal of Algorithms,* June 1985, pp. 163–180.

Knuth, D. E., Morris, J. H., and Pratt, V. R., "Fast Pattern Matching in Strings," *SIAM Journal on Computing.* June 1977, pp. 323–349.

Larson, P., "Expected Worst-Case Performance of Hash Files," *Computer Journal,* August 1982, pp. 347–352.

Liskov, B. H., and Zilles, S. N., "Specification Techniques for Data Abstractions," *IEEE Transactions on Software Engineering,* Vol. 1, No. 1, 1975.

Liskov, B. H., Snyder, A., Atkinson, R., and Schaffert, C., "Abstraction Mechanisms in CLU," *Communications of the ACM,* Vol. 20, No. 8, August 1977.

Lum, V. Y., Yuen, P. S. T., and Dodd, M., "Key-to-Address Transform Techniques: A Fundamental Performance Study on Large Existing Formatted Files," *Communications of the ACM,* April 1971, pp. 228–239.

MacLane, B., and Birkhoff, G., *Algebra,* Macmillan, NY, 1967.

Matick, Richard E., *Computer Storage Systems and Technology,* Wiley, NY, 1977.

Microsoft, Inc., *MS-DOS 2.0,* Microsoft, Bellevue, WA.

Mitchell, J. G., Maybury, W., and Sweet, R., "Mesa Language Manual," Version 5.0, CSL 79-3, XEROX, Palo Alto Research Center, Systems Development Department, Palo Alto, CA, 1979.

Motzkin, D., "Meansort," *Communications of the ACM,* April 1983, pp. 250–251.

MT Microsystems, *PASCAL/MT+ User's Guide,* Release 5 (CP/M-8080–Z80), MT Microsystems, 1981.

Myers, Glenford J., *Advances in Computer Architecture,* 2nd Edition, Wiley, NY, 1982.

Nievergelt, J., "Binary Search Trees and File Organization," *Computing Surveys,* September 1974, pp. 195–207.

OMSI Pascal-1 VI.2, *User's Guide,* Oregon Software, 2340 S.W. Canyon Road, Portland, OR, 1980.

Paice, C. D., "Information Retrieval and the Computer," *MacDonald and Jane's Computer Monographs,* London, 1977.

Pascal/MT+, "Language Reference and Applications Guide," Release 5.1.

Perlis, A. J., Sayward, F. G., and Shaw, M. (Eds.), *Software Metrics: An Analysis and Evaluation,* MIT Press, Cambridge, MA, 1981.

Poblete, P. V., and Munro, J. I., "The Analysis of a Fringe Heuristic for Binary Search Trees," *Journal of Algorithms,* September 1985, pp. 336–350.

Radke, C. E., "The Use of Quadratic Residue Research," *Communications of the ACM,* February 1970, pp. 103–105.

Reingold, Edward M., and Hansen, Wilfred, S., *Data Structures in Pascal,* Little, Brown, 1986.

Rivest, Ronald, "On Self-Organizing Sequential Search Heuristics," *Communications of the ACM,* Vol. 19, No. 2, February 1976.

Sack, J.-R., and Strothotte, T., "An Algorithm for Merging Heaps," *Acta Informatica,* June 1985, pp. 171–186.

Sale, A. H. J., "Strings and the Sequence Abstraction in Pascal," *Software—Practice and Experience,* Vol. 9, 1979, pp. 671–683.

Sebesta, R. W., and Taylor, M. A., "Fast Identification of Ada and Modula-2 Reserved Words," *Journal of Pascal, Ada, & Modula-2,* March/April 1986, pp. 36–39.

Sedgewick, R., "Implementing Quicksort Programs," *Communications of the ACM,* Vol. 21, No. 10, October 1978, pp. 847–856.

Sedgewick, R., *Algorithms,* Addison-Wesley, Reading, MA, 1983.

Shaw, Mary, "The Impact of Abstraction Concerns on Modern Programming Languages," Carnegie-Mellon University, Computer Science Technical Report CMU-CS-80-116, 1980.

Shen, V. Y., Conte, S. D., and Dunsmore, H. E., "Software Science Revisited: A Critical Analysis of the Theory and Its Empirical Support," *IEEE Transactions on Software Engineering,* Vol. SE-9, No. 2, March 1983, pp. 155–165.

Signum Newsletter, "The Proposed IEEE Floating-Point Standard," Special Issue of the ACM Special Interest Group on Numerical Mathematics, October 1979.

Sipala, P. "Optimum Cell Size for the Storage of Messages," *IEEE Transactions on Software Engineering,* January 1981, pp. 132–134.

Smit, G. De V., "A Comparison of Three String Matching Algorithms," *Software—Practice and Experience,* Vol. 12, 1982, pp. 57–66.

Sprugnoli, R., "A Single Probe Retrieving Method for Static Sets," *Communications of the ACM,* Vol. 20, No. 11, November 1977.

Stanat, D. F., and McAllister, D. F., *Discrete Mathematics in Computer Science,* Prentice-Hall, Englewood Cliffs, NJ, 1977.

Standish, T. A., *Data Structure Techniques,* Addison-Wesley, Reading, MA, 1980.

Stoll, R. R., *Sets, Logic, and Axiomatic Theories,* W. H. Freeman, San Francisco, 1961.

Tanenbaum, Andrew S., *Structured Computer Organization,* Series in Automatic Computation, Prentice-Hall, Englewood Cliffs, NJ, 1976.

Tyner, P., *iAPX General Data Processor Architecture Reference Manual,* Order No. 171860-001, Intel Corporation, Santa Clara, CA, 1981.

United States Department of Defense, *Reference Manual for the Ada Programming Language,* ANSI/MIL-STD-1815A-1983, 1983.

Vaucher, J., "Pretty Printing of Trees," *Software—Practice and Experience,* Vol. 10, 1980, pp. 553–561.

Vitter, J. S., "Implementations for Coalesced Hashing," *Communications of the ACM,* December 1982, pp. 911–926.

Vitter, J. S., "Analysis of the Search Performance of Coalesced Hashing," *Journal of the ACM,* April 1983, pp. 231–258.

von Neumann, 1946; see Burke, 1946.

Wainwright, R. L., "A Class of Sorting Algorithms Based on Quicksort," *Communications of the ACM,* April 1985, pp. 396–403.

Wiederhold, Gio, *Database Design,* 2nd Edition, McGraw-Hill, NY, 1983.

Wiener, R., and Sincovec, R., "Two Approaches to Implementing Generic Data Structures in Modula-2," *ACM SIGPLAN Notices,* Vol. 20, No. 6, June 1985.

Wirth, *Algorithms + Data Structures = Programs,* Prentice-Hall, Englewood Cliffs, NJ, 1976.

Wirth, N., *MODULA-2,* Report No. 36, Eidgenoessische Technische Hochschule, Institut für Informatik, Zurich, 1980.

Wirth, N., *Programming in Modula-2,* 2nd Edition, Springer-Verlag, NY, 1983.

Wirth, N., *Programming in Modula-2,* 3rd Edition, Springer-Verlag, NY, 1985.

Wirth, N., "Revisions and Amendments to Modula-2," *Journal of Pascal, Ada, & Modula-2,* January/February, 1985a, pp. 25–28.

Wirth, N., *Algorithms & Data Structures,* Prentice-Hall, Englewood Cliffs, NJ, 1986.

Wolverton, D. A., "A Perfect Hash Function for Ada Reserved Words," *ACM Ada Letters,* 4(1), 1984, pp. 40–44.

Wright, W. E., "Some Average Performance Measures for the B-Tree," *Acta Informatica,* March 1985, pp. 541–557.

Wulf, W. A., London, R. L., and Shaw, M., "An Introduction to the Construction and Verification of Alphard Programs," *IEEE Transactions on Software Engineering,* SE-2, No. 4, December 1976.

Yao, A. C., and Yao, F. F., "The Complexity of Searching an Ordered Random Table," *Proceedings of the Conference on the Foundations of Computer Science,* Houston, TX, October 1976, p. 173.

Index

Abstract data types, 7–8, 12–22, 442–443
  atomic, 12–16
  formal specifications, 453–460
  implementation, 23–25
  problem level, 449–453
  representation, 23, 34–35
  specifications, 12–22
Abstract model method, 459
Activation, procedure, 113–114
Ada, 446–449
Arrays, 54–69
  characteristics, 61–63
  descriptor record, 65
  dynamic, 68
  lower triangular, 66
  mapping function, 60–61, 63–65
  multidimensional, 58–60
  of pointers, 93–95
  of records, 93
  open parameters, 68–69
  row-major order, 64
  sparse, 66–67
ASCII code, 366–368
Assemblers, 10
Assembly language, 10–11
Assertions, 13
Available (procedure), 88

Backtracking algorithms, 355
Binary search, 163–169, 360–361
Birthday paradox, 335
Bit maps, 328–330

Capsule, 26
CDC code, 366–367

Character-valued keys (hashing), 339–340
Compilers, 10
Complexity, 27, 51, 298
Component, see Data elements

Data, 2
  integrity of, 27
  objects, 4
  visibility of, 26
Data elements, 2, 14, 29–30, 287
  atomic, 2
Data structures, 6–7, 33–34
Data type, 5, 103–104, 324
  generic, 104, 443–445, 447–449
  instance, 103–104
  opaque, 103–104
  ordinal, 324
Data types, 4–29
  abstract, 7–8, 12–16
  abstraction levels, 8
  atomic, 6–7
  bit, 45
  boolean, 44–45
  byte, 45–46, 368
  character, 45, 366–375
  common, 40–46
  integer, 40–42
  native, 9–11
  physical, 8, 36–46
  pointer, see Pointers
  real, 42–44
  structured, see Data Structures
  virtual, 8, 36–46
  word, 46
Data values, 2, 5
  atomic, 5
  decomposition, 2, 5

Digit selection (hashing), 336–337
Digraphs (letter pairs), 184
DISPOSE (procedure), 86–87
Division (hashing), 337
Domains, 14
Dynamic memory allocation, 86–88

EBCDIC code, 366–367
Embedded shift instructions, 369–371
Encapsulation, 26
Equivalence, 455
Existential quantifier, 455
EXPORT statement, 18, 20

Fibonacci search, 170–171
Fields, 30, 287
Files, 37, 180–183
Folding (hashing), 338–339

Garbage collection, 396
Generic data types, 104, 443–445, 447–449
Graphs, 400–439
  adjacency lists, 407–420
  adjacency matrix, 405–407
  breadth first search, 422, 425–426
  depth first search, 422–425, 427, 436
  directed, 403, 434–437
  directed acyclic graph, 436
  fragments, 433
  priority first search, 424
  shortest path, 432
  spanning tree, 402, 428–431
  terminology, 401–403
  topological sorting, 435–437

Graphs (*continued*)
  transitive closure, 434–435
  Warshall's algorithm, 435
  weighted, 403, 428

Hashing, 333–363
  bucket, 341
  clustering, 346–347
  collisions, 335
  coalesced chaining, 341, 352–353, 357–362
  deletions, 342, 352–353, 359
  double hashing, 348–350, 357, 361–362
  external chaining, 341, 350–353, 357–362
  functions, 334–340, 359–360
  linear rehashing, 341–348, 357, 361–362
  load factor, 340–341, 352, 357–358
  memory requirements, 358
  open address methods, 341–350, 358
  perfect functions, 333, 353–355, 516–517
  performance, 356–362
  quadratic rehashing, 348
  rehashing, 333, 335
  table, 333, 340–341
Heaps, 127, 264–272, 308–310
Hierarchies, *see* Trees
High-level languages, 10–11, 33–34, 39
Huffman codes, 372–375

Implication, 454
Index, 6, 57, 288
  array, 95, 288, 296
Information hiding, 19
InOut standard module, 542–544
Interfaces, 26, 28
Interpolation search, 169–170
Interpreters, 10
Items, *see* Fields

Letter frequency application, 183–189, 261–264, 359–362
Lexicographic order, 32
Linearity, 32–33, 139
Linked lists, 79–91, 407–420
  circular, 89
  doubly linked, 90
  multilinked, 90–91
  singly linked, 90

Linked structures, 35, 56, 77–91
Lists, 138–175, 332, 351, 357, 362–363
  chronological, 138, 158–160
  frequency-ordered, 138, 172–175
  ordered, 157–158
  self-organizing, 173–175
  sorted, 138, 161–171, 362–363

Machine, *see* Processors
Machine language, 8–9
Median of three, 306–307
Memories, 37–38, 47–48
  cache, 37
  direct access, 37
  random access, 37–38, 341
  register, 37
  sequential access, 37
Memory management, 111–114
Metrics, 46–47
Modula-2, 40, 354, 380–381, 444–445, 464–490
  assignment statements, 483
  block structure, 465
  CASE statements, 465
  comments, 465
  compound statements, 483
  constants, 468
  declarations, 466–467
  FOR statements, 487
  identifiers, 465
  IF statements, 484–485
  LOOP/EXIT statements, 486–487
  modules, 477–482
    definition, 480–482
    implementation, 482
    internal, 477–480
    program, 464–465
  procedure calls, 488–490
  REPEAT statements, 486
  RETURN statements, 488
  statement sequences, 483–484
  types, 469–475
    array, 471–472
    pointer, 470–471
    procedure, 474–475, 477
    record, 472–474
    set, 474
    simple, 470
    standard, 469
  variables, 475–476
  WHILE statements, 465–486
  WITH statements, 488
Modules, 4, 16–26, 442–443, 464–465, 477–482
  standard, 540–544

Multiplication (hashing), 337–338
Multiplicative search, 170

Networks (*see also* Graphs, weighted), 31
NEW, 86–87

Objects, 461
Operating systems, 39
Operations, 3
Ordered structure, 32
Orders of magnitude, 48–50

Packages, 446–449
Parity, 368
Partial order, 31
Partitioning, in quicksorts, 301–306
Performance, 38
Pointers, 46, 56, 77–91
Position (linear), 139, 287
Positioning and calculation, 34–35
Postconditions, 13, 21
Preconditions, 13, 21, 546–548
Predicate calculus, 454–460
Prefix property, 372
Priority queues, 100, 124–127, 271–272, 424, 429
Processors, 8–10, 38–40, 47–48
  physical, 8
  virtual, 8
PROCEDURE, 21
Proofs of correctness, 442, 460

Queues (FIFO), 100, 118–123, 422, 424

Random access, 58
Random number generator module, 517–519
Records, 54–56, 70–76
  characteristics, 73–74
  memory mapping function, 74
  of arrays, 92–93
  variant, 74–76
Recursion, 116, 169, 204, 215, 217, 220–221, 302, 307–308, 492–504
  alternatives to, 504
  depth, 493
  implementation, 500–503
  performance, 503–504
Rings, 138, 176–178
Run-time systems, 116

Scheduling (I/O), 128–134
   abstraction, 133–134
   disks, 128–133
   shortest seek time first, 129–130
   sweep/SSTF, 131–133
Semantics, 19–20
Sentinels, 145–146
Sequences, 138, 178–180
Sets, 324–363, 454
   atomic elements, 324–330
   bit maps, 328–330
   structured elements, 330–332
Simplicity, 26
Sort field, 288, 298
Sorting, 286–321, 333–334
   bubble sort, *see* Sorting, exchange
      sort
   distribution sort, 319
   exchange sort, 291–293, 296–299
   external, 286
   heapsort, 308–310, 313–314
   insertion sort, 293–299, 307, 313–
      314, 319–321
   internal, 286–287
   linked lists, 295–299
   meansort, 316
   mergesort, 310–314, 321
   quicksort, 297, 301–308, 313–314,
      319, 320–321
   performance, 297–299
   radix exchange sort, 320
   radix sort, 316–319, 321
   selection sort, 290–291, 296–299,
      321, 495–496
   shellsort, 315–316
   stability, 299
   treesort, 308
Sorts, in-place, 299
Stacks, 100–117, 215–218, 307, 422,
      424, 436, 444–445, 504
   pairs, 108–111

Standard element, 30
Storage media, 3
Storage standard module, 541–542
Streams, 182–183
Strings, 366–398, 506–517
   array representation, 381–393, 395–
      396
   Boyer-Moore algorithm, 387–389,
      392, 509, 512
   Knuth-Morris-Pratt algorithm, 385–
      387
   linked representation, 381–382, 393–
      396
   Modula-2, 380–381
   obvious algorithm, 384–385, 392, 509
   pattern matching, 379, 506–517
   substrings, 376
Structure, 2–3, 6, 30–33
   abstract, 3
   graph, 30–31
   linear, 30–33, 139, 195–196
   physical, 3
   set, 30–31, 324–325
   tree, 30–31, 195–197
Subscript, *see* Index
Syntax, 18, 20
SYSTEM standard module, 541

Timing studies, 167, 186–189, 261–264,
      297–298, 314, 359–362
Total order, 31
Traversal, 208, 421–427
Trees, 192–284, 357, 402
   degenerate, 243
   edges, 195
   expression, 204
   full, 243
   height, 199

Trees (*continued*)
   height-balanced, 251
   level, 199
   nodes, 194
   ordered, 194
   parse, 204
   paths, 197
   spanning, 402
   terminology, 194–195, 197–199
Trees, AVL, 250–260
Trees, B-, 273, 282, 519–527
   insertion, 519–525
   node splits, 274
   order, 274
   printing, 525–527
Trees, binary, 201–228, 528–538
   characteristics, 211–212
   complete, 265
   definition, 204
   Huffman codes, 372–375
   printing, 528–538
   shells, 216–218
   threaded, 226–228
   traversal, 215–218
Trees, binary search, 228–242, 308, 332,
      334, 362–363
   definition, 229
   element deletion, 236–239
   enumeration and performance, 243–
      249
   minimal height, 244
   node removal, 236–239
   random, 245
   search length, 245
Tuples, 454
Type, 5

Unique identification property, 30
Universal quantifier, 455